Government and Politics of
the Contemporary Middle East

D0025654

This exciting new book for students of Middle Eastern politics provides a comprehensive introduction to the complexities of the region, its politics and people. Combining a thematic framework for examining patterns of politics with individual chapters dedicated to specific countries, the book explores current issues within an historical context.

Presenting information in an accessible and inclusive format, the book offers:

- Coverage of the historical influence of colonialism and major world powers on the shaping of the modern Middle East.
- A detailed examination of the legacy of Islam.
- Analysis of the political and social aspects of Middle Eastern life: alienation between state and society, poverty and social inequality, ideological crises and renewal.
- Case studies on countries in the Northern Belt (Turkey and Iran); the Fertile Crescent (Iraq, Syria and Lebanon, Israel and Palestine); and those west and east of the Red Sea (Egypt and the members of the Gulf Cooperation Council).
- Extensive pedagogical features, including original maps and detailed further reading sections, which provide essential support for the reader.

A key introductory text for students of Middle Eastern politics and history at advanced undergraduate and postgraduate levels, this book will also be a significant reference for policy-makers and any motivated reader.

Tareq Y. Ismael is Professor of Political Science at the University of Calgary, Canada. He is the Secretary General of the International Association of Middle Eastern Studies and co-editor of the *International Journal of Contemporary Iraqi Studies*. His current research focuses on human rights and civil society in the Middle East, and he has written numerous books on ideologies in the Middle East and the international and domestic politics of Middle Eastern countries.

Jacqueline S. Ismael is Professor of Social Work at the University of Calgary, Canada. Her research interests and numerous publications lie in the areas of Canadian social policy, international social development, comparative welfare states, human rights and social change. She is one of the founding members of the International Association of Contemporary Iraqi Studies and is co-editor of the *International Journal of Contemporary Iraqi Studies*.

Government and Politics of the Contemporary Middle East

Continuity and Change

Tareq Y. Ismael
Jacqueline S. Ismael

With contributions from Shereen T. Ismael,
Glenn E. Perry and Ali Rezaei

Routledge
Taylor & Francis Group

LONDON AND NEW YORK

First published 2011
by Routledge
2 Park Square, Milton Park, Abingdon, Oxon OX14 4RN

Simultaneously published in the USA and Canada
by Routledge
270 Madison Avenue, New York, NY 10016

Routledge is an imprint of the Taylor & Francis Group, an informa business

Typeset in Times New Roman
by Keystroke, Tettenhall, Wolverhampton
Printed and bound in Great Britain
by CPI Antony Rowe, Chippenham, Wiltshire

British Library Cataloguing in Publication Data
A catalogue record for this book is available from the British Library

Library of Congress Cataloging in Publication Data
Government and politics of the contemporary Middle East : continuity and
change / Tareq Y. Ismael, Jacqueline S. Ismael ; with contributions from
Shereen T. Ismael ... [et al.].
p. cm.
Includes bibliographical references and index.
1. Middle East–Politics and government–1979– I. Ismael, Tareq Y.
II. Ismael, Jacqueline S. III. Ismael, Shereen T.
DS63.1.G68 2010
320.956–dc22
2010007850

ISBN: 978–0–415–49144–0 (hbk)
ISBN: 978–0–415–49145–7 (pbk)
ISBN: 978–0–203–84745–9 (ebk)

To our connections to the Kurdish people,
our uncles Hussein Mawlood Sherwani (1930–1972)
and Kakarash Haji Nabi Sherwani (1930–2003)

Contents

Illustrations

Maps

Tables

Contributors

Authors

Jaqueline S. Ismael is Professor of Social Work at the University of Calgary and is co-editor of the *International Journal of Contemporary Iraqi Studies*. She has published extensively on Canadian social policy and international social welfare, including *The Canadian Welfare State: Evolution and Transition* (1989) and *International Social Welfare in a Changing World* (1996). She has also written articles and monographs on social change in the Middle East and has co-authored a number of works with Tareq Y. Ismael, including *The Communist Movement in Syria and Lebanon* (1998) and *The Iraqi Predicament* (2004). Her latest work, with William Haddad, is entitled *Barriers to Reconciliation: Case Studies on Iraq and the Palestine–Israel Conflict* (2006).

Tareq Y. Ismael is a Professor of Political Science at the University of Calgary, Canada; the Secretary General of the International Association of Middle Eastern Studies; and co-editor of the *International Journal of Contemporary Iraqi Studies*. He has published extensively on the Middle East, Iraq and international studies. His most recent works include *Turkey's Foreign Policy in the 21st Century: A Changing Role in World Politics* (2003), *Iraq: The Human Cost of History*, with William H. Haddad (2004), *The Iraqi Predicament: People in the Quagmire of Power Politics*, with Jacqueline S. Ismael (2004), *The Communist Movement in the Arab World* (2005), *The Rise and Fall of the Communist Party of Iraq* (2008) and *Cultural Cleansing in Iraq: Why Museums Were Looted, Libraries Burned and Academics Murdered*, with Raymond Baker and Shereen Ismael (eds) (2010).

Contributors

Shereen T. Ismael is Associate Professor of Social Work in the School of Social Work, Carleton University. In addition to her book *Child Poverty and the Canadian Welfare State: From Entitlement to Charity* (2006), she is the editor of *Cultural Cleansing in Iraq: Why Museums Were Looted, Libraries Burned and Academics Murdered*, with Raymond Baker and Tareq Y. Ismael, and *Globalization: Policies, Challenges and Responses* (1999). She has published numerous articles on Canadian and international social welfare issues. Her latest journal articles have appeared in the *Journal of Comparative Family Studies*, *Arab Studies Quarterly* and the *International Journal of Contemporary Iraqi Studies*.

Glenn E. Perry received his Ph.D. in Foreign Affairs from the University of Virginia in 1964 and did further work in Arabic and Middle East Studies at Princeton. He has taught Political Science, particularly courses on the Middle East, at Indiana State University since 1970. He also taught at the American University in Cairo. Reflecting his interdisciplinary interests in the region, he has published several books – including *The Middle East: Fourteen Islamic Centuries* (1997) and *The History of Egypt* (2004) – and dozens of articles and chapters, all dealing with Middle Eastern politics, history and religion. In recent years, much of his work has focused on the paucity of Middle Eastern democracy.

Ali Rezaei worked as a journalist and social researcher in Iran in the 1980s and 1990s. He was on the editorial board of reformist newspapers *Sobh-e emrooz*, *Bahar* and *Doran-e emrooz*, and was a co-founder of *Aftab* magazine. All were banned by the Iranian authorities between 1998 and 2004. He is currently completing his Ph.D. dissertation at the University of Calgary in Canada.

Preface

This is our fourth textbook on the Middle East. Each volume has incorporated the findings of previous efforts along with a decade's worth of material recasting, reinterpreting and re-organizing the events that have unfolded, leading to a unique and fuller understanding of the region with every publication. One approach to the study of Middle East politics has always been that the patterns of activity over time reveal the meaning and nature of historical development at any particular juncture.

This volume is an attempt to make it possible for students, general readers, journalists and opinion-makers of Middle East politics to understand current events in the region as they unfold in the context of historical patterns that have evolved through time. In this context, *Government and Politics of the Contemporary Middle East* examines the interplay between governments and their societies, while looking at the Middle East of today in relation to the patterns of Middle East politics historically.

The organization of this volume reflects the effort to set events in the context of patterns of continuity and change throughout the region. Part I introduces the predominant dynamics of Middle East politics: history, particularly as embodied in the legacies of imperialism, as well as Islam in its religious, cultural and political dynamics. Chapter 2, "The Burden of History," is a survey of how historical encounters between the Middle East and the great powers, prior to and following the colonial era, have configured and continue to shape the nature of the contemporary Middle East states.

Chapter 3, "The Legacy of Islam," considers the political and social significance of the Islamic religion in Middle East society in three dimensions: first, it surveys the classical Islamic thought, Sunni and Shi'a, on the nature of politics and society; second, it evaluates the contemporary interplay, and occasional conflict, between the secular institutions of state and the prerogatives of Islamic thought; and third, it examines the rise of Islam as a force for political mobilization in the contemporary age, as embodied in the modern Islamist movements.

Part II surveys the conditions of politics and society in the most significant countries of the Middle East, interpreted through the thematic lens outlined in the first section of the book. As such, each chapter in Part II attempts to clarify the patterns of political dynamics that have evolved in the country being examined.

In this manner, the reader has the flexibility to study each chapter individually, as well as in reference to the ebb and flow of history.

This volume is intended to give the reader a comprehensive introduction to the complexities of the region, its politics and people. The principle of parsimony should encourage the reader to search bibliographic references in order to enhance their understanding and inform their further study of the region. Thus, unless the topic is controversial, the information is contentious, or a direct quotation has been used, notes have been eliminated. With the enormous resources available online, we would be remiss not to encourage the use of web-based material in the study of the region's politics, given the seemingly infinite scope of information available on the internet, which can often provide differing and broader perspectives than are available in mainstream journalism, including sources of information based in the Middle East region itself. Nevertheless, it is imperative to use critical judgment and to evaluate the credibility of available sources, as the open nature of the internet allows publication of both credible and suspect material.

The modern Middle East is colored by its colonial past, making a definition of the region problematic. Although it is distinguishable from Europe chiefly by religion and from most of Asia by culture, the Middle East as we know it today has no tangible geographic periphery. Historically, its meaning has been determined by political rather than geographic factors and therefore has changed in correspondence to the growth of Western interest and involvement in the area.

The delineation of the Middle East adhered to in this volume includes the countries in the Northern Belt (Turkey and Iran); the Fertile Crescent (Iraq, Syria and Lebanon, Israel and Palestine); and those west and east of the Red Sea (Egypt and the members of the Gulf Cooperation Council). The selection of case studies was restricted by space, leaving us to accord the most attention to what we consider the core states in the region.

There are many systems of transliteration from Middle Eastern languages, and no particular standards prevail. In an effort to aid the reader's recognition of names and places, the system of transliteration used in this book follows conventions that will be familiar to Western readers, as opposed to a formal system. Turkish names and words are spelled in their modern Turkish form.

This endeavor would not have been possible without the contributions and encouragement, sometimes beyond the call of duty, of friends and colleagues who graciously read drafts of each chapter. All offered valuable suggestions, comments and critical evaluations in a number of ways. However, the views expressed in this book, as well as any errors of fact or omission, are the responsibility of the authors alone.

The chapter on the State of Israel and the Palestinian Territories was co-authored by Glenn E. Perry of Indiana State University, whose attention to detail and scholarship cannot go unmentioned. Part I of the text was carefully examined by Moncef Khaddar of Eastern Mediterranean University, while the chapter on the Republic of Turkey was updated and revised a number of times by Ali Rezaei of the University of Calgary, who also co-authored the chapter on the Islamic Republic of Iran. We must thank Greg Muttitt and Ahmed M. Jiyad, both distinguished oil experts, for all of their advice and critical examination of the oil issues as presented in the introduction and the chapter on Iraq. Without their diligence and scholarship, this would not have been an easy task for the authors.

Fuat Keyman of Koç University in Istanbul and Tozun Bahcheli of the University of Western Ontario both graciously read over the many drafts of the chapter on the Republic of Turkey. Gilbert Achcar of the School of Oriental and African Studies at the University of London and Samer Abboud of Susquehanna University were indispensable in the revision of the chapter on the Syrian Arab and Lebanese republics. Both Norton Mezvinsky of Central Connecticut State University and Ghada Talhami of Lake Forest College applied their command of the subjects to tackle the sensitivities and complexities of the chapter on the State of Israel and the Palestinian Territories, while Mohammed Selim of the University of Kuwait offered invaluable advice on the Gulf Cooperation Council chapter. Colleagues from the American University in Cairo, Walid Kazziha and Manar Shorbagy, both pored over the chapter on the Arab Republic of Egypt. Finally, Reider Visser of the Norwegian Institute of International Affairs, Anne Alexander of the School of Oriental and African Studies of the University of London, Eric Herring of the University of Bristol, Mundher Adhami and Sami J. Albanna were our greatest critics for the complex chapter on the Republic of Iraq.

We also wish to acknowledge the contributions of the University of Calgary Research Grants Committee, and more particularly the Social Science and Humanities Research Council of Canada for their support of this project over the past decade in so many different ways. A word of appreciation should also be given to acknowledge the efforts of our research assistants – Chris Langille, who provided much-appreciated commentary and editorial assistance through the successive rounds of research and editing; likewise Candice M. Juby, whose diligence, commitment and patience deserve special thanks, especially during pre-publication; and Yousri Wagdy, Bassem Hafez and Gamal Selim, who were also indispensable, particularly when it came to translation and transliteration of Arabic sources. They have all proven invaluable during the many drafts and rewrites of the past four years, especially in tracking down footnotes and obscure details, updating, research, editing and the strategic condensation of the enormous volumes of material to an acceptable size.

Not to be forgotten is our dear colleague and friend, Andrew Johnson of Bishop's University, who courageously accepted our request to shepherd the final version of the book through to completion, first as a critic of content, language and logic and later as a sympathetic soul when the text was finally ready for Joe Whiting, our most patient and encouraging editor, to publish.

Tareq and Jacqueline Ismael
Calgary, Canada
10 August 2010

1   Introduction

Middle East politics in the twenty-first century: patterns of continuity and change

The Middle East as an area of study

Defining the Middle East is problematic. Although it is distinguishable from Europe chiefly by religion, and from the Far East by culture, the Middle East, located roughly between southwest Asia and the eastern Mediterranean, has no tangible geographic periphery. Historically, its meaning has been determined by political rather than geographic factors and therefore has changed in correspondence to the growth of Western interest and involvement in the area. Indeed, the term "Middle East" originates with Alfred Taylor Mahan (1840–1914), an American naval strategist, who coined it in 1902, and advised Britain on the importance of securing and maintaining the Gulf area en route to India. The term gained wide circulation during the Second World War when the Middle East Supply Center was established by the US and UK. However, the term did not initially have any definite geograph-ical boundary; for Mahan, it was the area between the Near East (Mesopotamia and the Nile Valley) and the Far East (China and Japan), and served as a flexible strategic concept reflecting the early twentieth-century geopolitical struggle between Britain and Russia. In other words, the Middle East was invented as a formulation of British security discourse, and later – during the Cold War era – the term became integral to Anglo-American security terminology. Nevertheless, as a modern conceptual and geographic unit, the Middle East is commonly delineated as: the Fertile Crescent, the Arabian Peninsula, the Nile Valley of Egypt and the Sudan, and – on the margins – the Northern Belt of Turkey and Iran, on one end, and the Arab Maghrib states of North Africa, on the other.

The politics of the Middle East vary in their particulars, state to state, though the region can be studied as a unit on the basis of shared thematic traits. First, the majority of Middle East states – minus Israel, Turkey and Iran – share an Arabo-Islamic heritage that defines cultural norms and colors the social environment. Indeed, these cultural forms have proven to be the most vital in terms of political and social mobilization, with first pan-Arabism and later Islamism forming powerful ideologies within the region. Second, all of the states of the Middle East – except Israel – share the burdens of post-colonialism; and, in varying forms, continue to struggle with the exigencies of imperialism and neo-imperialism. In this vein, modern state-building in the Middle East has been an attempt to elucidate national programs vis-à-vis the pressures of successive great powers, now embodied in the United States. In the ashes of the repressive infrastructure created by the former colonial regimes, the Middle East region has sustained – with little exception – patterns of oppressive rule.

The Middle East, as identified in the preceding definition, is a critical area of academic study, whose significance ranges from historic to religious/legendary to geostrategic. In the historic frame, the Fertile Crescent (more precisely, modern Iraq) is a site of agricultural revolution and human settlement – and later the world's first cities – perhaps as early as 10,000 BCE. The epic tale of Gilgamesh, the first known work of literature, similarly emerged in ancient Iraq. Likewise, the Fertile Crescent is the site of the world's earliest – preserved – legal codes, including the Laws of Eshunna, Mosaic Law and the Hammurabi Code. Finally, the Middle East region gave birth to monotheism as a coherent system of theology; it was the birthplace and remains the spiritual center of the world's core monotheist religions – Judaism, Christianity, and Islam – which today comprise over three billion believers. To this day, the region represents a major pilgrimage site for the world's monotheistic believers, with Arabia and historic Palestine featuring prominently. As the historic birthplace of organized monotheism, the early history of the Middle East has shaped the minds of people, nations and empires to this day. Nowhere does this ancient legacy more impose itself than in dueling historical/religious claims to Palestine/Israel. In premodern and modern history, the monotheistic religions of the Middle East have formed the ideational core of grand political projects, wars and social organization.

The significance of the contemporary Middle East, of course, is not merely in its historical contributions or religious legacy but in its worldly significance in matters geostrategic and economic. For much of human history, the Middle East, as the corridor between three continents, served as a nexus for human transit. And while the region's significance in this regard waned with technological developments in transport, its strategic significance re-emerged in the twentieth century with the discovery and exploitation of vast petroleum reserves. The region is a fulcrum of a world economy. Consequently, it has been a key battlefield – both literally and figuratively – in modern history. At present, the United States – as the last remaining superpower – has an unprecedented military and economic role in the region, with occupation of Iraq and a network of military bases scattered throughout the region. Moreover, three Middle East countries – Israel, Egypt and Jordan – are among the top-ten recipients of official US economic/military aid.

The academic study of the Middle East is all the more crucial given the vast degree of misinformation that permeates public culture in the West through the mass media. At the time of writing, the United States was deeply entrenched in a military occupation of Iraq, and yet, over six years since the initial invasion of Iraq, there continued to be much public confusion over the reality of the Iraq imbroglio. The claims which led the US to invade and occupy Iraq – possession of WMDs, ties to al-Qa'ida, nuclear ambitions, etc. – have proven to be objectively false; and yet, according to an October 2008 Harris Interactive poll, 52 percent of Americans believed that Saddam Hussein had strong links to al-Qaʻida and 37 percent believed Iraq had weapons of mass destruction at the time of the Anglo-American invasion. That so many Americans held to objectively false beliefs as late as 2008 reflects poorly on the public's under-standing of this crucial part of the world. The stubborn persistence of such beliefs reveals the efficacy of a concentrated campaign of prewar propaganda that amounted to – according to a 2008 report by the Center for Public Integrity – 935 false statements by President George W. Bush, Vice-President Dick Cheney, Condoleeza Rice and Donald Rumsfeld in the two-year period following the attacks of September 11, 2001.

Why study the Middle East? The region represents a point of origin for human civilization and dominant systems of thought (in the vein of monotheistic religion). Moreover, in an oil-dependent world, the Middle East has geostrategic para-mountcy that has resulted in deep Western involvement in the affairs of the region. Yet, for all the significance of the Middle East in world affairs and in light of some comprehensive Western interests in the region, misinformation and myth dominate much of the popular discourse.

This text is a presentation of the predominant themes of Middle East politics. Its thematic frames for the study of the Middle East, as introduced in the first part of this book, are: first, the "burden of history" – that is, a historical sketch of the Middle East generally, but more precisely a consideration of how historical encounters with the great powers and colonialism shaped and continue to shape the nature of post-colonial states and societies in the region; and, second, the role of Islam in Middle East society and politics, particularly in terms of how Islam has colored the social and political cultural backdrop of the region, and how Islam has interacted with modern efforts of state-building.

Part II of the text is a survey of the key states in the region, using the thematic framework provided in Part I.

Social geography of the Middle East: patterns of continuity

The predominant theme of Middle Eastern development in the twentieth century was a dedicated state-building project that attempted to mitigate the religious/ethnic particularities of society in favor of a nationalistic vision. This has been an admittedly uneven project as the claims of ethnoreligious nationalism have frequently been pitted against the claims of national minorities. Nevertheless, Middle East state-building – particularly in the case of secular nationalist regimes – achieved a significant measure of social cohesion, with a few notable exceptions.

There are three major linguistic/cultural groups in the region: Arab, Turkic and Persian; and a large number of secondary groups, including Jewish, Kurds, Berbers and Assyrians. In 2006, the population of the Middle East was estimated to be approximately 350 million, of which Arabs make up nearly two-thirds. The most significant non-Arab populations include Turkic people, largely represented in Turkey; Persians, who make up half the population of Iran; Berbers, concentrated in Algeria and Morocco; Kurds, who are spread across Turkey, Iraq and Syria; and Jews, concentrated in Israel.[1]

Among the five million-plus Jewish people living in the Middle East – the majority in Israel – there are several ethnic subdivisions: the Ashkenazim represent those Jews extracted from Germany ('Ashkenaz' being the medieval Hebrew name for Germany) who later expanded into Eastern Europe; the Sefaradim represent Jews extracted from the Iberian Peninsula, initially the Spanish provinces, until their expulsion following the Spanish *reconquista*, whereupon they resettled throughout Iberia, including the provinces of the former Ottoman Empire; finally, the Mizrahim, who represent those Jews settled in the Middle East and North Africa, Central Asia and the Caucasus. The Ashkenazim represent the majority of world Jewry, over two-thirds.

In order to understand the political dynamics of the Middle East, it is essential to discern the distinctions between groups as well as see their similarities. What determines ethnicity in the Middle East is the combined nomenclature of language in the region. On the other hand, what determines religious identification is a declaration of belief. Thus, Kurds are predominantly Muslims but not Arab; Christians may or not be Arab or Kurd; Jews are predominantly Ashkenazi but may be Arab, Kurdish, Turkish or Persian. The existence of Arab Jews and Arab Christians often confuses those new to the region, but the diversity is almost endless.

Religion has played an important role in the affairs of the Middle East for centuries and has provided not only a basis for national and cultural unity but a source of diversity. Islam, Judaism and Christianity, all of which originated in the Middle East, are the dominant religions; religion in the Middle East, as elsewhere, interacts with the social factors of race, ideology and nationality in often contradictory ways, both syncretic (e.g. Judaism and Zionism; Iran and Shi'ism) and oppositional (e.g. confessional politics in Lebanon and Iraq).

In the Middle East, Islam is numerically and socially the most influential religion. Since early in its history, it was divided into two major sects, the Shi'a and the Sunni. The Shi'a sect is found predominantly in Iraq, Bahrain and Iran, but also forms a significant minority in most other states and has a number of sub-sects (for example, Imami, Isma'illi and Zaidi). In addition, there are a number of Islamic heterodox and offshoot sects, which include the Druze, Ibadhi (modern Kharijite), Alawi and Ali-Ilahi/Ahl-I Haqq. With the overthrow of the Pahlavi dynasty in Iran in 1979, Shi'ism has risen to global political prominence. The Khomeini administration dismantled the last remnant of what was perceived as a Western-style and repressive monarchy. In its place, Iran was transformed into an Islamic republic in accordance with the Shi'ite school of thought.

It is the Sunni sect of Islam that predominates. This sect represents 90 percent of all Muslims in the world, and is the principal faith of Egypt, Syria, Jordan, the Arabian Peninsula, Turkey and the Maghrib. The Sunni branch of Islam is further divided into four schools of law: the Hanifite, the Malikite, the Shafi'ite and the Hanbalite. Each of these schools has its own distinct interpretation of scripture and tradition in forming the *corpus juris*; but there is agreement on the fundamentals.

Members of the Coptic Church in Egypt and the Greek Orthodox Church in Syria and Lebanon constitute the largest Christian sects found in the Middle East

in terms of number of followers. In addition, there are small groups of Nest
and Armenian and Syrian Orthodox scattered throughout the region. Orig.
the Coptic Church evolved in Alexandria, the Greek Orthodox in Constantin
and the Syrian or Jacobite in Antioch. The Roman Catholic Church is curre
represented in the Middle East by various Uniate churches, including Greek
Catholic, Coptic Catholic, Syrian Catholic and Chaldean, which first arose in
Rome.

The Jewish faith is the third most significant religion in the Middle East and,
aside from traces of the lost Samaritan and Daraite sects, generally follows the
traditional canons set forth by an orthodox rabbinate Judaism. The principal
canonical scripture is the Torah. Although there is disagreement over the precise
number of divisions in Judaism, it can be broadly divided into two major sects:
Orthodox and Reform. Jewish communities can be found in most Middle Eastern
states, but since 1948 the largest concentrations are in Israel. The creation of the
State of Israel may be viewed as a product of the politicization of Judaism in the
form of a national movement called Zionism.

Smaller religious communities are also scattered throughout the region,
including the Zoroastrians and the Baha'i in Iran, the Yazidi in northern Iraq, and
the Mandaens in southern Iraq and Khuzestan Province in Iran. In addition, there
is a host of more obscure religions and cults. Furthermore, the modern Middle East
has a significant history of secular tendencies and orientations, in which religious
identity is either discarded entirely or subjugated to ideological or ethnic identity.

The Middle East, while diverse in religious terms, is Muslim-majority in all
countries but Israel, and has an Islamized culture and history. This is most
prominent in artistic and intellectual traditions. The Islamic expansion from the
seventh century onwards resulted in an empire and a civilization that was notably
creative in art and architecture, calligraphy, philosophy, natural and physical
sciences. Islamic advances in these fields passed to Europe through Spain under
the Arabs in the Middle Ages. Muslim philosophers expanded upon Aristotelian
logic (abstract deductive thinking) and practiced Sufism (self-illumination) and
experimental learning (inductive thinking). With the break up and eventual eclipse
of the empire, empiricism receded and the Muslim powers became intellectually
uncritical. While Muslims fell into a religious torpor under Ottoman rule, empirical
learning, creative criticism and the development of technology were proceeding
at pace in Europe.

In the contemporary Middle East, Islamic activism has served to mobilize
populations for various ends, including resistance to imperialism. Since the 1967
Arab–Israeli war, Islamic activists have increasingly been the vanguard of anti-
Israel activity, including armed opposition. This is chiefly embodied in the
examples of Hamas in Palestine and Hizbollah in Lebanon. Conversely, Arab
regimes have manipulated Islamic justifications to perpetuate their rule and justify
unpopular measures; this trend is most notable in Saudi Arabia, where the official
'Ulama have served an explicitly political role, providing religious cover for the
regime's political preferences. At the societal level, Islamic political movements,
typified by the Muslim Brotherhood, have emerged as unofficial oppositions to

the ossified Arab regimes. However, given their social power, they are indulged by most of those regimes.

In practice, the ethnoreligious diversity of the Middle East has produced divergent outcomes. In the case of religiously oriented regimes, Islamic governance has engendered some degree of folk sectarian discrimination, with Saudi Arabia representing an extreme case. Ruled by an austere and heterodox form of Sunni Islam, since its inception Saudi Arabia has been at odds with the predominantly Shi'a populations of the al Hasa and Qatif regions, who have frequently been cast as pawns of Iran. In a different vein, the religious divisions of Lebanon, formalized with the 1943 "national pact," created an explicitly confessional state; the infusion of Palestinian refugees in 1948 further upset the ethnoreligious composition of society. The predominance of sectarian politics in Lebanon, institutionalized under the confessional system of governance, propelled continuous social conflict, up to and including civil war, as in 1975–1990.

As an exclusionary Jewish state, Israel represents an exceptional case. Established under the auspices of Zionist ideology in 1948, the State of Israel was built on the displacement of the indigenous Palestinian population. This has resulted in a state and society strained by contradictions: democratic rights for those granted Israeli citizenship, itself stratified along ethnic lines (Ashkenazi, Mizrahi, Beta Israel (Ethiopian Jews), Druze Israeli, Arab Israeli and so on) versus the captive peoples of the Palestinian territories, who have lived under military occupation and socioeconomic domination. The creation of Israel and the mass expulsion of Palestinians have had a permanent effect on regional politics, creating restive and second-class refugee populations – particularly in Jordan and Lebanon – and driving an unending process of regional militarization.

Finally, there is Iraq. After fourteen months of military occupation, initiated in 2003, the United States established a nominally democratic regime. In a condition of military occupation and social deconstruction, however, the so-called state in fact represents an engineered pastiche of ethnosectarian interests. Plagued by rampaging sectarian militias and occupying Anglo-American troops, the social fabric of Iraq has been torn asunder, with estimates of civilian fatalities ranging as high one million-plus; as many as two million external refugees; and 1.7 million internally displaced persons. Compounding the human tragedy of contemporary Iraq is the shadow of its potential. Over the course of the twentieth century, the process of state-building in Iraq followed a path of detribalization and secular nationalism. Fueled by vast national resources, the Iraqi state created health and education sectors without equal in the Arab world. Iraqi state-building, while an uneven and turbulent process, saw a state-centered national project that created a remarkable social cohesion, given the substantial diversity of the country's social mosaic.

Impact of global dynamics: patterns of change

The political dynamics set in motion at the end of the First World War by the collapse of the Ottoman Empire, on the one hand, and British/French occupation, on the other, catalyzed the process of structural social change in the Middle East.

This was manifested in two interrelated structural dynamics. First, the nominally independent states set up by the British and French imperial powers (Egypt, Iraq, Syria, Lebanon) had, at best, fragile legitimacy and authority among their respective populations. This was because the state was a product of international fabrication and British/French imposition, not of indigenous political processes. Thus, from the outset, there was an underlying tension between state and society. In these fabricated states, political elites were empowered by Western symbols of state sovereignty rather than by indigenous cultural symbols of social legitimacy.[2]

Second, the fabricated states established by Britain and France invested rural-based tribal and feudal elites with political authority mediated by external power. Closely related to this, the central mechanism of economic development was tied to the external markets of British and French imperialism, effectively marginalizing locally and regionally oriented economic elites, based primarily in urban centers. Thus, in the economic and political spheres, rural-based elites that were oriented toward Western economic and political institutions displaced the old-guard, urban-based elites of the Ottoman era.[3]

The structural tension between state and society, on the one hand, and between urban-based and rural-based elites, on the other, essentially bifurcated Arab societies into two solitudes: one, the segmented tribal-rural insular-oriented social systems cut off from each other and from the main flow of world history; the other, urban-based outer world-oriented social systems populated with a heterogeneous mix of disaffected old-guard elites; an emerging middle class of state functionaries, professionals and military staff; and a budding working class largely composed of marginalized peasantry immigrating into the urban centers for work.[4] Caught in the main currents of world history following the First World War – collapse of the Ottoman Empire and the retrenchment of Western imperialism – Cairo, Beirut, Baghdad and Damascus became centers where the ideas of modernity, independence, sovereignty, development, tradition, imperialism and exploitation were all juxtaposed against each other. It was in this tumultuous environment of ideas that the principles of liberation and development took root in the popular political culture of urban society.

The dynamics that were inherited in the aftermath of the First World War, and developed thereafter, form the contemporary system of the Arab state. Iran, Israel and Turkey – while integrally connected to the "Arab world" – themselves are not "Arab states"; nor do their histories follow the same trajectory. Modern Iran, save for a brief period during the Second World War, escaped direct colonial control, though it has scarcely been free of imperialist interventions (i.e. Operation Ajax and the overthrow of the Mossadegh government). Subsequently, the Western-backed Pahlavi dynasty collapsed under popular opposition, culminating with the Islamic revolution in 1979 under Ayatollah Khomeini. Current-day Iran represents a fusion of clerical rule (Velayet-e Faqih) and quasi-democratic elements. Outside the orbit of direct Western control, Iran currently represents the United States' primary competitor for hegemony in the region.

Likewise, in the aftermath of the First World War, Turkey represented an independent state under the leadership of Mustafa Kemal Ataturk and the Young

Turk movement, which – save for occasional military interventions and ethnic tension vis-à-vis Armenians and Kurds – has largely functioned as a secular democratic state. Modern Turkey, in both geography and self-conception, is a corridor between the Arab/Muslim world and Europe. This attempt at civilizational and socioeconomic fusion has engendered ideological/identity soul-searching and political conflict. Geostrategically, Turkey is a member of NATO and hopes to join the EU; hence it is solidly within the Western orbit of influence.

Finally, Israel came into being as an independent state in 1948 under the banner of Zionism, at the expense of mass displacement of the indigenous Palestinian population. Because of this displacement, Israel represents the nemesis of the Arab world. Its military prowess and massive support from Western powers have reinforced its isolation in the region as a colonial-settler regime. Israel is the primary recipient of US military/economic aid and, as such, represents an outpost of Western power and influence within the region.

It is useful to draw a distinction between political culture (representing the political values, norms and interests manifest in a society) and political discourse (representing the political values, norms and interests of the state) to identify how the principles of liberation and development catalyzed the dynamic of change in the Middle East. The distinction helps to identify the contradiction between political culture and political discourse manifest in the notion of the nation state. The idea of the sovereign state was manifest in political discourse, a discourse invested by imperialism. However, it was the notion of a sovereign nation state that gained widespread appeal in the robust political culture of the cities, especially among the nascent intelligentsia who vigorously debated the liberal, socialist, communist and nationalist ideas current in world affairs.[5] Already ingrained in Islamic culture was the principle of social justice and assumption of government responsibility for the social welfare of the Ummah (community).[6] For social activists, the young intelligentsia, and the budding middle and working classes, the construction of social equity had both cultural legitimacy and broad appeal as a means of nation-building in states fragmented by social inequity and inequality. It was in this context that the call for liberation and development fueled the dynamic of change throughout the region.

With the onset of the oil age, particularly post-First World War, the Middle East emerged as a preeminent strategic concern of the imperialist powers, where the Western powers provided the region's oil-rich sheikhdoms and kingdoms (Iraq, Iran, Saudi Arabia and the Gulf) with a security guarantee in exchange for the uninterrupted flow of oil. With the advent of the Cold War in the wake of the Second World War, oil production in the Middle East soon overshadowed any other global concerns with the region. For the industrialized nations in general, the uninterrupted supply of energy became a major concern. Writing in 1968, the preeminent American diplomat-scholar John S. Badeau observed, "The first and foremost [interest of America] is that the Middle East, or any part of it, shall not be occupied or controlled by a foreign power hostile to the United States and the free world. Such a power could either deny oil a passage to the West, or use access to them as diplomatic blackmail to force changes in Western policy."[7]

The oil cartel and the rise of the Organization of the Petroleum Exporting Countries (OPEC) in the aftermath of the 1973 Arab–Israeli War created a profoundly heightened and intensified interest in the region. Because Middle Eastern oil is key to the economy of the industrial world, and is a basic global resource, its continued availability is of vital economic and strategic importance. This strategic concern, which emanated from the dynamics of the Cold War, remains relevant in the post-Cold War era vis-à-vis rising powers that might challenge US regional hegemony (i.e. China or a European economic/political bloc). More importantly, however, US hegemony – and hence unfettered access to Middle East oil – is being challenged by popular insurgent movements and anti-US trends, as well as by Iran, which has emerged as a possible regional hegemon in the aftermath of the US invasion and occupation of Iraq in 2003.

As Table 1.1 illustrates, the US and its major Western allies account for more than 50 percent of global oil consumption, while the Middle East, which produced nearly 30 percent of oil and natural gas in the same years, consumed only 7.3 percent. The accumulation of petrodollars by the region's oil-producing countries has engendered lucrative economic opportunities, especially for the advanced industrialized nations. Consequently, the expansion of trade and commerce with the Middle East became increasingly important for the oil-consuming nations of the West.

The concentration of large oil reserves in the Middle East – proven reserves in 2007 of 755.3 billion barrels, 61 percent of the world's total[8] – and the questions of energy security and access have imposed vital political and strategic importance on the Middle East. The United States has considered the safety of the oil supply from the Gulf as a vital national security concern since the 1970s, establishing a

Table 1.1 World oil production and consumption (thousands of barrels/day), 2007

Region	Total	% Total
World	81,533 (production) 85,220 (consumption)	100.0
North America	13,665 (production) 25,024 (consumption)	16.8 (production) 28.7 (consumption)
Europe & Eurasia	17,835 (production) 20,100 (consumption)	21.9 (production) 24 (consumption)
China	3,743 (production) 7,855 (consumption)	4.6 (production) 9.3 (consumption)
Middle East	25,176 (production) 6,203 (consumption)	30.9 (production) 7.4 (consumption)
Japan	5,051 (consumption)	5.8 (consumption)
Africa	10,318 (production) 2,955 (consumption)	12.6 (production) 3.5 (consumption)

Source: Christof Ruhl, *BP Statistical Review of World Energy* (London: British Petroleum, June 2008).

permanent military presence in the region – first with Iran, then Iraq, and throughout this period with Saudi Arabia – which expanded greatly during and after the Gulf War of 1990–91; and henceforth, reached a crescendo with the invasion of Iraq in 2003, described as this century's "first resource war" by David King, formerly the British government's chief scientific advisor.[9]

While the United States is not directly dependent on Middle Eastern oil, which provides less than one-third of American domestic consumption, the preeminence of Middle Eastern producers within OPEC gives the region a dominant role in setting global prices and worldwide supply, upon which the US economy ultimately hinges. Consequently, the United States maintains a tight commercial and military grip on Middle Eastern oil, to protect the interests of its allies, ensuring the supply of energy to American commercial ventures, and to sustain the coherence of the world capitalist system, which depends upon the stability of oil supply.

Oil production in the Middle East continues apace, though worldwide demand might eventually outpace supply, barring significant developments in alternative energy. In 1963 Middle East crude oil production was recorded at 6.8 million barrels per day (mb/d). By 1973, this figure had tripled to 21 mb/d. Four years later, crude oil production reached 22.1 mb/d. Although production plummeted to a low of 9.7 mb/d in 1985 – as a result of the Iran–Iraq War as well as OPEC cuts in production in an attempt to stabilize collapsing prices – it jumped to 12.3 mb/d the following year. Thereafter, the upward trend continued – with a brief hiatus for the 1990 Gulf crisis[10] – reaching 21.6 mb/d in 2002 and 25.3 mb/d in 2005, before settling at 25.1 mb/d in 2007.[11]

The onset of the oil age in the Middle East has brought tremendous wealth, but it has also had profound effects on the economic and political structures in the region, namely in the fostering of vast state apparatuses whose predominance – at the expense of non-state forces – is seen in national economies, civil society and the labor sector. The intensity of this dynamic varies from country to country, though all are subject to these political and economic forces. The paradigmatic example of Kuwait is revealing. The private sector in Kuwait is limited by Kuwaiti law; and, as of 2008, it contributed only 30 percent to the country's GDP. Between 2005 and 2008, oil revenue represented, on average, approximately 90 percent of public revenue (in 2008, it was 93 percent). Finally, as with other major oil-producing states in the Gulf, Kuwait maintains a dualistic labor market, representing nationals versus expatriates; in 2009, just 40 percent of Kuwait's labour force was made up of Kuwaiti nationals.[12] The treatment and restriction of the rights of foreign laborers (largely from South Asia) are persistent problems in the Gulf Arab states, though some – notably Kuwait – have recently attempted to reform their labor laws.

Studying Middle East politics

The approach to the Middle East used by this text considers the long-term trends in Middle East politics and society more revealing than a straight chronology. The patterns of politics in the contemporary Middle East are: historical inheritance and burden – i.e. how successive encounters with imperialism shaped the Middle Eastern states and subsequent resistance; and the factor of Islam – which, while not providing complete explanation for political phenomena, colors the cultural and moral backdrop within which Middle Eastern politics operate.

These patterns were background factors in the dynamics of state-building in Middle Eastern politics throughout the twentieth century. In the twenty-first century, however, they are increasingly in disarray as the American occupation of Iraq has unleashed a political sectarian narrative – previously mollified through an ethic of secular nation-building – in Iraq and across the region. Moreover, the collapse of Arab nationalism as a governing ideology, the failure of the Arab states to resolve the Palestinian crisis – particularly in light of the 2008 Israeli assault on Gaza – and the failure of the governing to address the socioeconomic crises of the governed have additionally contributed to the delegitimization of the Arab state system, inviting challenge from popular forces (notably Islamists).

While the overriding patterns of Middle Eastern politics have remained, there is the threat of regional disruption and collapse, the consequences of which are scarcely clear. This threat, a great regional revision, lurks throughout this discussion of the region. In the last decade, the Middle East has been beset by a series of calamities: the continuing failure to engineer a humane settlement on the Israeli–Palestinian front, culminating in the 2008 destruction of Gaza; the consequential delegitimization of the Arab state system; the Iraqi disaster; and so forth.

Notes

1 Dan Smith, *The State of the Middle East: An Atlas of Conflict and Resolution* (Berkeley: University of California Press, 2006), p. 114.
2 George Lenczowski, "Radical Regimes in Egypt, Syria and Iraq: Some Comparative Observations on Ideologies and Practices," *Journal of Politics*, Vol. 28, No. 1 (1966), pp. 28–29; Percy Cox, *The Letters of Gertrude Bell* (London: Ernest Benn, 1927), II, pp. 523–525; and Zaki Sâlih, *Muqdamah fi Tarikh al-Iraq al-Mua'sir al-Iraq* (Baghdad: al-Rabitah Press, 1955), pp. 48–78.
3 Laith 'Abdul Hasan Jawad al-Zubaidi, *Thawrat 14 Tamuz 1958 fi al-'Iraq* (Baghdad: Dar al-Rashid, 1979), pp. 29–38; and Lenczowski, op. cit., pp. 28–29.
4 Tareq Y. Ismael, *Government and Politics of the Contemporary Middle East* (Homewood: Dorsey Press, 1970), pp. 100–121; and Manfred Halpern, *The Politics of Social Change in the Middle East and North Africa* (Princeton: Princeton University Press, 1963).
5 Tareq Ismael, *The Rise and Fall of the Communist Party of Iraq* (Cambridge: Cambridge University Press, 2007), pp. 1–59.
6 Majid Khadduri, *The Islamic Conception of Justice* (Baltimore: Johns Hopkins University Press, 1984); and Sayyid Qutb, *Sayyid Qutb and Islamic Activism: A Translation and Critical Analysis of Social Justice in Islam* (Leiden: E.J. Brill, 1996).
7 John S. Badeau, *The American Approach to the Arab World* (New York: Harper and Row, 1968), p. 22.
8 Christof Ruhl, *BP Statistical Review of World Energy* (London: British Petroleum, June 2008).

9   James Randerson, "David King: Iraq Was the First 'Resource War' of the Century," *Guardian*, February 12, 2009. URL: http://www.guardian.co.uk/environment/2009 /feb/12/king-iraq-resources-war.

10 Financial Times, *Oil and Gas International Yearbook* (London: Longman, 1995).

11 Ruhl, , op. cit.

12 Fahed Al Rasheed, et al., *Kuwait Competitiveness Report: 2008–2009* (Kuwait: Kuwait University, 2009); *CIA World Factbook: Kuwait* (2010). URL: https://www.cia.gov/ library/publications/the-world-factbook/geos/ku.html.

Further reading

The following represent general works on the Middle East, seminal works that serve as primers for the study of the region, as well as *sui generis* studies of the Middle East. These texts are works that should serve as: introductions for beginning students and reference guides for more experienced readers in the field; geographical surveys of the Middle East region; and methodological critiques of the Middle East as a field of study.

First, Dan Smith's *The State of the Middle East: An Atlas of Conflict* is a highly attractive and useful overview of conflict phenomena in the Middle East, drawn along axes including the legacy of imperialism, conflicts related to ethnicity and religion, resource management, including oil and water, and other factors. An essential and visual overview of the contemporary Middle East. As a comprehensive reference source, Dean, Holman and Canton's *The Middle East and North Africa 2009* is immensely useful – a massive, encyclopedic work detailing all aspects of the Middle East and North Africa.

Ewan Anderson and William Fisher's *Middle East: Geography and Geopolitics* is an update of Fisher's well-regarded 1978 work and provides an overview of the geography of the Middle East and its relationship to conflict. Ewan and Liam Anderson's *An Atlas of Middle Eastern Affairs* is a continuation of these themes, with commentary on the geopolitical concerns of water resources, the petroleum industry, conflict and boundary issues, and detailed analyses of the countries of the Middle East. Stephen Hemsley Longrigg's *The Middle East: A Social Geography*, though dated, remains a useful overview of the social, geographic and religious nature of the region, with additional commentary on industry, agriculture and climate. J. Malcolm Wagstaff's *The Evolution of Middle Eastern Landscapes* covers similar ground and is likewise useful.

For anthropological and cultural inquiries, Dale Eickelman's *The Middle East: An Anthropological Approach* is a dense and comprehensive synthesis of the extensive anthropological research on the Middle East and covers a breadth of topics. Also, Halim Barakat's *The Arab World: Society, Culture, and State* is useful as a provocative and critical reflection on the state of the Middle East, at the levels of culture, religion and society.

With relation to the Middle East as a field of study, Edward Said's *Orientalism* remains of profound import and is a critical inquiry into the nature of academic study, literature, power and discourse concerning the Middle East. Said continues to explore these themes in *Covering Islam*, a critical inquiry into the representation of Islam in Western media, academia and culture. Together, these represent the primary texts of methodological criticism of the field of Middle East studies.

References

Anderson, Ewan & Anderson, Liam (2009) *An Atlas of Middle Eastern Affairs*, University Paperbacks.

Anderson, Ewan & Fisher, William Bayne (2000) *Middle East: Geography and Geopolitics*, Routledge Press.

Barakat, Halim (1993) *The Arab World: Society, Culture, and State*, University of California Press.

Dean, Lucy, Holman, Catriona Appeatu & Canton, Ellen (eds) (2009) *The Middle East and North Africa 2009* (55th Edition), Europa Publications.

Eickelman, Dale (2001) *The Middle East: An Anthropological Approach* (4th Edition), Prentice-Hall.

Longrigg, Stephen Hemsley (1963) *The Middle East: A Social Geography*, Walter de Gruyter.

Said, Edward (1978) *Orientalism*, Vintage.

—— (1997) *Covering Islam* (Revised Edition), Vintage.

Smith, Dan (2008) *The State of the Middle East: An Atlas of Conflict* (2nd Edition), Earthscan Publications.

Wagstaff, J. Malcolm (1985) *The Evolution of Middle Eastern Landscapes*, Rowman & Littlefield.

Part I

Dynamics in Middle East politics

2 The burden of history

From empire to nation states

Although historians disagree over the exact location of the birthplace of civilization, they do agree that it originated in the Middle East, either in the Nile Valley or in Mesopotamia, along the Tigris and Euphrates rivers.[1] Historically, the area has been the crossroads of migrating peoples. Successive invasions of the Middle East, occurring between approximately 5000 BCE and the Roman conquest, helped to create a melting pot of races and cultures. The first of the invaders, the Sumerians, established city states between the Tigris and the Euphrates. Their agriculture-based social structure led to the growth of towns and more complex social organizations. Their advanced agricultural techniques allowed for sufficient surpluses to sustain large urban populations in the immediate area. Urbanization led to further innovations in terms of culture and governance. The Sumerians' technical achievements were matched by their cultural production, the most significant of which was the first known work of literature: the tale of Gilgamesh, ruler of Uruk.

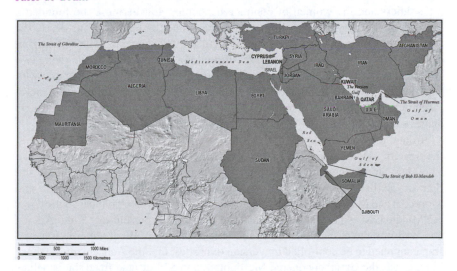

Map 2.1 The Arab world

Drawn by Ian Cool

The prosperity of these city states attracted Semitic peoples from the surrounding areas who founded the state of Akkad along the middle Euphrates around the beginning of the third millennium BCE. For a thousand years, Sumerian and Akkadian states competed with each other. The threat of outside invasion by the non-Semitic Elamites resulted in the unification of all Mesopotamia by Hammurabi of Babylon in about 1700 BCE. During this period, the Hamites, forming a monarchical state in the Nile Valley, were able to remain relatively undisturbed until about 500 BCE, when the Persians invaded Egypt and established an empire. Meanwhile, Semitic tribes from Arabia continued to fill the area between Sumeria and the Nile, establishing communities in the area known as the Fertile Crescent.[2]

From 1700 to 100 BCE, successive invasions brought waves of conquerors, each of whom extended the empire of their predecessor. Thus, the Persians, by 500 BCE, were able to establish an empire bordered by the Indus River, the Black Sea and the eastern border of Egypt. The Persian Empire, a monarchical state, was effectively administered by satraps in its territorial subdivisions, and by the use of spies who watched the satraps and reported directly to the emperor. The Persians also built a highway, the Royal Road, from Sardis on the Aegean Sea to their capital at Susa. This road was regularly policed, which facilitated East–West trade and ensured communication within the empire.

One of the major threats facing the Persian Empire was the expansionist tendency of the Greek city states. Ultimately, the failure to control the growth of Greek power was to have a dramatic impact upon the development of the Middle East. The conquests of Alexander the Great ushered in a new age for Greece and for the peoples of this ancient region. It had been Alexander's wish to blend the cultures of Greece and Persia. Before his death in 323 BCE, he was partially successful in Hellenizing the Middle East by encouraging intermarriage between his soldiers and the women of conquered peoples. Furthermore, he founded a number of cities styled after those of Greece. None the less, after his death, the empire broke up into a series of kingdoms ruled by his generals. The Hellenizing effects of his conquests were, however, more long-lasting. For the following two centuries under the Seleucid kings (named for Seleucus, the Greek general who founded the dynasty) and the Ptolemaic dynasty in Egypt (after the general Ptolemy), the Middle East continued to be an area rich in intellectual and artistic achievements, though it remained politically unstable.

Around the first century BCE, the Romans – then the most powerful people in the western Mediterranean – began to extend their influence into the Middle East. They had already conquered North Africa from the Semitic Carthaginians and Semitic–Berber native dynasties in Numidia (modern-day Libya, Algeria and Morocco) and Mauritania. Eventually, the Romans established political control over the Middle East as far east as Damascus, as far south as present-day Saudi Arabia, and well into the eastern portion of modern-day Turkey. What are now Iraq and Iran continued to be controlled by Persian dynasties, first the Achaemenids, whose king, Cyrus the Great, conquered Mesopotamia in 539 BC and freed the Israelites from Babylonian captivity; then the Parthians (*c*.200 BCE–220 CE); and finally the Sassanids (220 CE–637 CE). The eastern portion of the Roman Empire was very influential, with Alexandria in Egypt, Antioch in Syria and Caesarea in modern-day Israel noted as centers of learning and commerce.

Roman control of the Middle East, however, was rarely tranquil. The first centuries of occupation witnessed large-scale uprisings and continuous conflict with the Parthians and Sassanids. The furthest point of Roman expansion came in the early second century CE, when Emperor Trajan's armies plunged into Mesopotamia (modern Iraq). After a long period of civil war and repeated barbarian invasions, from the early fourth century onward the Roman Empire was divided into two portions: the Western Empire, with its capital at Rome; and the more affluent, populous and secure Eastern Empire, with its capital at Constantinople (modern Istanbul). The Western Empire collapsed from the combined pressure of a German invasion and internal dissent in the late fifth century: the last emperor in Rome was deposed in 476 CE by a Gothic warlord, Odovacar. The Eastern Empire survived and prospered. Its population primarily spoke Greek, and had adopted the Christian faith. Over time, the Eastern Empire transformed itself into the Byzantine Empire.

It might have been expected that the spread of Christianity throughout the Roman Empire would have brought unity in its wake, but it did not. From Constantinople to North Africa, each area developed its own sect of the religion, often closely related to indigenous culture and language. Christianity also developed a following outside the empire, in the Parthian and Sassanid lands. These Christians, mostly of the Nestorian sect, formed an influential group in Persia from the fourth century until the Muslim armies completed their conquest of Sassanid Persia in 637 CE. It has been suggested that the later Sassanid Empire was predominantly Christian, despite an overt attachment to the ancient Persian Zoroastrian religion.

The Byzantine and Sassanid empires were bitter rivals in the sixth and early seventh centuries CE. In 603, Khusro II Aparwez's Persian armies, ostensibly to intervene in a Byzantine dynastic struggle, marched across the Fertile Crescent and captured the great city of Antioch in 613. Jerusalem fell the following year, and Egypt was conquered in 619. Thus, the Persian army was virtually at the gates of Constantinople by 620. The Byzantine counterstrike, led by Emperor Heraclius, pushed deep into Persian territory to loot cities, towns and the estates of the Persian nobility. Ironically, Heraclius impoverished his own empire by pursuing this invasion. In the end, the war devastated the disputed territories: cities were left half deserted; harsh taxes stripped the wealth of the remaining people; and the Persian dynasty lost most of its armed might. Meanwhile, the Byzantines recaptured razed territory that produced no revenue and their finances were so depleted that they had to melt down the holy golden relics of their great churches in order to pay their mercenaries and Caucasian allies. Then the Muslim armies from the Arabian Peninsula plunged into this morass of political and religious strife.

Islam and the Islamic empire

By the seventh century, Mecca was the principal trade and cultural center of the Arabian Peninsula. It had become a wealthy and independent city and had achieved its eminent position by trade and through financial speculation in the Red Sea and eastern Mediterranean. The city maintained good relations with the tribes in the surrounding area but carefully kept itself neutral in the conflicts between the warring Sassanid and Byzantine empires through skillful diplomacy and able leadership. The city government consisted of a council of clan leaders, though each clan was independent of the council and responsible only to itself. There was a great breadth of religion in Mecca, from magic to pantheism. The Arabian Peninsula was rife with tribal rivalry and constant raiding.

In 610 Mohammad Ibn Abdullah, a forty-year-old native of Mecca, began preaching a monotheistic strand of Abrahamic belief called Islam in this chaotic environment. His message emphasized faith and trust in an all-merciful and all-powerful God. Initially, his movement drew converts mainly from the ranks of the poor. Although there were no defined religious prescriptions, the Meccan ruling elite was wary of the prophetic calling of Mohammad. To submit to the will of one sovereign God implied a divesting of political and economic privileges and a transformation of society as a whole. Accordingly, economic sanctions were imposed on the new converts, who became known as Muslims. Against a tide of persecution, the Prophet sent many of his followers to Christian Abyssinia (Ethiopia) until the hostile climate abated. However, as conditions in Mecca deteriorated, Mohammad regrouped the Meccan Muslims and led them to migrate to Medina in 622. Medina had invited Mohammad and his followers and accepted the Prophet as an arbitrator of clan conflict; he proceeded to consolidate his position and became the undisputed leader of the first Islamic city state. This migration, called the Hijra, became the first year of the Islamic calendar. Eight years of intermittent hostilities with Mecca ensued until finally Mohammad and the Muslims were able to return victorious. During this hostile period, Islam began to spread throughout the Arabian Peninsula and the social precepts of this new order were developed.

From the death of the Prophet Mohammad in 632 until the establishment of the Umayyad dynasty at Damascus in 661, the leading men of Mecca and Medina chose the Muslim leader or *khalifah* (caliph, or "successor"). Each of the four leaders chosen in this period – Abu Bakr, 'Umar, 'Uthman and 'Ali – presided over both religious and temporal affairs. During their years in power, these four leaders succeeded in entrenching Islam in the Arabian Peninsula and, with relatively little military effort, wrested the lands of modern Syria, Palestine, Egypt, Iraq and Iran from the Byzantine and Sassanid empires. The remnants of the Roman Empire, reconquered by the Byzantines, simply collapsed under the combined weight of the Muslim religious and military advance. Antioch fell in 637, followed by Alexandria in 642 and then a rebuilt Carthage (in what is now Tunisia) in 698. The Muslims and Byzantines remained implacable enemies for the next eight centuries, with only Constantinople standing between Islam and Europe, often defeating Islamic armies at its very gates. The Persians fought fiercely, but had nowhere to retreat after the Battle of Qadesiya in 637, where the rest of the Persian military nobility was crushed. Consequently, the Sassanid Empire had disappeared by the later half of the seventh century. Thus, the Islamic Empire became preeminent in the region.

During the reign of the third caliph, 'Uthman Ibn 'Affan (644–656), the Umayyad clan possessed considerable political clout once 'Uthman gave them governorships in the four principal provinces of the Islamic Empire (Basra, Kufa, Syria and Egypt), while saving the position of main counselor for his cousin, Marawan Ibn al-Hakam. 'Uthman's appointments were viewed by many in the Muslim community as nepotism and favoritism, acts that Islam formally decries. Social unrest eventually led to 'Uthman's assassination and 'Ali Ibn Abi Talib, Mohammad's cousin, becoming his successor in 661. After the subsequent assassination of 'Ali in 661, Mu'awia, from the Umayyad family, seized control of the Caliphate and established a dynasty with its base in Syria. This was to last for nearly a century.

The Umayyads left four marks on the Islamic world: they moved the imperial capital to Damascus; they enlarged the empire to include North Africa, Spain and parts of Asia; they reorganized and improved the imperial administration; and they changed the elective Caliphate to a hereditary monarchical system. The Umayyads at first partitioned the empire into five vice-royalties ruled by appointees; but due to the lack of qualified Arabs, they left the administration of each of these areas in the hands of pre-conquest administrators.

During the last half of the Umayyads' reign, however, the Middle East was again torn apart by civil strife, and charges of corruption were made against the Damascene rulers. In 750, Abu al-Abbas overthrew the Umayyads and founded the Abbasid dynasty. The Umayyads, however, retained control of Spain, which was the furthest Islamic advance into Western Europe. In 732, the Franks, under Charles Martel, halted the Muslim armies in what is now southern France. Fifteen years earlier, the Byzantines had defeated a Muslim fleet in the harbor of Constantinople, halting expansion to the northeast.

Following their rise to power, the Abbasids moved the capital to a new location, later named Baghdad. Establishing a system of *wazirs* (viziers), they ruled their steadily dwindling dominions, marking the return of Persian influence in the Middle East. While the Sassanids had fallen from power in Persia, the Persian language survived and became an integral part of the Abbasid court as Persian nobility and culture formed the backbone of the governing class.[3] Additionally, the disintegration of empire led to the establishment of an independent state in Morocco in 788, followed by subsequent gambits for independence across North Africa, including Tunisia around 800. Finally, in the tenth century, the Fatimids of Egypt established a western Muslim polity that stretched from Syria to the Straits of Gibraltar. In the East, all Muslim provinces in and near India fell away from Baghdad's control. In the eleventh century, the eastern Seljuk Turk invaders seized the last of the Abbasid Empire. However, a rich culture developed concurrently with the political decline of the Abbasids. Noteworthy contributions were made to philosophy and poetry, and a distinct Abbasid style of architecture developed, featuring tall minarets with complex geometrical designs. In this cultural milieu, the works of Greek scholars were translated, studied and supplemented, and original and lasting contributions were made to medicine, astronomy and geography.

In the eleventh century both the Seljuk and the Fatimid empires began to fragment into various minor states. Disunited and vulnerable, they stood by helplessly as Christian crusaders from Western Europe occupied Syria and Palestine during the twelfth century. However, Salah-al-Din al-Ayyubi (Saladin) succeeded in regrouping the splintered Muslim world, starting with Egypt and proceeding on to Syria, northern Iraq, Hijaz, Nubia and then to North Africa, thus extending his influence from the Nile to the Tigris. Disunity re-emerged after his death, however, and the crusaders regained territory that they were able to hold until the Mamluks, warrior slaves of different ethnic backgrounds, gained firm control of Egypt and established a feudal system as the new order in the region. However, as the Mamluks were driving the crusaders from the Middle East, a new threat emerged. Mongol hordes under Genghis Khan and his successors invaded from the East, conquering territories as far south as Damascus. They were finally defeated and repulsed from Syria by the Mamluk rulers of Egypt in 1260. However, the conquests of the Mongolian Turks, led by Timur Leng (Tamerlane), in the last part of the fourteenth century ended Mamluk control east of Egypt, resulting in a diminished Turkic state in Asia Minor, and a weak and dismembered Persia.

Of all the invasions of the Muslim world, the Western onslaught – the crusades – left an indelible stain on the collective memory of the Muslim people. Indeed, the term "crusader" remains a political epithet in Muslim political discourse, reappearing during the Arab independence movement in the twentieth century, the pan-Arabist movements of the 1950s and 1960s, and is replete in contemporary Islamist and secular discourse.

The Ottoman Empire and European involvement

From the time of the Seljuk invasions onward, the Turks dominated the Middle East, largely at the expense of the Byzantines. By the latter half of the twelfth century, the Seljuk sultanate in Asia Minor and the holdings of Salah-al-Din included the greater part of Muslim lands. The Mongol invasions, however, destroyed both. By approximately 1300 CE, Osman, a Turkish chieftain, had begun to consolidate, by conquest and alliance, numerous small towns in Asia Minor.[4] Although Osman died in 1324, the Ottoman Turks continued to expand their sphere of influence in the Middle East. In 1354, an earthquake destroyed the walls and fortifications of Gallipoli and thus enabled the Ottomans to cross the Dardanelles and gain a foothold in Europe. From there, aided by the mayhem created by the plague, they were able to extend their dominion into the Balkans. At the same time, they pressed south and east, establishing control over the greater part of Asia Minor. However, Tamerlane, the Turko-Mongol conqueror and founder of the Timurid Empire and dynasty, repulsed Ottoman expansion in the East. He defeated Bayezid I in 1402 at the Battle of Ankara and then conquered the West as far as the Mediterranean.[5] Rather than holding Ottoman territory directly, and in exchange for an oath of allegiance, Tamerlane divided the Ottoman conquests of Europe and the holdings of Osman and Orhan I (Osman's son) in Asia among Bayezid's sons.[6] Upon Tamerlane's death in 1405 the Ottoman emirs (leaders) asserted their independence from the Timurids (1402–1413) but the Ottoman state remained fragmented among Bayezid's four sons.[7]

A son of Bayezid, Mehmed I, reunited the Ottoman state and set it again on the path of further conquest. His grandson, Mehmed II, pushed into Hungary and southern Russia, completed the conquest of Asia Minor, and in 1453 captured Constantinople (henceforth Istanbul), laying the foundation of the Ottoman Empire. Selim I continued the conquest, adding Syria, Palestine, Egypt and Algeria, and then finally, toward the end of the seventeenth century, Tunisia, the west coast of Arabia and small holdings around the Black Sea and the Persian Gulf.[8]

The Ottoman Empire was ruled from the sultan's divan (council) in Istanbul, which met daily to make decisions on military and administrative affairs. Although the sultan was theoretically the absolute ruler of both the state and the Muslim community, local autonomy was entrenched proportionately in relation to distance from Istanbul: the longer the distance, the more autonomy. In addition, non-Muslim minorities, like Christians and the Jews, were given administrative autonomy, in conformity with earlier Islamic practice, from which an order of intercommunal cooperation evolved. Because the Turks were a minority within their vast empire, administrators were drawn from just about any source, including states outside the empire's borders. Officials could therefore be chosen on the basis of ability as well as according to loyalty to the sultan, rather than on the basis of racial or religious considerations, a process that was generally supportive of meritocracy.[9] Indeed, the corps of janissaries, the famed bodyguard of the sultans, was composed entirely of Islamized Christians.[10] Though bribery was not uncommon in the appointment of lower officials, a palace school was maintained for the education of those who might occupy high positions in government. After all, the sultan and his immediate circle of deputies had to make provisions to ensure that they were capable of ruling.

The Ottoman Empire exercised considerable influence in European affairs, partly because of encroachments into European territory and partly because of its control of East–West trade routes. As a consequence, European states and particularly their merchants had always aspired to break the Ottoman monopoly on trans-regional trade and to appropriate profits for themselves. In the second half of the fifteenth century, Portuguese expeditions reached the western coast of Africa; and beyond the sphere of Ottoman control, the Portuguese established stations that traded in spice, gold and slaves. Their considerable influence on trade was augmented by the discovery of the Cape of Good Hope when Vasco da Gama sailed around the apparent southernmost tip of Africa and reached the Indian Ocean in 1498. Spain soon followed the Portuguese to set up its own trading empire in Southeast Asia.

The discovery of the New World by Columbus in 1492 initiated the exploitation of minerals, agricultural commodities and slaves, bringing Spain incredible wealth. Soon the Dutch, the French and the British arrived to challenge the trading power of the Portuguese and to limit Spain's territorial expansion in the New World. In a contest of maritime expeditions for trade, profit and exploitation of the New

World, the Western states established a global network of trading activities, and eventually empires, throttling the Middle Eastern trans-regional trading economy that supported the Ottoman state. Additionally, the wealth extracted from the various colonies in the Americas created unprecedented capital in Western Europe, which, alongside improvements in sanitary practices, led to the elimination of various plagues. This encouraged immense population growth, especially in cities, which became powerful production and trading centers. The rapid advance of Europe and its reduced dependency upon Middle Eastern land trade routes, combined with Ottoman stagnation, altered the Ottoman economy for the worse. Inflation became common; there were recurring financial crises; and, ultimately, the Ottoman economy devolved into the exportation of raw materials to Europe and importation of manufactured goods, increasing Ottoman dependency on the West throughout the nineteenth century.[11] In addition, a combination of weak sultans, civil wars and Ottoman concessions to European states culminated in a European expansion that drove the Ottomans first from Europe and then from North Africa.

A new challenge to the Ottoman Empire's regional hegemony came about with the rise of the Safavid dynasty (1501–1722 CE) which emerged in Persia under the leadership of Ismail I and became its primary rival. They viewed one another not merely as military and political contenders, but as theological contenders. Ismail I quickly declared Shi'i Islam as the state religion and had reunited Persia by 1509. While initiated as a political institution, the Safavid dynasty had as its origins the Safaviya Sufi order founded by the mystic Safi-al-Din in the thirteenth century. However, by the time the Safavid emerged as a political movement, it had moved towards orthodox Twelver Shi'ism, confronting the dominance of the Sunni Ottomans, thus setting the foundation for Iran's status as center of Shi'ism. Under Ismail I, the Safavid dynasty saw tremendous territorial growth, extending as far as modern-day Iraq, transforming itself into an empire. The empire reached its territorial peak (including portions of modern-day Afghanistan, Turkmenistan and Uzbekistan) and under the reign of Abbas I (1587–1629), it became more centralized, initiated an expanded diplomatic campaign in Europe and experienced its most effective era of rule. Conflict between the two empires ranged from mass deportation of Shi'ites from Ottoman territories, to economic conflict and blockade, culminating in the Battle of Chaldrian (1514), which resulted in the Ottoman recaptaure of Anatolia and parts of modern-day Iraq, as well as the brief capture of the Safavid capital Tabriz.[12]

In the eighteenth century European expansion became even more evident. As governmental authority broke down in the Far and Middle East, France and Britiain sought to secure their positions in the global trade network by seizing territories in these regions. The first Ottoman defeat was at the Battle of Vienna in 1683. The resulting Treaty of Karlowitz (1699) reduced many Ottoman holdings in Central Europe, including Hungary. The territories under the control of the declining empire in Europe, North Africa and the Middle East became the preoccupation of the major European powers in their competition for greater influence and a larger share of territory after the eighteenth century.

The Anglo-Russian competition for the Ottoman territory and resources was known as the "Great Game." The Russo-Ottoman War of 1768–1774 ended in the military defeat of the Ottoman Empire and the destruction of its navy. In 1774, the Russian Empire imposed the Treaty of Kucuk Kaynarca on the Ottomans, forcing them to cede the Yedesian region that lay between the Dnieper and the Southern Bug rivers and to grant Russia access to a number of key Ottoman ports. The treaty also gave the Russian czar the right to protect Orthodox Christian Ottoman subjects.

The Russian Empire then fought two wars with Persia (1804–1813 and 1826–1828). Following Persian defeats, the Russians imposed the Treaty of Gulistan in 1813 and the Treaty of Turkmenchay in 1829. Again, the Persians surrendered vast tracts of land and sea and renounced claims on several khanates and territories while forfeiting their right to navigate in the Caspian Sea and its coasts. Furthermore, Persia granted Russia economic concessions, including war reparations and economic treaties favorable to Russian interests.

Britain also seized political power in large parts of the Far East and attempted to do the same in the Middle East. France countered in 1798 with Napoleon's expedition to Egypt. However, the defeat of the French fleet at Aboukir Bay checked French ambitions. Three years later, Napoleon withdrew his forces to Europe. This left Britain as the dominant power in the Middle East. However, the Egyptians had been impressed by the military efficiency of the French expeditionary force, so Mohammad 'Ali (1769–1849; r. 1805–1848) and his son Ibrahim Pasha (1789–1848; r. 1848) set the foundations for the modernization of Egypt. Under their leadership, Egypt rapidly expanded into the Sudan, Ethiopia, Palestine, Syria and Arabia. However, British collaboration with the Ottomans checked further expansion.

When Britain refused to modernize Egypt, Mohammad 'Ali and Ibrahim Pasha turned to France. The French responded by supplying trained administrators, military missions and assistance for the education and training of young Egyptians in French colleges. Half of Egypt's trade remained with Britain, though, and France's setback in the Franco-Prussian War of 1870–1871 meant the British remained dominant throughout the Middle East.

Nevertheless, in this era of imperial competition, the French left the most significant mark on Middle Eastern affairs. Capitalizing on a brief period of influence with the Ottoman Empire during the Crimean War, it was the French who pressed for permission to build the Suez Canal. This was granted after France secured the support of Russia and Austria. The canal opened in 1869, linking Asia with the West through the Middle East and initiating a new chapter in Middle Eastern–Western relations.

The lack of foresight and the extravagance of Mohammad 'Ali's successors in Egypt resulted in enormous indebtedness to European powers. By 1876, Egypt had already sold its shares in the Suez Canal Company to Britain. Three years later, France and Britain established *de facto* political control over Egypt to secure their investments and impose their jurisdiction over the canal. When the Egyptians resisted, the British occupied the country. British imperial authority then continued until the First World War. Although this helped reduce the Egyptian debt, the country itself did not improve materially.

Throughout the nineteenth century, the Ottoman Empire became one of the major areas of European competition. French Roman Catholics and Russian Orthodox Christians each claimed control of the Christian holy places in the Middle East. Russian expansionists wanted to secure an entrance to the Mediterranean through the Bosporus while Austria feared that Russia would outflank her from the south. Meanwhile, Britain was apprehensive about the effect Russian expansion into the Mediterranean would have upon its passage to India. In addition, both Britain and France were interested in Ottoman territory that lay astride the trade routes to their extensive commercial interests in the Orient. These nations waged a series of small wars over Ottoman territory; and while none of them managed to exert complete domination over the region, the Ottoman Empire was justifiably referred to as the "Sick Man of Europe."

In 1872 a serious threat to Anglo-French interests in Turkey appeared when the Ottomans secured German investment and engineering expertise to build the Balkan railway system. During the next thirty years, the Germans increased their influence in Turkey through the extension of the railway as well as through trade agreements. Furthermore, the discovery of oil in Persia in 1908 initiated a dramatic increase in European interest in the region because it was recognized that control over that valuable energy resource could ensure economic and military supremacy in Europe and throughout the world. In other words, oil heightened European ambitions and rivalry in the region.

Turkification and the collapse of the Ottoman Empire

The intense European intervention in the Middle East during the nineteenth century unintentionally augmented the collective sense of nationhood in the Arabo-Islamic territories, while the oppression and absolutism of the Ottoman sultan and the winds of change from Europe spurred the growth of Turkish nationalism. In 1889, students at the Istanbul Military Medical College, led by an Albanian student, Ibrahim Temo, organized the Committee of Progress and Union (CPU). This was a secret society modeled on the Italian Carbonari societies. It soon penetrated and won adherents in the Military Academy, the Naval Academy, the Artillery and Engineering School, the Veterinary School and the Civil College. With the blessing and support of the major ethnic and religious groups, the CPU led a revolution in 1908. Its objectives were the centralization of admin-istration and "Turkification" of the empire. These objectives also incited nationalist acts outside Turkey and heightened nationalism in the various urban centers of Syria and Iraq. By 1909, however, conflict within the CPU had divided its members along national lines and resulted in the growth of extremism on all sides. In the Arab world, secret societies advocating complete independence shot up everywhere. Moreover, Turkish nationalism had grown proportionately with German influence. Germany's *Drang nach Osten* (drive to the East) led to German aid in Turkish modernization, development of the Berlin–Baghdad railway, and the eventual emergence of Turkey as Germany's military ally in the First World War.

There was little combat in the Middle East during the first months of the war, but in October 1914 the British instigated a revolt in Arabia. In the correspondence between al-Sharif Hussein of Mecca and Sir Henry McMahon, British High Commissioner for Egypt and the Sudan, McMahon promised the creation of an independent Arab state at the conclusion of the war in return for an Arab revolt against their Turkish masters. The proposed state was to encompass the area demarcated to the north by a line from Alexandretta to the Iranian frontier and thence southward to the Persian Gulf, to include the entire Arabian Peninsula with the exception of Aden. Yet, at the same time, the Allies were negotiating the division of Turkish and Arab land among themselves. The Constantinople Agreement of March 1915 gave Russia the right to annex parts of Asia Minor and Thrace while guaranteeing the French and British certain interests in Turkey and Iran. In addition, the Treaty of London, signed in April 1915, satisfied Italy's territorial claims in North Africa and Asia Minor. Then, in May 1916, the secret Sykes–Picot Agreement defined the exact territories to be taken over by Russia, France and Britain, and recognized the spheres of British and French influence in the Arab territories. However, both the McMahon promises and the Sykes–Picot Agreement were undermined by the Balfour Declaration of November 2, 1917, which stated that "His Majesty's Government [of Britain] views with favour the Jewish people." Although this was not a guarantee of British support for a Jewish state, it paved the way for Zionists to start lobbying for the establishment of one in Palestine. In doing so, it set the stage for a crisis in the Middle East that lasts to this day.

Precipitated by the Young Turks' declaration of martial law in Syria and by the execution and deportation of Arab nationalists, the Arab revolt began on June 5, 1916. While hardly successful in mobilizing mass support among the local population, this rebellion was immensely helpful to the British by diverting Turkish reinforcements from the British advance through Palestine, ending German propaganda in Arabia, and forestalling the possible establishment of a German submarine base on the Red Sea coast.

Between the two World Wars

Arab assistance during the First World War had been secured with promises of an independent Arab state after its conclusion. However, the secretive nature of British negotiations and the multiple offers made to divergent interests for the same territory meant that these promises were never going to be kept. The Treaty of Sevres, which was forced on the Ottoman sultan on August 10, 1920, led him to renounce all claims to Arabia, Egypt, Mesopotamia and Syria. Britain was given a protectorate in Egypt, a mandate over Palestine, and tutelage over nominally independent Mesopotamia. Syria was placed under a French mandate. The rulers of Arabia were granted nominal independence.

So the end of the war left the Allies in possession of much of today's Turkey, which Greece occupied at the behest of the Allies until they could determine its fate. However, the Turks, led by Mustafa Kamal, raised the banner of revolt in 1920. After two years of warfare, they forced the withdrawal of the Greek occupying force. The Turks established a new government, deposed the Ottoman sultan, and voided the legislation of his government. In 1922–1923 they met the Allies at the Lausanne Conference to determine Turkey's future. This conference severed the last remnants of Ottoman rule from Turkey, leaving the Turkish Republic an independent state. In 1923 Mustafa Kamal was elected president. A year later, he declared the official dissolution of the Ottoman Caliphate. Until his death in 1938, he directed the modernization of Turkey, and encouraged the resolution of the two principal problems that had concerned foreign interests: the demarcation of the Iraqi–Turkish frontier in Mosul Province; and foreign use of the Dardanelles and the Bosporus. The first issue was resolved by awarding Mosul to Iraq, for which Turkey received £500,000 from the Iraqi government as well as a guarantee of 10 percent of all oil royalties paid to Iraq by the concessionaire for the next twenty-five years. An international agreement that allowed Turkey to fortify the straits settled the second issue.

The dismemberment of the Ottoman Empire resulted in the proliferation of nominally independent and mandatory states whose boundaries were drawn by the British and French colonial powers. This, in turn, gave rise to conflicting territorial claims: Iraq's intermittent claim to Kuwait; Syria's rejection of Lebanese independence; and the Kurdish challenge to the full sovereignty of Turkey, Iraq, Iran and Syria. Successive riots and wars followed. Despite these border disputes, though, Arab states would initiate state-building processes with varying degrees of success.

In the Fertile Crescent, the French established a governorship in Lebanon. In 1936, they agreed to make Lebanon an independent state, but later refused to sign treaties that would have granted independence. In Syria, also under French mandate, independence was again promised and later denied; and tensions arose between the French administrators and Syrian leaders over Syria's loss of Lebanon, Alexandretta and the Jabel Druze.

The British occupation of Iraq was met with such resistance that in 1921 Britain was forced to establish a nominally independent kingdom. However, full independence was not achieved until Iraq became a member of the League of Nations in 1932. Just as it is now, oil was the greatest issue in inter-war Iraqi politics.

Palestine, also occupied by the British, was torn through conflict by the competing territorial claims of the Arabs and Jews. According to the 1931 census, Arabs constituted approximately 90 percent of the population. But Jewish immigration and effective Zionist lobbying reinforced Jewish strength. Jewish settlements in Palestine flourished with the immigration of skilled European Jews and with massive financial aid from sympathizers around the world. British rule over Palestine was a failed attempt to aid the Jews while still protecting the rights of Christian and Muslim Arabs.

After the First World War, Egypt remained a British protectorate under martial law. The British stationed most of the Egyptian army in southern Sudan after its reconquest in 1898, to isolate the armed forces from their popular Egyptian base and the upsurge in Egyptian nationalism. The Egyptian Army College and army command structure were also kept under British supervision until 1936.[13] In that year, strong nationalist resistance forced promises of eventual independence, and the Anglo-Egyptian Treaty set the process in motion. However, in the late 1930s, internal political instability, Britain's preoccupation with other matters and Allied concerns over the Suez Canal made granting Egyptian independence untenable.

Elsewhere, Britain maintained its influence on the southern coast of the Persian Gulf and Ibn Sa'ud consolidated the Arabian Peninsula under his rule in 1927, proclaiming himself King of the Hijaz and Najd, which were unified as the Kingdom of Saudi Arabia in 1932.

Iran, an independent state at the start of the First World War, successfully resisted British attempts to incorporate it into the British Empire after the war and foiled Russian attempts to secure some of its territory. Then, in 1920, Reza Khan overthrew the government and attempted to establish a republic modeled on Mustafa Kemal's Turkey. Religious opposition prevented him from doing so, but in 1925 he became shah and initiated several reforms: the power of Iran's religious institutions was reduced; 15,000 miles of roads and the Trans-Iranian railway were built; irrigation and agricultural methods were improved; and a number of industries were supported by state capital. Finally, oil concessions to Britain were reduced, and domestic control over the petroleum industry was established. In international affairs, Iran sought closer ties with Germany to protect itself from British and Russian encroachments. However, this would come to an end during the Second World War.

Initially, most Middle Eastern peoples saw the Second World War as a European affair that would have little impact on them. But they were soon disabused of that. Britain and the Soviet Union occupied Iran, deposed Reza Shah, and forced Iranian cooperation with the Allies. Meanwhile, the collapse of France weakened French control in Lebanon and Syria, and attempts by both the wartime Vichy government and later the liberated French administration to reassert that control were met by strong British and indigenous opposition. Iraqi nationalists endeavored to capitalize on Britain's weakness in the early part of the war by staging a revolt, but they were ultimately unsuccessful. In Palestine, Arabs remained unconcerned by the war. However, Nazi atrocities against European Jews led to the creation of a Zionist Brigade, and Jewish immigration to Palestine dramatically increased. All of this led to intensified hostilities between Arabs and Jews.

Arab nationalism

Nationalism as a political ideology is a fairly recent phenomenon in the Middle East; it was still in its embryonic phase in the early twentieth century. Since then, though, it has burgeoned and has proved to be both constructive and destructive. On the one hand, reform and modernization have often been primary goals of indigenous Middle Eastern nationalist movements (Turkish, Arab, Iranian), and have contributed to civil and social improvements. On the other hand, the primal factors of race, language and territoriality tend to be integral to nationalism and these have engendered conflict. This section considers Arab nationalism generally. Individual state nationalism is examined in each of the chapters in Part II.

Islam was instrumental in bringing about political unity among Arabs in the Arabian Peninsula. As Muslim power expanded into new lands and encountered foreign cultures, an Arab feeling of distinctness, based on language and culture, emerged while still remaining subordinate to the overriding religious tenets of the equality of all Muslims. For several centuries, Arabization and Islamization went hand-in-hand, creating a community of language and culture in the core lands of the Middle East. Like most civilizations, Islamic civilization was founded in urban centers and financed by the surplus profits that accrued from long-distance trade.[14] The merchant–warriors who ran the long-distance trade, not feudal overlords, were the catalyst for unifying the contiguous Arabo-Muslim territories. Islamic civilization thrived on the preservation and integrity of a vast commercial network. However, over time, the unifying power of the merchant–warriors was seriously undermined by a series of destructive events that fragmented the Islamic empire into conglomerates of related ethnic groups.

Arabs were deprived of their commercial intermediary role by the crusades, the swing of commerce to the Italian cities, and the widespread destruction of the Mongols, followed by the Ottoman conquest in the sixteenth century, which shifted Mediterranean trade to Atlantic routes.[15] Under the Ottoman aegis there was a slow but continuous process of cultural – mainly linguistic – assimilation of non-Arab and non-Muslim populations in the Middle East. The adoption of Arabic as the lingua franca for cultural expression and literary production was a notable outcome of this assimilation. However, Jewish minorities, unlike Christian Arabs, shielded themselves from acculturation and chose to live in an exclusively Hebrew environment. The Ottoman system enabled them to do so by introducing the *millet* system, which accommodated the various ethno-religious minorities. Under this system, each religious community enjoyed internal autonomy in the discharge of its affairs, which tended to reduce inter-denominational friction. Thus, religious communities had separate schools and professional apprenticeships until the late eighteenth century, when the interplay of domestic and foreign dynamics forced change in the social order.[16] Inter-communal autonomy had its political counterpart in the Ottoman government of Arab territories, where such provinces as Egypt, Greater Syria, Mosul, Baghdad and Basra retained a form of administrative autonomy. This not only augmented the power of local notables and dignitaries but fostered the emergence of local identities that arose from the decline of the Islamic civilization and centuries of provincialism. The local identities were molded by the historical experience of ethnic Arabness and religion, with the latter defining social norms and prescribing ethical standards.

In the core lands of the Ottoman Empire, military defeats of the Ottoman army prompted the introduction of a state educational system that ran in parallel with traditional teaching in order to train new officers in innovative military strategies. It was not foreseen that an advanced military education would be accompanied by alien Western ideas and a concomitant evaporation of inter-communal social order. The *Tanzimat* (or reorganization) of 1839–1876 ushered in European-style legal, administrative and financial innovations. For example, the Islamic *jyzia* (or poll-tax) was abolished and all Ottomans were declared to be equal, regardless of religion. Thus, Christians, much to their dismay, were now required to serve in the Ottoman army, a duty from which they had previously been exempt. Group identity, preached by native Christian schools and missionary educational agencies, became a source of disloyalty to the Ottoman government and to the communality of an Ottoman common fatherland.[17] Non-Arab Christians identified with Europe, but Arab Christians suffered due to their conflicting loyalties to foreign missionary influence and to their primal sense of "Arabness." Thus, while missionary education aggravated sectarian separatism, the European annexation of Muslim lands augmented suspicion of European intentions, reignited religious polemics and provoked the pan-Islamic movement in the late nineteenth century. The pan-Islamic movement later mutated into an Arab resistance movement against European aggression, in which Arab Christians joined forces with their Muslim counterparts. The works of several nineteenth-century Muslims and Christians – such as Refa'a al-Tahtawi in Egypt and Butrus al-Bustani in Syria – promoted Arabic nationalism. Later, the likes of al-Afghani, Mohammad 'Abdu in Egypt, Adib Ishaq and Rashid Rida in Syria, Farah Antoun in Lebanon, and 'Abd al-Rahman al-Kwakibi endeavored to develop the hazy notion of nationhood and the love for the *Watan* (or fatherland) that had been proposed by al-Tahtawi and al-Bustani. Indigenizing European ideas of nationalism, they made their work accessible to local and less educated people. Hence, a fluid mixture of religious nationalism, regional nationalism and ethnic nationalism evolved and this persists to the present day.[18]

In Syria, educational societies were organized to facilitate inquiry into Arab history, art and literature. The Society of Arts and Sciences was created in 1847 with the help of American missionaries, while Jesuits organized the Oriental Society in 1850. Generally, however, Muslim Arabs refused to join these two groups because of their foreign Christian missionary affiliations. In 1857 the Syrian Scientific Society was established on a non-sectarian basis, and under its auspices Christians and Muslims united to foster and develop their common Arabic heritage. From this society came Ibrahim Yaziji's rallying cry, "Ode to Patriotism," a poem appealing to the Arabs to join forces and revolt against Turkish oppression. (It has been noted that "contemporaries, however, including the Christian Lebanese 'Selim Sarkis,' assigned the poem's authorship to a noted Muslim Sheikh he did not name, probably as a protective measure against the Turkish censor."[19])The first organized response to Ibrahim Yaziji's appeal for unity and revolt came in the form of secret societies in Beirut, Damascus, Tripoli and other cities. Their primary activity was to post placards that urged Arabs to revolt. These groups were unsuccessful and short-lived, but they were significant because they made specific demands that served as models for later Arab political programs. These included calls for the independence of Syria, in union with Lebanon; the recognition of Arabic as a national language; an end to censorship; the removal of other restrictions on freedom of expression; and the use of only locally recruited units for military service.[20] In the second half of the nineteenth century – in response to large-scale centralization by the Ottomans, Western encroachment and Ottoman inability to protect Arab provinces – Arab leaders called for autonomous Arab governments in Arab provinces within the Ottoman Empire. Before 1908, only very few Muslims and the Christians of Mount Lebanon – who were immersed in French culture and political thought – even countenanced the idea of complete independence.

In Egypt, a pronounced sense of identity expressed itself in the concept of Ibn al-Balad (son of the homeland), which was commonly used to foster a sense of belonging vis-à-vis resident non-Egyptians. During the French invasion of Egypt (1798–1801), three uprisings took place and a war of attrition against the French expedition erupted, despite general Egyptian approbation for French material progress and scientific technology. As a result, Sheikh Hasan al-Attar, a teacher from al-Azhar, was asked by the French to visit their newly established scientific laboratory. After he had been thoroughly acquainted with French science, he urged his fellow Muslims to learn and apply it to their endeavors. The Egyptian collective drive to modernity was also given impetus by reforms to the education system, sustaining programs, and the establishment of a modern standing army during the reign of the founder of the new Egypt, Mohammad 'Ali Pasha, whose dynasty ruled the country until 1952.

The ascendancy of Mohammad 'Ali to power in Egypt in 1805 wrested independence from Istanbul. His principal goal for the education system was to create the necessary technical and professional staff for a preconceived bureaucratic state that would champion modernization projects in agriculture and industry while satisfying the needs of the national army. Thus, a bureaucratic–military formation emerged and acted, in the absence of a powerful middle class, as a means to bring about a modern nation state. This ultimately led to the army's revolt, commonly known as the 'Urabi Uprising, against the ruling Khedive Tawfiq in 1882. However, British forces put down the uprising and occupied Egypt that year.[21] Efforts at modernizing Egypt during the reign of Mohammad 'Ali culminated in what became known as the Arab *Nahda* (renaissance), which was reflected in his two-level education system – one prospective and the other retrospective. The former involved sending student missions to the West, particularly to France, to learn modern science and technology, and inviting foreign instructors in those fields to teach in Egypt. The latter involved reviving and printing[22] Arabo-Islamic scholarly works and translating classic Western works. Mohammad 'Ali's conceptualization of modernization, education and *Nahda* was intended to safeguard the integrity of Arabo-Islamic culture and maintain Egyptian national identity in the midst of a multifaceted Western onslaught. However, his successors did not follow his policies, which made Egypt vulnerable to Western cultural penetration.

In the early twentieth century and in opposition to Turkification, numerous Arab societies came together to disseminate notions of Arab nationhood. The Literary Club of Istanbul was founded in 1909. Its objectives were ostensibly cultural rather than political, and it operated publicly, eventually boasting a membership in the thousands, with branches in Syria and Iraq.[23] Another public group, the Ottoman Decentralization Party, was founded in Cairo in 1912 for the purpose of winning equality and autonomy for the Arab provinces within the Ottoman Empire.

Branches were established throughout Syria and close contact was maintained with other Arab nationalist associations. This organization provided Arabs with their first extensive political machinery, capable of coordinating their activities and maintaining concerted and continuous pressure to achieve a specific political program. In addition, al-Kahtaniya, a secret society founded in 1909, had a well-defined program that advocated the creation of a Turko-Arab empire on the Austro-Hungarian model. It attempted to attract Arab officers who were serving in the Turkish army into the Arab nationalist movement, but it was short-lived.

Al-Fatat, a clandestine society organized by Muslim Arab students in Paris in 1911, fully rejected the idea of collaboration with the Turks and integration into a decentralized empire. Instead, it worked for the creation of a sovereign Arab state, and it soon became an effective and widespread force. The society convened the first Congress of Arabs in Paris, drawing representatives from most of the Arab nationalist organizations, under the sponsorship of the Ottoman Decentralization Party. The resulting "Paris Platform" was a moderate program, calling for reform within the empire and more local autonomy for Arabs and other non-Turkish nationalities. To placate Arabs, Istanbul claimed to accept this program but nothing was done to implement it.

Al-'Ahd, another secret society, was organized by an Egyptian major on the Ottoman general staff – Azziz 'Ali al-Misri – who had been one of the founders of al-Kahtaniya. The new society's program was essentially the same as al-Kahtaniya's. In 1914 the Turks arrested al-Misri on a trumped-up charge of treason during the Italian campaigns in Libya and sentenced him to death. Although the British subsequently pardoned him after intervening, al-Misri's arrest and trial outraged both Arab elites and the masses, thus ending hopes for Arab–Turkish cooperation. The Arab nationalist movement then fully united in a drive for an independent Arab state, although it lacked support from all levels of society. With the outbreak of the First World War, Arab nationalism manifested itself through the alliance between Britain and the Emir of Mecca, al-Sharif Hussein. The Damascus Protocol was delivered in 1915. It embodied demands for an independent Arab state that would encompass all of the culturally and linguistically Arabic lands of western Asia. Sir Henry McMahon, the British High Commissioner of Egypt, accepted the conditions of the protocol on behalf of the British government, and consequently the Arab revolt was launched.

When the Paris Peace Conference convened in 1919, al-Sharif Hussein's son, Prince Faisal, attended as the representative of a people who had made a significant contribution to the Allied war effort. Armed with several Allied promises of Arab independence – the Hussein–McMahon correspondence, Britain's "Declaration to the Seven" (a reaffirmation of Britain's pledge made to seven Arab leaders in Cairo in June 1918), President Wilson's Fourteen Points and the Anglo-French declaration of November 1918 (which again reaffirmed Allied promises) – Faisal demanded the fulfillment of those promises. But Britain had made other treaties and agreements that conflicted with Arab aspirations, most notably the Balfour Declaration of 1917 and the Sykes–Picot Agreement of 1916. In an attempt to forestall British and French designs to dismember the Middle East to their own advantage, Wilson sent the King–Crane Commission to Syria and Iraq to deter-mine the wishes of the people regarding their political future. Two recommenda-tions, both directly relevant to these agreements, were strongly urged in the report to the peace conference. The first emphasized a "maximalist" vision of Syria, including today's Syria, Lebanon, Jordan and Palestine, on the basis that "the territory concerned is too limited, the population too small, and the economic, geographical, racial, and language unity too manifest, to make the setting up of independent states within its boundaries desirable, if such division can possibly be avoided. The country is very largely Arab in language, culture, traditions, and customs."[24] The second de-emphasized the establishment of a Jewish national home, reporting that the "anti-Zionist feeling in Palestine and Syria is intense and *not likely to be flouted*."[25] It recommended that the Zionist program be greatly reduced because it could be carried out only by force of arms.

Realizing that the French and British intended to disregard their aspirations and pinning their hopes on the King–Crane Commission, Arab nationalist leaders in Syria organized elections and convened the first Arab Parliament on July 2, 1919. Known as the General Syrian Congress, its resolutions may be summarized as follows:

(a) Recognition of the independence of Syria, including Palestine, as a sovereign state with the Emir Faisal as king; recognition of the independence of Iraq.
(b) Repudiation of the Sykes–Picot Agreement and the Balfour Declaration and of any plan for the partition of Syria or the creation of a Jewish common-wealth in Palestine.
(c) Rejection of the political tutelage implied in the proposed mandatory systems; but acceptance of foreign assistance for a limited period provided it does not conflict with national independence and unity, with preference being given to American or – failing American – British assistance.
(d) Rejection of French assistance in any form.[26]

In March 1920, the congress declared Syria and Iraq to be independent and demanded the evacuation of foreign troops. However, the following month, the Allied Supreme Council, meeting at San Remo, disregarded the congress's decisions, Allied promises and the King–Crane report. The council divided the Arab provinces into several mandates: Syria and Lebanon under France; and Palestine, Transjordan and Iraq under Britain. The Balfour Declaration, which was abhorrent to the Arabs, was reaffirmed. The Arabian Peninsula, comprising five principalities, remained independent, and was unified by 'Abd al-Aziz al-Sa'ud in 1926.

As a result of the mandate system, the Arab territories under foreign occupation became thoroughly preoccupied with liberation and independence, and separate struggles to achieve these goals began in each country. However, these made it difficult to formulate a theory of pan-Arab nationalism. None the less, Zionist designs on Palestine, challenged by the Palestine–Arab revolt of 1936, sub-ordinated the specifics of nationhood to higher considerations of supporting and preserving an entity for fellow Arabs. Thus, the Palestinian problem, in time, became the catalyst for the popularization of Arab nationalism. Committees for the defence of Palestine were organized throughout the Arab world and, in 1938, the various groups merged to form the World Inter-parliamentary Congress of Arab and Muslim Countries for the Defense of Palestine.

The Middle East in the aftermath of the Second World War

Five major turning points have characterized the Middle East since the end of the Second World War. First, in 1948, Zionist Jews living in the British mandate of Palestine declared the independent State of Israel. This ushered in strong sentiments of military-centered nationalism and engulfed the entire region in war. Following the 1967 defeat of Arab military forces in the Arab–Israeli War, it became clear that the military nationalists had failed to provide answers to the most pressing issues of the region, including social and economic disparities, the Israeli occupation of more Arab territory, and the questions of civil society. The second turning point was the resurgence of Islamism in the 1970s and the reappearance of foreign (primarily American) troops on Arab lands. The third comprised the Camp David Accords (1978), which led Egypt and Israel to make peace in 1979. The fourth was the Israeli invasion of Lebanon in 1982. And the final turning point consisted of the structural changes brought forth by the Madrid and Oslo peace processes (1991 and 1992), which have altered the political landscape of the entire region.

During the Second World War, unrest continued throughout the Arab lands, resulting in the aborted coups of Rashid 'Ali al-Gilani in Iraq and General Aziz 'Ali al-Misri in Egypt. In recognition of nationalist dissatisfaction, Anthony Eden, the British Foreign Minister, declared in May 1941 that Britain realized that "many Arab thinkers desire for the Arab peoples a greater degree of unity than they now enjoy . . . His Majesty's Government for their part will give full support to any scheme that commands general approval."[27] In response to Eden's declaration, Nuri al-Sa'id, the Iraqi Prime Minister, circulated his own plan for the creation of a Greater Syria to include Syria, Lebanon, Palestine and the Transjordan, as well as a League of Arab States to include any Arab state that might wish to join. The concept of a Greater Syria was opposed, but the idea of a League of Arab States gathered support and by 1945 the Arab League Pact was formalized with Iraq, Syria, Lebanon, Transjordan, Saudi Arabia and Egypt as its members. Each Arab state subsequently joined as it achieved independence, and by 1977 the league had twenty-two members. Its aim was to promote cooperation among the member states in communications, health, economics and extradition as well as in social and cultural matters. It guaranteed each member's sovereignty and could force no member to take any action. However, although the league initially generated enthusiasm, its failure to organize the Arab states in opposition to Zionism during the first Palestine War severely damaged its credentials among Arab nationalists.

The establishment of the State of Israel in May 1948 created more than one million Palestinian refugees. The Zionist victory led many youthful nationalists to condemn Arab society as a whole, and, within a decade of the Palestine War, nationalist–military takeovers occurred in Syria, Jordan, Iraq, Lebanon and Egypt. Today, all Arab states with the exception of Palestine have achieved national independence.

The military–nationalist movements which arose in the 1950s and 1960s were dedicated to the concept of Arab unity as a means of regaining control over the course and pattern of Arab development. These nationalists were more aggressive and ideologically committed in outlook than the old nationalists had been: they were dedicated to restructuring the regional and domestic environments. As the most technological and modern institution within Middle Eastern society, the military quickly became the principal recruiting ground for the nationalists. With the involvement of a generation of young military officers, the armed forces were soon politicized. Military coups took place throughout the region: Syria in 1949, Egypt in 1952, Iraq in 1958, Yemen in 1962 and Libya in 1969.

Meanwhile, the Palestinian liberation movement became increasingly indigenous, a movement unto itself rather than an outgrowth of Arab nationalism. In 1964, the Palestinian Liberation Organization (PLO) was formed out of a League of Arab States summit in Cairo, declaring its objective as the liberation of Palestine through armed struggle. The goals of the umbrella movement were elucidated in the Palestinian National Covenant. In the aftermath of the 1967 defeat of the Arab states, and the subsequent damage to the credibility of the pan-Arabist cause, the PLO became an increasingly independent organization, tactically organized along the concepts of guerrilla warfare. The PLO was hence identified by the United States and Israel as a terrorist organization until the 1991 Madrid Conference. With the subsequent Oslo Agreement and the popular rise of the Hamas organization, the nationalistic cachet and credibility of the PLO gradually receded.

The Organization of the Islamic Conference (OIC) was formed in 1969 as a political embodiment of the Muslim Ummah, with the aim of promoting solidarity throughout the Muslim world and cooperation across a range of shared concerns. The Islamic countries of the Middle East make up more than a third of the membership of the OIC. Moreover, Arab states constitute more than half of its membership. The OIC has permanent observer status at the United Nations, and while it has never managed to become a collective voice for the whole Muslim world, it has been used as a tool to punish Islamic states that deviate from preeminent political concerns. For example, it temporarily expelled Egypt after the latter normalized relations with Israel.

In 1979, two momentous events changed the landscape of the Middle East. First, the Camp David Accords saw Egypt publicly acknowledging the legitimacy of the State of Israel. This left Egypt open to challenge as the leader of the Arab nationalists, a position which Iraq then attempted to assume. With Egypt's exit from the Arab nationalist project, Arab fragmentation once again became the status quo. Second, the Iranian Islamic revolution, toppling the Shah's pro-West regime, engendered anxiety in the US that the Soviet Union would seize the opportunity to establish a stronghold in oil-rich Iran. Such fear, according to the national security advisor of the Carter administration, Zbigniew Brzezinski, led the US to support

Afghanistan in the Soviet–Afghan War (1979–1989), which would exhaust the Soviet economy.[28] Iraq was also encouraged to pursue an eight-year war (1980–1988) against the new Islamic regime of Iran, which depleted both countries' resources. It also led to an economic and political crisis in Iraq, which eventually manifested itself in further aggression against Kuwait from 1990 to 1991.

In 1987, the first Palestinian Intifadah erupted against a backdrop of ongoing Israeli occupation and the inability of the PLO or Palestine's Arab neighbors to represent the Palestinian people. The Intifadah broke out in the Jabalia refugee camp but rapidly spread to the rest of Gaza and the West Bank. It was a comprehensive and popular resistance movement that incorporated civil disobedience, general strikes, boycott of Israeli goods and organized military resistance. As a result, a mutual aid network was established by various Palestinian organizations.

In an attempt to reassert itself through the Intifadah, the PLO established the United National Leadership of the Uprising, consisting of the local leadership of the PLO sub-organization in the occupied territories. The legitimacy of the PLO was challenged, however, by Hamas and Islamic Jihad, and by the fact that PLO headquarters were in Tunis. The Intifadah played a significant role in changing the politics of the Middle East. First, it exposed the Israeli occupation as unacceptable and untenable, and indicated that the Palestinians were no longer content with Arab representation. Second, the Palestinians set up their local leadership in the occupied territories and resisted *en masse*, which was very costly for Israel to suppress and deprived it of cheap Palestinian labor. Third, the Palestinian issue re-emerged internationally and forced its way back on to the UN table. Fourth, the impotence of Arab regimes was fully exposed, which generated increased domestic disapproval and heightened the appeal of militant Islamic movements.

Saddam Hussein was desperate to deflect responsibility for the economic and political crises that afflicted Iraq in the aftermath of its war with Iran.[29] Kuwait became a convenient target for three reasons. First, it refused to adhere to its quota set by OPEC, aggravating Iraq's economic recovery. Second, it was no military match for Iraq. Third, it had provoked Iraq over a number of diplomatic issues, such as refusing to rent Iraq island space for deep sea ports and demanding that Iraq repay loans made during the war with Iran. (Saddam apparently believed that these loans were war subsidies to stop Iran's advance into the Gulf area.) Iraq invaded Kuwait on August 2, 1990, forcing the monarchy to flee Kuwait. Saddam then installed a puppet regime.

However, the collapse of the USSR had encouraged the US to be more aggressive in its policies toward the Middle East. George Bush Senior's administration now feared that Iraq might become a regional hegemon, challenging US interests in the oil-rich Gulf area and potentially threatening the world's oil supply. The US immediately orchestrated UN-imposed sanctions on Iraq and initiated plans to expel Iraq from Kuwait with military force. A US-led coalition of thirty-four countries crushed Iraqi defenses, retook Kuwait and re-installed the old Kuwaiti ruling family. The US then deepened its presence in the Gulf by permanently establishing military bases in Saudi Arabia. At this point, Osama Bin Laden, a rich Saudi businessman, made public his disapproval of the US military presence, which he viewed as sacrilege. In response, the Saudi rulers drove him into exile, and ultimately stripped him of his nationality. However, the majority of Arabs in the Middle East agreed with Bin Laden and were angered by the stationing of US troops in Saudi Arabia (which includes both Mecca and Medina).

The first Gulf War and the subsequent UN sanctions debilitated Iraq and seriously weakened the ruling Ba'th regime. Two uprisings broke out in the south and north of Iraq, but the US did not support the rebels, which meant that the remnants of Iraq's military forces were able to crush them, leaving thousands dead and tens of thousands homeless.

In 1993 the US-sponsored Madrid Conference was followed by the Oslo Agreement, which brought into existence the ineffectual and corrupt Palestinian Authority (PA), headed by Yasser Arafat, in the Gaza Strip and parts of the West Bank. The agreement did not address the central issues of the Palestinian refugees, the status of East Jerusalem or the right of return. Further, construction of Israeli settlements in the West Bank and confiscated Palestinian land continued unabated. Ultimately, Arafat's political movement, Fatah, and the whole secular discourse of national liberation movements were discredited. Moreover, the military success of Hizbollah against Israel and Hamas's successful resistance encouraged the rise of religiously based national resistance movements throughout Middle East.

Although a resurgence of Islamism had begun prior to the 1970s, it gained vigor and vitality after the US destruction of Iraq, in protest against the failure of the Arab regimes to protect their people from Western and Israeli encroachment. Therefore, Islamism is not only a vocal protest against American domination of the Middle East and Israeli aggression but a proposed alternative to the failed programs of incumbent regimes.

Post 9/11 Middle East and the new world order

George W. Bush's administration capitalized on the terrorist attacks of September 11 to legitimize an aggressive drive in the Middle East that attempted to secure US strategic interests by redrawing the map of the region. The US invaded and occupied Afghanistan and Iraq in 2001 and 2003, respectively. In the case of Iraq, the invasion was carried out despite numerous international protests and without UN support.

Under the rubric of a "war on terror," the Americans initiated a propaganda campaign accusing Iraq of possessing weapons of mass destruction (WMD), of having links to al-Qa'ida, and of sponsoring terrorism. The Iraqi regime was portrayed as an existential threat to the region, the US and, indeed, the whole world. The international community was far from convinced of these claims, but it was unable to prevent Anglo-American forces from invading Iraq on March 19, 2003 and occupying the country soon after. The US established the Coalition Provisional Authority (CPA) from April 2003 to June 2004 in an attempt to engineer and legitimize a political system that had sectarianism as its base. Under proconsul Paul Bremer, the Transient Administrative Law (TAL) superseded Iraq's existing laws, initiated privatization of nationalized industries and paved the way for long-term foreign ownership of Iraq's energy resources. However, US reconstruction projects were generally substandard and often unfinished. Approximately $13 billion of Iraqi money was lost in fraudulent practices, which only compounded the chaos and misery experienced by ordinary Iraqis after the invasion.

Meanwhile, Israel began the twenty-first century by erecting a "security wall" that now encircles the Israeli settlements in the West Bank. In 2003, Prime Minister Ariel Sharon dismantled the few Israeli settlements in Gaza but then allowed more to be built in the larger territory of the West Bank. Gaza became a politically autonomous territory, but it was beleaguered by apartheid-like walls and the constant threat of Israeli military intervention. In January 2005, a Palestinian election was held in which Hamas – a political and social welfare organization, as well as paramilitary movement – emerged victorious. Both the US and Israel refused to recognize the new government and continued to support the defeated Fatah, now headed by Mahmoud Abbas. This resulted in an armed conflict between Hamas and Fatah that ended with Hamas firmly establishing itself as the ruling power in Gaza in 2007. Subsequently, Israel unilaterally imposed a trade blockade on Gaza. At the same time, Egypt closed its border crossing at Rafah, which further aggravated the situation. In late 2008/early 2009, Israel launched a concentrated air assault against Gaza, nominally to end rocket attacks from the territory but principally to undermine the Hamas administration. Over 1,300 Palestinians were killed.

Conclusion

The Middle East suffers the burdens of its colonial history and political misfortunes, leaving it in a present state of political disarray, weakness and illegitimacy. What remaining credibility the Arab state system had at the end of the twentieth century was lost by its continued failure to address the Palestinian question adequately, culminating with the Israeli assaults on Gaza in 2008 and 2009; and its failure to counter Western domination, particularly by its compliance with the US invasion and occupation of Iraq and generally by its inability to develop truly national programs that correspond to the aspirations of its population. Islamists have therefore been able to offer an alternative by capitalizing on the people's sense of religious identity and disenfranchisement from their political environment.

At the international level, the Western world and the Middle East are experiencing levels of mutual mistrust and discord that were not witnessed even at the height of the colonial era. During the eight years of the George W. Bush administration there were Western encroachments into the region, resulting in a high toll of death and destruction in occupied Iraq, the resurgence of sectarianism regionally, and the humiliation of being lectured on "democracy" while suffering under Western-backed tyranny. With the change in the US administration in 2009, President Barack Obama was greeted with optimism and was seen as a break from the belligerence of the preceding era. Indeed, Obama has made rhetorical gestures toward a settlement with the Middle East. In his first post-election interview with *al-Arabiya*,[30] he emphasized his desire for reconciliation and noted his own familial connection to the Islamic world. But at the time of writing Obama had yet to demonstrate willingness to resolve the Iraqi and Israeli issues, both of which must be addressed if he is to appease even the most moderate elements in the Middle East. Accordingly, conditions for improved East–West relations are not especially auspicious.

Notes

1   David Fromkin, *The Way of the World: From the Dawn of Civilizations to the Eve of the Twenty-first Century* (New York: Knopf, 1999), pp. 28–37.
2   For a survey of general Arab history, see Bernard Lewis, *The Arabs in History* (London: Hutchinson, 1950); Hamilton R. Gibb, *The Arab Conquests in Central Asia* (London: Ams Press, 1923); Peter Mansfield, *The Arabs* (Harmondsworth: Penguin, 1978); Sydney Nettleton Fisher, *The Middle East: A History* (New York: Knopf, 1979); and Albert Hourani, *A History of the Arab Peoples* (2nd Edition) (Cambridge, MA: Harvard University Press, 2003).
3   The language spoken in Persia, and modern-day Iran, is Farsi.
4   Ismail Hakki Uzuncarsili, *Osmanli Tarihi* (6th Edition) (Ankara: Turk Tarihi Kurumu Basimevi, 1994), I, pp. 123–124.
5   Ibid., pp. 309–316.
6   For Timur's policies, see ibid., pp. 326–328.
7   Ibid., pp. 328–345.
8   Andrew Wheatcroft, *The Ottomans* (New York: Viking, 1993), pp. 195, 259.
9   For detailed information on the Ottoman state administration, see Uzuncarsili, op. cit., pp. 501–506.
10   For information on janissaries, see Ibid., pp. 510–513.
11   Zachary Lockman, *Contending Visions of the Middle East* (Cambridge: Cambridge University Press, 2004), pp. 49–50, 52–53.
12   Rudi Mattee, "Safavid Dynasty," *Encyclopedia Iranica* (28 July 2008), http://www.iranica.com/articles/safavids.
13   Yunan Labib Rizk, "An Issue of Identity," *Al-Ahram Weekly*, November 22–28, 2001. URL: http://weekly.ahram.org.eg/2001/561/chrncls.htm.
14   Samir Amin, *The Arab Nation* (London: Zed Press, 1978), pp. 12, 14.
15   Ibid., pp. 81–82.
16   'Abd al-Latif al-Tibawi, *Arabic and Islamic Themes* (London: Luzac & Co., 1976), pp. 100–101.
17   Ibid., pp. 102–104.
18   Ibid., p. 109.
19   Mansfield, op. cit., pp. 75–82.
20   Ibid., p. 174.
21   Samir Amin, *Unequal Development* (London: Monthly Review Press, 1976), pp. 302–304.
22   The Egyptian Press (Boulaq Press) was founded in 1822 as a result of these initiatives.
23   Fisher, op. cit., pp. 109, 282.
24   Ibid., pp. 282, 445.
25   Albert Hourani, *A History of the Arab Peoples* (New York: Warner Books, 1991), pp. 319–320.
26   Fisher, op. cit., pp. 282, 293–294.
27   Mansfield, op. cit., pp. 65–67.
28   *Le Nouvel Observateur*, January 15–21, 1998, p. 76. See also URL: http://www.global research.ca/articles/BRZ110A.html.

29   Thabit A.J. Abdullah, *Dictatorship, Imperialism and Chaos: Iraq since 1989* (London: Zed Books, 2006), pp. 52–56.
30   "Obama Tells *al-Arabiya* Peace Talks Should Resume," *al-Arabiya*, May 6, 2009. URL: http://www.alarabiya.net/articles/2009/01/27/65087.html.

Further reading

There is a wealth of historical material concerning the Arab people and the Middle East region, including its political, social and economic development. We list the seminal texts below, as well as works of more recent interest.

There are a great many histories of the Arab people, including pre-modern and pre-Islamic. Albert Hourani's *A History of the Arab People* remains a seminal work and it is a thorough treatment of Arab thought, social practice, religion and historical experience from the seventh century to the present. Likewise, Ira M. Lapidus's *A History of Islamic Societies* is a thorough but readable survey of the development of Islamic society and states, from the advent of Islam to Islamic revivalist movements in the twentieth century. Peter Mansfield's *The Arabs* and *History of the Middle East*, James L. Gelvin's *The Modern Middle East: A History* and Martin Bunton and William L. Cleveland's *A History of the Modern Middle East* are useful historical surveys of the Arab people, the Arab world and the Middle East generally. Charles Issawi's *Arab World's Legacy*, written over three decades, is a collection of historical and analytical essays covering economics, political development, cultural and demographic history and the formative periods of Islamic civilization.

First published in 1938, George Antonius's *The Arab Awakening* remains the classic account of the rise of Arab nationalism and has served as a primary text for successive generations of students.

Beyond broad histories of the Middle East region, there are many works dealing with sub-regional and sub-discipline themes of historical development in the Middle East. Roger Owen's *The Middle East in the World Economy, 1800–1914* examines the profound shifts in Middle East economies during the growth of European power, culminating in the collapse of the Ottoman Empire. Likewise, Halil Inalcik and Donald Quataert's *An Economic and Social History of the Ottoman Empire 1300–1914* is a massive, two-volume economic history of the Ottoman Empire, from infancy to death.

Wadad Makdisi Cortas's *The World I Loved: The Story of an Arab Woman* serves as an important personal memoir of an intelligent and accomplished Lebanese woman who evokes the larger Arab homeland to which she is fiercely attached – a homeland ravaged by Western imperialism, the Zionist project in Palestine, and the betrayal of corrupt and authoritarian Arab regimes. Through all the wars and tragedies, she nevertheless evokes the underlying unities of Arab history and culture that shaped the world she loves and might yet produce something better than the fractured, disjointed and diminished realities that currently define so much of the Arab world.

At the sub-regional level, Ahmad Mustafa Abu Hakima's *History of Eastern Arabia 1750–1800: The Rise and Development of Bahrain, Kuwait and Wahhabi*

Saudi Arabia is an historical account of the formative period of the region that later constituted the center of the Arab Gulf states. Charles Issawi's *The Fertile Crescent 1800–1914: A Documentary Economic History* and *The Economic History of Iran, 1800–1914* are economic histories of the Middle East during a period of European political and cultural expansion.

References

Antonius, George (2001) *The Arab Awakening*, Simon Publications.

Bunton, Martin & Cleveland, William L. (2008) *A History of the Modern Middle East* (4th Edition), Westview Press.

Cortas, Wadad Makdisi (2009) *The World I Loved: The Story of an Arab Woman*, Nation Books.

Gelvin, James L. (2005) *The Modern Middle East: A History*, Oxford University Press.

Hakima, Ahmad Mustafa Abu (1988) *History of Eastern Arabia 1750–1800: The Rise and Development of Bahrain, Kuwait and Wahhabi Saudi Arabia*, International Book Centre.

Hourani, Albert (2003) *A History of the Arab People* (2nd Edition), Harvard University Press.

Inalcik, Halil & Quataert, Donald (eds) (1994) *An Economic and Social History of the Ottoman Empire 1300–1914*, Cambridge University Press.

Issawi, Charles (1971) *The Economic History of Iran, 1800–1914*, University of Chicago Press.

—— (1981) *Arab World's Legacy: Essays*, Darwin Press.

—— (1988) *The Fertile Crescent 1800–1914: A Documentary Economic History*, Oxford University Press.

Lapidus, Ira M. (2002) *A History of Islamic Societies* (2nd Edition), Cambridge University Press.

Mansfield, Peter (1992) *The Arabs* (3rd Edition), Penguin.

—— (2004) *A History of the Middle East* (2nd Edition), Penguin.

Owen, Roger (1993) *The Middle East in the World Economy, 1800–1914*, I.B. Tauris.

3   The legacy of Islam
Continuity and change

An historical survey of Islamic political history reveals a continual project to adapt the formal doctrines of Islam to the exigencies of modern political life. Islam, though frequently portrayed as both static and monolithic, has proven to be a dynamic socio-political force, and adaptable to a changing environment. The contentious relations between the Muslim world and the West throughout the past century, first through colonialism, then through socialist and nationalist state-building projects, and most recently through a confrontation with neo-colonialism in the guise of democratization, has left Islam as the least

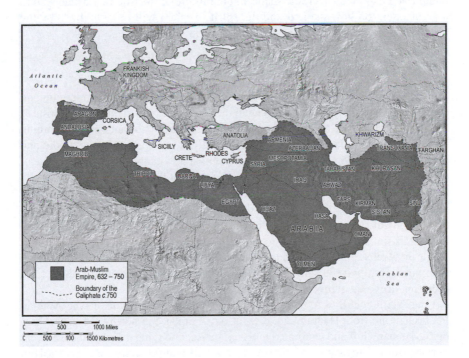

Map 3.1 Islamic expansion

Drawn by Ian Cool

compromised socio-political force in the region. Appropriately, today's Islamic activism is a potent political force, having the authenticity and popular legitimacy that unelected autocracies lack.

The Islamic empire began around 622 CE, during the lifetime of Mohammad, the Prophet of Islam (569–632). The nucleus of the emergent socio-political/ religious project was the city state of Medina (Yathrib). Over the succeeding ten years, the empire expanded at a rate of 274 square miles per day. When Mohammad died, the Islamic empire ruled over more than a million square miles, with a population of approximately a million people. Islam did not only spread by force. Quite the contrary, the faith proliferated and became a major world religion primarily because of its ability to accommodate, absorb and integrate cultural diversity.

The primary political unit in the Muslim world today is the nation state, not the erstwhile Ummah – the Muslim community that was historically the basic unit in the vast territories during the Golden Age of Islam. The Muslim community was an active socio-political force in the early days of Muslim expansion, though, today, this term refers only to a vague religio-cultural bond. None the less, in the Middle East today Islam assumes political prominence and social relevance of such magnitude that modern states in the region have, without exception, responded in a way that suppresses or coopts almost all forms and symbols of Islamic activism. However, the shape and the future of the Middle East depend to a great extent on how the text and the spirit of Islam will be revitalized by the imaginative creativity of devout Muslim thinkers.

Pre-Islamic Arabia

For many decades before Mohammad was born, Mecca had been undergoing an economic transformation that challenged the socio-political identity of the tribe as the primary unit of Bedouin society. The Bedouin inhabitants of the Arabian Peninsula, present-day Saudi Arabia, consisted of two categories: nomadic and settled tribes. The nomadic Bedouins were almost inevitably in a perpetual state of conflict, given the exigencies of desert life. This led them to enter into mutually beneficial alliances, either to fend off or to initiate aggression. The Bedouin Arabs, whether nomadic or settled, possessed strong intrinsic kinship, with its concomitant notions of racial purity and extreme genealogic separation. This encouraged civic seclusion, which, in turn, precluded a stable and inclusive political unity. While the Arabs spoke the same language, observed the same customs, more often than not worshiped the same gods and, above all, aspired to unity, their civic seclusion drove them toward decentralization.[1]

In the sixth century CE, there were two main land trade routes in the Arabian Peninsula: one from Hadramawt, present-day Yemen, ran northward to al-Ahsa' on the Persian Gulf and continued to Syria; the second ran parallel to the Red Sea. Services for trading caravans, like camel markets and protection squads, evolved along these routes. Additionally, sedentary Arab tribes, like the Quraysh in Mecca, participated heavily in trade,[2] which brought them ever-increasing prosperity.

Polytheism formed the primary religious orientation of pre-Islamic Mecca, with the Ka'ba, the House of God, a principal pilgrimage site. Meccan society was dominated by the Quraysh clan. As the custodians of the Ka'ba, they commanded universal respect among the other Arabs of the peninsula. In addition, they enjoyed the privilege of maintaining the spring of Zamzam. With such advantages, the people of Mecca, particularly the Quraysh, initially set themselves up as collectors of "transient taxes" from trade caravans. However, as capital accumulated from these taxes (one-tenth of the total value of goods), the Meccans engaged in their own trade activity, which increased over time. This growth in economic activity occurred after they had built a network of trade routes, and instituted twelve all-year markets by concluding pacts or obtaining charters from the rulers of Syria, Abyssinia, Persia and Yemen.[3]

In contrast to this economic confederacy, the political system in Mecca was oligarchical. The hereditary heads of the ten principal tribes administered the municipal functions of the town, and formed a municipal council, where the Ummayyad, the richest house, were assigned the War Banner, the most prestigious of the municipal functions. It is not known whether decisions were based on deliberation or on individual judgment.[4] The emergent hierarchy in Mecca's social structure resulted from increased financial wealth and trade, and dislocated the old tribal bonds of equality, communal ownership of tribal assets and unwavering individual loyalty to the tribe. It also accentuated wealth-based stratification within and among the tribes, dislodging the tribe as the socio-political and economic unit in the Arab Bedouin society, particularly in the Hejaz. Before the establishment of Islam, the Ummayyads were so rich that by 623 they financed 80 percent of a trade caravan. The annual value of fragrant goods alone was estimated at one hundred million dirhams.[5] (The dirham was a silver coin that weighed 3.906 grams; in 1960 silver prices, one hundred million was equivalent to £15,060,000.[6])

Despite intense trading with the Gnostic Christian Lakhmids (Lakhmid was an Arab vassal city state of Persia) and the Jacobite Christian Ghassanids (Arab vassals of Byzantium), the materialist outlook of the pagan Arabs was not tempered by the monotheistic teachings of Christianity, notwithstanding gatherings where monks and priests would discuss Christian theology in the presence of Arab traders.[7] The Arabs remained idolaters and so metaphysics did not make much of an impression on their thinking and daily lives. In the words of Sir William Muir, "the tide of indigenous idolatry . . . setting strongly from every quarter towards the Ka'ba, gave ample evidence that the faith and worship of Mecca held the Arab mind in a rigorous and undisputed thralldom."[8]

In the patriarchal society of pagan Arab tribes, a woman's status was, at best, undefined. The institution of marriage was indeterminate in the sense that it permitted unlimited polygamy and also the marrying of two sisters simultaneously. Marriage to a stepmother was permitted and she was inherited as part of the patrimony of the deceased. Amid the constant hardships of desert living, and the relatively physical frailty of women, the social bearing of a woman tended to suffer to the point where infant daughters were buried alive. A female was perceived to be a liability in such a male-dominated society.[9] Historical annals on pre-Islamic

Arabia have, however, recorded instances of women of exceptional power and higher status than that of many men around them. Hind bint Utba, the wife of Sufyan bin Harb, and Leila, mother of Amr bin Kalthum, are prominent examples. Nevertheless, their status and power stemmed from being born into a powerful clan or tribe, and being related to chiefs through marriage or descent. Hind, who persecuted Mohammad and his followers severely, was married to the chief of the Ummayyad clan in Mecca; while Leila was the mother of the chief of Taghlib, a powerful tribe, and was descended from a long line of chieftains.

Pre-Islamic Yathrib

Centuries before Islam, Jewish settlements appeared in Yathrib as clients of the two major tribes, the Aws and Khazraj. They made a name for themselves as skilled blacksmiths, silversmiths, goldsmiths and weapons makers, as well as farmers and moneylenders. The social inequalities experienced as a result of their client status led to their emphasizing that they were the "Chosen People" in accordance with their religion, and that a prophet, or messiah, would one day elevate them to the highest distinction.[10] In the meantime, an internecine war raged for generations between the Aws and Khazraj, which led to the exhaustion of both parties and a persistent search for a peaceful solution.

In sum, there was no dominant form of government in the Arabian Peninsula. Nor was there a central authority for the Arabs of the desert, who experienced many forms of rule, ranging from the plutocratic oligarchy of Mecca to relative anarchy in Medina. By the beginning of seventh century, both towns were experiencing the weakening of the tribe as the primary unit in the social fabric of Arab society.

The Advent of Islam

When Mohammad was born in 569, Mecca had sunk into corruption on two levels. First, the Ka'ba was no longer the House of One God that Abraham built, according to Muslim belief. At that time it housed about 360 idols, catering to every religious belief of visiting pilgrims. Second, the Spartan work virtues of the desert Arabs had given way to gambling, with the people of Mecca speculating on rates of exchange, the prices of commodities, the arrival or loss of trade caravans, and the spoils of war. Arrogance replaced honor, while the old chivalric code of protecting the weak waned, and was finally denied to foreigners.[11]

Mohammad was born into the noble Hashimite branch of the Quraysh. He was orphaned soon after, at which point his grandfather, the head of the Hashimite clan, took care of him. However, he died shortly afterwards. Thereafter, raised by a wet-nurse in the desert, Mohammad spent most of his time as a shepherd boy. These circumstances meant that he did not undergo the social conditioning usually exercised by parents, and he had no formal schooling – his education consisted of life experiences in desert society.[12] At the age of twenty, he undertook trading enterprises, and five years later he was married to a wealthy widow from a prestigious background, Khadija b. Khuwailed. A respected member of his community, he became known for his generosity and good sense, and he was expected to become one of the more influential elders of Mecca in due course. He was a businessman and belonged to a community that tended to take a practical view of things, regarding spiritual extravagance with suspicion. His future seemed assured.[13]

However, all this changed in 609, when, according to Muslim religious belief, God told Mohammad that he was His messenger and ordered him to preach His Word, first to his family and close associates and later to the wider community. Quraysh hostility to the monotheistic call of Islam and its ethical content escalated from mockery and insults to physical violence to economic starvation of Mohammad's clan. In 622, repression of the new community culminated in a plot to assassinate Mohammad, at which point he and his followers sought refuge in Medina. For thirteen years, Mohammad and his people suffered many forms of persecution without raising a hand in self-defence. The pagan rulers in Mecca viewed the Muslims as a state within a state because they seemed to defer to Mohammad rather than to the municipal council of the town. They even had their own law, the Qur'an, although this had not yet been finalized.[14]

The Qur'an was written over a twenty-three-year period – thirteen in Mecca and ten in Medina. It consists of 114 chapters and over 6000 verses. More often than not, the verses expound teachings in response to specific situations, and sometimes a ruling may span a number of verses spread across several chapters. Therefore, Qur'anic studies, including exegesis, constitutes a discipline in itself. The centrality of the Qur'an in Muslim life is attributed to its multidimensionality and its symbolic, multi-layered text. These two hallmarks make intelligible the Qur'anic accommodative capacity for societal change. For example, *Fiqh*, or Islamic jurisprudence, evolved from the need to find solutions to legal questions; Qur'anic metaphysics gave shape to the development of Islamic scholastics; and meditating on the afterlife gave substance to Islamic ethics and asceticism. Moreover, reflections on Islamic governance gave birth to political thought, and contemplation of the beauty of the language of the Qur'an gave rise to Arabic linguistics.[15] Islam is intended to address not one but many generations, so its language is necessarily versatile, communicating in images compacted with layers of concealed ideas for the believer to discover.[16]

Mohammad in Medina

When the Prophet arrived in Medina its population was an estimated 10,000. There was no central municipal organization in the town, and in this heterogeneous community religion was largely an apolitical, private affair. Mohammad faced the following urgent issues:

1   Defining his own status in relation to the rights and duties of the local inhabitants.
2   Arranging the rehabilitation the Meccan Muslims.

3   Reaching an understanding with non-Muslims, particularly the Jews.
4   Securing compensation for the loss suffered by the Meccan Muslims.

He entered into a free public dialogue with the people of Medina, which resulted in a written charter of rights and obligations that came to be known as the "Covenant of Medina." This institutionalized the Islamic city state and laid down the code for its administration. While Mohammad assumed the multiple roles of messenger of God, arbiter and military leader, the injunctions ordained for the people in the Covenant were equally applicable to himself as an individual. This document, which has been preserved in its entirety, was revolutionary in the sense that it provided people with a central institution for justice and administration that not only superseded tribal structures but ended the chaos of tribalism. It also provided a basis for both the emergence of the Muslim community as a political entity and the development of the concept of the Islamic welfare state. After the Muslims' victory over the Meccan pagans in the Battle of Badr in 624, Jews entered into the Covenant.[17] Thus, in less than two years, the first and the third issues had been resolved.

With respect to the second issue, the number of the Meccan Muslims who arrived in Medina was small – just a few hundred – but they hailed from several tribes and clans, including some from Iraq, Abyssinia and Persia. Mohammad treated this multiracial group as a supraracial and supranational unit that transcended race, color and language, thus putting in practice the beginning of an Islamic ideal: equality among all humans.[18] In a general meeting, he suggested fraternization between each well-to-do Medinan Muslim and a Meccan refugee. The families of the two would work together, live together and even inherit each other's possessions. In this way, the Medinans and the Meccans increased their wealth and became self-sufficient.[19]

For the Muslim believer, brotherhood is a core concept of the faith. The Qur'an teaches that mankind descends from the same couple who were created from the same substance (4:1, 49:13). This descent makes all human beings brothers and sisters, differentiated only by accidental attributes of color, language, skills, talents and personal gifts. Observable differences, from the Qur'anic viewpoint, are not causes for inherent superiority or pride amid one group over another (30:22). Therefore, absolute toleration must be maintained (2:62, 5:69, 29:46, 16:125). The specific fraternity of Muslims, which the Qur'an encourages, made this state of brotherhood more distinct and gave Muslims a deep sense of solidarity and organic unity (49:10).

Following the conclusion of the Covenant of Medina, around 623, Mohammad persuaded non-Muslim tribes around Medina to enter into an alliance with the city state, establishing a *cordon sanitaire* so that the Meccan trade caravans to Syria, Iraq and Egypt could not pass. This was an attempt to resolve the fourth of Mohammad's pressing concerns – securing Meccan reparation for the losses suffered by the Muslim community. Rejecting negotiation, the Meccans chose force, which led to three battles between 624 and 627 and their ultimate defeat. The successful consolidation of Arabia under the banner of Islam was a remarkable achievement, especially given its comparatively bloodless nature, and this model of empire-building was largely replicated later. While a subsequent war with the Persian and Byzantine empires led to the expansion of Islam to the east and west, the Muslim faith was not imposed by force on the conquered people as the Qur'an forbids such religious coercion (2:256). As a normative practice, Muslim rule allows religious minorities to practice their faiths unmolested, on condition of paying a poll-tax (*jyzia*) in lieu of conscription to military service (which was obligatory for Muslims). The *jyzia* ranged from 12 to 48 dirhams per month, depending on the wealth of the person. The poor, women, children, the unemployed and the disabled were all exempt.

The words of the Qur'an, and the teachings of the Prophet, were instrumental in extricating Arabia from generations of warfare. They were also the catalyst to transform the peninsula into a centralized authority whose administration protected the rights of religious minorities, a policy which the Ottomans later transformed into the "*millet* system." In the words of William Montgomery Watt, "On the whole Muslim regimes behaved very fairly towards their minorities and did not oppress them. The worst that could happen was that in time of crisis a mob could get out of hand and attack minorities, but this was rare."[20] Nevertheless, religious minorities certainly felt themselves to be second-class citizens and they faced social discrimination.

War and *Jihad*

In the West, it is very common to refer to *Jihad* erroneously as a "holy war." As an Islamic concept, it has a broader and more complex meaning. All references to war in Islam use the word "killing" (*qital*). The Qur'an uses this term when referring to war and to delimit the context and conduct of war. First, war should never be waged aggressively (2:190). Second, differences of religion or culture are not justifications for war (60:8–9). Third, war ceases when the opposing side seeks peace (9:7). Ethical and criminal responsibility is based on individual choice in Islam. Thus, engaging civilians or non-combatants in arms is strictly prohibited in the Qur'an (2:190). The Prophet even prohibited the destruction of an enemy's property.[21] The literal meaning, and orthodox understanding, of *Jihad* is self-exertion. The word is mentioned in the Qur'an thirty-two times, emphasizing, from different perspectives, that self-exertion on the path to God is the process of self-realization, as is the realization of "*Tawhid*." This noun derives from the root "*wah-hada*," which means to bring unity to what is diverse by a conscious and strenuous human effort. By *Tawhid*, the dualities of the body and soul, heavenly and worldly kingdoms, the material and the spiritual world, as well as the tension between ethics and politics, merge into balanced proportion and unity. The ongoing individual process of transforming the physical into the contemplative spiritual is what Mohammad referred to when he said, "There are no monasteries in Islam," because the walls of monasteries are demolished by *Tawhid*. The Qur'an (28:77) also alludes to the unity of the mundane with the Kingdom of Heaven through conscious acts by human beings. Because the unity of God and the unity of creation are basic themes in Islam, human beings – God's vice-regents on earth (Qur'an, 2:30–38) – are in a state of perpetual *Jihad*. Since Mohammad educated Muslims by living and practicing the principles of Islam, his life, according to the Qur'an (33:21), is the ultimate example for Muslims to follow on the path to God – *Jihad*.

The record of Mohammad's deeds is called the Sunna – trodden path. As a religious term, it means "the Prophet's way of life in terms of his statements and actions that explain and apply the principles and tenets of the religion of Islam."[22] As such, the Sunna is indispensable, not only for understanding Islam but for legislation, because it can explain terse injunctions in the Qur'an.[23] It can also restrict what appears to be Qur'anic general principle and establish a ruling on a condition that is not addressed by the Qur'an. For Muslim jurists, the Sunna is the second source of legislation after the Qur'an. There are a number of compilations of the Sunna, known as the Hadith, the six best known of which were compiled by Bukhary, Muslim, al-Nisa'i, Abu Dawud, al-Termidhi and Ibn Maja. The rigor of the criteria for authenticating the statements and actions of the Prophet tend to vary among the authors of the Hadith books. However, there is agreement among all authors that for a Hadith to be accepted, the credibility and personal probity of each narrator must be established. The credibility criterion, however, goes a step further to ensure that the morality of each narrator has not been questioned throughout his or her life. Second, the text of the Hadith that the narrators attribute to the Prophet must never be contradicted by the Qur'an or by demonstrable scientific laws. In this regard, the word *Shari'a* is related to *Fiqh*, which literally means "understanding" and is commonly used to refer to the Islamic corpus of law.[24]

Pillars of Pax Islamica

The fundamental pillars of the Golden Age of Islamic society were erected in the doctrines of Islam, but they took on greater meaning as Muslims sought to implement them in their lives. Professor 'Ali Mazrui has argued that the foundations of Muslim society in historical experience were established on the following grounds:[25]

1 Retaliation to aggression was permitted, while maintaining a tolerance for differences of views, and forgiveness when it is within human capacity to endure affliction.
2 Optimization of the economic well-being of society was permitted through the encouragement of the market, along with transcultural trade with Islam supporting profit, while being against the charging of interest. Other Islamic specifics regarding economic institutions sprang up for the benefit of civil society, such as *al-awqaf* (endowments) whose beneficiaries could include schools, clinics, social clubs and even graveyards for the poor.
3 Celebration of human diversity was encouraged by understanding oneself, learning about the differences of other people and studying the environment

in order to bridge the geographic, religious and national barriers that separate humankind, and thus increase the chances for cooperation and reduce tension between groups and so strengthen the chances for lasting peace (Qur'an, 13:49).

4 Gender equality is guaranteed both in the Qur'an and by Mohammad's practice. None the less, sexism, understood as drastic discrimination against women, resulting in sexual exploitation, economic marginalization and political disempowerment – although formally rejected by Islam – is practiced in many Muslim as well as in non-Muslim countries.

Jurisprudence in Islam

Historical experience and the diversity of opinion that arose within the dual context of political opposition and freedom of expression gave rise to two main socio-political forces within Islam: the Sunni majority and the Shi'ite minority. In legal matters, both use almost the same legislation. However, different emphasis in legal reasoning can lead to contrasting rulings. Furthermore, majority and minority legal rationale appears to diverge when political thought and government become the issue. Here, we shall consider only the Sunni school of legal thought because it represents the majority.

Islam is theocentric, rather than theocratic, and emphasizes individual responsibility (Qur'an, 2:281, 3:25, 14:51, 36:54, 74:38). Additionally, the Muslim articles of faith are simple and do not require theological speculation/interpretation. Muslims aspire to know what to do under all circumstances in order to proceed steadily on the path of *Tawhid*. Hence, jurisprudence is of primary importance. However, there were theological schools which speculated on the conception of God in relation to His creation, such as the Mu'tazilites and the Maturidis, advancing a rational defense of Islam. In addition, the Ash'arite school challenged Aristotelian logic. Yet, as Islamic theology became systematized over time, it gave rise to the science of comparative religion and 'Ilm al-Kalam, or dialectic Islamic scholastics.

Muslims have generally remained uninterested in theology and philosophy, considering them to be irrelevant to daily life and the hereafter. The Qur'an places great importance on thought processes, logical reasoning and knowledge, fearing that faith degenerates in their absence into fanaticism and superstition.[26] In other words, the Qur'an urges all Muslims to reason and to use available knowledge in pursuit of truth without prejudice. The 'Ulama, or jurists, assumed prominence in Muslim communities and labored on law codification independently of the state apparatus. The process of legal reasoning is commonly referred to as *ijtihad*, which literally means applying human judgment to a question. In its technical sense, it refers to reaching a judgment based on methodical reasoning of legal sources and precedents.

The main legal sources, in descending order, are the Qur'an, the Sunna, the consensus of religious scholars (*Ijma'*) and *Qiyas*. The last refers to a logical analogy between the constitutive elements of a precedent and a new situation. If a

similarity between the elements of both precedent and the new situation is established, then a ruling of the precedent is attached to the situation. There are two
other legal sources that have enriched the legal corpus over time – the *al-Masalih
al-Mursala* (public interest) and *'Urf* (social conventions), which are grounds for
a legal ruling if they do not contravene Qur'anic ordinances.

The Qur'an set out 228 ordinances to oversee the main areas of human association.[27] Surprisingly, Muslim jurists used this small number of ordinances to
legislate for every situation as it arose in the extremely sophisticated civilizations
of Persia and Byzantium, which were absorbed by Islam. They were able to do this
because the symbolism of the Qur'anic text allows for flexible accommodation in
accordance with the religious scholar's depth of learning and the level of accumulated experience. Second, the Qur'an proclaims some edicts, supported by reasons,
which facilitate the use of *Qiyas*. Third, Qur'anic ordinances are, more often than
not, general principles, or constants, whose procedural details and execution are
allowed to vary over time and place, but within a general religious framework of
easing of hardship and pursuing justice (Qur'an, 4:58, 5:8, 42:15, 5:6, 22:78).[28]

The Sunna, along with the Qura'n and *ijtihad*, constitutes the Islamic *Shari'a*.
Because the corpus of Hadith is much larger than the Qur'an, much of the law is
based on the Sunna. In this respect, jurists may disagree over the standing of an
injunction in the Sunna – that is, over whether it is specific and private or general
and public. Whatever the case, methodical reasoning and human judgment have
been indispensable in forming Islamic jurisprudence.

Shortly before his death, Mohammad appointed Mu'adh Ibn Jabal, one of his
closest and most learned companions, as governor and judge of Yemen (which, at
the time, was a more sophisticated society than either Mecca or Medina). In order
to fulfill this role, Mu'adh said that he would first search the Qur'an for guidance
and then consult the Sunna. If he could not find adequate guidance in either source,
he would exercise his own good judgment. The Prophet approved of this
procedure.[29]

With the expansion of the Muslim commonwealth, the companions of the
Prophet spread throughout the region and taught the tenets of Islam and the
practice of the Mohammad. They then founded schools of legal thought that
adapted to the variable needs of the Muslims. The schools soon multiplied as their
students became qualified to teach.[30] Four schools of thought emerged – the
Hanifite, the Shafi'ite, the Malikite and the Hanbalite – but their legal thought is
not as disparate as is often suggested.

Notwithstanding the good intentions of the jurists, their decisions had far-
reaching effects. The dynamism of history and the constant development of
societies brought into relief a frozen expression of the collective intellectual life of
the Muslim community. Future generations of religious scholars (the 'Ulama)
became no more than imitators of, commentators on, and abridgers of the earlier
literature of previous generations of Muslim jurists. Worse, some clerical classes
in later Muslim society betrayed the intentions of their predecessors by providing
religious authority for their temporal authorities. This environment encouraged an
intellectually complacent attitude that was further aggravated by the progressive

decline in the empirical or experimental method of discovery and understanding, which Muslim scientists, like al-Khawarizmi, Ibn al-Haytham and Ibn Hayyan, had employed during the zenith of Islamic civilization, from the eighth to tenth century.[31] Centuries of intellectual lassitude gave rise to a rigidity of outlook that was intolerant of critical religious thought.

The complacent and self-defeating religious outlook coexisted with the emergent multiplicity of power centers in the Muslim commonwealth – Baghdad, Egypt, North Africa, Spain and Mughal India – all of which were in decline. Further, this ossified intellectual outlook continued even after a series of foreign invasions – the crusades, which began in the twelfth century, the Mongol invasions in the mid-thirteenth century and, finally, the Ottoman invasion that conquered the eastern Muslim lands in the early sixteenth century.

The Ottomans ruled as self-proclaimed caliphs – that is, as successors to the Prophet. They instituted their own cultural customs, such as the veil for women and the sacrilege of a woman appearing in public, and the ethos of the warrior-dervish as the accepted mode of conduct.[32] During the colonization era and the carving up of Muslim territory into nation states, Islam prompted political action until the epoch of political independence in the aftermath of the Second World War, when the two spheres of action, the religious and the political, took separate turns. The religious sphere was subordinated to the interests of a nationalist, secularist state until very recently. The anachronism of a stagnated body of religious thought with a simultaneous insistence on the temporal relevance of the body of legal corpus compelled a prominent Egyptian intellectual to state: "If no *Ijtihad*, then no prescripts."[33] In mid-2004, an Islamic conference was held in the United Arab Emirates and concluded that a dynamic understanding of the Qur'an and *Shari'a* must be revived by applying the accumulated reservoir of scientific facts to the symbolism of the text. At the time of writing, this momentous task was still in progress.

The heritage of Islamic political thought

During his lifetime, Mohammad was messenger and explicator of the Qur'an, the supreme justice and the military commander of the Muslim state, which he established in Medina and expanded to include all of Arabia. However, his infallibility was confined only to the first of these roles. He could err just like anyone else in the rest of his functions, and politically he was subject to the same laws as the rest of the community.

The Sunni and Shi'a schools of thought agree on the following matters:

1 The Islamic state is not a theocracy although it is theocentric.
2 The Islamic state is nomothetic in its pursuit of justice whose socio-economic aspect is realized through state-sponsored welfare as well as individual acts of charity, which the Qur'an enunciated (9:60) and Sunna implemented;[34] the earliest nomothetic welfarist model was the Islamic state, which was first established by the Covenant of Medina.

3   The head of the state should be able-bodied and in possession of sagacity,
     reasoning capacity and knowledge.

The Sunni school calls the state leader *khalifa* – successor to the Prophet – that is,
a caliph – while the Shi'a school prefers the term *Imam*, which translates as
"leader" and confers upon him extra human qualities.

Sunni political thought

Throughout the Qur'an the main address is made to *al-Nas* – the people, or
specifically the masses, those without any particular class or racial privileges or
distinguishing social form. In Islam, therefore (Qur'an, 8:53, 13:11), the people
are the conscious and fundamental factor in changing society and in making
history.[35] Hence, the Sunni school conceptualized political sovereignty in the inter-
relation between *Shari'a* and the people, commonly called the Muslim community.
Such dual sovereignty theoretically sets the Islamic political system apart from
theocracy, autocracy, nomocracy and democracy.[36] Sunni political thought features
the evolutionary historical experiences that have been cast in legally reasoned
principles linked to the ethical foundation of Islamic justice and the people's well-
being, as laid out in the Qur'an and Sunna.[37]

Mohammad died without appointing either a successor or a method for the
selection of the ruler. Nor did he specify the length of term of the political office of
the head of the Islamic state. The formalities of the system of governance were left
to the decisions of the people, which can vary over time and place. The substance
of governance was already, however, a part of the *Shari'a*, which the Qur'an
(4:58–59) and Sunna made explicit. The Qur'an, in these two verses, refers to all-
encompassing justice and safeguarding of the well-being of Muslims as the
cornerstones of government, and establishes itself as the ultimate reference for
resolving public disputes that might arise between the ruler(s) and the people. In
other words, the law, to which the ruler and the ruled are both subject, is the final
arbiter, as was the case in the city state of Medina. The Qur'an (3:159, 42:38)
defined the nature of the state in Islam as one that is based on deliberation with
respect to issues that impact on the public because the ruler, whether the Prophet or
any other human, can err in the management of civil, political, military and judicial
affairs. The Qur'anic command for deliberation is intended as a safeguard against
tyranny that, from a Qur'anic perspective, breeds corruption (89:11), which Islam
endeavors to eradicate[38] (8:25; 11:59,113; 71:21; 43:54). Indeed, there were revolts
and rebellions attempting to restore the political principles from these perspectives,
such as the revolt of Imam Zayd during the reign of the Ummayyads, as well as
many other Shi'a revolts against the Abbasid rulers who did not conform to Islamic
principles of governance. The failure of these rebellions left behind a toll in blood,
bitterness and human suffering because the early Muslim jurists, who were in
agreement on the Islamic principles of governance, did not ponder, let alone
develop, a doctrine that could be translated into a defined political system. Neither
the instruments for the selection of the ruler nor the roles of the people in installing

or removing him were systematized. For example, the first *khalifa*, Abu Bakr, was publicly elected; the second, 'Umar Ibn al-Khattab, was appointed by his predecessor and only then publicly ratified; the third, 'Uthman, was appointed by a majority vote among a limited panel of candidates. The Ummayyads, the Abbasids and the Ottomans, however, maintained dynastic hereditary rule. Muslim jurists came up short in another aspect of the political realm, too. While they agreed that it was legitimate to remove a ruler who was corrupt, tyrannical, habitually disregarded the law or continually caused harm to the Muslim people,[39] they did not codify the procedures for a process of impeachment and peaceful removal.

Two other types of Muslim thinker, philosophers and civil counsellors, however, made Islamic governance a constituent part of their intellectual construction. Though these thinkers' disposition to philosophical thinking could be said to have arisen from reflection on the Qur'an, which gave rise to rational theology, they remained distinct from exponents of Greek philosophy, such as al-Farabi (d.950 CE) and Ibn Sina (Avicenna) (d.1037 CE). Greek philosophy made an impression on a few wealthy or highly placed individuals, not on the middle and lower echelons of society.[40] The works of the Muslim disciples of Greek philosophy remained personal achievements in the wider intellectual realm, but did not permeate the collective consciousness of the Muslim community as a whole because they did not relate to the daily experiences of the masses, in contrast, for instance, to the works of the 'Ulama. Further, when the question of governance and the nature of the state arose, Muslim philosophers did not elaborate on questions of sovereignty, rights and the relationship of the ruler to the ruled, nor did the philosophers advocate any single particular system of government.[41]

While Ibn Sina was a famous physician by profession, he was a multitalented scholar whose interests extended into a number of scientific disciplines. However, when he cast his gaze on to politics and the state, the result was no more than a personal cogitation on how a society is sustained by the division of labor and a balanced interdependence of differentiated societal formations.[42] Abu al-Nasr al-Farabi hailed from a respectable Turkish family who were recent converts to Islam, and he received his first education under the Christian teacher Yuhanna Ibn Haylan. al-Farabi pursued multifarious scientific interests but he was, above all, a logician and metaphysician who sought to found a school of political philosophy among the Arabs. Two of his books, *Kitab al-Siyasa al-Madaniyya* (*Book of Civil Politics*) and *Kitab Ara' Ahl al-Madina al-Fadhila* (*Book of the Opinions of the Inhabitants of the Virtuous City*),[43] expounded his political philosophy, which proposed a utopian ideal by which one might judge the good states from the bad.[44] Al-Farabi also supported Plato's concept of the philosopher king, or more accurately the prophet king. He described such a ruler as one who is both a philosopher and a prophet, who draws upon both his intellect and his imagination to interpret the wisdom of the divine, and called him Ra'is Awwal – Peerless or Unprecedented. Conspicuous in his discursive reasoning is the influence of the Neoplatonist notion of *Fayd*, or Emanation, that connects the Unprecedented with God. Ra'is Awwal, by "his very nature and up-bringing, does not need to be instructed by others. He has the inherent capacity for observation and of conveying his sense to others."[45] Al-Farabi listed twelve attributes of Ra'is Awwal, but admitted that it is very difficult to find all of these attributes in one person. Consequently, he proposed that the state could be virtuous if ruled by an oligarchy of those who possess the necessary attributes or by rulers who maintain and interpret the laws of the founding Caliphate. In the ideal state, men should be organized by the ideal ruler in service departments that are in accordance with their nature, upbringing and suitability for the job. Nevertheless, Ra'is Awwal would not take orders from any individual. In al-Farabi's scheme, society should be divided into classes with common property to which all class members would have equal rights.[46] At the other end of the virtuous, or the utopian, state there were societies that had no knowledge of the good, and were founded on force or held together by common characteristics of descent and language, which al-Farabi called Madinat al-Taghallub or Madinat al-Jahiliya.[47] One can easily read in al-Farabi's notion of Ra'is Awwal an implicit censure of the intellectual landscape, political miasma and common royal and administrative malaise of his time. What remain unclear in his political philosophy are the ability of such a political system founded on a combination of rulers actually to function, the method for the selection of these rulers and the modalities necessary to ensure that their attributes would be harmoniously integrated. However, his political philosophy marks a watershed between the dual sovereignty of the people and *Shari'a* as advanced by the 'Ulama and the sovereignty of al-Farabi's self-acting ruler(s).

The works of the civil counsellors, which began to appear in the ninth century and continued until the ascendancy of the Ottomans, are too many to be listed.[48] These writings express the interests of those who serve the powerful in order to maintain their positions while serving one dynasty after the other. The dangers of absolute rule are highlighted, with solutions ranging from a counsel of perfection to principles of statecraft, the education of princes and the careful choice of officials. In this category of political literature, it is not uncommon to find self-serving ingratiation in the rationalization of the corruption of powerful ruler(s).[49]

Shi'ite political thought

The political doctrine of Shi'ism evolved in three distinct stages. The first stage saw the appearance of the term "Shi'ite," which referred to communities that lived among the Sunni majority in the seventh century after the death of al-Hussein, the son of 'Ali Ibn Abi Talib, the fourth caliph and the husband of Fatima, the daughter of the Prophet. Shi'a, at that time, meant those who preferred 'Ali over and above all others, particularly his Ummayyad adversaries and their supporters, who eventually murdered al-Hussein. The term simply meant supporters of 'Ali, and did not initially carry any great religious significance. The second stage, in the eighth century, witnessed the development of the concept of the Imamate, literally meaning de jure leadership, which proposed that 'Ali and his descendants were infallible and appointed by writ from the time of the Prophet. The infallibility of the Imam is borne out of the belief that Mohammad's impeccable knowledge was transmitted to 'Ali, who, in turn, bequeathed it to the lineage of his son, al-Hussyan. The third stage began in the tenth century and continued until the Iranian revolution of 1979. This stage marked the birth of the term "Twelvers," which refers to a chain of twelve Imams, the last of whom went into occultation (disappeared)[50] but would reappear to resume his religio-political leadership and restore justice and truth in the world. The twelfth Imam, though his birth is doubted, was Mohammad Ibn al-Hasan al-'Askari,[51] who is believed to have gone into occultation around 951. The Shi'ite Twelvers have been in the "Period of Awaiting" ever since, with significant socio-political repercussions.[52] Khomeini's political theory of *Wilayet al-Faqih* (which is the Arabic translation of the Persian term velayat-e faqih) – the guardianship of the jurist-consult – brought to the fore a new perspective on state and society.

The insistence of the Shi'ite Twelvers on the concept of the Imamate unwittingly brought about their self-imposed exile from the Muslim community for the period of occultation while they awaited the return of the infallible Imam. Politically, the Twelvers dissuaded followers from revolting against state oppression or, for that matter, conducting any war against the internal enemies of Islam. Thus, the concept of the Islamic state disappeared from their literature, even when the rulers of the Muslims were Shi'ites, as was the case under the Bu'ids during the tenth and eleventh centuries and the Safavids during the fifteenth century. Economically, they suspended collection of all state taxes, except *zakat* (a tax of 2.5 per thousand levied on annual profit or unused capital for a whole year), though they left the dispensation of revenues to the discretion of Shi'ite Muslim individuals. From the late eleventh century, they went as far as to prohibit Friday communal prayer – which the Qura'n explicitly enjoins (62:9) – because the leader of the prayer, according to their theory of the Imamate, must be the infallible Imam.[53]

However, the ever-changing reality which gives rise to new needs, experiences and questions forced the Shi'ite jurists to adapt their theories. Accommodating change in legal thought began in the eleventh century, when the concept of the vice-regency of the jurisprudents, or Wilayat al-Fuqaha', was formulated. In other words, the collective body of religious scholars that had reached the rank of *Mujtahid* could represent the absent Imam. The activities and power of the Shi'ite scholars remained within socio-economic and religious boundaries, but this concept gained prestige during the fourteenth and fifteenth centuries, which led ruling monarchs, and even the Qajar dynasty in the nineteenth century, to bow to the jusrists' influence and seek their support. Now, the notion of Wilayat al-Fuqaha' has given the organized hierarchy of the Shi'ite 'Ulama immeasurable power among the Shi'ite masses for the following reasons:

1   Wilayat al-Fuqaha' underlines a polarity between the 'Ulama and the laity; the latter must obey the former.[54]
2   The Shi'ite 'Ulama has built into the collective consciousness of the masses that they represent the absent Imam, which bestows implicit sanctity on the religious collectivity.[55]
3   The Shi'ite 'Ulama have imposed and collected one-fifth of the profits and capital accrued from business-people since the twelfth century, which has

given the religious hierarchy not only economic power but tangible independence from the state.[56] They have used this tax and the revenue from other sources, such as the endowments and charity, to support the poor and themselves (to the point of occasionally amassing great personal wealth), build mosques and fund education – activities that have made the 'Ulama not only the linchpins of Shi'ite society but the arbiters of right and wrong, truth and falsehood in the historical experience of the people, as well as a mobilizing apparatus of public opinion.

Khomeini's role in the Iranian revolution is well known. But his attempt to formulate an Islamic political theory is less understood. While 'Ali Shariati – a sociologist engaged in constructing Islamic social categories of meaning – emphasized the role of the masses in effecting change, hence the sovereignty of the people, Khomeini attempted to blend popular sovereignty with the Qur'anic ordinances. This would be articulated in the Iranian Constitution of 1979. Thus, a binary political structure emerged: a parliament and prime minister elected by the people and an eighty-six-member "Assembly of Experts," also elected by the people, to ensure the compatibility of governance with *Shari'a*. However, the historical experience of Wilayat al-Fuqaha' had such a conditioning impact on Khomeini's mindset that the sovereignty of the people was subordinated to the leadership of the twelve-member Council of Guardians, who can, in their jurisdictional capacities, revoke parliamentary decisions. In a public communiqué in 1988 Khomeini argued for the jurisdictional supremacy of a class of religious interpreters, the "Guardianship of Islamic Jurists" (*Welayat-e Faqih*), and bestowed upon the elected religious council virtually absolute powers. This political doctrine nevertheless remains the first conscious attempt to synthesize religious thought with popular democracy.

Islamic revivalism

In the contemporary Middle East, and the Islamic world more generally, two forces predominate in the shaping of thought and the behavior of the people: foreign intervention and Islam, both of which have been in continuous interaction. Islam, understood as a force for social justice, equality and economic well-being, has been an inheritable dynamic in the collective consciousness of the inhabitants of the Middle East. But it has changed over history, with Islamic reawakenings usually as diverse as the countries in which they originate and colored by domestic political circumstance. Yet, all forms of Islamic revival have had at least two common elements: opposition to foreign domination; and defense against perceived internal threats to the values and well-being of the Muslim community. Islamic movements, thus, have emerged in response to both domestic and foreign threats.

The Wahhabbi movement of Saudi Arabia is one such case. Wahhabbism owes its name to its founder, Mohammad Ibn 'Abd al-Wahhab (1703–1792). By the end of the seventh century, the Arabian Peninsula had already begun to decline in relation to the intellectual and civilizational influences of the newly founded Islamic capitals in Syria and Iraq, and later the Sublime Porte (today's Istanbul), and hence came to embody a political/economic periphery on the edge of the Islamic world. By the eighteenth century the Bedouins in the vast desert expanse of the Arabian Peninsula had reverted to polytheistic religious practices, which spread to every town and oasis, from Mecca and Medina to Jeddah, Najd and Najran.[57] Economically, greed and avarice ruled supreme.[58] Politically, the region was in a state of recidivistic tribal atavism and perpetual violence, particularly when it came to finding an heir on the death of a tribal chieftain.[59]

Restoration of Islam's pillars, particularly the externalities of monotheism, prayer, modest dress, *zakat*, etc., was the stated preoccupation of 'Abd al-Wahhab. However, unlike the Prophet, he refused dialogue, education and persuasion with those he considered to be apostates, or unbelievers. His personality and thought process had been forged by experiences of intellectual retrogression, intra-tribal factional wars and brutal force. The implements of his restorative mission were force and rationalization by extensive dependency on Hadith or Prophetic traditions without, however, the intellectual correlate of fully authenticating the Hadith. The use of Hadith in his religious venture served two purposes. First, in an illiterate society of Bedouins, the aura of the Sunna could relate the Bedouin to the demands of 'Abd al-Wahhab without the need for much explanation. Second, by calling the followers of his thought the "People of Hadith," or "Salafiyya" (the way of the good Muslim predecessors), he provided a linkage to an earlier epoch (1263–1328) when it was argued and believed that only adherents to the Sunna and Hadith would be redeemed.[60] Thus, the core teachings of Wahhabbism became the sole road to salvation.

The uncritical use of Hadith and the self-exculpatory reference to edicts from the past – without reasoned assessment of the context that gave rise to such edicts, particularly those of Ibn Hanbal – placed the movement on a retrospective trajectory that necessarily robbed it of the forward-looking orientation, intellectual vigor, or accommodative thought that characterized normative Islam. Human intelligence and reasoned judgment were marginalized and in time excluded, and, as a consequence, gave the movement its rigidity and parochialism. Given the core goal of Wahhabbism – the restoration of monotheism – 'Abd al-Wahhab probably believed he did not have the opportunity or time to engage in formulation of any political theory or system of government. The hereditary rule within a family, which he experienced throughout his life, remained the basis of his politics, and contemporary Saudi Arabia continues to demonstrate this.

Wahhabbism, through alliance with the Sa'udi clan from 1744 onward, became the religio-political framework of Saudi Arabia; it was borne of obscurantism and some violence. These tendencies persist, particularly in relation to the Shi'a minority within Saudi Arabia and the Saudi orientation toward the larger Shi'a community globally. Saudi chronicler 'Uthman Ibn 'Abdullah Ibn Bishr (as translated by Hamid Algar) provides an illustrative, matter-of-fact account of the Wahhabbis' orientation towards the Shi'a community:

In the year 1216 [1802 CE] . . . Sa'ud set out with his divinely supported army . . . He made for Karbala and began hostilities against the people. The

Muslims [i.e., the Wahhabbis] scaled the walls, entered the city by force, and killed the majority of its people in the markets and in their homes. Then they destroyed the dome placed over the grave of al-Husayn by those who believe in such things . . . They took everything they found in the town: different types of property, weapons, clothing, carpets, gold, silver . . . He had the booty assembled in front of him. He deducted one fifth for himself and then distributed the rest about the Muslims [Wahhabbis].[61]

By the nineteenth century there was some waning in the luster of the traditional system of religious studies in the Ottoman Middle East because of the influence of Western scientific disciplines in education. Yet, the religious educational system and the Sufi orders continued to be powerful channels for forming and articulating the collective consciousness of Muslims. Therefore, the governments in the Middle East attempted to exercise more control over the Sufi orders and religious teachings, though without much appreciable success, particularly in the rural areas and in the wilderness of the desert, where the mosque was the center of learning and Sufi orders flourished.[62] It was in these desolate areas that the Mahdi and the Sanusi movements erupted.

Mohammad Ahmad (1844–1885) founded the Mahdi movement in Sudan. Mohammad Ibn 'Ali al-Sanusi (1787–1859), who was born in Algeria, founded his sect in Cyrenaica (modern-day Libya). Both founders adhered to the Sufi path, and aspired to revive the ideal community according to the teachings of Islam, which, they both claimed, had deteriorated under Ottoman rule and the penetrating influence of the West. This belief was made clear by the Sanusi aphorism "I am against the Ottomans and the West."[63] However, there were differences between them, too. Mohammad Ahmad did not acquire a deep religious education, and his capacity to reconcile the modern forces of change to religious concepts was meager. Nevertheless, he and his followers among the poor and the dervishes fought the foreign presence between 1881 and 1885 and won quick victories.[64] By 1899, though, his movement had fallen apart because of its lack of an integrated religio-intellectual framework.

Al-Sanusi, on the other hand, was a religious scholar, and so versed in the Malikite School of Islamic legal thought that he modified its legal corpus by addition and omission in accordance with the needs of his time. Furthermore, his movement survived him. The main instrument of the Islamic revival efforts that al-Sanusi attempted to employ was the *Zawya*, a form of religious retreat from urban centers, where Muslims congregated to partake of religious education and logical reasoning, and to learn fighting methods and agriculture. It was a self-sufficient and charitable structure, devised from the early model of the city state of Medina. Al-Sanusi set up 188 such *Zawya* alongside caravan routes or close to caravan parks, as well as at strategic locations for defense. These promoted religious awakening, sharpened fighting skills, and propagated Islam deep into western Africa and Chad. The spirit, and training, of the *Zawya* constituted the nucleus of resistance to the French military in Mali, the Italian army in Libya and Christian missionary activity in Africa.[65] However, al-Sanusi's movement failed to provide its many followers with any advances in Islamic political theory. Its focus was on immediate threats, and the tool employed was adaptive borrowing from the Islamic heritage that had conditioned the thought processes of al-Sanusi himself.

While organized movements developed along the periphery of the Ottoman Empire, high-caliber religious intellectuals, like Mohammad Jamal al-Din al-Afghani (1838–1897) and his disciple, Mohammad 'Abdu (1849–1905), sparked an Islamic political awakening in Istanbul and Cairo, respectively, where the pervasive influence of the government was most felt. Al-Afghani was born in Kabul, Afghanistan.[66] Traditional religious disciplines, as well as modern European sciences, forged his intellectual orientation. Moreover, his frequent travels in the Ottoman lands, as well as Ottoman institutional complacency with its divisive professional rivalry and his direct experience of British methods of control in India, led him to believe in revolution as a tool of political change, and in the political education of the people for rational emancipation. His political thought and practice evolved during his stay in Egypt between 1871 and 1879.[67] There, the breadth and depth of his knowledge attracted young intellectuals of all disciplines, and his home became their special school. Here al-Afghani's profundity and the galvanizing clarity of his expression imbued revolutionary political ideas with religious undertones in his newly found followers, who included Mohammad 'Abdu, Ahmad 'Urabi (who led a revolt against Egyptian royal repression), al-Baroudi, Abdullah Nadim, Adib Issac and many others.[68]

Although the concept of pan-Islam had preceded al-Afghani and was exploited by both foreign and indigenous rulers to serve their interests, al-Afghani took it further and added new political dimensions of anti-imperialism, anti-sectarianism and pro-nationalism. He consistently emphasized that pan-Islam did not mean just the Office of the Ottoman Caliphate. Rather, it meant liberation from all forms of subjugation to foreigners, whether political, cultural or economic, and solidarity among Muslims, whether Sunnis or Shi'as. His opposition to sectarianism ensued from his principled belief that monotheistic religions share the same religious norms; hence, equality and solidarity among different religious adherents in a given territory should be the basis of socio-political cohesion. His advocacy of nationalism as a component of pan-Islam seems to be an echo of his era, when emergent nationalism was formative of new nation states. He reconciled nationalism with Islam pragmatically by arguing that historical and linguistic specifics identify a nation, while Islam is a wider container of faith and destiny that can accommodate many types of nationalism. Hence, many Muslim nation states can coexist in solidarity under pan-Islam. The methods he employed for the praxis of his political ideas ranged from public meetings, public addresses, a secret political organization (al-Hizb al-Watani al-Hur) in Egypt, publishing in existing papers and setting up new papers to stir the public to revolt against Western imperialism. Al-Afghani even suggested the use of popular armed resistance in order to attain the ultimate goal of freely elected constitutional government in the East.[69] He may not have formulated a distinct treatise of political theory, but he was no mere political agitator. Rather, he was a multifaceted leader who practiced what he preached; he taught revolution to the masses and the promising young because he had personally experienced the opportunism and selfish ruthlessness of rulers who succumbed to foreign domination. Al-Afghani campaigned relentlessly against despotism, tyranny and disunity, whether practiced by Muslims or non-Muslims. The spirit of his pan-Islam is now being recast by Muslim intellectuals in twenty-first-century Egypt.

One of his most promising followers was Mohammad 'Abdu, known to many Egyptians as the Imam. Al-Afghani and 'Abdu shared the same goals: the attainment of a freely elected government subject to the constraints of a popularly approved constitution, and freedom from foreign domination. But each championed his own methods. 'Abdu, unlike al-Afghani, was cautious about the inevitability and desirability of revolution, perhaps because he had not been similarly conditioned by extensive experience of rulers' opportunism. Instead, he emphasized reform and education of the public.[70] He also sought to free religious understanding from the blind imitation and superstition that had endured for hundreds of years by returning to the Qur'an, and by attempting to reconcile Islam with science. 'Abdu distinguished between the essential doctrine of Islam, the social teachings and the law. He argued that the doctrine is established and can be defended by reason. Law and socio-moral order, however, are applications to certain circumstances of general Qur'anic principles, which are deduced by human reasoning. Applications of Qur'anic principles would accommodate changing social circumstance. The task of human reason, from an Islamic perspective, he taught, is to relate temporal change to the unchanging principles.[71] 'Abdu set out to ponder the Qur'anic imagery and its relationship to contemporary understandings of the Islamic principles as they reasonably relate to the circumstances of the modern time. However, he died shortly thereafter, having achieved little.

'Abdu conceptualized religious reform at the macro level in order to expedite the process of public enlightenment. The focus of reform included the religious material study and teaching methods in al-Azhar – the oldest religious university in the Arabo-Muslim world – and the restructuring of religious courts and the system of religious endowments, *al-awqaf*. A reform of such magnitude might have been possible in a different political milieu, but Egypt was, at that time, occupied by the British and torn apart by factions who were loyal to the Khedive of Egypt and other wealthy, self-serving groups. 'Abdu's activism and activities were undermined by British imperialism, the Khedive and the economic elite. He did not foresee that, given the political situation, his conceptualized religious reform could not succeed without a comprehensive, radical program.[72] Politically, he espoused pan-Islamism and argued that normative Islamic politics could never be theocracy. The ruler was chosen by the people, who could subsequently depose him. Thus, for 'Abdu, sovereignty lay with the people, who were politically equal, irrespective of religion or lineage.[73] He did not elaborate, however, on the concept of political sovereignty, perhaps because his life, though rich and full, was so short. His influence was powerful, though, and he attempted to open people's minds to the problems of blind religious imitation. A hundred years later a vanguard of Muslim religious intellectuals – many of whom would later form the Muslim Brotherhood – would tread his contemplative path in an attempt to formulate an Islamic political doctrine proper.

The Muslim Brotherhood

Much like Mohammad 'Abdu, Hasan al-Banna (1906–1949), who founded the Muslim Brotherhood in 1928, believed in the importance of Islamizing the public by way of education and organization. Unlike 'Abdu, though, al-Banna chose to educate personally, by setting an example among his followers. His educational orientation toward religious awakening, much like 'Abdu's, was a return to the Qur'an, because the leaders of various Sufi orders, schools of legal thought, philosophy and theologians had unwittingly sown seeds of dissension in the Muslim community. Although al-Banna did not possess 'Abdu's erudition, he had a galvanizing personality and an easily comprehensible teaching method, which soon attracted many followers. His goal was to cultivate the kind of faith that integrates the spiritual, temporal and intellectual; and drives the transformed Muslim to renounce pretentiousness and prejudice, and to fight oppression and domination selflessly.[74]

During the first year of his call, al-Banna recruited over seventy followers via public sermons in coffee shops, social and sports clubs and various prayer spaces where the common people congregated.[75] The rapid spread of his teachings and growth of his organization can be attributed, among other things, to the interconnected networks that united the associations in public society. In other words, a physician in the Muslim Brotherhood would spread the teachings and the goals of the movement not only among his fellow physicians but in his family, his neighborhood, and even among some of his patients. The Muslim Brotherhood was built on two parallel structures: the general and the special. The former consisted of three levels of membership that addressed the varying spiritual and intellectual needs of the members; the latter, formed in 1940, was a military faction formed to fight foreign enemies whenever the time was right, particularly the occupying British and the Zionists in Palestine.[76] None the less, the strategy of the movement, according to al-Banna, was acceptance of all Muslims as they were into the fold and the peaceful Islamization of society through penetration of Egypt's social institutions and state apparatus. He consciously avoided open confrontation with the state, and sought to change it through social transformation. Moreover, he avoided a political Islamic discourse because of his limited formal training and his social, rather than explicitly political, goals.

Military confrontation was forced inopportunely upon the Brotherhood. First, there was the war of 1948 in Palestine, after which many members remained in Gaza and other occupied territories, cut off from the organization's base in Egypt. Second, there was the Egyptian military *coup d'état* in July 1952, which the Muslim Brotherhood initially supported. However, the coup's leaders, led by Nasser, saw the movement as a potential threat to their rule, and maneuvered to dissolve it in a new popular formation – the National Rally – which they designed. Finally, in 1954, an executive decree banned the Muslim Brotherhood.[77]

Discourses on nationalism and pan-Arabism from the top could not, however, replace the Islamic element in the collective consciousness of the masses, and this secular trend was eventually discredited, particularly after the military defeat of the Arab armies in 1967. The perceived failure of these secular experiments generated a number of crises in Arab society: one in identity, another in legitimacy, a third in penetration, and a fourth in distribution and participation. Such multidimensional fissures in the fabric of society gave weight – in one way or another – to the Islamic discourse of the Brotherhood. Al-Sadat, on taking office, allowed a margin of freedom to migrate for the previously repressed movement, largely in an attempt to counterbalance the power of the Nasserites and the leftists. The movement has ebbed and flowed over the years, but recently it has been very prominent in Egyptian social projects and unlicensed political agitation. Its discourse, in both Muslim and non-Muslim territories, focuses on repudiation of violence and the peaceful message of Islam. There has been inter-generational friction within the movement, often manifested in the selection of its leadership.[78] None the less, it now has a presence in at least sixty countries, and the fact that it has survived for over eighty years, usually in harsh political circumstances, is testament to its resilience and adaptability.[79]

However, the movement has not yet presented a comprehensive political reform program that can meet the needs of society domestically, regionally or globally. In March 2004, it published its reform initiative, which, among other propositions, highlighted its political outlook of people's sovereignty, peaceful change of political authority, freedom of conscience, thought and expression, freedom of assembly, peaceful protest, the right to form political parties without hindrance and the depoliticization of the army and police.[80] Furthermore, though the movement has recently advocated gender equality, it has not elaborated on the socio-political ramifications of such equality in unambiguous terms. Nor has it explicitly supported the right of both Muslim and non-Muslim individuals to occupy the office of the presidency.[81]

John Walsh argues that the Brotherhood has used a threefold strategy since Mubarak's ascent to power to gain a foothold in Egypt's socio-political institutions:[82] first, it sought to gain elected representation in the Egyptian parliament, largely through coalitions with other small opposition parties, or by fielding "independent" candidates; second, it has taken control of many NGOs, professional organizations and student associations through conventional electoral processes; and third, it has established a network of social services in neighborhoods and villages, which has given it a tangible degree of popular support without directly challenging the government. Mubarak has responded to these successes with consistent repression.[83]

In October 2006, Human Rights Watch reported that 792 Brotherhood members had been arrested and held without charge since March that year. Among them were 'Issam al-'Irian, chair of the Muslim Brotherhood Political Bureau, and Mohammad Mursi, former Member of Parliament and Executive Bureau member. The Egyptian government has yet to present a convincing justification for the continued ban on the movement (which has never been lifted since being imposed in 1954). Rather, it continues to trample on the political rights of its citizens and to arrest members of the political opposition, particularly the Brotherhood.[84] Underlying the repression of the Brotherhood in Egypt is the crisis of legitimacy in the Arab regimes, evidenced most clearly in their failure to counter Israeli violence against Palestinians – peaking with its Gaza assault in January 2009. The Egyptian regime, in particular, has been charged by the masses not only with inactivity but with complicity, cooperating formally and informally with Israeli violence against the Palestinians. Appropriately, with the outbreak of the Gaza War in early 2009, the Brotherhood was at the forefront in organizing massive demonstrations against Israeli belligerence and Egyptian inaction, drawing a reported 15,000 people north of Cairo on 16 January 2009. Consequently, the Egyptian regime increased its repression, allegedly arresting an additional 860 members of the movement.[85]

Militant activism

The two most prominent militant Islamic movements in the contemporary Arab world are Hizbollah in Lebanon and Hamas in the occupied Palestinian territories. They both took their inspiration and form from the Muslim Brotherhood and to some degree the Da'wah Party of Iraq. They have become Western bywords for "radical Islam."

Hizbollah, which emerged in reaction to Israel's occupation of southern Lebanon between 1982 and 2000, is a multidimensional movement that articulates the interest of Lebanon's historically disenfranchised Shi'a Muslim community. In Lebanon, government power rests on a confessional distribution of eighteen ethno-religious sects, of which the Shi'a people have been historically under-represented, despite their rapidly growing population. Funds for welfare and social development are tied to representation, which has contributed to the poverty of the Shi'a community. Attempts in the 1970s to mobilize in order to alleviate poverty did not bring about any significant gains.

From the beginning of the Israeli occupation of southern Lebanon in June of 1982 small, armed groups of young Shi'ites mobilized in the Beka' Valley and the suburbs of Beirut to repel the Israeli forces under the banner of Islam. Iran provided the initial military training and equipment for these militias. Over time, they came together to form Hizbollah. Sayyid Hasan Nasrallah, who became the secretary-general of Hizbollah in 1992, was still its leader at the time of writing. He had studied at the center of Shi'a studies in Najaf, Iraq, and became a follower of Ayatollah Khomenei, the then spiritual leader of Iran. Since Israel's withdrawal from southern Lebanon in June 2000, Hizbollah has committed itself to working within the state system and it now participates in the country's elections, a decision that alienated some of its more revolutionary-oriented leaders. In the "Cedar Revolution" of 2005, Hizbollah won 28 seats in the Lebanese parliament, and two cabinet positions.[86] In the election of 2009, it gained only 14 seats.

Hizbollah's gradual integration into the Lebanese state and the concurrent routinization of its politics raised the possibility that it would shed its more revolutionary dimension. However, Israel's invasion of Lebanon in the summer of 2006 halted this possibility. Precipitated by Hizbollah's capture of Israeli border patrollers, the Israeli campaign had the goal of destroying Hizbollah as a national movement and putting an end to its threats toward Israel's regional strategy. However, Israel was unable to accomplish either of these aims. In fact, Nasrallah emerged from the conflict as a lionized figure throughout the region, having achieved what the most powerful Arab states have not – forcing an Israeli military withdrawal by military action. Yet, for all the military rigor of Hizbollah, its day-to-day activities occur in the spheres of parliamentary politics and social welfare. In 2009, it published a comprehensive statement of political beliefs, its first since 1985, which expressed a practical political vision rather than the religious fanaticism that had marked its earlier statement.

Hamas is the historical embodiment of Muslim Brotherhood activism in the Gaza Strip since 1948. Although formally established only in 1987, its activities can be traced back to the 1970s, when its founder Ahmad Yassin returned from Cairo and established several charitable organizations, most notably an "Islamic University" in Gaza City. The image of the movement, fostered by its members' daily activities, is incorruptibility and self-sacrifice. Israel had perceived this brand of Islamic activity as harmless to its existence, viewing it more as a challenge to Fatah, Israel's main protagonist in the occupied territories. However, spurred on by the first Palestinian Intifadah of 1987, Hamas emerged politically and the movement expanded its activities to include military resistance and employed the tactic of suicide bombings. Over time, the organization gained solid popularity in the occupied territories, which stemmed from its being considered "the voice of Palestinian dignity and the symbol of the defence of Palestinian rights at a time of unprecedented hardship, humiliation, and despair."[87] When Israel pursued a collective punishment policy and ruination of the infrastructure of the occupied territories, it unwittingly created favorable circumstances for Hamas to become an indispensable socio-political movement. It pursued a policy of aid and assistance based on need rather than creed or political affiliation, which made it representative of all Palestinians.[88] Due to this, Hamas was able to gain 74 out of 132 seats in the Palestinian parliamentary elections of January 2006, assuming power as the elected government soon thereafter.

In mid-2008, Hamas was ousted from power by a coalition of Fatah and independent politicos, leaving it isolated and in control of only the Gaza Strip, its stronghold. Then, in late December 2008, Israel launched an intense bombing campaign and a ground offensive into Gaza, nominally to halt Hamas's haphazard rocket attacks but also to restrict access into and out of the enclave. The civilian population bore the brunt of Israel's attacks: "at least 1,300 Palestinians were reported killed, including 410 children and more than 100 women," while another 5,000 had been injured by mid-January 2009.[89] It is further estimated that the Israeli assault damaged the area's infrastructure to the tune of $1.9 billion.[90] In a post-conflict report, Amnesty International noted:

> Much of the destruction was wanton and resulted from direct attacks on civilian objects as well as indiscriminate attacks that failed to distinguish between legitimate military targets and civilian objects. Such attacks violated fundamental provisions of international humanitarian law, notably the

prohibition on direct attacks on civilians and civilian objects (the principle of distinction), the prohibition on indiscriminate or disproportionate attacks, and the prohibition on collective punishment.[91]

Hamas simultaneously represents a socio-political movement and a paramilitary challenge to Israel. It is nevertheless portrayed in the Western media and treated by Western political elites, particularly American, as irreconcilably terrorist in nature, with its core aim the destruction of Israel. Given this dominant perspective, it is instructive to consider the actual opinion of Hamas and its supporters, not merely that which is reported in the West. In research conducted by the Ramallah-based Near East Consulting Institute, 77 percent of Hamas supporters responded in favor of a negotiated settlement to the conflict;[92] moreover, Hamas has frequently accepted, in principle, the existence of Israel as delineated by its 1967 borders,[93] and has dropped the call for the destruction of Israel from its manifesto.[94] When asked whether Hamas would abandon the destruction of Israel as part of its platform, Mahmoud Zahar, one of its "hard-line" leaders, answered: "If Israel is ready to tell the people what is the official border, after that we are going to answer this question."[95] Khalid Meshal, Hamas's political bureau chief, admitted in 2008 that he and his fellow leaders are "realists" who recognize the existence of an "entity named Israel." Pushed further, he continued that Hamas accepts "the national accord for a Palestinian state based on the 1967 borders." More specifically, another Hamas leader, Ghazi Hamad, said in January 2009 that Hamas would be satisfied with the minimalist goals of reclaiming the West Bank, the Gaza Strip and East Jerusalem (the territories lost in 1967), thereby implicitly accepting Israel's pre-1967 borders.[96]

Hamas's increasingly conciliatory tone owes much to the evolution of the movement, particularly since its emergence as a formal player within the infrastructure of the Palestinian Authority and its accompanying responsibilities of governance. Due to this, it has continued to engage in Egyptian-brokered reconciliation talks with the rival Fatah movement, in the hope of forging a truly democratic Palestinian Authority. Hamas's continuous shift toward formal politics and an accompanying withdrawal from its original maximalist goals of an Islamic project have been noted by former Israeli Mossad chief Ephraim Halevy, who commented that Hamas has undergone a transformation "right under our very noses" and suggested that "its ideological goals [are] not attainable and will not be in the foreseeable future."[97] The formalization of Hamas's politics offers a possibility for reconciliation with Fatah, and, more importantly, a beginning of genuine discussions toward a final resolution with Israel. However, this will be difficult to achieve, given that Hamas is still largely treated as a pariah by the United States, Europe and Israel, which will only encourage it to revert to its previous form. The Israeli assault on the Gaza Strip was emblematic of the pressures that might eliminate Hamas from any good-faith negotiations.

The US and the spread of religious influence

The US-led invasions of Afghanistan and Iraq have removed Iran's adversaries in the East (the Taliban) and the West (Saddam Hussein's oppressive, though secular, regime). In Iraq, a politically sectarian government has emerged, with its dominant components paramilitary parties nurtured by Iran. Furthermore, the failure of the Israeli wars against Hizbollah in Lebanon from July to August 2006 and December 2008 to January 2009, which the US firmly supported, has boosted Iran's influence in that country. Moreover, Western denial of aid to the elected government in the occupied Palestinian territories resulted in a closer relationship between Hamas and Iran. Thus, if Iran's influence has expanded, it is as a direct result of US policy in the region. In addition, the Saudis perceive the rise of Iran as a threat to their brand of religious conservatism and power in the region. Even the liberal and secular Prince El Hasan bin Talal of Jordan fears that the welfare network and social policies of Hizbollah and Ayatollah Khomeini galvanize and recruit the poor and disenfranchised, because such social networks are able to meet people's needs much more effectively than governments can. Iran has built a vast aid network that covers the whole region, bringing Shi'ite groups together and even linking to Sunni groups.[98]

The phrase "Shi'ite Crescent" was first introduced in official Arab discourse by Egyptian President Hosni Mubarak in December 2005; King Abdullah II of Jordan and the Saudi Foreign Minister, Sa'ud al-Faisal, echoed the sentiment soon after. It came into widespread use after June 2006, once the US-based think-tank the Council on Foreign Relations had adopted it without considering its implications. Geographically, it could portray the spread of Iran's Shi'ite influence into Iraq, Syria, Lebanon and Saudi Arabia (10 percent of Saudis are Shi'ites). The concern in the West, particularly in the US, is not the rise of the power of Shi'ites *per se*, but how such a rise will affect domestic policies in countries with visible Shi'ite populations, as well as the overall balance of power in the Middle East. An excellent example of this was the 2009 Lebanese election, where regional powers, mainly Saudi Arabia and Iran, poured millions of dollars into political campaigns in an effort to have their "side" gain the upper hand.[99] In late 2009, Saudi Arabia forced itself into direct conflict with Shi'a militancy when it intervened militarily against the Houthi Shi'a rebels of northern Yemen. The Iranian experience has transformed Shi'ism from the "quietist denomination to a dynamic political force that engages the lives of the people."[100] It therefore poses a threat to the rigid, conservative political regimes of Sunni populations.

Conclusion

Within the wide swath that makes up today's Islamist movement, from reformist to radical, the most popular and active strain is found in the intellectual vanguard of the "New Islamists." Their discursive platform assumes a middle course – *Wasatiyya* – between historical Islam and modernity. The New Islamists aim to revive Islamic society based on the pursuit of social justice by utilizing the

Western processes of representation and free elections. Their ongoing project is laying the educational and cultural underpinnings of plurality and unrestricted deliberation to achieve an Islamic polity that has justice as its core value and democracy as its vehicle of realization. This is deemed necessary because, at the moment, there is no comprehensive Islamic constitutional thought.[101] The project has echoes of the Scandinavian political experiment that blended socialist values with the political mechanisms of democracy. According to 'Ali Mazrui, such a positive outcome is possible because Islamic heritage includes democratic principles, like *ijtihad*, *shura* (deliberation), and the Ottoman *millet* system that was devised to guarantee the autonomy of minorities. Should such a blending be successfully formulated, truly Islamic politics may evolve. The result would be "Islamocracy" – a synthesis of Islam and democracy. Iran, despite a heavy clerical element at the top, has attempted to achieve this.[102] However, given Western suspicion, if not downright opposition to Islamic alternative discourse, and the American support for Arabo-Muslim tyrannical regimes, it is difficult to conceive how the Islamic civilization project of the New Islamists could be implemented if it were ever formulated.

Even in Iran, which is a sovereign nation state, the natural course of historical development has been diverted by the unrelenting hostility of the US, which has imposed economic sanctions and threatened regime change ever since 1979. It will not be surprising if, in such a context, the instinct for survival propels the Iranian regime toward entrenchment and bellicosity rather than openness and finding a proportionate balance between the people's sovereignty and *Shari'a*. Taking the other route – whether in Iran, Palestine, Lebanon or elsewhere – requires regime stability, a sense of security and freedom from foreign hegemony. Unfortunately, however open and moderate the current generation of Islamists might be, the combination of domestic oppression and international isolation could preclude the development of Islamocracy and force a return to radical exclusionary politics.

Notes

1 Mohammad Hamidullah, *Muslim Conduct of State* (7th Edition) (Lahore: Ashrah, 1977), p. 51.

2 Afzal Iqbal, *Culture of Islam: The First Hundred Years* (4th Edition) (Chicago: Kazi Publications, 1990), pp. 11, 13.

3 Hamidullah, op. cit., pp. 53, 57.

4 Mohammad Hamidullah, *The Prophet's Establishing a State and His Succession* (Islamabad: Pakistan Hijra Council, 1988) pp. 20–21.

5 Saiyyid Maḥmûd al-Qimnî, *Ḥurûb Dawlat al-Rasûl* (Cairo: Sina, 1993) pp. 12, 16–17.

6 For details on coins, see Hasan Ibrahim Hasan, *Islam: A Religious, Political, Social And Economic Study* (Baghdad: University of Baghdad, 1967) , pp. 433–434.

7 Iqbal, op.cit. pp. 25, 28.

8 William Muir and William Muammad, *The Life of Mahomet* (Edinburgh: Nabu Press, 2010), p. xcvii.

9 Iqbal, op.cit., p. 5.

10 Ibid., p. 22.

11 Charles Gai Eaton, *Islam and the Destiny of Man* (Albany: SUNY Press), p. 113.
12 'Ali Shariati, *On the Sociology of Islam: Lectures* (Berkeley: Mizan Press, 2000), pp. 55–57.
13 Eaton, op. cit., pp. 115–116, 119.
14 Hamidullah, *The Prophet's Establishing a State*, op. cit., pp. 22–23.
15 Alî Sâmî al-Nashâr, *Nash'at al-Fikr al-Falsafî fî al-Islâm* (Alexendria: Dar al-Ma'arif, 1965), pp. 226–227.
16 Shariati, op. cit., pp. 71–72.
17 Mohammad Hamidullah, *The First Written Constitution in the World* (Chicago: Kazi, 1986), pp. 14–16, 18–19, 26–27.
18 Hamidullah, *The Prophet's Establishing a State*, op. cit., p. 34.
19 Mohammad Hamidullah, *Mohammad Rasululah: A Concise Survey of the Life and Work of the Founder of Islam* (Hyderabad-Deccan: Stockists, Habib, 1974), p. 62.
20 William Montgomery Watt, *Muslim–Christian Encounters: Perceptions and Misperceptions* (London: Routledge, 1991) p. 61.
21 Muḥammad 'Abd-ul-lah Idrîs, *Madkhal Ilâ al-Qur'ân al-Karîm* (Dubai: Dâr al-Qalam, 1980) pp. 60–64.
22 Yûsuf al-Qaradâwî, *Madkhal li Dirâsat al-Sunnah al-Nabawiyyah* (Beirut: Mu'assasat al-Risâlah, 2004), pp. 8, 12.
23 For example, the mandatory rites, commonly referred to as the pillars of Islam, which the Qur'an enjoined, could not be understood or performed without the explication of the Prophet. These are al-Shahada (the Muslim's conviction in the oneness and unity of a single God), the five daily prayers, fasting during the month of Ramadan, the calculation and the timing of giving *zakat* (a social tax) and the rituals of pilgrimage.
24 Yûsuf al-Qaradâwî, *Madkhal li Dirâsat al-Sharî'ah al-Islâmiyyah* (Beirut: Mu'assasat al-Risâlah, 1993), pp. 21–22.
25 'Ali A. Mazrui, "Pax Islamica and the Seven Pillars of Wisdom," Fifth Annual Conference, Center for the Study of Islam and Democracy, Washington, D.C., May 28–29, 2004.
26 Eaton, op. cit., p. 180; Shariati, op. cit., pp. 28–29.
27 Muṣṭafâ Abû-Zaid Fahmî, *Fan al- Ḥukm fî al-Islâm* (Cairo: al-Maktab al-Maṣrî al-Hadîth, 1981), p. 416.
28 Ibid., pp. 417–419.
29 Mohammad Hamidullah, *The Emergence of Islam* (Delhi: Adam, 1993) pp. 68, 85.
30 Adam Mez, *The Renaissance of Islam* (London: Luzac & Co., 1937) p. 212.
31 Muḥammad al-Ghazâlî, *Al-Ṭarîq min Honâ* (Cairo: Dâr al-Bashîr, 1987) pp. 25–31.
32 Warrior-dervish ethos refers to the founding Turkoman tribes of the Ottoman Empire, which translated their Sufi fraternity orders into political-administrative organization by the use of force and territorial expansion.
33 Abbâs Maḥmûd al-'Aqqâd, *Al- Dîmuqrâṭiyyah fî al-Islâm* (4th Edition) (Cairo: Dâr al-Ma'ârif, 1971), pp. 110–111.
34 Hamidullah, *The Prophet's Establishing a State*, op. cit., pp. 94–99.
35 Shariati, op. cit., p. 49.
36 Muḥammad Dîyâ-ul-Dîn al-Raiyyis, *Al-Nadhariyyât al-Siyâsiyyah al-Islâmiyyah* (Cairo: Dâr al-Turâth, 1952), p. 385.
37 Ibid., pp. 17–19.
38 Yûsuf al-Qaradâwî, *Min Fiqh al-Dawlah fî al-Islâm* (2nd Edition), (Cairo: Dâr al-Shurûq, 1999), p. 96.
39 Al-Raiyyis, op.cit., pp. 337–342.
40 D.M. Dunlop, *Arab Civilisation to AD 1500* (New York: Praeger, 1971), p. 173.
41 Al-'Aqqâd, op. cit., p. 157.
42 Ibid., pp. 151–152.
43 Dunlop, op. cit. pp. 186–187.

44 Albert Hourani, *The History of the Arab Peoples* (Cambridge, MA: Harvard University Press, 1991), p. 145.
45 Haroon Khan Sherwani, *Studies in Muslim Political Thought and Administration* (Philadelphia: Porcupine, 1977), pp. 80–84.
46 Ibid., p. 148.
47 Ibid., pp. 77–79. See also Hourani, op. cit., p. 145.
48 Sherwani, op. cit., pp. 158–171. Some analysis of the nature of these works is found in these pages.
49 Ibid., p. 172. See also Hourani, op. cit., p. 146.
50 In Shi'ite terminology, "occultation" refers to the supernatural or esoteric disappearance of the Imam.
51 For an excellent overview of Shi'a Islam and the Twelfth Imam, see Moojan Momen's *An Introduction to Shi'i Islam* (New Haven: Yale University Press, 1985), pp. 161–171.
52 Ahmad al-Kâtib, *Tatawwur al-Fikr al-Siyâsî al-Shî'î min al-Shûrâ Ilâ Wilâyat al-Faqîh* (Beirut: al-Dâr al-'Arabiyyah lil 'Ulûm, 2005), pp. 9–12, 205. The author is a Shi'ite Iraqi who provides in this work a critical analysis of the Shi'a political thought in historical context.
53 Ibid., pp. 13–15. See also the Shi'a website, URL: http://alkatib.co.uk/thirdprint.htm.
54 Mûsâ al-Mûsawî, *Al-Shî'ah Wa al-Tashih* (n.p., 1988), pp. 63–64.
55 Al-Kâtib, op. cit., p. 330.
56 Al-Mûsawî, op. cit., pp. 66–69.
57 Mahmûd Mitwallî, *Tawâ'if al-'Âlam al-Islâmî: Ru'yah Mu'âsirah* (Cairo: Nah'dha Bookshop, 1985), pp. 73–76.
58 Ibid., p.76
59 Ahmad al-Kâtib, *Al-Fikr al-Siyâsî al-Wahhâbî* (2nd Edition) (London: Dar al-Shura London, 2004), p. 61.
60 Ibid., pp. 15–30, 40–41, 51, 71.
61 Hamid Algar, *Wahhabism: A Critical Essay* (Oneonta: Islamic Publications International, 2001), pp. 24–25.
62 Hourani, op. cit., pp. 311–312.
63 Mitwallî, op. cit., pp. 118–119, 126, 131.
64 "Dervishes" is an umbrella word for all the local Sufi fraternities that flourished in Sudan at that time.
65 Mitwallî, op. cit., pp. 128–130.
66 It is often mentioned that Afghani was born in Iran–Asadabadi. However, other sources stipulate that he was born near Kabul in Afghanistan.
67 Muhammad 'Imârah, *Jamâl-u-Dîn al-Afghânî: Al-A'mâl al-Kâmilah* (Beirut, al-Mu'assasah al-'Arabiyya lil Dirâsât wa al-Nashr, 1979), I, pp. 28–31, 33.
68 Ibid., p. 35.
69 Ibid., pp. 35, 58, 63–81.
70 Muhammad 'Imârah, *Al-A'mâl al-Kâmilah lil Imâm Muhammad 'Abduh* (Beirut, al-Mu'assasah al-'Arabiyya lil Dirâsât wa al-Nashr, 1972), I, pp. 38–40.
71 Hourani, op. cit., p. 308.
72 'Imârah, *Al-A'mâl al-Kâmilah lil Imâm Muhammad 'Abduh*, op. cit., pp. 80–81.
73 Ibid., pp. 104–109, 362–366.
74 Yûsuf al-Qaradâwî, *Al-Tarbiyah al-Islâmiyyah wa Madrasit Hasan al-Bannâ* (Cairo: Wahba Book Store, 1992), pp. 9–14.
75 Al-Saiyyid Yûsuf, *Hasan al-Bannâ wa Binâ' al-Tandhîm* (Cairo: al-Mahrûsah, 1994), pp. 148–53, 161.
76 Ref'at al-Saiyyid Ahmad & 'Amr al-Shubakî, *Mustaqbal al-Harakât al-Islâmiyyah ba'd September 11* (Damascus: Dâr al-Fikr, 2005), pp. 240–245.
77 Salâh Shâdî, *Hasâd al-'Umr* (3rd Edition) (Cairo: al-Zahrâ', 1987), especially pp. 253–260.

78 *Dalîl al-Ḥarakât al-Islâmiyyah fî al-'Âlam* (Cairo: al-Ahram Center for Political & Strategic Studies, 2006), pp. 28–32. See also Shâdî, op. cit., pp. 120–125.
79 Israel Elad-Altman, "Democracy, Elections, and the Egyptian Muslim Brotherhood," in *Current Trends in Islamist Ideology* (New York: Hudson Institute, 2006), III, p. 28.
80 *Dalîl al-Ḥarakât al-Islâmiyyah fî al-'Âlam*, pp. 32–33, 40.
81 Rashwân, op. cit.
82 John Walsh, "Egypt's Muslim Brotherhood: Understanding Centrist Islam," *Harvard International Review*, Vol. 24, No. 1, 2003. URL: http://hir.harvard.edu/articles/1048.
83 Ibid.
84 Human Rights Watch, "Egypt: Crackdown on Muslim Brotherhood Deepens," October 26, 2006. URL: http://www.hrw.org/english/docs/2006/10/24/egypt14433.htm.
85 Human Rights Watch, "Gaza Crisis: Regimes React with Routine Repression," January 21, 2008. URL: http://www.hrw.org/en/news/2009/01/21/gaza-crisis-regimes-react-routine-repression?print.
86 Robert Pape, "Ground to a Halt,", *International Herald Tribune*, August 3, 2006. URL: http://www.iht.com/articles/2006/08/03/opinion/edpape.php; Lara Deeb, "Hizbollah: A Primer,", *Middle East Research and Information Project*, August 3, 2006. URL: http://www.globalresearch.ca/index.php?context = viewArticle&code = DEE2006 0803&articleId = 2897.
87 Neve Gordon, "Why Hamas Won and What it Means,", *Z Magazine*, February 7, 2006. URL: http://www.zmag.org/content/showarticle.cfm?ItemID = 9686.
88 Ibid.
89 Jeffrey Fleishman, "A Battle over What Happened in Gaza," *Los Angeles Times*, January 23, 2009. URL: http://www.latimes.com/news/nationworld/world/la-fg-gaza-aftermath23–2009jan23,0,2503152,print.story.
90 Amira Hass, "Palestinian Estimates: Fighting Caused $1.9 Billion in Damage to Gaza Strip," *Haaretz*, January 20, 2009. URL: http://www.haaretz.com/hasen/spages/1056951.html.
91 Amnesty International, "Israel/Gaza Operation 'Case Lead': 22 Days of Death and Destruction." URL: http://www.amnesty.org/en/library/asset/MDE15/015/2009/en/8f299083–89a74-4853-860f-0563725e633a/mde150152009en.pdf.
92 "Despite Hamas Win, Palestinians Want a Peace with Israel," Agence France-Presse, January 30, 2006. URL: http://www.reliefweb.int/rw/RWB.NSF/db900SID/VBOL-6LJDSG?OpenDocument.
93 Arnon Regular, "Hamas Recognizes 1967 Borders for the First Time," *Haaretz*, January 21, 2006. URL: http://www.israelpalestineforum.com/content/view/27/30.
94 Chris McGreal, "Hamas Drops Call for Destruction of Israel from Manifesto," *Guardian*, January 12, 2006, p. 17.
95 Rahul Mahajan, "Hamas and Palestinian Democracy," *Z Magazine*, February 5, 2006. URL: http://www.zmag.org/content/showarticle.cfm?ItemID = 9667.
96 Fawaz Gerges, "The Transformation of Hamas," *The Nation*, January 7, 2010. URL: http://www.thenation.com/doc/20100125/gerges/print.
97 Ibid.
98 Olivia Ward, "Iran Gives New Global Muscle Workout," *Toronto Star*, December 30, 2006. URL: http://www.thestar.com/News/article/166401.
99 See Robert F. Worth, "Foreign Money Seeks to Buy Lebanese Votes," *New York Times*, April 23, 2009. URL: http://www.nytimes.com/2009/04/23/world/middleeast/23lebanon.html?_r = 1&pagewanted = print. "Lebanon's Post Election Fate Tied to Region," Reuters, June 8, 2009. URL: http://www.independent.co.uk/news/world/middle-east/lebanons-postelection-fate-tied-to-region-1699828.html. Robert Fisk, "The Mysterious Case of the Israeli Spy Ring, Hizbollah and the Lebanese Ballot," *Independent*, June 1, 2009. URL: http://www.independent.co.uk/opinion/commentators/fisk/robert-fisk-the-mysterious-case-of-the-israeli-spy-ring-hizbollah-and-the-lebanese-ballot-1693844.html. Robert Fisk, "Biden's Real Mission Is to Stop Hizbollah,"

Independent, May 23, 2009. URL: http://www.independent.co.uk/opinion/commentators/
fisk/robert-fisk-bidens-real-mission-is-to-stop-hizbollah-1689778.html.

100 Council on Foreign Relations, *The Emerging Shia Crescent Symposium: Implications
for US Policy in the Middle* East, August 2006. URL: http://www.cfr.org/publication/
10866/emerging_shia_crescent_symposium.html.

101 Raymond W. Baker, *Islam without Fear* (Cambridge, MA: Harvard University Press,
2003), pp. 170–173.

102 'Ali Mazrui, "Islamocracy: In Search of a Muslim Path to Democracy," Fourth Annual
Conference, Center for the Study of Islam and Democracy, Washington, D.C., May
16, 2003.

Further reading

The following is a compilation of seminal works on the question of Islam,
including the foundational texts of the religion, inquiries in Islamic law, and
commentaries on contemporary phenomena, including Islamic revivalism and
political movements.

As to the Qur'an itself, (Mohammad) Marmaduke Pickthall, an Anglican
convert to Islam, produced a Qur'anic translation in 1920 that is both a faithful
religious effort as well as a significant literary achievement of poetic quality.
Relating to the Hadith, the sayings and traditions of the Prophet of Islam, Thomas
Clearly's *The Wisdom of the Prophet: The Sayings of Mohammad* is a well-
regarded and rich collection of hadiths, chosen for their universal appeal.

Hamilton Alexander Rosskeen Gibb's *Mohammadanism: A Historical Survey*
and *Islam: A Historical Survey* are fine pieces of Orientalist scholarship that survey
the origins and development of Islam. Karen Armstrong's *Islam: A Short History*
is a highly accessible work of popular history and useful as an introduction to
Islam. Likewise, William M. Watt's *Mohammad at Mecca* is a fair-minded and
broad biography of the Prophet of Islam during his life in Mecca and remains
accessible and useful; his *The Majesty that was Islam* is a thorough account of
Islamic heritage at its cultural, economic and political zenith.

Concerning traditions of Islamic jurisprudence, Bernard G. Weiss's *The Spirit
of Islamic Law* is a concise and lucid analysis of Islamic law as a system, including
an analysis of historical debates in matters of Islamic jurisprudence. It is an
accomplished distillation of the principles of Islamic law.

For an historical account of Islam's political mobilization, Nikki Keddie's *An
Islamic Response to Imperialism: Political and Religious Writings of Sayyid Jamal
ad-Din "al-Afghani"* is a good starting point, with accessible translations of al-
Afghani's writings and thoughts and commentary on this early Islamic encounter
with imperialism. Concerning contemporary debates and the question of Islamist
political movements, Graham E. Fuller's *A Sense of Siege: The Geopolitics of
Islam and the West* (with Ian Lesser) and *The Future of Political Islam* (with
Joanne Myers) are substantial treatments of the geostrategic and political questions
surrounding the emergence of politicized Islam. Richard P. Mitchell's *The Society
of Muslim Brothers* is the standard English-language account of the origins and
development of the Egyptian Muslim Brotherhood. Raymond William Baker's

Islam without Fear is a useful addendum, detailing the developments in theory and organization of Egypt's Muslim societies, particularly the mainstream centrist trend of Islamist movements.

Finally, as a broad representation of contemporary Muslim opinion on a range of political, economic and social questions, John L. Esposito and Dalia Mogahed's *Who Speaks for Islam? What a Billion Muslims Really Think* – drawn from Gallup World's extensive data – is a concise but informative overview of the Muslim world's reaction to and interpretation of the questions of the contemporary world.

References

Armstrong, Karen (2002) *Islam: A Short History*, Modern Library.

Baker, Raymond William (2006) *Islam without Fear*, Harvard University Press.

Clearly, Thomas (translator) (2001) *The Wisdom of the Prophet: The Sayings of Mohammad*, Shambhala.

Esposito, John L. & Mogahed, Dalia (2008) *Who Speaks for Islam? What a Billion Muslims Really Think,* Gallup Press.

Fuller, Graham E. & Lesser, Ian O. (1995) *A Sense of Siege: The Geopolitics of Islam and the West* (5th Edition), Westview Press.

Fuller, Graham E. & Myers, Joanne J. (2004) *The Future of Political Islam*, Palgrave Macmillan.

Gibb, Hamilton Alexander Rosskeen (1953) *Mohammadanism: A Historical Survey*, Oxford University Press.

—— (1999) *Islam: A Historical Survey*, Pan.

Keddie, Nikki (1968) *An Islamic Response to Imperialism: Political and Religious Writings of Sayyid Jamal ad-Din "al-Afghani"*, Cambridge University Press.

Mitchell, Richard P. (1993) *The Society of Muslim Brothers*, Oxford University Press.

Watt, William M. (1990) *The Majesty that Was Islam*, Palgrave Macmillan.

—— (1993) *Mohammad at Mecca*, Kazi Publications.

Weiss, Bernard G. (2006) *The Spirit of Islamic Law*, University of Georgia Press.

Part II

Major governments and politics

The Northern Belt

4   The Republic of Turkey

The migration of the Turkic people south-westward from their ancestral homeland in Central Asia, where they had lived for centuries as tribal nomads, had an immense impact on the Middle Eastern region as well as substantial parts of Africa and Europe. In 1055, they seized the capital of the Islamic Caliphate, Baghdad, founding the Seljuk dynasty, which would rule over a major swath of the Islamic world. By the thirteenth century, the power of the dynasty had waned, due mainly to weak leadership and defeats at the hands of Mongolian warriors. From the crumbling Seljuk Empire arose a new Turkic ruling class who would greatly expand upon the lands the Seljuks had conquered. The Ottoman Empire was the last great Islamic civilization free from foreign exploitation. Emerging in the thirteenth century, it reached its zenith in the fifteenth century with the conquest of Constantinople (today's Istanbul) and the dismantling of the Byzantine Empire. It would continue to rule much of the Middle East until the twentieth century. However, at the close of the First World War, with the empire carved up between European powers, Turkish nationalists established the modern – and secular – Republic of Turkey.

The encroachment of the Turks into the Middle East had been facilitated by their superior abilities as warriors; in the ninth century they were hired by Abbasid caliphs as mercenaries and "warriors of the faith" (*ghazis*). However, these warriors seldom limited their role to the defense and expansion of the Caliphate, and eventually took power themselves. The Caliphate, which was centered in Baghdad, was overthrown by an Oguz Turk – Tugrul Bey – who proclaimed himself Sultan and established the Seljuk dynasty. Oguz, one of the Turkic tribes, is the group from which modern Turks claim descent. These warlike tribesmen migrated from east to west up to the frontiers of the Byzantine Empire, across which they made raids into the lands of Christendom. A doomed effort was made by the Byzantines, crippled by their own internal divisions and ironically aided by Turkish mercenaries, to defeat the Muslim Turkish invaders. In the Battle of Malazgirt in eastern Turkey in 1071, Seljuk forces triumphed, defeating the Byzantine armies and capturing the Emperor, which gave them control over much of Anatolia.

In the middle of the thirteenth century, the Seljuk dynasty began to decline as the invasions of the Mongol armies of Genghis Khan reached its eastern frontier.

With this conquest more Turks migrated westward, drastically altering the character of Anatolia through settlement, intermarriage and conversion to Islam, leaving the area to be dominated by the Turks. In spite of this Islamic-Turkish dominance, the indigenous Greek and Armenian populations were allowed to retain their religions.

The Mongols destroyed the central authority of the Seljuk Sultan but a number of his princes survived as independent chieftains. These leaders of *ghazis*, whose reputation and livelihood depended on the waging of holy war (*Jihad*) against "infidels," extended the Turkish presence up to the Anatolian coastline and irrevocably transformed it into a Turko-Muslim culture.[1] One such prince, Osman, founded the Ottoman Empire. His principality was the closest to the Byzantine capital of Constantinople and was well defended. Bursa, which was conquered by Osman's son Orhan in 1326, served as the capital of the Ottoman state for several decades. The Ottomans successfully expanded their empire, and in 1352 their forces crossed the Bosporus into Europe, subduing the fortifications of Gallipoli. A decade later, Sultan Murad I (r.1362–1389) occupied Adrianople (Edirne) and made it the new capital of the empire. In 1380 he created an embryonic empire that consisted of vassal principalities in both Anatolia and Rumelia, and this was eventually transformed by Sultan Bayezit I (r.1389–1403) into a true empire ruled by a centralized administration.[2] Mehmet, "The Conqueror," captured Constantinople in 1453 and renamed it Istanbul, which was a transliteration of the Greek *eis tein polein* (the city). (In the ninth and tenth centuries, Constantinople had been the largest city in the world, and was simply referred to as such.) After capturing his new capital, Mehmet claimed all the lands once previously ruled by the Byzantines, establishing a mandate for later Ottoman sultans to extend the boundaries of the empire. At its height in the seventeenth century, the Ottoman dominion included the Balkan Peninsula, the Crimea, Iraq and the western shores of the Persian Gulf, Syria, Palestine, west and south Arabia, Egypt, Libya, Tunisia and Algeria.[3]

However, the Ottoman Empire's authority in the Middle East began to recede in the eighteenth century under a variety of pressures. Turkish administration had become highly centralized in Istanbul, with only a network of feudal overlords and governors serving as provincial governments. The latter were encouraged to increase their autonomy, allowing non-Turkish populations to nurture nationalistic feelings. In addition, the whole Ottoman bureaucracy was tainted with nepotism and corruption, which paralyzed the work of government. Further weakening the empire was the penetration of European colonial powers into the Middle East. In the economic sphere, this had a particularly damaging impact because of the system of capitulation. Capitulations were originally unilateral concessions granted to selected Western powers and could be withdrawn by the Sultan. However, as the balance of power shifted decisively in favor of the European powers, they ceased to be given voluntarily and became mechanisms for the exploitation of Ottoman territory.

Some historians note that the first capitulations granted to France in 1535 were intended to support that country in its competition with the Habsburgs, who controlled territory on the expansion route of the Ottomans and sought to unify Europe under Catholic Christianity. Under the system of capitulation, foreigners were granted special privileges as an act of goodwill and to encourage trade. They exempted foreigners from Turkish law and taxes, and granted the power of arrest and deportation over foreign nationals to ambassadors.[4] Through them, the region's economy was opened to Western capitalism, with the direct result of stifling the industrialization of the local manufacturing sector, which in turn relegated the region to a producer of raw materials for European industry. This curtailed the central government's ability to raise revenues, which led to borrowing from foreign banks and governments in an effort to meet any shortfall in the budget. The first loan was contracted in 1854, and by 1877 the public debt had reached £190,997,980 (plus interest of £61,803,905), which forced the Ottoman state to declare bankruptcy.[5]

In the eighteenth century, with Ottoman imperial control in the Balkans and the Crimean Peninsula faltering, domestic reforms were initiated. The Turkish imperial administration had been highly centralized in Istanbul, with a network of feudalistic overlords and governors controlling the provinces. This led to two problems. First, the governors, who were generally geographically distant from the administrative center, made repeated attempts to increase their autonomy. Second, the provinces remained predominantly non-Turkish in terms of population and culture, and over time they developed nationalist ideologies. The central government also began to decline. The sultans had long had the prerogative of appointing personal favorites to ministerial posts, often after accepting lavish bribes. So long as the sultan was the only one operating in this manner, little harm resulted, but when the entire bureaucracy began following this practice, the government became paralyzed by nepotism and corruption.

The Ottoman Empire was a multi-ethnic and multi-religious state. Religious communities were called *millets*, and each *millet* was recognized as internally autonomous in the administration of its religious and personal laws as long as it remained loyal to the sultan. Russian expansion eastwards toward the Black Sea in the eighteenth century politicized these ethnic and religious communities. After the defeat of the Ottoman Empire in the first major Russo-Turkish War (1768–1774), Russia gained control of two ports in the Crimean Peninsula and, for the first time, access to the Black Sea and the Dardanelles. From this point on, the protection of Orthodox Christian *millets* in Ottoman lands became a pretext for further Russian, and later other European, interference in Ottoman politics on behalf of non-Muslim minorities. The Treaty of Kuchuk Kaynarja, signed after this war, gave Tartars of the Crimea political independence from Ottoman rule, but "they were to remain somehow linked to the Ottoman sultan in his capacity as 'Grand Caliph.'"[6] Article III of the Treaty states: "As to the ceremonies of religion, as the Tartars profess the same faith as the Mahometans [i.e. Muslims], they shall regulate themselves, with respect to His Highness, in his capacity of Grand Caliph of Mahometanism, according to the precepts prescribed to them by their law, without compromising, nevertheless, the stability of their political and civil liberty."[7] Article XIV gives the Russian Emperor the right to protect Orthodox

Christian subjects of the Ottoman Empire: "After the manner of other Powers, permission is given to the High Court of Russia, in addition to the chapel built in the Ministers residence, to erect in one of the quarters of Galata, in the street called Bey Oglu [in Istanbul], a public church of the Greek ritual, which shall always be under the protection of the Ministers of that Empire, and secure from all coercion and outrage."[8]

European military penetration in the Middle East, and later the presence of missionaries and commercial interests, brought with it Western culture. Symbols of this culture, such as dress and manners, were adopted by many educated people in the urban centers, but of far more importance was the influx of Western thought, which sparked a Turkish intellectual revolution. One of the fruits of this renaissance was a new literature that transformed the nationalist ideas of European liberals into local and regional political programs. During this period of European expansion into the Middle East, Turkish leaders were given ample opportunity to observe the more efficient Western administrative machinery and compare it with their own institutions. This comparison made it clear to some of those leaders that administrative reform was both possible and necessary. Two schools of reform emerged within the empire, both influenced by Europeans. The idealists felt that the adoption of Western governmental procedures (along with the philosophy underlying those procedures) would lead to such economic and industrial development that Turkey would eventually gain equality with the Western nations. The realists felt that technological development was necessary first and that this would then force governmental change. The Ottoman administration attempted to follow both programs, endeavoring to introduce the use of modern and predominantly Western tools and techniques at all governmental levels, with direction from the top of the administrative pyramid. In order to achieve this, the government's first task was to break the power of conservative elements in the military. Consequently, a special artillery unit, loyal only to Sultan Mahmoud II, was formed. This unit surrounded the barracks of the famed Janissary Corps in Istanbul, the stronghold of conservatism, and annihilated them in 1826. Then it traveled throughout the country and purged the rest of the military in a similar manner. Once the conservative elements had been eliminated, a new army was created, one that supported the government's reform program.[9]

Backed by its modern army, the government was able to issue two decrees: 1839's *Tanzimat Fermani-Gülhane Hatt-i Sherif* and 1856's *Islahat Fermani-Hatt-i Humayun*. Limiting its own powers, it gave non-Muslims equal protection under the law, and it reorganized corrupt governmental agencies. Although neither decree was ever fully implemented and the pressure for reform waxed and waned periodically, these measures managed to increase governmental efficiency. Going hand in hand with them, government support was provided for fledgling newspapers and publishing houses, and the number of schools was increased with the express purpose of raising literacy.[10]

Finally, in 1876, Midhat Pasha, the Grand Vizier and the last of the nineteenth-century reformers, promoted an Ottoman state in which the citizens would be subject to only one legal system in an effort to overcome existing religious and ethnic differences that made the country virtually impossible to govern. Hence the idea of Ottomanism emerged as an alternative to the old *millet* system.[11] Pasha succeeded in introducing a constitution, *Kanun-i Esasi* (literally Fundamental Law), in 1876 and established a two-chamber parliament. However, Sultan 'Abdul Hamid II used the Russo-Turkish War of 1877–1878 as a pretext to regain absolute control of the state through the emergency powers clause of the new constitution. The parliament was rendered powerless and Pasha and the rest of the reformers were dismissed and then murdered.

Nevertheless, by then, the Ottoman armed forces had been modernized through the adoption of European training, tactics, equipment and organizational structure. And it was anticipated that reformist ideas would gradually spread from the military to the political, economic and cultural spheres. Indeed, many of those lobbying for change would see their sentiments echoed in the Young Turks, who were trained in the new, Western-style military academies of the empire. Furthermore, the return to despotism was followed by the proliferation of a network of secret societies, most often centered on Turkish nationalism. These societies were divided between those that favored a continuation of central rule and those advocating decentralization. In 1907, at the Ottoman Liberal Congress in Paris, these groups were united under the Committee of Union and Progress (CUP), which consisted mostly of army officers, government officials and professional men, and was dominated by the concepts of Ottomanism and centralization. It adopted a program opposed to the government of 'Abdul Hamid II, and in 1908 the Young Turks, who were inspired by nationalist and ethnic concerns rather than social justice,[12] led a rebellion against the Sultan's government. The committee forced a return to parliamentary government and sponsored a resurgence of the programs of modernization and reform and the opening of the second constitutional period. The CUP became the dominant political party in the parliament at the April 1912 elections, even though the Young Turk revolutionaries had declared themselves to be a political party in April 1909.[13] However, reform efforts were constrained by a number of factors, most importantly continued fighting in the Balkans, which led to the loss of the few remaining Ottoman possessions in Europe.

In 1914, Turkey entered the First World War on the side of the Germans, which ultimately brought about the collapse of the Empire four years later. The armistice agreement, signed by Turkish and British representatives, placed all Ottoman territories in the Arab and African regions under Allied control, as well as the Dardanelles and Black Sea fortifications. On November 2–3, 1918, several prominent leaders of the CUP fled to Berlin, while Vahdettin (known as Mehmed VI) became Sultan. He was keen to accede to all the demands of the Allied powers as long as his own position was secured, which brought him into sharp conflict with Turkish nationalists.

On November 13, a fleet of Allied ships anchored at Istanbul and Allied forces entered the city. To allay well-placed fears and suspicion, the commander of the force assured the Turks that no occupation of Ottoman territory was intended. However, in a series of secret agreements, the Allied powers had carved up the

Ottoman territories between themselves. French forces landed in Istanbul on February 8, 1919 to an enthusiastic welcome by the non-Turkish population of the city and a great deal of resentment from Turkish nationalists. The arrogance of the victorious powers spurred on Turkish nationalism and in all parts of the country patriotic societies sprang up, with one of the earliest being the Ottoman Defense Committee of Thrace. "Weakened by years of war, despised by their former subjects, betrayed by their leaders, the Turks had suddenly begun to find themselves."[14] The nationalist spirit became militant when Greek forces, with Allied naval support, invaded Izmir on February 15, 1919. Local Turkish inhabitants were massacred as the Greek forces pushed into the interior, and an armed resistance was born. Mustafa Kemal Pasha harnessed this militant nationalism to found an independent Turkish state. In acknowledgment of his achievement, he was given the name Atatürk ("Father of the Turks") by the Turkish Grand National Assembly in the 1930s.

Turkish nationalism

Throughout the reform period,[15] concepts of nationalism were developed, the terms for "fatherland" and "nation" began to acquire specific definitions in relation to the Ottoman state, and Ottomanism developed increasingly patriotic overtones. Thus, in 1860, Sinasi, an Ottoman journalist, wrote an article that discussed the interests of the "fatherland" and spoke of an Ottoman "nation" within the Ottoman state. Namik Kemal, a gifted contemporary of Sinasi, also wrote of an Ottoman nation within the empire, but he wanted that nation to be Islamic as well as Ottoman. He firmly believed that Muslim values and traditions would be reconciled with his own concepts of nationalism, parliamentary democracy and individual freedom. He was, in fact, so anxious to preserve the best of the Islamic tradition that he suggested that the tie of Islamic brotherhood should become the means of implementing modernization, not just in Turkey but throughout Asia and Africa.

A number of secret societies were established following the return to despotism at the end of the first constitutional movement, and these proponents of nationalist ideology gained adherents from all sectors of society. Many of them espoused pan-Turanism, a belief that the Ottoman Turks were part of a larger Turanian race that occupied swaths of Russia, Central Asia and China. The pan-Turanists fostered racism by concentrating on the ancient history of Turkey and the original Turkish language. Pan-Turanism, however, was countered by Ottomanism, a concept that stressed the equality of all subjects of the empire, regardless of race, nationality or religion. The secret societies were also divided between those who favored the continuation of centralism and those advocating a movement toward decentralization.

The next notable factor in the growth of Turkish nationalism was the outstanding performance of the Turkish military during and immediately after the First World War. The Turkish success in repelling the Allies at Gallipoli, and later in driving out the Greek army of occupation, were viewed as great triumphs. The people began to regard themselves proudly as Turks, rather than as citizens of the more cosmopolitan Ottoman Empire.

However, the complete formulation of Turkish nationalism, as it would develop under Atatürk, was derived from the ideas of the sociologist Ziya Gökalp.[16] Gökalp drew the idea of society as a reified concept from the philosophy of the French sociologist Emile Durkheim. He rejected a multinational society in favor of a Turkish one, for he held that any state that consisted of two or more cultures would disintegrate when those cultures were allowed to reassert themselves. For the same reason, he made a distinction between Western culture and Western civilization, rejecting the former while accepting the latter. Gökalp's program of pan-Turkism consisted basically of two elements. First, he advocated a conscious return to a pure Turkish culture. The Turkish language was to be used, particularly in prayer, and there should be a return to the supposedly superior morality of the ancient Turks in the areas of national patriotism and family relations. The second element was Gökalp's plan for the modernization of the country. He stated that the power of the religious courts had to be curtailed in order to deliver Turkey from theocracy and clericalism. And he championed "economic patriotism," which would seek to attain the prosperity of the ancient Turks through industrialism and capitalism, with occupational unions and guilds becoming leading players in the system. It was assumed that government aid would be necessary for the development of industry. Atatürk adopted many of these notions, although he and the founders of the republic rejected romantic nationalistic adventures in Central Asia, restricting their goals to Turkey's existing boundaries.

Thus, as the Ottoman Empire was on its deathbed, the intellectual and political foundations necessary for the development of a modern Turkish state were already in place. It was on these secular and nationalistic foundations that Atatürk would build the Turkish Republic. Born in Salonika in 1881, Mustafa Kemal was a professional soldier who progressed to the rank of *pasha* during the Ottoman period. In the course of the First World War he served first as an officer in the Gallipoli campaign, where he distinguished himself as a daring and popular leader, and was then given command of the Ottoman forces on the Syrian front, where he dramatically improved morale and prevented collapse of the Turkish forces. By the end of the war, he had won the admiration of many demoralized Turkish soldiers and was something of a national hero. As such, he was a prime candidate to lead the nationalist struggle.

However, immediately after the war, the nationalists' cause seemed hopeless. They were weak and poorly organized, and they faced a variety of external and internal opponents. Chief among these were the victorious Allies, who were determined to conclude a peace treaty with the Sultan's government. What came to be known as the Treaty of Sévres, signed on August 10, 1920, would have ended the dream of an independent and united Turkish republic, had it been implemented. As Atatürk stated:

> That Treaty is a sentence of death [for Turkey], so fatal for the Turkish nation that we request that its name should not be pronounced by mouths which

claim to be friends. It is impossible that Europe should be ignorant of our National Pact; perhaps it is ignorant of the text, but Europe and the whole world, seeing us spill our blood for years, must certainly reflect upon the reasons which have provoked such bloody conflicts.[17]

When it was passed, the treaty gave impetus to the nationalist struggle.

The initial Greek advances of 1919 and 1920 were partly facilitated by disunity in the ranks of the nationalist leaders. But as the nationalist forces organized under the command of Atatürk, the tide of the war turned in their favor. On June 4, 1920, the Caliphate's forces were routed; the Greeks were pushed back to Bursa on January 10, 1921; and, in the East, the Armenians were defeated. (During the war, hundreds of thousands of Armenians had been expelled from Anatolia, which had led to great suffering. And when an independent Armenia had appeared in the Soviet Union, relations between the Christian Armenians and the Muslim Turks and Kurds had deteriorated further. This had signaled the end of many years of peaceful coexistence in the Ottoman Empire.)

The French and the nationalists signed the Franklin–Bouillon Agreement, which brought to an end hostilities on the southeastern front. Then the final push against the Greeks liberated Izmir on September 9, 1922. An armistice was signed at Mudanya on October 11 in which the Allied powers conceded to all of the nationalists' demands, and all foreign forces had left Turkey a year later. On July 24, 1923, a treaty was signed at the Lausanne peace conference that fulfilled all of the demands of Atatürk's nationalists.

The previous year, on November 1, 1922, the Grand National Assembly (GNA) of Turkey had abolished the sultanate, but the last Ottoman sultan retained the title of Caliph. Nevertheless, he placed himself under British protection on November 17 and left the country.[18] The GNA declared itself the true government of Turkey and all executive powers were vested in an executive council under the leadership of Atatürk. To cope with the security situation facing the nascent state, he was also voted commander-in-chief of the armed forces, a post that carried extensive powers. On October 13, 1923, the GNA made Ankara the permanent seat of government, since its strategic location made it less vulnerable to foreign assault. This choice also symbolized a break with the Ottoman past, whose political center had been Istanbul for almost five centuries. On October 29, a national referendum approved both the republican constitution and Mustafa Kemal as its first president.

Atatürk immediately initiated a sweeping program of secularization and Westernization, concepts that had already gained popularity among Ottoman elites. In March 1924, he pushed a series of radical reforms through the GNA. These abolished the Caliphate and banished all members of the imperial family, closed religious schools, prohibited wearing of the fez, and abolished the Ministry of Holy Law (*Sha'ria*) and of Pious Foundations. In November 1925, all dervish orders (mostly mystics of the Sufi sect) were suppressed and Muslim shrines were closed. New penal and civil codes based on the Swiss model were adopted, and European styles of dress could be legally enforced. Finally, an adapted form of the Latin script officially replaced the Arabic alphabet in 1928. These far-reaching reforms were hastily implemented and Atatürk had no qualms about forcing compliance. The new constitution, adopted on April 24, 1924, vested sovereignty in an elected parliament, but Atatürk, as President, was still allowed to select the cabinet.

Political development and issues

System of government

Since its foundation in 1923, Turkey has been a republic. Its political system is based on the separation of powers among the three branches of government: the legislature, executive and judiciary. Over the years, this system has been subjected to a number of strains that have contributed to its overall development. Sovereignty in the country still rests in the Grand National Assembly of Turkey, whose membership currently stands at 550. Elections to the assembly are normally held every five years, based on a system of proportional representation. After the military *coup d'état* of 1980, in order to avoid the political chaos of the 1970s that was partly blamed on this electoral system, some modifications were introduced in the 1982 constitution. A party is now required to obtain a national minimum of 10 percent of the popular vote in order to be represented in the assembly. Parties organized on communist, sectarian, fascist or theological doctrines were also prohibited.

The assembly elects a president, who is the head of state, to a seven-year term (although this will be reduced to five years once the current incumbent, Abdullah Gül, has served his term). The powers of the president were significantly increased by the new constitution, generally at the expense of the other branches of government. The presidential purview now includes calling an election when there is deadlock between government and parliament, appointing prime ministers and accepting the resignations of government officials relatively independently of the assembly, vetoing legislation, and declaring states of emergency.

The executive branch of government is headed by the prime minister, who is the leader of the largest party in the legislature that is able to form a government. Most Turkish governments since the Second World War have taken the form of coalitions between several parties – a prospective prime minister must first assemble a parliamentary majority willing to support his candidacy. Approval of a new government must be sought from the assembly, whose term is fixed at five years.

A special branch of the judiciary known as the administrative justice (administrative courts, regional courts and Council of State) plays an important role in checking the power of the other two branches of government. Administration of justice in the country and all of the judiciary, including the Constitutional Court, is independent. Turkey is a unitary state comprised of 80 provinces, the governors of which are state appointees, and about 634 districts. Mayors in the metropolitan areas and municipalities are popularly elected, and there are also village heads and councils of elders.

Party politics and the military

As we have seen, the military played a key role in the founding and the development of the Turkish Republic, and since independence it has intervened to change the government four times – 1960–1961, 1971–1973, 1980–1983 and the "soft coup" of 1997. The justification advanced for each of these actions was the reestablishment or safeguarding of democracy and/or preserving the secular character of the state.[19] According to Turkey's 1982 constitution (formulated primarily by the military), the National Security Council (NSC) is an advisory body to the government. It is currently composed of six civilian members (including the president) and five from the military – the chief of the General Staff, the chiefs of the three branches of the Turkish armed forces and the head of the Gendarmerie. The NSC is the most powerful body of state authority and has assumed the role of the "guardian" of Turkey's secularism. It was created by Law No. 2945 on November 1, 1983 in accordance with Article 118 of the constitution, which was ratified during the tenure of General Kenan Evren as head of state. According to Article 4 of Law 2945, the NSC

> determines measures that are deemed necessary for preserving the constitutional order, maintaining the national unity and integrity, orienting the Turkish nation around the national ideals and values in accordance with Atatürk's Principles and Reforms. In order to eliminate threats directed against these principles of the state, both internal and external, the Council determines basic strategies, principles, opinions on planning and implementation of necessary precautions.

Since 2002, the ruling Justice and Development Party (AKP) has successfully pushed for constitutional reforms aimed at curtailing the power of the NSC and the involvement of the army in politics. According to a 2003 amendment to Law 2945, the NSC now takes

> advisory decisions on issues pertaining to the formulation, establishment and implementation of the national security policy of the State, and shall provide its views with a view to ensuring the necessary coordination; it shall submit these advisory decisions and views to the Council of Ministers, and fulfill duties given by laws.

Seeing themselves as the primary and most important defenders of Turkey's independence, the armed forces' basic missions are the defense and protection of the nation and the republic, as well as the fulfillment of Turkey's NATO duties. To perform these roles, they have developed into a modern force with an array of weapons systems that are well up to international standards.

The military was an important element in Turkish society long before the foundation of the republic. In fact, Turks have been well known for their military prowess ever since their entry into the Middle East, which led Arab Muslim monarchs to rely on their services as mercenaries. During the Ottoman era, too, the slave–mercenary army known as the janissaries – which was also composed of Christians, Kurds, Slavs and others who could not aspire to high office – occupied a special place in the hierarchy of the state. Although the janissaries themselves sometimes attempted to depose the sultan, they were more often an important bulwark against the interminable intrigues of the court. However, when they became an obstacle to the rejuvenation of the declining empire, they were disbanded. In their place there emerged a modern military force, which continued to play an important political role in the Ottoman state. The officer corps, which had been influenced by reformist ideas, played an indirect role in the upheavals of the late nineteenth century; and later, Mustafa Kemal relied on his military ability and prestige to advance the political ambitions of the new Turkish modernizing elite. When he became the first president of Turkey, he made his trusted deputy, Ismet Inönü, the first prime minister. It was largely the unwavering support of the military that allowed Atatürk to implement his far-reaching reform program.

Atatürk established the Republican People's Party (RPP) that won all the national elections held between 1923 and 1943. He allowed the first opposition party to organize in 1924, and encouraged another in 1930, but both were suppressed and dissolved within a few months of their formation, having become too vocal in their criticism of state policy.

The traditional, republican Turkish political elite backed the regime of Atatürk and Inönü (who succeeded Atatürk as president in 1938) and in return it continued to occupy a comfortable position in the system. However, when the Democrat Party (DP), under the leadership of Celal Bayar and Adnan Menderes, emerged victorious in the election of 1950, power shifted slightly against the military and the political elite. Representation in the assembly, when broken down on occupational lines, indicated a shift in favor of lawyers, traders, commercial and banking entrepreneurs and against the traditional political elite and civil bureaucrats.[20] Throughout the rest of the decade, government policies further eroded the privileges and power of the political elite and civil bureaucrats, while entrepreneurs and businessmen, as well as regional elites, saw their political fortunes rise.

However, the DP's policies, particularly those concerning the economy, began to cause unease among much of the population. Soaring inflation wreaked havoc on personal incomes and caused deep resentment. Opposition to the DP government gained momentum, and in response it adopted a tough stance, including the suppression of democratic freedoms. Unhappy with the authoritarian nature of the regime, nineteen deputies broke away from the government in February 1955 to form a new party called the Freedom Party. In early 1960, tension between the DP and the opposition came to a head. In early February, the police broke up a meeting organized by the veteran leader of the RPP, Ismet Inönü. On 10 February, the DP voted to convene a powerful commission to investigate the opposition. This triggered riots, and the government declared martial law in Istanbul and Ankara. The military, which had stayed out of the confrontation up to this point, now decided the time had arrived for it to intervene. Under the leadership of General

Cemal Gürsel, a bloodless coup was staged on May 27. The DP was disbanded and its leaders, including the entire parliamentary delegation, were imprisoned. Menderes and two of his colleagues were eventually tried and hanged, and a National Unity Committee (NUC) was formed to run the country.

However, the NUC, which included members with widely divergent ideologies, proved unwieldy. This caused a split in the ruling military junta between the older, senior moderates and the more radical junior officers, which was resolved by the expulsion of fourteen radicals.[21] A new constitution was adopted in 1961, which, in essence, sought to prevent the reemergence of an authoritarian partisan regime legitimized by a majority in parliament.[22] A number of significant checks and balances, such as the introduction of a bicameral parliament, a presidential veto over legislation, a constitutional court, and granting of autonomy to such institutions as universities, were incorporated into this constitution. In effect, this reduced the powers of the government while increasing civil and social rights, which resulted in such advances as a new law legalizing the right of strike action in 1963. However, the checks and balances created a stalemate in the political system that was to exert a negative impact on politics in the future.

When a general election was held in 1961, no party was able to achieve an electoral majority. The new Justice Party (JP) had been formed to fill the void left by the disbanded DP. Under the aging İnönü, the RPP entered into fragile coalition governments with the JP and other, smaller parties. In the 1965 general election, the JP won an overall majority under its young and dynamic leader, Süleyman Demirel. This heralded the return of stable government, which lasted for six years, but the RPP entered a state of turmoil during this time. Differences over policy occasioned a split in its ranks in 1967, when breakaway deputies formed the Reliance Party. In the 1969 election, the JP increased its majority in the lower house of parliament.

However, the JP also had problems within its ranks, as was evidenced by the formation of a splinter Democratic Party in 1971. Leftist groups also became more active during this time, benefiting from the liberal atmosphere created under the 1961 constitution. A polarization of politics began to take shape as violent clashes between extreme left and extreme right groups increased in frequency in 1971. The issues under dispute were basic, revolving around standard of living, social justice and democratic freedom. This rising violence led the military to intervene for the second time on March 12. The "coup by memorandum" forced the government to resign and a non-partisan cabinet was installed in its place. Martial law was imposed, and free elections were not held again until 1973.

In that year, the RPP and the JP emerged as the major parties in the new assembly, but neither held an overall majority. Consequently, throughout the rest of the 1970s, the two parties were obliged to court smaller parties in order to form coalition governments. The result was a series of shaky governments that saw Demirel and Bülent Ecevit, the new leader of the RPP, changing places at the head of the government according to who was able to forge a coalition. The rise and fall of these short-lived coalitions was based entirely on political maneuvering, with no consideration for either the desires of the population or the smooth transaction of governmental business. Public confidence in politicians of all parties declined steeply.

The 1970s witnessed several crises, including oil price rises and a US–Iran embargo following the Cyprus intervention, which dramatically affected the Turkish economy. Strikes and other factors, such as an inability to import much-needed oil, brought the economy to a state of stagnation, with inflation soaring as unemployment rose and basic consumer goods often unavailable. Running in parallel to these economic problems were continued clashes between leftists and rightists, with students, state employees and Islamists all involved. Street fights and terrorist activities claimed several thousand lives each year and were the military's main justification for its third intervention into politics, when, on September 12, 1980, General Kenan Evren intervened to restore order.

The military leaders outlawed all political parties that had existed prior to the coup. Parliamentarians were banned from politics for five years, and party leaders for up to a decade. (However, these restrictions were later revoked by a national referendum.) The military men established the National Security Council and a new constitution was passed by referendum in 1982, with Evren elected to a seven-year presidency. The constitution increased the powers of the presidency and made cabinet responsible to the elected parliament. The junta then encouraged the formation of only two political parties in place of the numerous old ones: the National Democracy Party, under retired General Turgut Sunalp, was earmarked as the ruling party; while the Populist Party, under Necdet Calp, a career civil servant, was cast in the role of loyal opposition. However, the military's plan came unstuck in the first election to be held after the coup, when the Motherland Party (ANAP), under Turgut Özal, won a landslide victory in 1983. Furthermore, in subsequent elections, the old parties emerged, albeit under new names (the Social Democratic Populist Party instead of the RPP, and the True Path Party (DYP) instead of the JP) and new leaderships.

State, religion and Islamic parties

In Turkey, as in other Middle Eastern countries, religion has played a key role in politics. The relationship between Islamic political activism and domestic politics has been scrutinized due to Turkey's secular, democratic, republican status, which is unique in the Islamic world. The success of Islamists in recent elections has triggered fears that Atatürk's legacy might soon unravel, a prospect that could persuade the ever-vigilant military back into the political arena.

Tracing the role of religion in the development of the nation requires taking stock of the situation before the founding of the modern state. Ever since the Turks first converted to the Islamic faith, they have lived as Muslims while maintaining many of their ancestral folk traditions. For centuries, the Turkish–Ottoman governmental system ensured that the state could operate independently from the influence of religious-based political associations.[23] However, this changed in the sixteenth century, when the Ottoman sultan assumed the title of caliph and accepted the responsibility of being "the leader of all Muslims." There was a clear demarcation between the secular powers of the sultan and the religious domain under the tutelage of the 'Ulama. But the religious establishment was very successful in inculcating the Islamic tradition in the minds of the Turkish conquerors and, consequently, religion became a powerful force among both urban and rural populations.

When Atatürk enacted his massive cultural, legal and social reform program between 1923 and 1935, with the view of turning the nation from religion to secularism and promoting Westernization, the impact on many average Turks, particularly in rural areas, was minimal. For instance, discouragement of Islamic styles of dress could be effectively implemented only in the urban areas, while life in the countryside continued in the traditional fashion. Consequently, Islamic traditions survived in spite of the state-sponsored drive toward secularization. Moreover, before the introduction of multiparty politics in 1945, the country was run by an authoritarian single party (the RPP), which thwarted the development of civil society. As a consequence, Islam was the only channel for expressing dissent.[24] For instance, the Sufi orders played an active role in the political arena, resulting in their increased suppression by the government.

The introduction of multiparty politics, and the government's commitment to democracy, diluted the militant secularism that had dominated the new republic in its early years. Aware of the strong appeal of religion among the population, especially those in the periphery, opposition politicians tailored their platforms to appeal to the traditional and Islamic character of the electorate. Even members of the DP (including Prime Minister Menderes) played on religious themes to win over voters. More significantly, a party dedicated to the promotion of Muslim consciousness – the National Order Party (Milli Nezam Partisi, MNP) – was launched on January 26, 1970. However, it was disbanded by order of the Constitutional Court on May 20, 1971, two months after the *coup d'état*, on the grounds that it was a threat to the secular nature of the Turkish state. Its successor, the National Salvation Party (Milli Selamet Partisi, MSP) was formed on October 11, 1972, but it faced a similar fate after the 1980 coup. However, with the foundation of the Refah (Welfare) Party in 1983, a self-defined Islamic party finally became a permanent feature of Turkish domestic politics.

The turbulent political climate of the 1970s had propelled Islamists to the forefront of national politics. In 1975, Demirel included the National Salvation Party in his center-right coalition government, which enabled them to push through some reforms in the realm of religious affairs, notably an increase in the number Qur'anic (*imam-hatip*) schools, in which the standard curriculum was mixed with religious education in order to train clerical personnel for mosques and other religious roles, all of which are under state control.

The military coup of 1980 boosted Islamic sentiment in the country, initially through the deliberate encouragement of the junta, who wished to counter influential leftist and communist movements, and later in response to the difficult socio-economic conditions. Free market policies were introduced (with the blessing of the military) by the civilian government that came to power in 1983, but these resulted in a lowering of living standards as inflation rose and real wages plummeted. Concurrently, the gap between the rich and the poor widened, creating fertile ground for the Islamic organizations. Consequently, there was a significant increase in the number of Islamic publications and schools. For instance, the Ministry of Education estimates that there were 72 *imam-hatip* schools in 1970, 374 in 1980, 416 in 1992 and 558 in 2002.[25] Many of the graduates of these schools received further education in the national universities, after which they went into the civil service and other positions of responsibility and influence.

A direct beneficiary of these developments was the Refah Party, which attracted disgruntled former supporters of the governing parties. It quickly increased its electoral support, much to the alarm of many secularists. In the 1987 election, it won just 7.1 percent of the national vote, far short of the 10 percent required for representation in the assembly, but the ANAP, which emerged as the winner in the election, soon began to lose support because of the worsening economic situation. Local election results in 1989 and 1994 indicated the increasing popularity of the Refah Party, while the governing parties saw a reduction in their public approval ratings.[26] The same trend was evident in general elections. In 1991, the Refah Party and two smaller allied parties won 16.8 percent of the national vote. Four years later, the Refah Party emerged with 21.4 percent of the vote, giving it 158 seats in the assembly and making it the largest single party. The DYP came third with 19.19 percent of the vote and 135 seats, with the ANAP second with 19.65 percent of the vote (although the peculiarities of the electoral system meant it gained slightly fewer seats than the DYP – 132). The remainder of the seats in the 550-member assembly were shared between two center-left parties – the Democratic Left Party (DSP), with 14.64 percent of the vote, and the Republican People's Party (CHP), with 10.71 percent. Thus, for the first time since the founding of modern Turkey, an Islamist party was given the mandate to form the government. However, Refah was unable to find a coalition partner, so the mantle passed to the leaders of the centre-right secular parties, Mesut Yilmaz of ANAP and Tansu Çiller of DYP. However, they initially failed to form a government, too, largely because of personal animosity between the two leaders. In desperation, Çiller attempted to forge a coalition with Refah, but she was forced to abandon this plan when her own party members started to voice their concerns. Refah embraced democracy and stopped short of advocating the implementation of *Shari'a*. It also promised to scrap interest rates, form an Islamic common market, withdraw Turkey from NATO and renegotiate the agreed Customs Union with the European Union.[27] These policies provoked considerable fear among Turkey's secularist establishment as well as the country's Western allies, so when the two large center-right parties finally overcame their differences and agreed to form a coalition, the news was greeted with relief in many quarters. Effectively, the Islamists had been denied power at the last moment.

The compromise that was reached between the ANAP and the DYP stated that Yilmaz would become prime minister in March 1996, would hold the post for a year, and would then hand the premiership over to Çiller. She would serve for the next two years, before handing back to Yilmaz for another one-year term. However, the government collapsed after a series of no-confidence votes in early June 1996. Once again, as the largest party, Refah tried to form a coalition, but once again it failed. Then Çiller was unable to form a secular coalition. So, in late June, she approached the Islamists again. A new coalition government was finally announced in July: for the first time in its republican history, Turkey had an Islamic party as the main partner in government.

Necmettin Erbakan – the leader of Refah since its inception – was named prime minister, with Çiller becoming foreign minister. After surviving a no-confidence vote only a few days after it had been formed, the government's first major act was to raise the pay of civil servants, whose wages had been frozen throughout the recent period of high inflation, resulting in poverty for many. Next, Erbakan tried to defuse a worsening Kurdish situation by promising to allow the return of deported Kurds to their ancestral homelands in the east of the country. This concession displeased the military and led to fears of a coup. Economically, Erbakan promised to reevaluate the country's drive toward Westernization, which was seen as having impoverished many of Refah's supporters. This also attracted criticism, with the argument being that Turkey's economy would suffer if the country did not press ahead with modernization and increase its economic connection to a prosperous Europe.

Ultimately, the military felt unable to stand by and allow Erbakan to challenge the secular state, so its leaders engineered an opposition coalition of the ANAP, DSP, CHP and the Democratic Turkey Party (DTP). All of these parties felt that radical Islamic movements, which had begun to spring up around the country, were posing a threat to the Turkish state. Islamic supporters of Refah were threatened when a debate over compulsory eight-year elementary education was brought on to the national political agenda, with the schools' funding challenged on grounds of universality and secularism. Islamists feared this would lead to the closure of the middle sections of *imam-hatip* schools and would thereby challenge their way of life.

It was widely believed that the military was orchestrating this opposition to the government, but army intervention became more explicit in repsonse to a series of mostly symbolic moves by the members and supporters of Refah. During November 1996, some Refah mayors in Anatolian towns refused to participate in events commemorating Atatürk's legacy. Then, on February 2, 1997, the mayor of the small town of Sincan near Ankara organized a protest against the occupation of East Jerusalem by Israel in which the Iranian ambassador was present as a guest. The event was in fact a protest against the Military Cooperation and Training Agreement signed between Israel and Çiller's government in February 1996. The army reacted by sending tanks to the city and arresting the mayor, while the Iranian ambassador was recalled by Tehran. Finally on February 28, the National Security Council, under direct pressure from the army, asked the Erbakan government to implement an eighteen-point plan to ensure the preservation of the secular nature of the republic. This plan included mandatory extension of public schooling which amounted to the closure of the middle level of *imam-hatip* schools, investigation of the financial resources of religious institutions, terminating the employment of Refah members in government bureaucracies, and ending warm relations with Iran. The army published long lists of corporations, radio and TV stations, publications and student organizations who were supporters of Refah and placed them under investigation. In April 1997, it announced its revised concept of national security threats and stated that the main threats to Turkey came from Islamists (the "internal" threat) and the Workers' Party of Kurdistan (PKK) (the "external" threat), with the former the more dangerous.[28] As a result of increased tension and the possibility of a military coup, Erbakan resigned on June 18. This is known in Turkish political literature as the "February 28 process" or the "soft coup." President Demirel then appointed the ANAP's leader, Mesut Yilmaz, as prime minister at the head of a new coalition government composed of the ANAP, DSP and DTP.[29] This government received a vote of confidence in the assembly on July 12, having secured the support of the CHP.

Anti-secularist Islamists have likened the military's 1997 intervention to a "postmodern coup." Political Islam in Turkey was marginalized from the mainstream discourse as the military felt that their intervention was required to save the republic's secular, democratic and nationalist character. Senior military officers were alarmed by what they perceived as attacks against the legacy of Kemal Atatürk, the attitude of pro-Islamist politicians to secular institutions of state, the increasing appearance of religious symbols with political overtones, such as robes and headscarves, Refah's plans to open a road traffic route for would-be pilgrims to Mecca – circumscribing the government quota system, which was maintained by permitting only air travel to Mecca – some calls for Muslims to be tried not by the secular judicial system but under *Shari'a*, and finally the increased sales of pump-action shotguns, which were thought to be ending up in the hands of violent Islamists.[30]

Yilmaz's new government introduced several bills that were designed to appease the military's concerns. For instance, religious education was significantly undermined, civil service supporters of the Islamists were dismissed, religious propaganda was banned, and firearm sales were restricted. Even more importantly, the new government and its policies facilitated a sharp rise in "secular awareness" throughout Turkey.[31]

The rise in political tension after the "soft coup" led many MPs from the former coalition government, especially from the DYP, to resign in protest from their party. This altered the distribution of seats in the Grand National Assembly, and by mid-1997 it was as follows: Refah 150; ANAP 138; DYP 93; DSP 67; CHP 49; DTP 20, Great Unity Party (BBP) 8; Nationalist Action Party (MHP) 2; plus 21 independents and 2 vacant seats. On January 16, 1998, the Constitutional Court accused Refah of "actions against the principles of the secular republic,"[32] banned seven of its leaders, including ex-Prime Minister Erbakan, from political activities for five years, and then banned the party itself because it had used religion for "political purposes."[33] Former Refah parliamentarians subsequently joined the newly founded, Islamic-oriented Virtue Party (FT), which, in effect, simply took the place of the banned party.

At the end of November 1998, Yilmaz was forced to resign over a scandalous privatization deal after the CHP joined with the DYP and the FT to pass a vote of no-confidence in the government. Deputy Prime Minister Ecevit of the DSP was installed as prime minister of a caretaker government in preparation for the upcoming general election.

The 1999 general election

The results of the April 18 general election, held at a highpoint of nationalistic fever after the arrest of the PKK's leader, Abdullah Ocalan, resulted in a major shift in Turkish politics because, for the first time in many years, a clear victor emerged: Ecevit won 22 percent of the votes cast, an increase for the DSP of nine points since the last election.[34] The MHP also had a successful campaign: with 18 percent of the vote, it doubled its 1995 result and became the second-largest party in the assembly. The big losers were the ANAP and the DYP, both of which lost around 6 percent of the popular vote, while the pro-Kurdish Democratic People's Party (HADEP) was unable to pass the 10 percent hurdle required to gain parliamentary representation. (However, HADEP enjoyed broad support in the mainly Kurdish areas of southeast Turkey and managed to win control of several mayoral posts.) Meanwhile, Deniz Baykal's CHP, if it is viewed as the direct descendant of Atatürk's party, failed to gain any parliamentary representation for the first time since independence. One of Baykal's election slogans had been "Don't keep the party of Atatürk out of parliament."[35] The Islamists of the FP lost votes mainly as a direct result of a massive campaign of intimidation by the military,[36] which had not let up since 1997. The army made it clear that it would simply not tolerate an FP victory in the election, even though the party consistently swore its loyalty to the state and the official policy of secularism.

A month after the election, for the first time since the 1970s and only the second time in the history of modern Turkey, the extreme nationalist MHP joined the government as a main partner of a coalition.[37] Ecevit, a long-serving social democrat and confirmed Kemalist, remained as prime minister, and his DSP–MHP–ANAP government soon proved to be one of the most active in Turkish history. With a substantial majority of 351 out of the 550 seats in parliament, in its first eight months it passed 113 new laws and 2 constitutional amendments.[38] On July 18, 1999, it amended the constitution and removed the military judge of the State Security Court (DGM) in an attempt to forestall foreign criticism of the trial of the recently arrested Abdullah Ocalan. The government was also kept busy dealing with the 1999 and 2000 budgets, social security reform, banking laws and taxation laws, not to mention the cost of the 1999 earthquakes. The coalition also took steps to alleviate inflation by entering into agreements with the IMF and further liberalizing the economy,[39] and explored ways of enhancing Turkey's chances of gaining full entry to the European Union.[40] Improving the country's human rights record and normalizing relations with the Kurds appeared to be at the top of the government's agenda. When it was announced in December

1999 that Turkey had been granted EU "candidate status," the government rapidly set about making conciliatory moves toward the Kurdish movement.[41]

The general progress toward democratic consolidation and secularization clearly motivated the parliament's decision on May 5, 2000 to elect the reformist and staunchly secularist judge Ahmet Necdet Sezer as Turkey's next president. This also indicated a willingness to open the political process to outsiders, as Sezer – who had never served in a political office but was a chief justice of the Constitutional Court – was unanimously supported by all of the party leaders. As the first judge to be elected president – six out of the previous nine had been military generals – Sezer's election also signaled only the third peaceful transfer of power in the republic since 1980. He is on record as calling for constitutional changes to overturn alterations made during the 1980–1983 period of military rule, a clear indication that he believes the current constitution restricts basic rights and freedoms. His election also continued the evolution of consensus politics in Turkey's parliament, a rejection of its past feuding and plot-riddled culture. Sezer was committed to continuing the modernization efforts driven by Turkey's pursuit of EU membership, as well as the secularization of both politics and society.[42] He said that "state and society cannot be organized along the rules of religion" but must abide by the rule of law, democracy and a welfare state.[43] His election was seen as both a commitment to the secularization process which reaffirmed the military's vision of the republic and the drive for EU membership and as a goodwill gesture to generate support among Turkey's minority communities.[44]

The FP was declared unconstitutional by the Constitutional Court in 2001, and was subsequently banned. However, out of its ashes emerged the Justice and Development Party (AKP), a centre-right Islamic party. While having an undeniable Islamic heritage, the AKP has consistently taken a moderate position on questions of religion and secularism, and, moreover, has advocated Turkey's pursuit of EU membership. Nevertheless, its critics accuse the party of harboring a secret "Islamist agenda." However, on September 12, 2007, the deputy head of the European Union's Directorate-General for Enlargement Turkey Team, Jean-Christophe Filori, said, "they had never been in a position to report on any fundamentalist trends of the AK Party to institutionally change Turkey's structure," and added, "One of the stakes of this process is to demonstrate to Europe that Islam and democracy are perfectly compatible and at the same time to demonstrate to the Muslim world that being Muslim is not an obstacle for EU membership."[45]

Poor economic performance, double-digit inflation, and a general sense of government corruption allowed the AKP to gain power in the 2002 general election, with 34.28 percent of the popular vote. Recep Tayyip Erdogan, previously mayor of Istanbul, became prime minister. His government improved the economy and made further progress toward joining the EU, including joining the European People's Party (EPP) – a centre-right grouping in the EU parliament – as an observer member. But the AKP could stand its ground against the West, too, for instance when it denied the United States permission to launch its attack on Iraq from Turkey.

In the July 2007 election, the AKP won 46.7 percent of the popular vote, which translated into 341 of the Turkish parliament's 550 seats and allowed it to form a single-party government. It was opposed in the assembly by just two main opposition parties, the CHP and MHP, which achieved 20 and 15 percent of the vote, respectively. There are several reasons for this remarkable electoral success. The AKP can certainly count on the support of Islamists, but its rise to political dominance can be explained much more fully by the party's sound stewardship of the economy and its expansion of rural social services, which have proved highly popular with Turkey's poor. Moreover, it has distanced itself from the racial chauvinism of the secular "state parties" by reaching out to the Kurdish minority and emphasizing that it respects the Kurds' identity and distinct culture. Erdogan was the first Turkish prime minister to acknowledge that "the state made mistakes about the Kurdish issue."[46] That is not to say that his line has been entirely conciliatory, though: for instance, Turkey has continued to make sporadic air strikes against PKK targets in northern Iraq.

The AKP's candidate, Abdullah Gül, was elected president on August 29, 2007, much to the consternation of his secular foes. However, in his inaugural speech, Gül mentioned Atatürk's name twice and took the opportunity to pay "tribute with the utmost respect to the first President of our Republic Mustafa Kemal Atatürk." He also praised secularism as "one of the core principles of our Republic, [which] is as much a model that underpins freedom for different lifestyles as it is a rule of social harmony."[47] Nevertheless, while Gül dedicated himself to Turkey's secular tradition, praising it for guaranteeing personal freedoms, and claimed to have abandoned religious politics long ago, his inauguration was boycotted by the officer corps – who by tradition attend the signing-in of all new presidents – and by members of the CHP. His election seems to have intensified the division between religion and the secular state. The outgoing, fiercely secular President Sezer had previously vetoed 400 official appointments by the AKP.

Gül reaffirmed his commitment to seeing Turkey join the EU. Also, in contrast to the nationalist and secular parties, he suggested that he would like to see a weakening of the law against "insulting Turkishness," which had previously been invoked against writers and journalists, including the Nobel Prize-winner Orhan Pamuk. According to Article 301 of the Turkish Penal Code, "A person who explicitly insults being a Turk, the Republic or Turkish Grand National Assembly, shall be imposed a penalty of imprisonment for a term of six months to three years." Those who "explicitly" insult "the Government of the Republic of Turkey, the judicial bodies of the State, the military or security organization" will be jailed for "six months to two years." Pamuk was charged under this article after making the following statement to a Swiss newspaper in 2005: "30,000 Kurds and a million Armenians were murdered. Hardly anyone dares mention it, so I do. And that's why I'm hated."[48] (The case against Pamuk was eventually dropped on a technicality.) Finally, Gül reaffirmed his party's conciliatory position towards the Kurdish minority, echoing Erdogan's earlier acknowledgement that "mistakes" had been made on the Kurdish question.

While the AKP has deliberately engaged with Turkey's secular parties and society, and consistently denies any intention to "Islamicize" Turkish society, it continues to run the risk of clashing with the country's fiercely secular military. In the spring and summer of 2007, the army tried a new tack to influence politics – what might be termed a "cyber coup." On April 27, after Gül was nominated for president by the AKP, an unsigned memorandum was posted on the army website which threatened to interfere if the election went ahead. Other statements posted on the same website called for street demonstrations against Gül's candidature, which were launched before the election. However, the sweeping victory for the AKP at the polls made Gül's presidency almost a formality.

Another round of serious confrontation between the secularist elite and the AKP began in January 2008, when the parliament amended the constitution in order to lift a ban on female students wearing the headscarf on university campuses. On March 14, 2008, Abdurrahman Yalçınkaya, the chief prosecutor of the Supreme Court of Appeals, filed a lawsuit with the Constitutional Court to disband the AKP, accusing it of "being a hotbed of anti-secular activities." Yalçınkaya also demanded "a five-year ban from involvement in politics for 71 senior AK Party administrators, including Prime Minister Erdogan and President Abdullah Gül."[49] On June 5, before this lawsuit was heard, the Constitutional Court annulled the parliament's amendment.

Since its founding in 1963, the Constitutional Court has closed down twenty-four political parties, representing various Kurdish, communist and Islamist constituencies. But this was the first time in the history of modern Turkey that a ruling party, with both the prime minister and the president among its members, faced being banned. On July 30, six of the eleven Constitutional Court judges voted in favor of closing down the AKP, but this was one short of the required majority to enforce the order. However, in its final verdict the court announced that "the head of the party, Recep Tayyip Erdogan, party member and former Parliament Speaker Bülent Arınç [and] Education Minister Hüseyin Çelik . . . were involved in determined and intense activities, which were against the Article 68 of the Constitution." For this reason, the party was fined, losing half of its public funding for election campaigns, which amounted to YTL 47 million in 2007.

The Kurdish insurgency and human rights

Kurds in Turkey, who number between ten and twenty million (population figures are disputed), have worked to promote their own separate nationalism through both peaceful and violent means, provoking harsh treatment from the political and military establishment. Eastern Turkey, the traditional homeland of Kurds, has been embroiled in severe civil strife involving armed Kurds, government security forces and local militia. The impact on human life and property has been devastating and both human rights organizations and foreign governments have expressed concern about the actions of both the Turkish government and separatist guerrillas.

Among the Kurdish groups that proliferated in the 1970s, the banned Kurdish Workers' Party (PKK) evolved as the most radical and violent. Founded in 1979 and led by Abdullah Ocalan, it was established in eastern Turkey and proclaimed an armed struggle against the Turkish government and the feudal Kurdish leaders who supported it.[50] Its program, a mix of Marxism–Leninism and extreme nationalism, aims to create a greater independent Kurdistan incorporating the Kurds of Turkey, Iraq and Iran. Generally, it has employed violence in a bid to achieve this, with its guerrillas accused of carrying out summary executions, bombings and the destruction of civilian property in order to dissuade people from cooperating with the Turkish authorities. In 1986, the government initiated a policy of arming villagers to resist the guerrillas, but this only made matters worse by inviting more PKK attacks against those civilians who were deemed to be unsympathetic to the Kurdish cause.

Another strategy the authorities have attempted is to assimilate the Kurds into Turkey's secular society. The view that Kurds do not have a separate identity has been persistently promoted and some have asserted that the Kurds are just "mountain Turks" who have lost touch with their Turkish origins. Not surprisingly, the academic works of İsmail Beşikçi, who claimed that the Kurds constituted a nation with a distinct language, culture and heritage, earned him a prison term.[51] The country's penal code has also been used to stifle Kurdish nationalism in a number of respects, including several prohibitions against political activity and the formation of public associations, which have been invoked against both individuals and groups. Since 1980, the authorities have arrested and tortured many alleged separatists, repression that has raised the concerns of human rights organizations worldwide. Many Kurds have been killed or displaced from their homes in the traditional Kurdish regions in the east of the country and Human Rights Watch has estimated that more than 30,000 people have been killed since 1984. Security forces launched a massive counter-insurgency campaign against PKK guerrillas in eastern Turkey in 1993, and many Kurdish civilians were forced to flee their homes. The Constitutional Court outlawed the Kurdish-based Democracy Party (DEP) in June 1994, and eight parliamentarians who had been stripped of their immunity that March were charged with treason and separatism because of alleged collaboration with the banned PKK. Once again, this provoked widespread condemnation from human rights organizations. In the parliamentary power struggle of spring 1996, the power vacuum led to outbursts of violence, such as when youth members of HADEP tore down a Turkish flag at a political convention and replaced it with the banner of the PKK. Unidentified gunmen killed several HADEP members, and in retaliation a Kurdish woman detonated a bomb, killing herself and nine Turkish soldiers. This signaled the beginning of a new and unpredictable phase of Kurdish activism, which had previously been limited to the PKK's guerrilla operations.

Throughout the imposition of the no-fly zones in Iraqi Kurdistan, which provided some measure of cover for Kurdish organizations, the Turkish military made repeated incursions into northern Iraq in pursuit of PKK guerrillas. Up to 35,000 ground troops were deployed on these missions in 1995, 1997 and 1999.

However, the Iraqi government did not strongly protest against these challenges to its sovereignty, as much of northeastern Iraq was under the control of autonomous Kurdish authorities, which the regime in Baghdad was happy to see humbled. There was little international outcry either, which indicated a lack of Western interest in the Kurds, rather than any specific support for Turkey. Ankara also accused Syria of supporting the PKK, and threatened to invade Syria if this (completely unproven) support did not cease. Tension between the two countries escalated sufficiently to bring them to the brink of war. On October 4, 1998, Turkish troops massed on the Syrian border and President Demirel warned Syria, "I am not only warning the world. This cannot continue . . . the situation is serious. Turkey has suffered for many years and it no longer wants to suffer."[52]

This pressure led to the expulsion of the PKK from Syria in October 1998, forcing its leader Abdullah Ocalan to seek refuge, first in Russia, then, in mid-November, in Italy, as a political refugee.[53] Ocalan was apprehended in Nairobi on February 15, 1999, leading to violent Kurdish demonstrations in Turkey and throughout the world. He was caught hiding in the Greek ambassador's residence by Kenyan officials and then handed over to the Turkish government at Nairobi airport.[54] The nature of his capture raised questions about possible US or even Israeli intelligence cooperation with the Turkish authorities. He eventually stood trial on the island prison of Imrali in the Marmara Sea and was convicted for his role in leading the PKK's insurgency in Turkey's southeast. He was sentenced to death, but this was eventually commuted to life imprisonment when the death penalty was abolished in Turkey in 2002.

While Ocalan's undoubted complicity with a large number of violent acts, including many against fellow Kurds, left much of Turkey rejoicing over his imprisonment, many others have questioned whether his punishment is turning him into a martyr for the Kurdish cause. This seems unlikely, though, as he did everything he could to save himself during his trial, separating the Kurdish cause from his own fate, which prompted some Kurdish leaders to disassociate themselves from him.

Meanwhile, Western human rights advocates have questioned both Ocalan's prison conditions and the fairness of his trial. Many observers have gone so far as to link the treatment he has received with Turkish acceptance into the European Union.[55] To some extent, it was inevitable that the Turkish criminal justice system would be put on trial while it tried one of the most wanted terrorists in Turkey.[56] Indeed, on March 11, 1999, President Demirel announced that he favored amending the 1982 constitution to remove military judges from courts in order to make the judicial system fully independent (a military judge sat on the bench in Ocalan's trial).[57]

Despite the successful prosecution of Ocalan, there is still a "Kurdish problem" in Turkey's southeastern provinces, and this has only intensified since the Anglo-American invasion and occupation of Iraq in 2003. Northern Iraq – or "southern Kurdistan" – has emerged as a de facto autonomous state, and PKK militants have sheltered themselves within the safe harbor of Iraqi Kurdistan. At last report, it was estimated that over 4,000 Kurdish militants operate out of northern Iraq.[58] The emergence of a PKK enclave in Iraq has led to frequent artillery strikes, air raids and ground operations by the Turkish army. However, during the summer and autumn of 2007, Prime Minister Erdogan repeatedly stated his preference for diplomacy over war. On the domestic front, he did not want to alienate Turkey's Kurdish population, whose vote was crucial in the electoral victories of the AKP and whose support was vital in the party's power struggle with the Turkish military. The army has used the "Kurdish terrorist threat" as a tool to mobilize public opinion behind a "nationalist agenda" aimed at undermining the broad electoral base of the AKP and its main source of power.

After the political upheavals of the summer of 2007, the "Kurdish terror" issue has become the main battleground over which the power struggle is fought in Turkey. Ultra-nationalist parties like the MHP and influential circles within the old secularist elite have used PKK attacks as indicators of the government's "lack of patriotism" and ineffectiveness. The AKP, however, has played the foreign policy card wisely by reaching a tacit agreement with the United States on conducting cross-border air raids into Iraqi territory against PKK guerrilla camps without getting involved in large-scale military operations and large troop deployments. On November 5, 2007, Erdogan urged George W. Bush to take "concrete steps" against the PKK. This led to "information sharing" arrangements between the two countries regarding PKK positions inside Iraqi territory. There were subsequently several rounds of Turkish air raids against guerrilla positions in December. On the 17th, the chief of staff of the Turkish army, General Yasar Buyukanit, announced that these operations had been made possible because of information provided by the US; and he promised that they would continue for as long as was necessary.[59]

For a while, these moves by the government seemed to have been successful, and the criticism from the army and the ultra-nationalists subsided. However, the picture changed as PKK attacks resumed, and the army finally managed to win the argument for launching ground operations, which began on February 21, 2008. Several units of the Turkish army attacked PKK hideouts up to sixteen kilometers inside northern Iraq. The US put pressure on Ankara to conclude this operation for fear of alienating Iraqi Kurds and jeopardizing the security of the autonomous Kurdish region, the only stable part of Iraq, and the Turkish army withdrew after just two weeks.

This operation did not stop PKK attacks. For instance, on October 3, 2008, a military post in Aktütün, Hakkari Province, was attacked and seventeen soldiers were killed. The government was again fiercely criticized for its weakness in the face of terrorism by ultra-nationalist and militant Kemalist media outlets and politicians. However, a week later, the liberal newspaper *Taraf* published aerial imagery taken by an unmanned plane showing that the military had information of the guerrillas approaching the post hours before the attack occurred. *Taraf* also claimed that the military had received information about plans for this attack in advance. The daily *Zaman* (which supports the AKP) later presented evidence that the military knew about the terrorist operation ten days before it was launched and yet did nothing to stop it.[60]

Disturbingly, then, it seems that both the PKK and the army are happy to see the Kurdish–Turkish conflict escalate. On October 28, 2007, the veteran British journalist Patrick Cockburn said that nobody wants to see the war in southeastern Turkey continue,

> apart from the PKK and militant factions within the Turkish army . . . The PKK was defeated in its battle for independence or at least autonomy for Turkey's 15 million Kurds after a bloody war fought between 1984 and 1999. A Turkish invasion might enable it to regain its political popularity among Turkish Kurds. The Turkish army, or at least some of its leaders, also has a vested interest in escalating the long-running struggle. This is the army's strongest card in trying to maintain its authority in the state in opposition to the moderate Islamist government of Prime Minister Tayyip Erdogan, whose AK party was re-elected in July. There is no doubt that the PKK did carry out last Sunday's attack. But the Iraqi Kurds believe – and it is a view supported by diplomats in Ankara – that at least some of the recent attacks on Turkish security forces were the work of an extreme faction within the Turkish army. The PKK denies, for instance, that it carried out a raid in which 12 village guards – a pro-government home guard – were shot dead in Beytussebap recently. The Iraqi Foreign Minister, Hoshyar Zebari, also points out that the PKK is notoriously riddled with Turkish agents.[61]

The crux of the matter is that the shift of the AKP towards embracing the idea of EU integration – as a means to curtail the intervention of the military in politics and ensure broader freedoms and political participation by Islamic and Kurdish constituencies through democratic reform – threatens the traditional position of the army as the final arbiter in Turkish politics. The army and the Kemalist elites see the democratic reforms encouraged by the EU accession process since 2005 as a threat to their traditional superior position in Turkish society. Hence the upsurge in inter-elite political contestation of recent years. The government's major policy in Kurdish affairs has been the launch of a five-year "grand socio-economic development strategy" for the southeastern parts of the country, announced in May 2008 and known as South-East Anatolia Project. The government claims that the plan aims to tackle the root causes of the Kurdish problem – poverty, underdevelopment of infrastructure, high unemployment, discrimination and denial of cultural rights.

In spite of all the talk showing good intentions toward the "Kurdish problem" on the part of the government at least, political reality does not encourage much optimism. In 2007, the only political party representing Kurdish interests in Turkey, the DYP, was investigated by the Constitutional Court on charges of "activities against the unity and integrity of the country." These charges were laid on November 16, 2007 and demanded the closure of the party and the banning of 221 of its members from political activity for five years.

In order to meet the deadline for reforms required for accession talks leading to full membership of the European Union, Turkey has been forced to adopt a number of institutional measures to promote human rights. Legislation forcing all government ministries and related institutions to abide by human rights norms and standards in line with those in Western Europe is being finalized. It will establish governmental and nongovernmental organizations that will be independently responsible for monitoring torture, illegal arrests and other violations of human rights within Turkey. The country has already established a Human Rights High Coordination Board Secretariat that has investigated Turkey's police and gendarmerie for human rights abuses. It found that detainees were being routinely tortured, that police holding facilities and penitentiaries were generally below acceptable standards, and that there was a general lack of access to duty lawyers (public defenders). It is now investigating two other sensitive issues that might damage Turkey's entry into the EU: the subordination of the Turkish military to civilian authority, especially the powerful National Security Council; and the treatment of Turkey's minorities, with special emphasis on the Kurds.[62]

On paper, membership of the NSC is shared equally between military and civilian representatives. Chaired by the country's president, it consists of the prime minister, the chief of the General Staff, the defense minister, the minister of interior affairs, the minister of foreign affairs, the land forces commander, the air force commander and the general commander of the gendarmerie. However, the military members have increasingly dominated the NSC's agenda and decision-making process, especially since 1997, when the Islamic coalition government challenged the military's traditional vision of a secular and nationalist Turkish state. The firm assertion of civilian control over such policy creation and imple-mentation processes is seen by the EU as a benchmark of Turkey's commitment to democracy.

It is hoped that the Board Secretariat will be successful in implementing the changes necessary to improve Turkey's human rights record. In the past, Turkey has implemented changes to the structure of the State Security Courts and lowered the custody period from fifteen days to four. However, Turkey remains a leader in the number of cases heard before the European Court of Human Rights in Strasbourg. This court is not an appeal court or a court of first instance, but rather produces case law, which can then be adopted by the contracting state to amend legislation and promptly change its implementation of the rule of law. However, unlike European Union members, which tend to change their domestic legal and administrative systems after test cases, Turkey has been slow to adopt such measures.

Freedom of speech has emerged as a significant issue as dissent has been stifled through the arrest of a number of prominent intellectuals, opinion makers, activists and even politicians. Some of the most celebrated cases include the incarceration of ex-Prime Minister Necmettin Erbakan; Human Rights Association president and activist Akin Birdal; and the founder of the secular Rebirth Party (YDP), Hasan Celal Guzel, who had served for over thirty years in many top government posts. Guzel, like Erbakan and Birdal, was charged with "provoking hatred and enmity among people on the basis of religious and racist discrimination," as stipulated by Article 312 of the Penal Code, when delivering a speech in 1997 entitled "Where on the road to democracy does Turkey stand?" He was sentenced to one year in prison by the Ankara State Security Court and later lost his appeal to the Supreme Court, even though no acts of violence or public disorder could be attributed to his speech.[63]

The expansion of Turkey's understanding of democracy to include notions of freedom of speech, thought and expression, rather than merely competition between political parties, will mark its move into the Western discourse on the development of a civil society. Certainly, signaling a maturity of its appreciation of such values will be required for its admission to the EU. The freedom of association clauses in the Turkish constitution have often been neglected in secularization and security-promotion efforts. Indeed, notions of "public" institutions in Turkey are almost exclusively state-centered and political in nature. Such limitations must be abrogated in order that the associations and social groupings required of a true civil society may develop.

However, the domestic conflicts mentioned above have slowed the pace of reform that has been under way since the accession negotiations started in 2005. According to the European Commission's *Turkey 2008 Progress Report*, the country's progress toward meeting its obligations has been far from impressive. Although the report mentions notable improvements in judicial reform, prison administration, combating torture in detention centers and economic and trade-related reform, there are several outstanding issues that make Turkey's prospects for entry into the EU bleak. Out of a total of thirty-three points raised in 2005, only one (science and research) has been satisfactorily resolved. The main issue raised by the report is the delay in revising the 1982 constitution. The report notes that a group of academics has been asked to begin the revision process, but that "no draft [for a new constitution] has been presented either to the public or to parliament, and no clear timetable has been set for discussing it."[64] To gain the approval of the EU, the revision must include changes favoring the rule of law, civil and political liberties, minority political and cultural rights and, especially, civilian control over the military establishment, many of which the Kemalist establishment would wish to avoid. On the role of the military, the report states:

> the armed forces have continued to exercise significant political influence via formal and informal mechanisms. Senior members of the armed forces have expressed their opinion on domestic and foreign policy issues going beyond their remit, including Cyprus, the South East [i.e. Kurdistan], secularism, political parties and other non-military developments . . . overall, no progress has been made in ensuring full civilian supervisory functions over the military and parliamentary oversight of defence expenditures.[65]

On the foreign policy front, the AKP government faces increasing pressure from the EU to accelerate legal–political reforms. The Cyprus problem is a principal issue. In spite of some recent moves aimed at reducing tension with Greece, Turkey still enforces a partial embargo on Cyprus and, according to the EU report, "Turkey has made no progress on normalizing bilateral relations with Cyprus.

Turkey continues to veto Cyprus's membership of several international organizations and of the Wassenaar Agreement on the Code of Conduct on Arms Exports and on Dual-Use Goods."[66]

The Turkish economy

Aware of the need to bring about a fast improvement in the living conditions of the people, Atatürk and the leaders of the new republic met in February 1923 in the first Economic Congress at the recently liberated town of Izmir. The gathering of some 1,100 delegates representing farmers, traders, industrialists and laborers aimed to formulate the government's economic policy. Two issues were hotly debated: the extent of the government's role in planning the economy, and the use of foreign capital in the economic development of the republic. This preoccupation with economic matters was understandable, given that Turkey was extremely underdeveloped and heavily burdened with debts inherited from the Ottoman era as well as those amassed during the war for independence. The bulk of the citizens lived in poverty; and agriculture, the key sector in the economy, was backward and dominated by feudal landlords who exploited the peasantry. Furthermore, the ravages of war had led to the flight or massacre of much of the Greek and Armenian populations, depriving the economy of much-needed professional and technical skills just as it was attempting to develop.

Between 1930 and 1950, the regime assumed a leading role in the development of the economy. During the 1930s, the government adopted the *etatist* principle of economic development to improve production. Although theoretically vague, *etatism* has in practice amounted to the assumption that the state had a major responsibility for undertaking industrial development, even at the expense of private sector development.[67] Thus, within the context of this policy, the government carried out a massive nationalization program of foreign firms throughout the 1930s to address the country's balance of payments predicament. In 1933, the first development plan (to be implemented between 1934 and 1938) was outlined, and the Soviet Union, which had proposed several industrial projects to be implemented in this phase, gave Turkey an interest-free loan of $8 million to finance the plan. The Second World War interrupted the second industrialization plan, prepared in 1936 for implementation between 1939 and 1943.

In the agricultural sector, the government focused on the introduction of reforms benefiting landless farmers; large tracts of land, formerly under public ownership, were divided among the landless. However, big landowners continued to block land reform plans involving private property. The parliament passed a land reform bill in May 1945, but its impact on the big landowners proved marginal. Only when multi-party politics emerged was real attention paid to the peasants, as their numbers gave them a newfound leverage within the democratic system.

Etatism failed to improve living standards, which opened it to criticism from both Turkish and foreign observers, who faulted the system for its concentration on heavy industrialization projects while paying little attention to the agricultural sector, which was the backbone of the economy. DP politicians won a great deal of public support by exposing the weaknesses of the *etatist* system. Not surprisingly, when they came to power in 1950, their economic policies differed from those of their predecessors. Much attention was paid to the neglected rural farming populations and the private sector was encouraged. However, the economy continued to grow at a modest pace, and rising inflation reduced income, causing widespread discontent. On the positive side, the encouragement of the private sector led to increased investment by entrepreneurs, which resulted in a sharp rise in industrial production.

Between 1960 and 1978, GNP grew at an encouraging annual average of 6.2 percent. This vigorous growth was partly due to remittances sent home by Turkish emigrants working abroad. In 1974 earnings sent home by Turkish workers in Western Europe alone were in excess of $1.45 billion.[68] As the 1970s drew to a close, the economy slowed down dramatically due to a shortage of hard currency, reduced remittances and poor leadership from fragile and indecisive coalition governments (in 1979, GNP grew at a meager 1.7 percent). Ordinary people's economic situation worsened when the civilian government assumed power in 1983 and continued to liberalize the economy. Growth in the rest of the decade was limited by persistently high inflation – between 60 and 100 percent annually – and by the burgeoning national debt. The gloomy economic profile continued into the 1990s, leading to the devaluation of the Turkish lira by some 28 percent in 1994.

The devaluation and mounting foreign debt (which reached in excess of $100 billion[69]) forced the government to adopt even tougher austerity measures, a move that further alienated many citizens. Public sector salaries remained almost stagnant amid rampant inflation, impoverishing many workers. Unemployment increased in urban areas, peaking at 13 percent, with the devaluation crisis alone putting an estimated 600,000 Turks out of work.[70] Nevertheless, the various coalition governments of the mid-1990s pressed on with their free-market policies, which generated support for the more welfarist Islamists.

At the end of twentieth century, Turkey's economy was at a crossroads, with the country increasingly dependent upon its ties to the European Union. It experienced an average annual growth rate in excess of 4 percent during the 1990s, but also labored under crippling inflation. Economic reality finally caught up with Turkey on the eve of the new century as high interest rates of 40 percent began to impact on growth. Turkey's massive public debt also left its economy highly vulnerable to external shock, and the government was left with no option but to commit the country to suggested International Monetary Fund (IMF) reforms.

In exchange for some $4 billion from the IMF, the government agreed to an extensive three-year program. Reforms made it harder to qualify for a public pension and agricultural subsidies. Government spending cuts and tax increases were accompanied by privatization and a new and more open exchange-rate system in 2001. In spite of the restrictions placed upon government spending, the increasingly competitive markets surrounding banking and capital growth as well as the development of a number of monopolistic moguls, Turkey's economy has since displayed a certain dynamism. The impossibly high cost of borrowing and the capricious nature of interest rates have driven off foreign investors, but the reforms appeared to be working as inflation started to decrease and interest rates stabilized. Such stability encouraged increased foreign investment as well as some normalization of Turkey's black economy, which is reported to be as large as the official one. More recently, particularly under the leadership of the AKP since 2002, the Turkish economy initially showed significant improvement. The inflation rate fell from 68.5 percent in 2001 to 10 percent in 2006, and the economy grew at a consistent rate: 7.9 percent in 2002, 5.9 percent in 2003, 9.9 percent in 2004, and 7.6 percent in 2005. IMF estimates for GNP growth in 2006 and 2007 were 6 percent and 5 percent, respectively.[71] However, GDP growth slowed to just 0.9 percent in 2008, and then plunged to -5.6 percent in 2009, owing to the global economic crisis.[72]

Foreign relations

Turkish foreign relations are centered on its role as a regional power within the Balkan–Caucasus–Middle East triangle. In December 1999, at the European Union's Helsinki summit, Turkey was granted candidate status, successfully concluding decades of diplomatic effort and giving rise to hopes for a strong future within a secular Western and Mediterranean order. Similarly, improved strategic cooperation with the United States, Israel and the European Union, the successful laying of the Ceyhan pipeline, and improved opportunities for peaceful resolution of the longstanding and highly divisive conflicts with Greece in Cyprus and its own Kurdish population allow for guarded optimism. With the ending of the Cold War, Turkey's role as the southeastern flank of the North Atlantic Treaty Organization (NATO) diminished in value. Nevertheless, its location between the democracies of Western Europe, the mayhem of the Balkans and the Caucasus, and the dictatorships of the Arab region continues to sustain its central position in the geopolitical thinking of the West. In effect, Turkey is a bridge between East and West and a pivotal player in the new world order.[73] Thus, the central tenets of Turkey's Cold War foreign policy have largely survived, although with some alterations in emphasis.

The country has generally been closely aligned with the Western powers, in particular the United States and the European Union. The development of this orientation can be traced to the last years of the Ottoman Empire, which by virtue of its large possessions in Europe had evolved into more of a European power than an Asiatic one. Before the empire collapsed, the Ottomans embraced reforms that introduced structures, social norms and customs characteristic of the West. Then Atatürk launched a cultural revolution that secularized and further Westernized Turkish society. The republican government was determined to integrate the country into the modern Western, and more precisely European, world.[74] The Turkish leaders who followed in the footsteps of Atatürk pressed Turkey down a similar secularist and pro-Western development path. The country joined NATO, the European Economic Community (as an associate member), the Organization of Economic Cooperation and Development, the Council of Europe, the Conference on Security and Cooperation in Europe, the Western European Union (again as an associate member) and a Customs Union with the European Union. In 1987 the country applied to join the European Union as a full member, but this provoked heated debate within the Union. Concerns were expressed regarding Turkey's human rights record, the tremendous scale of economic development yet to be undertaken, and the eventual impact of allowing such a large and poor country to join the EU. (If allowed to join, Turkey would be the third most populous and the poorest state in the Union.) The principal concern is that Turkey's accession will result in massive relocation of Turkish workers to more favorable economic environments in the rest of the Union. This has already occurred to some extent, with most European states – especially Germany – accommodating steadily growing Turkish populations, who in many cases fill jobs that the local populations consider "beneath" them. Right-wing nationalist groups in many European states have long campaigned against this type of economic immigration, and public sentiment in some circles is violently hostile to foreigners. Many Turkish workers who have returned to Turkey after working in Western Europe vividly remember the hostility they faced, and this has fueled a degree of anti-European sentiment. Debate also swirls around the impact of a predominantly Muslim nation joining the Union, especially one with a such a dominant Islamic party as the AKP running the country. In September 2004, French Prime Minister Jean Marie Raffarin said, "We are not doubting the good faith of Mr Erdogan, but to what extent can today's or tomorrow's government make Turkish society embrace Europe's human rights values? Do we want the river of Islam to enter the riverbed of secularism?"[75] Frits Bolkestein, a former EU commissioner and head of Dutch Liberal Party, warned that Europe might become predominantly Muslim if Turkey joined the EU, and added pointedly that the "relief of Vienna [from an Ottoman army siege in 1683] will have been in vain."[76]

Turkish society will be forced to initiate some fundamental changes if it wishes to assuage European fears and guarantee its entry into the Union. Constitutional amendments will need to address human rights and economic and individual freedoms of expression, enterprise and thought.[77] Continued disagreement with Brussels over the fate of Cyprus has proven to be a further irritant. However, progress on human rights has been made, as the government removed military prosecutors and judges from State Security Courts, made it more difficult to ban political parties, enacted legislation to punish the use of torture by state police and the military forces, increased the freedom of the press, passed a repentance law – granting immunity from prosecution for many Kurdish guerrillas – and increased civil service accountability.[78]

Nevertheless, the issue of Kurdish language and broadcast rights remains unresolved. The debate continues over whether allowing Kurdish language broadcasts would improve Turkish unity or promote divisiveness in society and promote Kurdish independence. But it seems certain that the EU will continue to insist that allowing such broadcasts is a precondition for Turkey's entry.[79]

Turkey has generally enjoyed a close relationship with the United States, based on the US desire to maintain Turkey first as a base against the USSR and the

Warsaw Pact, and more recently as a moderate, democratic Muslim state in the turbulent Middle East. This has led the US to support Turkey in regard to issues related to the PKK, the EU and construction of oil pipelines. The two countries' relationship has been mostly military in nature, and has brought Turkey a great deal of military assistance. However, most of the equipment given to the Turks is fast becoming obsolete, and recently relations have become strained. Turkey's refusal to host US troops prior to the 2003 invasion of Iraq and its frustration with the US's failure to control PKK militants operating in northern Iraq have both undermined the relationship. Moreover, with the US mismanagement of the Iraq occupation, Turkish public opinion has turned against the US to an unprecedented degree: a poll conducted in June 2006 showed that only 12 percent of Turks viewed the United States positively.[80]

Turkey's determination to become a full member of the EU has been consistently frustrated by its longstanding conflict with Greece. Although the two countries are both members of NATO, neither side has been willing to back down over Cyprus or other territorial issues. The Cyprus dispute came to a head in July 1974 when the Turkish military intervened on the island in the aftermath of a military coup engineered by the Greek junta then ruling in Athens. Since then, Cyprus has been divided into two zones, and occasional summits have not come close to resolving the dispute. Relations became further embittered when Greece landed forces on and claimed sovereignty over the uninhabited Kardak (Imia) Islets, which are just four nautical miles from the Turkish mainland.

The confrontation between the two countries has been a source of friction in US–Turkish relations. Between 1975 and 1978, the US Congress attempted to force the withdrawal of Turkish forces from northern Cyprus by imposing an embargo on military assistance to its NATO ally. In retaliation Ankara closed specifically US bases on Turkish territory, while maintaining those belonging to NATO. However, the US embargo was lifted in 1979 after it had proved ineffectual and costly. Relations improved thereafter, especially when Turkey joined the US-led 1991 Gulf War coalition. Turkish bases were used by Western planes to launch missions against Iraqi targets, and the country strictly enforced the UN-imposed embargo on Iraq. However, twelve years later, Turkey refused to allow US planes to use its bases for the second Gulf War.

While mindful of not damaging its long-term, generally good relations with the West, Turkey has cultivated ties with other nations in recognition of the changed international climate since the end of the Cold War. Recently, it has actively sought to build links with some 60 million Turkic-speaking people in the former Soviet republics of Central Asia, and this has helped it to form new relationships with nations in that region. For instance, agreement was reached with Azerbaijan over the Baku–Ceyhan pipeline, which has brought enormous economic and political benefits to both countries. Some Turkish politicians and academics have viewed this foreign policy initiative as setting the foundations for a "Greater Turkish World" stretching into Central Asia. In March 1998, Turkey invited all of the newly independent Central Asian republics to a conference. Some observers interpreted this as an attempt by Turkey to capitalize on the cultural, linguistic and historical ties it has with the Asian republics and thereby extend Turkish hegemony into Central Asia. However, it has some serious competition in that respect, most notably from Russia, Iran and even its ally the United States.

Relations with Russia have improved since the days of the Cold War, and Turkey has even turned to Russia as an alternate source of arms, as Moscow does not tend to ask troublesome questions about human rights. Nevertheless, a degree of animosity remains, not least because of Turkey's tacit support for Chechen rebels in the Caucasus. Chechen groups have been free to raise funds in the country's major cities and have been permitted to use Turkey as a point of transit for both arms and sympathetic volunteers from Afghanistan to enter Chechnya. The Turkish government is unwilling to restrict these activities on its soil as there is a sizable Chechen minority in the country.

Turkish aspirations were manifested in November 1999 when US President Bill Clinton visited Turkey and several new agreements were reached regarding Caspian energy reserves, such as the construction of pipelines to transport Kazakh oil and Turkmenistan gas to the West. These decisions to transport oil and gas by pipeline into Turkey rather than by sea through the Turkish straits could be seen as attempts to isolate Russia.[81] Certainly they bolster Turkey's position in the region.

Turkey has also tried to restore its trade links with Iraq (formerly the country's second-largest trading partner). If successful, this is bound to bolster the already strong position the country occupies in the Middle East region. The Turkish position was confirmed by its participation in the Israeli–Arab multilateral negotiations. Furthermore, Turkish–Israeli agreements on increasing trade and joint armament manufacture, as well as strategic military and intelligence-sharing cooperation,[82] which were signed in February 1996, were conceived and proposed by Turkish generals, who had ultimate control over the country's foreign policy at the time. In the absence of the Soviet threat, the generals feared the marginalization of their status and sought to find a new role within the framework of US and European strategic interests in the Middle East and the Gulf. By designating Islamic activism as the "enemy within," Turkey made itself a component of the West's anti-Iranian strategy; and by allying itself with Israel, it could obtain sophisticated military technology while bypassing the pressure of the US Congress, human rights organizations and the strong lobby of Greeks and Armenians in both the US and EU. In fact, for some time after the end of the Cold War, it seemed that Turkey, through its alliance with Israel, had succeeded in enlisting the strong support of the Israeli lobby in the US Congress to neutralize Greek and Armenian pressure.[83] Of course, this led to considerable disquiet in the Arab world. At a summit in Cairo in June 1996, Arab leaders called on Turkey to reconsider its military agreement with Israel because they saw it as a threat to their own security. Nevertheless, the coalition government which came to power in Turkey in 1999 (ANAP–DSP–DTP) went even further than its predecessors by signing a military training cooperation agreement with Israel.

Turkey's relationships with both Syria and Iraq are complicated by the continued development of massive dam projects in southeastern Turkey, known as the Southeastern Anatolia Project. By damming the Tigris and Euphrates with a series of twenty-two dams, Turkey hopes to produce enough hydroelectric power to support the country's advanced industrial development as well as irrigation water for agriculture. However, the environmental effects downstream, throughout the Mesopotamian Plain, will dramatically affect the people and economies of both Iraq and Syria. Two treaties regulate the flow downstream: a 1987 protocol between Turkey and Syria guaranteeing a minimum flow of 500 cubic meters per second) in the Euphrates at the Turkish–Syrian border; and an Iraqi–Syrian pact splitting that amount in a 58:42 ratio. However, all three countries need most water during the dry summer growing season, and drought in 1999 highlighted the extent to which Syria and Iraq are dependent on the two rivers. As it controls almost all of the water in the Euphrates and half that in the Tigris, Turkey has been afforded the luxury of being able to force both Arab states to react to its initiatives. Furthermore, the destruction of Iraqi society after ten years of warfare, ten years of draconian economic sanctions and now an Anglo-American occupation has left it in no position to protect its rights. Syria, too, can exert little leverage, and it also has to consider the water implications of its negotiations with Israel over the Golan Heights region.[84]

Nevertheless, with the political shift in Turkey, the collapse of US credibility in the Middle East and the strains on US–Turkish relations, Turkey has attempted to re-engage with the Middle East. In 2004, Prime Minister Erdogan visited Iran and the two countries signed a join security agreement, designating the PKK as a "terrorist group." Concurrently, Syria's fear of Kurdish nationalism on its home soil, as well as Turkish pressure, compelled it to drop its support for the PKK, and coordinate with Turkey on the "Kurdish question." All of this has contributed to Turkey reviewing its strategic relationship with Israel.

Between 2007 and 2008, Turkey mediated several rounds of "indirect talks" between Syria and Israel. In April 2008, Erdogan visited Damascus and conveyed a message from the Israeli government of Ehud Olmert concerning a willingness to "withdraw from the Golan Heights in return for peace." After the visit, Erdogan said, "in this respect, there is a request from Syria and in the same way a request from Israel . . . The peace diplomacy we carry out will have a positive contribution . . . whether in Iraq, between Syria and Israel or between Israel and Palestine."[85] Similarly, following the Palestinian elections of 2006, Hamas representative Khalid Mashaal made an official visit to Turkey, suggesting Turkey's desire to mediate the Israeli–Palestinian conflict.[86]

With the election of the AKP, Turkish–Israeli relations gradually declined over the first decade of the twenty-first century. Prime Minister Erdogan condemned Israeli policy towards the West Bank and Gaza as "state terror" and the Turkish government was highly critical of Israel's assault against Lebanon and Gaza. Following the Israeli invasion of Gaza in 2008, Turkey escalated its condemnation, which peaked in a heated exchange between Erdogan and the Israeli President Perez at the World Economic Forum in Davos in 2009. After the debate, Erdogan left the meeting in protest. Turkish–Israeli relations perhaps reached their modern nadir, however, in the aftermath of the May 2010 flotilla incident. On May 30, 2010, a six-ship flotilla of pro-Palestinian activists attempted to break Israel's embargo on the Gaza strip by shipping supplies into the beleaguered territory. The flotilla, whose chief organizer was the Turkish *Foundation for Human Rights and Freedoms and Humanitarian Relief* (IHH), was assaulted by Israeli commandos, resulting in the death of nine activists (eight Turks and one Turkish-American). In the aftermath of the flotilla incident, Turkish–Israeli relations chilled significantly, with Erdogan once more condemning Israel for its lawlessness and practicing "state terror."

Turkey has derived much of its international status from the fact that it is the only Muslim state with a moderate, secular political system. The "Turkish model" of secular democracy is now being promoted as a viable alternative to the "Iranian model" of "fundamentalist theocracy" in the Muslim world. For instance, in a speech at Oxford University on November 18, 2008, Israeli President Shimon Peres stated: "Many Muslims will have to make their choice between the Iranian school of domination and the Turkish school of cooperation."[87]

Turkey's recent shift toward "Islamic" government has not stunted US–Turkish relations, mainly because the ruling AKP, despite its Islamic credentials, has maintained a pro-American posture. The greatest threats to US–Turkish relations will arguably center on the Iraqi situation and its corollary of ascendant Kurdish power. Meanwhile, Turkey's full participation in Middle Eastern affairs will continue to be constrained by the Arab states' suspicion of their northern neighbor – the inevitable legacy of Turkey's Ottoman past.

Notes

1 Andrew Mango, *Turkey and the War on Terror: For Forty Years We Fought Alone* (New York: Rutledge, 2005), pp. 17–18.
2 Martin Heper, *The State Tradition in Turkey* (Huntingdon: The Eothen Press, 1985), p. 22.
3 Bernard Lewis, *The Emergence of Modern Turkey* (Oxford: Oxford University Press), p. 31.
4 Ibid, p. 37.
5 Berch Berberoglu, *Turkey in Crisis: From State Capitalism to Neocolonialism* (Westport: Lawrence Hill & Co., 1982), p. 4.
6 L. Carl Brown, *Religion and State: The Muslim Approach to Politics* (New York: Columbia University Press, 2000), p. 109.
7 J. C. Hurewitz, *Diplomacy in the Near and Middle East: A Documentary Record* (Princeton: Princeton University Press, 1975), I, p. 94.
8 Ibid., p. 96.
9 Sydney Nettleton Fisher and William Ochsenwald, *The Middle East: A History* (Columbus: McGraw-Hill, 1996), I, pp. 274–276.
10 Halil Inalcik, *The Ottoman Empire: The Classical Age 1300–1600* (London: Phoenix Press, 2001), pp. 53–56.
11 Jorge Blanco Villalta, *Ataturk* (translated by William Campbell) (Ankara: Türk Tarih Kurumu Basimevi, 1979; originally published Buenos Aires: Editorial Claridad, 1939), p. 25.
12 Heper, op. cit., p. 46.
13 Berberoglu, op. cit., p. 5.
14 Lewis, op. cit., pp. 31, 65.

112 *Major governments: the Northern Belt*

15 Roderic H. Davison, *Reform in the Ottoman Empire 1856–1876* (Staten Island: Gordian Press, 1973).
16 Gokalp, *Turkish Nationalism and Western Civilization: Selected Essays of Ziya Gokalp* (Abingdon: Greenwood Press, 1981).
17 Villalta, op. cit., p. 278.
18 Niyazi Berkes, *The Development of Secularism in Turkey* (New York: Routledge, 1998), p. 460.
19 Frank Tachau, *Turkey, the Politics of Authority, Democracy, and Development* (Abingdon: Praeger, 1984), p. 18.
20 Frank Tachau, *Political Elites and Political Development* (Hoboken: John Wiley & Sons, 1975), p. 554.
21 C.H. Dodd, *Democracy and Development in Turkey* (Huntingdon: The Eothen Press, 1979), p. 136.
22 Tachau, op. cit., p. 22.
23 Jenny White, "Islam and Democracy: The Turkish Experience," *Current History*, Vol. 94, No. 588 (January 1995), pp. 7–12.
24 Ibid., p. 7.
25 M. Hakan Yavuz, *Islamic Political Identity in Turkey* (Oxford: Oxford University Press, 2003), p. 124.
26 White, op. cit., p. 10.
27 John Doxey, "Turkey: Post-Election Uncertainty," *The Middle East*, March 1, 1996, p. 14.
28 Omer Taspinar, "Kemalist Identity in Transition: A Case Study of Kurdish Nationalism and Political Islam in Turkey," Ph.D. Dissertation, Johns Hopkins University, 2001, pp. 232–234.
29 A small party led by Cindoruk that was established by the MPs who had resigned from the DYP over their dissatisfaction with the insistence of Tansu Çiller to remain in the RP–DYP coalition.
30 Aryeh Shmuelevitz, *Turkey's Experiment in Islamist Government, 1996–1997* (Tel Aviv: Moshe Dayan Center, May 1999).
31 Ibid.
32 Stephen Kinzer, "Turks' High Court Orders Disbanding of Islamic Party: Leader Appeals for Calm", *New York Times*, January 17, 1998, p. A1.
33 "Turkish Islamic Party Officially Dissolved," *New York Times*, February 23, 1998, p. A5.
34 Kemal Balci, "Rebirth of the Gray Wolves," *Turkish Daily News*, April 20, 1999, p. A1.
35 "CHP's Baykal, the Bitter Loser," *Turkish Daily News*, April 20, 1999, p. A1.
36 "Islamists Defeated in Parliamentary Polls, Successful in Local Elections," *Turkish Daily News*, April 20, 1999, p. A1.
37 "Official Tally out, Parliament to Convene Sunday," *Turkish Daily News*, April 28, 1999, p. A1.
38 "Parliament Breaks Record," *Turkish Daily News*, December 31, 1999, p. A3.
39 "A Century-Long Journey from a Closed Farm Economy to a Troubled, Semi-Liberal System," *Turkish Probe*, January 2, 2000, p. 1.
40 "The Apo Reports," *Turkish Daily News*, January 5, 2000, p. B4.
41 "Mixed Signals from Turkey to Europe," *Turkish Daily News*, January 7, 2000, p. A3.
42 "Overwhelming Support for the President-Elect," *Turkish Daily News*, May 8, 2000, pp. 1–2; "Sezer: Democratic, Secular Republic," *Turkish Daily News*, May 17, 2000), pp. 1, 9; "A New Era: President Sezer," *Turkish Probe*, May 8, 2000, pp. 1, 4.
43 "President Sezer's Rule of Law Pledge," *Turkish Probe*, May 22, 2000, p. 3.
44 "President Sezer Receives Full Support from Politicians of Kurdish Descent," *Turkish Daily News*, May 22, 2000, p. 5.
45 Selcuk Gultasli, "EU: No Proof of Islamic Agenda," *Today's Zaman*, September 12,

2007. URL: http://www.todayszaman.com/tz-web/detaylar.do?load = detay&link = 122014.

46 Mustafa Akyol Diyarbakir, "Winning Kurdish Hearts and Minds," *Turkish Daily News*, July 28, 2007. URL: http://www.thewhitepath.com/archives/2007/07/winning_kurdish_hearts_and_minds.php.

47 "Gül era at Çankaya Palace Begins," *Today's Zaman*, August 29, 2007. URL: http://www.todayszaman.com/tz-web/detaylar.do?load=detay&link=120593.

48 For a translation of this article, see URL: http://www.osce.org/documents/rfm/2005/03/14223_en.pdf. See also Amnesty International's Public Statement: "Turkey: Article 301 is a Threat to Freedom of Expression and Must be Repealed Now!," AI Index: EUR 44/035/2005 (Public), News Service No: 324, December 1, 2005. URL: http://web.amnesty.org/library/index/engeur440352005.

49 Ibon Villelabeitia, "Ex-Turkish Army Chief Says 'E-Coup' Justified," Reuters, March 8, 2009. URL: http://www.reuters.com/article/idUSTRE5471UQ20090508.

50 Michael M. Gunter, "The Kurdish Problem in Turkey," *Middle East Journal*, Vol. 40, No. 3 (Summer 1988), p. 395.

51 A conclusion supported by virtually all scholarship outside Turkey. See Michael M. Gunter, *The Kurdish Problem in Turkey* (Houndmills: Palgrave Macmillan, 2007), p. 400.

52 Elisa Munoz, "Ismail Besikci," in *Scientists Clash with the State in Turkey* [e-book] (New York: AAAS, 1998). URL: http://shr.aaas.org/scws/cs4.htm.

53 "Ocalan Caught in Italy: Nowhere to Run," *Turkish Probe*, November 15, 1998, p. 9.

54 "Human Rights Diary," *Turkish Probe*, March 14, 1999, p. 4.

55 "Turkey and Abdullah Ocalan: Both on Trial," *The Economist*, July 5, 1999, p. 36.

56 Ibid., p. 16.

57 "Demirel Backs Abolishing Courts with Military Judges," *Turkish Probe*, March 14, 1999, p. 4.

58 Patrick Cockburn, "Turkish PM Threatens to Invade Iraq," *Independent*, July 21, 2007. URL: http://www.independent.co.uk/news/world/middle-east/turkish-pm-threatens-to-invade-northern-iraq-458094.html.

59 "Operation Success Built on Diplomacy," *Zaman*, December 18, 2007. URL: http://www.todayszaman.com/tz-web/detaylar.do?load = detay&link = 129664.

60 "Targeted Newspaper Taraf Rejects 'Threats' from military," *Today's Zaman*, October 16, 2008. URL: http://www.todayszaman.com/tz-web/detaylar.do?load = detay&link = 156068.

61 Patrick Cockburn, "Turkey Reluctantly Prepares for Attack on Kurds," *Independent*, October 28, 2007. URL: http://news.independent.co.uk/world/middle_east/article 3104682.ece.

62 Commission of the European Communities, *Turkey 2008 Progress Report*, SEC(2008)2699 (May 11, 2008), p. 6.

63 "Addressing Human Rights Problems Awaits government Will," *Turkish Daily News*, May 1, 2000, p. 1; "Renewed Claims of Torture," *Turkish Daily News*, May 10, 2000, p. 3; "Parliamentary Human Rights Initiatives Documented," *Turkish Daily News*, May 27, 2000, p. 5.

64 Commission of the European Communities, op. cit., p. 6.

65 Ibid., p. 9.

66 Ibid., p. 28.

67 William Hale, *The Political and Economic Development of Modern Turkey* (London: Croom Helm, 1981), p. 55.

68 Ibid., p. 132.

69 *The Economist*, November 19, 1994, p. 23.

70 Ibid., p. 24.

71 International Monetary Fund, *IMF Country Report No. 07/161* (May 2007), p. 31.

72   *CIA World Factbook: Turkey* (2010). URL: https://www.cia.gov/library/publications/
      the-world-factbook/geos/tu.html.
73   International Monetary Fund, op. cit., p. 23.
74   Eric Rouleau, "The Challenges to Turkey," *Foreign Affairs*, November/December
      1993, p. 116.
75   "Turkey's Francophiles Wounded by French EU Doubts," *Turkish Daily News*,
      September 12, 2004, as quoted in P. Kubicek, "Turkish Accession to the European
      Union: Challenges and Opportunities," *World Affairs*, Vol. 168, No. 2 (Fall 2005),
      pp. 67–78.
76   "In 1683 Turkey Was the Invader; in 2004 Much of Europe Still Sees It That Way,"
      Guardian, September 22, 2004. URL: http://www.guardian.co.uk/world/2004/sep/
      22/eu.turkey.
77   "Main Opposition Leader Recai Kutan Speaks out: We Cannot Get into European
      Union with a Prohibitive Constitution," *Turkish Daily News*, November 19, 1999,
      Special Section: Turkey at the OSCE Summit, p. 1.
78   "Times Are Changing, but All for the Better," *Turkish Daily News*, November 19, 1999,
      Special Section: Turkey at the OSCE Summit, p. 1.
79   "Language: To Go for 'National Unity' or Integration with Europe?," *Turkish Probe*,
      November 7, 1999, p. 3.
80   Pew Research Center, "America's Image Slips, but Allies Share US Concerns
      over Iran, Hamas, 15-Nation Pew Global Attitude Survey," June 13, 2006. URL:
      http://pewglobal.org/reports/display.php?ReportID = 252.
81   "Oil: United States Diplomacy Prevails," *Turkish Daily News*, November 21, 1999,
      p. 5.
82   *Middle East Times*, April 21–27, 1996, p. 6; North Atlantic Council Declaration, *The
      Istanbul Declaration: Our Security in a New Era*, June 28, 2004. URL: http://www.
      nato.int/docu/pr/2004/p04-097e.htm.
83   Alain Gresh, "Turkish–Israeli–Syrian Relations," *Middle East Journal*, Vol. 55, No. 2
      (Spring 1998), pp. 190–191.
84   "Sharing Mesopotamia's Water," *The Economist*, November 13, 1999, pp. 45–46.
85   http://news.bbc.co.uk/go/pr/fr/-/2/hi/middle_east/7368551.stm Published: 2008/04/26.
86   F. Stephen Larrabee, "Turkey Rediscovers the Middle East," *Foreign Affairs*,
      July/August 2007, pp. 103–114.
87   http://www.todayszaman.com/tz-web/detaylar.do?load = detay&link = 159248.

Further reading

In this section we mention a very small sample of useful sources that can be
consulted as either background material or as key positions in theoretical debates.

Two books stand out as the major works on Ottoman economic, social and
political history in English: the edited volume by Halil Inacik and Donald Quataert,
An Economic and Social History of the Ottoman Empire, 1300–1914, and Kemal
Karpat's *Studies on Ottoman Social and Political History*. In recent years Donald
Quataert has added a revised edition of his history, *The Ottoman Empire,
1700–1922*, to the collection. Together, these works provide a wealth of information about the Ottoman state, its tax base, bureaucracy, population, army and the
question of ethnic and religious minorities. A good knowledge of Ottoman history
is crucial for understanding current conflicts in the Middle East and these books
provide a good historical background.

The writings of Serif Mardin, the most eminent scholar of Turkey as a modern
state, are indispensable reading for any deep knowledge of modern Turkish

history. He is a prolific author, but his classic *The Genesis of Young Ottoman Thought: A Study in the Modernization of Turkish Political Ideas* is still a great source for understanding the origins of secularism as state ideology. His *Religion, Society and Modernity in Turkey* is also a good source of historically informed analysis and insight into the complex relationship between religion and the state.

Modern Turkey has emerged as a major economic power and a model for multiparty politics and democratization in the Muslim world. Yet, conflicts centered on secularism and the public role of religion, the civil–military relations and the question of its large Kurdish minority have divided the polity and impeded its accession into the European Union.

On the question of the secularism versus public religion debate there are a number of major works. Niyazi Berkes's sympathetic account of the origins and rise of secularism, *The Development of Secularism in Turkey,* is a rich history of the emergence of an aggressive secular ideology partly as the outcome of the encounter between the Ottoman Empire and Western colonial powers from the eighteenth century onward.

M. Hakan Yavuz's study, *Islamic Political Identity in Turkey*, is a theoretically informed critique of secularism as state ideology and its consequences in terms of exclusion and the widening of the gap between Kemalist elites and large segments of Turkish society. Yavuz has pursued a rigorous research program of deconstructing secular authoritarianism. His latest book, *Secularism and Muslim Democracy in Turkey,* explores the possibility of "liberalizing" a political party with religious roots and thereby expanding the confines of the democratization process and political participation.

The entry of a new capitalist class with religious provincial-town roots into mainstream Turkish politics has intensified polarization in the secularism debate. Esra Ozyurek's *Nostalgia for the Modern: State Secularism and Everyday Politics in Turkey* is a rich ethnography of the simultaneous transformation of the state and religion in Turkey.

A very useful source that addresses various aspects of this transformation in chapters by prominent scholars of contemporary Turkey is Sibel Bozdogan and Resat Kasaba's *Rethinking Modernity and National Identity in Turkey*.

More than three decades of armed conflict with the Kurdish rebels in the southeast has left thousands dead and displaced. The marginalization of Kurdish identity and human rights violations that have accompanied this are major sources of conflict in Turkey today. Recently the AKP government has launched a "Kurdish initiative" which aims at integrating the Kurdish regions of the country into the mainstream political process. According to the government, this is a program that combines major economic investment with a more genuine recognition of Kurdish cultural rights. Omer Taspinar's *Kurdish Nationalism and Political Islam in Turkey: Kemalist Identity in Transition* traces the origins of the conflict to Kemalist efforts to create a homogenized Turkish state. In the 1980s, following General Kenan Evren's *coup d'état*, Kurdish nationalism was defined as an "existential threat." Metin Heper's *State and Kurds in Turkey: The Question of Assimilation* casts the Kurdish issue within a theoretical framework that he describes as acculturation as opposed to assimilation. Finally, 'Ali Kemal Ozcan's *Turkey's Kurds: A Theoretical Analysis of the PKK and Abdullah Ocalan* is a work that adds new material from the radical Kurdish perspective to the debate.

Constantine Arvanitopoulos's *Turkey's Accession to the European Union: An Unusual Candidacy* discusses the integration of Turkey into the European Union from different viewpoints. It also covers economic issues and political and cultural consequences of the accession in a comprehensive manner. Esra Lagro's *Turkey and the European Union: Prospects for a Difficult Encounter* is a more systematic, though somewhat dated, analysis of the problems associated with the accession and its prospects. It covers the major legal reforms, economic changes and political changes that should pave the way for Turkey's accession.

References

Arvanitopoulos, Constantine (2009) *Turkey's Accession to the European Union: An Unusual Candidacy*, Springer.

Berkes, Niazi (1999) *The Development of Secularism in Turkey*, Routledge.

Bozdogan, Sibel and Kasaba, Resat (1997) *Rethinking Modernity and National Identity in Turkey*, University of Washington Press.

Heper, Metin (2007) *State and Kurds in Turkey: The Question of Assimilation*, Palgrave Macmillan.

Inacik, Halil and Quataert, Donald (eds) (1994) *An Economic and Social History of the Ottoman Empire, 1300–1914*, Cambridge University Press.

Karpat, Kemal (2002) *Studies on Ottoman Social and Political History*, Brill.

Lagro, Esra (2005) *Turkey and the European Union: Prospects for a Difficult Encounter*, Anthem Press.

Mardin, Serif (2000) *The Genesis of Young Ottoman Thought: A Study in Modernization of Turkish Political Ideas*, Syracuse University Press.

—— (2006) *Religion, Society and Modernity in Turkey*, Syracuse University Press.

Ozcan, 'Ali Kemal (2005) *Turkey's Kurds: A Theoretical Analysis of the PKK and Abdullah Ocalan*, Routledge.

Ozyurek, Esra (2006) *Nostalgia for the Modern: State Secularism and Everyday Politics in Turkey*, Duke University Press.

Quataert, Donald (2005) *The Ottoman Empire, 1700–1922*, Cambridge University Press.

Taspinar, Omer (2004) *Kurdish Nationalism and Political Islam in Turkey: Kemalist Identity in Transition*, Routledge.

Yavuz, M. Hakan (2003) *Islamic Political Identity in Turkey*, Oxford University Press.

—— (2009) *Secularism and Muslim Democracy in Turkey*, Cambridge University Press.

5 The Islamic Republic of Iran

With Ali Rezaei

Contemporary Iran has a land area of 1,648,000 square kilometers, only 8.72 percent of which is arable. In March 2008 its population was estimated to be 71.5 million people. According to the 2006 census, 68.5 percent of the population lived in urban areas; 99 percent of rural Iranians resided in villages; and there were 240,000 nomads.[1] The UN forecasts the proportion of people living in urban areas to rise to three-quarters of the total inhabitants of the country by 2025. Tehran already has a population of over 10 million, and is the largest city in the Middle East after Cairo.

Iran, or Persia, has been the seat of eastern empires for twenty-seven centuries. The Persians are Indo-Europeans who migrated to what is now Iran in the second millennium BCE. The Iranians appear in historical records as the Aryans who invaded India, the Scythians and Saka of Western history, and the Yueh-Chi on the northwest frontiers of China, exploding out of Central Asia from the twelfth century BCE onwards. Being nomadic herders who raised horses and cattle, their way of life was characterized by mobility, and they were renowned for their skills as mounted archers and warriors. The character of Persian history is one of a tradition of centralized state systems, the rise and fall of pre-capitalist states based on tribal armies, territorial expansion and militarism. By the end of the Safavid dynasty (1502–1722 CE), there existed among the population a perceptible sense of unswerving pride in Persian culture and civilization.

When the Muslim Arabs overtook Persia in 640 CE, there already existed a rich legacy and civilization that a number of kingdoms and dynasties had developed and recorded. Among these founders of the Persian Empire and civilization are the Achaemenids (550–330 BCE), the Parthians (247 BCE–228 CE) and the Sassanids (224–640 CE).

Traced back to the Achaemenids are the development of governmental administration, the appearance of literature written in cuneiform, the spread of Zoroastrianism (a dualistic system of belief that has survived since time immemorial) and a great flourishing of Persian art and architecture. The Parthian kingdom stands out for defeating the post-Alexander Seleucids, building Parthia into an Eastern superpower, reviving the greatness of the Achaemenid Empire and counterbalancing Rome's hegemony in the West. The Sassanids overthrew the Parthians, revived the traditions of the Achaemenids, and reestablished

Map 5.1 Iran

Drawn by Ian Cool

Zoroastrianism as the state religion, which resulted in a persecution of Christians, and led to wars with Byzantium, ultimately exhausting both empires, and leaving them open to the Muslim conquest of the seventh century. Nevertheless, Persian language and literature survived the Arabization process, and even prospered under the Arabo-Muslim rule. The courtly culture of the Sassanids attended to much of the pomp of the Abbasid protocols of governance, and distinguished it from the earlier simplicity of the Muslim caliphs.

The Sassanid epoch witnessed the highest achievement of Persian civilization, and its influence was felt far beyond its political boundaries. Sassanid motifs found their way into the art of Central Asia and China, the Byzantine Empire and even Merovingian France. Indeed, the developments of Zoroastrianism, and those of its various sects, greatly influenced Eastern Christianity. Zoroastrianism survived as a major religion in Persia and India for another millennium, and Central Asian peoples incorporate many elements of its ritual into their cultural Islamic rites and Nestorian Christianity. Although not popularly tolerated, Nestorian Christianity was well received among the Sassanid elites.

The Mongols who swooped down on the lands of the Islamic Empire in the 1220s ultimately embraced Islam and ruled over Persia for almost a hundred years. For almost three centuries, Iran went through a period of decentralization and fragmented political rule under the dynasties of Ilkhanid (1256–1334) and Timurid (1337–1495), offshoots of the Mongol invasion. The Safavid dynasty traced its ancestry to the seventh Shi'ite Imam, Musa al-Kazim (d. 805), a connection which linked it to the Prophet's family. Most historical sources written at or close to the time of Sheikh Safi al-Din Ardebili (1252–1334), the founding ancestor of the Safavid dynasty, dispute this claim. Sheikh Safi was a powerful Sufi patriarch whose brotherhood or *Tariqat* monastery, *Khanegegh*, was a powerful institution in Ardebil in northwestern Iran. According to Mostowfi's *Nozhal-ul Gholoub*, written in 1340, "a majority [of Ardebil's population] belong to the Shafei School [of Sunni Islam] and are followers of Sheikh Safi al-Din."[2] Ahmad Kasravi, the renowned historian of the Iranian Constitutional Revolution, provides a variety of sources and historical evidence to refute the claim to Imam ancestry by the Safavid kings and their court historians.[3] Although Safi al-Din's allegiance to 'Ali – the Prophet Mohammad's son-in-law and the first Shi'a Imam – has been mentioned in some historical sources, it was some time between the time of Safi al-Din and the crowning of Ismael I as the first Safavid king in 1501 that Safavid Sufis fully embraced Shi'ism and finally turned it into the state religion in Iran at the beginning of the sixteenth century. This seemed to be in response to a history of numerous popular, mainly Shi'a, rebellions against various Sunni rulers of Turkic origin allied with the caliphs in Baghdad or Damascus, on the one hand, and the uprisings against the devastating effects of various Mongol, Ilkhanid and Timurid dynasties ruling over different parts of Iran between the thirteenth and sixteenth centuries, on the other.

An interesting historical comparison can be made with the historical developments that led to the rise of the modern state in Western Europe. After the second fall of the empire in Iran as a result of Mongol invasion, and the rise of a fragmented structure of political rule with many contending centers of power in Iranian provinces, the absence of a centralized ecclesiastical hierarchy comparable to the Catholic Church in Western Europe contributed to the strength of Sufi brotherhoods and their institutional power in various parts of Iran. In a period that stretches over six generations of Safavid Sufis from Safi al-Din to Ismael, they are transformed into full-blown Shi'a *murshid*s, Sufi saints, and prince-like temporal rulers possessing huge material and symbolic resources. It is Sheikh Jonayd, Ismael's grandfather, who clearly displays this unification of spiritual and temporal authority as the simultaneous head of a Sufi order and a provincial lord for the first time.

At a time when the power of Ottoman sultans was expanding beyond eastern Anatolia, and the Byzantine Empire was desperately resisting its final doom, only a year or two before the fall of Constantinople in 1453 Jonayd married the sister of Ozun Hasan, the king-chief of the "White Sheep" Turkmen dynasty and the main ally and son-in-law of the last Byzantine emperor. Hasan had just won control over Iraq and contemporary Azerbaijan to the west and Turkestan on the northeastern border of Iran, all lands lying between Iran and the Ottoman Empire and their Uzbek allies to the east. In fact, Ismael's father, Sheikh Heydar, married Martha, the granddaughter of that last emperor of Eastern Christianity. The drive to politicize Shi'ism and turn it into an established religion, then, was partly due to the need for an ideological counterweight against Ottoman sultans whose armies had already conquered Constantinople and were threatening the holy cities of Shi'a Islam in present-day Iraq.

The Safavid monarchs imposed on the population – which, up to that time, had been predominantly Sunni – the Twelvers Shi'ite creed, and ruled, according to the sovereign's discretion, without any Shi'ite political theory of government, which as yet had not been developed. They presided over a decline in Persian power, as the caravan routes of Central Asia were surpassed in importance by sea routes through the Indian Ocean, which linked the Mediterranean world and Western Europe with China and Southeast Asia through the Middle East. This, of course, was mainly due to the fall of Constantinople and Ottoman supremacy in the Mediterranean and the Black Sea.

The Safavid dynasty was brought to a close in 1722 when its capital, Isfahan, was overrun by the tribal army of Mahmoud "the Afghan," who then ruled over a rapidly disintegrating Persian society. Persia entered a period of decay and anarchy, from which it did not emerge until the ascendancy of the Qajar dynasty (1794–1925) in the late eighteenth century.

Russian expansion eastwards into Iranian territory dates back to the early eighteenth century. The first serious military invasion came at the time of the fall of the Safavid dynasty. With Isfahan under the occupation of Afghan tribes, the armies of Czar Peter the Great made inroads into the northwestern shores of the Caspian Sea and occupied the Iranian town of Darband (in today's Azerbaijan) in 1723.[4] The Russian drive toward "warm waters" into the Caucasus and Central Asia and the consolidation of British colonial rule in India in the second half of the eighteenth century gradually shaped the struggle for the control of Central Asia, dubbed the "Great Game" the following century. Lord Curzon, the viceroy of India, described this Great Game in very clear terms: "Turkestan, Afghanistan, Transcaspia, Persia – to many these words breathe only a sense of utter remoteness, or a memory of strange vicissitudes and of moribund romance. To me, I confess they are pieces on a chessboard upon which is being played out a game for the domination of the world."[5] The rivalry between the two imperial powers, Britain and Russia, that shaped the Great Game in this vast area of land stretching from Georgia and the Caucasus to Transoxiana and territories bordering China's western frontiers, led to the cessation of huge former Iranian provinces north of the Caspian Sea and parts of present-day Afghanistan.[6] Between 1779 and 1794, Agha Mohammad Khan, a leader of the Qajar tribe, succeeded in reunifying Iran. He established his capital at Tehran, which has remained the capital of Iran ever since. His successor, Fath 'Ali Shah (1797–1834), fought two disastrous wars with Russia, which ended in ceding Georgia, Armenia, Azerbaijan and most of the north Caucasus region to the expanding Russian Empire. Moreover, his reign witnessed the emergence of intense diplomatic rivalries between Russia and Britain over the geostrategic position of Iran, which ensued from their respective imperial designs. British and Russian territorial encroachment resulted in the Russian conquest of present-day Turkmenistan and Uzbekistan, and in the severing of historic Iranian ties to the cities of Bukhara and Samarqand. Further, Britain annexed Herat (1851) and incorporated it into Afghanistan in order to extend eastward the buffer between its Indian territories and Russia's expanding empire.[7]

During the reign of Naser o-Din Shah (1848–1896) the state started to modernize Iran by introducing a standing army, Western science, technology, and modern educational methods. During the tenure of Mirza Taghi Khan, Iran's army was reorganized and modernized, growing from a force of no more than 2,000 troops at the end of Mohammad Shah's (1834–1848) reign into a relatively disciplined army of around seventy organized units.[8] Amir Kabir started a more comprehensive modernization effort by building small military industries, modern factories and schools and initiating legal reforms. These efforts did not lead to much positive social transformation, however – Amir Kabir was dismissed in November 1851 and was killed by order of the Shah two months later.

In 1890 Iran granted a full monopoly of tobacco production for fifty years to a British businessman who, in turn, sold the concession to Britain's Imperial Tobacco Company. This caused a mass rebellion against the concession and merchants in major cities formed alliances with religious leaders, the 'Ulama, to boycott the use of tobacco as long as the monopoly concession lasted. The boycott even extended into the Shah's royal court after the leading Shi'a scholar of the time, Mirza Shirazi, issued a decree (*fatwa*) from Najaf, Iraq, forbidding the use of tobacco by Muslims. Large-scale protest forced the Shah to cancel the concession. This rebellion clearly indicated the rising power of the Shi'a clergy as an institution, and the importance of the bazaar–mosque alliance. The bazaar has traditionally been a socio-religious and economic center of active popular forces to which the 'Ulama lent their protective care. The 'Ulama were next in rank to the princes and nobility in Qajar social stratification, and comprised a hierarchy consisting of a wide spectrum of groups that were connected though vertically identifiable and assumed educational, cultural, economic and political functions which permeated every strata of society, thus availing themselves of formidable socio-political power, from which the idea of Wilayat al-Fuqaha' (custodianship of the jurists) developed. The 'Ulama, while economically independent of state control, were publicly acknowledged to be the spokesmen for the commoners, a link to the government machinery and an upward communication conduit.[9]

The tobacco rebellion was a prelude to the constitutional revolution of 1906.[10] The Shah had to contract large loans with British banks to pay the penalty for the cancellation of the concession. This was followed by a series of concessions to other Europeans. The low customs tariffs and municipal tax exemption for Western merchants combined with the commercialization of agriculture and certain handicrafts to exacerbate the gulfs between owner and worker, peasants and landlords, notables and commoners, and the powerful and the weak. Thus, the peasantry's discontent overlapped with the grievances of displaced urban craftsmen to kindle the spirit of resistance.[11]

What remained relatively intact, however, was the bazaar structure, with its traditional small-scale bourgeoisie, the banking trade, brokers, artisans and merchants, whose combined opposition to the customs tariff was not heeded by the government. The origins of the idea of a constitution and a constitutional government in Iran date back to the mid-nineteenth century and a group of statesmen around Fath 'Ali Shah's crown prince, Abbas Mirza, who attempted to modernize the army and the administration after Iran's defeat in the Russo-Persian Wars. Amir Kabir rose to prominence within the administration of the crown prince in Tabriz before becoming prime minister in 1847. According to an unpublished treatise written by a confidant, Mirza Ya'qoob, after Amir Kabir's death, he "had the idea of constitution in his head" but the "greatest obstacle" in his way "was the Russians."[12] These statesmen and many of their intellectual allies were influenced by the demands for a constitutional government in the Ottoman Empire that started around 1840s. The first Ottoman constitution was drafted in 1876 and lasted only two years before being revoked by Sultan Abdulhamid II. The Iranian constitutional revolution of 1906 in turn influenced the rebellion of Young Turk officers in 1908, which restored the constitution of 1876. The victory of Japan – an Asian country with a constitution – over Russia – a European country without a constitution – in their 1905 war also encouraged the opponents of despotic rule in Iran to press their demands for a constitution, which, at the time, was perceived to be the basis of Western governments' strength. The defeat had started a constitutional revolution in Russia, and a vast population of Iranian émigrés working in the oilfields of Baku and other Russian industries had transmitted news of this to their homeland. This was welcomed by modernist intellectuals and a majority of senior clergy in Iran, who saw in a parliamentary constitution the means to curb the autocratic power of the monarchy and empower the popular forces. In fact, these groups had been circulating literature on constitutionalism for decades.[13] In the face of these demands, the Shah signed a constitution that was modeled on Belgium's on December 30, 1906, set up a Majlis (the equivalent of a parliament) and promptly died five days later. The Supplementary Fundamental Laws, approved in 1907, provided, within limits, for freedom of press, speech and association, and for the security of life and property. However, the revolution was opposed by the monarchy, large landowners and tribal chiefs, as well as the Anglo-Russian bloc.

In 1911, when Russian forces had entered into northern Iranian cities of Rasht, Anzali and Mashhad, and British forces had occupied parts of southern Iran, disagreements between the two major parties in the parliament over who should be the next prime minister led to armed clashes in Tehran between militias loyal to the two parties, the center-left Democrats (Fergh-e democrat) and the conservative

Etedaliyoon. Bakhtiari chiefs supporting the current prime minister, Mostowfi, ordered their militia to occupy the parliament building, dissolved the parliament and suspended the constitution on December 20, 1911. (Bakhtiaries are members of a large tribe from the Lur ethnic group living in a vast area in central and southern Iran, comprising parts of the provinces of Khuzistan, Isfahan, Kohgilooyeh va Booyer Ahmadi and Lurestan.)

During the constitutional revolution, oil was discovered in southern Persia, and the Anglo-Persian Oil Company (APOC) was established. In traditional British imperial style, the British government set out to establish the company's virtual sovereignty in its areas of operation by supporting the autonomy of local chiefs against the central authority of Tehran. APOC began constructing pipelines, refineries and port facilities at Abadan, and in 1912 the first oil shipment was exported to England. After converting the Royal Navy from coal to oil in 1913, the British government became strategically dependent on Iranian oil, so, in 1914, just before the outbreak of the First World War, it acquired a 51 percent stake in APOC. Britain's policy towards Iran was now dictated by its strategic interests, and the country was fiercely contested during the war, with Russian, British and Ottoman troops all occupying parts of it at various times.

In the aftermath of the 1917 Bolshevik revolution, Britain became the sole dominant foreign power in Iran. In 1919, the British government imposed an agreement on Iran, known as the Anglo-Persian Agreement, which gave Britain the right to build railroads according to its needs, send military and technical advisors to Iran at the expense of the Iranian government, and exercise some control over the Iranian army. The idea behind this agreement was to strengthen the buffer between Russia and British India and the warm waters of the Persian Gulf and Indian Ocean. In a passage that sounds like a harbinger of the Cold War, Curzon expressed the essence of the British attitude toward Iran:

> If it be asked why we should undertake the task at all, and why Persia should not be left to herself and allowed to rot into picturesque decay, the answer is that her geographical position, the magnitude of our interests in the country, and the future safety of our Eastern Empire render it impossible for us . . . to disinherit ourselves from what happens in Persia. Moreover, now that we are about to assume the Mandate for Mesopotamia, which will make us coterminous with the western frontiers of Asia, we cannot permit the existence between the frontiers of our Indian Empire and Baluchistan and those of our new protectorate, a hotbed of misrule, enemy intrigue, financial chaos, and political disorder. Further, if Persia were to be alone, there is every reason to fear that she would be overrun by Bolshevik influence from the north. Lastly, we possess in the southwestern corner of Persia great assets in the shape of oil fields, which are worked for the British navy and which give us a commanding interest in that part of the world.[14]

The regimes of Reza Shah and Mohammad Reza Pahlavi Shah

In 1921, Reza Khan, a colonel serving in the Cossack Brigade, instigated a *coup d'état*, and seized power alongside a pro-British journalist, Seyyed Zia el-din Tabatabaie. In response, Ahmad Shah, who remained the titular Qajar monarch, appointed Reza Khan as commander of the army and Seyyed Zia as prime minister.

Reza Khan used his position to consolidate the military and police forces under his control, and then used those forces to secure the frontiers and quell Iran's restive tribes. In November 1923 the government of Moshir al-Doleh fell, and Reza Khan was appointed prime minister. Over the next year a temporary alliance was formed in the Majlis between the Western-oriented modernist deputies, known as the "modernity faction," and pro-Soviet deputies led by Suleiman Mirza, who wished to establish a republic. This alarmed Ahmad Shah and he demanded a change in government. Reza Khan temporarily resigned but returned triumphantly after a massive campaign by his supporters in the Majlis and threats of army commanders in provinces to march on Tehran. All this had the potential to return Iran to the chaos and insecurity of 1911 and the occupation of the country during the First World War.[15] Both the progressive parliamentary deputies, led by Seyyed Hasan Moddares (later killed on Reza Khan's orders), and the leading clergy sensed Reza Khan's hidden agenda and his drive towards a fully consolidated dictatorship. Given the measures taken by Mustafa Kemal against religious institutions in Turkey and his aggressive secularism, the Iranian 'Ulama were fearful that establishing a republic with a powerful president would result in a similar secularization drive in Iran and significant loss of their power.[16] However, this meant the perpetuation of a monarchical dictatorship in which there was no legal or institutional right to vote the head of state out of power.

Against this background, in 1924, Reza Khan attempted to establish a secular republic, but he was strongly opposed by clerical opposition. Consequently, in 1925, he took a different track by ousting Ahmad Shah and assuming the title of Shah himself. However, his authority was severely limited by the British stranglehold on Iran's economy. His efforts to negotiate better terms for Iranian oil resulted in the Oil Agreement of 1933, which granted the British a preeminent role in the Iranian oil industry for the next sixty years.[17]

Reza Shah was able to centralize power as he ruthlessly eliminated opponents and potential rivals. Religious and tribal leaders came under intense pressure, and although the Majlis was allowed to continue, its power was greatly reduced. As in the Qajar dynasty, the central pillars of power were the military, the bureaucracy and the royal court. Rapid Westernization was attempted through improvements in communications and education. In the economic sphere, Reza Shah promoted industrialization, with a view to modernizing and diversifying the economy. Infrastructure enterprises, such as the construction of roads and railways, as well as government-owned factories, were given priority. However, little attention was paid to the agricultural base of the economy in a country where 85 percent of the population lived in rural areas, and the burden of Reza Shah's policies fell on the populace as taxes rose.

The Shah adopted a number of secular reforms in the social and cultural domains whose aim was partly to curtail the influence of the 'Ulama. Men and women were compelled to adopt Western styles of dress, and from 1936 women were forbidden from wearing the traditional veil: shops were ordered not to serve veiled women, and those wearing veils were forbidden to appear in public or to board public transportation. Some restrictions were imposed on men's traditional dress as well. The judiciary was also affected by the secularization drive. On December 27, 1936, the Majlis passed a law requiring all judges to obtain a degree from the University of Tehran's law faculty, or a foreign university, and to have completed additional years of secular legal training. This legislation had a direct impact on the 'Ulama, who saw their traditional hold on the judiciary decline.

Unsurprisingly, many Iranians were unhappy about Reza Shah's modernization policies. The unveiling of women caused uproar among the 'Ulama, and prior to the Second World War Reza Shah began to establish ties with Nazi Germany. German technicians were brought to Iran to organize governmental administration, agriculture and industry; German teachers were secured for Iranian schools; many Iranian students were sent to German schools for advanced education; and commercial ties were developed between the two countries. By 1939, more than a third of Iran's foreign trade was with Nazi Germany.

Although there were opponents to all of this, they did not have the strength to alter the secularization drive while Reza Shah was at the helm. However, once he was removed from power in August 1941, the drive waned dramatically. His removal came when Britain and Russia invaded Iran in an effort to ensure the free flow of oil for their war efforts and to safeguard supply routes to the Russian forces that were bearing the brunt of the fighting against Germany. The Shah's army quickly collapsed in the face of the joint British–Soviet action and Reza was forced to abdicate in favor of his twenty-one-year-old son, Mohammad Reza Pahlavi. Reza Shah died in South Africa in 1944.

On assuming the throne, the young ruler had to cultivate his own political and economic power base, an uphill task in the turmoil of the war. His immediate job was to repair Iran's severely compromised sovereignty. In the north of the country, Soviet forces had continued to occupy Iranian territory in violation of earlier withdrawal commitments. In the areas occupied by these forces, two "autonomous republics" – Azerbaijan and Kurdistan – had been established, and Tehran feared this was a prelude to their eventual incorporation into the Soviet Union. However, under intense diplomatic maneuvering from the Iranians and pressure from the US and Britain, Iran regained these territories and the Soviet forces finally withdrew.

Next, the government set out to capitalize on its immense oil reserves. While the Anglo-Iranian Oil Company (AIOC) secured huge revenues from its Iranian operation, only about one-sixth of its profits remained in Iran.[18] According to the concession originally granted to William Knox D'Arcy in 1903, Iran's share of the revenues was set at 16 percent of the company's net profit. The problem was that the amount of money Iran received fluctuated considerably year by year. It was £1.4 million in 1926, £530,000 in 1928 and just £310,000 in 1931, although it bounced back to £1.53 million in 1932. This caused major problems since oil revenues now accounted for one-third of all government spending.[19] Reza Shah ordered his cabinet to annul the concession in 1932, and after a lengthy series of negotiations a new agreement was reached in 1933 which granted rights to the AIOC to produce oil in Iran for another sixty years. This time the company agreed to pay a fixed amount of four shillings per barrel of oil produced.[20] This was dubbed the "shameful agreement" and was used as a weapon in the publicity campaigns of the Iranian opposition against the regime over the next four decades.

Reza Shah's abdication and the relatively free political atmosphere that followed his departure in 1941 opened up the old wounds again, and it was no surprise that oil and the 1933 agreement became issues of hot public debate. Around this time, Dr. Mohammad Mossadegh returned to Iran from self-imposed exile. Educated at the Ecole des Sciences Politiques in Paris and the law school of Neuchatel University in Switzerland, Mossadegh had held various government positions from an early age and had been a member of parliament from 1924 to 1927. However, under British pressure, Reza Shah had forced him into an early retirement that had lasted from 1928 to 1941. Despite the interference and fraud perpetrated by Mohammad Reza Pahlavi, who was obsequious to the British, Mossadegh and a group of nationalists were elected to the Majlis in the parliamentary elections of 1943. In the 1950 elections, Mossadegh and seven others won seats under the banner of the "National Front" and formed a small but vocal opposition in the Majlis. Earlier, on July 30, 1949, the government had introduced a bill to amend the 1933 agreement with AIOC, but this was rejected due to the efforts of the nationalist deputies, so it was left to the 1950 Majlis to decide on the question of oil.

The next bill preserved AIOC's near-colonial authority, and caused outrage over the government's seeming inability to negotiate better terms. A Majlis committee demanded the nationalization of Iran's petroleum resources by March 9, 1951, throwing the government into crisis. While the Shah and his cabinet, on behalf of AIOC, attempted to force their bill through the Majlis, the demand for nationalization gained increasing public support, and the Oil Nationalization Law was passed by the Majlis on March 15, 1951. The Senate followed suit five days later. During March and April, there were mass demonstrations in Tehran in support of nationalization. Oil workers in Iran's southern provinces went on strike at the same time. To forestall open rebellion, the Shah did not veto Mossadegh's election as prime minister on April 29, when the National Front, despite its minority status in the Majlis, managed to secure a majority vote. Undaunted by palace and foreign pressure, his first act as prime minister was to implement the new Oil Nationalization Law and terminate British control over Iran's oil industry. Britain responded with a lawsuit against Iran in the International Court of Justice, and a complaint to the United Nations Security Council. Mossadegh personally defended Iran's rights at both the UN and the International Court of Justice in Hague and secured victory for the people of Iran. Thus, he was able to dissolve the Anglo-Iranian Oil Company, 50 percent of whose stocks belonged to the British government, and abolish all its legal rights, and established the National Iranian Oil Company (NIOC), the first national oil company in the Middle East.[21]

The British government retaliated by imposing sanctions on Iran and starting military maneuvers in the Persian Gulf. By the summer of 1951, these had developed into a near-complete blockade of Iran.

The success of the nationalization gave the Majlis more power than it had ever possessed. The popularity and patriotism of Mossadegh propelled the office of prime minister to such power that Britain – and, later, after the election of President Eisenhower in late 1952, the US – decided to intervene covertly to topple him and his government in order to secure a vassal state and regain Western control of Iranian oil. The operation, code-named Ajax, was executed in the summer of 1953.[22] This was a joint effort between the CIA and MI6. The core of the plan was to cause mob riots and buy the loyalty of the army, the Royal Guard and the police to remove Mossadegh. C.M. Woodhouse, Britain's top spy in the British Embassy in Tehran, conceived the blueprint of the coup, which received the approval of John Foster Dulles, the US Secretary of State. Woodhouse flew guns to Iran from Habbaniya, the British air force base in Iraq, and buried them for later use. He then handed a few million Iranian riyals to the Rashidian Brothers, who were the mob organizers. This group had been cultivated by the British diplomat Robin Zaehner, who coordinated with the CIA's station chief in Tehran, Roger Goiran. Shortly before the coup, in August 1953, Kermit Roosevelt arrived secretly in Tehran in a supervisory capacity. Earlier, in April, General Afshartous, the nationalist chief of the Iranian police force, had been kidnapped and murdered under MI6 supervision. Around mid-August, the coup began when Iranians working for the CIA, although posing as communists, harassed religious leaders and bombed a cleric's home to turn the country's Islamic community against the government. Meanwhile, the Shah reluctantly signed a CIA-drafted royal decree to remove Mossadegh, change the government and appoint General Fazlollah Zahedi as the new prime minister. Zahedi had already been bought off by the Anglo-American intelligence services. Mossadegh made his refusal to quit public, and in a few hours massive rioting erupted throughout Iran, indicating his widespread support. The Shah fled the country on August 16, and the protests and demonstrations continued for two days, with the people pulling down statues of the current Shah and his father all over Iran. The CIA arranged for the Shah's twin sister, Princess Ashraf Pahlavi, and General H. Norman Schwarzkopf (the father of the Desert Storm commander) to act as supportive intermediaries to keep the Shah from succumbing to the pressure.

With the first stage of the coup having failed, Kermit Roosevelt launched the second stage, whereupon a column of tanks led by Zahedi moved through Tehran, surrounded the residence of Mossadegh and attacked the demonstrators. In a few hours 300 were dead, thousands were wounded and Mossadegh was forced to surrender. Woodhouse returned to Britain to become the MP for Oxford, and Zaehner later became Professor of Eastern Religions at Oxford. On August 19, the Shah was restored.

The fall of Mossadegh began a new era of US intervention, and growing hostility toward the US among the awakening forces of Iranian nationalism.[23] As Behrooz puts it: "The long-term consequence of this intervention can partially explain the 1979 revolution in Iran and the ongoing crisis in Iran–US relations."[24] The new oil agreement drafted after the coup gave US oil corporations almost a 40 percent share of Iran's oil.[25] Mossadegh was under house arrest from 1953 until his death on March 4, 1967. The coup changed the political landscape in Iran for the next twenty-five years in fundamental ways. It took away whatever political legitimacy the Shah's regime could have claimed up to that point based on the constitution of 1906 and its amendments. A new generation of younger political activists, within the National Front and the Tudeh Communist Party, began to emerge, and they did not believe that playing the parliamentary game within the current regime could lead to any meaningful political change and social improvement. The coup also significantly increased the US's military and security presence in Iran and linked the latter firmly with the southern belt of containment around the Soviet Union, transforming Iran into a central ring (the Central Treaty Organization) that linked NATO to Southeast Asian military arrangements (the South East Asian Treaty Organization) against the Soviet Union and China. This "partnership" imposed a heavy burden on the Iranian economy in the form of massive spending on arms and other items that were needed if the Shah were to succeed in becoming a regional power. Therefore, together with the suppression of the June 1963 rebellion in support of Khomeini, the 1953 coup transformed the discourse of the Iranian opposition into one of revolution, as it focused on changing the entire regime by violent means.

Following the coup, the United States, with the willing collaboration of the Shah, emerged as the most powerful influence in the country. By the time Amir Abbas Hoveida, one of the Shah's most trusted and loyal confidants, was made prime minister in 1965, the Shah's position had been consolidated. Hoveida remained in office until 1977, as his unquestioning loyalty to the royal house facilitated the furtherance of the executive power of the Shah, and the progressive erosion of other power centers, most notably the Majlis, leaving the monarch in sole possession of political authority. Hoveida ultimately paid for his unquestioning loyalty with his life. At the height of the revolutionary upheaval in the autumn of 1978, the Shah used him as a scapegoat to stem the rising revolutionary tide and save himself. Hoveida was arrested on charges of corruption on November 8 and remained in jail even after the Shah's departure later that month. He was then tried in a revolutionary court after the fall of the Pahlavi regime and was executed on March 8, 1979.[26]

Other factors also helped the Shah to consolidate his power. He received massive military and economic assistance from the United States because he was regarded as a valuable asset during the Cold War. With this US support and the absence of any significant opposition after the repression that followed the 1953 coup, he embarked on an extensive reform of the institutions of the state and the economy.

Occupying a central position in the absolutist regime was an overwhelming bureaucracy, which played an integral role in the maintenance of the Shah's regime. It was also the organ that planned and carried out the many government programs and initiatives aimed at modernizing the country. Government ministries maintained extensive networks of offices which penetrated even the most remote parts of the country to implement government programs. Nevertheless, the ability of the bureaucracy to carry out the designated tasks was frustrated by several inherent weaknesses. It was tainted with layers of corruption and overt inefficiency, ills that were also rampant in the royal court itself. The modernization projects and the secularization of Iran polarized the country into a very opulent minority and a rapidly growing class of urban poor, mostly recent migrants from equally impoverished rural areas that were adversely affected by the land reform of the 1960s.[27]

From 1953 until his exile in 1978, the Shah dramatically expanded the armed forces in line with his determination to turn the country into a regional power. In 1978, the Iranian armed forces were reported to be one of the largest military institutions in the world.[28] This was made possible by increased oil revenues and by the Nixon–Kissinger doctrine, whose aim was to develop regional powers under American patronage. Obsessed with the Soviet threat, Iran was most willing to be promoted to regional power status under this arrangement. Thus, it was second only to Israel in receiving American military hardware, loans and other assistance. It received modern naval vessels, armored vehicles, advanced F-14 interceptors and numerous other pieces of equipment, all of which enabled Iran to survive the sanctions that were enforced during the devastating war with Iraq in the 1980s.

The former chief CIA analyst in Iran, Jesse J. Leaf, is reported to have said that the Iranian security apparatus, SAVAK, which the CIA helped set up in 1957, was trained in the German torture techniques of the Second World War.[29] The Israeli intelligence service, Mossad, undertook the training of SAVAK personnel, whose main task was to control all facets of the political life of the Iranian people, both domestically and abroad.[30] An extension of SAVAK was the Censorship Office, which was established to monitor journalists, literary figures, academics, labor unions and peasants' organizations throughout the country. Over the years, SAVAK became a law unto itself, with enough authority to arrest, detain, brutally interrogate and torture suspects indefinitely without any checks. Further, SAVAK operated its own prisons in Tehran, such as the Qezel-Qalaeh and Evin facilities.[31] It had many full-time case officers running a network of informers and infiltrators who watched 30,000 Iranian students on US college campuses. The head of the SAVAK agents in the United States was officially an attaché at the Iranian Mission to the United Nations, although the FBI, CIA and State Department were all fully aware of his real role.[32] The brutality of SAVAK toward its victims generated extensive condemnation from human rights organizations and governments around the world. However, the Shah, with the US on his side, was able to ignore all of their protests.

In the political arena, the Shah tried to legitimize his rule and concentrate all power under his personal command. After the 1953 coup, only two political parties, the Nationalist Party (Melliyoon) and the People's Party (Hezb-e mardom) were allowed to operate. In the 1960s, the Nationalist Party developed into the New Iran Party, which was headed by Prime Minister Hoveida. Although both parties were extremely loyal to the Shah and under his command, in 1975 he dissolved them and formed the Rastakhiz (Resurgence) Party to act as the sole ruling party. On March 3, 1975, the Iranian newspaper *Keyhan International* quoted the Shah as saying:

> One who does not join the new political party has two options. Such a person either belongs to an illegal organization or to the [banned communist] Tudeh Party, or, in other words, he/she is a traitor. Such a person deserves to be in one of Iran's jails, or if he/she so wishes he/she can leave the country without paying exit duties [at the airport]. They can go wherever they wish, for they are not Iranians, they don't belong to the nation and their activities are against the law and entitled to punishment.[33]

This all-embracing party was expected to solicit support for the regime in both urban areas and the countryside. However, the party organization soon turned to suppressing the masses politically, rather than mobilizing them.[34] When the revolt against the regime ultimately took shape in 1978, Rastakhiz was a predictable target.

Cultural and social reforms started by the Shah's father were continued, in spite of opposition from the 'Ulama and other groups. The Shah was in a less difficult position than his father, who had to initiate economic development and infrastructure-building from scratch, without large-scale foreign assistance. The latter Shah's package of long-term plans and reforms was called the "White Revolution" and comprised six elements: land reform; nationalization of forests; sale of state-owned enterprises to finance the land reform; a workers' profit-sharing plan; a new election law and female suffrage; and the creation of a literacy corps.[35] To justify the reforms, a national referendum was organized in early 1963, in which the government attempted to orchestrate a resounding "yes vote." The main opposition parties, the National Front and the Liberation Movement, issued radical criticism and their leaders were arrested and sent to jail. High-ranking clergy headed by Khomeini declared the reform package a "colonial scheme," and the regime had to resort to discredited propaganda by declaring that the referendum had been approved by 99.9 percent of the voters.

The only part of the "White Revolution" that had far-reaching consequences related to the reallocation of land. Opposing this land reform were strong traditional landowners and some clerics. In the aftermath of the Cuban revolution, during President Kennedy's administration in the US, land reform in developing countries was considered a deterrent against communism, as it would theoretically transfer resources from the rural sector to the nascent urban industrial sector, create a large urban consumer market for new industries and a growing middle class, and placate the peasant masses that resented traditional landowners. Thus, the United States sponsored, and provided foreign assistance to encourage, this type of reform in many developing countries, as a counterbalance to the perceived communist threat. Iran found itself compelled to adopt the reform, which benefited the Shah because it increased American support to his regime. He also sponsored the measure because it eroded the power of the landlords and generated support among the several million landless peasants within the countryside. In addition to the US and the Shah, the other major players in the land reform project were Prime Minister 'Ali Amini and Minister of Agriculture Hasan Arsanjani.

By this stage, the Iranian political landscape had changed significantly. The National Front had been reorganized and had the indirect backing of Mossadegh, which gave it a significant popular base. The student movement, inspired by revolutionary changes in Cuba and Algeria and the anticolonial movements in many parts of the Third World, was strong and had become very active in support of political reform and ending corruption and dictatorial rule. Amini was the grandson of the Qajar king who had signed the Constitution Edict of 1906, and he had served for a brief period in Mossadegh's government as minister of economic affairs. Then he was the minister of finance in the first cabinet after the 1953 coup, so he was the person to sign the agreement with the oil conglomerates. Later, he was Iran's ambassador in Washington.[36] All of which had allowed him to establish good connections with the new Kennedy administration in the US, but he also enjoyed the support of a significant group of reform-minded elite technocrats who were opposed to both communism and the Shah's dictatorship. In August 1960, there were widespread protests against election rigging orchestrated by the Shah's court after the results of parliamentary elections were announced. Amid large-scale protests by university students, the Shah agreed to a new round of elections in Tehran in January 1961, and then he reluctantly agreed to Amini's premiership in May 1961.

Amini came to power in the midst of a severe economic recession. Huge balance of trade problems and a budget deficit had forced Iran to agree to an IMF-dictated stabilization policy the previous year. Strict monetary measures were put in place to curb inflation and government spending. This brought schoolteachers into the equation. They went on strike and subsequent demonstrations led to clashes with police in which a teacher was killed. Amini promised effective reform and a more open political atmosphere. The main plank of his reform package was land reform. However, the court used many different tactics to paralyze the government of Amini, including employing the Rashidian Brothers' services. The National Front leaders also refused to work with Amini's government because he would not commit himself to holding free elections. Student protests continued and the Shah used army commando units to storm Tehran University campus, classes and offices in order to weaken the government further. Finally, the Shah paid a visit to Washington in April 1962 and promised that he would lead the reform program himself. Amini was forced to resign in July.[37]

In the forefront of the opposition to the Shah's land reform and modernization plans were the 'Ulama, many of whom had long been critical of the Shah's leadership. The first serious confrontation between the two sides occurred with the introduction of a local council election bill in October 1962, which gave women the right to vote and eliminated the mandatory oath of office on the Qur'an (instead, the bill referred to any "Holy Book"). After a series of heated public exchanges between the leading clergy in Qom and the Shah and his new prime minister, Amir Asadollah Alam, the government revoked the bill and Ayatollah

Khomeini, as the most radical and vocally critical opponent of the government, emerged as a new political leader. His main active social base was a group of second-rank bazaar merchants gradually forming into an orthodox Islamic group, later known as the United Islamic Societies, and his politically motivated young theology students.[38] Khomeini's radical stance was also welcomed by a radical wing of Mossadegh supporters who had recently formed the Iranian Freedom Movement, led by Mehdi Bazargan.

Khomeini and the Iranian revolution

Khomeini, who had been born into a religious family in 1902, stood out for his opposition to the Pahlavis. After learning Arabic and the basics of Shi'ism, he went to Arak in central Iran in 1920 to study under 'Abdul Karim Hae'eri-Yazdi and become a *mujtahid* (expert jurist). 'Abdul Karim was himself a leading *marja-e taqlid* (literally, a source of emulation) in the Shi'a faith. He moved to Qom in 1922 to establish a seminary that later developed into the main theology center of Iran, the *Hozeh-ye Elmi-ye Qom*. Khomeini moved to Qom with his teacher, and in 1926 completed his qualifications to become a *mujtahid*. As a young jurist, he witnessed the damage done to the power and privileges of the 'Ulama by Reza Shah's secularization drive and expressed his opposition to these measures in his writing. However, the repressive nature of the regime thwarted any overt action on the part of the 'Ulama to halt the secular authoritarian forces.

Khomeini would come to prominence around the time of the referendum on the "White Revolution." He opposed it heartily and campaigned actively against it. The confrontation between the Shah's regime and Khomeini came to a head in June 1963, during the month of Muharram, when Shi'ites commemorate the martyrdom of the grandson of Prophet Mohammad. In an earlier incident, in January, army commandos in civilian clothes had stormed the Feyziya Seminary in Qom. One person was killed and hundreds were injured, and thereafter Khomeini's criticism of the regime had taken a harsher tone. On June 3, referring to this attack, he made a speech in which he accused the Shah's regime of being fundamentally against Islam and the Qur'an and of collaborating with Israel to uproot the clergy and Islam. He also reiterated his opposition to the "White Revolution."[39] Khomeini was arrested late the next day and transferred to a prison in Tehran. News of this arrest of a leading *marja-e taqlid*, which was unprecedented in Shi'a history, caused demonstrations in the capital and some other cities on June 5. These clashes resulted in several hundred deaths, a state of emergency was declared, and the army moved out of its barracks for some weeks to restore order.

Khomeini's last confrontation with the Shah came on October 26, 1964. A month earlier, the Majlis had passed a "capitulation bill" which, by extending the diplomatic immunity provisions included in the Vienna Convention of April 1961, gave US military personnel in Iran judicial immunity. This inspired memories of the much-resented capitulation privileges that had been imposed on Iran after its defeat in the second Russo-Persian War of 1828, which had only been annulled in 1921. Now, after more than forty years, it seemed that the United States was imposing similar strictures on Iran.[40] In another fiery speech, Khomeini attacked the new law and accused the government of "selling the country's independence" to the US. Then, as if predicting his own fate, he asked: "If this country is occupied by America, it should be announced and then we should be expelled from this country."[41] He was arrested on November 4 in Qom, was taken directly to the airport in Tehran, and was sent into exile in Turkey. A few months later, he moved to Najaf in Iraq, where he lived until 1978, before moving to Paris en route to a triumphant return to Iran in February 1979.

The unraveling of the Pahlavi regime accelerated as the forces arrayed against it joined ranks under the leadership of the 'Ulama. Although Khomeini was in exile, the June 1963 uprising had transformed him into a hero. "Khomeini's themes of anti-Americanism, fervent opposition to Zionism, opposition to the Shah's autocracy, and an emphasis on Islam attracted a large audience, which cut across class distinctions and ideological persuasions."[42] But it was his charismatic appeal that ultimately united the opposition, which consisted of several groups of various ideological persuasions, all working to bring down the Shah's dictatorial rule: the 'Ulama, secular political parties, guerrilla organizations and the intelligentsia.

Among the opposition political parties were the Tudeh Party – the communist party that had been formed in 1941 – and the National Front. The Tudeh Party, which developed a monolithic organization, came to prominence due to international geopolitical factors, but these also brought about its demise. The overtly pro-Soviet line of the party allowed its leadership some measure of popular support throughout the 1940s, when intense anti-British sentiment prevailed in Iran and people viewed the Soviet Union in positive terms. But when Tudeh supported the Soviet-backed secessionist movement in Azerbaijan in 1945, most of its support was lost.

The National Front was composed of a number of parties united by a strong sense of nationalism. After its formation, it evolved into a major challenge to the regime and the Tudeh Party. As we have seen, it reached its zenith between 1951 and 1953, when Mossadegh served as prime minister. However, after the coup of 1953, the National Front lost much of its support base as a result of severe repression by the SAVAK.

In the 1960s and 1970s, with these opposition parties existing virtually in name only, two left-wing guerrilla movements emerged: the Organization of People's Mujahedeen (Sazman-e Mujahedin-e Khalgh – MEK) and the Organization of People's Fedayi Guerrillas (Sazman-e Cherik haay-e Fadayee-e Khalgh), each founded by dissatisfied members of the two traditional opposition parties, who had lost faith in the peaceful struggle against the Shah.

Meanwhile, intellectual opposition against the regime rose as a consequence of its authoritarian, state-building and socio-economic policies. By the end of 1960s and throughout the 1970s, the more socially dominant intellectual current focused on the politicization of Islam, blurring the distinction between secular and religious opposition to the regime.[43]

This helped the 'Ulama to play the leading role in the revolution. They were able to utilize their extensive network of mosques, religious schools and seminaries scattered across the country, as well as their allies in the bazaar, to mobilize mass action against the Shah's rule. The guerrilla organizations had been incapacitated by the SAVAK by 1977, while the intelligentsia had been marginalized as heavy-handed censorship did not allow them to publish their views. Moreover, all public spaces – except, crucially, for religious ones – were occupied and controlled by the state. In such circumstances, few intellectuals dared to speak out against the Shah, and even when they did their message was limited to venues that were inaccessible to many Iranians.

By contrast, the regime's efforts to tame the 'Ulama were never successful. When Khomeini was expelled, it was believed that his deportation would curtail the 'Ulama-led agitation in the country – and, indeed, for a short time, Khomeini was inactive. However, he soon resumed his anti-regime agitation. Once he had settled in Najaf, teaching jurisprudence in one of the most respected centers of Shi'a learning, he came into close contact with other Iranian 'Ulama who were studying there. His role as a teacher gave him the opportunity to influence younger clerics, cement his relationship with the older religious establishment and build a wider network to communicate his political ideas.

In an effort to tarnish his image, the regime began slandering his name in the state-controlled press. But this failed and his popularity and prestige continued to rise. On October 26, 1977, Khomeini's elder son died suddenly in Najaf. Rumors circulated that he had been killed by the Shah's secret agents. Such claims were never substantiated, but they were turned into yet another weapon against a regime that was deeply resented by the majority of its people. Open letters and communiqués expressing sympathy for Khomeini were published, and he responded by issuing a statement thanking the "Iranian people." He also attacked the regime's "open political atmosphere" as a fraud that was intended to "deceive the people" and condemned the regime's "cooperation" with Israel and the United States.[44]

The rise of Khomeini occurred against the backdrop of an historically unprecedented political scene. The huge increase in oil prices in 1973 had quadrupled revenues, and the share of oil in the GDP had risen from 12.3 percent in 1963 to 50.6 percent in 1973.[45] This enabled large state-sponsored investments in urban infrastructure and industry, and heavy subsidies in foodstuffs and fuel. The land reform of the early 1960s had benefited modern, large, capital-intensive enterprises and small landowner families. This had created huge waves of migration of landless peasants to large urban centers. But these peasants had to settle in squalid neighborhoods and shanty towns on the margins of large cities like Tehran, Isfahan, Tabriz and Mashhad. Illegal urban settlements built on public land outside the official city limits grew rapidly in the early 1970s. This displayed the huge poor–rich gap that oil-powered rapid economic growth had brought about. There were clashes in 1976 between municipal authorities, the riot police and inhabitants of these poor neighborhoods, who illegally tapped water and electricity off the public city water lines and power grids in Tehran and some other large cities. Early forms of what Asef Bayat calls the "quiet encroachment of the ordinary" and "street politics" developed during these years.[46] The infrastructure could not keep up with the rapid growth and large cities suffered from traffic jams and air pollution, while there were frequent power outages. The oil boom had created wealth, but the new industrial bourgeoisie, merchants and entrepreneurs with good political connections that facilitated access to cheap loans, as well as the affluent middle classes, were the only real beneficiaries. All this created mass social discontent that needed only a more open political atmosphere to turn into political protest. Two developments helped bring about precisely that more open political environment.

First, in January 1977 US President Jimmy Carter took office. Carter's administration set out to restore the US's credibility in the wake of defeat in Vietnam, the Watergate scandal and US interventions in support of ruthless dictatorships such as Pinochet's regime in Chile. It also aimed to support political dissidents in the Soviet Bloc. Nevertheless, Carter abandoned the Nixon–Kissinger doctrine of "containment (of communism) at all costs," and human rights emerged at the forefront of US foreign policy. Although the new president sought to maintain the valuable geopolitical role of Iran, he also wanted a dramatic improvement in the human rights record of the Shah's government. American–Israeli complicity in the notorious SAVAK was well known, not only among its Iranian victims but around the world. For this reason, the US called for liberalization that would reflect positively on the American–Israeli image as protectors of the regime. The Shah knew he could not resist this pressure and started to initiate changes that amounted to a controlled liberalization and loosening the grip of SAVAK and Rastakhiz. General Abbas Gharabaghi, the Shah's last chief of staff of the armed forces, recalls this policy in his book on the causes of the revolution:

> With the election of Mr. Carter as US President (20 January 1977) and the victory of the Democratic Party and the announcement of Human Rights as the cornerstone of America's International policy, there came changes in His Majesty's policies and that of the government of Mr. Amir Abbas Hoveida . . . This change took a more public form with the resignation of Mr. Hoveida after 13 years of premiership and the formation of the government of Mr. Jamshid Amouzgar, and [at this stage] a policy called "creation of open political atmosphere" and handing gradual freedom to people began.[47]

Gharabaghi quotes the Shah explaining the new policy in a meeting with top military commanders:

> After the events of September 1941 . . . [the abdication of Reza Shah] and assuming the throne, I had to deal with a lot of troubles and problems. In order that these troubles will not be repeated again and the state is handed over smoothly to the Crown Prince [his son Reza] measures must be taken and you should be informed of the upcoming developments. Up to now, the circumstances necessitated that the country should be run in this way, and this was done and we achieved notable success. But with current developments in the world we cannot continue in this way and running the affairs of the state should be in line with today's requirements and the world's developments

... It is on this basis that We have decided that people should be given freedom, so that when the country is handed over to the Crown Prince he will not face the same political difficulties. You should know that the changes that you observe are what We have decided and considered necessary.[48]

This leads to the second factor that prompted the Shah to act: by 1977, he had been diagnosed with leukemia.[49] Perhaps this explains why the crown prince's succession was weighing so heavily on the Shah's mind when he met with his military commanders.

Mass social discontent, a corrupt and inefficient administration unable to handle the mounting economic and social problems, a misreading of Carter's human rights policy, and the Shah's terminal illness therefore combined to force Iran's ruler to open up his political system. However, as events over the next couple of years would prove, repressive regimes that have exhausted their political legitimacy always take this step too late. The opponents of such regimes realize that the concessions are being forced on the ruler and there is no genuine will to reform the system, so they invariably become more vocal and bold in their opposition.

This is precisely what happened in Iran between 1978 and 1979. A number of opposition forces, from across the political spectrum, both religious and secular, published open letters of protest against government corruption and lack of freedom of expression. Then they started to hold meetings, organize public performances by poets and writers who had hitherto been banned, and commemorated "political prisoners and martyrs." All formerly banned opposition forces, including the National Front and Iran's Freedom Movement, as well as supporters of underground movements of the early 1970s, gradually became active; and as circumstances increasingly changed in their favor, they intensified their activities. However, it was the bazaar–'Ulama alliance that was most effective in mobilizing dissent and leading the protest in the direction they desired. The historical alliance between the two led to the financial independence of the 'Ulamas as the bazaaris paid their alms (*khoms*) to their choice of 'Ulama. By late 1977, the mosques were packed with people from all walks of life and social classes, and in some meetings slogans were chanted in support of Khomeini. Meanwhile, gatherings in Tehran's main universities ended in clashes with security forces, and intellectuals and students were beaten up by the authorities.

The turning point came on January 7, 1978, with the publication of an article against Khomeini in a regime-supporting newspaper. Only a week before this, President Carter had visited Iran and given assurances to the Shah of continuing US support. Carter said Iran was an "island of stability" under the Shah in one of the most unsettled regions of the world.[50] Spirited by these assurances, the Shah had directly ordered the publication of the article against Khomeini.[51] It was a fiercely personal attack, calling Khomeini the "Indian Seyyed" who acted as an instrument of "black and red colonialism" and labeling him the large landowners' agent in opposing land reform and the liberation of women.[52] In the protests that followed the publication of the article fourteen people were killed by the police in Qom. This, in turn, led to a series of commemorations in major Iranian cities on the fortieth day after their deaths (a traditional pattern of mourning among Iranian Muslims). Each gathering turned into a street demonstration and ended in more violent clashes between security forces and demonstrators that resulted in even more deaths. On March 6, the Shah stated, "Nobody can overthrow me. I have the support of 700,000 troops, all the workers, and most of the people. I have the power."[53]

Khomeini had moved to Paris on October 7, 1978. While there, he gained the support of a growing number of intellectuals and began to be seen as the only individual capable of overthrowing the dictatorial regime in Iran. Soon, a cluster of revolutionaries formed around him, creating a movement that would tailor his message to suit both Iranian and world opinion, and eventually directing the course of the revolution. (Most of these revolutionaries eventually fell out of favor with Khomeini's regime and were persecuted.) Within Iran itself, the political situation was approaching complete collapse, as public demonstrations and antigovernment actions escalated. During December, millions of people were on the streets, chanting: "Death to the Shah." Strikes, particularly those targeting oil production facilities, were meanwhile damaging the economy. The Shah tried to introduce reforms in an effort to calm the situation and maintain power, but his moves came too late and only encouraged opposition forces. He then sought counsel from his American allies. However, in an odd mixture of pragmatism, principle and indecision, the Carter administration was unwilling to offer public support to the teetering and internationally unpopular Pahlavi regime. Furthermore, it was unclear what the Americans could possibly do to save the Shah.

In January 1979, the Shah fled the country and a member of the National Front, Dr. Shapour Bakhtiar, was appointed prime minister. The National Front subsequently expelled Bakhtiar for joining the Shah's regime.

Meanwhile, in Khomeini's camp, a secret council, which evolved into the Council of the Islamic Revolution (CIR), was formed to coordinate the activities of the Islamic opposition with the popular demonstrations taking place within the country. This council was not well received by some within the opposition parties and affiliated organizations, as they were clearly excluded from it. Nobody seemed able to agree on what should happen once the old regime was overthrown, as now seemed inevitable.

In a final bid to retain power, Bakhtiar's government immediately implemented a number of reforms: the dissolution of SAVAK, the release of many political detainees and an unsuccessful attempt at a rapprochement with Khomeini. The advancing religious tide of the revolution continued onward, and Bakhtiar's position became more precarious after the triumphant return of Khomeini on February 1. Khomeini immediately declared that Bakhtiar's appointment to the premiership had been "illegal" and asked Mehdi Bazargan, leader of the Iranian Freedom Movement, to form a provisional government. With the country in turmoil and the military disunited, fighting once again erupted on the streets. When calm was restored by the military declaring its neutrality, power was effectively handed to the revolutionaries. Bakhtiar went into hiding, and Bazargan appointed a new military chief of staff, having fired several top commanders who were known to be loyal to the Shah. Elections to a new Majlis were held in March, followed by a referendum to establish an Islamic republic. This proposal was approved by 98.2 percent of the electorate. On April 11, 1979, Iran duly became an Islamic republic.

The Islamic Republic of Iran

The new ruling coalition, united only by hatred of the Shah and respect for Khomeini, was divided by ideology, generation, socio-economic factors and educational achievement, which made its collapse inevitable. Sharing in the spoils of the victory became the main objective of a variety of groups and led to fierce antagonism between fundamentalists, Islamic liberal nationalists, leftist parties and secular liberal nationalists. In the end, by 1981, the fundamentalists emerged as the dominant faction in Iranian politics. That victory, however, was won at a heavy cost in human life and national unity.

Although the revolution was effective in removing the stalwarts of the overthrown regime, a key ingredient of Iranian political culture – authoritarianism – survived. The Islamist regime that initially replaced the Shah was even more socially restrictive than the Shah's had been. Khomeini gathered a group of loyalists around him, all of whom shared his particular understanding of Shi'a politics, and they consistently attempted to imprint this on the post-revolutionary era. To achieve this, they relied on three mechanisms: Friday prayer meetings, the Islamic Republican Party (IRP) and the Majlis. The prayer meetings facilitated the propagation of Khomeini's ideas, while discrediting opponents or people whose loyalty was in doubt. By appointing Friday prayer imams, Khomeini brought the clerics under his control. The IRP was founded in February 1979 by a small group of the clergy and the laity expressly to consolidate the political power for the 'Ulama. Under the leadership of Ayatollah Beheshti, the party gained prominence in government and the trust of Khomeini. It came to dominate the Majlis, which was elected in March 1980, as well as the Assembly of Experts, which comprised eighty-three members and was elected in August 1979 to draw up the country's new constitution. As such, the IRP was a useful tool in coalescing pro-Khomeini forces and challenging the power of rival revolutionary forces.

Reflecting the intensity of the jockeying for power and the frustration over the erosion of the power of the religious nationalists, Bazargan's provisional government resigned on November 5, 1979, a day after the American Embassy in Tehran had been occupied by radical students. The IRP-dominated Majlis then appointed Mohammad 'Ali Rajai as prime minister, against the objections of President Abolhassan Bani-Sadr, a veteran activist of the National Front. Bani-Sadr was impeached by the Majlis on June 10, 1981 (on the grounds of incompetence) and fled to France to form an opposition party.

Thereafter, the revolutionary forces managed to mobilize Iranian society in support of theocentric government, according to Khomeini's political vision.

The nature of the "just society"

"Just society" is central to Islamic political thought. The primary concern of an Islamic government is the implementation of divine social legislation. To this end Khomeini stated:

> The Qur'an verses concerned with society's affairs are numerous compared to the verses concerned with private worship. In any of the detailed Hadith books, you can hardly find more than three or four sections concerned with regulating man's private worship and man's relationship with God . . . The rest is strongly related to social and economic [affairs], with human rights, with administration and with the policy of societies.[54]

According to Khomeini, a just society is one in which, "governing is not an end in itself . . . if sought as a goal, and if all means are used to attain it, then it degenerates to the level of a crime, and its seekers come to be considered criminals."[55] And government has no right to undermine the private property of individuals arbitrarily.[56] The Qur'an does not proscribe enjoyment of material wealth. An Islamic government must ensure that Islamic laws are applied without privilege or discrimination. The taxation system and the alms system as legislated in the Qur'an guarantee that there will not be an excess of either wealth or poverty, and the legal system guarantees that wealth is not secured through exploitation.

The separation of economic and political power was central to Khomeini's view of society. Mechanisms ensuring that political office did not result in privilege, favor or material gain required that office-holders would have to live humbly and piously.[57] Khomeini saw in the accumulation of material wealth and conspicuous consumption by political office-holders manifest indicators of corruption.[58] It was not necessary for the holders of political office to be religious leaders, but it was incumbent upon them to emulate the Prophet and pious Imams in their lifestyle. The just society, then, is the society where divine law is implemented without privilege or discrimination and where both the transgressor and the transgressed upon are secure in their knowledge of swift, equitable application of the law.[59] It is axiomatic for religious believers that God's law is inherently just. It is man's interpretation and application of the law that leads to injustice. Consequently, injustice must be guarded against in the structure of government during the period of the absence of the "infallible imam" (the Mahdi). In this period there is a great danger that "laws and rules would be changed and the heretics would add to them and the atheists would detract from them."[60]

Thus, the structure of the Iranian Republic was derived from Khomeini's concept of *velayat-e faqih* (which is the Persian translation of the Arabic term Wilayet al-Faqih) – the rule of the religious jurist that has served as the central pillar of Iran's theocratic system since the revolution. Concentrating executive power in the hands of a single man, the jurists allowed the supreme leader – appointed by the Assembly of Experts – absolute authority over matters of state. Thus, as supreme leader, this individual has final say on all matters of governance – from foreign relations to domestic policy – and most importantly he is given control over all vehicles of authority, including the army, the police and the judiciary. Since Khomeini's death in June 1989, the supreme leader has always represented the conservative religious faction of Iranian society, which has allowed the religious hierarchy to maintain control.

Post-revolution national politics

The Islamic Republic of Iran has a governmental structure based on an executive and a 290-member, unicameral parliament, with several additional bodies filling roles created by the adoption of Islam as the guiding philosophy of society and state. The highest authority in the state is the supreme leader – as laid out in *velayat-e faqih* – who should posses the "scholarly capacity to issue edicts in all areas of Islamic jurisprudence, justice and piety as required for the leadership of the Islamic Ummah, the right political and social vision, prudence, courage, administrative capability and adequate capacity for leadership."[61]

This position – initially held by Khomeini – was held at the time of writing by Seyyed 'Ali Khameini. On paper, the position is incredibly powerful, incorporating general supervision of all government policy, command of the armed forces and the power to declare war and peace, the power to recognize the president and dismiss him, and monitoring of the relationship between the executive, the legislature and the judiciary. The Assembly of Experts elects the supreme leader, while the people elect the eighty-six members of the Assembly for eight-year terms. All of these members are clerics, and the Assembly sits just once a year, as its only tasks are to appoint and (at least theoretically) supervise the supreme leader. All candidates running for the Assembly should be approved by the Guardian Council, whose members are selected by the supreme leader. Of course, this creates a loop that makes any real supervision of the leader impossible, and he is above the law. Another assembly, the Constitutional Assembly of Experts, is charged with matters of constitutional amendment.

The president is elected in a national election and serves a four-year term, with a limit of two consecutive terms in office. He is responsible for the administration of the civil service and the appointment of ministers, who are then accountable to the Majlis and may be removed only by a vote of no-confidence. The president can also be impeached by a vote of no-confidence, requiring a two-thirds majority of the Majlis. The main legislative body is the Majlis, which has 290 members who are elected by direct popular vote every four years. The seats are allocated to the administrative districts of the provinces in proportion to population, including one seat each for the small Jewish and Zoroastrian minorities and three seats for the rather larger Christian Armenian and Assyrian minorities. The Majlis has powers similar to those in any other democratic legislature, debating all national affairs and forming committees to examine policy and table bills for discussion. But its power is severely limited as all candidates running for parliament and all of its legislation must be approved by the Guardian Council. Here, again, the supreme leader exerts substantial influence through the Guardian Council. The executive branch may also table bills. The Majlis is also responsible for approving all international agreements.

The Guardian Council examines all legislation approved by the Majlis, based on the principles of the constitution as well as Islamic law and practice. It consists of six Islamic canonists appointed by the supreme leader, and six civil jurists elected by the Majlis from candidates proposed by the head of the judiciary, who is himself appointed by the supreme leader. The Guardians have tended to be extremely conservative, to such an extent that another body, the Council for the Determination of Expediency of the State, was formed by Khomeini in February 1988 in order to break the legislative deadlock that had arisen between the Majlis and the Guardians. The Council, whose members are yet again appointed by the leader, passes binding arbitration on disputes between the two other bodies.

The Iranian judiciary is led by the chief justice, who is appointed by the leader for a five-year term to work with the Ministry of Justice. He then appoints the head of the Supreme Court. The judiciary is divided into several subsections of civil and criminal courts, as well as clerical tribunals (for punishing offenses by clergy), revolutionary tribunals (for charges of terrorism and offenses relating to national security, such as espionage), and administrative tribunals, which deal with complaints of citizens against government organs or officials.

This whole system of government had barely begun to take shape before Iraq launched its invasion of Iran.

The Iran–Iraq War

On September 22, 1980, Saddam Hussein ordered the Iraqi army across the border into Iran. He was hoping for a quick victory over a nascent regime in order to gain effective leadership of the Arabs now that Egypt had concluded a peace agreement with Israel. However, the Iranian people and their army rallied behind the new regime and inflicted tremendous losses on the Iraqis. By early 1982, Iraq was on the defensive in what would become the longest conventional war of the twentieth century.

There had been unresolved differences between Iran and Iraq for a long period of time. The borders between the two states were disputed, especially the Shatt al-Arab waterway that marked the southern part of their mutual frontier. Through the 1960s and 1970s, Iran had been an American client state while the regime in Baghdad had leaned toward the Soviet Union. In addition, Iraq accused Iran of supporting Kurdish rebels in their long conflict with the Iraqi government. Finally, Iraq's substantial Shi'a population looked to Iran as their spiritual center, and to Khomeini, who in 1979 had called for the overthrow of Hussein's Ba'thist regime. Hussein had oppressed millions of Shi'as, many of them ethnic Persians, in Iraq and executed their leaders. He also had the support of the rich Gulf states, which feared the populist implications of the Iranian revolution for their own authoritarian regimes.

The specter of a possible Iranian victory frightened most Arab states and the West, so finance from the rich Gulf states and military aid from the West flowed into Iraq. Until 1986, there were no negotiations between the combatants and no ceasefires, and the international community remained silent while continuing to support Iraq with money and arms.

In 1987, both sides were exhausted. Iraq was in deep financial debt; Iran had suffered about 300,000 dead and many more injured, and without international support it had little sophisticated military hardware left. In 1988, pressure from the government and military leaders expressing the impossibility of a military victory in the war, given the dire economic situation, the severe shortage of advanced military hardware and failure to mobilize adequate volunteers to join the war effort – in addition to increasing US involvement in support of Iraq – after a three-month campaign of aerial bombardment and missile attacks against major Iranian cities, including Tehran, forced Khomeini to accept a UN-sponsored ceasefire based on UN Security Council Resolution 598, which took effect in August that year. There were also rumors that Iraq had developed missiles capable of delivering chemical warheads, and these probably played a part in the decision to end the war.

The Iran–Iraq War was one of the most brutal and senseless wars in recorded history. The fighting destroyed much of both countries' infrastructure and resulted in heavy losses among their young male populations. Kamran Mofid has estimated that the economic cost of the war was $644.3 billion for Iran and $452.6 billion for Iraq.[62] These figures exceed the total oil revenues earned by both countries in their entire history of oil production prior to September 1980. During the war, Iraq used 100,000 chemical shells against Iranian targets.[63] Estimates of the number of dead vary, but it is thought that Iran lost about 300,000 and Iraq between 160,000 and 240,000.[64] Both countries suffered massive destruction, and Iraq was plunged into a crippling debt to the Gulf states.

Ironically, Hussein actually helped cement the Iranian regime's position, as the war proved a very useful tool against internal opposition. Any criticism of Khomeini or his regime was labeled treason, and punishment was severe. Moreover, Iran financed its war effort entirely from its own reserves, which naturally created tremendous economic hardship for its people, but also led to a sense of unity and self-reliance – of having defeated the invader through a monumental effort that was theirs and theirs alone. It also prevented Iran from falling into the same massive debt trap that had swallowed Iraq.

The death of Khomeini

The ageing Ayatollah Khomeini held the system together in the face of immense difficulties. However, he failed in one respect: appointing a successor. His first choice, Ayatollah Hussein 'Ali Montazeri, was politically ostracized after criticizing the human rights record of the regime. Montazeri was the most influential supporter of Khomeini inside Iran during the latter's years of struggle against the Shah, and had a leading role in incorporating the principle of *velayat-e faqih* in the constitution against opposition from all secular and nationalist religious forces in 1979. But he fell out of favor because of his principled opposition to mistreatment of political detainees in Iranian prisons after the revolution and, most notably, the mass execution of political prisoners in the summer of 1988.[65] Over the years, Montazeri distanced himself, in theory and practice, from the Islamic Republic regime. He remained under house arrest for most of the 1990s, after his son-in-law's brother was executed on charges of acting against national security in 1988, and many of his theology students were imprisoned thereafter.

Although Khomeini did not manage to appoint a specific successor, he at least set the tone for the succession by allowing a constitutional revision to restructure the political system so that it was not dependent on the charisma of another *marja-e taqlid*. Accordingly, a plebiscite was held in 1989 to amend the 1979 constitution. Among the changes introduced were a redefinition of the powers of the supreme leader, and the annulment of the post of prime minister, giving executive power to a popularly elected president as the manager of state affairs. The day after Khomeini's death on June 3, 1989, the Assembly of Experts selected President 'Ali Khamenei, a religiously conservative cleric, to succeed Khomeini as supreme Leader. Akbar Hashemi Rafsanjani, the speaker of the Majlis, replaced Khamenei as president, while Mahdi Karroubi succeed Rafsanjani as speaker.

Rafsanjani's administration was guided more by pragmatism than dogmatism. In order to rebuild the country from the ruins of the Iran–Iraq War, he favored market-oriented reforms including privatization, made IMF-friendly structural adjustments and accepted foreign loans. Moreover, he introduced changes in the administration to emphasize "competence and skill." Until 1993, leftists opposed these economic policies, while the conservative bazaar supported them. However, after 1993, the positions of the two factions reversed, which ultimately resulted in a *de facto* coalition between Rafsanjani and the center-left in the Majlis election of 1996 and the presidential election of 1997. Meanwhile, conservative elements in the Majlis made their opposition to this state of affairs well known.

Iran experienced economic growth between 1992 and 1996, with improvements in industry and international trade. However, while the government increased its revenues and provided basic employment, and all Iranians saw some degree of stabilization in economic policies, the poor and those who had been mobilized during the war with Iraq, for the most part, did not experience real improvements in their standard of living. The privatization and liberalization policies of Rafsanjani during 1989–1993 mainly benefited the rich and an emerging state-sponsored capitalist class comprising bureaucrats with privileged access to cheap loans from the state-owned banking system. In addition, there was dissatisfaction over ceding government price controls, the raising of controlled prices, and the lack of access of the large rural population to basic goods and services. In urban areas, especially in the continually growing Tehran, life was more affluent but there was also serious pollution, poor infrastructure planning, and an increasing penetration of Western culture and influence, in both the public and private spheres, which some found disturbing.

During Rafsanjani's second term in office as president, inflation hit a 49.4 percent high and Iran accumulated around $30 billion of foreign debt. This caused riots in several major cities. In the same period, the Ministry of Intelligence, control of which Rafsanjani had relinquished to the supreme leader, started a campaign of assassinating opponents of the regime – including the Shah's last prime minister, Bakhtiar – both inside the country and abroad. Rafsanjani was humiliated and discredited among the people by the time his second term came to an end in 1997.

Moderate forces were given a further boost by the election of the reform-minded Mohammad Khatami (ex-minister of Islamic guidance and culture) as the new president in May 1997. The rightist coalition had been confident of the victory of its candidate, 'Ali Akbar Nategh-Noori, and had hoped the election would legitimize their rule. However, they were defeated by reformist factions and independent activists who formed a broad coalition that became known as the May 23 Reform Movement. Subsequently, it appeared that the Islamic Republic was moving toward a more pragmatic foreign policy and more freedom in both social and political life inside Iran. The various political factions continued to vie for influence, but Iran seemed to be set on a course of continued economic development, combined with a policy of rapprochement with the West. However, in the October 1998 election to the Assembly of Experts, Iran's conservative factions reaffirmed their control, in effect stymying the forces of liberalization. Soon after the election, dissidents, journalists, intellectuals and even reformist cabinet ministers were being harassed by the conservatives and taken to (conservative-led) courts on charges of corruption, endangering state security and insulting Islam. Just over a year into Khatami's presidency, four prominent opposition figures – two members of the Writers' Guild and two leaders of the National Front – were murdered by agents of the Ministry of Intelligence, and a massive campaign of sabotage was staged to destabilize Khatami's government.

Dissent and organized opposition

There appears to have been little organized political opposition to the Islamic government inside Iran. The opposition to the Shah's regime consisted of three main currents: nationalists, whose main concern was full sovereignty and independent control of Iran's natural resources, especially the oil industry; various socialist groups, who wanted social justice and a classless society; and Islamist groups, who wished to establish cultural independence and Islamic government. The revolution gave Iran full political independence and a firm control of its natural resources and energy industry.

US military advisors and intelligence personnel left the country and the new Iranian government withdrew from every regional and international alliance that the former regime had joined. Then the new regime started a campaign of purging the country and its educational system of all manifestations of "Western culture." Bars, casinos, foreign cultural and educational institutes, and pro-Western publications were either banned or severely restricted. The army, the bureaucracy, professional organizations and trade associations, universities, colleges and even schools were purged by "cleansing committees" (*paksazi*), mainly made up of young, inexperienced, recently converted revolutionaries who were connected to the leading clergy and their political allies. Women were forced by law and social pressure to cover their heads and observe the state-imposed codes of "decent dressing."

This Islamization drive, together with the chaotic situation that followed the crumbling of the security apparatuses of the old order and the passionate outcries of the various young revolutionary groups for social justice "here and now," virtually paralyzed the country in the two years that followed the fall of the Shah. In practice, this meant that unrestrained forces loyal to the new regime violated fundamental civil and political rights on a large scale. The narrow-minded drive toward "cultural authenticity" based on a restrictive, and in many instances impractical, clerical outlook created widespread discontent among the modern middle class and the educated strata of Iranian society. These groups became the main social bases of support for various radical opposition groups. With the dictatorship and its foreign supporters gone, Iranians of various ideological persuasions had become each other's enemies. By the time Iraq invaded Iran in September 1980, a mini-civil war was being fought in Iranian Kurdish provinces by the newly formed Revolutionary Guards and some regular army units against several Kurdish and leftists groups. Armed clashes between government forces and some leftist parties had also erupted in Turkmen areas bordering the Soviet Union, and there were daily labor strikes, street demonstrations and clashes between state-sponsored vigilantes and opposition supporters. On June 20, 1981, the leftist MEK Islamic group started an armed campaign of assassinations and bombings in an effort to reverse the clerical takeover. This campaign and the war provided the pretext for a gradual but massive reorganization of the security apparatuses and the armed forces of the new state. By the time the war with Iraq ended, all opposition forces had been repressed, silenced or forced to flee the country. Meanwhile, the regime had developed into a two-faction structure that comprised two heterogeneous coalitions: the Islamic left, which had substantial control over the state bureaucracy, the judiciary and the intelligence apparatus; and the conservative, rightist faction, which comprised the majority of the clergy and some bazaar merchants in control of prisons and revolutionary courts, and other activists in control of various civil and military-intelligence bureaucracies.

The only significant opposition party that did not go underground or leave Iran altogether after 1981 was the Freedom Movement of Mehdi Bazargan. For a short period in the early 1980s, this group was allowed to publish its newspaper, *Mizan* (the *Scale*), and hold regular meetings, mainly in party members' homes. But when it voiced its opposition to expanding the war into Iraqi territory after all occupied Iranian land was liberated, its leaders were arrested and its publications were banned. During the same period, some members of the Writers' Guild published two monthly magazines, *Adineh* (*Friday*) and *Donya-ye Sokhan* (*Universe of Discourse*), that did not follow the official regime line and contained some mild criticism. The National Front, except for a small party led by the Dariyush Forouhar, was not active inside Iran, but some of its old activists sporadically issued statements from exile. In late 1980s, a number of former Freedom

Movement members, together with other religious intellectuals, student activists and some other veteran activists of the struggle against the Shah, formed a nationalist–religious coalition that has remained a critical voice inside Iran. Its members have often been arrested and have served lengthy jail terms.

In the early 2000s, a broad coalition of exiled secular parties of the left and some smaller nationalist groups formed an umbrella organization called the Union of Nationalist Republicans. Mainly consisting of activists from the 1960s-era Confederation of Iranian Students, former radical opposition groups who had been active against the Shah's regime and some independent political activists, this looked promising for a while, but it has suffered from internal division and lack of a clear vision for Iran's future.

The armed opposition still consists of the MEK, some Kurdish regional parties and a number of new terrorist groups in Iran's ethnic regions. The MEK moved into Iraq in 1983, set up guerrilla camps close to the Iranian border and formed a military alliance with Saddam Hussein. Its forces were used by Hussein to gather military intelligence against Iran and to crush the Iraqi Kurdish and Shi'a rebellions that followed the second Gulf War in 1991. It was added to the US State Department's list of terrorist organizations in the mid-1990s and remains in Iraq to this day. However, it was under the protection of the US military until 2009, and its representatives have held press conferences in Washington, D.C. Supervision of their main camp in Iraq, "Ashraf City," has recently been passed on to the Iraqi government. This transfer led to clashes between Iraqi security forces and members of the MEK which left at least seven people dead. The MEK has had links with Israeli intelligence since the mid-1990s and has been used by the Israelis to gather information about Iran's nuclear program since 2002.[66]

The Tudeh Party was banned after its entire leadership were arrested in 1983 on charges of espionage and treason; some of its members in the armed forces, including the former commander of the Iranian navy, were executed. The Organization of People's Fedayi Guerrillas, the main Marxist guerrilla organization, with a strong base in Iranian universities throughout the 1970s, had split into at least three factions by 1983, and all of its major leaders were forced underground and/or had to leave the country after that date. All the smaller Marxist groups were defeated during the war in Kurdistan by 1988.

By the end of the 1980s, most surviving Iranian opposition forces were settled in Western Europe or the United States. This exiled opposition has had very little success in influencing the course of events inside Iran.

Since the end of the Iran–Iraq War, the Kurdish areas of Iran have remained relatively calm. However, the Kurdistan Democratic Party (KDP) lost two of its general secretaries, Abdolrahman Ghasemlou and Sadeq Sharafkandi, in terrorist attacks organized by the Ministry of Intelligence during the 1990s. The party maintains an armed presence in northern Iraq and remote areas of Iranian Kurdistan, but it has not engaged in armed struggle against the government in recent years. This is partly because it has been weakened by internal divisions and splits. It still fights for Kurdish autonomy within a "federal Iran," but it has not entered into any political alliance with the Workers' Party of Kurdistan (PKK) –

which was declared a terrorist organization by the US State Department in the 1980s and is fighting an ongoing civil war in neighboring Turkey. Since 2004, a group calling itself Pejak, an Iranian offshoot of the PKK, has conducted raids into Iranian Kurdistan from its bases in northern Iraq. Heavy clashes were reported between Iranian armed forces and Pejak guerrillas across the northernmost section of the Iran–Iraq border in 2007 and 2008, and there have been several reports of US and Israeli aid going to Pejak.[67]

In 2006, another organization started an armed campaign against government forces in Iran's southeast Baluchistan Province, bordering Pakistan. Called Jundallah, this group has captured and killed Iranian military personnel and provincial government officials. The leader of the group, Abdolmalek Rigi (b.1984), has posted video footage of himself beheading an Iranian border guard on the internet.[68] According to Seymour Hersh:

> Robert Baer, a former CIA clandestine officer who worked for nearly two decades in South Asia and the Middle East, [reported that Jundallah] are Sunni fundamentalists who hate the regime in Tehran, but you can also describe them as Al Qaeda . . . These are guys who cut off the heads of nonbelievers – in this case, it's Shiite Iranians. The irony is that we're once again working with Sunni fundamentalists, just as we did in Afghanistan in the nineteen-eighties.[69]

In May 2007, ABC news reported that "the United States has supported and encouraged an Iranian militant group, Jundallah, which has conducted deadly raids inside Iran from bases on the rugged Iran–Pakistan–Afghanistan tri-border region."[70] According to Hersh, "these operations, for which the [US] President sought up to four hundred million dollars, were described in a Presidential Finding signed by Bush, and are designed to destabilize the country's religious leadership."[71]

Jundallah continued its attacks inside Baluchistan throughout 2008. In one attack the group disarmed a border police station near the Pakistani border and kidnapped seventeen Iranian soldiers before demanding the release of Rigi's jailed brother. Early in December, the Iranian Ministry of the Interior confirmed that the hostages had been killed. Although there have been some reports of clashes between Pakistani government forces and Jundallah guerrillas, and Pakistan agreed to the extradition of a Jundallah suspect to Iran, the Iranian government has repeatedly complained about Pakistan's lack of cooperation in combating terrorism.

Jundallah claimed responsibility for an explosion in a mosque that killed twenty-five people in Zahedan, the provincial capital of Sistan and Baluchistan, in May 2009. The Iranian government executed three people in connection with this bombing a few days after the explosion, but there were street clashes in Zahedan in early June. Then, on July 14, thirteen alleged Jundallah members who were said to have been involved in the explosion were hanged in the same city. In November, a Jundallah suicide attack killed two top commanders of the Revolutionary Guards as well as several tribal leaders and bystanders in a gathering in Baluchistan.

Abdolmalek Rigi was arrested by the Iranian authorities in February 2010, and at the time of writing was awaiting trial.

The new opposition inside Iran

Today's Iranian society is vastly different from the one that brought about the removal of the Shah. In the early 1990s, increasing literacy and large investment resulted in a huge increase in the number of university graduates.[72] By 2008, literacy had risen to 97.2 percent among the nation's youth (6–29-year-olds), who now make up a very significant proportion of the overall population (25 percent of Iranians are under the age of 15 and 37.5 percent are under 20). This young, well-educated sector of society has been a force to be reckoned with at times over the last twenty years.

Since the early 1990s, and especially after the 1997 presidential election victory of Khatami, new political forces that are more connected to a broader social base have gradually emerged. Iran certainly allows more freedom of expression than most Arab states, and the increasingly open political atmosphere during the eight years of Khatami's presidency provided space for critical expression and a limited degree of development for gender-, class- and profession-based groups. As a result, four social movements are emerging through a new brand of democratic activism that focuses on specific rights for women, workers, students and professional groups, such as teachers and nurses. These, together with courageous journalistic activism, have transformed Iranian politics in very significant ways. In contrast to the Leninist discourse of the pre-revolutionary activists who were obsessed with conquering "state power" by violence to transform property relations, and emphasized "communist hegemony" in the struggle to create a socialist system, the new movements do not subscribe to grand narratives of political change and violent overthrowing of the regime.

For instance, the women's movement, ever since its early days in mid-1980s, has focused on achieving legal equality for the sexes. Women's issues were publicly debated in a number of women's magazines published by religious female activists who could not be discredited by the government as "un-Islamic" or pro-Western in the 1990s. These publications have played a very important role in two respects: first, they politicized women's issues and gender inequality in family and inheritance laws, education and employment; second, they increasingly provided outlets for secular critics of the gender laws and policies of the Islamic Republic, and over time they have been instrumental in the formation of cross-ideological alliances among different groups of women inside Iran. By creating a public space for democratic debate in which both religious and secular women have participated, to some extent they have bridged the gaps between these groups and have helped to create broad coalitions of female activists.[73] Recently, a broad coalition of Iranian women that includes secular, religious, left and liberal groups has started a campaign to gather one million signatures in support of changing all discriminatory laws that adversely affect women in Iran.[74] Prominent women's rights activists such as Nobel Peace Prize-winner Shirin Ebadi, Mehrangiz Kar and Shahla Sherkat, editor-in-chief of the most important women's journal, *Zanan* (*Women*), are among those leading this campaign. However, since the election of Mahmoud Ahmadinejad as president in 2005, women's publications and NGOs have come under intense pressure and many female activists have been arrested and received prison sentences. *Zanan* was closed down by Ahmadinejad's government in January 2008 after sixteen years of successful publication.

Another area of democratic opposition activity is the labor movement. Iran's Labour Law does not allow independent workers' unions to form. But in recent years there has been a resurgence of strikes in protest against low wages and unacceptable working conditions in many industrial sites and urban services. At the forefront of this new wave of labor activism is the Syndicate of Workers of Tehran and the Suburbs Bus Company. Its members have staged a number of "informal" strikes since December 2005 for better wages and working conditions.[75] Mansour Osanlou, the secretary general of the syndicate, has been beaten up by paramilitary gangs, arrested and has faced several court cases. He was kidnapped by plain-clothed security agents on July 10, 2007 while riding on a public bus in Tehran and was placed in solitary confinement in Tehran's Evin Prison. Nevertheless, the labor movement, freed from its Cold War ideological constraints, is a growing movement in Iran, and continues to demand the right to form independent unions and pursue collective bargaining.

Iran's public education system employs more than one million teachers and support staff. Public schoolteachers have organized informally since the mid-1990s and have staged sit-in campaigns and gatherings in front of the Iranian parliament building in Tehran on several occasions to demand better wages and benefits. During March and April 2007, teachers organized a nationwide campaign to demand better pay and representation on government committees that decide their salaries. Several leaders of teachers' organizations were arrested after the Ministry of the Interior ordered the closure of their professional organizations and the Supreme National Security Council ordered newspapers to stop publishing news of the teachers' protests in May 2007.[76] Dozens of teachers across Iran have received jail sentences or have been exiled in recent years.

Under the leadership of Khomeini, human rights were ignored and oppressive measures were largely accepted because of the real threat from Iraq and the perceived threat from a hostile United States. However, from 1989 to 1997, the regime was forced to face the issue of how a country that is a regional power and has global economic connections could retain a genuine Islamic character. There were signs that the growing middle class and many of the inhabitants of relatively cosmopolitan Tehran felt constrained by the strict Islamist laws on dress and conduct, and generally ignored them in private. Women's issues came to the fore when Rafsanjani's own daughter, Fa'ezeh, a leading moderate publisher of the *Zan Daily* newspaper, was elected to the Majlis in 1996 (without his public support). She campaigned on what might be described as Iran's version of a feminist platform, which included increased political and economic rights for women. However, despite significant increases in female literacy, and attempts to carve a larger role in society, many women still find themselves estranged from the conservative political leadership. Fa'ezeh herself lost popular support as soon as she defended her much-derided father's record. Seizing their chance, the conservative judiciary then shut down *Zan Daily*.

Nevertheless, despite this predictable conservative backlash against liberal-ization and those who advocated it, led by the clerically dominated judiciary, Khatami's reforms enjoyed popular support, certainly for a while. Ataollah Mohajerani, the minister of culture and Islamic guidance, who was principally responsible for increasing the freedom of the press and artistic expression, was able to stave off an impeachment accusation in 1999. By persuading parliament of the merits of such freedoms in an Islamic society, he did his best to preserve the much more open cultural atmosphere that had been ushered in by Khatami. However, Mohajerani was forced to resign in 2000 when he came head to head with the supreme leader.

In the summer of 1999, reform-minded students in Tehran clashed with security forces and hardline activists. The students were motivated by the closure of an opposition newspaper, a police raid on a Tehran University dormitory (one student was killed) and the absolute clerical control of Supreme Leader Ayatollah 'Ali Khameini. In other words, they were reacting to the activities of the government, not against the principles of the revolution. The demonstrations spread to at least eight other cities and towns – Yazd, Khorram-Abad, Zanjan, Mashhad, Isfahan, Urumiyeh, Shahroud and Tabriz – and highlighted the widespread support for the reform movement.[77] Conservative elements in the government had to respond, so they altered their tactics in the following year's parliamentary election campaign. Their candidates appeared more secular, in a bid to indicate that they had taken on board popular discontent with clerical rule. However, they also used their power in the Guardian Council to stop several leading lights of the reform movement from standing against them in the election.[78]

Khatami himself came to symbolize a melding of progressive reform with a democratic Islamic tradition. His clerical credentials and status as a popularly elected leader gave him legitimacy as well as greater latitude to create and implement policy than was granted to other leaders of the reform movement. The reformers promised that political development and greater freedom would top their agenda. Changes to press and election laws were planned to ensure that further conservative interference in the electoral process would be curtailed.

In spite of the obstacles that had been put in their way, supporters of Khatami and their reformist allies swept to an overwhelming majority in the Majlis election: only 20 percent of the conservative-dominated former parliament was re-elected. Mohammad Reza Khatami (the president's brother and a leading reformist figure in the new parliament) promised that all legislation would be in line with the Iranian constitution, but this was clearly a great opportunity for the reformers. He went on to say that his Participation Front was committed to guaranteeing personal and social rights and freedoms. Basically, the reformists were confident that they could push through their plans with or without the support of other groups.

Their main base of support was among the urban middle class, women, journalists, intellectuals and students. The burgeoning independent press also provided a critical space for political expression, and a significant number of human rights and women's NGOs and associations had recently been formed. However, the reform movement never possessed a united leadership structure, and it suffered internal divisions because of the huge variety of factions and groups that it encompassed. Khatami felt that he was unable to perform the dual (perhaps impossible) role of reform-movement leader and president of the established state, and there was no mass-based political party to guide the movement, either.

This gave the right-wing, conservative opposition, via the security forces and the judiciary, the chance to regroup and counterattack. By 2002, the reform movement had largely lost the support of the population and it was cruising toward its demise. In that year's local council elections, most of those who had supported the reformists two years before stayed at home on election day. Consequently, the well-organized right-wing coalition won council seats in all of the major cities. The overall voter turnout was just 49.2 percent. In Tehran, where only 12 percent of those eligible to vote did so, the fifteen-member city council was dominated by supporters of the supreme leader. They selected Mahmoud Ahmadinejad as the capital's next mayor. The following year, a majority of members of the Majlis, paralyzed by the Guardian Council and unable to pass even the annual budget without prolonged conflict and haggling, staged a sit-in to protest against the disqualification of 80 percent of reformist candidates who wished to run in the upcoming 2004 national election. This generated a lot of fiery speeches and a threat of mass resignation by the reformist deputies, but it did not reverse the tide of conservative consolidation. The previous year, Khatami had tried to change the balance of power by introducing two major bills to reduce the power of the Guardian Council and increase the discretionary powers of the president. Of course, neither had made it through the Guardian Council barrier.

With the official adoption of the "Axis of Evil" regime-change policy by the Bush administration and the invasion of Iraq in March 2003, Khatami was caught between the demands of the Iranian people for genuine political change and the prospect of a US-led invasion and disintegration of the state in Iran. The dilemma of the "choice" between domestic despotism and foreign invasion, which had been faced by several generations of Iranian intellectuals and reformists over the previous two centuries, had displayed its ugly face again. In a bitter and humiliating step-by-step retreat in the face of mounting pressure from the conservative right, the president was forced to backtrack on almost all of his major promises of reform and transparency. His government, divided and demoralized, agreed to hold the Majlis elections in February 2004 under current laws due to the extralegal intervention of the military and the supreme leader. With low participation rates in major urban centres again, and most reformist candidates disqualified by the Guardian Council, the conservatives won the majority of seats. The overall participation rate dropped to 51.2 percent of eligible voters, down from 67.3 percent in 2000. By the end of the year, the reform movement had been defeated and the scene was set for another conservative victory, this time in the presidential election.

Ahmadinejad's first presidential term

In June 2005, for the first time in the history of the Islamic Republic, the presidential election went to a second vote. In the first round, Mahmoud Ahmadinejad had come second with just 19.2 percent of the total votes. Four reformist candidates together won close to 57 percent of the votes in that first round. Rafsanjani came first with 21.1 percent. The run-off was a highly polarized contest between a symbol of the establishment, Rafsanjani, and the relatively unknown Ahmadinejad. The latter won decisively with 67 percent of the votes cast. However, out of a total of 46.78 million eligible voters, Ahmadinejad won just 17.2 million votes, or about 38 percent of the total, compared with just over 10 million for Rafsanjani. That meant the overall participation rate was 59.8 percent, down 20 percent on the election that had brought Khatami to power eight years before.

There were many complaints of election rigging and the involvement of the military in the election. Reza Khatami said: "What we saw [in the first round of the presidential election] was a showdown between civilian parties and organizations and a Garrison Party . . . And now [after the election] this Garrison Party has turned into a military–security cabinet."[79] There were reports of the organized involvement of the Revolutionary Guards and the Basij volunteer militia in Ahmadinejad's drive to power. One Revolutionary Guard commander, affiliated with right-wing factions of the government since the 1980s, Baqer Zolghadr, said after the election that the new president's victory was the result of a "multi-layered" effort by the "system." The voters turned away from reformist politics in favor of a populist, right-wing revolutionary candidate who focused on the problems of housing and poverty. The low turnout showed the public distaste for lethargic reform and their disgust for corrupt politicians, while their support for Ahmadinejad indicated a preoccupation with economic concerns among the lower classes and a nationalist surge against perceived unfair international pressure being applied on Iran, especially on the issue of nuclear technology. Ahmadinejad portrayed himself as a humble, righteous underdog who would fight for the ordinary people. However, he was not as law-abiding as he made out. He entered the Ph.D. program in Tehran's Science and Industry University in 1993 and graduated in 1997. During that time, he was the governor of Ardebil Province, some 1,200 kilometers from Tehran, and advisor to the minister of science and higher education. According to Iranian law, state employees cannot be full-time students.[80]

Ahmadinejad's Ph.D. supervisor, Dr. Behbahani, later became minister of roads and transportation even though he had no record of civil service activity. Another minister in his cabinet, Sadegh Mahsooli, was involved in oil-swap arrangements with former Soviet republics during his friend's term as governor of Ardebil. Apparently, the deals were very profitable, since Mahsooli's assets exceeded $160 million at the time of his appointment as minister of the interior, which led some Majlis deputies from the conservative coalition supporting the government to vote against his appointment. However, it was eventually approved by a margin of just one vote. The previous interior minister in Ahmadinejad's cabinet, Avazali

Kordan, was impeached by parliament for lying about his educational qualifications. He attained a two-year higher national diploma, yet he had provided his former employer, the state-run radio and television network IRIB, with a fake Oxford University Ph.D. and was at the same time employed in Iran's Free University as a law professor teaching and supervising Ph.D. students. As for Ahmadinejad's financial record, during his term as Tehran's mayor (2002–2005), $300 million of the city's funds were classed as "undocumented expenses" and could not be traced after his departure. According to some press reports, these funds were used by Ahmadinejad to buy support from a variety of groups during his presidential election campaign.[81]

Ahmadinejad's weakest point has been his economic policy. Iran's oil revenues reached $81.764 billion in 2007/2008 compared with $27.355 billion in 2003/2004, the last full year that Khatami was in power. This was due to exceptionally high energy prices during that period. Each $1 per barrel increase in the price of oil adds $1 billion to Iran's annual income and a $10 increase per barrel translates into 7.5 percent growth in Iran's GDP.[82] However, with at least $270 billion in oil reveues during his first term as president, the Ahmadinejad government's economic performance was not even close to satisfactory. Iran's imports in 2008 were 91 percent higher than they had been in 2003/2004, reaching $56.582 billion.[83] This is an historical record that has led to a wave of bankruptcies and serious slowdown of local industrial production. Textile, apparel and food industries have been hit especially hard and thousands of workers have been laid off. Imports of items such as fresh fruit and sugar soared as tariffs were lifted or reduced drastically overnight. Iran imported 270,000 tons of sugar in 2008 and fresh fruit imports reached $1.1 billion. As a result of these policies, investment in related agricultural sectors dropped and sugar refineries and citrus producers suffered heavy losses. According to Mohsen Safayee Farahani, a former deputy finance minister, a mere ten large importers now dominate the sugar trade in Iran, and most have strong ties to the government.[84] It is a similar story with the major fruit importers.

Ahmadinejad's policies in the banking sector also had a number of disastrous consequences. With inflation around 20 percent, he forced the central bank and all state-owned banks to reduce their interest rates to 12 percent. This created a huge demand for bank loans, and those with political connections borrowed heavily to invest mainly in the booming real estate market or lent at higher rates on the black market. Many people in less affluent parts of cities and a significant number of rural residents borrowed from the banks to add one floor on top of their homes or to build new houses. This, in turn, created a strong upward surge in the price of homes and commercial real estate. Housing prices increased by at least 100 percent in major urban areas during 2007 and the first half of 2008. The rush of capital away from the uncertain stock market and into real estate created a huge housing bubble. When this bubble burst in mid-2008, the construction sector and all its related industries, including cement and steel, came to a halt. Large and small firms could not pay back their loans and the value of unpaid loans reached a staggering 20–25 percent of available banking sector credit. In response to the chaos, the government changed its expansionary fiscal policy and curtailed distributing cheap credit in the form of small mortgage loans in the housing market. The governor of the central bank, Tahmasb Mazaheri, resigned after trying in vain for several months to bring the president and his minister of labor to their senses about distributing cheap credit. Both believed that increased liquidity injection in an economy under international sanctions and suffering from dwindling levels of investment in the manufacturing sector would not lead to inflation. The debate also led to the resignation of the finance minister, Davood Danesh Jafari, at a time when the inflation rate had reached 24.9 percent, around March 2009. The outome of all this has been rising unemployment and a deep recession. While Iran needs one million new jobs each year to keep the unemployment rate at its 2008 level, on average just 300,000 jobs were created annually during Ahmadinejad's first term in office.

With the June 2009 presidential election approaching, Ahmadinejad implemented policies to try to win the hearts and minds of lower-income groups. These will certainly have major long-term consequences. As part of a "privatization" drive, the government started distributing "justice shares" dividends among close to five million recipients two months before the election. According to the fourth five-year development plan, adopted in 2004, and a law authorizing the sale of some state-owned industries, banks and insurance companies to private investors and the "transfer" of some of the resulting shares to "vulnerable groups," passed in the autumn of 2007, the government has distributed documents that are assumed to be "shares" in several undisclosed companies. However, nobody knows these companies' names, their account balances or whether they are currently making any profit. It is also unclear how the shareholders are represented in the decision-making processes regarding the operation of these firms, investment and the distribution of profits. Ahmadinejad also increased public sector pensions in the month before the election.

These were desperate measures by a president under severe pressure. Rampant inflation caused by short-sighted economic policies, heavy-handed repression of Iranian youth and women, and foreign policy failures that have led to Iran's isolation and the passing of four UN Security Council resolutions against the country (which, in turn, have caused even more inflation) all contributed to a deep disillusionment with Ahmadinejad and his government. In the most recent local government (2007) and Majlis elections (March 2008), the ruling coalition had lost to more pragmatic political forces within the Iranian right. Out of a total of 290 parliament deputies, only 80 were now supporters of the president. A majority of the rest formed a more moderate coalition of Iran's conservatives, including factions headed by three former Revolutionary Guard commanders: 'Ali Larijani (the former negotiator on the nuclear issue with the European Union and the UN Security Council), Bagher Ghalibaf (the mayor of Tehran) and Mohsen Rezaie (the former commander-in-chief of the Revolutionary Guards). Reformist parties close to former president Khatami and former speaker of the parliament Mahdi Karroubi won at least thirty seats (most reformist candidates were again disqualified by the Guardian Council, so reformers could compete for less than a third of the total seats). Another fifty seats were won by "independent" candidates with no clear party loyalties.

The tenth presidential election

As we have seen, Ahmadinejad won the 2005 election mainly as a result of the low turnout by supporters of reformist candidates. The overall participation rate was about 60 percent and many intellectuals and political activists boycotted the election in reaction to the Khatami government's failure to bring about genuine changes in the power structure and his retreat in the face of the conservative backlash. But four years of Ahmadinejad brought international sanctions and economic hardship, as well as political repression. The government closed down more than forty publications and jailed several leaders of labor unions, teachers' professional organizations, lawyers and civil rights activists. While claiming to promote the cause of the poor, the government did not allow workers to form unions, clamped down on teachers demanding the right to engage in collective bargaining and arrested activists for signing a petition in favor of changing laws that discriminate against women.

Another reformist boycott would inevitably lead to four more years of this. At the same time, several leaders of Ahmadinejad's coalition, the supreme leader and some commanders of the Revolutionary Guards made it clear that they would not allow a reformist to come to power "at any price." Nevertheless, from the autumn of 2008, a younger generation of activists, mainly university students, and several older reformists started a campaign in support of former president Khatami, even though he had expressed doubts over whether Iran's power arrangements could be changed, given the provisions of the constitution and the influence of the supreme leader and the Guardian Council. After months of hesitation, Khatami finally announced his candidacy for the presidency on February 5, 2009. According to some reports, he met with Supreme Leader Khameini to inform him of his decision, and Khamenei tried to dissuade him from running. On February 12, the *Keyhan* newspaper (considered to be very close to Khameini) publicly warned Khatami that he should take heed of the fate of Benazir Bhutto.[85]

Earlier, Khatami had said that he wanted Mir Hussein Mousavi, a prime minister in the 1980s, to run as the reformist candidate. Mousavi had kept quiet for twenty years, aside from rare interventions in some public debates. Many reformists even considered him old-fashioned, conservative and too close to the clerical leadership of the Islamic Republic in its early days. Khatami, however, insisted that Mousavi was an honest politician who was against the monopolization of power by a minority of hardline clergy and closed groups who controlled the security–military apparatus. Another point in his favor was that, given his revolutionary credentials, the hardliners could not accuse him of being too liberal, Western-oriented or a supporter of some sort of "velvet revolution." Mousavi subsequently announced his decision to run in the election, which allowed Khatami to withdraw and pledge his support. After a few days of confusion within the reformist camp, the activists who had supported Khatami switched their allegiance to Mousavi. Then, as had happened in all presidential election campaigns since 1997, the small wave grew into a mass movement in a matter of three to four weeks. The backbone of this campaign was a network of mainly young activists who knew how to use "small media" to spread their message and connect people in a variety of settings. Their skillful use of the color green as the symbol of a collective identity formed in protest against despotism created an easily available marker that facilitated communication among the movement's supporters and signaled their growing numbers to potentially sympathetic onlookers.

However, Mousavi started his campaign very slowly. He said he was concerned about Iran's future and deeply worried that a second term for Ahmadinejad would deal a final blow to the ideals and the true spirit of the 1979 revolution. He also criticized Ahmadinejad for isolating Iran internationally through unnecessary provocation, such as denying the Holocaust, and lambasted the government over its attempts to buy political loyalty among the poor while granting lucrative contracts and transferring state-owned companies to supporters who were already in high positions of power. He said his aim was to revive the repressed ideals of the revolution, such as freedom from fear, freedom of thought, independence and justice. In a matter of weeks, a vast coalition of intellectuals, young activists, artists, journalists and opposition politicians had joined forces to support Mousavi in their publications, blogs, meetings and street gatherings. Supporters of all candidates roamed the cities in great numbers after sunset, but the "green wave" was the most visible. People wore green clothes or tied green bands around their wrists, cars sported green flags and youngsters carrying some green symbol or other formed human chains along miles of streets and roads. The other reformist candidate, Mahdi Karroubi, received support from a smaller number of pro-democracy groups, such as the main student association, Tahkim Vahdat (Consolidation of Unity), and some disillusioned former supporters of Khatami. Nevertheless, Karroubi was instrumental in formulating the demands of the whole reformist campaign because he was bold and echoed the opinions of many dissidents and opposition figures.

Ahmadinejad's campaign replicated his 2005 rhetoric of confronting the "nexus of money and power" – borrowed from the presidential campaign of Vladimir Putin in Russia. However, now, of course, he was the very embodiment of that power, publicly supported by the very core of power in the Islamic Republic – Ayatollah Khamenei and the leadership of the Revolutionary Guards. During his first term in office, Ahmadinejad had made many speeches about the "Mafia in Iran's Oil Ministry" as well as corruption in state-owned banks and on the stock market, and had promised to put an end to these practices. However, not a single employee of the Oil Ministry or the state-owned banks was brought to court during his first four years in office, and his oil minister, Kazem Vaziri Hamaneh, publicly stated that he could find no trace of a "Mafia" in the Ministry of Oil. It was obvious that the "crusade against corruption" was actually little more than a propaganda campaign against political opponents, primarily the more moderate factions within the political elite.

The presidential election of June 12, 2009 was a turning point in the confrontation between right-wing hardliners and the rest of Iranian society. According to official results announced less than four hours after the polling stations had closed, about 84 percent of eligible voters, close to 39 million people, voted; and Ahmadinejad received 63 percent of their votes. Mousavi won 34 percent, with the other two candidates sharing the remaining 3 percent. These results were announced with a speed that was unprecedented in the thirty-year history of the Islamic Republic. Less than twenty-four hours before voting day, the text-messaging system on mobile phones had been blocked. Opposition candidates had trained more than 50,000 observers to use text-messaging codes to report any voting irregularities or fraud to a central monitoring system located at Mousavi's campaign headquarters. The landline system that was hastily put in place as an alternative (and less effective) monitoring system (faxing reports of cheating to Mousavi's headquarters) was also cut off around 1 p.m. on election day. The night before the election, Mousavi's campaign headquarters had been attacked, his internet TV station had been raided and several of his campaign activists had been arrested. One hour before the end of voting, the security forces had announced an "authority maneuver" on the streets of Tehran. There were several reports of election rigging on a massive scale.

The announcement of Ahmadinejad's victory in such a tense atmosphere and after weeks of heated electioneering shocked many people. There were huge demonstrations on the streets of Tehran and other major urban centers. The rallies in Tehran were comparable to the huge demonstrations in 1979 that led to the fall of the Shah. Two weeks of demonstrations and clashes between unarmed civilians and riot police, the Basij and plain-clothed security forces resulted in several deaths and thousands of arrests. According to official figures, twenty people were killed, but human rights organizations and independent observers put the figure above a hundred. Resistance to the government continued in many different forms, including people chanting, "God is great!" from rooftops at night, despite the severe crackdown by government forces.

Mousavi and Karroubi – as well as two former presidents, Khatami and Rafsanjani – announced that they did not consider the government legitimate and insisted that the election be declared null and void. The Islamic Republic and supreme leader have experienced the worst legitimation crisis of the past thirty years, and for the first time a significant portion of the Iranian people seem prepared to confront the state in a sustained way, even if they have to pay a heavy price for their actions. The question is: what makes paying such a hefty price in terms of delegitimization acceptable for a state that has always based its legitimacy on the "popular vote"? The only plausible answer seems to be: acquiring a deterrent that guarantees the survival of the state without the need to legitimize power through the popular vote. Ahmadinejad seems to be precisely the right man for this task.

The economy

Iran's economy has long relied on its oil reserves, which, during the time of the last Shah, facilitated the establishment of an elaborate, mainly urban, infrastructure while maintaining a high economic growth rate. Between 1960 and 1977, Iran's annual growth rate was 9.6 percent, double the average of countries in its development category.[86] Its real GDP fell by about 11 percent in the first decade after the revolution, but had started to bounce back to its 1976 level by 1996.[87] The initial decline can primarily be explained by the eight-year war with Iraq, which destroyed much of Iran's infrastructure and led to a labor shortage because of the heavy losses incurred by the young male population. US sanctions on Iran have also had adverse effects on the Iranian economy since the revolution.

Nevertheless, Iran's GDP rose by an annual average of 3.3 percent during 1995–2000, and this increased to 5.5 percent annually over the next five years.[88] While the regime of the Shah heavily invested in strengthening the military to allow the country to become a regional power, the military expenditure of the Islamic Republic has been around 4.5 to 5.8 percent of its GDP since 2000, amounting to $9.057 billion in 2005 and $9.849 biillion in 2006.[89]

Oil production was 3.6 million barrels per day in 1994, and 3.962 million barrels per day in 2004, of which 2.5 million were exported. In March 2005, Oil Minister Bijan Namdar Zanganeh said that Iran's oil production capacity had risen to 4.2 million barrels per day. And Oil Minister Gholam Hussein Nozari announced that Iran was producing 4.085 million barrels per day in September 2007. [90] In 2003, natural gas production was 79 billion cubic meters, with proven reserves estimated at 26.7 trillion cubic meters the following year.

However, Iran still suffers a number of economic and social problems that are partly the result of the war with Iraq and its consequences. Poverty rates are high in less developed regions of the country. Estimates put the percentage of the population living on less than $2 per day over the period 1990–2004 at 9.3 percent.[91] Concomitant with the high rate of poverty is a high rate of unemployment – 10.6 percent for the Iranian year ending March 20, 2007 – and an inflation rate of 18.4 percent for the same year.[92] Moreover, the inflation rate had officially reached around 30 percent by the end of September 2008,[93] and independent economists believe the true figure is considerably higher.[94]

The economic vision of the Islamic Republic was set out in the constitution of 1979. The document as a whole prescribes an ideal model wherein the state is entrusted with the task of providing for the "basic needs" of the population: "shelter, food, clothing, health, education and providing all with the necessities of forming a family."[95] The state controls all of the major sectors of the economy: heavy industry, banking, insurance, foreign trade and public utilities. The constitution envisions a strong "cooperative" sector and a private sector that "complements economic activities of the government and cooperatives." [96]

In line with this, all major industries were taken over by the government after the revolution. Banking, insurance and thousands of firms were nationalized. As part of Islamizing the economy, legislation outlawing the collection of interest was adopted in 1982. However, after the end of the war with Iraq in August 1988 and especially following the death of Khomeini in 1989, new policies of economic pragmatism developed. In the wake of Rafsanjani's election to the presidency, a five-year development plan (1989/1990–1993/1994) was adopted which was designed to encourage a move toward a market economy. Concern shifted to such issues as reform of the economy, inflation, job creation, joint ventures with foreign companies, and management of the country's debts. This was spurred, in part, by a public sentiment that the Iranian people had "earned" some degree of prosperity and economic and social well-being after the terrible sacrifices they had made in the Iran–Iraq War. Iran also continues to pursue the recouping of hundreds of millions of dollars' worth of Iranian assets seized by the United States following the revolution.

Although the government has always deplored its over-reliance on the oil sector, it has struggled to diversify the economy, although the economic policies of Rafsanjani, labeled postwar reconstruction, opened the door for some economic liberalization. Meanwhile, Iran's agricultural sector has been growing steadily since 1979. Agriculture now accounts for 10.4 percent of GDP, with industry at 17.1 percent, the hydrocarbon sector at 26.5 percent, and services at 46 percent.[97] GDP per capita for 2006 was $2,802, with the poverty rate an estimated 20.9 percent. According to the 2006 census, 70 percent of the population was between the ages of 15 and 64, giving Iran the largest workforce in its history.[98] The country's GDP was $188.9 billion in the 2005 fiscal year, and grew to $222.9 billion the following year.[99]

Iran has attempted to attract foreign firms to invest in its oil and other sectors. Although the United States has led a move to isolate Iran economically and prevent further development, this was unsuccessful up to early 2007 due to a lack of cooperation from the US's economic allies in the European Union and Asia, as well as Russia, China and the Central Asian states. On November 6, 2004, the *Asia Times* reported that a gas deal between Beijing and Tehran worth $100 billion had been signed. Negotiations then began on a similar oil agreement with China, worth roughly the same amount. The gas deal entails the annual export of some 10 million tons of Iranian liquefied natural gas over a twenty-five-year period, as well as China's participation in exploration and drilling, petrochemical and gas industries, pipelines and energy services.[100] On January 7, 2005, the *Financial Times* reported that India had signed a preliminary agreement with the National Iranian Oil Company that was unofficially estimated to be worth $40 billion, which committed India to import liquefied natural gas and develop two Iranian oilfields and a gas field.[101] Iran, however, faces a very uncertain future in its economic dealings with the outside world, including the contracts mentioned above, because it has been forced to operate under a UN-imposed regime of economic sanctions that seriously affects foreign investment in its energy sector.

Since August 2002, when a representative of the armed MEK opposition group provided information on Iran's nuclear program to the Israeli intelligence service, Iran has been under international supervision. The United Nations' International Atomic Energy Agency (IAEA) has been closely monitoring Iran's nuclear sites since October of that year.[102] Iran acquired equipment and started building facilities to enrich uranium in the mid- to late 1990s, and some of these activities were not divulged to the IAEA, thereby violating the terms of the

Nuclear Non-Proliferation Treaty, to which Iran is a signatory. The main issue concerns acquiring centrifuge equipment through the black market and introducing nuclear material bought from China in 1991 into that equipment without the prior knowledge of the IAEA.[103] Rounds of intense negotiations with the IAEA and the European Union, especially since Ahmadinejad's government took control in 2005, failed to resolve the issue, and Iran's case was referred to the UN Security Council in 2006. Since then, six resolutions have been issued against Iran: 1696, 1737 (both 2006), 1747 (2007), 1803 and 1835 (both 2008) and 1929 (2010). Resolutions 1737, 1747 and 1803 have imposed sanctions that cover a wide range of trade, technology transfer and financial transactions with Iran. Resolution 1737 demanded that Iran should immediately suspend "all enrichment-related and reprocessing activities including research and development." Iran was also told to suspend "work on all heavy water-related projects." Resolution 1747 "calls upon all States and international financial institutions not to enter into new commitments for grants, financial assistance, and concessional loans, to the government of the Islamic Republic of Iran, except for humanitarian and developmental purposes." A number of banks, companies and individuals claimed to be connected with Iran's nuclear energy and defense industries have been put on an international watch list, and this has led to serious doubts over the prospects of investment in Iran. Due to US and Israeli diplomatic pressure, a number of major agreements reached with Japanese and European companies to invest in Iran's oil and gas industries have already been suspended or canceled. Russia has delayed the completion of the Bushehr nuclear power plant, which was supposed to be operational by 2006.

Resolution 1803

> calls upon all States, in accordance with their national legal authorities and legislation and consistent with international law, in particular the law of the sea and relevant international civil aviation agreements, to inspect the cargoes to and from Iran, of aircraft and vessels, at their airports and seaports, owned or operated by Iran Air Cargo and Islamic Republic of Iran Shipping Line, provided there are reasonable grounds to believe that the aircraft or vessel is transporting goods prohibited under this resolution or resolution 1737 (2006) or resolution 1747 (2007).

This gives the international community the right to inspect ships and aircraft carrying goods to and from Iran. The resolution also calls upon all states to "exercise vigilance" in entering into trade with Iran or extending loans and credit to Iranian banks that might contribute to the development of Iran's nuclear energy program or "weapons delivery systems." Resolution 1929 targets more banks, defense industry companies and RGC commanders and restricts selling conventional arms, such as tanks and helicopters, to Iran.

Under the Non-Proliferation Treaty, Iran has the right to enrich uranium for non-military purposes and IAEA reports have so far not indicated the existence of a military nuclear program. Iran insists today, as it did during the Shah's time, that

it will need a nuclear energy production capacity to meet its industrial requirements once its oil resources start to deplete,[104] and it has allowed inspection of its
nuclear sites by the IAEA. The main problem, however, is the question of a "secret
military program," mainly suggested by Israel – which has its own nuclear military
capability which is not under IAEA or indeed any other international supervision
– and the United States.

At the time of writing, Iran has been unable to build trust with the international community and the United Nations about its nuclear intentions, and
Ahmadinejad's harsh rhetoric has further complicated matters. However, Iran
reached a working agreement with the IAEA on resolving all remaining issues
related to its nuclear program on August 21, 2007, when a "work plan" was
finalized with the IAEA "which includes understandings between the Secretariat
and Iran on the modalities, procedures and timelines for resolving [all] the
remaining safeguards implementation issues, including the long outstanding
issues."[105] Based on this agreement, the director general of the IAEA, Mohammad
El-Baradei, urged the US and a number of European states – most notably France,
which has taken an aggressive stance toward Iran since the election of President
Nicolas Sarkozy in 2007 – to give diplomacy a chance to resolve the dispute. In an
interview with the German magazine *Der Spiegel*, El-Baradei said: "For the first
time, we have agreed, with the Iranians, to a sort of roadmap, a schedule, if you
will, for clarifying the outstanding issues. We should know by November, or
December at the latest, whether the Iranians will keep their promises." But he
warned: "If they don't, Tehran will have missed a great opportunity – possibly the
last one."[106]

A series of interesting developments since November 2007 has given a
new twist to the Iranian nuclear issue. In that month, the Office of the Director
of National Intelligence in the United States issued a new national intelligence estimate (NIE) of Iran. According to this document, Iran had halted
its military nuclear program in the autumn of 2003 and had not resumed it by
mid-2007. The document adds that while Iran had a military program prior to
2003, the intelligence community in the United States continues "to assess
with moderate-to-high confidence that Iran does not currently have a nuclear
weapon."[107]

The publication of this document met with strong opposition in Israel and
among US neoconservative political circles because, as the Israeli newspaper
Haaretz stated, "The report does not dismiss the Iranian threat – though it does
not substantiate it – but it snatches an important strategic asset from Israel. No
longer can Israel play the regional power that charts the map of global strategic
threats; the state that mobilized the world against Iran will now assume the role
of nudnik."[108]

On February 22, 2008, El-Baradei issued a report on the status of Iran's nuclear
program after months of deliberations between IAEA technical staff and their
Iranian counterparts and a final visit by El-Baradei to Tehran that included
meetings with the supreme leader, the president and the foreign minister. In this
report, the IAEA cleared Iran on issues pertaining to "sources of contamination"

in Iranian research and industrial facilities, some past procurement activities, activities related to polonium-210 research and "the complex arrangements governing the past and current administration of the Gchine uranium mine and mill." However, the report raised some new issues pertaining to "alleged studies concerning the conversion of uranium dioxide (UO_2) into uranium tetrafluoride (UF_4) (the green salt project), high explosives testing and the design of a missile re-entry vehicle, which could have a military nuclear dimension and which appear to have administrative interconnections, and in view of their possible link to nuclear material." [109] The report states that information on these issues was passed to the IAEA by "other member states." According to the report, Iran claimed that "such allegations were baseless and that the information which the Agency had shown to Iran was fabricated."[110] Nevertheless, the report formed the basis for Security Council Resolution 1803, which requested the director general of the IAEA to submit a report on the status of negotiations with Iran within ninety days. This report was duly issued on May 26, 2008. It is mainly concerned with "studies on the green salt project, high explosives testing and the missile re-entry vehicle project" allegedly carried out by Iran. The report maintains that the information regarding these issues "was provided by several member states," although "much of this information" was received "only in electronic form" and the IAEA "was not authorized to provide copies to Iran." Iran's reply was that the documents were "forged" or "fabricated," and it repeated that it does not have "any nuclear weapon program."[111] The report concludes that the IAEA requires clarification from Iran regarding the alleged studies and states that it "has not suspended its enrichment related activities."[112]

Another report was issued by the IAEA on September 15. This led to UN Security Council Resolution 1835, which reaffirmed the previous resolutions and called upon Iran to comply with their requirements. A further report of November 19 reiterates concerns over the suspected military diversion of some of Iran's nuclear activities and its non-compliance with the Security Council's call to suspend its uranium-enrichment program.[113]

Iran and the Security Council seemed to have reached an impasse, in spite of the diplomatic efforts of EU foreign policy chief Xavier Solana, Russian President Vladimir Putin and others. While Iranians have expressed their willingness to negotiate directly with the United States over a range of regional security issues (including the nuclear issue, Iraq and Afghanistan), the US has insisted that Iran must abandon its uranium enrichment program before any meeting can be held. With "regime change" being US government policy during the Bush administration, Iran placed a high value on its "nuclear card" for most of the 2000s, and it is now reluctant to give it up cheaply, even though Barack Obama is now in the White House. Obama stated his willingness to engage in direct negotiations with Iran without preconditions during his presidential campaign, but his tone changed after winning the election. Now, the stance he has taken regarding the conflicts in the Middle East and the composition of his foreign policy team would seem to indicate that a major breakthrough in the Iran–US confrontation is unlikely in the near future.

Many observers see the issue of Iran's nuclear energy in a wider context of regional and international rivalry for power and dominance in the Middle East. Iran's current government has certainly used the nuclear issue to mobilize the Iranian people to resist the policy of regime change that has been actively implemented by the US and Israel.[114] It has also used this threat to divert attention from its poor economic performance and to repress domestic opposition and civil society activism.

Iran requires an estimated $2 billion investment in its oil industry to keep production around the 4 million barrels per day mark, but it faces increasing difficulties in reaching agreements with foreign investors for all the reasons outlined above. On March 24, 2007, US Under-Secretary of State Nicholas Burns said that the new sanctions against Iran were designed to cause "financial strangulation."[115] In addition to the UN sanctions, the US has imposed unilateral sanctions and has convinced many European and Asian banks to cut their ties with Iran. Spearheading this effort was Stuart Levy, under-secretary for terrorism and financial intelligence at the Treasury Department. According to a *New York Times* report, Levy "has since [February 2006] made more than 80 foreign visits of his own to talk to more than five dozen banks" in order to persuade them to sever their links with Iran.[116] Since 2006, beginning with Bank Saderat, Iran's largest bank, nearly all of the country's banks have been blacklisted by the US government. The EU, Australia, Japan, China and even Muslim countries have all followed suit, albeit to a lesser extent. A *New York Times* reporter who has investigated the US Treasury's efforts to isolate Iran notes that threats were used to make foreign banks comply with these efforts; "foreign bankers, however, insisted that threats were always implicit."[117] The efforts to strangulate Iran financially took a new turn on October 16, 2008, when the Financial Action Task Force (FATF), representing the thirty-two largest economies in the world, warned for a fourth time about problems in Iran's anti-money-laundering and counter-terrorist-financing measures. (FATF is the world's preeminent organization in the fight against money laundering and non-transparent fund transfers.) This prepared the ground for the most severe action against Iran's economy by the United States. On November 6, the US Treasury Department revoked the "U-turn" general license which had allowed US financial institutions to transfer funds on behalf of Iranian parties initiated by non-American banks. This, in the words of the Treasury Department, "applies not only to state-owned Iranian banks and the Central Bank of Iran, but also to privately-owned Iranian banks, Iranian companies, and the settlement of third-country trade transactions that involve Iran." The Treasury Department has recently turned its attention to Dubai, which provides an indirect route of trade to Iran.[118] (Trade between the two countries reached nearly $14 billion in 2008.[119])

Foreign relations

Iran occupies a unique global position. It is simultaneously a Middle Eastern, a Central Asian and a South Asian nation. It has been both the seat of empires and the coveted possession of imperial powers. In the immediate aftermath of the Islamic revolution, ideological zealots attempted to export their version of the revolution and lent support to radical movements in other countries. This ultimately earned Iran many enemies in the world. However, Iranian foreign policy, even during the time of Khomeini, was influenced by ideological and pragmatic considerations, along with traditional Iranian foreign policy positions and the world-view generated by the revolution.[120] Elements of traditional Iranian foreign policy positions include balancing major forces against one another, building a bloc against a threatening state and invoking what Mossadegh termed "negative equilibrium" – that is, avoiding falling under the pressure of one of the major international powers.[121] Since the late 1980s, a pragmatic tendency has become more evident. Iran did not let the Syrian repression of the Muslim Brotherhood strain their warm political relations, and it maintained good relations with the United Arab Emirates during the war with Iraq as the UAE was an important staging-post for imports to Iran. Further, Iran did not seek influence within the ex-Soviet Islamic republics, nor has it heaped criticism on Russia for its suppression of Muslims in Chechnya. As before, it has continued to view itself as a regional power, stressing the centrality of its great history, resources, strategic position and Islamic credentials.[122] It was the government of Rafsanjani which first adopted a conciliatory foreign policy based on presenting Iran as a responsible, "respectable" international citizen, despite US opposition to the Tehran regime. This was pursued through close involvement in international organizations such as the Non-Aligned Movement, the Red Crescent (the Islamic counterpart of the Red Cross) and the Organization of the Islamic Conference. Iran has subsequently acted to improve relations with its neighbors and the rest of the world, and still hosts a very large number of Iraqi and Afghani refugees.

At the same time, Iran continues to be the official seat of Shi'ism, and exercises conspicuous influence over a significant number of Muslims all over the world. Indeed, it is the fifth-largest Muslim country in population after Indonesia, Pakistan, Turkey and Egypt. It is also the most advanced and stable nation in Central Asia, a region which is only now emerging from the shadow of the dismantled Soviet Union. Finally, Iran is, by a factor of four, the most populous Persian Gulf state, and the one with the longest coastline. With these advantages, the nation is well placed to be a regional leader in several areas. It has therefore influenced, and continues to influence, both overtly and covertly, the populations of both its neighbors and more distant countries.

American antagonism

Iran's most significant opponent in the foreign policy area is the United States. American hostility began with the US Embassy hostage saga in 1979, and has continued unabated ever since. On November 4, 1979, a group of Iranian students invaded the American Embassy and then held fifty-two people hostage for 444 days, during which time the American military attempted a rescue that failed abysmally because of an unpredictable desert storm. The students acted in response to the ousted Shah's arrival in New York in September, which stirred up suspicions that the Americans were planning to reinstate the monarch. They were so convinced about this that they spent thousands of hours in the embassy piecing together shredded secret papers that eventually showed the depth of US involvement in Iranian domestic and regional policies.[123]

The United States applied sanctions against Iran immediately after the embassy siege began. The intensity of conflict between the two countries increased as a result of US involvement in the eight-year war between Iran and Iraq, when America overwhelmingly supported the latter (although it supplied weapons to both sides – see below). By the summer of 1982, the Iranian armed forces had pushed the Iraqi invaders back from most parts of Iranian territory. Iran then went on the offensive, at a time when Israel had invaded Lebanon and had laid a siege around Beirut. The prospects of an Iranian victory led to the formation of a *de facto* international and regional alliance that included the US, Israel and some Arab allies of Washington – mainly Saudi Arabia, Kuwait and Egypt. The main purpose of this alliance was to support the regime of Saddam Hussein against Iranian offensives and, crucially, to prevent the emergence of a definitive winner in the war. The ultimate aim was the mutual exhaustion and weakening of both countries, so that Israeli supremacy in the regional balance of power could be maintained. From 1982 onward, the US government simply decided that it "could not afford to allow Iraq to lose the war to Iran."[124] Howard Teicher, a high-level National Security Council member during Reagan's presidency, stated:

> President Ronald Reagan decided that the United States would do whatever was necessary and legal to prevent Iraq from losing the war to Iran ... The United States actively supported the Iraqi war effort by supporting the Iraqis with billions of dollars of credit, by providing US military intelligence and advice to the Iraqis, and by closely monitoring third country arms sales to Iraq to make sure that Iraq had the military weaponry required. [125]

Teicher "attended meetings in which CIA Director Casey or CIA Deputy Director Gates noted the need for Iraq to have certain weapons such as cluster bombs and anti-armor penetrators to stave off the Iranian attacks."[126] In February 1982 (four months *before* the start of Iranian military operations across the border) Iraq was removed from the US State Department's list of states supporting international terrorism. Thereafter, the US supplied Hussein's regime with military intelligence concerning Iranian troop positions and provided military hardware and credit to the Iraqis. In 1983, Iraq started to use chemical weapons against Iranian troops and in its own Kurdish areas. In the 1990s, Iraq admitted that its armed forces "had used about 100,000 chemical shells" during the Iran–Iraq war.[127] When Iran took the issue to the UN Security Council in 1984 and requested an investigation, the US used its influence to prevent the matter going any further. It did this even though Secretary of State George Shultz, in a memorandum dated November 1, 1983, had stated: "We have recently received additional information confirming Iraqi use of chemical weapons. We also know that Iraq has acquired a CW production capacity, primarily from Western firms, including possibly a

US foreign subsidiary." The same document mentions "Iraq's almost daily use of CW."[128]

In the aftermath of the Israeli invasion of Lebanon, in 1983 a US marines barracks in Beirut was attacked and sixty-three people were killed. As a result, the US State Department, citing Iranian logistical support for the attack, added Iran to its list of states that support terrorism. This meant non-provision of US bank credits and strict licensing of all trade with Iran. In December, Donald Rumsfeld, then the CEO of the pharmaceutical multinational G.D. Searl, visited Baghdad as a "special envoy" of President Reagan and met with Saddam Hussein and other top Iraqi officials to convey the US government's willingness to support Iraq in the war. A State Department summary of Rumsfeld's meeting with Iraqi Foreign Minister Tariq Aziz stated that "the two agreed the US and Iraq shared many common interests: peace in the Gulf, keeping Syria and Iran off balance and less influential, and promoting Egypt's reintegration into the Arab world."[129]

Nevertheless, the policy of "no winner" – the prolonged mutual destruction of Iran *and* Iraq – was pursued in various ways. According to a telegram sent to the State Department by the US Embassy in Ankara in November 1980, "substantial quantities of Israeli goods also transit Turkey for [both] Islamic belligerents." The same document quotes an undisclosed source as admiring "Israeli business acumen in selling to both sides."[130] However, according to Howard Teicher, by 1984,

> the Israelis concluded that Iran was more dangerous than Iraq to Israel's existence due to the growing Iranian influence and presence in Lebanon . . . The Israelis approached the United States in a meeting in Jerusalem that I attended with Donald Rumsfeld. Israeli Foreign Minister Ytizhak Shamir asked Rumsfeld if the United States would deliver a secret offer of Israeli assistance to Iraq. The United States agreed.[131]

However, Teicher mentions that the Iraqi side then refused to accept the secret Israeli letter.

Richard Sale reported:

> the CIA regularly sent a team to Saddam to deliver battlefield intelligence obtained from Saudi AWACS surveillance aircraft to aid the effectiveness of Iraq's armed forces . . . [but one] former official said that he personally had signed off on a document that shared US satellite intelligence with both Iraq and Iran in an attempt to produce a military stalemate. "When I signed it, I thought I was losing my mind," [the former official remembered].[132]

When Kuwaiti ships supplying Iraq with fuel and other commodities became targets of Iranian attacks, the Americans not only provided military escorts but hoisted US flags on Kuwaiti and Iraqi oil tankers. In 1987, when the confrontation was at its peak in the Persian Gulf, an Iranian mine-layer was captured and sunk by US forces, and US ships bombarded an Iranian oil platform on the Gulf. Moreover, a civilian Iran Air jet carrying more than 200 passengers was hit by a US missile, killing everyone on board. Before then, however, the US had secretly smuggled some military equipment to Iran in the hope that the latter might be able to secure the release of American captives held by Islamic militia in Lebanon. At the same time, they continued to supply Iraq with a massive arsenal of weapons. Before long, these weapons would be used against US forces and their allies during the second Gulf War. The embarrassment surrounding these issues was key in the defeat of George Bush Senior in the 1992 US presidential election.

Under President Clinton's administration, the "dual containment" policy continued, with the aim being to isolate Iran economically and politically. But with traditionally hawkish Republicans dominating the US legislature from the mid-1990s to 2006, even tougher action against Iran was demanded. In December 1995, the House of Representatives passed legislation for a secondary boycott of Iran. In addition, Newt Gingrich, the speaker of the House, announced that the CIA should mount an $18 million covert operation to overthrow the government in Iran. In response, in January 1996, the Majlis announced a $20 million fund to combat the activities of the "Great Satan." However, since then, Iran has been careful to refrain from any action that could be construed as provocative by the United States. This is hardly surprising, given the considerable US military presence in the Persian Gulf, which could be mobilized at very short notice against Iran.

When George W. Bush assumed office in 2001, he intensified the negative rhetoric against Iran, labeling it a member of the "Axis of Evil," alongside Iraq and North Korea. The Bush administration repeatedly accused Iran of supporting "terrorist" organizations, including Hizbollah. Iran, in continuing to resist the Israeli occupation of Palestinian territory, also lends support to Hamas, another "terrorist" organization, according to the United States, in spite of being the democratically elected government of the Palestinian National Authority (PNA).

Iran and Europe, Russia and Central Asia

The American government's antagonism towards the Iranian government, particularly evidenced in its economic sanctions against Iran, has not been well received by all members of the European Union, which favors a policy of critical dialogue and strongly opposes the extraterritorial application of US legislation.[133] The EU and Iran's annual trade in the mid-1990s amounted to some $14 billion. The US boycott resulted in a boon for some European companies, with Total (France) picking up a $1 billion oil deal that US firm Conoco was forced to abandon. However, the current impasse over Iran's nuclear-enrichment program has pushed the EU closer to the US. In September 2007, under pressure from the French government, Total announced that it had withdrawn from major investments in Iran's energy industry.

Iran has also worked to develop links with Eastern European states, especially Ukraine and Belarus. These, combined with Iran's influence in the Central Asian republics, which are suppliers of some low-cost consumer goods and military equipment to Iran, allow Iran rail access – and, more importantly, natural gas pipelines – directly to Europe. Iran has also developed a close relationship with Russia. The two countries have mutual economic interests, especially in exploiting the mineral resources of the Caspian Sea area and preventing Western penetration of the region. Russia is now an immense source of technological support to Iran, and a counterbalance to the United States. They also share a mutual interest in minimizing Turkish influence in Central Asia, and containing unrest in the former Soviet republics. For Russia, Iran is an important customer for high-technology industrial equipment and arms, and has symbolic importance to nationalistic Russians who view close relations with Iran as a means of cementing Russia's dominance in Asia against the West. The two countries, moreover, have co-operated on developing legal regimes for resource development in the Caspian Sea. However, once again, this relationship has been affected by Iran's insistence on its right to enrich uranium. Russia voted for sanctions against Iran along with the other members of the UN Security Council in 2006 and 2007.

Iran's new pragmatism is nowhere more evident than in Central Asia. In its quest to develop a "sphere of influence," it has abandoned the Islamist card when dealing with Central Asian states, most of which are ruled by their former communist masters under new names. Iran enjoys good relations with Armenia, despite the latter's occupation of Azeri territory in the Republic of Azerbaijan (a Shi'a-majority country neighboring Iran). These authoritarian leaderships are deeply suspicious of political Islam, and their populations, while professing Islam, are equally influenced by folk beliefs as well as approximately seventy years of state atheism. Iran has acted to help these states improve their economic infrastructures and provide trade opportunities in the region, as it has the nearest access to the sea. In 1996 a rail line running through Uzbekistan, Turkmenistan and Iran to the port of Bandar Abbas on the Persian Gulf was opened. Iran was also involved in negotiations to end the civil wars in Tajikistan and Afghanistan (which pushed numerous refugees into Iran), and has established close diplomatic and cultural links with the states of Central Asia.

Close ties with Pakistan have also been cultivated, which, despite US support through the Cold War as a counterweight to Soviet-leaning India, is sliding into instability. The Pakistani government and especially the military have very strong Islamist sympathies, stemming in no small part from their continuing confrontation with India. Thus Iran and Pakistan's common rhetoric is based on Islamic brotherhood. This has strong military implications, but at the same time Iran's continued friendly overtures to India have paid off economically.

Iran and the Middle East

On the regional scene, Iran has been viewed with suspicion, particularly during the first decade after the revolution, owing to a complex of regional and foreign dynamic forces, which construed (or more often misconstrued) the new regime's ideology as hazardous to the stability of the regional system. However, from the 1990s, Iranian caution and pragmatism began to dispel earlier fears among Arab states. Initially, these states were concerned about Iran's rhetoric and its support for the mismanaged Islamic government in Sudan as well as the violent opposition movements in Egypt and Algeria. In Bahrain, Iran was accused of fomenting opposition among the Shi'ite majority to the Sunni minority governing elite. Iraq also accused Iran of supporting its Shi'ite population and working to bring down the government. In response, the Iraqis supported opposition groups (such as the MEK) fighting the Iranian regime. Moreover, Iranian relations with the UAE have been dogged by sovereignty disputes over three small Gulf islands – Abu Musa, Lesser Tunb and Greater Tunb. This dispute is two centuries old and based on the fact that members of the Arab Qawasim tribe, which inhabited parts of what is now the UAE, also lived on the islands and on the Iranian coast under Persian sovereignty. Nevertheless, Iranian–UAE relations improved throughout the 1990s in both the economic and political spheres.[134] The present Iranian policy is based on improving relations with all countries except Israel, which, according to Iran, has usurped Palestinian land and inflicted an oppressive occupation on the Palestinian people.

Both Iran and Saudi Arabia claim regional influence in the Gulf, which has led to mutual competition and suspicion. This has been amplified by US efforts to isolate Iran, and maintain its dominance in the region. However, when Khatami became president in 1997, his pursuit of a less ideological foreign policy paved the way for rapid expansion of ties between Iran and Saudi Arabia. This resulted in stable and friendly relations as well as a series of security, economic, political and educational bilateral agreements.[135]

However, the Anglo-American invasion and occupation of Iraq in 2003 caused a dramatic shift in the regional balance of power. Accordingly, all Arab states (save for Syria, which has always maintained a good relationship with Iran) have relaunched their verbal campaigns against Iran, seeing the rise of an Iranian-affiliated government in Iraq as a sign of an incipient "Shi'a crescent." Certainly, Iran has been the major (perhaps the sole) victor in the Iraq imbroglio.

Iran's threat as a regional power has been widely discussed. Militarily, it has acquired MiG-29 fighter aircraft from Russia, giving it a measure of air defense capability, as well as several Russian-built diesel-electric submarines of the Kilo class.[136] These vessels are limited in their reach, but they are very effective in the Persian Gulf, as they are difficult to detect. Nevertheless, Iran is unable to project any naval force very far from its coast.[137] On the ground, Iran has Chinese- and Russian-built missile launchers and armored vehicles, as well as domestically made equipment based on American designs from the pre-revolution period. It has also installed Chinese-built surface-to-surface missiles (SSMs) in its coastal defense batteries.[138] However, its entire stock of SSMs does not equal the firepower of a single American frigate. The real problem, from the US perspective, is that Iran has installed its missile launchers in underground tunnels, with camouflaged, dummy and hidden entrances, making them difficult to identify and attack.

The US and Israel have accused Iran of attempting to develop nuclear weapons at the Bushehr power plant. This project was launched in 1974 under the Shah's regime, but was damaged during the Iran–Iraq War. Thereafter, Iran could not persuade Siemens, the original contractor, to return to finish the project after the US put pressure on Germany. In 1995, amid more US objections, Iran signed an $800 million deal with Victor Mikhailov, chief of Minatom, the Russian Ministry of Atomic Energy, to complete the project. However, Russia would not provide Iran with the gas centrifuge technology it wanted, so instead the light water reactor had to be fueled with low enriched uranium (LEU), which is unsuitable for use in warheads. Russia also agreed to store the exhausted LEU to reduce the risk of a diversion of plutonium to military use.[139] Iran has invited the IAEA to set up a permanent office at the Bushehr complex and has allowed it to visit Bushehr and other sites. In February 2003, the IAEA reported no violations, and in 2008 it verified that no nuclear material had been diverted to military ends.[140]

There are two political reasons why Iran would want to have a nuclear reactor and associated technology, the first being prestige. Iran portrays itself as the leader of the Islamic world, and as the "first citizen" of Central Asia and the Persian Gulf. As a regional leader, it feels it must have the appropriate signs of technological advancement. Second, Iran wants to be a respected member of the world community in general. In possessing nuclear technology, it would rank alongside such states as Japan and Germany, or, at a lower level, Sweden and Canada, which enjoy international respect without the taint of an imperialist past. Iran would thus be able to present itself as fiercely independent of "imperialism" on the world stage while enjoying the global support of many Muslims.

However, Iran's continued development of nuclear technology is an open provocation to the United States. If Iran were to construct a nuclear warhead, the US would surely waste no time in crushing the Islamic regime, having finally been given the pretext it has long desired.

Terrorism

The most common attack leveled against Iran is that it supports violent Islamic fundamentalist movements. In the past, Iran has supported Islamic Jihad for the Liberation of Palestine, Hizbollah, various groups in Afghanistan and Tajikistan and, to a lesser extent, Hamas and the Islamic regime in Sudan. It has also been accused of supporting groups in Algeria, Bahrain, Egypt, Saudi Arabia and virtually every other state where an Islamic activist element exists. Currently, it is accused of sponsoring insurgent attacks against US troops in occupied Iraq.

In the 1980s, partly to break its international isolation, Iran supported various liberation movements in order to gain leverage, as it was cut off from the normal channels of diplomacy. In addition, it sought to implement its ideological commitment to anti-imperialism and the spread of Islamic revolution. In the late 1990s, however, despite US propaganda to the contrary, Iran has been neither particularly isolated nor particularly committed to the export of Islamic revolution. Indeed, it now appears to accept the notion that overt support for violent groups could backfire and cause Iran significant economic and political damage. Within Iran, especially during Khatami's presidency, there was friction between parochial religious leaders who vocally supported Islamic groups and their impulsive radical attacks on the US and Israel and more pragmatic members of the government who wanted Iran to be able to operate on the international stage as an accepted member of the global community.

Iran used the summit of the Organization of the Islamic Conference that was held in Tehran in December 1997 to step back from state support of terrorism, while reaching out to its regional adversaries. Overtures were made to the Gulf countries, the PNA and Yasser Arafat, and Iraq, while reconciliation was couched in a strong condemnation of the US policy of containment (specifically the Iran and Libya Sanctions Act of 1996 and US Executive Order 13059 of 1997, which hampers US investment in Iran).

Relations with Iraq after 2003

In July 2005, Iraq's Shi'ite prime minister, Ibrahim al-Ja'fari, and eight high-powered cabinet ministers paid an extremely friendly visit to Tehran, where oil pipelines, port access, pilgrimage, trade, security and military assistance were all discussed, and economic and security treaties were signed. The economic deal involved Iran paying for three pipelines that would stretch across the southern border of the two countries, and Iraq shipping 150,000 barrels of light crude each day to be refined in Iran, which will then ship back processed petroleum, kerosene and gasoline. It was hoped that the project would be operational within a year. In addition, it was agreed that Iran would supply electricity to Iraq and would sell it 200,000 tons of wheat. Moreover, Iran offered Iraq the use of its ports, along with $1 billion of aid. It also promised to step up cooperation in policing the borders of the two countries.

The Iraqi government solemnly assured Tehran that it would not allow Iraqi territory to be used as a base for any attack on Iran. Then the Iranian leaders raised the question of the continued presence of the MEK in Iraq. (Saddam Hussein had used the MEK to foment trouble within Iran, as had the US more recently.) Al-Ja'fari promised that members of the MEK would be disarmed, and would not be allowed to conduct terrorist raids from Iraqi soil.[141]

Al-Ja'fari was replaced by Nouri al-Maliki in Iraq's 2006 elections. Since then, al-Maliki and other top Iraqi officials have paid several visits to Iran and have emphasized the government's desire to maintain close relations with Iran. Both al-Ja'fari and al-Maliki belong to a coalition of Shi'a groups that are considered to be Iran's long-term allies. The Iraqi Shi'a and Kurdish opposition forged strong ties with Iran during the 1980s and 1990s, and during the Iran–Iraq War Iran supported these groups by supplying and organizing their military units. The current Iraqi government is mainly composed of the leaders of those groups.

During 2006 the insurgency in Iraq intensified, and attacks by al-Qa'ida and Sunni extremist groups on Shi'a religious sites and civilians led to a vicious cycle of sectarian killings and acts of revenge throughout southern and central Iraq. The

United States intensified its rhetoric against Iran's involvement in this violence, with top military and political officials accusing Iran of training Shi'a militias and smuggling arms and explosives that were subsequently used against American troops. In January 2007, President Bush announced the "surge," to provide security in Baghdad and cleanse the city of both Shi'a and Sunni insurgents. This was a package of military, political and economic measures, including revision of the de-Ba'thification laws (which had been hastily passed after the invasion) to give more power to Sunni political factions, a $10 billion investment in "reconstruction and infrastructure projects" to create jobs, and an increase of pressure on al-Maliki to act against Shi'a militias that had infiltrated the police and security forces. The United States also increased its number of troops in Iraq to about 168,000 and exerted pressure on Iran both in Iraq and on the international scene by enforcing sanctions and encouraging allies to halt investment and trade. Bush accused Iran of backing violence against US soldiers and authorized American commanders to "confront Iran's murderous activities."[142]

Meanwhile, two rounds of talks at ambassadorial level were conducted in Iraq between Tehran and Washington. These achieved no tangible results. In December 2008, the US–Iranian confrontation intensified as the UN's authorization that foreign troops could be stationed in Iraq ran out. Washington reached agreement with Baghdad over the continued presence of US troops in Iraq, but this topic was hotly debated by all of Iraq's political parties. Initially, capitulation privileges, exempting American soldiers from Iraqi justice, were contained in the agreement and it was unclear whether the US would have permanent military bases in Iraq. Another important issue was whether US forces in Iraq could launch attacks from there against a third country. There was opposition to all of these issues from both Shi'a allies of Iran and Sunni factions. Of course, Iran supported the Iraqi opposition, and in the final agreement that was ratified by the Iraqi parliament in late November 2008, it was specified that Iraqi soil could not be used by the US to attack another country.

Nevertheless, at the time of writing, Iran could not feel secure in relation to the United States. Dan Plesch and Martin Butcher have contemplated what might happen in the near future. They suggest that US policy toward Iran remains regime change through political means but "prevention of nuclear weapons acquisition by all means." To achieve these ends, the United States would embark on a "full-spectrum approach" to "reduce" Iran to "a weak or failed state."[143]

It is clear that US policy toward Iran is a continuation of the post-Second World War strategy of controlling the Middle East to secure a continuing flow of cheap oil and guarantee the supremacy of Israel as the hegemonic regional power. The policy of "reducing" Iran's power echoes the policy that was pursued so vigorously by the US toward Iraq in the twelve years that followed the first Gulf War. Only time will tell whether Iran will suffer the same ultimate fate as its neighbor.

Notes

1 *CIA World Factbook: Iran* (2010). URL: https://www.cia.gov/library/publications/the-world-factbook/geos/ir.html.
2 Hamdallah, *Nozhat al-Qolub* (edited by Mohammad Dabir Sayyaqi) (Tehran: Tahuri, 1957), p. 92.
3 Ahmad Kasravi, *Sheikh Safi va Tabarash* Publishers (Tehran: Firdaws, 1976).
4 Saeed Nafisi, *Social and Political History of Iran* Publishers (Tehran: Ibn Sina, 1982), I, pp. 86–87.
5 George Curzon, *Persia and the Persian Question* (London: Frank Cass, 1966), I, pp. 3–4.
6 Karl Meyer and Shareen Brysac, *Tournament of Shadows: The Great Game and the Race for Empire in Asia* (London: Abacus, 2001).
7 "History of Iran," http://www.iranchamber.com/history/qajar/qajar.php.
8 Jahangir Ghaem-Maghami, *Tarikh-i Tahavolat-e Nezam–e Iran* (Tehran: 'Ali Akbar Elmi, 1947), pp. 69–70.
9 Ahmad Ashraf and 'Ali Banuazizi, *The Qajar Class Structure*. URL: http://www.iranchamber.com/history/articles/qajar_class_structure.php.
10 Nikki R. Keddie, *Religion and Rebellion in Iran: The Tobacco Protest of 1891–1892* (London: Cass, 1966) and *An Islamic Response to Imperialism: Political and Religious Writings of Sayyid Jamal ad-Din "al-Afghani"* (Berkeley and Los Angeles: University of California Press, 1968), pp. 28–29.
11 Keddie, *An Islamic Response to Imperialism*, op. cit., pp. 617–620.
12 Fereydoun Adamiyat, *Articles on Iranian History* (Tehran: Shabgir, 1974), p. 88.
13 Keddie, *An Islamic Response to Imperialism*, op. cit., pp. 622–623.
14 Quoted in Stephen Kinzer, *All the Shah's Men: An American Coup and the Roots of Middle East Terror* (New York: Wiley Press, 2003), pp. 39–40.
15 Homa Katouzian, "State and Society under Reza Shah," in Touraj Atabaki and Erik J. Zurcher (eds), *Men of Order: Authoritarian Modernization under Ataturk and Reza Shah* (London and New York: I.B. Tauris, 2004), p. 21.
16 Ibid., p. 21; Arnold J. Toynbee, *Survey of International Affairs 1925 (The Islamic World since the Peace Conference)* (Oxford: Oxford University Press, under the auspices of the Royal Institute of International Affairs, 1927), I.
17 "Dr. Mohammad Mossadegh: The Iranian National Hero." URL: http://www.angelfire.com/home/iran/mossadegh.html.
18 Homa Katouzian, *The Political Economy of Modern Iran* (London and New York: Macmillan and New York University Press, 1981), p. 183, Table 9.2.
19 Ibid., p. 117, Table 6.3.
20 Ibid., p. 118.
21 Ibid.
22 Mark Gasiorowski, "The 1953 Coup D'état in Iran," *International Journal of Middle East Studies*, Vol. 19 (1987), pp. 261–286. Mark Gasiorowsky and Malcolm Byrne, *Mohammad Mosaddeq and the 1953 Coup in Iran* (Syracuse: Syracuse University Press, 2004); and US State Department, *Foreign Relations of the United States, 1952–1954*, Volume X: *Iran 1951–1954* (edited by Carl N. Raether and Charles S. Sampson) (Washington, D.C.: State Department, 1989).
23 James Risen, "Overthrow of Premier Mossadegh," *New York Times*, June 18, 2000. URL: http://www.nytimes.com/library/world/mideast/041600iran-cia-index.html. Robert Fisk, "Another Fine Mess." URL: http://www.informationclearinghouse.info/article4588.htm. "The CIA Destroyed Files on 1953 Iran Coup D'état," *New York Times*, May 29, 1997. URL: http://www.nytimes.com/1997/05/29/us/cia-destroyed-files-on-1953-iran-coup.html?pagewanted=all. James Risen, "Secrets of History: The CIA in Iran," *New York Times*, April 6, 2000. URL: http://www.nytimes.com/2000/04/16/world/secrets-history-cia-iran-special-report-plot-convulsed-iran-53-79.html?

scp=1&sq=New%20York%20Times%20Special%20Report:%20The%20C.I.A.%20in %20Iran&st=cse.
24 Maziar Behrooz, "Tudeh Factionalism and the 1953 Coup in Iran," *International Journal of Middle East Studies*, Vol. 33 (2001), p. 363.
25 Gasiorowski, "The 1953 Coup D'état in Iran," op. cit., p. 275.
26 Abbas Milani, *Mo'amma-ye Hoveida* (Tehran, 2001). (Persian translation of *The Persian Sphinx: Amir Abbas Hoveida and the Riddle of the Iranian Revolution* (Washington, D.C.: Mage Books.)
27 Alî Fahmî, *Al-Jughrâfyâ al-Siyâsiyyah lil Naft* (Cairo: Dâr Sînâ lil Nashr, 1991), p. 42.
28 Mehran Kamrava, *Revolution in Iran: The Roots of Turmoil* (London: Routledge, 1990), p. 25.
29 US Senate, *US Security*, March 5, 1992. URL: http://www.globalsecurity.org/intell/ library/reports/gao/920300-train.htm.
30 Library of Congress, *Country Studies: Iran*, December 1987. URL: http://lcweb2.loc. gov/cgi-bin/query/r?frd/cstdy:@field%28DOCID+ir0187%29.
31 Ibid.
32 Ibid.
33 Gholam Reza Nejati, *Tarikh-e Siyasi-ye Bist-o Panj sal-e-ye Iran: az Coup d'etat ta Enghelab* (Tehran: Rasaa, 1992), I, p. 296.
34 Kamrava, op.cit., p. 22.
35 Mohsen M. Milani, *The Making of Iran's Revolution* (Boulder: Westview Press, 1988), p. 85.
36 Nejati, op. cit., I, p. 173.
37 Ibid., pp. 193–194.
38 Baqer Moin, *Khomeini: Life of the Ayatollah* (New York: St. Martin's Press, 1999), pp. 75–80; Nejati, op. cit., pp. 222–224; Asadollah Badamchian and 'Ali Banayie, *Hei'at ha-ye Mo'talefeh-ye Eslami* (Tehran: Awj, 1983), p. 127.
39 Nejati, op. cit., I, pp. 228–230.
40 Ibid., p. 303.
41 Ibid., p. 307.
42 Milani, op. cit., p. 99.
43 Kamrava, op. cit., p. 66.
44 Emaduddin Baghi, *A Study of the Iranian Revolution* (Tehran: Sarayee, 2004), p. 225.
45 Homa Katouzian, *The Political Economy of Modern Iran: Despotism and Pseudo-Modernism, 1926–1979* (New York: New York University Press, 1981), p. 159, Table 13.1.
46 Asef Bayat, "Activism and Social Development in the Middle East," *International Journal of Middle East Studies*, Vol. 34 (2002)pp. 1–28.
47 Abbas Gharabaghi, *The Truth about the Crisis in Iran* (Paris: 1987), p. 22, quoted in Baghi, op. cit., p. 203.
48 Gharabaghi, op. cit., p. 24.
49 William Showcross, *The Shah's Last Ride: The Fate of an Ally* (London: Simon & Schuster, 1988).
50 Pierre Salinger, *America Held Hostage* (Garden City: Doubleday, 1981), pp. 4–5.
51 Baghi, op. cit., pp. 229–233.
52 The text of the article is reproduced in Nejati, op. cit., II, pp. 61–62
53 Sasan Fayazmanesh, "Iran and the Experts," *Z Magazine*, July 25, 2005. URL: http://www.zmag.org/content/showarticle.cfm?SectionID = 67&ItemID = 8371.
54 Rohallah al-Khomeini, "Al-Hukuma al-Islamiyya," in *Macmillan Reference Encyclopedia of Islam and the Muslim* (Houndmills: Macmillan, 2004).
55 Ibid.
56 Ibid.
57 Ibid.

58 Ibid.

59 Ibid.

60 Ibid.

61 Article 109, Constitution of the Islamic Republic of Iran.

62 Kamran Mofid, *The Economic Consequences of the Gulf War* (London: Routledge, 1990), p. 139.

63 Anton La Guardia, "Weapons Are Secret of Saddam's Survival," *Daily Telegraph*, September 17, 2002. URL: http://www.telegraph.co.uk/news/main.jhtml?xml =/news/2002/09/18/wirq118.xml.

64 "Iran Iraq War: 1980–88," *Global Security*. URL: http://www.globalsecurity.org/ military/world/war/iran-iraq.htm.

65 Ervand Abrahamian, *Tortured Confessions: Prisoners and Public Recantations in Modern Iran* (Berkeley: University of California Press, 1999), ch. 5. Human Rights Watch, *Ministers of Murder: Iran's New Security Cabinet*, December 15, 2005. URL: http://hrw.org/backgrounder/mena/iran1205/iran1205.pdf. Hussein 'Ali, Ayatollah Montazeri, *Khaterat*, 1997. URL: http://www.amontazeri.com.

66 Scott Ritter, *Target Iran: The Truth about the White House's Plans for Regime Change* (New York: Nation Books, 2006), pp. xxv–xxvi, 60, 91–93.

67 Reese Erlich, *The Iran Agenda: The Real Story of US Policy and the Middle East Crisis* (Sausalito: PoliPoint Press; 2006); "The Next Act: Is a Damaged Administration Less Likely to Attack Iran, or More?," *New Yorker*, November 27, 2006, p. 94; Seymour Hersh, "Preparing the Battlefield: Iran's Nuclear Program," *New Yorker*, July 7, 2008, p. 61.

68 Ibid.; Brian Ross, "The Secret War against Iran," ABC, April 3, 2007. URL: http://blogs.abcnews.com/theblotter/2007/04/abc_news_exclus.html.

69 Hersh, op. cit.

70 Brian Ross, "Bush Authorizes New Covert Action against Iran," ABC, May, 22 2007. URL: http://blogs.abcnews.com/theblotter/2007/05/bush_authorizes.html.

71 Hersh, op. cit., p. 61.

72 Since 1998 the number of women entering Iranian universities has exceeded that of men, but male graduates still significantly outnumber females in engineering, science and medicine.

73 Elaheh Rostami Povey, "Feminist Contestations of Institutional Domains in Iran," *Feminist Review*, No. 69 (Winter 2001), pp. 44–72; Ziba Mir-Hosseini, *Islam and Gender: The Religious Debate in Contemporary Iran* (Princeton: Princeton University Press, 2000); Valentine Moghadam, "Islamic Feminism and its Discontents: Toward a Resolution of the Debate," *Sign: Journal of Women in Culture and Society*, Vol. 27, No. 41 (2002), pp 1135–1171.

74 "*Zanan*, Iran's Leading Women's Magazine, Shut Down by Government," *Women's Learning Partnership*, February 8, 2008. URL: http://learningpartnership.org/ en/advocacy/alerts/zanan0208.

75 International Transportation Workers' Federation, "Tehran Busses." URL: http://www.itfglobal.org/urban-transport/tehranbuses.cfm.

76 http://sedaye-moalem.blogfa.com.

77 Jonathan Lyons, "Hard Liners Set for Showdown with Protestors," *Globe and Mail*, July 14, 1999), p. A7.

78 "Conservative Courts Muzzle Iranian Reformers," *Turkish Daily News*, November 28, 1999), p. A1.

79 Mohammad Reza Khatami interview with Dariush Sajjadi, Homa Satellite TV, October 27, 2005.

80 "Qananoun-e Mamnouat-e Idamah-e Tahsil-e Kagazaran Keshvar Dar Sa'at-e Edari." URL: http://www.dadkhahi.net/page.php?op = showpage&pid = 64.

81 "Az 300 Milliard Tuman ta 300 Milliard Dollar." URL: http://emruz.biz/ShowItem. aspx?ID = 21815&p = 1. "Nagahi bar do Parvandeh ye Naft Ardibil va 200 Milliard

Tuman Pol gomshodeh dar Shaharadari Tahran Dar Zaman Ahmadinejad." URL: http://www.mizanpress.com/index.php?option = com_content&view = article&id = 1729:2009-06-10-19-19-42&catid = 6:2009-04-01-10-24-33&Itemid = 66.

82 Mohammad Reza Farzanegana & Gunther Markwardt, "The Effects of Oil Price Shocks on the Iranian Economy," *Energy Economics*, Vol. 31, No. 1 (January 2009), pp. 134–151.

83 Central Bank of the Islamic Republic of Iran, *Annual Review 1386* (2007–2008), p. 16.

84 Shirin Karimi, "When Did Ahmadinejad Get His Doctorate?," *Rooz*, June 7, 2009. URL: http://www.roozonline.com/persian/news/newsitem/article/2009/june/07//-91559cd93b.html.

85 Quoted in "Khatami Should Learn from the Fate of Benazir Bhutto," *Sarmayeh*, February 15, 2009. URL: http://www.sarmayeh.net/ShowNews.php?35103.

86 Jahangir Amuzegar, *The Dynamics of the Iranian Revolution* (Albany: State University of New York, 1991), p. 414.

87 Hamid Zangeneh, "Socioeconomic Trends in Iran: Successes and Failures," *The Muslim World*, Vol. 94 (October 2004), pp. 481–493.

88 International Monetary Fund, "IMF Executive Board Concludes 2006 Article IV Consultation with the Islamic Republic of Iran," Public Information Notice No. 07/29, March 5, 2007.

89 SIPRI, *SIPRI Military Expenditure Database*. URL: http://first.sipri.org/non_first/milex.php.

90 http://www.irna.ir/en/news/view/line-18/0508011351184531.htm; and http://www.farsnews.com/newstext.php?nn = 8606250497.

91 United Nations Development Program (UNDP), *Human Development Report* (Washington, D.C.: UNDP, 2006), p. 292.

92 Central Bank of Iran, *Summary of Economic Developments during March 21, 2007–March 20, 2008* (Tehran: Central Bank of Iran, 2008), pp. 1, 3.

93 Central Bank of Iran, *Consumer Price Index in Iran's Urban Areas, June 2007* (Tehran: Central Bank of Iran, 2007), p. 1; "According to the Central Bank Inflation is Close to 30 percent," *Etemad*, October 10, 2008. URL: http://www.etemaad.com/Released/87-07-18/133.htm#116967.

94 "Conflicting Statistics on Inflation in Iran," Deutsche Welle Persian Service, February 1, 2010. URL: http://www.dw-world.de/dw/article/0,,5200233,00.html.

95 Article 43, Constitution of the Islamic Republic of Iran.

96 Article 44, Constitution of the Islamic Republic of Iran.

97 http://devdata.worldbank.org/external/CPProfile.asp?PTYPE = CP&CCODE = IRN.

98 Statistical Center of Iran, *General Results of the 2006 Census: Country-Level Results* (Tehran, 2008), No. 1, Table 1; Central Bank of Iran, *Summary of Economic Developments*, op. cit.; http://www.cia.gov/cia/publications/factbook/geos/ir.html.

99 International Monetary Fund, *Islamic Republic of Iran: 2006 Article IV Consultation – Staff Report; Staff Statement; Public Information Notice on the Executive Board Discussion; and Statement by the Executive Director for the Islamic Republic of Iran*, IMF Country Report No. 07/100, March 2007, p. 23; International Monetary Fund, *Islamic Republic of Iran: 2008 Article IV Consultation – Staff Report; Public Information Notice on the Executive Board Discussion; and Statement by the Executive Director for Islamic Republic of Iran*, IMF Country Report No. 08/284, August 2008, p. 6.

100 Kavah L. Afrasiabi, "China Rocks the Geopolitical Boat with Iran Oil Deal," quoted in *Z Magazine*, December 2, 2004. URL: http://www.zmag.org/content/showarticle.cfm?SectionID = 67&ItemID = 6783.

101 Ray Marcelo, "India Looks to Russia and Iran for Energy," *Financial Times*, January 7, 2005. URL: http://news.ft.com/cms/s/5298223e-6079-11d9-af5a-00000e2511c8.html.

102 Scott Ritter, *Target Iran: The Truth about the White House's Plans for Regime Change* (New York: Nation Books, 2006).

103 Ibid., pp. 58, 62.

104 Amir Asadollah Alam, *The Diaries of Asadollah Alam*, Volume V: *1354/1975* (edited by Alinaghi Alikhani) (Tehran: Saales, 2003), pp. 490–492.

105 IAEA, Report by the Director General, "Implementation of the NPT Safeguards Agreement in the Islamic Republic of Iran." URL: http://www.iaea.org/Publications/Documents/Board/2007/gov2007-48.pdf.

106 "We Are Moving Rapidly towards an Abyss," *Der Spiegel*, September 3, 2007. URL: http://www.spiegel.de/international/world/0,1518,503841,00.html.

107 Office of the Director of National Intelligence, *National Intelligence Estimate; Iran: Nuclear Intentions and Capabilities* (Washington, D.C.: National Intelligence Council, 2007).

108 Zvi Bar'el, "They Stole the Threat from Us," *Haaretz*, December 11, 2007. URL: http://www.haaretz.com/hasen/spages/932413.html.

109 IAEA Board of Governors, *Implementation of the NPT Safeguards Agreement and Relevant Provisions of Security Council Resolutions 1737 (2006) and 1747 (2007) in the Islamic Republic of Iran*, GOV/2008/4, February 22, 2008.

110 Ibid.

111 IAEA Board of Governors, *Implementation of the NPT Safeguards Agreement and Relevant Provisions of Security Council Resolutions 1737 (2006), 1747 (2007) and 1803 (2008) in the Islamic Republic of Iran*, GOV/2008/15, May 26, 2008, p. 4.

112 Ibid., p. 5.

113 IAEA, Board of Governors, *Implementation of the NPT Safeguards Agreement and Relevant Provisions of Security Council Resolutions 1737 (2006), 1747 (2007),1803 (2008) and 1835 (2008) in the Islamic Republic of Iran*, GOV/2008/59, November 19, 2008.

114 Ritter, op. cit. Seymour Hersh, "The Redirection: Is the Administration's New Policy Benefiting Our Enemies in the War on Terrorism?," *New Yorker*, March 5, 2007. URL: http://www.newyorker.com/reporting/2007/03/05/070305fa_fact_hersh. Seymour Hersh, "The Iran Plans: Would President Bush Go to War to Stop Tehran from Getting the Bomb?," *New Yorker*, April 17, 2006. URL: http://www.newyorker.com/archive/2006/04/17/060417fa_fact. Seymour Hersh, "Last Stand: The Military's Problem with the President's Iran Policy," *New Yorker*, July 10, 2006. URL: http://www.newyorker.com/archive/2006/07/10/060710fa_fact. Seymour Hersh, "The Next Act: Is a Damaged Administration Less Likely to Attack Iran, or More?," *New Yorker*, November 27, 2006. URL: http://www.newyorker.com/archive/2006/11/27/061127fa_fact. Seymour M. Hersh, "The Iran Game," *New Yorker*, December 3, 2001. URL: http://www.newyorker.com/archive/2001/12/03/011203fa_FACT.

115 Nicholas Burns, "Conference Call Briefing with Members of the Press, Washington, D.C.," March 24, 2007. URL: http://www.state.gov/p/us/rm/2007/82163.htm.

116 Robin Wright, "Stuart Lev's War," *New York Times*, November 2, 2008. URL: http://www.nytimes.com/2008/11/02/magazine/02IRAN-t.html.

117 Ibid.

118 US Treasury Department, "Fact Sheet: Treasury Strengthens Preventive Measures Against Iran." URL: http://www.treas.gov/press/releases/hp1258.htm.

119 Wright, op. cit.

120 Shaul Bakhash, "Iran's Foreign Policy under the Islamic Republic, 1979–2000," in L. Carl Brown (ed.), *Diplomacy in the Middle East: The International Relations of Regional and Outside Powers* (New York: I.B Tauris, 2001), p. 251.

121 Ibid., p. 256.

122 Ibid., pp. 251, 256, 258.

123 Kavitha Rao, "The Great Satan," *Middle East*, April 26, 2000. URL: http://www.worldtrek.org/odyssey/mideast/042600/042600kavispies.html.

124 Joyce Battle (ed.), *Shaking Hands with Saddam Hussein: The US Tilts toward Iraq, 1980–1984*, National Security Archive Electronic Briefing Book No. 82, Doc 61. URL: http://www.gwu.edu/~nsarchiv/NSAEBB/NSAEBB82/.

125 "The Teicher Affidavit: Iraq-Gate." URL: http://www.informationclearinghouse. info/article1413.htm.

126 Battle, op. cit., Doc. 61.

127 La Guardia, op. cit.

128 Any account of Western and US involvement in Saddam Hussein's war against Iran remains far from comprehensive since only a very limited number of documents have been unclassified so far, and sensitive parts of the unclassified documents published by the National Security archives are excised: Battle, op. cit., Doc. 24.

129 Ibid.

130 Ibid., Doc. 1.

131 Ibid., Doc. 61.

132 Richard Sale, "Exclusive: Saddam Key in Early CIA Plot," UPI, International Intelligence Analysis, April 10, 2003.

133 As quoted by Juan Cole, "For Whom the Bell Tolls: Top Ten Ways the US Enabled Saddam Hussein," December 30, 2005. URL: http://www.juancole.com/2006/12/for-whom-bell-tolls-top-ten-ways-us.html.

134 "Kharrazi: Iran–UAE Relations Growing," *Turkish Weekly*, July 27, 2005. URL: http://www.turkishweekly.net/news.php?id = 15861#.

135 Hooman Peimani, "The Ties that Bind Iran and Saudi Arabia, *Asia Times*, August 16, 2002. URL: http://www.atimes.com/atimes/Middle_East/DH16Ak01.html.

136 Iran's military budget is less than 50 percent of Canada's, according to the Stockholm International Peace Research Institute (URL: http://milexdata.sipri.org/result.php4), or 57 percent of Canada's, according to the *CIA World Factbook* (URL: https://www.cia.gov/library/publications/the-world-factbook/geos/ca.html; https://www.cia.gov/library/publications/the-world-factbook/geos/ir.html).

137 See, for example, the naval inventory complied by GlobalSecurity. URL: http://www.globalsecurity.org/military/world/iran/ships.htm.

138 Iran publicly displayed its SSMs in 2002. In 2009 Iran reportedly tested SSMs that had the potential to reach Israel. See Julian Borger, "Iran Test Fires Missiles Capable of Reaching US Bases or Israel," *Guardian*, May 20, 2009. URL: http://www.guardian.co.uk/world/2009/may/20/iran-test-fires-missile-israel.

139 Mark Gaffney, "Will Iran be Next?", May 8, 2003. URL: http://informationclearing house.info/article3288.htm.

140 See IAEA, "Safeguards Statement for 2008 and Background to Safeguards Statement." URL: http://www.iaea.org/OurWork/SV/Safeguards/es2008.pdf, pp. 9–10.

141 Juan Cole, "The Iraq War is Over, and the Winner Is. . .Iran," July 21, 2005. URL: http://www.salon.com/news/feature/2005/07/21/iran/index_np.html.

142 "President George W. Bush's Address on Iraq," January 11, 2007. URL: http://news.bbc.co.uk/go/pr/fr/-/2/hi/americas/6250687.stm.

143 Dan Plesch and Martin Butcher, "Considering a War with Iran: A Discussion Paper on WMD in the Middle East," School of Oriental and African Studies, University of London, September 2007, p. 7.

Further reading

Literature on the Iranian revolution and the developments that followed the fall of the monarchy is varied and voluminous. The following is a small selection of sources that address different aspects of Iranian politics and society. Ervand Abrahamian's *A History of Modern Iran* is a broad historical survey of Iranian history, from the Qajar dynasty to the Islamic revolution, treating in detail the successive waves of upheavals and intrigues. For particular focus on the Qajar dynasty, Nikki Keddie's *Qajar Iran and the Rise of Reza Khan, 1796–1925* provides a concise historical review of the cultural and political environment of the Qajar era and the conditions which gave rise to Reza Khan and the Pahlavis.

The conflict between the Shi'a clergy and the modern authoritarian state has shaped a good part of twentieth-century Iran. Hamid Algar's *Religion and State in Iran 1785–1906* is a study of the state–clergy relations during the important period of Iran's major confrontation with colonial powers up to the constitutional revolution.

Keddie's *Modern Iran: Roots and Results of Revolution* gives a comprehensive view of a century of political protest in the midst of authoritarian modernization and state-building efforts. It serves as a good historical introduction to the developments that led to the 1979 revolution. Abrahamian's *Iran between Two Revolutions* is probably the best account of the social bases of political conflicts in the twentieth century. This work studies the links between social forces and political actors in Iran in great detail.

Two other major works are Said Arjomand's *The Turban for the Crown* and Misagh Parsa's *Social Origins of the Iranian Revolution*. Arjomand's book is a major scholarly work using Weberian concepts of political authority and legitimacy to study the revolution that changed the course of history in the region. Parsa's book is a pioneering study of the social bases and mobilizing structures of the political protest that replaced the Western-oriented monarchy with an Islamic republic.

Charles Kurzman's *The Unthinkable Revolution in Iran* is a thorough study of the major sources published on the Iranian revolution. This work is a major criticism of the theoretical approaches to the study of revolution and emphasizes its historical specificity and uniqueness.

The new state has been built in an atmosphere of war, intense domestic conflicts and international sanctions. In a region where a tradition of authoritarian "development" models has existed for at least a century, beginning with the Turkish modernization drive that was finally crystalized in Ataturk's "Turkish paradigm," the crisis atmosphere of the past thirty years has best served a dominating state in subordinating the interests of all social forces to its uninterrupted rule. The "security imperative" has left its imprint on all aspects of state–society relations, creating serious problems in the management of the economy, providing jobs and welfare, implementing the rule of law and protecting civil and political liberties.

Hooshang Amirahmadi's *Revolution and Economic Transition: The Iranian Experience* is a summary of economic changes and the devastation of the eight-year war with Iraq.

The edited volume by Parvin Alizadeh, *The Economy of Iran: The Dilemma of an Islamic State*, has provided another critical survey of the economy and the performance of various sectors. Various authors point to the problems created by the effects of the enlarged role of the government in the economy, budget deficits and high inflation. More recently, three International Monetary Fund economists,

Jbili et al., have published *Islamic Republic of Iran: Managing the Transition to a Market Economy*. This book is important in its explication of the strategic choices ahead of a government grappling with the dilemma of making long-overdue decisions: from removing huge, unsustainable energy subsidies to privatizing state-owned firms that consume about half of the annual government budget and the specter of massive unemployment and possible social unrest that follow such decisions.

A well-written book that explains the evolution of the state structure and its modes of governance is Arang Keshavarzian's *Bazaar and State in Iran: The Politics of the Tehran Marketplace*. Keshavarzian shows how the bazaar, as a major mobilizing network during the 1970s, was transformed as a result of the revolutionary state's strategy, rendering it ineffective. This book addresses the very complex question of how an apparently "traditional theocracy" transforms historically enabling traditional social resources into depoliticized, divided aggregates.

'Ali Ansari's *Confronting Iran: The Failure of American Foreign Policy and the Next Great Crisis in the Middle East* puts the current impasse in US–Iran relations into the historical context of mutual antagonism that has the potential to result in a military confrontation. This book covers the period between the 1953 Anglo-American-engineered coup to the aftermath of the invasion of Iraq in 2003.

Ray Takeyh's *Hidden Iran: Paradox and Power in the Islamic Republic* studies the current standoff over Iran's nuclear program and explains the rationale behind Iran's foreign policy. Takeyh's study is a major critique of the "regime-change" policy pursued by the George W. Bush administration in the early years of the twenty-first century.

Finally, the edited volume by Anoush Ehteshami and Mahjoob Zweiri, *Iran's Foreign Policy: From Khatami to Ahmadinejad*, includes chapters by experts on Iran's relations with the Arab world, the West and Iraq.

References

Abrahamian, Ervand (1982) *Iran between Two Revolutions*, Princeton University Press.
—— (2008) *A History of Modern Iran*, Cambridge University Press.
Algar, Hamid (1969) *Religion and State in Iran 1785–1906*, University of Berkeley Press.
'Alizadeh, Parvin (ed.) (2001) *The Economy of Iran: The Dilemma of an Islamic State*, I.B. Tauris.
Amirahmadi, Hooshang (1990) *Revolution and Economic Transition: The Iranian Experience*, SUNY Press.
Ansari, 'Ali (2007) *Confronting Iran: The Failure of American Foreign Policy and the Next Great Crisis in the Middle East*, Basic Books.
Arjomand, Said (1988) *The Turban for the Crown*, Oxford University Press.
Ehteshami, Anoush & Zweiri, Mahjoob (eds) (2008) *Iran's Foreign Policy: From Khatami to Ahamadinejad*, Ithaca Press.
Jbili, A., Kramarenko, V. & Bailen, J. (2007) *Islamic Republic of Iran: Managing the Transition to a Market Economy*, International Monetary Fund.
Keddie, Nikki (1999) *Qajar Iran and the Rise of Reza Khan, 1796–1925*, Princeton University Press.

—— (2006) *Modern Iran: Roots and Results of Revolution*, Yale University Press.

Keshavarzian, Arang (2007) *Bazaar and State in Iran: The Politics of the Tehran Marketplace*, Cambridge University Press.

Kurzman, Charles (2004) *The Unthinkable Revolution in Iran*, Cambridge University Press.

Parsa, Misagh (1989) *Social Origins of the Iranian Revolution*, Rutgers University Press.

Takeyh, Ray (2007) *Hidden Iran: Paradox and Power in the Islamic Republic*, Holt Paperbacks.

The Fertile Crescent

The Fertile Crescent

6   The Republic of Iraq

With Shereen T. Ismael

Iraq, an ancient Sumerian word meaning "country of the sun," is a relatively new state situated on ancient land. It is roughly the size of the US state of California and, prior to the Anglo-American invasion of 2003, the population was estimated to be 26 million,[1] growing at an annual rate of 2.8 percent. Outside of North Africa, Iraq is the most populous country in the Arab world and it is second only to Saudi Arabia in geographical size. It is situated at the northern end of the Persian Gulf, and shares borders with two non-Arab states, Turkey and Iran. Iraq is composed of four distinctive geographical regions: desert in the west, rolling uplands on the central plains of the upper Tigris and Euphrates rivers, highlands in the north and marshland in the south. The central plains are the most agriculturally productive regions of the country. However, agriculture has declined in importance over the course of the past century as oil became Iraq's economic lifeblood. Iraq officially has the third-largest proven oil reserves in the world,[2] although recent seismic data suggests that it may in fact have the largest oil reserves, as high as 350 billion barrels.[3]

Arabic and Kurdish are the official languages. However, Aramaic (including its dialects Assyrian, Chalden and Syriac), Turkish, Armenian and Farsi are all commonly spoken by their respective communities. The relationship between the dominant Arab majority and the Kurdish minority has greatly affected Iraqi history. The population is estimated to be 75–80 percent Arab and 15–20 percent Kurdish, with small minorities of Turkoman, Assyrians and others forming the remainder. The division of the population into the usual social, economic and regional groups is complicated by fragmentation according to religion, sect and nationality. Arabs are evenly distributed throughout the country, while the Kurds are concentrated in the mountainous northern region, with a significant presence in Baghdad as well. The Kurds speak a different language, belong to a separate ethnic group and have developed a distinct culture; moreover, they form a distinct subnational segment in three other Middle East states, in addition to Iraq: Syria, Iran and Turkey. The majority of the population of Iraq is Muslim, divided into the two major Islamic sects, Sunni and Shi'ite (individual degree and type of religious observance varies), while religious minorities include Zoroastrians, Christians, Mandaeans, Yazidis, the Shabak and Jews. The presence of such distinct and culturally insulated minority groups, while adding stress to the process of national integration, has been a secondary factor in comparison with the larger issues of the urban/rural divide, the Arab/Kurd split, and Sunni/Shi'i tensions.

Map 6.1 Iraq: ethnic

Drawn by Ian Cool

Finally, secular, if not outright atheistic, tendencies have long had currency in Iraq, especially in progressive circles.

The contemporary state of Iraq dates back to 1921, with the formation of the "Kingdom of Iraq," while Iraq was granted official independence in 1932. However, Iraq (or Mesopotamia) has ancient roots. The Greek word Mesopotamia means "the land between the two rivers" and refers to the lands surrounding the alluvial plain created by the Tigris and Euphrates. This area is commonly acknowledged as one of the first cradles of civilization. Ancient peninsular Arabs used the word "Iraq" for the same area – meaning "the land close to the water," "the fertile land," and variations thereof. A Kish document from the twelfth century BCE referred to the area as "Eriqa," a term which the Sassanids (226 BCE–637 CE) later popularized.[4]

The history of this area has been tumultuous since its ancient beginning. Yet it is believed that this was the first region of the world to practice centralized

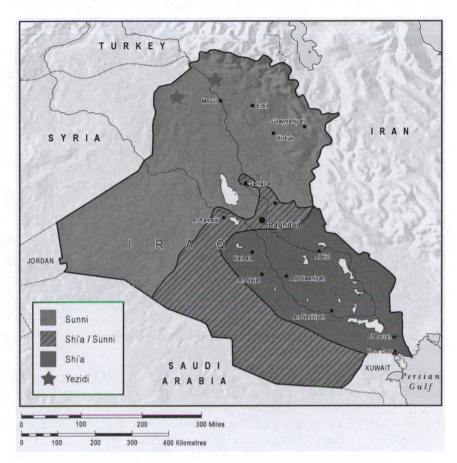

Map 6.2 Iraq: religious sects

Drawn by Ian Cool

government and it developed a flourishing, literate culture. The agricultural revolution began and thrived in the fertile valley of the Tigris and Euphrates and true commerce prospered.[5] In turn, a constant interchange of people, products and ideas was fostered. Numerous city states burgeoned in antiquity but tended to compete with each other and even go to war over the spoils related to protection, dominance and territory. Later, empires – some indigenous, others originating in neighboring lands – emerged and faded, marking the rise and fall of successive civilizations: Sumerian (*c*.2900–2350 BCE), Akkadian (*c*.2350–2159 BCE), Babylonian (*c*.1894–1594 BCE), Kassite (*c*.1680–1157 BCE), Assyrian (*c*.953–605 BCE), Sassanid (*c*.226 BCE–637 CE) and Arab (633–1258 CE).

Arab armies arrived in Mesopotamia in 633 CE and the region was one of the first conquests of the rapidly expanding Arab Empire, which was emerging from the Arabian Desert under the banner of Islam. Following the death of the Prophet

Mohammad in 632, the center of the empire shifted from Arabia to the Fertile Crescent, first in Damascus (661–750). Then, in 762 the reigning caliph, Ja'far al-Mansur, founded Baghdad as his capital, and for the next five centuries the Abbasid dynasty (*c*.750–1258) ruled an extensive empire. In 1258 the Mongol destruction of Baghdad and much of the Abbasid cultural edifice reinforced the emergent principalities until the whole territory of the Arab–Islamic Empire had been integrated into the Ottoman Empire in the sixteenth century.

From the mid-eighteenth century onward, the Ottoman Empire slid into a steady decline, and European influence gradually expanded throughout the Middle East. In the early nineteenth century Britain began supplanting Ottoman hegemony in the region in order to protect, consolidate and expand its own empire, which was centered in India. It extended its influence in Iraq in the middle of the century, and finally occupied the country in 1918.

It is important to note here that the territory of Iraq – as it was constituted following the First World War under British rule and later as it became independent – was not determined by Western statesmen. The boundaries that were applied to modern Iraq, though modeled upon Ottoman design, were remarkably similar to those that had been in existence since the time of the Sargon of Akkad (r. *c*.2270–2215 BCE).

British occupation and the creation of the modern state (1918–1958)

An historical sense of Arab and Islamic heritage, tempered by a long process of intercultural exchange, has shaped Iraq and its identity in the modern era. Iraq has long been marked by cultural plurality and this plurality has historically played a dynamic rather than a divisive role. The continuously evolving dynamic of Iraq developed into a national consciousness in the twentieth century.

Between 1908 and the First World War, waves of nationalism – Arab and otherwise – took form in response to historical and structural developments, the most important of which was foreign domination.[6] During the last years of the Ottoman Empire, Iraq fell under the influence and eventual control of Great Britain, which invaded in 1914 and formalized its designs on the state with the 1916 Sykes–Picot Agreement but was unable to occupy the country fully until 1918. As part of the settlement claims proffered by the Sykes–Picot Agreement, France agreed to forgo its claim to Mosul and to recognize the British right to rule in the former Turkish *vilayets* (provinces) of Baghdad, Basra and Mosul, in return for British withdrawal from Syria. The League of Nations subsequently legitimized the occupation by formally placing Iraq under the "British Mandate of Mesopotamia" at the San Remo Conference on April 24, 1920. A British-engineered plebiscite in December 1918, purportedly demonstrating Iraqi support for the mandate, was used as justification. While the mandate called for Britain to provide administrative advice and assistance to help the country develop its own self-government, Iraqis perceived it to be a hollow rationalization for occupation.

At the same time, the British began to restructure Iraqi society by creating institutions to support its rule. First, in the urban areas, they cultivated the religious elite into the new system of government. Second, the system of sheikhdom in the rural areas was reconstituted and aligned with British colonial interests so that the sheikhs were more powerful than ever, while acting as British agents.[7] Tribalism was built into the nascent institutions of state from the initiation of the British state-building enterprise. In 1918, the British enshrined tribal customary law into the penal code. This utilization of the underlying tribal ethic was aptly described by a distinguished Iraqi anthropologist as similar to the system that had been engineered by Robert Sandeman (1835–1892), the district officer of Dera Ghazi Khan in Baluchistan, India.[8] The British authorities formally recognized the sheikhs, who were "authorized to keep order, protect communication lines, and collect taxes, and provided them arms and funds, paid them salaries and granted them land."[9] By the time the British had established the governing council, the sheikhs had amassed enough power and resources to be included in the new elite as partners with the religious leadership. The sheikhs took on new responsibilities, too. As paramount authorities in their tribes, they regulated tribal relations and adjudicated in disputes, legally and autonomously.[10] These provisions would be enshrined in the country's first constitution.

However, before then, the Iraqis rebelled against Britain's attempt to reformulate Iraqi society according to its colonial objectives. Diverse social actors and institutions converged to express a nascent Iraqi consciousness that was manifest across the range of Iraq's religious, cultural and social orientations. In a spirit of national solidarity, Arab nationalists and clerics of all religious persuasions joined the rebellion. The "Great Iraqi Revolution," with its roots in the armed struggle in Najaf of March 19, 1918, began in the middle Euphrates area on June 30, 1920.[11] A bond was created between Sunnis and Shi'as, and "a new process set in: the painful, now gradual, now spasmodic growth of an Iraqi national community."[12]

The Hashimite monarchical period (1921–1958)

Superior British firepower ultimately suppressed the revolt that had engulfed the entire country. Nevertheless, Iraqi nationalism had become so substantial as to compel Britain to seek an alternative to direct control. In October 1920, British High Commissioner Sir Percy Cox started to implement his government's plan to establish a national government in Mesopotamia – a scheme that had been hatched more than two years earlier by Britain's India Office.[13] A truce was called, and representatives of the nationalist forces and other prominent Iraqis were invited to cooperate in establishing an independent state. Thus, a Council of State was established that month, headed by 'Abdul Rahman al-Gailani (1841–1927), the Naqib al-Ashraf (head of notables of Baghdad). This Council of State was a provisional body that was to be supplemented by a General Elective Assembly, which would be "representative of, and freely elected by, the population." It was Cox's "duty to prepare, in consultation with the General Elective Assembly, the permanent organic law."[14] However, the British "had no intention of transferring actual administrative power either in the provincial or in the central administration any faster than practical conditions demanded. Until fuller confidence in the provisional Government had been established, until it was working comparatively smoothly and had consolidated its authority."[15] Essentially, then, this new governmental structure was constructed to ensure continued British dominance.

Faisal Ibn al-Hussein (1883–1933), the son of al-Sharif Hussein (the leader of the Arab revolt against the Ottoman Empire in 1916), had been installed as King of Syria earlier in 1920 by Syrian nationalists, but he had reigned for only six months before being deposed by the French. However, the British then selected him to rule the newly independent Iraq. A plebiscite administered by the British authorities saw him receive 98 percent approval, and he reigned as King Faisal I from August 23, 1921. The following July, the Council of State proclaimed that the Iraqi monarchy should be "constitutional, representative and democratically . . . limited by law."

In Britain's grand geostrategic design, Iraq was now considered "the keystone of the upper arch of the overland route to the East, H.M. Government had evolved the policy of creating a state . . . as part of a chain of friendly countries between Europe and the borders of India . . . to be administered according to the wishes of the inhabitants of the country insofar as they coincided with strict British tutelage and control."[16] The British then sought to legitimize and consolidate their control over Iraq through a series of treaties between the two countries. In October 1922 the first of these laid out the basic features of the Iraqi government while disguising British influence and safeguarding British interests. The treaty incorporated all of the mandatory provisions and imposed on Iraq repayment of all of the costs of British occupation and mandatory rule, including the costs incurred by the British during the 1920 revolution (between £30 million and £40 million).

Iraq's constitution was ratified in 1924 by a Constituent Assembly comprising delegates who were not elected by the population but rather selected by a small group of British officials and their newly installed Iraqi ruling elite (a nascent oligarchy). It vested major powers in the monarch, while limiting the power of parliament and leaving executive powers vague. British financial interests in Iraq were removed from the ambit of parliament by vesting the power to initiate all financial legislation in the cabinet. The monarch and his cabinet (drawn from the new elite), without effective popular legislative scrutiny, were therefore to determine Iraq's destiny. All promulgations and regulations issued by the British high commissioner in Iraq were to be abrogated or amended only by a legislative act. In effect institutionalizing sectarian interests into the architecture of the state, the constitution recognized religious communities as autonomous entities, formally recognized the existence of the Islamic religious sects, the Shi'a and Sunni, and granted each the right to practice its tenets. At the same time, the constitution established separate court systems that adjudicated on personal law (from marriage to inheritance) according to each sect's precepts. Christian churches and Mandaean *mandi* (religious centers) had jurisdiction in the civil matters of their constituents, including marriage, divorce and inheritance. The churches and temples also registered births and deaths, but the certificates had to be authenticated by the government.[17] Although permitted, political parties were restricted and scrupulously controlled by the executive.

The October 1922 treaty, which was also approved in 1924, left most instruments of power in British hands, to much popular resentment. The main purpose of the treaty was to guarantee Britain's economic, strategic and military interests within the country for twenty-five years following independence, including access to Iraqi oil and unconditional rights for the British to deploy troops within the country. The British High Commission in Baghdad also retained a great deal of power, including the ability to appoint "advisors" to the Iraqi government. Although most of the lower-level civil servants were Iraqi, the top administrative posts were occupied by British nationals whose duties included training the Iraqi army; protecting foreigners in accordance with the tenets of English law; advising Iraq on fiscal and monetary policy; and managing Iraq's foreign relations.

More Anglo-Iraqi treaties followed in January 1926, December 1927 (drafted but not ratified by the Chamber of Deputies) and June 1930, all of which circumscribed some of the British control over the country. For instance, under the terms of the 1930 treaty, British advisory privileges were terminated and the Iraqis were granted authority to initiate diplomatic representation abroad and conduct their own foreign policy, independent of Britain. However, British military bases and military transit privileges were maintained, Britain continued to train and equip Iraq's military, and regular consultations between the two countries' foreign offices were to continue. The 1930 treaty came into effect on October 3, 1932, upon Iraq's admission into the League of Nations, and this is cited by many sources as the official date of Iraqi independence.[18]

In this formative period of the Iraqi state, King Faisal I encountered competing visions of nation-building. One centered on pan-Arabism and the greatness of a united Islamic civilization; another celebrated Iraqi nationalism as an ancient civilization, predating the Arabs and the emergence of Islam, while simultaneously paying tribute to the nation's Arab and Islamic heritage; and a third promoted unconditional independence under a cleric-based Islamic government. Faisal ultimately sided with the second vision. However, overall, his reign fluctuated between a desire to accommodate the British and an attempt to satisfy the demands of Iraq nationalists. Faisal viewed education and the military as the crucial instruments for the inculcation of Iraqi nationalism. Under the slogan "Religion is for Allah, but the homeland is for everybody," he built schools so that state-sponsored education could nurture national sentiment, common feeling and common purpose, and help in the creation of a nascent middle-class intelligentsia to act as the social vehicle to advance an Iraqi national ethos. Moreover, Faisal attempted to bridge the urban–rural gap by placing promising rural youths from the northern and southern provinces into training programs to bring them into the national government and the military's officer corps. Conscription into the Iraqi army also bolstered education and employment opportunities. A genuine Iraqi army was viewed as a necessary instrument for nation-building. It was to be a showpiece for the mutual accommodation and unity of the country's ethnic and religious groups, and thus an agent of national identity that transcended sect and race.

Two domestic issues highlighted the army's presence in Iraqi politics – the Assyrian rebellion and the Kurdish uprisings. Both resulted from colonial meddling with the social fabric and the disruption of the organic development of Iraq's diverse population.

The Assyrians have ancient roots in the country, but their population had increased markedly since the beginning of the First World War – through immigration from Turkey and Iran – as a result of a British promise of an Assyrian homeland, centered in the Nineveh Plain, around present-day Mosul. Such promises were made to all of the peoples in the Ottoman lands in a bid to foment rebellion during the war, resulting in inevitable conflicts over land and power. In 1920 the Assyrian leadership refused to swear allegiance to Faisal, which earned them the animosity of the new regime. Thirteen years later, the Assyrian population revolted, demanding the establishment of an independent state, but they were brutally suppressed by the Iraqi army. Kurdish revolts were similarly suppressed. These "victories" bolstered the army's self-confidence and popularity among Iraqis, and conferred on it a degree of credibility as a national institution. Before long, the army had become a locus of political activity, orchestrating many coups, the first of which occurred in 1936.

In spite of the army's success in suppressing the revolts, Kurdish nationalism remained an intractable feature of the Iraqi polity, and the Hashimite government failed to design a policy that fully integrated the intensely nationalistic Kurds within the Iraqi state-building project. The Barzani rebellion (summer 1931–fall 1932), led by Sheikh Ahmad of Barzan (1896–1969), was a response to the penetration of the Iraqi army into Kurdish territory and the Anglo-Iraqi sponsorship of aggressive Assyrian settling near Barzani tribal territories. Sheikh Ahmad's attempts to resolve these issues diplomatically had failed, which precipitated the revolt. Ultimately, he and his younger brother, Mulla Mustafa Barzani (1903–1979), were apprehended and confined to the city of Sulaymaniya.[19]

In 1943 Mulla Mustafa escaped from confinement and returned to the Barzan region. He assumed leadership of the nationalist movement and started to build alliances with the surrounding Kurdish tribes. When he felt sufficiently powerful, he demanded cultural, economic and administrative autonomy from the central government, except in matters pertaining to the army and police. The government refused these demands and the Kurdish movement subsequently collapsed amid a series of tribal rifts. As a result, in 1945 Mulla Mustafa fled to the short-lived Republic of Mahabad (officially the Republic of Kurdistan) in Iran and became its minister of defense.[20] However, following the withdrawal of the Soviet Union from Iran, the Iranian army descended upon Mahabad and restored Iranian sovereignty over the territory. Mulla Mustafa retreated first to Iraq and then to the Soviet Union.

Despite the inherent contradictions between Iraqi nationalism and British imperialism, Faisal I was able to maintain a precarious balance between his obligations to British authority and the demands of Iraq's domestic nationalist constituency. However, he died suddenly in 1933, whereupon his young son, Ghazi, succeeded him. He reigned for only six years before dying in an automobile accident, leaving his four-year-old son, Faisal II, to inherit the throne. A maternal uncle, 'Abd al-Illah (1913–1958), was appointed regent and crown prince. Conspiracy theorists have long claimed that both Faisal I and Ghazi were murdered by the British and their Iraqi protégés.

Nuri al-Sa'id (1888–1958) served 'Abd al-Illah in successive cabinets, leading a quarter of them (fifteen out of sixty) and performing a prominent role in more than half. Both men were staunchly pro-British and came to symbolize British power in Iraq. Al-Sa'id ruled with an iron fist and suppressed all political opposition. In May 1941 Iraqi nationalists temporarily replaced pro-British politicians in the Iraqi government through a bloodless coup. However, Britain moved swiftly to reinstate its proxies in powerful positions, and to integrate Iraq into its war effort. Iraq was subsequently pressured to declare war against the Axis in the fall of 1943. The May 1941 episode and the execution of the four colonels who had led the coup effectively ruined the Iraqi army's relationship with the monarchy and planted the seeds for the revolution of 1958.

With the end of the war, the Iraqi government began to show signs of political relaxation. In April 1946 it officially licensed five moderate political parties, while other, more radical parties were forced to continue their activities underground. Between March 1946 and January 1948, negotiations between Baghdad and London led to a new Anglo-Iraqi treaty to replace the unpopular agreement of 1930. However, populist mobilization against the new treaty, led by all political parties, including the underground ones, prevented it from being ratified.

To deal with the unrest, on November 23, 1952, the chief of staff of the army, General Nur al-Din Mahmoud, was called upon by Crown Prince 'Abd al-Illah to form a new government. Mahmoud declared martial law, banned all political activities, including political parties, and promised to alleviate the problems of the poor, reduce taxes and create a new electoral law.[21] Although Mahmoud had banned the political parties, they defied him and continued their activities openly. They were emboldened by the popular support they received and the emergence of new social forces that were changing Iraq's political landscape. These new forces came not only in the form of new political movements – Ba'th, the Arab National Movement, the Peace Partisans – but in the emerging civil society which rose with the optimism following the Second World War – comprising professional, women's and students' associations – that was ready to confront and challenge the old-guard's ruling oligarchy. The civil society enthusiastically embraced the promise of a democratic shift. However, a blatantly fraudulent election was held in January 1953, resulting in the return of the same oligarchy to parliament. Another caretaker government was appointed and all pretense of a liberal or democratic shift was eliminated.

In May 1953, King Faisal II came of age and assumed the reins of power. The population was jubilant over the prospect of a new order under the young king; however, it became apparent that he was still under the mentorship of his uncle, who had retained his hold of the country and the king. A glimmer of hope emerged in September 1953 when the widely respected educator and liberal Fadhil al-Jamali was appointed prime minister. His new government "lifted martial law, ended press censorship"[22] and found a legal loophole to expunge the ban on political parties.[23] However, the oligarchy frustrated al-Jamali's reform efforts (over land and taxation in particular), forcing him to resign in April 1954. With this, Nuri al-Sa'id managed to return to power in August 1954. In an official communiqué of September 28, he again banned all political parties, including his own (which he had formed in 1949).[24]

With the advent of the Cold War, the United States sought to fill the Middle East power vacuum created by the decline of British and French influence in the region. A mutual defense alliance, the Baghdad Pact of 1955, was designed to link security arrangements in the Middle East with the North Atlantic Treaty Organization (NATO) and with Southeast Asia Treaty Organization (SEATO), in an effort to isolate the USSR. The Pact's membership included Britain, Turkey, Iran, Pakistan and Iraq, with al-Sa'id leading the last into it in February 1955, despite popular opposition to what many viewed as a Western-sponsored strategy to stem the rising tide of Arab nationalism. Eventually, domestic opposition to the Pact would be a significant factor in the 1958 revolution, and Iraq would withdraw from it the following year.

Throughout the monarchical period, the interrelated factors of increased oil revenues and rapid migration to urban centers damaged traditional agriculture and rural society, leaving social conditions to deteriorate, poverty to run rampant and social cleavages to increase. According to official Iraqi statistics in 1957, the average life expectancy ranged from thirty-eight to forty years; 50 percent of the population was below the age of twenty; the cost of living had increased fivefold since independence; 80 percent of the population was illiterate; and there was only one doctor for every 6,000 Iraqis.[25] Moreover, 75 percent of agricultural land was owned by less than 1 percent of the population, and 85 percent of the peasants were landless.[26] During the bulk of the Ottoman period, land ownership had been based on a communal system in which the cultivated land was regarded as belonging jointly to all members of the settled tribes who also shared the crops. However, in 1858, the Ottoman Empire introduced the Land Code, requiring land to be registered in the names of the owners. The British then built upon this policy to leverage the creation of a land oligarchy derived from loyal tribal sheikhs. Thereafter, land tenure became the basis of social and political power in the country as the majority of the population was tied into an economic relationship in which they were subjugated to the will of semi-feudal landlords.

After independence, the state, citing Islamic law, claimed ownership of all land except that which had been granted to individuals under the Land Code as a form of inheritable tenancy. Therefore, most land was owned by the state (in 1950, 65 percent of surveyed land was state-owned), but in reality it was used by powerful sheikhs who claimed ownership and demanded settlements of their respective rights. Most of these disputes were settled on the side of the sheikhs because of their personal influence. The failure of the government to recognize tribal communal rights served to consolidate and concentrate large properties in the names of a few influential sheikhs. By 1959, of the total surveyed cultivatable land, half was owned by 250,000 individuals, while the other half was owned by just

2,480 landlords.[27] Two prominent sheikhs each owned in excess of a million dunums and six others each owned more than half a million dunums.[28]

Popular discontent rose as the monarchy failed to improve living conditions or address the humiliation of foreign domination. In addition, the rise of Nasserism and pan-Arab nationalism had popular appeal throughout Iraq, particularly among military officers. The frustration with foreign domination within army circles was exacerbated by the distasteful role they had to play in suppressing the riots of January 1948 and November 1952, as well as in the aftermath of the Arab–Israel War (1948). Although Iraq had gained independence before all of the other Arab states (Egypt, Syria, Lebanon, Jordan and the Gulf states), it appeared less autonomous in the mid-twentieth century. Consequently, the four main opposition parties, the National Democratic Party (NDP), the Iraqi Communist Party (ICP), the *Istiqlal* (Independent) Party and the Ba'th Party (all of which were illegal and functioning underground), coalesced to form the National Unity Front (NUF) on March 9, 1957. Its immediate aims were declared as: removal of Nuri al-Sa'id from power; withdrawal of Iraq from the Baghdad Pact; freedom for all political prisoners; removal of all restrictions against political parties; and support for the non-aligned movement. By articulating public sentiment, the NUF was the ideological expression of popular dissatisfaction. Sixteen months later, on July 14, 1958, the army toppled the monarchy and the oligarchic government of al-Sa'id, and Iraq was declared a republic.

The 1958 coup and its aftermath

The formation of the United Arab Republic (UAR) in February 1958 was a triumph for the forces of pan-Arab nationalism in the Middle East, but it posed a serious threat to the conservative monarchies of the region, particularly in Iraq, as its unpopular and oppressive regime had failed to address the fundamental socio-economic problems of the majority of the citizens. In response to the political and ideological challenge posed by the formation of the UAR, the Iraqi government joined with the Jordanian monarch a couple of weeks later to form the Arab Hashimite Federation, a union in which the two Hashimite kingdoms pledged to support one another in a form that was somewhat similar to the structure of the UAR. Shortly thereafter, the political polarization of Lebanon between Lebanese nationalists and Arab nationalists developed into widespread civil strife. The Arab nationalists were supported by Syria, which was part of the UAR, in their fight against President Camille Chamoun and his pro-Western Maronite Christian government. With events in Lebanon reaching crisis proportions during the summer of 1958 and threatening to spill over into Jordan, al-Sa'id argued that Iraq had to fulfill its pledge to support King Hussein. Therefore, he ordered Iraqi army units into Jordan. However, Colonel 'Abd al-Salam Arif (1921–1966), a member of the clandestine Free Officers' Movement, instructed his units not to enter Jordan but instead to head to Baghdad, and on the morning of July 14 the al-Sa'id government was toppled. Baghdad was jubilant at his downfall and residents celebrated in the streets. Scores of members of the establishment, including King

Faisal II, Crown Prince 'Abd al-Illah and Nuri al-Sa'id, were killed in the mob violence that ensued. When order was restored on the evening of July 16, the country was under the firm control of a military junta. A republic was proclaimed, and a new government was formed under the leadership of Brigadier General 'Abd al-Karim Qasim (1914–1963), the founder and chief of the Free Officers' Movement.

During the five years of his government, Qasim endeavored to consolidate his power and implement a progressive national program by supporting progressive factions, neutralizing competing ideological platforms, such as pan-Arabism, Marxism and Ba'thism, and accelerating a program of multi-ethnic and multi-sect state-building. Under the country's new constitution, all Iraqis were declared equal under the law, regardless of race, language or religion. Indeed, a significant number of the regime's ruling council were Kurdish or Shi'ite. A progressive program of nationalization was also pursued, including the nationalization of Iraq's oil industry, which would subsequently serve as a fulcrum for national development. Likewise, the first meeting of OPEC convened in Baghdad in 1960, "in response to a 1960 American law that forced quotas on Venezuelan and Persian Gulf oil in favor of the Canadian and Mexican oil industries."[29] In addition, Qasim implemented a series of land-reform policies, partially in an effort to undercut the tribal power bases of patron–client relationships that had undermined the emergence of a modern Iraqi society.

It was obvious that the revolution of 1958 would reorganize the land tenure system, and, indeed, the Agrarian Reform Act of 1958 was promulgated to accomplish political, economic and social goals. The political goal was to reduce the power of the sheikh class by limiting their agricultural holdings. The government would confiscate lands held above a certain limit in return for compensation. The act stated that the expropriation of land would be completed within five years, beginning with the largest holdings, which amounted to 8.5 million dunums, one-third of which was held by just ninety-five landlords.[30] The economic goal was to create a class of small landowners and raise the standard of living for the majority of peasants. Ultimately, it was hoped that it would lead to an increase in agricultural production, which, in turn, would help increase the country's GDP. The social goal was to discourage internal migration from the rural areas to urban centers.[31]

In 1959, the regime passed the Personal Status Law 188, which delineated civil rights that were unprecedented for the region. Family law and laws on the status of women, previously dictated by institutionalized religious authorities, were radically transformed. The laws prohibited polygamy, challenged inheritance law, eased the requirements for divorce and set the minimum age for marriage at eighteen. The Personal Status Law replaced the Sunni and Shi'a legal courts with a national and secular-oriented system that also accommodated progressive interpretations of Islam. The expansion of women's rights in Iraq was accompanied by a general expansion of women's social and political activity, earning Qasim's regime the wrath of traditional reactionary forces, namely the religious and tribal elites. In 1959, the government also licensed the communist-dominated

"League for the Defense of Iraqi Women's Rights," which saw its membership grow from 20,000 to 42,000 in a single year. A thriving civil society emerged, and was reflected in a "world of government functionaries, intellectuals, teachers, journalists, artists, the modern sectors of business, traders and financiers and the professions and, in some instances, extending to sectors of the organized elements of the working classes who consciously linked themselves to the national and international situation."[32]

Qasim's regime also initiated a "tectonic" shift in foreign policy. Within a few hours of the revolution, he announced that the new republic's foreign policy would be based on neutralism and non-alignment, a notable break from the Baghdad Pact, which, inter alia, had represented the legacy of British domination of Iraqi affairs. In accordance with its neutral policy, Iraq established relations with the Soviet Union and the People's Republic of China as well as with other Socialist Bloc states. Subsequently, there were many commercial, technical and cultural agreements with the Socialist Bloc. A major technical and economic cooperation agreement was signed with the USSR in March 1959. Through this the Soviet Union was able to extend loans and provide engineering and technical staff to build factories in Iraq. Despite Britain's announcement two months later that it intended to provide Iraq with arms and military aircraft, Iraq withdrew from the Sterling Area in June and refused offers of US military aid. Throughout the Qasim regime (July 1958–February 1963), Iraq continued to increase technical, political, economic and cultural relations with the Socialist Bloc, while relations with the Western Bloc continued to cool.

In opposition to these measures, conservative groups – such as the Islamists – began to organize themselves, and gradually the mosques in Iraq became political hubs. The Hizb-ul Tahrir al Islami (Islamic Liberation Party), an offshoot of the Muslim Brotherhood, emerged in this period as the mouthpiece for the Sunnis while the Islamic Da'wa Party served the same purpose for the Shi'ites. The opposition of conservative and traditional forces within Iraq to Qasim's government increased with his rejection of pan-Arabism, his flirtation with leftist parties, and the nationalization of oil land concessions. The Ba'thists made an attempt to assassinate Qasim in 1959 in retaliation for his own execution of officers implicated in a failed coup earlier in the year. Iraqi society under Qasim was rife with competing ideologies, including Iraqi nationalism, pan-Arabism, socialism, communism, Nasserism and Ba'thism, all of which coexisted within the traditional strata that were governed by the "sentiments of community, whether of tribe, religion, ethnicity, village or region, as well as groupings of bazaar, guilds and patronage networks."[33]

Against this backdrop of political and social dissatisfaction, three events in 1961 significantly undermined Qasim's government. First, early in the year, the Kurdish leader Mulla Mustafa Barzani launched a rebellion against Qasim's regime, and by September 1961 the rebels controlled some 250 square miles of territory in northern Iraq. The government began an offensive against the rebellion but the Kurds maintained their position. The war became quite bloody and with the apparent inability of government forces to bring it to a successful conclusion, there was much dissatisfaction among many army officers. The Ba'thists, strengthened in Syria by the fall of the UAR, capitalized on the army's dissatisfaction and found a receptive audience for their militant and dogmatic ideology. As a result, Qasim's hold on the army, whose loyalty was essential to the maintenance of his regime, began to wane.

The second event occurred on June 25, when Qasim announced his intention of annexing newly independent Kuwait. Not only was this action vigorously denounced throughout the world, but it was strongly condemned by all members of the League of Arab States, who the same year welcomed Kuwait as a member of their organization. In retaliation, Iraq withdrew from the League's meetings.

Third, between October and December, Qasim restarted two-year-old negotiations with the Iraqi Petroleum Company (IPC), the most powerful symbol of British interests in monarchical Iraq, to increase Iraq's ownership to 20 percent of the company. When the IPC resisted Qasim's demands, he enacted Law 80, which nationalized 99.5 percent of the company's territorial holdings, leaving it only with oilfields currently under production. Law 80 also established the Iraq National Oil Company, which would explore and exploit the newly nationalized territory.[34]

Internally and diplomatically isolated, Qasim found himself in a precarious position. However, his opposition was also highly fragmented, so Qasim was able to maintain his hold, albeit unsteadily, until early 1963. Significantly, the Ba'thists used the interim period to organize a coalition of all nationalist and independent groups in an anti-communist and anti-Qasim front. The American CIA, likewise, was deeply involved during this tumultuous period:

> American agents marshaled opponents of the Iraqi regime. Washington set up a base of operations in Kuwait, intercepting Iraqi communications and radioing orders to rebels. The United States armed Kurdish insurgents. The CIA's "Health Alteration Committee," as it was tactfully called, sent Kassem [Qasim] a monogrammed, poisoned handkerchief, though the potentially lethal gift either failed to work or never reached its victim.[35]

Ba'thist forces and army officers, in collaboration with the CIA, overthrew Qasim on February 8, 1963, and installed Colonel 'Abd al-Salam Arif as the figurehead leader of their National Revolutionary Command Council and nominal president. However, real power resided in the hands of the inexperienced Ba'thists. According to the party's secretary general, 'Ali Saleh Sa'di, "We came to power on a CIA train." Robert Komer, a National Security Council aide, wrote to President Kennedy the day of the takeover that it was "Almost certainly a gain for our side."[36] However, a split in the Ba'th Party allowed 'Abd al-Salam Arif to assume genuine control in November 1963, whereuon he appointed his brother, 'Abd al-Rahman, as the army's chief of staff to secure his control over the military.[37] Arif purged the upper levels of the administration of the Ba'thists, and replaced them with his own followers.

Upon assuming complete power, Arif immediately announced that the armed forces would govern the country. However, in both domestic and foreign policy, his regime was erratic. His personal admiration for Nasser's domestic socialist policies led him to nationalize Iraq's financial institutions capriciously. This led to a shortage of financial expertise that, in turn, disrupted economic development. Then he vacillated between pursuing political union with Egypt and breaking ties with that country. He ended up persecuting Nasserites. In addition, his Arab nationalist prejudices precipitated the rekindling of the Kurdish uprising in northern Iraq.

All this came to an abrupt end in April 1966, when 'Abd al-Salam died in a helicopter crash and his brother 'Abd al-Rahman was installed as president with the approval of the military and the cabinet. He did not possess sufficient influence or political experience to fill his brother's shoes, and increasingly deferred to the military. Not surprisingly, from 1963 to 1968, Iraq did not possess a coherent national ideology, nor did it project clearly conceived domestic or foreign strategies.[38] Paradoxically, though, the country witnessed a flourishing of arts and literature, and even the revival of civil society organizations, which was aided by the regime's abandonment of execution and torture and its inclination toward the rule of law.

Ba'thist Iraq (1968–2003)

In 1968, in the aftermath of the 1967 Arab–Israeli War, the Ba'th Party seized power in Iraq under the leadership of Ahmad Hasan al-Bakr, the general secretary of the Regional Command of the Ba'th Party in Iraq (as well as a former premier and vice-president in Arif's regime). However, Saddam Hussein, a party functionary and a member of al-Bakr's clan from the village of Tikrit, gradually emerged as the real power within the Ba'th Party, and a power-sharing arrangement between al-Bakr and Hussein divided executive responsibilities between the two men. Hussein concentrated his efforts on domestic security and policing, while al-Bakr took over the military, became nominal head of state as president, and was installed as chairman of the Revolutionary Command Council (RCC). During this period, Hussein consolidated his power by assuming the posts of vice-chairman of the RCC, assistant secretary general of the Regional Command of the Ba'th Party and assistant secretary general of the National Command of the Ba'th Party.

The Ba'th regime would become the most ruthless and oppressive, yet stable, regime of the republican era.[39] In 1979, al-Bakr, either by choice or through coercion, stepped down as president after granting Hussein the military rank of general. Hussein then assumed all leadership posts formally held by al-Bakr. (In July 1990, he was proclaimed "president for life" by the National Assembly of Iraq, a 250-member façade that functioned to legitimize and pass the policies of the RCC by automatically approving Hussein's decisions.)

By the time Hussein assumed the presidency in 1979, the Ba'th Party was awash with oil wealth and had already established a totalitarian regime through control of a command economy, the army and the media and other means of communication. The totalitarian state's unquestioned and pervasive oppressiveness was grounded in its status as the largest employer by virtue of its ownership of the public sector, including, most importantly, the oil sector. The state did not have to rely on income from taxes on economic activity because of phenomenal oil price increases following the growth in influence of the Oil Petroleum Exporting Countries (OPEC) and the Arab oil embargo of 1973. Oil revenue helped the party create a political economy of patron–client relations in which personal relationships and cronyism were the driving forces of the ruling clan–class.[40] Unchecked by financial constraints, and inflamed by a toxic combination of international geopolitics, heady regional nationalism and tribal parochialism, the Ba'th Party in general, and Saddam Hussein in particular, sought aggrandizement of the state through extravagant military expenditure. By 1987, this had increased to 30.2 percent of GNP (from 7.3 percent in 1960).[41]

Hussein and his associates attained total control of the Ba'th Party apparatus, the state and then Iraqi society through a combination of ruthless coercion, financial cooptation and a complex web of security agencies spying on the population and each other. Civil society and any scarce remnants of a culture of civic participation were drained of their vitality and, ultimately, their viability. Regionally, the Hussein regime sought leadership of the Arab world by championing Arab issues, especially the Palestinian question. Next, it sought to fill the geopolitical vacuum created by the collapse of the Shah's regime and the emergence of the Islamic state in Iran by invading the latter with the tacit encouragement of the United States and the West in general. The subsequent eight-year war exposed the military establishment's delusions of grandeur, strategic naiveté and ineptitude, especially given Iran's superior armaments and manpower. The seemingly interminable war also exhausted the state financially, and bankrupted it ideologically. In November 1982, in consequence of the war, the anti-Ba'thist Supreme Council of the Islamic Revolution in Iraq (SCIRI) was created as an umbrella organization that would:

> encompass all Shi'a Islamic parties, mainly the Da'wa Party, the Organization for Islamic Action, and the Mujahideen Movement, as well as the Turkmen and Kurdish Islamists, such as the Hizbollah grouping led by Mulla Khalid Barzani, brother of Mulla Mustafa Barzani . . . Throughout the period of the Iran–Iraq War, SCIRI acted as an adjunct to Iranian objectives and plans. It mobilized a number of Iraqi prisoners of war (the so-called *tawabin*, or penitents) into an organized and well-equipped military unit – the Badr Corps – that was initially led by officers from the Iranian Revolutionary Guard.[42]

The economies of both Iraq and Iran were severely damaged during the war. Moreover, their economic problems were exacerbated by a steady decline in petroleum revenue that began in 1980 and resulted in a 75 percent decline in petroleum revenue by 1986. Following the 1979 energy crisis, there was a reduction in demand at the same time as there was a surge in production.

The damage to Iraq's infrastructure during the war amounted to at least $120 billion – more than the total value of the country's oil exports since 1973. In 1988, at the end of the war, Iraqi oil revenue was between $13 billion and $15 billion, while civilian imports were $12 billion, debt service was $5 billion and another $1 billion was needed for the salaries of guest workers who had been recruited to fill the positions of those who were performing military service.[43] The total economic cost of the war has been estimated at $644 billion on the Iranian side and $453 billion on the Iraqi side.[44] The GDP per capita in Iraq declined from $6,052 in 1977 to $2,944 in 1988.[45] In addition, at the conclusion of the war, Iraq had accumulated a foreign debt officially estimated at $42 billion, excluding interest.[46] Iraq was drowning in debt, and was attempting to secure even more foreign loans to sustain itself by undertaking economic liberalization. In the political sphere, regional and international pressures toward liberalization were also evident. Liberalization included the privatization of certain state industries, the abolition of socialist-inspired labor laws, and the deregulation of private enterprise.

In addition to the debt problem, the country's economy was burdened with large imports of staple and luxury consumer goods. Iraq's major trading partners – Japan, Italy, France, West Germany and Turkey – secured a long-term loan of $20 billion for Iraq. In addition, the United Kingdom, Australia and even the United States granted Iraq substantial agricultural credits. Nevertheless, "Iraqis faced 50% inflation, empty pantries and a shortage of jobs for soldiers demobilized from the war with Iran. The gap between rhetoric and reality was widening, as foreign creditors balked at further loans."[47]

Invasion of Kuwait

Iraq's economy was in tatters. An increase of oil revenue was the only recourse, but even this was hampered by low prices on the world market. Lack of compliance with the oil production quotas agreed by OPEC was partly to blame for the fall in prices, and the overproducers – particularly Kuwait and the United Arab Emirates – increasingly came under attack from Iraq for the glut.[48] Hussein claimed that Gulf countries, prompted by the United States, were conspiring to keep down prices through overproduction. Indeed, "in the weeks prior to the invasion, Kuwait had raised its oil production from 1.5 million barrels/day – the OPEC quote – to 1.9 million barrels/day."[49] The standoff between Iraq and Kuwait, and the fear of an Iraqi military onslaught, led Kuwait to put its armed forces on a state of alert in July 1990. Attempts to resolve the disagreement diplomatically failed, and on August 2 Iraq invaded, annexing Kuwait six days later and making it the nineteenth province of Iraq.

At the regional level, the invasion exacerbated ideological tension in the Arab world between the conservative Gulf states, led by Saudi Arabia, and nationalist groups. It also precipitated the collapse of organized Arab opposition to Israel and forced an acceptance by Arab regimes of American military bases on their territory. Previously, the Ba'th Party had championed the cause of Arab unity and the Palestinian cause. With Iraq's near collapse after the first Gulf War, Israel's regional position was strengthened, culminating in 1994 with the Israeli–Jordanian peace treaty and the fragmentation of Arab nationalist opposition to the Israeli state.

A few days after the occupation of Kuwait, the US deployed forces to Saudi Arabia, and these were followed within the next three months by armed contingents from other countries in the coalition, including several Arab countries. Between August 2 and November 28, the UN Security Council (UNSC) passed eleven resolutions to sanction Iraq for its occupation of Kuwait in an effort to force withdrawal. The sanctions ranged from mild to extreme – that is, from condemnation to an economic embargo. Resolutions 661 and 665 were the most overtly coercive of the resolutions: 661 imposed stringent sanctions on all trade to and from Iraq, including the freezing of some $4–6 billion in global assets; while 665 sanctioned the use of limited naval force to ensure compliance with the embargo, including the right to inspect cargo.

Except for medicine and foodstuffs, UN sanctions prohibited all dealings with Iraq by UN member states. However, the US and Britain enforced sanctions so rigorously that even food and medical supplies were prevented from being imported, with dire consequences for the Iraqi population.[50] Turkey and Saudi Arabia, through which 90 percent of Iraqi oil passed for export, complied with the sanctions, effectively stopping the export of Iraqi oil. Within a month of the imposition of the embargo, Iraq had suffered a loss of over $1.5 billion in potential oil revenues, while Saudi Arabia had increased its oil production and global exports to compensate for the shortfall. The economic toll on an economy that was already facing major difficulties after the devastating war with Iran was very high indeed.

The American-led and later UN-sanctioned coalition would settle for nothing less than the immediate total withdrawal of Iraqi forces from Kuwaiti territory. Thus, on November 29, the UNSC passed Resolution 678, which authorized military action against Iraq. On January 17, 1991, Operation Desert Storm was launched with an aerial bombardment of Iraq. Coalition forces dropped some 88,000 tons of bombs on Iraq, the equivalent of one Hiroshima-sized atomic bomb, each week for seven successive weeks. This amounted to more explosives than were dropped on Europe in the entire Second World War. The operation was directed by the US military. Its air force took center stage for the first 1,000 hours of the war. Air superiority was established in the initial salvos, and thereafter coalition control of Iraqi airspace was complete and total. The ground offensive was initiated on February 24 and lasted only 100 hours as the Iraqi army, cut off from supply lines and communications as a result of the bombing campaign, was quickly overwhelmed. US President George Bush Senior duly announced the cessation of offensive operations on February 28.

The direct human cost of the war and its aftermath has been estimated at 158,000, with 86,194 men, 39,612 women and 32,195 children dying. Soldiers accounted for just 40,000 of these deaths.[51] The bombing campaign also decimated Iraq's water treatment and sanitation facilities, fertilizer and power plants, oil facilities, hospitals, bridges, storage facilities and industrial infrastructure. Soon after the end of the war, a series of rebellions broke out. Those in the south of the country were spontaneous, while those in the north seem to have been planned and organized by Kurdish nationalist parties. All were swiftly crushed by the Hussein regime. At the same time, no-fly zones (NFZs) were established by the US, France and Britain in the north and south in order to protect humanitarian projects. These were enforced from the 36th parallel northwards and the 32nd parallel (and, from 1996, the 33rd parallel) southwards. They remained in place until the Anglo-American invasion and occupation of Iraq in March 2003.

UNSC Resolution 687 of April 3, 1991 called for an end to the sanctions when Iraqi compliance was established by the Security Council. However, President Bush rejected the primary purpose of this resolution and barred even the relaxation of the sanctions as long as Hussein was in power. His successor, President Bill Clinton, later concurred, and Secretary of State Warren Christopher announced in 1994 that Iraqi compliance was not enough to lift the embargo, thereby unilaterally changing the substance of the UNSC ruling.[52]

Immediately after the war, per capita income in Iraq fell to just $627, and it had decreased to $450 by 1995.[53] Numerous surveys and reports conducted by the government of Iraq and UN agencies during the 1990s revealed a deepening of the complex humanitarian crisis that had been precipitated by the war and exacerbated by the sanctions.[54] The 1999–2000 Report of the UNDP Iraq Country Office summarized the situation as follows:

> Iraq's economy has been in crisis since the imposition of economic sanctions in 1990. Despite the Oil-for-Food program, the country continued its decline into poverty, particularly in the south. Food supplies continue to be inadequate in the centre and south of the country; the prevalence of general malnutrition in the centre and south has hardly changed. Although the rates have stabilised, this happened at "an unacceptably high level." In the area of child and maternal health, in August 1999, UNICEF and the Government of Iraq released the results of the first survey on child mortality in Iraq since 1991. The survey showed that under-five child mortality had more than doubled from 56 deaths per 1000 live births in 1984 to 131 deaths in the period 1994–99. At least 50% of the labour force is unemployed or underemployed; a shortage of basic goods, compounded by a drought, has resulted in high prices and an estimated inflation rate of 135% and 120% in 1999 and 2000 respectively . . . Most of the country's civil infrastructure remains in serious disrepair. GDP per capita dropped to an estimated US$715 [from $3508 before the Gulf War], which is a figure comparable with such countries as Madagascar and Rwanda.[55]

Food production and availability were major factors exacerbating the problem of increasing morbidity and mortality in Iraq under the sanctions regime. Shored up by plentiful oil income in the 1970s and 1980s, the Ba'th Party had substituted importation of foodstuffs from the international market for domestic economic development. As a result, the agricultural and domestic industrial sectors were not only underdeveloped but languished as markets were deluged with imported goods. Under the embargo imposed by the sanctions regime, oil revenue precipitously declined, and food importation was seriously curtailed. In addition, replacement parts for repairs to civil infrastructure destroyed by the aerial bombardment and components essential to increase agricultural production were embargoed. As a result, average intake had decreased from 3,120 to 1,093 calories per person per day by 1995, with women and children deprived more than men.[56]

In response to the growing humanitarian crisis, the UNSC passed Resolutions 706 in 1991 and 986 (the "Oil-for-Food" program) in April 1995. The latter was implemented following a memorandum of understanding with the Iraqi government in 1996. Notwithstanding the sanctions resolutions, Iraq was permitted to export oil up to a value of $1 billion in a period of ninety days (this figure would increase with Resolution 1153 of 1998 to $5.2 billion per ninety days), in exchange for "medicine, health supplies, foodstuffs, and materials and supplies for essential civilian needs."[57] The program was administered by the UN Office of the Iraq Program, which ensured that the Iraqi government would fully comply with the provisions of the resolutions. However, against a UN target of 2,463 calories and 63.6 grams of protein per person per day, the Oil-for-Food program did not manage to exceed 1,993 calories and 43 grams of protein per person per day. Meanwhile, the rate of inflation after the imposition of the sanctions regime increased from 18 percent in 1975 to 2000 percent in 1992,[58] and the exchange rate of the Iraqi dinar to the US dollar dropped from 1:3 in 1972 to 180:1 in 1993. In other words, the dinar was worth considerably less than 1 US cent.[59]

Prior to the start of the Oil-for-Food program, the government had been distributing 1,300 calories per day to the population by way of food rations and foodstuff subsidies.[60] The prevalence of malnutrition in Iraqi children under five almost doubled between 1991 and 1996: from 12 to 23 percent. Acute malnutrition in the center and southern regions rose from 3 to 11 percent for the same age bracket. Indeed, the World Food Program (WFP) indicated that by July 1995, average shop prices of essential commodities stood at 850 times the July 1990 level. The Oil-for-Food program successfully staved off mass starvation, but the level of malnutrition within Iraq remained high and directly contributed to the high morbidity and mortality rates.[61] In 1999, a UNICEF report estimated that sanctions had caused the deaths of half a million Iraqi children.[62] In March 2000, UN Secretary General Kofi Annan acknowledged in his report that the prices of essential food items were beyond the reach of most Iraqis.[63] The 2003 *Report on the State of the World's Children*, issued by UNICEF, agreed, stating that "Iraq's regression over the past decade is by far the most severe of the 193 countries surveyed."[64] The impact of the sanctions regime on Iraq was overwhelming and multifarious. While it pauperized the Iraqi people, it strengthened the grip of the Hussein regime over a population that had become fully dependent on the state's food-distribution system.[65]

Under the auspices of the UNSC, Iraq lost control of its airspace in the north and south while maintaining territorial jurisdiction in the center and the south, and nominal power in the north, where the Kurds enjoyed *de facto* autonomy under American protection. In this context, the Iraqi people, excluding the Kurds, suffered in a cynical game of brinksmanship between the Hussein regime and the Anglo-American-led UNSC, with the US especially insisting that the Iraqis possessed weapons of mass destruction. Bombed back to a near pre-industrial stage of development by Desert Storm, the people reverted to pre-industrial social patterns for survival in the aberrant socio-political and economic situation of the sanctions regime. Tribal, religious and ethnic bonds of community reciprocity and exchange reemerged to provide personal and social security.

Subsequently, the second US military defeat of the Iraqi regime (April 9, 2003) intensified the sense of defeat among many Arabs, who perceived it as a major indicator of the bankruptcy of their regimes after three generations of nation-building. The toll of sanctions on the Iraqi people, and the perceived collusion of Arab regimes in the destruction of Iraq, fed into rising anti-Western sentiment throughout the Arab world and sharpened and widened the schism between Arab states' governments and their populations.[66]

The US occupation and the unraveling of Iraq

From Iraq's emergence in 1921 as a modern nation state, it underwent a program of secular state-building and social infrastructure development. Accordingly, by the 1970s, it had the most advanced health and education systems in the Arab world. Moreover, Iraq's fervent support of the Palestinian cause had established it in the vanguard of Arab nationalism (particularly with Egypt's forfeiture of this traditional role after Camp David). However, these material gains, fueled by vast oil wealth, were coupled with the accumulation of state power by Saddam Hussein's dictatorial regime, with its layers of parasitic military and security apparatuses. Additionally, Iraq's real social gains were undermined by the foreign policy adventures of the regime, culminating in the invasion of Kuwait in 1990 and the subsequent imposition of crushing economic sanctions.

Shock and awe

The destruction of Iraq in 1991 was motivated by the US's desire to maintain its regional hegemony and to enhance the regional influence of Israel and the Gulf oil states. Thirteen years of brutal sanctions then destroyed Iraq's social and economic infrastructure from within. In the early 1990s, the George Bush Senior administration tasked Paul Wolfowitz and Zalmay Khalilzad at the Department of Defense to develop a plan for global garrisoning through military redeployment and high-tech weaponry in what came to be known as "defense transformation" or the "Global Posture Review." The Middle East was a crucial territory for US interests, both economic and geostrategic, in this plan. The design of the Global Posture Review rested on strategically positioning US hardware and troops in foreign areas where nationalist ideologies, antipathy toward the US and energy reserves existed.

Structural changes in the global political economy of oil and the collapse of the USSR in 1991 set in motion the political dynamics that eventually culminated in the US invasion of Iraq. US strategic goals in the Gulf region were outlined in the document *Rebuilding American's Defenses: Strategies, Forces and Resources*, published in 2000 by a neo-conservative think-tank – Project for a New American Century.[67] The report argued that "American power and presence" were essential for Gulf security and singled out Iraq and Iran as major threats to US strategic interests in the region.[68] Richard Clarke, who served as national coordinator for security and counter-terrorism in the Clinton and George W. Bush administrations, reported: "in 2001 more and more the talk was of Iraq, with CENTCOM [Central Command] being asked to plan to invade."[69]

According to a study by the Center for Public Integrity in January 2008,[70] in the absence of any legal or moral grounds for the war, the Bush administration invaded Iraq on the basis of 935 misstatements and mischaracterizations of the Hussein regime and the inferred threat it posed to the US and the West. According to "Phase II" of the US Senate Report on Pre-war Intelligence on Iraq (2008), this vast collection of misstatements and mischaracterizations "presented intelligence as fact when in reality it was unsubstantiated, contradicted, or even non-existent. As a result, the American people were led to believe that the threat from Iraq was much greater than actually existed." The fantastical claims made by the Bush administration in the United States were doubled by equally dubious "doomsday scenarios" presented by the British government under Tony Blair.[71] And beyond the highly questionable intelligence proffered in justification for the Anglo-American invasion, the legality of the invasion itself was internally questioned in the run-up to the venture. In a hitherto unpublished letter provided to the Chilcot Inquiry on the Iraq War, Lord Goldsmith – the British attorney-general in 2002 – advised Blair that an invasion of Iraq would constitute a serious breach of international law. Goldsmith warned that while international law permitted "military intervention on basis of self-defense," those conditions did not apply to the Iraq case, concluding that Britain could not "do it [invade Iraq]." Goldsmith then reportedly reversed his opinion under political pressure and provided a brief and perfunctory legal approval for the war. The Anglo-American invasion commenced eight months later in direct violation of Chapter VII of the UN Charter.[72]

Apart from primary war justifications concerning Iraq's possession of weapons of mass destruction and Hussein's links to al-Qaʻida (which regional experts, from the beginning, viewed skeptically), the Anglo-American campaign portrayed the impending invasion as a humanitarian intervention to save the Iraqis from a dictatorial leader who had killed around 300,000 innocent people to sustain his regime. It was rarely mentioned that most of the regime's oppression, repression and extermination campaigns had occurred during the 1980s, when Iraq had been a client state of the US, whose patronage had included critical battle planning assistance during the Iraq–Iran War.[73]

By the end of the twentieth century, as a consequence of misrule, war and crushing economic sanctions, Iraq was certainly in no position to threaten its neighbors militarily; nor did it have the capacity to attack its Western adversaries. Furthermore, the regime's purported connections to al-Qaʻida were easily debunked. The 2006 US Senate Report on Pre-war Intelligence on Iraq concluded that Saddam Hussein was deeply "distrustful of al-Qaʼida and viewed Islamic extremism as a threat to his [secular] regime, refusing all requests from al-Qa'ida to provide material or operational support."[74] Furthermore, pre-war contacts between the Hussein regime and Ansar al-Islam – an Islamist group based in Iraqi Kurdistan that the US had alleged was collaborating with the Iraqi regime – were, in fact, attempts to spy on the movement, rather than collaborate with it. Needless to say, repeated implications that Hussein was complicit in the 9/11 terrorist attacks on the United States, which are still widely believed by Americans, have subsequently been rejected by the CIA, the National Security Agency (NSA) and the Defense Intelligence Agency (DIA). In sum, the Hussein regime, while tyrannical, was militarily irrelevant both regionally and internationally.

The US invasion of Iraq, initiated on March 18, 2003, added military occupation to Iraq's already subaltern status. The US vision of transforming the country into a utopian free-market democracy has been discussed in a number of works. However, rather than a utopian society, the occupation has resulted in outright plunder.[75] Inaugurated with a campaign of "shock and awe" against a captive and vulnerable nation, the opening salvo of the US assault was an aerial bombardment that destroyed much of what remained of Iraq's civilian infrastructure. Thereafter, the invasion directly assaulted Iraq's cultural heritage, social infrastructure and social stability. First came the mass looting of the country's historical legacy, whose significance cannot be overstated. In the opening phase of the occupation, over 32,000 items were looted, including 15,000 invaluable Mesopotamian artifacts from the National Museum in Baghdad, and 17,000 priceless objects from 12,000 archaeological sites.[76] Calls from archaeologists, historians and concerned citizens (including employees of the various museums) to protect these antiquities were ignored, as the occupying forces focused on guarding the Ministry of Oil rather than cultural relics.[77] The Geneva Convention states that an occupation army should use all means within its power to guard the cultural heritage of a defeated state,[78] but as this was ignored "legions of antiquities looters" were able to establish smuggling networks to transport Iraq's plundered historical patrimony to the US, Europe and the Gulf region.[79]

In an investigative report, Naomi Klein wrote that the mass destruction initiated under military occupation created the conditions for the application of economic shock tactics, reversing the historical trend of national development driven by public industry. Iraq became a test case for the application of extreme neoliberal principles in the Gulf region, a "utopia" of free-market economics that could be penetrated by multinational interests. According to Klein, "Two months before the invasion, USAID drafted a work order . . . to oversee Iraq's transition to a sustainable market-driven economic system, and to take appropriate advantage of the unique opportunity for rapid progress in this area presented by the current configuration of political circumstances."[80]

Occupation profiteering

In the 2009 annual report from Transparency International, Iraq was ranked as the fifth most corrupt country in world, exceeded only by Somalia, Afghanistan,

Myanmar (Burma) and the Sudan. In a June 2008 investigation by the BBC, it was estimated that over $23 billion had been stolen or lost or was unaccounted for as a result of profiteering by private contractors, leading US Representative Henry Waxman to label the Iraq imbroglio as "the largest war profiteering in history." Indeed, a culture of corruption has enveloped the enterprise of Iraq's recon-struction. Lawyer and anti-corruption advocate Alan Grayson, subsequently elected in 2008 to the US House of Representatives, characterized the aftermath of the Anglo-American invasion as an environment where "American law was suspended, Iraqi law was suspended, and Iraq basically became a free fraud zone . . . In a free fraud zone, you can steal anything you like. And that is what they did."[81] Profiteering has become a growth industry, particularly among former occupation authorities with extensive local connections. Zalmay Khalilzad, the former US ambassador to Iraq, has, according to the *Financial Times*, opened branch offices of his consulting firm (Khalilzad Associates) in Baghdad and Erbil, and has made "several trips to the country this year" for undisclosed purposes. Likewise, Robert Kelley, a former advisor to US diplomats in Iraq, is "the chief executive officer of the Summit group which is building a $100m hotel in Baghdad." And General Jay Garner was serving on the board of Vast Exploration when, in 2006, the company purchased a 36 percent stake in the Qara Dagh oil block in Kurdistan. He currently serves as an advisor to the company. According to a Vast spokesman, "Jay is very well known in Kurdistan and Iraq and it was useful to the company. . .we needed a military guy with connections internally."[82]

However, the most prominent allegations of profiteering target Peter W. Galbraith. A long-time advocate for Iraqi Kurdish interests, he served as advisor to the Kurdistan Democratic Party (KDP) and the Patriotic Union of Kurdistan (PUK) between 2003 and 2005, assisting in negotiations with the view that the "Constitution of Kurdistan, and laws made pursuant to the Constitution, is the supreme law of Kurdistan. Any conflict between laws of Kurdistan and the laws of or Constitution of Iraq shall be decided in favor of the former."[83] In other words, he was an advocate for a decentralized political environment in Iraq favorable to Kurdish *de facto* autonomy. In October 2009, the exact scope of Galbraith's interests in Iraqi Kurdistan came under scrutiny when Norwegian investigative journalists uncovered documents linking him to drilling rights fees for

> negotiating a potentially lucrative contract that allowed the Norweigan oil company DNO to drill for oil in the promising Dohuk region of Kurdistan . . . When drillers struck oil in a rich new field called Tawke in December 2005, no one but a handful of government and business officials and members of Mr Galbraith's inner circle knew that the constitutional provisions he had pushed through only months earlier could enrich him so handsomely.

Galbraith, for his part, stands to earn "perhaps a hundred million or more dollars as a result of his closeness to the Kurds," his relationship with DNO, and "con-stitutional provisions he helped the Kurds extract." Feisal Amin al-Istrabadi, "a principal drafter of the law that governed Iraq after the United States ceded control to an Iraqi government," summarized many Iraqis' deepest fears, lamenting that "an oil company [through their apparent proxy Galbraith] was participating in the drafting of the Iraqi Constitution."[84]

Deconstructing the state

In January 2003, Major General Jay Garner was appointed to lead the reconstruction efforts by the Bush administration. Two months later, he announced his plans to hold elections within ninety days, and to embark immediately on negotiations with all of the political forces in Iraq – bringing together 100 leaders from across the country in what he called the "Big Tent" on April 15. The pronounced purpose of the Big Tent was to bring about national reconciliation, and to take the first steps toward building a political infrastructure to sustain democracy and stability. However, Garner's vision of Iraq's political reconstitution was quickly sidelined, as he was replaced on April 21 by L. Paul Bremer as the head of the Coalition Provisional Authority (CPA), which was formed as a transitional government following the invasion.[85] Bremer set out to accomplish two goals: to apply free-market shock therapy to Iraq's economy, opening its markets to foreign penetration; and to ban the Ba'th Party and purge its members from their posts within the government. Bremer's first order was to disband the national army, which had long served as the chief institution for the inculcation of national identity, especially among young adult males. Next, Iraq's state and bureaucratic infrastructure was dismantled, under the banner of "De-Ba'thification." Bremer dismissed approximately 500,000 soldiers and thus contributed heavily to a skyrocketing unemployment rate of 60–70 percent.

These two moves resulted in the collapse of the Iraqi infrastructure. The purging of these institutions created a security and social vacuum that was filled by sectarian-inclined parties and their militias. The chief parties rushing to fill the vacuum were the Supreme Council for Islamic Revolution in Iraq (later dubbed the Islamic Supreme Council of Iraq, or ISCI), accompanied by its Badr Brigade militia, and the Da'wa Party. Both of these Shi'ite parties had been trained and armed by Iran in the context of the Iran–Iraq War. Traditional social institutions (the tribal, religious and communal formations that had reemerged under the sanctions regime) were the only loosely structured groups left to fill the security vacuum caused by the loss of administrative control precipitated by Bremer's actions. The United States, viewing Iraq through the narrow lens of sectarianism, facilitated the political dominance of these and other sect-based parties in post-occupation Iraq. On May 18, 2004, Deputy Secretary of Defense Paul Wolfowitz recommended to the Senate Foreign Relations Committee that militias should be accepted rather than disarmed.[86]

Bremer also arranged for the largest state liquidation sale of economic enterprises since the collapse of the Soviet Union.[87] While he opened borders to unrestricted imports, he obstructed domestic production by introducing a set of laws in September 2003 aimed at encouraging transnational corporations to move into Iraq. Accordingly, Order 37 dramatically lowered the corporate tax from 40 to 15 percent. Order 39 permitted foreign companies to own 100 percent of what had previously been Iraqi assets, and allowed investors to transfer profits made in Iraq abroad. Moreover, reinvestment and taxation conditions were not imposed on investments, and foreign national corporations could lease Iraqi assets for up to forty years. In addition, Order 40 created favorable capital investment and transfer terms for foreign banks. Furthermore, the old regime's laws restricting collective bargaining and trade unions were left untouched, so organized labor continued to be suppressed while Iraq's capital assets and resources were sold off.

The US liquidation of the Iraqi state apparatus, and the attempt to reconstruct the Iraqi environment, was a major factor in the escalation of armed resistance. In the first four months after Bremer's arrival, 109 US soldiers were killed and 570 were wounded. When Bremer's shock therapy began to take effect in the subsequent four months, the number of American casualties almost doubled.[88] Bremer's policies resulted in half a million job losses practically overnight, and resistance to the US occupation became a compelling alternative to unemployment. Moreover, the wholesale plundering of Iraq by multinational interests, as facilitated by the foreign investment laws, represented an imminent threat to small and medium business owners. They therefore started to finance the armed rebels as a desperate act of self-preservation. The influx of foreign products and workers into Iraq further fueled the resistance.[89]

The cost of the second Gulf War for American taxpayers has been substantial. As of December 2009, according to the think-tank National Priorities Project, the second Gulf War had directly cost the United States $700 billion. But the total cost, including hidden expenses, must have been much higher. A Congressional Budget Office report released in late 2007 estimated the total long-term cost of the Iraqi mission to be $2.4 trillion, $1.9 trillion of which would be spent in Iraq itself.[90] Joseph Stiglitz, a Nobel Prize-winner in economics and former chief economist at the World Bank, concluded that the Iraq and Afghanistan wars would ultimately cost $3 trillion.[91] The human cost to the United States has also been substantial. As of December 2009, it had suffered over 4,300 fatalities and over 31,500 wounded.[92] However, this figure is paltry when weighed against what has been inflicted on Iraq.

The human consequences of invasion and occupation

The assault upon Iraqi society has had devastating consequences. The Iraqi death rate prior to the invasion was 5.5 per thousand people per year. The invasion in March 2003 raised the average figure to 13.2 for that year, but both US and Iraqi researchers found that the death rate then rose with each successive year of occupation. In 2006, according to a study published in the *Lancet*, the death rate was 19.8 per thousand people, a near-fourfold increase over pre-invasion levels.[93] The study estimated that the invasion caused the deaths of 650,000 Iraqi civilians, or 2.5 percent of the country's population.[94] Subsequently, the Opinion Research Business Group conducted a comprehensive survey of war-related deaths, and found that about a million Iraqis had died by the end of 2007 – about 4 percent of the population in just four years.[95] The American Civil War, by comparison, produced 970,000 casualties, or 3 percent of the population.

Since the onset of the invasion and occupation (as of January 2009), an estimated 2 million Iraqis have become external refugees, with 1.2 million in Syria, 450,000 in Jordan, 155,000 in Egypt, Lebanon, Iran and Turkey, and 150,000 in the Gulf states. Similarly, it is estimated that 2,650,000 Iraqis have been internally displaced as a result of sectarian violence and criminality. By 2009, a mere 96,380 of the latter and a paltry 25,440 refugees had resettled.[96] In 2008, the NGO Global Peace Index continued to score Iraq – on a variety of aggregate measures – as the "least peaceful" country in the world. Reflective of the social chaos in Iraq, a survey conducted in 2007 revealed that over 25 percent of the population has experienced or witnessed the murder of a family member (34 percent among Shi'as), while 12 percent had seen a friend or colleague murdered.[97]

As is typical of armed conflict, vulnerable groups in Iraq have been targeted by both violence and national restructuring. In 2003, with the onset of mass violence, and with the subsequent passage of the Iraqi constitution in 2005, women's status and rights have been under attack. The Law of Personal Status of 1959, which had defined the status of women in Iraq, outlawed polygamy, revised inheritance laws, eased restrictions on divorce, and set the minimum age for marriage at eighteen. In effect, this progressive law superseded the traditional codes associated with the Sunni and Shi'a legal courts and lessened the control of tribal and traditional authority. Under the occupation, however, this progressive attitude has been undermined: the 2005 constitution resurrected some of the legal powers of traditional authorities; subsequent legislation reaffirmed tribal power; and the general environment of widespread violence has left women particularly vulnerable.

Likewise, sexual minorities have been widely victimized. Homosexual Iraqis certainly faced social, cultural and folkloric discrimination and violence prior to 2003, largely due to the rise of Islamic fundamentalism. However, since the occupation, homosexuals – particularly men – have increasingly been harassed, tortured and murdered. According to a Human Rights Watch report released in 2009, "A killing campaign moved across Iraq in the early months of 2009 . . . death squads started specifically singling out men who they considered not manly enough . . . Iraqi police and security forces have done little to investigate or halt the killings . . . Human Rights Watch heard accounts of police complicity in abuse."[98] All of this has proceeded even though homosexuality is not illegal in Iraq, as relevant laws – contained in the 1969 Criminal Code and successive amendments – concern only rape, sexual harassment and public immodesty or licentiousness, with no explicit reference to sexual orientation. While it is impossible to know the numbers killed by waves of anti-homosexual violence, a "well-informed official at the United Nations Assistance Mission for Iraq (UNAMI) told Human Rights Watch in April [2009] that the dead probably already numbered 'in the hundreds.'"[99]

Finally, the technocratic and intellectual classes that had been nurtured and developed through decades of state-building have increasingly come under attack, draining Iraq of vital talent for reconstruction and rehabilitation. Prior to 2003, there were an estimated 34,000 doctors in Iraq; since then, 20,000 have fled the country, 2,000 have been murdered and an estimated 250 have been kidnapped. And while it is estimated that there are now 2,250 graduates of Iraqi medical schools each year, 20 percent plan to work outside of the country.[100] Academics were also vulnerable during the chaos; by late 2005, the Monitoring Net for Human Rights in Iraq reported that police records showed that over 1,000 Iraqi academics and scientists had been assassinated. Between February and October 2006, 180 professors were killed. In late 2006, the Ministry of Higher Education estimated that no fewer than 3,250 academics had fled the country.[101]

Oil in Iraqi politics

The status of Iraq's oil sector is an extraordinarily sensitive issue in the country's politics. Since the nationalization of the oil sector in the 1970s, Iraqi national development and economic independence have been premised upon a state-run oil sector that financed relatively progressive and redistributive social, health and educational sectors, creating social institutions that were without peer in the Arab world. However, Iraq's ongoing development was interrupted by the military adventures of the Ba'th regime, which derailed economic and social advance. Oil revenues decreased and the oil industry infrastructure degraded as a result of the economic sanctions of the 1990s. Consequently, Hussein's regime was forced to shift from its tradition of development funded by the state oil sector. Instead, it made oil concessions in the form of production sharing agreements (PSAs) to the Russian and Chinese governments, though these agreements never exceeded a 10 percent profit percentage when a barrel of oil was priced at less than $25.[102] In the aftermath of the Anglo-American invasion in 2003, the dynamic of a publicly controlled oil sector as the engine of social development was undermined in an unprecedented way.

In view of the historical orientation of the US toward the state oil sector in the oil-rich Gulf, and indeed the history of Iraqi oil, the specter of a foreign oil grab and economic domination by transnational oil giants weighed heavily on the minds of many Iraqis. These worries were reinforced with American-backed efforts to push a hydrocarbon law through the Iraqi parliament that would have upended Iraq's historical development model. If passed, this law would have greatly reduced the state's role in the oil sector, in terms of revenue as well as national planning. It would also have given the provinces the ability to grant PSAs to interested transnational entities, independent of the central government. As of 2010, however, attempts to pass the law have continued to fail due to opposition from labor unions, Iraqi oil industry professionals, and political disagreement as well as general public opinion.[103]

However, the absence of a formal law to establish a legal framework for the Iraqi oil industry and PSAs did not prevent the (re)entry of the world's oil giants into the Iraqi market. The political decentralization imposed upon Iraq by occupation edicts has allowed the Kurdish Regional Government (KRG) to grant oil concessions to smaller oil interests, including Norway's DNO International,

Turkey's Genel Enerji and Canada's Addax Petroleum, reportedly at 10 to 15 percent of the total profits, though the KRG has failed to make the contract details public. Iraq's central government, with limited influence in the Kurdish north, has been unable to void these contracts, even though the Iraqi Oil Ministry continues to insist that contracts signed since September 2007 are illegal. Nevertheless, the Iraqi government has "given the Kurds permission to ship oil to the outside world by connecting to a pipeline that runs through neighboring Turkey. In return, Baghdad gets a major share of the revenue from the piped oil."[104] This concession, theoretically, applies only to oil contracts signed prior to September 2007.

In 2008 Iraqi Oil Minister Hussain al-Shahristani "unilaterally invited oil companies to bid on contracts."[105] This measure, though widely criticized, culminated with the June 2009 nationally televised auction of Iraqi oil and gas fields, which was attended by representatives of the world's most significant oil companies. At the conclusion of the auction, only a single venture had been agreed: the granting of twenty-year development rights in the Rumaila oilfield to a British Petroleum (BP)–China National Petroleum Company (CNPC) joint venture. According to an estimate from energy consultant firm Wood Mackenzie, under the terms of the agreement, BP "must spend $15 billion to $20 billion overhauling Rumaila [oilfields], including a $500 million signing fee [interest-bearing loan] to the government [paid within thirty days of the agreement]," while the Iraqi government will pay the joint venture $2 per barrel produced, a far cry from the $3.99 per barrel initially desired by BP.[106] Total reserves in these fields are estimated at 17 billion barrels.[107]

The televised auctions – though a practical failure – were presented as a popular victory for Iraqi national pride. Shahristani claimed that he had sent a message to the world "that there are people in Iraq who are protecting Iraq's wealth."[108] However, 'Ali Balou, the Kurdish head of Iraq's parliamentary Oil and Gas Committee, challenged the legality of the auction: "We advised Shahristani to work with parliament to provide legal cover for these contracts. Shahristani turned his back on parliament."[109] Samuel Ciszuk, an energy consultant for IHS Global Insight, characterized the proceedings as a disaster: "The expectations at the Iraqi oil ministry of a rush of supermajors and national oil companies with an international appetite fighting over each field no matter what terms Iraq would offer were deeply misplaced ... Iraq's oil production development strategies are in tatters, with no clear 'Plan B' visible."[110] The initial auctions hence failed to solicit technical expertise and large-scale funding from the transnational oil companies at rates favorable to Iraq, with one exception: the BP–Chinese joint venture. Shahristani's subsequent appeals to Iraqi national pride and independence have the character of *ex post facto* justification for the near failure of his government's oil strategy. The second round of oil auctions resulted in far more substantial activity. In December 2009, the Oil Ministry's second round of bidding rights secured ten agreements with international oil companies, with the short-term aim of increasing oil production by 4.765 million barrels/day and a longer-term goal (within a few years) of producing 12 million barrels/day. Oil contracts were granted to foreign oil interests as varied as Russia's Lukoil Holdings and Statoil Hydro (at a proposed fee of $1.15/barrel), a consortium of Royal Dutch

Shell (at a proposed remuneration fee of $1.39/barrel), China National Petroleum (at a proposed fee of $1.39/barrel) and the Japanese consortium Japex (at a fee of $1.49/barrel).[111] These developments, pending approval (at the time of writing, the issue was before the Federal Court), chart a path that reverses the country's historic national-development model. The new model, provided by Shahristani, introduces two categories of contracts for the development of natural resources: "Model Gas Service Development and Production Contracts" (GSDPC) and "Model Producing Oilfield Technical Service Contracts" (PFTSC). These initially concerned oil developments in the northern gasfields of Akkas and Mansuriya, but now constitute a model for future development. One Iraqi critic, Ahmad Jiyad, a prominent international oil consultant, has raised several concerns about these agreements and also about natural resource concessions:

1   Contract duration, as per the production contracts, can be open-ended, but no less than 20 years, binding Iraqi parties to a fixed long-term contract.
2   Geographic scope granted to International Oil Companies (IOCs) could include not only "producing reservoirs" but "discovered but underdeveloped reservoirs" as well as "undiscovered potential reservoirs;" the granting of such a concession would give winning IOCs great sway over future developments in these fields and would limit the freedom of Regional Oil Companies to develop these fields. Moreover, IOCs may come to have "exclusive right" over these potential developments.
3   Provisions of such contracts would weaken national control over petroleum policy and undermine any future attempt to develop a coherent national petroleum policy. The role of the state partner in these contracts is vague, and portions of the contracts imply that the state partner would become a minority "shareholder" within the agreements, with the IOCs having a combined voting right of at least 70% in such contracts. Specific clauses in both the GSDPC and the PFTSC could reduce the state partner into a mere coordinator within the agreements. Such a trend would reverse the state's historic role in the oil sector and, hence, the effectiveness of the oil sector as a tool for national development.
4   The contract mandates negotiations on the principle of "competitive basis," hence international competition, inevitably results in the inability of indigenous industry to participate in private–public ventures. Likewise, these contracts stipulate little or no participation by Iraq's banking sector, with most banking functions related to these contracts performed by international banks. This, again, calls into question the role of Iraq's oil industry as a tool to finance the country's economic sectors, in this case the financial sector.[112]

Furthermore, 'Issam al-Chalabi, a former Iraqi oil minister and oil analyst interpreted the actions of Shahristani from another perspective in a televised interview,[113] arguing the following:

•   Since the First World War, Iraqi oil has been central to the international power competition, and control agenda, of oil giants. Iraqis suffered this intolerable situation for about fifty years, until the oil industry was fully nationalized in 1972. Iraqi hydrocarbon wealth undergirds modern Iraq and the future of Iraqis.

- The pre-invasion hydrocarbon laws are still legally operative and binding; developing the oil sector, according to the laws, is the responsibility of the Iraqi state through direct investment, not partnership with oil giants, which would require exemption or a new law by the Iraqi parliament.
- Without international bidding, the Iraqi Oil Ministry has signed a memo-randum of understanding worth billions of dollars with Dutch Shell to acquire 50 percent of revenue in return for taking charge of an oil project whose infrastructure and operation facilities had already been constructed since 1980s. This oil project needs only some rehabilitation and technical upgrading which Japan offered to undertake and finance, but the Iraqi government refused.
- Despite the dire living standards due to sanctions, the Russian oil company Lukoil signed an agreement with Iraq in 1997 to service and upgrade the Qarna oilfield through direct investment, as did the Chinese oil company CNPC with respect to al-Ahdab oilfield. PSAs, even under the extreme conditions of the UN sanctions, were considered a national taboo.
- Given the intricate international situation at those times, neither the Russian nor Chinese companies could fulfill their contractual obligations. The Iraqi government therefore rescinded their contracts.
- The Iraqi Oil Ministry renegotiated the existing Chinese contract for al-Ahdab oilfield and rejected out of hand Lukoil's request for equal treatment. The reason may very well lie in the unprecedented corruption in Iraqi and Anglo-American pressure to isolate Russia as far as possible from access to energy sources.

In the presence of multinational oil interests, and Anglo-American advisors, oil production in Iraq is – at the time of writing – roughly at pre-invasion levels of 2.5 million barrels/day.

The sectarian foundations of the new state

The standard account of Iraqi political culture in Western media analysis is the framework of political sectarianism. This has been treated not merely as a present-day reality foisted on to Iraq by war and occupation, but as the interpretative lens to view the whole of Iraq's political history, hence the clichéd and deceptive model of Sunni versus Shi'a and Arab versus Kurd. Political sectarianism is, in fact, not the natural order of political life in Iraq. The bulk of modern Iraqi history featured an intensive and largely successful program of modern state-building that integrated the country's disparate ethnic/religious communities into a national program. Iraq under occupation has, unfortunately, had the logic of political sectarianism foisted upon it; and in the Anglo-American destruction of Iraq's socio-political infra-structure of national institutions, the organized forces of political sectarianism have redefined the basis of Iraqi politics. In fact, the logic of political sectarian rule that came to define post-invasion Iraq had been presaged by Anglo-American policy at least as early as the immediate aftermath of the first Gulf War.

In the aftermath of the 1991 war, the United States embarked upon a policy of economic strangulation of Iraq, embodied in the UN sanctions regime. Implicit in the US's dedication to the crippling sanctions regime was a desire to render Iraq ungovernable by the Ba'thist Party, with regime change the desired outcome. In conjunction with the enforcement of the sanctions regime, and the frequent air attacks in the nominal enforcement of the no-fly zones (notably Operation Desert Fox), in 1998 the United States Congress passed the Iraq Liberation Act, which was subsequently signed into law by President Clinton, explicitly declaring that "it should be the policy of the United States to seek to remove the Saddam Hussein regime from power in Iraq," authorizing, among other aspects, "military education and training" for designated (sectarian militia) groups.[114] These groups included the Supreme Council for Islamic Revolution in Iraq, the two primary Kurdish factions (Patriotic Union of Kurdistan (PUK) and Kurdish Democratic Party (KDP)) and the Islamic Movement of Iraqi Kurdistan, alongside secular (though highly unrepresentative) factions, including Ahmad Chalabi's Iraqi National Congress. The stated policy of the United States, as evinced by the Iraqi Liberation Act – "regime change" backed by *matériel* support for sectarian militia parties – came to fruition with the 2003 Anglo-American invasion, with the US-supported parties parachuted into the void left by the destruction of the Iraqi state and its infrastructure. The subsequent ascendancy of the sectarian militia parties was, at the very least, entirely predictable under these circumstances.

According to Hasan Al-'Alawi, an analyst and prominent figure of the Iraqi opposition,[115] Western nurturing of sectarian parties predated the US policies of the 1990s. He claims that, during the 1980s, the British attempted to foster an alternative center of Iraqi Shi'a authority, as "the seminaries [*howzas*] of Sayyedah Zainab [in Damascus] were removed of their leaders and teachers . . . [and] hosted in London . . . it appears they [British Intelligence] were preparing for the post-Saddam era and building a reservoir of Iraqi 'Ulama"[116] favorable to British influence. The school of Shi'a 'Ulama manufactured during this period reappeared in post-invasion Iraq within the sectarian milieu generated by the occupation environment. Much like policy during the mandate period, Britain (and later the US) engaged in a project to engineer a pliable class of traditional leaders to form the core of the future (post-Saddam) Iraqi state.

In terms of occupation policy and the operationalization of a political sectarian environment, the intentions of the Anglo-American authorities were clear from the early phase of occupation. On July 13, 2003, the CPA handpicked and imposed a twenty-five-member Interim Governing Council (IGC) on Iraq. Its composition was overtly sectarian with little popular base, little in common with ordinary Iraqis, and no bureaucratic apparatus for decision-making. It was the US, not the Iraqi people, who created the IGC, stirring "ethnic and religious conflict, long absent from Iraqi society."[117] The first act in the establishment of an Iraqi government as a sectarian body became the framework for future developments in Iraqi politics, hence establishing the Iraqi state as a sectarian – rather than a national and unified – institution. The International Crisis Group characterized the IGC as:

> A gathering of political leaders with weak popular followings, very little in common between them, no bureaucratic apparatus and a clumsy nine-person rotating presidency at its helm, it is doubtful that it can become an effective decision-making body. The principle behind the Interim Governing Council's composition also sets a troubling precedent. Its members were chosen so as to mirror Iraq's sectarian and ethnic makeup; for the first time in the country's history, the guiding assumption is that political representation must be apportioned according to such quotas. This decision reflects how the Council's creators, not the Iraqi people, view Iraqi society and politics, but it will not be without consequence. Ethnic and religious conflict, for the most part absent from Iraq's modern history, is likely to be exacerbated as its people increasingly organize along these divisive lines.[118]

Subsequent elections in Iraq only reinforced the sectarian state. The first parliamentary elections in occupied Iraq took place in 2005. Voting blocs were constituted on the basis of sect: the United Iraqi Alliance represented the Shi'a Arab parties (Supreme Islamic Iraqi Council, Da'wa, Badr Organization, etc.); the Democratic Patriotic Alliance of Kurdistan represented the Kurdish parties (Patriotic Union of Kurdistan and the Kurdish Democratic Party); the Iraqi Accord Front represented the Sunni Arab parties; and other groupings were represented in smaller electoral blocs. Although the nature of political alliances in Iraq has shifted since 2005, particularly with the emergence of the Sadrist faction, the pattern of sectarian governance remains fixed. In the latter part of 2009, squabbles over a new election law for the forthcoming election nearly plunged the Iraqi political system into collapse, as Iraqi Vice-President Tariq al-Hashimi, the self-styled representative for Iraqi Sunnis, particularly the Sunni refugee population, vetoed successive election laws that he felt underrepresented his Sunni constituency. Finally, a new electoral law amenable to the assorted sectarian factions was approved, expanding the Iraqi parliament from 275 seats to 325, with 310 of those seats allotted to Iraq's 18 provinces and the remainder reserved for Iraqis living outside the country. The approved electoral law allowed for a round of national elections to take place in 2010, and underscores the inexorably sectarian nature of contemporary Iraqi politics. Electoral and political coalitions within contemporary Iraq remain based not on traditional ideological contrasts, functional competencies or citizenship, but on political sectarian interests. Indeed, even after the new electoral law had been largely agreed, "lawmakers were still haggling over such issues as how the Christian minority would be represented."[119]

A second round of national elections occurred on March 7, 2010, with the results (at the time of writing: mid-August 2010) being 91 seats for Iyad Allawi's generally secular al-'Iraqiya coalition; 89 for Nouri al-Maliki's State of Law (SOL) coalition; and 70 for Ammar al-Hakim's Iraqi National Alliance (with the

Sadrists accounting for 40 of these). Yet, although the Allawi bloc won a plurality of the parliamentary seats, the Iraqi political system was frozen in a state of inertia, as al-Maliki asserted that there had been irregularities in the electoral process and demanded a manual recount. At the time of writing, an Iraqi government had yet to be formed, with contradictory reports emerging.

On May 7, 2010, it was announced that an Iranian-engineered coalition government would be formed under the leadership of SOL and the Iraqi National Alliance, a Shi'a coalition that would effectively squeeze Sunni and secular parties out of government. Allawi denounced the proposed coalition, and hinted that such a maneuver would lead to violence.[120] Moreover, the Iraqi National Alliance, which is dominated by Sadrists, would seem ill-disposed to ally with the SOL, as al-Maliki is despised by Sadrists for leading a military assault against Basra and Sadr City in 2008. However, some reports suggested that the Iranian Embassy in Baghdad had placed extreme pressure on the Sadr bloc to join the coalition. Conversely, it was also suggested in *al-Hayat* that the next prime minister might be chosen by a simple up-and-down vote.[121] While the end result remains unknown at the time of writing, the paralysis that followed the March 2010 election, and the subsequent maneuverings by internal and external forces, vividly highlighted the fundamentally sectarian orientation of contemporary Iraqi politics and the failure of the political process to generate a truly national, non-sectarian, political system.

The failure of Iraq's contemporary politics to generate a coherent party system, as opposed to a pastiche of sectarian flanks, owes much to the erasure of the country's national institutions. Both the Iraqi army and the social infrastructure were decimated by the occupation authorities. In their place, a sectarian governing council was installed – and thereafter a sectarian government – that was unresponsive to Iraqi nationalist impulses and bound to its own narrow constituencies and patrons. In May 2003, under occupation reengineering, the US Office for Reconstruction and Humanitarian Assistance appointed Noah Feldman, an assistant professor at New York University Law School, as a "Senior Constitutional Advisor to the Iraqi Constitutional Process" to help frame a new constitution for Iraq. Reflecting on this, the late Edward Said, in a critical commentary in *al-Ahram* in 2003, observed:

> [Feldman] has never practiced law in the Arab world, never been to Iraq, and seems to have no real practical background in the problems of post-war Iraq. What an open-faced snub not only to Iraq itself, but also to the legions of Arab and Muslim legal minds who could have done a perfectly acceptable job in the service of Iraq's future . . . [T]he contempt is thick enough to cut with a knife.[122]

The constitution installed in 2005 reinforced the sectarian logic of the "new Iraq," declaring in Article 2, Chapter 1 that Islam is the fundamental source for legislation and that no law should contravene the verities of Islam. The majority of the Iraqi Constitution Drafting Committee belonged to the Shi'ite United Iraqi

Alliance faction (28 of the 55 members of the committee), followed by those from the Democratic Patriotic Alliance of Kurdistan (15 members). In effect, the "religious provisions" bolstered the authority of the Shi'ite clerics.

Paramilitary politics and sectarian warfare

The reengineering of Iraq's social and state institutions from national and Iraqi to loose and sectarian created a socio-political vacuum that was readily filled by the militias of the beneficiaries of occupation policy – most notably the Badr Brigade of the Islamic Supreme Council of Iraq (ISCI) militia – and the Da'wa Party. The power of the Badr Brigade was reinforced with the appointment of John Negroponte as ambassador to Iraq (June 2004–April 2005). Negroponte has been described as "a man who has had a career bent on generating civilian death and widespread human rights abuses, and promoting sectarian and ethnic violence," illustrated by his role in conceiving and implementing the "El Salvador Option" in Honduras.[123] Supporting this description, Negroponte brought in his right-hand man from the "El Salvador Option," Colonel James Steele, who assumed the post of "counselor for the Iraqi security forces." Negroponte's presence in Iraq coincided with the emergence of an Iraqi government under Ibrahim al-Ja'fari (Da'wa Party). During this period, under the supervision of the occupation authorities, Shi'a militias were integrated into the military, police and intelligence service.[124]

A further entrant into this mélange of sectarian politics and paramilitary activity was the Mahdi Army, under the leadership of Muqtada al-Sadr. His family can boast a number of religio-political martyrs: his father, sister, two brothers and father-in-law were all assassinated by the Hussein regime. With the fall of Hussein, al-Sadr took the leadership position among a mass of destitute Shi'ites which he eventually marshaled into the well-organized al-Sadr Movement, primarily based in "Sadr City," a section of Baghdad slums that was previously the location of "Revolution City" under Qasim before being known as "Saddam City." It is also well represented in southern Iraq, particularly in the city of Basra. The Mahdi Army has approximately 60,000 volunteers, who are involved in social welfare, policing, religious enforcement and paramilitary activities.

Muqtada al-Sadr and the Mahdi Army have proven to be problematic in contemporary Iraqi politics. With a position of uncompromising opposition to the Anglo-American occupation, al-Sadr presented himself as a pious Muslim and Iraqi nationalist. His ties to the Iranian regime, relative to those of the ISCI and the Da'wa Party, are not extensive; hence the Mahdi Army is less open to accusations of being an Iranian puppet. Conversely, and in spite of al-Sadr's nationalist claims, the Mahdi Army has been implicated in sectarian violence. In the aftermath of the bombing of the Shi'ite Imam Mohammad al-'Askary Mosque in February 2006, the Mahdi Army – along with the Badr Brigade – was implicated in widescale retributive killings. The period of 2005 through 2006 represented the height of the intercommunal violence, particularly in Baghdad, where Shi'ite paramilitaries waged a violent terrorist campaign, effectively purging Sunni populations from mixed communities and transforming Baghdad into a Shi'ite-majority city carved into homogeneous enclaves based on sect. However, in 2008, the prominence of the Sadrist Movement began to decline as it came into direct conflict with the Iraqi army, mainly its Badr forces, who assaulted the Mahdi bastions in Basra from March 25 to 30, with the aid of Anglo-American firepower. A ceasefire was brokered by Iran and shortly afterwards US planes bombarded Sadr City and intensified efforts to eliminate al-Sadr and his army. Iran arranged a second ceasefire, providing evidence of its prodigious influence within Iraq.

Amid the mayhem of intercommunal violence that threatened to make Iraq ungovernable, American occupation authorities went ahead with a new strategy of "military surge," which saw a reinforcement of US troop levels in Iraq. At the internal level, the surge policy involved the cooption of indigenous forces into the American orbit, namely the so-called "awakening councils" of al-Anbar – a network of Sunni-based tribes – who were armed by the occupation authorities to form a 90,000-plus force of "Iraqi Security Volunteers" (ISVs). In 2008, the US budgeted $150 million to distribute among the Sunni tribal groups. Their cooption brought initial security gains, but these forces have traditionally undermined Middle Eastern state-building through tribalism, warlordism and sectarianism. Indeed, even as the surge was being celebrated as a turning point in the occupation, a senior US military advisor conceded that "We're not thinking through the impact of abetting further corruption and perpetuation [of] tribal power."[125] In the analysis of Chas Freeman, former US ambassador to Saudi Arabia, the policy "Essentially [provided] support [for] a quasi-feudal devolution of authority to armed enclaves, which exist at the expense of central government authority . . . Those we are arming and training are arming and training themselves not to facilitate our objectives but to pursue their own objectives vis-à-vis other Iraqis. It means that the sectarian and ethnic conflicts that are now suppressed are likely to burst out with even greater ferocity in the future."[126] Hence, a policy ostensibly designed to curb sectarian violence created a heavily armed tribal faction, further reinforcing the complex of sectarian militias as the basis of party politics in Iraq. Indeed, in the elections conducted in January 2009, the political wing of the awakening militias won a plurality of the seats in Anbar Province, reinforcing the tribal/sectarian composition of Iraqi politics.

As for the much-vaunted "success" of the surge, research conducted by the University of California suggests that much of this has been achieved through ethnic violence – that is, the "cleansing" of Iraq's formerly mixed neighborhoods reduced available targets, so the number of killings declined: "If the surge had truly 'worked,' we would expect to see a steady increase in night-light output over time . . . Instead, we found that the night-light signature diminished in only certain neighborhoods, and the pattern appears to be associated with ethno-sectarian violence and neighborhood ethnic cleansing."[127]

In any case, while violence has decreased from its apocalyptic levels of 2005–2006, conditions on the ground remain extremely volatile and mass terror attacks continue to abound. In October 2009, twin car bombs were detonated at the Iraqi Ministry of Justice and the Baghdad Provincial Council building, killing 155 and injuring over 700. The Islamic State of Iraq group claimed responsibility, although, as with much violence in Iraq, the credibility of this claim has been contested.[128] Government infrastructure was targeted again on December 8, as multiple car bombs exploded near the Finance, Foreign and Justice ministries, killing 127 and injuring over 400.[129]

The process of retribalization represents an extension of the scope of sectarianism embodied in the occupation policy of legitimizing and empowering dogmatic and rigid social groups. From the constitution of the "sovereign" Iraqi government to the tribal cooption embodied in the surge, this policy has established the framework for the political dynamic of occupied Iraq. Indeed, in June 2009 the Iraqi parliament initiated a process to formalize this retribalization, drafting a bill to revise Article 45 of the constitution, which would reactivate the formal legitimacy of the clans and tribal chiefs, potentially providing legal authority for tribal administration in matters concerning religion and law. According to Minister of Tribal Affairs Mohammad Abbas al-'Ureybi, the 1,150 tribal chieftains would be integrated into the processes of "security," state-building and the establishment of a constitutional framework for tribal power.[130] Iraqis' attitudes toward tribalism appear ambivalent, especially as many tribal leaders are educated and members of wider professional associations and older civil networks. The contemporary function of the tribe is focused on social solidarity and welfare in the absence of a functioning state. The central government, weak as it may be, is accordingly concerned by the reemergence of the tribe and its effects on the macro-level of governance. These same reasons make them acceptable (or the lesser evil) to many secular Iraqi nationalists, especially as tribes cross sectarian and even ethnic divides and have largely transcended basing themselves on old genealogies alone. One view that is gaining credence centers on the notion that any future democratic state should take into account the need to incorporate, rather than eliminate, the tribal infrastructure.

Kurdish nationalism and the creation of the Kurdish Regional Government

The Kurds constitute about 20 percent of Iraq's population. They are a non-Arab community and form a distinct cultural enclave concentrated in Iraq's northern provinces. Since the foundation of the Iraqi state in 1921, their integration into the national project has been a major challenge. The state recognized the Kurds' cultural differences and enshrined the right to use the Kurdish language in schools and the media in some of its earliest policies and constitutional arrangements. However, the challenge to integrate the Kurds within the Iraqi national project has frequently been undermined by the parochial and ethnocentric dogmatism of Arab nationalism. This was marked by successive clashes between the Arab and Kurdish nationalist drive in the second half of the twentieth century. Under the hegemony of various Arab nationalist regimes, Kurdish nationalism was increasingly inflamed by the state's arrogance and oppression. This clash between Kurdish nationalism and the prerogatives of the Iraqi state reached its peak during Saddam Hussein's reign, culminating in the brutal Anfal operations of 1987–1988. The

Anfal campaign left between 150,000 and 200,000 people killed or missing, while 1,000 villages were razed and hundreds of thousands were displaced.

Following the First World War, officials in Baghdad agreed to honor League of Nations recommendations that the Kurds should be allowed cultural freedom if they agreed to become part of the newly independent state of Iraq. Nevertheless, since 1927, the Iraqi Kurds have been in a state of revolution, on and off, calling for secession, independence or various degrees of autonomy. Baghdad, lacking experience and tolerance, vacillated on putting any guarantees to the Kurds in writing, and elements of a Kurdish national movement, in alliance with Kurdish tribal leaders, began to appear in the 1930s. As we have seen, the movement was suppressed by the central government, before being rekindled for a short time in the 1940s by Mulla Mustafa Barzani. He was invited to return in 1959 after the Qasim revolution, and his Kurdish Democratic Party (KDP) successfully articulated, for the first time, a clear program for the development of the Kurdish areas and called for increased Kurdish representation in the important educational and governmental apparatus of the young Iraqi state. Thus, the Kurds attempted to seize the opportunity to speed the pace of change by cooperating with the new regime. To some extent, this was successful, as Qasim went further than preceding governments in granting and recognizing certain Kurdish rights. The Iraqi provisional constitution of 1958 declared that Arabs and Kurds were partners in the Iraqi nation, and the permanent constitution guaranteed the national rights of Kurds within the framework of the entity of Iraq. Furthermore, Qasim legalized the KDP in February 1960, and expressed a desire to improve relations through a continuing dialogue. The government's platforms and program paid lip-service to democratic principles and expressed support for Kurdish political rights. Meanwhile, the KDP continued to be led by tribal conservatives who kept its activities within the geographical boundaries of modern Iraq while expanding contacts with the West.

Friction between Qasim and Barzani, initially of a personal nature, spilled over into a political confrontation over local autonomy within Iraq. Qasim responded with oppression, which was met with armed Kurdish resistance in September 1961. Thus began more than a decade of escalating violence between Kurdish nationalists under Barzani and successive Iraqi governments. The conflict intensified with Turkish, Iranian and even Israeli support for Kurdish elements in Iraq in a bid to undermine the central government in Baghdad.

The Kurds and the Ba'th Party have therefore had a long, stormy and often violent history. Each has intensely distrusted the other's motives and intentions: the Ba'th Party distrusted the Kurds because of their specific demands and secessionist desires; and the Kurds were fearful of the party's pan-Arab ideology, especially the proposal to enter a tripartite union with the UAR and Syria after 1963. At the same time, though, the Ba'thists offered more to the Kurds than any previous regime had.

When the Ba'thists returned to power in 1968, the resolution of the conflict by peaceful means was declared a major goal of the regime, but the mutual suspicion outweighed any constructive efforts on either side. The Ba'thists sided with an anti-Barzani faction of the KDP, while Barzani received support from Iran, Israel and the US. Thus, the Kurdish problem developed important international dimensions. Through the late 1960s, the conflict became bloodier, more intense and increasingly entrenched. By 1970, the squabbling within the KDP and the war-weariness of the Kurds forced Barzani to accept Ba'th peace proposals. An agreement was drawn up in March 1970 that gave the Kurds autonomy in their areas, including their own executive and legislature, as the central government began a rebuilding process. It also called for a three-year transitional period, which saw the regime establish a firm grip over the entire country, albeit amid further internationalization of the Kurdish issue. By the conclusion of the transitional period, in March 1973, Baghdad, now confident of its grip on domestic politics, attempted to expand its control in Kurdish areas.

Iran, the US and Israel urged Barzani to demand more than the Ba'th were prepared to give. A number of arguments developed, such as Baghdad's refusal to consider Barzani's candidate for vice-president and difficulties concerning the exact boundaries of the autonomous Kurdish territory. These tensions erupted into open hostilities, leading to Baghdad's unilateral implementation of the agreement in March 1973. By establishing the legislature and the Kurdish Executive Council, and by filling both with members who supported closer ties with the Ba'th government, the central government forced the hand of Barzani. He rejected the government's actions and retreated to his mountain stronghold to organize resistance. Full-scale conflict began in April 1974. With heavy American, Israeli and Iranian moral, financial and materiel assistance to the KDP, the conflict proved to be bloody and costly, with both sides suffering large casualties over the next two years. The Algiers Agreement of March 1975, signed by the new Iraqi vice-president Saddam Hussein and the Shah of Iran, left the Kurds isolated, with no outside help with which to face the Iraqi regime. It gave Baghdad the time it needed to extend its influence over northwestern Iraq, which it subsequently succeeded in doing.

The central government attempted to resettle entire Kurdish communities southward into Arab areas, while moving Arabs northward in an effort to create a *cordon sanitaire* between Kurdish areas and Iraq's borders with Iran and Turkey. While the exact number of Kurds that were resettled is unknown, it is clear that tens of thousands of people were removed from their villages, which were subsequently destroyed. This and army actions (including the use of gas and numerous human rights violations) heightened Kurdish nationalist sentiment. However, with Barzani forced to leave the country in 1975, his death in the US in 1979 and the Iranian revolution, the Kurdish leadership found itself in disarray and unable to mount effective opposition to government measures.

The Iran–Iraq War gave the Kurds an opportunity to press Baghdad once more on the issue of autonomy, because Kurdish military action against the government diverted troops from the main front against Iran. At the time, the KDP had fragmented, but one of its offshoots, the Patriotic Union of Kurdistan (PUK), led by Jalal Talabani, gradually emerged as the main Kurdish opponent to Iraq's centralized rule. By 1983, the PUK and the Ba'th Party were weary of fighting each other, and they entered into a ceasefire agreement. Baghdad agreed to some PUK demands for halting the Arabization of Kurdish areas and agreed to discuss others. However, it seems that both Talabani and Hussein viewed the agreement as nothing more than short-term breathing space.

The Kurdish nationalist movement of the late 1980s continued to be full of division and internal wrangling. The loss of the charismatic leadership of Barzani and the coopting of Kurdish elements by the Ba'th Party destroyed the movement's unity and, to a certain extent, its strength. However, massive Iraqi army operations, including the use of poison gas in 1987 and 1988, which resulted in thousands of deaths, further radicalized dissent among the Kurds and drew the opposing groups together. In May 1988, the Iraqi Kurdistan Front, a coalition of seven parties dominated by the PUK and KDP was formed.

The occupation of Kuwait in 1990, and the consequent relocation of men and equipment there to face the UN coalition, relieved the Kurdish areas of the heavy military deployment that had been stationed in the north. Taking advantage of this, the Kurdish guerrillas were able to remobilize and set up cell networks in the Kurdish towns to harass Iraqi forces and reestablish a Kurdish presence in the urban areas. When the Iraqi army left Kuwait in defeat and the rebellion against Hussein's rule took shape in the south, the Kurdish guerrillas occupied several key towns and advanced on the oil-rich city of Kirkuk. The pro-government Kurdish militia switched sides in support of the new Kurdish coalition. However, the uprising lacked outside support (except for indirect help from Iran) and failed to solicit massive army defections, so it proved a short-lived affair. In spite of its recent crushing defeat at the hands of the coalition, Hussein's regime still possessed a multi-layered secret police, the 500,000-strong "People's Army," the 15,000 hand-picked men of the Presidential Guard, and the third of the army that was not deployed in Kuwait. These forces quickly regained control of the Kurdish urban areas, sending the guerrillas into the mountains bordering Turkey and Iran and displacing several hundred thousand civilians.

UN Security Council Resolution 688 was adopted in response to this action, which authorized the US, Britain and France to impose a no-fly zone above the 36th parallel and establish a "safe haven" in Kurdish areas. The Iraqi army was forced to withdraw from Kurdish towns and much of the countryside. They were followed in turn by state security and Ba'th Party officials. Thereafter, the Kurds lived largely outside of Hussein's control, although they had to endure his economic blockade and his constant threats that he would regain control of the north. In May 1992, the Iraqi Kurdistan Front organized elections for a Kurdish legislature. These resulted in a virtual dead heat between the two major parties, leading to the formation of a coalition government. Real power, however, continued to rest with the two party leaders, Massoud Barzani (who had assumed leadership of the KDP on his father Mulla Mustafa's death in 1979) and Talabani, and their respective militias. Following the elections, the two leaders jointly controlled Iraq's Kurdish enclave. However, the region, and their relationship, proved highly unstable. Despite nominal support from Western air forces, the Kurds had to deal with Iraqi ground forces attempting to reestablish Baghdad's sovereignty over the region, Turkish army raids against PKK rebels who would slip across the border from Turkey, as well as communal fighting between forces allied to the two main factions. Joint administration proved tenuous, and collapsed entirely in 1994 amid increased factionalism. Disagreements centered on the distribution of KDP border revenues from an illicit diesel fuel trade with Turkey, and control of the capital Erbil, as well as control over development of the region economically and politically. Barzani's forces even fought alongside Iraqi troops in order to retake the capital from Talabani's forces, which had managed to capture it in August 1996. Further complicating matters, the KDP aligned itself with the Turkish forces attacking PKK strongholds in the region. Ultimately a ceasefire agreement brokered by Western diplomats and the Turkish government paved the way for negotiations between Turkey, Barzani and Talabani.

Subsequently, Barzani and Talabani were invited to Washington in September 1998. In an effort to reconcile the two factions, US Secretary of State Madeleine Albright facilitated their signing of the Washington Agreement. This allowed them to take steps toward a joint federal administration in northern Iraq. However, the secret talks in Washington did not address Turkish concerns nor clearly out-line the Western position on the future of the region. Iraqi sovereignty was not respected, and the Turkish government was so upset about being left out of the process that it demanded a further round of negotiations in Ankara. These resulted in a joint statement by London, Ankara and Washington in November 1998. The statement cemented the Washington Agreement and recognized Turkey's sensitivity to the affairs of northern Iraq and the two countries' Kurdish populations. The principal problems Turkey had expressed with the Washington Agreement – Turkish exclusion and talk of a federated Iraq in which Kurdish autonomy would be assured – were addressed as Ankara was centrally involved in the second round of negotiations and American and KDP negotiators assured the Turkish government that such a federation would not be placed on the agenda until a democratic government was in place in Iraq. With Turkish fears assuaged, and the weakening of the PKK with the Turkish capture and trial of its leader Abdullah Ocalan in November 1998, a period of calm and reconciliation appeared at hand.

However, the major factions have not made progress toward creating a more stable political union or democratizing their respective movements. The launch of KurdSat TV by Talabani in January 2000, to counter the KDP's Kurdistan TV, which began broadcasting in 1998, continued the fragmentation of Iraqi Kurdish society. By the end of March 2000, both the Foreign Ministry in Ankara and the Turkish army were expressing continued concern to a visiting KDP delegation over the possible emergence of a Kurdish state in northern Iraq. Stressing the importance of Iraq's unity, the Foreign Ministry "reiterated that the problem of the northern Iraqi Kurds should be solved within the national territory of Iraq."[131]

Meanwhile, Talabani was not only lobbying the US to overthrow Saddam Hussein but was seeking US support for a federated Iraq in which Kurds would enjoy *de facto*, if not *de jure*, independence from Baghdad. This finally materialized in the new Iraqi constitution of 2005, which outlined the legal framework for a federal Iraq in Articles 113–127.[132] However, while a federal Iraq may safeguard Kurdish society from the high-handedness of the Baghdad government that the Kurds have endured since the early 1960s, the Kurds' territory remains not only landlocked but surrounded by powerful states with their own large Kurdish minorities – Turkey, Iran and Syria. Therefore, to shore up Iraqi Kurdistan's autonomy, Kurdish leaders – particularly Talabani – have campaigned intensively to present themselves as reliable allies of the West and the US. Talabani's position was inadvertently strengthened by Turkey, when its government denied the use of its territory to wage war against Hussein's regime. Instead, the US used Iraqi Kurdistan as its launching point, and then enlisted the assistance of Peshmerga fighters, who captured Kirkuk and Mosul from Hussein's troops during the US invasion.[133]

In the arena of Iraq's politics, an alliance of Kurdish parties came second in the national election held in January 2005, winning 77 seats in the newly formed parliament. In April, Talabani was elected president of Iraq by MPs; two months later, Barzani became president of the Kurdish autonomous region. At the end of the year, the Kurdish Regional Government (KRG) openly welcomed foreign firms who wished to exploit the region's oil resources. This announcement raised suspicions among both Sunnis and Shi'ites in Iraq (as well as within Turkey) of Kurdish secessionist designs.[134] Some Kurds, such as Foreign Minister Hoshyar Zebari, occupy important cabinet offices in the federal Iraqi government. However, real influence and power still rest with those in command of the militias, such as the Badr Corps, the tribal armed councils of Nouri al-Maliki and the Peshmerga, the highest-ranking military personnel, and the heads of security and intelligence apparatuses – that is, those who have access to arms.

Both Talabani and Barzani are pushing the claim to make oil-rich Kirkuk part of Kurdistan. If this were to happen, 40 percent of Iraq's oil production[135] would be lost to an autonomous Kurdistan. The KRG has been busy reversing Hussein's attempt to swamp the area with non-Kurdish migrants by forcing Arabs and other non-Kurdish elements out of Kirkuk in anticipation of a "status referendum" on the Kurdish regions within the disputed provinces. These efforts have disturbed Turkey, which sees itself as a guardian of the Turkman community in Kirkuk, and thus has set the stage for conflict. The situation worsened when al-Maliki visited Ankara and signed a Memorandum of Understanding with Prime Minister Recep Erdogan on August 7, 2007. The Memorandum identified the PKK as a terrorist organization that must be fought by the cooperative efforts of Iraq and Turkey.

Economically, Iraqi Kurdistan has profited greatly from US intervention ever since the 1991 war. The standard of living has been raised, foreign investment increased and modern infrastructure built to attract oil executives, foreign politicians and even tourists to the region. Foreign investment was estimated to be $6 billion in 2007, 80 percent of which belongs to 380 Turkish companies out of a total of 500 foreign investors. Two modern airports, in Erbil and Sulaymaniya, have been constructed by Turkish companies. They cost $350 million and $300 million, respectively. Turkey is also building a new university campus in Sulaymaniya at a cost of approximately $260 million.[136]

Politically, however, Iraqi Kurdistan remains tribal. President Barzani's powers are so poorly defined that his authority is quite arbitrary, which has led to a lack of accountability and restrictions on freedom of the press. Tales of corruption, abuse, mismanagement and nepotism continue to raise eyebrows in the West, across the Middle East and even in politically jaded Iraq. Barzani's nephew, Nechervan Barzani, became the prime minister of the KRG, overseeing about forty ministries, while his son, Masrour Barzani, became head of intelligence. The PUK has displayed similar nepotism: Talabani's wife, Hero Khan, runs the satellite TV station, one of his sons manages intelligence operations of the PUK, and the other represents the KRG lobby in Washington. Meanwhile, in the Iraqi cabinet, Barzani's uncle, Zebari, is the foreign minister, and Talabani's brother-in-law heads the Ministry of Water Resources.[137]

However, owing to dissatisfaction with the political status quo, a dramatic shift took place in Iraqi Kurdistan's parliamentary and presidential elections in August 2009. Breaking the tradition of political domination by the PUK and the KDP, the two groups' alliance won only 57 percent of the vote, a historic low. Newshirwan Mustafa's "Change List," won 24 percent of the vote and 25 out of 111 assembly seats. (Mustafa was previously Talabani's deputy and second in command.) Other parties, including Islamists, Turkmen and independent leftists, took the remainder. This election marked the first challenge to PUK–KDP regional hegemony since the establishment of the KRG in 1992. It is likely that the Iraqi central government will attempt to capitalize on the political shift, with reports suggesting that Prime Minister al-Maliki courted the Change List to exert leverage in negotiations with the PUK–KDP leadership.[138]

The legal system of Iraqi Kurdistan is compromised owing to the existence of five parallel judicial systems: the regular courts, state security courts to try political offenses, military courts with jurisdiction over Peshmerga forces, KDP and PUK party courts known as *komalayati* (social) courts, and tribal courts with jurisdiction over members of specific tribes. They are all convenient legal devices, except for the regular courts, which apply Iraqi laws. Appointments to the courts are mediated among politicians, and this process seems to have brought the judicial system into some disrepute. The current judge of the Cassation Court (roughly equivalent to a Supreme Court) in Iraqi Kurdistan, Rizgar Hama, for instance, has expressed his profound concern about the degree of political interference in the system as it "seriously endangers the integrity of courts."[139]

From its inception in 1992, the KRG has pursued a foreign policy based on close ties with the United States. At the regional level, the Kurds began to explore ties with Israel. Such ties, while controversial, have been widely reported since the onset of the occupation. It was reported that Israel provided *matériel* support and training for Kurdish Peshmerga forces in order to "penetrate, gather intelligence on, and then kill off the leadership of the Shiite and Sunni insurgencies in Iraq," and to aid in Israeli efforts "to install sensors and other sensitive devices that primarily target suspected Iranian nuclear facilities."[140] Unsurprisingly, Talabani denied reports of an Israeli presence in Iraqi Kurdistan, dismissing them as "total fabrication."[141] Nevertheless, in 2006, the BBC *Newsnight* program broadcast videos of former Israeli special forces soldiers – now members of the Israeli security firm Interop – training Peshmerga troops in military tactics.[142]

In 2006, Massoud Barzani – during an official visit to Kuwait – commented that, in principle, "it is not a crime to have relations with Israel," since important Arab countries such as Egypt and Jordan already had such relations. He continued: "Should Baghdad establish diplomatic relations with Israel, we could open a consulate in Erbil."[143] This sentiment – an accommodation with Israel – was emphasized on July 1, 2008 with a brief meeting and a public handshake between Jalal Talabani and Israeli Defense Minister Ehud Barak during the 23rd Congress of the Socialist International.[144] In addition, Qubad Talabani, the KRG representative to the United States, attended the American Israeli Public Affairs Committee meeting on May 5, 2009. However, Kurdish overtures toward Israel remain extremely risky, as they go against the Arab nationalist project of anti-Zionism, and subject the KRG to intense domestic and regional scrutiny.

Conclusion

In the American desire to exploit Iraq's massive oil reserves, and increase its geostrategic position within the Gulf, Iraq has been subjected to economic shocks, with the extensive state sector rapidly privatized. The high levels of unemployment and the abandonment of service provisions for the majority of the population, along with the collapse of basic infrastructure, represent products of deliberate policies that have marked the Anglo-American occupation. Such a process of economic devastation and social fracturing is inhumane and against international laws and norms. The nationalist ethos and tradition in Iraq have been severely undermined by these developments.

Against this backdrop of destruction, however, there have been sputtering signs of national resistance. The draft oil law has met fierce resistance from the public, especially from the Federation of Oil Unions in Iraq, which has frequently threatened to launch a general strike. The law has been viewed as such an affront to national dignity and a reversal of the historic national development trend that it has remained impossible for the current regime to pass it. Yet, while a formal oil law establishing the legal conditions of Iraq's oil industry, including PSA agreements, has failed to come into effect, the Iraqi government pushed ahead in late 2009 with the signing of contracts worth billions of dollars.

A year earlier, the Status of Forces Agreement (SOFA) had been signed. The occupation authorities had hoped this agreement would allow for the establishment of permanent US military bases in Iraq, US control of Iraqi airspace, immunity for private contractors in Iraq, and permission for the US to launch military operations without consultation or approval from Iraqi authorities.[145] However, the final SOFA fell short of all these measures:

> American troops in Iraq will withdraw from cities, towns and villages by June 30, 2009 and from all of Iraq by December 31, 2011. The Iraqi government will take over military responsibility for the Green Zone in Baghdad, the heart of American power in Iraq, in a few weeks time. Private security companies will lose their legal immunity. US military operations and the arrest of Iraqis will

only be carried out with Iraqi consent. There will be no US military bases left behind when the last US troops leave in three years' time and the US military is banned in the interim from carrying out attacks on other countries from Iraq.[146]

Formal approval of the SOFA had been tentatively contingent on popular approval through a national referendum, originally scheduled for July 30, 2009. This was subsequently rescheduled for March 7, 2010. However, as this date passed, the promised referendum again went without a vote. The subsequent election controversies and the failure (at the time of writing) to form an Iraqi government has apparently left the matter in a state of flux.

Even after waves of cultural waste, the historical memory of Iraqis remains strong. Appropriately, the machinations of the Anglo-American occupation raise unpleasant analogies in the popular Iraqi mind, harkening back to the British mandate and the Anglo-Iraqi treaty of 1930. In the aftermath of the First World War, declaring his country's intentions upon invading Iraq, British general Stanley Maude announced that Britain did "not come into your cities and lands as conquerors or enemies, but as liberators."[147] Subsequent to "liberating" the Iraqi masses, Britain endeavored to reengineer Iraqi society through the cultivation of traditional elites (religious and tribal) into a compliant façade of indigenous authority before ultimately – in 1920 – installing a Council of State and a General Elective Assembly, again as a chimera of independent Iraqi rule. While the Anglo-American invasion and occupation of Iraq in 2003 may have been perceived by its architects as profoundly different in kind and motivation from the imperial machinations of the British Empire, the specter and memory of foreign domination echo powerfully among the Iraqis themselves. For the Iraqi public, the analogies between British domination and the contemporary occupation are legion. Subsequent to declaring their intentions to liberate the Iraqi public, the occupation authorities facilitated the empowerment of the formerly exiled party militias, first through the installation of the caretaker Iraqi Interim Government and subsequently through the Iraqi Transitional Government. Further, Proconsul Paul Bremer's role and personality can be compared to that of British High Commissioner Sir Percy Cox. The contours of the "new Iraq" have been sectarian from the outset, and with the dismantling of Iraq's national institutions, forces of sectarianism have formed the primary political institutions of occupied Iraq. Moreover, the drafting of the 2005 constitution – in which Noah Feldman played an ambiguous role as advisor – raised the ugly memory of the British role in the drafting and imposition of a constitution in 1925, which persisted until the 1958 revolution. The 2005 constitution undermined the progressive components of the 1958 interim constitution, particularly in relation to women's rights and the role of the traditional religious and tribal forces.

While the SOFA foresees the exit of American forces by December 31, 2011, an out-clause is built into it for renegotiation. Indeed, as per the SOFA, American forces should have left Iraqi cities by July 2009. As of early 2010, 3,000 troops were still based in Forward Operating Base Falcon, in the outskirts of Baghdad. Moreover, "city lines are redrawn, to the convenience of US military" operations.[148] Other aspects of the SOFA raise concerns, too. Just as the Anglo-Iraqi treaty of

1930 provided occupying forces "immunity and privileges in jurisdiction and fiscal matters, including freedom from taxation," the SOFA exempts Anglo-American occupying authorities from "any taxes, duties, or fees." Even more problematic are issues relating to Iraqi authority and sovereignty within the country's borders. Article 12, Section 5 of the SOFA requires that "Members of the United States Forces and of the civilian component arrested or detained by Iraqi authorities shall be notified immediately to United States Forces authorities and handed over to them within 24 hours." Beyond raising questions of Iraqi authority over the prosecution of potential crimes committed within its borders, the phrase "civilian component" implies private military contractors, notably Xe Services – formerly Blackwater.

While the final SOFA was edited down from its initial design, limiting the scope of US power within Iraq, there remains significant popular suspicion and concern about it. This is bolstered by the bilateral signing of the Declaration of Principles for a Long-Term Relationship between the Republic of Iraq and the United States of America; the Strategic Friendship Agreement of 2007; and the Strategic Framework Agreement (SFA) of 2008, which fundamentally replaced Chapter VII of the UN Charter. The Friendship Agreement and the SFA suggest vague yet broad privileges for the United States. These could include the United States being tasked to confront armed factions at the request of the Iraqi government, beyond the withdrawal date outlined by the SOFA. In other words:

> the United States will provide "security assurances and commitments to [Iraq] to deter foreign aggression against Iraq that violates its sovereignty and integrity of its territories, waters, or airspace." The Declaration [SFA] also states that the Iraqi government is combating "terrorist groups, at the forefront of which is Al Qaeda, Saddamists, and all other outlaw groups." This language might be interpreted as requiring US support for the Iraqi government against both external and internal security threats without regard for whether or not the Iraqi government has made efforts to address the sources and causes of the threat, or whether or not the threat is pursuing a legitimate grievance against the Iraqi government.[149]

Moreover:

> The November 2007 Declaration states that the United States will support Iraq "in defending its democratic system against internal and external threats." If the elected Iraqi government were to be forced out by violence, this language might be interpreted to require the United States to intervene to restore the elected government or to oust a government – even a stable government – that came to power through un-democratic means.[150]

In light of the above, and the role the United States currently plays in Iraq, there is popular apprehension that the *relatively* mild language of the SOFA could be overruled by subsequent agreements. For instance, many critics doubt that the promise of a complete exit of American troops by the end of 2011 will be kept. The burden of Iraq's historical experience with occupation powers weighs heavily in the popular mind, so promises of liberation and freedom from foreign interference are met with disbelief.

Notes

1 The latest official census was carried out in 1997; none has taken place since the US invasion in 2003. The demographics in the 1997 census became questionable under US military occupation that resulted in approximately 5 million displaced Iraqis, both internally and externally, in addition to nearly a million civilian deaths. None the less, according to a UN press release of August 8, 2003, the Iraqi population was 22 million in 1997; estimated at 23 million in 2000; and 26 million in 2003. URL: http://www. un.org/News/briefings/docs/2003/iraqdemobrf.doc.htm. The current official estimate, made for the purpose of the 2011 elections, assumes the population is over 30 million. URL: http://www.un.org/News/briefings/docs/2003/iraqdemobrf.doc.htm.
2 However, many oil experts argue that Iran's figures are debatable and unreliable, leaving Iraq to have the second-largest proven oil reserves in the world. See the Organization of Oil Exporting Countries "Annual Statistical Bulletin" at URL: http://www.opec.org/library/Annual%20Statistical%20Bulletin/interactive/FileZ/Main.htm and Dr Faleh Al Khayat, "Speech in the European Parliament, 18 March 2009," at URL: http://www.brusselstribunal.org/AlKhayat180309.htm.
3 Sonia Verma and Sharm el-Sheik, "Iraq Could Have Largest Oil Reserves in the World," *The Times*, May 20, 2008, at URL: http://business.timesonline.co.uk/tol/business/industry_sectors/natural_resources/article3964957.ece and "Iraqi Oil Reserves: 350 billion barrels", *Al-Quds Al-Arabi*, April 29, 2008.
4 Haifa Zangana, *An Iraqi Woman's Account of War and Resistance* (New York: Seven Stories Press, 2007), pp. 13, 153 footnote 3.
5 See Edwin Black, *Banking on Baghdad: Inside Iraq's 7,000-year History of War, Profit, and Conflict* (Hoboken: Dialog, 2008).
6 See Philip W. Ireland, *Iraq: A Study in Political Development* (London: Jonathan Cape, 1937), pp. 239–265.
7 For more details, see Imâd Ahmad al-Jawâhirî, *Târîkh Mushkilat al-'Arâdî fî al-'Irâq wa Dirâsah fî al-Tatawwurât al-'Âmmah: 1914–1932* (Baghdad: Dâr al-Hurriyyah lil Tibâ'ah, 1978).
8 'Abd al-Jalil Al Tahir, *Al 'Asha'ir Al Iraqiyah* (Baghdad: al-Muthana Press, 1972), pp. 40–41.
9 Ibid.
10 See Tareq Y. Ismael and 'Abdul H. Raoof, "Iraq," in Tareq Y. Ismael (ed.), *Government and Politics of the Contemporary Middle East* (Homewood: Dorsey Press, 1970), p. 185.
11 For details on the Najaf rebellion, see Zakî Sâlih, *Muqaddimah fî Târîkh al-'Irâq al-Hadîth* (Baghdad: Matba'at al-Râbitah, 1953), p. 27 and Hasan Al-'Alawi, *al-Shi'a wa al-Dawlah al-Qwamiyah fi al-'Irâq 1914-1990* (2nd Edition) (London: n.p., 1990), pp. 93–105.
12 See Hanna Batatu, *The Old Social Classes and the Revolutionary Movements of Iraq: A Study of Iraq's Old Landed and Commercial Classes and of its Communists, Ba'thists, and Free Officers* (Princeton: Princeton University Press, 1978), p. 23.
13 See Ireland, op. cit., pp. 177–200.
14 *Compilation of Proclamations, Notices, etc...Relating to...Mesopotamia*, Announcement No. 49, dated June 17, 1920 as quoted by ibid., p. 221.
15 Ibid., p. 288.
16 Ibid., p. 178.
17 Thanks to Sami Albanna for pointing this out.
18 Others, including official sources, cite the first Anglo-Iraqi treaty of October 1921, which created the state organization.

19 Wadie Jwaideh, *The Kurdish National Movement: Its Orgins and Development* (Syracuse: Syracuse University Press, 2006), pp. 219–229.
20 Ibid. pp. 230–239.
21 Ṣâlih, op. cit., p. 131.
22 Charles Tripp, *A History of Iraq* (3rd Edition) (Cambridge: Cambridge University Press, 2007), p. 130
23 Al-Saiyyed 'Abd-ul-Razzâq al-Ḥasanî, *Ta'rîkh al-Wizârât al-'Irâqiyyah* (Baghdad: Âfâq 'Arabiyyah, 1988), IX, pp. 58–59.
24 Ibid, p. 113.
25 General Director of Census, *Results of 1957 Census* (Baghdad, 1958).
26 Ibid.
27 For more on this, see Tareq Y. Ismael, *Governments and Politics of the Contemporary Middle East* (Homewood: Dorsey Press, 1970), pp. 184–186; Iraqi Ministry of Economics, *Report on Agriculture and Livestock Census of Iraq, 1958–59* (Baghdad, 1961), p. 7.
28 Ismael, op. cit., p. 184.
29 John C.K. Daly, "Analysis: Russia and OPEC Deepen Ties," *UPI*, September 10, 2008. URL: http://www.upi.com/Science_News/Resource-Wars/2008/09/10/Analysis-Russia-and-OPEC-deepen-ties/UPI-15401221090735/.
30 Dr Mohammad Salman Hasan, *Dirasat Fi al-Iqtisad al-'Iraqi* (Beirut: Dar al-Tali'ah, 1966), p. 45.
31 Ismael and Raoof, op. cit., pp. 185–186.
32 Sami Zubaida, "The Rise and Fall of Civil Society in Iraq," May 2, 2003. URL: http://www.opendemocracy.net/conflict-iraqwarquestions/article_953.jsp.
33 Sami Zubaida, "The Rise and Fall of Civil Society in Iraq," in Haldun Gulalp (ed.), *Citizenship and Ethnic Conflict: Challenging the Nation State* (London and New York: Routledge, 2006), p. 117.
34 See Phebe Marr, *The Modern History of Iraq* (Boulder: Westview Press, 1985), pp. 173–175.
35 Roger Morris, "A Tyrant Forty Years in the Making," *New York Times*, March 14, 2003. URL: http://www.globalpolicy.org/component/content/article/169-history/36407.html.
36 Ibid.
37 Seán Mac Mathúna, "CIA Helps Baath Party to Power in 1963." URL: http://www.fantompowa.net/Flame/cia_iraq.htm.
38 Library of Congress Country Studies, "Iraq Coups, Coup Attempts and Foreign Policy." URL: http://workmall.com/wfb2001/iraq/iraq_history_coups_coup_attempts_and_foreign_policy.html.
39 'Abdul Wahab Hamid Rashid, *al-'Iraq al-Mu'asir* (Damascus: al-Mada, 2002), pp. 164–166.
40 Faleh A. Jabar, "Post Conflict Iraq: A Race for Stability, Reconstruction, and Legitimacy," US Institute for Peace – Special Report 120 (May 2004). URL: http://www.usip.org/pubs/specialreports/sr120.html.
41 R.L. Sivard, *World Military and Social Expenditures* (Washington, D.C.: World Priorities, 1991, 1993).
42 'Ali A. Allawi, *The Occupation of Iraq: Wining the War, Losing the Peace* (New Haven and London: Yale University Press, 2007), p. 44.
43 Tareq Y. Ismael, *Middle East Politics Today: Government and Civil Society* (Gainesville: University of Florida Press, 2001), pp. 216–217.
44 Geoff T. Harris, *Recovery from Armed Conflict in Developing Countries* (London and New York: Routledge, 1999), p. 18.
45 See Tareq Y. Ismael and Jacqueline S. Ismael, "Wither Iraq? Beyond Saddam, Sanctions and Occupation," *Third World Quarterly*, Vol. 26, Nos. 4–5, 2005, p. 613.
46 Abbas Alnasrawi, "Iraq's Odious Debt," *Middle East Economic Survey*, March 29, 2004. URL: http://www.globalpolicy.org/component/content/article/168/37419.html.
47 "Worse is Better," *The Economist*, August 11, 1990, p. 22.

48 Youssef M. Ibrahim, "Iraq Said to Prevail in Oil Dispute with Kuwait and Arab Emirates," *New York Times*, July 26, 1990, p. A1.
49 Robert Fisk, "Gulf War Legacy Flares as 'Stingy' Kuwait Puts the Squeeze on Iraq," *Belfast Telegraph*, July 29, 2009. URL: http://www.belfasttelegraph.co.uk/opinion/columnists/robert-fisk/robert-fisk-gulf-war-legacy-flares-as-stingy-kuwait-puts-the-squeeze-on-iraq-14436277.html.
50 See Eric Herring and Glen Rangwala, *Iraq in Fragments: The Occupation and its Legacy* (Ithaca: Cornell University Press, 2006).
51 "Toting the Casualties of War: Beth Osborne Daponte Talks about how her Estimates of Iraq's Gulf War Dead got her into Deep Trouble with the White House," *Business Week*, February 6, 2003. URL: http://www.businessweek.com/bwdaily/dnflash/feb2003/nf2003026_0167_db052.htm.
52 Noam Chomsky, *Hegemony or Survival: America's Quest for Global Dominance* (New York: Henry Holt and Company, 2003), p. 30.
53 United Nations, *Report of the Second Panel Established Pursuant to the Note by the President of the Security Council of 30 January 1999 (S/1999/100), Concerning the Current Humanitarian Situation in Iraq*. URL: http://www.casi.org.uk/info/panelrep.html.
54 Tariq Y. Ismael and Jacqueline S. Ismael, *The Iraqi Predicament: People in the Quagmire of Power Politics* (London: Pluto Press, 2004), pp. 126–165.
55 United Nations Development Program Iraq Country Office, "1999–2000 Report." URL: http://www.iq.undp.org.
56 United Nations, op. cit.
57 United Nations Security Council Resolution 986, at URL: http://www.uncc.ch/resolutio/res0986.pdf and United Nations Security Council Resolution 1153, at URL: http://www.uncc.ch/resolutio/res1153.pdf.
58 Abbas Alnasrawi, *The Economy of Iraq Oil, Wars, Destruction of Development and Prospects, 1950–2010* (Westport: Greenwood Press, 1994).
59 Faleh 'Abd al-Jabbar, *Al-Dawla, al-Mugtama 'al-Madani wa al-Tahawul al-Demokrati fi al 'Iraq* (Cairo: Markaz. Ibn Khaldoun li al-dirasat al-Inma'iyya, 1995), pp. 168–169.
60 United Nations Office of the Iraq Program, "Oil-for-Food, Basic Figures," May 18, 2002. URL: http://www.un.org/Depts/oip/background.
61 Ibid. URL: http://www.un.org/Depts/oip/cpmd/roleofoip.
62 Tareq Y. Ismael & Jacqueline S. Ismael, "Whither Iraq? Beyond Saddam, Sanctions and Occupation," *Third World Quarterly*, Vol. 26, Nos. 4–5 (2005), pp. 609–629.
63 Kofi Annan, "Report of the Secretary-General Pursuant to Paragraphs 28 and 30 of Resolution 1284 (1999) and Paragraph 5 of Resolution 1281 (1999)," March 10, 2000. URL: http://daccessdds.un.org/doc/UNDOC/GEN/N00/331/13/PDF/N0033113.pdf?OpenElement.
64 Chomsky, op cit., p. 126.
65 Ibid., p. 127.
66 Ismael and Ismael, *The Iraqi Predicament*, op. cit., pp. 9–38.
67 Thomas Donnelly et al., *Rebuilding America's Defenses* (Washington, D.C.: PNAC, 2000).
68 Ibid., 5.
69 Richard Clarke, *Against All Enemies: Inside America's War on Terror* (New York: Free Press, 2004), p. 265.
70 Charles Lewis and Mark Reading-Smith, "False Pretenses," January 23, 2008. URL: http://www.publicintegrity.org./WarCard/Default.aspx?src = home&context = overview&id = 945. On the same issue of disinformation, see Yahoo News, at URL: http://news.yahoo.com/s/afp/20080123/wl_mideast_afp/usiraqwarpolitics.
71 Andrew Sparrow, "45-Minute WMD Claim 'May Have Come from an Iraqi Taxi Driver,'" *Guardian*, December 8, 2009. URL: http://www.guardian.co.uk/politics/2009/dec/08/45-minutes-wmd-taxi-driver.
72 Richard Norton, "Lord Goldsmith Told Tony Blair to Topple Saddam Would be

Illegal," *Guardian*, November 29, 2009. URL: http://www.guardian.co.uk/uk/2009/nov/29/iraq-war-lord-goldsmith-letter.

73 Patrick E. Tyler, "Officers Say US Aided Iraq in War Despite Use of Gas," *New York Times*, August 18, 2002.

74 Warren P. Strobel, "Exhaustive Review Finds No Link between Saddam and al Qaida," *McClatchy* Newspapers, March 10, 2008. URL: http://www.mcclatchydc.com/2008/03/10/29959/exhaustive-review-finds-no-link.html

75 Naomi Klein, *The Shock Doctrine: The Rise of Disaster Capitalism* (New York: Metropolitan Books, 2007).

76 Cara Buckley, "Rare Look Inside Baghdad Museum," *New York Times*, December 12, 2007. URL: http://www.nytimes.com/2007/12/12/world/middleeast/12iraq.html?em&ex = 1197522000&en = 30bbb59d472df2fb&ei = 5087%0A.

77 See Raymond W. Baker, Shereen T. Ismael and Tareq Y. Ismael, *Cultural Cleansing in Iraq: Why Museums Were Looted, Libraries Burned and Academics Murdered* (London: Pluto Press, 2010).

78 Simon Jenkins, "In Iraq's Four-Year Looting Frenzy, the Allies Have Become the Vandals," *Guardian*, June 8, 2007. URL: http://www.guardian.co.uk/Iraq/Story/0,2098273,00.html. Robert Fisk, "Another Crime of Occupation Iraq: Cultural Heritage Looted, Pillaged," *Independent*, September 17, 2007. URL: http://www.alternet.org/waroniraq/62810/.

79 Ibid.

80 Naomi Klein, "Baghdad Year Zero: Pillaging Iraq in Pursuit of Neocon Utopia," *Harpers* Vol. 309, No. 1852 (2004), p. 44.

81 Quoted in Gwynne Dyer, *The Mess They Made: The Middle East after Iraq* (Toronto: McClelland & Stewart Ltd, 2007), p. 17.

82 Roula Khalaf and Kevin Sieff, "War Veterans Make Iraq their Business," *Financial Times*, November 9, 2009. URL: http://www.ft.com/cms/s/0/1d91103e-cd55-11de-8162-00144feabdc0.html.

83 Peter Galbraith, *The End of Iraq: How American Incompetence Created a War without End* (New York City: Simon & Schuster, 2006), pp. 160–161.

84 James Glanz and Walter Gibbs, "US Advisor to Kurds Stands to Reap Oil Profits," *New York Times*, November 12, 2009. URL: http://www.nytimes.com/2009/11/12/world/middleeast/12galbraith.html?_r = 1&pagewanted = print.

85 Greg Palast, "Unreported: The Zarqawi Invitation," June 9, 2006. URL: http://www.truthout.org/cgi-bin/artman/exec/view.cgi/61/20385. BBC News, "General Jay Garner Speaks to BBC," April 15, 2003. URL: http://news.bbc.co.uk/2/hi/middle_east/2948907.stm. David Leigh, "General Sacked by Bush Says He Wanted Early Elections," *Guardian*, March 18, 2004. URL: http://www.guardian.co.uk/world/2004/mar/18/iraq.usa.

86 Gareth Porter, "How Neocon Shi'ite Strategy Led to Sectarian War," *IPS*, February 6, 2007. URL: http://ipsnews.net/news.asp?idnews = 36461.

87 Klein, "Baghdad Year Zero," op. cit.

88 Ibid., pp. 44, 48.

89 Ibid., pp. 48–49.

90 "US CBO Estimates $2.4 Trillion Long-term War Cost," *Reuters*, October 24, 2007. URL: http://www.reuters.com/article/politicsNews/idUSN2450753720071024.

91 Joseph Stiglitz and Linda Blimes, "The Three Trillion Dollar War," *Times Online*, February 23, 2008. URL: http://www.timesonline.co.uk/tol/comment/columnists/guest_contributors/article3419840.ece.

92 The details of US casualties were initially given by the Brooking Institution's *Iraqi Index* (Washington, D.C.: Brookings Institution, 2009), as part of a comprehensive coverage of the security, economic and social situation. At the height of the Iraqi insurgency (the umbrella title for the Iraqi resistance groups which are comprised of some seemingly nationalist forces allied with fractious local and tribal groups), over 110 armed attacks per day were recorded. The attacks varied by province, and over

time they become mixed with attacks by sectarian militias, atrocities in markets and mosques, and the mass expulsion of people due to sectarian identity. In 2007 the US initiated local truces with groups who turned against the religious hardliners, which served as a breakthrough. At the same time the US initiated dialogue with any resistance group willing to negotiate, something the Iraqi government opposed. It is difficult at present to analyze the struggle in Iraq objectively, due to the "fog of war" which has been created by all parties. This has resulted in the association of terrorism with the grassroots resistance movement which is aimed against illegal foreign occupation; that is permitted by the UN and customary international law. See Phil Shiner and Andrew Williams (eds), *The Iraq War and International Law* (Oxford: Hart Publishing, 2008).

93 Richard Horton, "Counting the Cost," *Guardian*, March 27, 2007. URL: http://commentisfree.guardian.co.uk/richard_horton/2007/03/counting_the_cost.html.
94 Debora MacKenzie, "Enormous Death Toll of Iraq Invasion Revealed," *New Scientist News Service,* October 11, 2006. URL: http://environment.newscientist.com/channel/earth/dn10276.
95 "Iraq Conflict Has Killed a Million, Says Survey," *Reuters*, January 30, 2008. URL: http://wiredispatch.com/news/?id = 26001.
96 Brookings Institution, op. cit., p. 26.
97 Ibid., p. 55.
98 Human Rights Watch, *They Want Us Exterminated: Murder, Torture, Sexual Orientation, and Gender in Iraq* (August 2009).
99 Ibid., p. 5.
100 Brookings Institution, op. cit., p. 41.
101 Aaron Glantz and Salam Talib, "Iraq Violence Leading to Academic Brain Drain," October 5, 2006. URL: http://www.antiwar.com/glantz/?articleid = 9791.
102 Ahmad Janabi, "Row over Iraq Oil Law," *Al Jazeera*, May 5, 2007). URL: http://english.aljazeera.net/news/middleeast/2007/05/200852518577734692.html.
103 "Iraq's Oil: Now Comes the Hard Part," *UPI*, December 16, 2009. URL: http://www.upi.com/Science_News/Resource-Wars/2009/12/16/Iraqs-oil-Now-comes-the-hard-part/UPI-47361260987000/.
104 Stanley Reed, "Iraq's Unsold Oil Fields," *Business Week*, July 2, 2009). URL: http://www.businessweek.com/magazine/content/09_28/b4139030321275.htm.
105 Gina Chon, "Big Oil Ready for Gamble in Iraq," *Wall Street Journal*, June 24, 2009. URL: http://online.wsj.com/article/SB124579553986643975.html.
106 Reed, op. cit.
107 "Update 1 – Iraq to Sign Deals for Rumaila, Zubair with BP, Eni," *Reuters*, October 29, 2009. URL: http://www.reuters.com/article/idUSLT27803720091029.
108 Timothy Williams, "At Iraqi Oil and Gas Auction, Bargaining is Contentious," *New York Times*, June 30, 2009. URL: http://www.nytimes.com/2009/07/01/business/global/01iraqoil.html?bl&ex = 1246593600&en = 7d023adc5bfa733a&ei = 5087.
109 Suadad al-Salhy and Ahmad Rasheed, "Flop to Some Iraq Oil Sale May be Victory to Others," *Guardian*, July 1, 2009. URL: http://www.guardian.co.uk/business/feed article/8587048.
110 Tamsin Carlisle, "Iraq Seeks Plan B after Auction," *The National*, July 2, 2009. URL: http://www.thenational.ae/article/20090701/BUSINESS/707019958/1005.
111 "Factbox – Details on Bidding for Iraqi Oilfields," *Reuters*, December 13, 2009. URL: http://www.reuters.com/article/idUSGEE5BA13S20091213?type = marketsNews. It is important to note that this fee is subject to a 35 percent Corporate Income Tax and 25 percent share of the Iraqi partner in each of these deals. What Iraq will actually pay is only 48.75 percent of the reported fee. Thanks to Ahmad M. Jiyad for pointing this out.
112 Ahmad M. Jiyad, "Preliminary Assessment of the GSDPC," June 22, 2009. URL: http://www.iraq-enterprise.com/rep/jiyad62009.htm.
113 *Russia Today*, July 8, 2009.

114 H.R. 4655, *To Establish a Program to Support a Transition to Democracy in Iraq*. URL: http://thomas.loc.gov/cgi-bin/bdquery/z?d105:HR04655:@@@L&summ2 = m&.

115 Hasan al-'Alawi is a well-known writer and journalist. He served as editor of the well-known Iraqi journal, *Alif ba* and as Saddam Hussein's press secretary until they had a dispute and al-'Alawi entered exile in Damascus. He joined the opposition and contributed to their newspapers, and served as editor of one of them. In 2004, he was appointed as the new Iraqi ambassador to Syria, but resigned soon after.

116 Hasan al-'Alawi, *Shî'at al-Sulṭah wa Shî'at al-'Irâq: Ṣirâ' al-Ajnâs* (London: Dâr al-Zawrâ', 2009). pp. 80–89.

117 The International Crisis Group, "Governing Iraq," Middle East Report No. 17, August 25, 2003. URL: http://www.crisisgroup.org/home/index.cfm?l = 1&id = 1672.

118 Ibid.

119 Marc Santora & Riyadh Mohammad, "After Delays, Deal Set on Iraq Election Law," *New York Times*, December 6, 2009, p. A6.

120 Oliver August, "Fear of Bloodshed in Iraq as Iran-Backed Bloc Tries to Take Power," *The Times*, May 7, 2010. URL: http://www.timesonline.co.uk/tol/news/world/iraq/article7118609.ece.

121 Juan Cole, "Parliament as a Whole May Have to Choose Iraqi Prime Minister," *Informed Comment*, May 7, 2010. URL: http://www.juancole.com/2010/05/parliament-as-a-whole-may-have-to-choose-iraqi-prime-minister.html. Uday Hatem, "Al Khilafat dakhil tahaluf al I'tlafian al shi'ian," *Dar Al Hayat*, May 7, 2010. URL: http://international.daralhayat.com/internationalarticle/138550.

122 Kareem Fahim, "Have a Nice Country," *Village* Voice, June 22, 2004. URL: http://www.villagevoice.com/2004-06-22/news/have-a-nice-country/.

123 Dahr Jamail, "Managing Escalation: Negroponte and Bush's New Iraq Team," January 8, 2007. URL: http://www.globalresearch.ca/index.php?context = viewArticle&code = JAM20070108&articleId = 4383.

124 Ibid.

125 Steven Simon, "The Price of the Surge: How US Strategy is Hastening Iraq's Demise," *Foreign Affairs*, Vol. 87, No. 3 (May/June 2008). URL: http://www.foreignaffairs.com/articles/63398/steven-simon/the-price-of-the-surge.

126 Nir Rosen, "The Myth of the Surge," *Rolling Stone*, May 6, 2008. URL: http://www.rollingstone.com/politics/story/18722376/the_myth_of_the_surge/print.

127 "Study: Surge of Violence Led to Peace in Iraq," *Foreign Policy: Passport*, September 19, 2008. URL: http://blog.foreignpolicy.com/posts/2008/09/19/study_surge_of_violence_led_to_peace_in_iraq.

128 Anthony Shadid, "Bombings Rock Iraq's Political Landscape," *Washington Post*, October 26, 2009. URL: http://www.washingtonpost.com/wp-dyn/content/article/2009/10/25/AR2009102500811.html.

129 "Baghdad Car Bombs Cause Carnage," *BBC News*, December 8, 2009. URL: http://news.bbc.co.uk/2/hi/middle_east/8400865.stm.

130 "The Approaching of Legislating a Special Law for the Iraqi Tribes," *Al-Sabaah*, April 30, 2009. URL: http://www.alsabaah.com/paper.php?source = akbar&mlf = inter page&sid = 85183.

131 Clarke, op. cit., p. 164.

132 "Profile: Jalal Talabani," *BBC* News, November 26, 2002. URL: http://news.bbc.co.uk/2/hi/middle_east/2480197.stm. See also, "Text of the Draft Iraqi Constitution," *USA Today*, August, 25, 2005. URL: http://www.usatoday.com/news/world/iraq/2005-08-24-iraqi-constitution-draft_x.htm.

133 Chris Kutschera, "Kurdish Autonomous Zone." URL: http://www.answers.com/topic/kurdish-autonomous-zone.

134 "Iraqi Kurds: A Chronology of Key Events," *BBC News*, March 10, 2009. URL: http://news.bbc.co.uk/1/hi/world/middle_east/country_profiles/2893067.stm.

135 Rod Nordland, "Now it's a Census that Could Rip Iraq Apart," *New York Times*, July 25, 2009, pg. WK4.

136 Soner Cagaptay & H. Akin Unver, "Iraqi Kurds and the Turkish–Iraqi Memorandum against the PKK," *Washington Institute for Near East Policy*, August 21, 2007. URL: http://www.akinunver.com/scholar/?p=9.

137 Michael Rubin, "Is Iraqi Kurdistan a Good Ally?," American Enterprise Institute – Middle Eastern Outlook, January 2008. URL: http://www.meforum.org/1822/is-iraqi-kurdistan-a-good-ally. Kamal Said Qadir, "Iraqi Kurdistan's downward Spiral," *Middle East Quarterly*, Summer 2007, pp. 19–26. URL: http://www.meforum.org/1703/iraqi-kurdistans-downward-spiral.

138 Ranj Alaaldin, "Can Democracy Survive in Kurdistan?," *Guardian*, August 9, 2009. URL: http://www.

139 Qadir, op. cit.

140 Seymour Hersh, "Plan B," *New Yorker*, June 28, 2004. URL: http://www.newyorker.com/archive/2004/06/28/040628fa_fact?printable = true.

141 "Kurds Deny 'Israeli Infiltration,'" *BBC News*, June 22, 2004. URL: http://news.bbc.co.uk/2/hi/middle_east/3829413.stm.

142 "Kurdish Soldiers Trained by Israelis," *Newsnight*, September 20, 2006. URL: http://news.bbc.co.uk/2/hi/programmes/newsnight/5363116.stm.

143 Institut Kurde de Paris, "Iraqi Kurdistan Unifies its Administration with a Single Government, Institut Kurde de Paris No. 254 (May 2006), p. 2. URL: http://www.institutkurde.org/en/publications/bulletins/254.html.

144 "Historic Handshake: Barak Meets Iraq's President in Athens," *Haaretz*, July 1, 2008. URL: http://www.haaretz.com/hasen/spages/997941.html. For a critical assessment, see Ramzy Baroud, "The Not-so-Historic Barak–Talabani Handshake," *Counterpunch*, July 11, 2008. URL: http://www.counterpunch.org/baroud07112008.html.

145 URL: http://www.independent.co.uk/news/world/middle-east/revealed-secret-plan-to-keep-iraq-under-us-control-840512.html.

146 Patrick Cockburn, "It's Official: Total Defeat for US in Iraq." URL: http://www.alternet.org/waroniraq/112768/it%27s_official:_total_defeat_for_US_in_iraq/.

147 Sir Stanley Maude, "The Proclamation of Baghdad", March 19, 1917, reproduced by *Harper's Magazine*, May 2003. URL: http://www.harpers.org/archive/2003/05/0079593.

148 Dahr Jamail, "US Occupation of Iraq Continues Unabated," July 6, 2009. URL: http://dahrjamailiraq.com/us-occupation-of-iraq-continues-unabated.

149 John Isaacs and Travis Sharp, "A Permanent Presence? Dangers of a Long-Term US Security Commitment to Iraq," Center for Arms Control and Non-Proliferation, January 29, 2008.

150 Ibid.

Further reading

There is a voluminous library of high-quality research on Iraq, in disciplines ranging from history to political science and from economics to anthropology. Beyond academic treatments of the Iraqi experience, there is a significant body of quality journalistic and popular accounts of Iraq.

For broad histories of Iraq, Charles Tripp's *A History of Iraq* is one of the most serious and comprehensive historical treatments of Iraq. Now in its third edition, it covers the history of the country from the Ottoman-era provinces of Basra and Baghdad through to the emergence of Iraq as a modern nation state, detailing the various political intrigues along the way, ending with the Anglo-American occupation. Incredibly comprehensive, but highly readable, it is an ideal primer on Iraqi history. Thabit Abdullah's *A Short History of Iraq: From 683 to the Present* is likewise a useful historical survey, covering a vast swath of history, from the spread of Islam to Iraq to the height of the Abbasid Empire seated in Baghdad, from the Ottoman Empire to the emergence of modern Iraq. His *Dictatorship, Imperialism and Chaos: Iraq since 1989* is a continuation of this historical inquiry, focusing on the period from 1989 that saw the deconstruction of Iraq through war, economic sanctions and, finally, military occupation and the restructuring of Iraqi nationhood.

At the more subtle and discreet level of analysis, Hanna Batatu's *The Old Social Classes and the New Revolutionary Movements of Iraq* remains the seminal work of Iraqi political sociology, providing a densely researched account of the emergence of the revolutionary movements within Iraq, chiefly the Iraqi Communist Party, prior to 1958. Though primarily focusing on the new revolutionary movements, Batatu provides a wealth of information on the traditional ruling classes of Iraq, and the interaction of the divergent movements within the country. It remains a fundamental study of modern Iraqi history.

'Ali al-Wardi's *Understanding Iraq: Society, Culture, and Personality* is a fascinating and probing analysis of the Iraqi social and cultural environment, and an analysis of the habits of mind that the conflict between Bedouinism and urbanism imparted. Wardi's text is additionally relevant in the context of the collapse of the Iraqi state and the reemergence of traditional sources of social power. Conversely, Eric Davis's, *Memories of State: Politics, History, and Collective Identity in Iraq* is a unique analysis of the attempt of the Iraqi Ba'thist regime to reengineer the nation's history and cultural project for the purposes of, first, serving party ideology and, second, undermining a traditional Iraqi identity that emphasized cultural pluralism, an inclusive Iraqi nationalism and social justice.

Yitzhak Nakash's *The Shi'is of Iraq* and *Reaching for Power: The Shi'a in the Modern Arab World* are comprehensive and careful accounts of the history of the Arab Shi'a, in general, and the Iraqi Shi'a, in particular. Attention is paid to the acculturation process that occurred during the mass conversions of Arab tribes to Shi'ism from the late eighteenth century onward and the development of religious, political and cultural customs as the Shi'a Iraqi related to the Iraqi state in the twentieth century. Patrick Cockburn's *Muqtada al-Sadr and the Battle for the Future of Iraq* is an admirable journalistic treatment of the social and cultural environment that gave rise to the Sadrist Movement and the Iraqi strain of Shi'a activism.

For the intervening period between the 1991 and 2003 wars, Hans C. Von Sponeck, the former UN humanitarian coordinator for Iraq, and Celso N. Amorim's *A Different Kind of War: The UN Sanctions Regime in Iraq* is a thorough and well-informed analysis of the social, economic and political developments during the era of comprehensive economic sanctions. Likewise, Geoff Simons's *The Scouring of Iraq: Sanctions, Law and Natural Justice* is an impassioned examination of the human costs of power politics during a similar timeframe.

The motivations for the Anglo-American invasion and occupation of Iraq remain a subject of significant debate, in which the question of oil remains ever present. As to the general question of oil and US strategy, Ian Rutledge's *Addicted to Oil: America's Relentless Drive for Energy Security* and Michael T. Klare's *Blood and Oil: The Dangers and Consequences of America's Growing*

Dependency on Imported Petroleum are useful primers. Greg Muttitt is a credible expert on oil policy and his *Fuel on the Fire: Oil and Politics in Occupied Iraq* provides a piercing viewpoint. At the more general level, John Ehrenberg's *The Iraq Papers* is a comprehensive and well-organized collection of documents and commentaries tracing, first, the intellectual and strategic origins of the US's Iraq strategy and the doctrine of "preemption" and, second, the history of US occupation policy post-2003, including an account of the US's dealings with successive Iraqi governments and its relationship to the Iraqi populace.

Treatments of Iraq post-occupation are plenty and vary in quality. 'Ali Allawi, a former trade and defense minister under the US-imposed Iraqi government and former supporter of the occupation plan, has written *The Occupation of Iraq: Winning the War, Losing the Peace*, which details his gradual disillusionment with the Anglo-American project in Iraq, and his attempts to interpret the failures and missteps of the occupation planners and authorities. While self-serving to a degree, it is nevertheless an insightful insider's account of the post-war period. Eric Herring and Glen Rangwala's *Iraq in Fragments: The Occupation and its Legacies* serves as an academic interpretation of the failures of the Anglo-American occupation, chiefly the failure to generate a stable political project that commanded cooperation and participation from the population. The occupation is perceived as a failure of regime legitimation, hence generating a counter-reaction of resistance and non-compliance. Mark Danner's *Torture and Truth: America, Abu Ghraib, and the War on Terror* provides vast documentary evidence of the abuse that took place at the American-run Abu Ghraib prison and the political conditions that gave rise to a culture of abuse. It is also a useful corrective to the "few bad apples" narrative that has become conventional wisdom.

The *Washington Post*'s Rajiv Chandrasekaren's *Imperial Life in the Emerald City: Inside Iraq's Green Zone* is a journalistic exposé of the endemic corruption and incompetence that has characterized the administration of Iraq, with the "green zone" representing a physical and mental cocoon, deaf and isolated from the external reality of the "red zone" (Iraq). Likewise, Dahr Jamail's *Beyond the Green Zone: Dispatches from an Unembedded Journalist in Occupied Iraq* and Nir Rosen's *The Triumph of the Martyrs: A Reporter's Journey into Occupied Iraq* are accomplished and penetrating accounts of the Iraqi occupation from two independent journalists, who provide unfiltered accounts of Iraq's descent into mass violence, documenting the social degeneration of Iraq and the accompanying plethora of individual human tragedies. Blunt and uncompromising, these books are valuable accounts of the human cost of the Anglo-American occupation.

Joseph Stiglitz, a Nobel Prize-winning economist and former president of the World Bank, collaborated with Harvard economist Linda Blimes to write *The Three Trillion Dollar War*, a meticulous audit of the full cost of the American war in Iraq, accounting for direct costs as well as opportunity costs and hidden costs. While material costs cannot be weighed morally against human costs, the final calculation of $3 trillion is nevertheless sobering.

Finally, the human cost of the occupation and its aftermath is detailed in the edited book by Raymond W. Baker, Shereen T. Ismael and Tareq Y. Ismael, *Cultural Cleansing in Iraq: Why Museums Were Looted, Libraries Burned and*

Academics Killed. The authors argue that the invasion aimed to dismantle the Iraqi state and remake it as a client regime. They painstakingly document the consequences of the occupiers' willful inaction and worse, which led to the ravaging of one of the world's oldest recorded cultures. Targeted assassination of over 400 academics, kidnapping and the forced flight of thousands of doctors, lawyers, artists and other intellectuals add up to cultural cleansing.

References

Abdullah, Thabit (2003) *A Short History of Iraq: From 683 to the Present*, Longman.
—— (2006) *Dictatorship, Imperialism and Chaos: Iraq since 1989*, Macmillan.
Allawi, 'Ali (2007) *The Occupation of Iraq: Winning the War, Losing the Peace*, Yale University Press.
Baker, Raymond W., Ismael, Shereen T. & Ismael, Tareq Y. (eds) (2010) *Cultural Cleansing in Iraq: Why Museums Were Looted, Libraries Burned and Academics Murdered*, Pluto Press.
Batatu, Hanna (2004) *The Old Social Classes and the New Revolutionary Movements of Iraq* (Reprint), Saqi Books.
Chandrasekaran, Rajiv (2007) *Imperial Life in the Emerald City: Inside Iraq's Green Zone*, Vintage.
Cockburn, Patrick (2008) *Muqtada al-Sadr and the Battle for the Future of Iraq*, Scribner.
Danner, Mark (2004) *Torture and Truth: America, Abu Ghraib, and the War on Terror*, New York Review Books.
Davis, Eric (2005) *Memories of State: Politics, History, and Collective Identity in Iraq*, University of California Press.
Ehrenberg, J. Patrick McSherry (2010) *The Iraq Papers*, Oxford University Press.
Herring, Eric and Rangwala, Glen (2006) *Iraq in Fragments: The Occupation and its Legacies*, Cornell University Press.
Jamail, Dahr (2008) *Beyond the Green Zone: Dispatches from an Unembedded Journalist in Occupied Iraq*, Haymarket Books.
Klare, Michael T. (2004) *Blood and Oil: The Dangers and Consequences of America's Growing Dependency on Imported Petroleum*, Metropolitan Books.
Muttitt, Greg (2010) *Fuel on the Fire: Oil and Politics in Occupied Iraq*, The Bodley Head.
Nakash, Yitzhak (2003) *The Shi'is of Iraq* (Revised Edition), Princeton University Press.
—— (2007) *Reaching for Power: The Shi'a in the Modern Arab World*, Princeton University Press.
Rosen, Nir (2008) *The Triumph of the Martyrs: A Reporter's Journey into Occupied Iraq*, Potomac Books.
Rutledge, Ian (2006) *Addicted to Oil: America's Relentless Drive for Energy Security*, I.B. Tauris.
Simons, Greg (1998) *The Scourging of Iraq: Sanctions, Law and Natural Justice* (2nd Edition), St. Martin's Press.
Sponeck, Hans C. Von & Amorim, Celso N. (2006) *A Different Kind of War: The UN Sanctions Regime in Iraq*, Berghahn Books.
Stiglitz, Joseph and Blimes, Linda (2008) *The Three Trillion Dollar War: The True Cost of the Iraq Conflict*, W.W. Norton.
Tripp, Charles (2007) *A History of Iraq* (3rd Edition), Cambridge University Press.
Wardi, 'Ali (2008) *Understanding Iraq: Society, Culture, and Personality* (translated by Fuad Baali), The Edwin Mellon Press.

7   The Syrian Arab Republic and the Lebanese Republic

From ancient times, and more recently during the Ottoman Empire, Syria has encompassed the geographic area along the Eastern Mediterranean between Turkey and Egypt. After the peace settlement following the First World War, this region was broken up into the political entities of Syria, Lebanon, Palestine and Transjordan, and after the 1948–1949 Arab–Israeli War, Palestine and Transjordan emerged as today's states of Israel and Jordan. Under Ottoman rule, from 1516 to 1918, Syria was divided into the three *villayets* (roughly the equivalent of cantons in the Swiss Republic) of Aleppo, Damascus and Beirut, and the two *mutasarrifiyyahs* (governorships) of Jerusalem and Mount Lebanon, with the last having more autonomy than any of the other four administrative units. Following the Maronite–Druze civil war in 1860 which resulted in the European imposition of the International Protocols of 1861 and 1864, special autonomy was guaranteed to the Christian Maronites of Mount Lebanon within the Ottoman Empire. Under the Ottoman *millet* sectarian system, Mount Lebanon, a Christian enclave, was administered by a Christian governor, appointed by Istanbul with local input through an administrative council representing all the various religious segments but dominated by the Christian sects. This *millet* system was abolished by the Young Turks half a century later but its influence on Lebanese politics has continued to this day.

Following the First World War, British and French forces controlled the coastal areas, and Arab forces the interior. The latter, under the command of Sharif Faisal of Hijaz, sought the creation of an independent and united Arab state, beginning with historically devised Syria under the terms of the Hussein–McMahon correspondence of October–November 1915. After the collapse of the Ottoman Empire in autumn 1918, Faisal set up an Arab national government in Damascus which lasted from November 1918 to July 1920. During its tenure, an Arab nationalist party, Hizb al-Istiqlal al-'Arabi (Arab Independence Party) took up the banner of nationalism from al-Fatat (a leading Arab nationalist party in Istanbul during the last years of the Ottoman Empire). Hizb al-Istiqlal al-'Arabi rallied nationalist forces around Sharif Faisal, giving the Arab national government a base of support among Arab nationalists. In March 1920, a Syrian General Congress was held in Damascus, with eighty-five delegates drawn from all over historically devised Syria, and proclaimed Sharif Faisal of Hijaz King of Syria.

Under the guise of the League of Nations mandate system, Arab territories of the Ottoman Empire were turned over to colonial powers for administration. The mandate system was presaged by earlier colonial machinations, as the French and British had prearranged the dismemberment of the region into zones of influence in the secret Sykes–Picot Agreement of May 1916. The San Remo Conference of May 1920, at which the victorious Allied powers settled the fate of the Arab provinces of the Ottoman Empire, allotted the northern half of historically devised Syria (which encompassed the territories subsequently known as Syria and Lebanon) to France and the remainder (i.e., Palestine) to Britain.

In Syria, the French administration set out to quash nationalist aspirations for independence and unity. At the Battle of Maisaloun on July 24, 1920, the French routed King Faisal and his nationalist forces, after which they divided Syria into a number of administrative units under military authority. The separation of Lebanon from Syria was followed by the formal establishment of the state of Greater Lebanon on August 30, 1920, which six years later became the Republic of Lebanon. The pre-war Maronite governorship of Mount Lebanon was enlarged to incorporate all the Muslim areas it could safely dominate, almost doubling its population and area, despite the objections of its inhabitants. According to the Basic Law introduced by the French on November 23, 1920, the French high commissioner, stationed in Beirut, was responsible to the French foreign minister; and the French government was the intermediary between the high commissioner and the League of Nations. By 1925, the high commissioner had ordered the promulgation of a constitution for Lebanon. It was drafted by the Representative Council of Lebanon and formally proclaimed in May 1926. However, it was suspended in 1932, allowing the French government to rule directly until 1941, when Vichy rule fell to British and Free French forces.

In 1924–1925, the Druze initiated an uprising against French rule. This spread throughout Syria, and threatened to spill over into Lebanon, but after Damascus was twice bombarded it was suppressed in 1926. The French continued their policy of separating Syria from Lebanon, and in 1928 a Constituent Assembly gathered in Damascus to formulate a constitution. This was proclaimed in 1932, but suspended two years later in response to further nationalist agitation for independence and unity with Lebanon. In 1936, nationalist-led mass demonstrations and strikes forced the French to negotiate a treaty promising some movement toward independence. However, the French socialist government of Leon Blum that negotiated this agreement fell shortly thereafter, and Syria, like Lebanon, remained under direct French rule until 1941, when the French mandate came to a formal conclusion with the victory of the Allied and Free French forces.[1] General Charles de Gaulle's forces installed pro-French governments promising independence to Syria and Lebanon; and, accordingly, in 1943, elections were allowed to take place. The pro-French candidates lost and nationalist leaderships came to the fore in both Lebanon and Syria. A year later, the French handed over local government and services to the newly elected national governments, and in 1945–1946 France reluctantly withdrew its troops from both countries. This concluded nearly a quarter of a century of colonial control, under the guise of a League of Nations mandate, and both countries moved toward full independence.

Syrian Arab Republic

With a land area of 185,180 square kilometers and a total population of just under 23 million people, history has bestowed on Syria a unique position in Middle East politics. It was the epicenter of the modern Arab political awakening and has continued to play a pivotal role in pan-Arab nationalism.

In the historical evolution of the country, geography has played a crucial role. Its strategic location sitting between three continents has exposed it to continuous movements of diverse peoples, whose impact has altered the socio-cultural heterogeneity of the region. Lacking any natural integrating factor, such as the river systems of Egypt and Iraq, segmentation developed into a salient feature of Syrian society. Geography has also had a significant impact on another aspect of the country – its economy. A complex geography of mountains, plains and desert has produced a differentiated ecological base for economic activities. Agriculture is the main occupation in the country while other important economic activities are trade and nomadic pastoralism.

About half of the country's territory is considered arable land. Farming is constrained by scarcity of precipitation with hopes for increasing acreage resting on irrigation. In addition, the government has constructed dams to replace the traditional but now obsolete waterwheel, on which local people have relied for centuries. In the more arid parts of the country, nomadism is widely practiced by Bedouins. However, the government is encouraging the settlement of these people, whose numbers are decreasing.

Another phenomenon partly attributed to the geography of the country is the expansion of urban life. Location aside, important commercial routes encouraged the development of commerce in the country, and the surplus extracted from these activities contributed to the establishment of cities and towns. With the growth of cities, nationalism and politics in general became the monopoly of the urban centers, to the political detriment of the rural areas, particularly in the nationalist period of the 1930s and the early years of independence. The urban areas became important centers of industry, wealth, politics and administration while the rural population continued to be impoverished, exploited and, thus, marginalized. This marginalization may help explain how these underprivileged segments of Syrian society came to feel that their only avenue for social mobility was via the army. Military education and the power resulting from a senior officer's position allowed them entry into Syrian politics, and eventually control of the army in the 1960s, and for the expansion of their influence to the economy, political culture and society at large in the 1970s, radically restructuring Syrian life.

Independence and nationalism

The country gained independence in 1945, at a time when it was ill-prepared to tackle the myriad problems facing it. The necessary institutional base was too weak. Moreover, the opposition to French imperial rule had exhausted the urban leadership of the country. As a consequence, independence was accompanied by a period of instability when one government followed another in rapid succession. The military played a major role in the post-independence carousel of regimes, which was finally arrested when the Ba'thists came to power in 1963.

The immediate task for the politicians who took over from the French – mostly Sunni Muslims from landowning and merchant classes – was to forge unity in the face of ethnic, social and religious discord. Syrian society has long been characterized by strong sectarian divisions, as is shown in Table 7.1.

While the Sunnis and Christians are dispersed, the Alawis, Druze and Ismailis are compact communities forming regional majorities. Most of the Alawis live in the northwestern Latakia region, with the Druze in the southern province of Suwayda (also called Jabal al Duruz – Mountain of the Druzes) and the Ismailis in the districts of Masyaf and Salamiyah in the central province of Hama. The Sunnis dominate the city populations and the remaining provinces.

During the mandate era, minorities were accorded autonomous status and were recruited in large numbers into the armed forces. Though it definitely had a role, the domination of the military by minorities in later years cannot entirely be explained by the French discriminatory recruitment practices. More plausible reasons are the inclination of Syrians from poorer backgrounds (where minorities dominated) to seek a career in the army for social advancement, and to encourage relatives to do the same; as well as the post-war reformulation of the Syrian armed forces, which pushed out much of the old military establishment.[2]

In the early years of independence, it was not surprising that the Sunni leaders of the country moved swiftly to break the independent power bases of the Alawites and Druze. By 1953 communal representation in the parliament had been abolished. Nevertheless, the minority groups increased their power and influence in both politics and the military. The emergence of the Ba'th Party provided an excellent opportunity for these groups, particularly the Alawites, eventually to come to dominate the political life of the country a decade later, and the newly expanded national army became one of the main avenues for social mobility.

Table 7.1 Sectarian division in Syrian society

Sunni Muslims	68.7 %
Alawis	11.5 %
Druze	3.0 %
Ismailis	1.5 %
Christians	14.1 %

Source: Nicholas S. Hopkins and Sa'd Eddin Ibrahim, *Arab Society: Class, Gender, Power and Development* (Cairo: American University in Cairo Press, 1998), pp. xv, 185–187.

The army in politics

The nationalist leadership which assumed power on independence lacked a vision of governance. When the first parliamentary election took place in 1947, corruption and election irregularities were rampant and by the time of the Palestine defeat in 1949, public dissatisfaction with the government was already high. As a result, when the first coup by army officers occurred on March 30 of that year, led by the chief of staff, Colonel Husni al-Za'im, public support was substantial, although military support was marginal. Nevertheless, the coup ushered in a new political era. The old nationalist center of power, composed largely of the landed aristocracy and rich merchant families, collapsed. A political vacuum was created, and a succession of coups followed, none surviving more than a few months.

The parliament continued to function within this environment with factions jockeying for influence with the leadership of each new coup and the General Staff counterbalancing and manipulating the parliament. Consequently, true power shifted completely from an elected body to the military. Thus, when a new election took place in November 1949, managed by the new chief of staff, Colonal Adib al-Shishakli, parliament blessed it and approved a new constitution put forward by the army. Following this, several governments rotated, with none of them powerful enough to satisfy either the army or the parliament. On November 29, 1951, the army overthrew the government, dissolved parliament, banned all political parties and gave the military-appointed head of state direct legislative and executive powers to rule through decree. Shishakli, involved in all previous coups, now began preparing the ground for his political ascendancy to the presidency by building a popular power base of support, first by the establishment in August 1952 of a populist organization known as the Arab Liberation Movement, which advanced some Arab nationalist slogans and progressive social and economic programs. Then, in July 1953, a new constitution was enacted ratifying Shishakli as president, while allowing the previously banned political parties to operate and prepare for a new round of elections, scheduled for October.

New forces had begun to gain more prominence on the political scene soon after independence and these gradually acquired genuine popular support based on clear political ideologies and social programs while traditional political parties were on the wane. One of these new forces, the Syrian Social Nationalist Party (SSNP), called for a unified, centralized, progressive state that would unite the entire Fertile Crescent. Another, the Arab Ba'th Socialist Party, supported a progressive semi-socialist (though non-Marxist) program, and advocated the establishment of a unified Arab state that would encompass all the Arab people from the Atlantic to the Persian Gulf. Meanwhile, the well-organized Communist Party of Syria supported a traditional Marxist–Leninist approach. The Syrian branch of the Egyptian Muslim Brotherhood propagated a unified Islamic world to counteract the influence of Western and European imperialism, and advanced a conservative social program with an avowed anti-leftist and anti-liberal orientation. The remnants of the traditional urban leadership of al-Kutla al-Wataniayah (the National Bloc), the Shaab (People's) Party and the Watani (National) Party, both with very conservative programs and waning popular support, particularly among the youth, operated primarily in the urban areas. In this environment, Shishakli saw to it that his popular Arab Liberation Movement won the election. However, amid charges of corruption, all the other parties mobilized demonstrations to protest against the election results, leading to a challenge to Shishakli from within the military itself. Shishakli was forced to flee the country on February 25, 1954, first to Lebanon and then to Argentina, where he was assassinated less than two years later.

For the seven months after his departure, the country was run by a provisional government whose mandate was to oversee a truly free election. The National and People's parties subsequently lost seats, while the leader of the Communist Party was elected to parliament for the first time in the party's history. Half of the seats were won by independent nationalist and progressive candidates, although the Ba'thists, holding a quarter of the seats, emerged as the strongest party and secured the support of a coalition of all progressive and leftist groups, including the communists. This gave the Ba'thists a dominant position in Syria. By July 1956, they had gained control of the most important positions in the cabinet and the leadership of parliament.

Union with Egypt

The popular appeal of Nasserism, particularly after the British–French–Israeli invasion in the Suez fiasco of November 1956, encouraged Arab nationalists in Syria to seek political union with Egypt. This had first been mooted in October 1955, when a military pact between the two countries was signed. The domestic circumstances within Syria – particularly the growth of what was perceived as an increasing communist threat with the dismissal of the conservative army chief of staff in the autumn of 1957 and the appointment of his deputy, the communist sympathizer General 'Afif al-Bizri – induced all the non-leftist, conservative and nationalist forces to unite amid fears of a loss of their power in the face of the increasing popularity of the Soviet Union in the region. These fears were buttressed by the ascendance of Khalid Bakdash – the leader of the Communist Party and a charismatic and popular figure in Syrian politics – and the emergence of the Communist Party itself as a political power, especially after the demise of the SSNP. The anti-leftist Ba'thist and Arab nationalist bloc saw their salvation from civil chaos in a union with Egypt. In addition, the emergence of Nasser as the symbol of Arab nationalism gave impetus to the movement for union as the nucleus of a pan-Arab state envisaged by the Ba'thists and espoused by other Arab nationalist groups. A marriage of ideological convenience ensued between Nasser and all nationalist groupings, including the Ba'thists, with the latter able to bask in Nasser's popularity. External threats, such as Turkey, Israel and Iraq, as well as internal dissention from Beirut also pushed the parties together. Thus, the Ba'th campaign for a union with Egypt became a cardinal principle of their National Front government, which was formed at the end of 1956. By 1957, Nasser and the Ba'th had become the most prominent forces in Syrian politics.[3]

Just prior to the union, the climate within Syria was politically unstable, characterized by much jockeying for power among the politicians, on the one hand, and between politicians and the military, on the other. The Ba'th Party had emerged as a strong political force and had joined the government of national unity formed in 1956. Unity with Egypt for the Ba'thists was an important step toward their grand goal of uniting the Arab peoples. Fearing the increasing popularity of the communists and other leftist organizations, the party's leadership saw in Nasser's popularity in Syria and the Arab world an opportunity to check the communist ascendance and to fulfill one of its main ideological tenets by espousing union with Egypt, which was at that time a popular notion among the army's younger officers, especially as the military now controlled the political balance of power, despite the fact that the chief of staff was now a Marxist. The Ba'th Party pushed for the union to bolster its position at home and to combat the rise of the left. Thus, when a high-ranking Syrian army delegation went to Cairo in January 1958 to ask for the union, the party quickly endorsed the move.

In the negotiations that followed, Nasser was in a strong position and his demands – total union, a disbanding of all political parties, the formation of a Syrian National Union modeled on his Egyptian counterpart, and the withdrawal of the military from politics – were fully accepted by the Syrians. On February 1, 1958, Presidents Nasser and Quwatli proclaimed the unity of the two countries under the name of the United Arab Republic. A referendum in both countries endorsed the move and Nasser was overwhelmingly elected president of the new republic. However, the constitution of the new state vested enormous power in the presidency and generally favored Egypt. Eventually, these two factors would become fatal flaws in the new arrangement.

During the union era, politicized Syrian army officers, including Ba'thists, were transferred from the Syrian region, assigned less sensitive military and police functions in Egypt and carefully watched by the UAR intelligence agencies. In the military, party members and Ba'thist sympathizers were forced to sever their formal party connections in order to survive in the new environment, but they solidified their personal relationships, transforming their party ties into more clandestine political–social relations. In early 1960, five young, disgruntled Syrian army officers in Egypt, most of whom were from minorities, chiefly Alawite, created a secret organization known as the Military Committee. Captain Hafez al-Assad, Major Salah Jadid and Lieutenant Colonel Mohammad Umran, who by virtue of having the highest rank served as its *de facto* chair, were the most active members of the committee, whose professed aim was to save the union from the corrupt cliques around Nasser, which they considered to be responsible for the growing failure of the UAR.

Soon the halcyon days of the union ended and the underlying contradictions within the UAR increasingly became a source of discontent in Syria. Merging the different political systems – an unstable and fragmented multi-party Syria and the single-party and stable Egypt – became problematic. Moreover, Nasser's imposition of the Egyptian system of government dissatisfied many Syrians, and the nationalization measures of July 1961 alienated the bourgeoisie and the commercial classes. Landowners protested against agrarian reforms, and politicians who found themselves left out of the new system were resentful, as were army officers who had been dismissed because of their political allegiances. The political insensitivity of the Egyptian upper echelon of military officers sent to Syria was another factor that fueled discontent. At the height of the worsening climate, in a right-wing putsch supported by the pro-Western, conservative Saudi Arabia and Jordan (who were worried about the popularity of progressive, nationalist Nasserism) and by the resentful business elite in Syria,[4] army officers stationed outside Damascus marched into the city on September 28, 1961 at the head of a coup. The union between the two countries came to an end and the Syrian Arab Republic was reborn.

The rise of the Ba'th

At its inception, the Ba'th Party's guiding slogan and principles were, and have remained, unity, freedom and socialism. For Syria's minorities, this slogan was appealing, for it promised secularism and social justice. Consequently, although the party was under the direction of urban middle-class intellectuals, it had a large following among the rural minority groups, many of whom had joined the army in the 1950s as a means of social mobility and who, as middle-ranking and junior officers, had formed cliques within the army during the period of union, slowly gaining prominence in the military and, eventually, in Syrian politics. However, the urban upper classes – many of them Sunnis – refrained from joining, since the party platform worked directly against the interests of the landed aristocracy, the merchant class and industrialists. Consequently, minority groups, particularly the Alawites, Druze and Ismailis, dominated both the army and the party.

Immediately after the breakup of the UAR, the Ba'th Party was in disarray, especially after several of its leaders denounced Nasser and the union and gave their blessing to the secessionist movement in a published manifesto. In this environment, various army cliques struggled to assert their power in the party, leaving the country in confusion. At the same time, the old civilian leadership also tried to regroup and take command of the party, which was essentially leaderless and chaotic.

With the demise of the union, the members of the Military Committee, except for Mohammad Umran, were immediately arrested by the Egyptian authorities, who eventually deported them back to Syria, where they were decommissioned and given civilian assignments. However, the Military Committee continued to recruit junior army officers, particularly those who had Nasserite and nationalist sympathies.

By the winter of 1962, secret negotiations between Umran, Jadid and al-Assad (the youngest of the group) and conservative, high-ranking nationalist army officers resulted in the formation of a junta which successfully staged a military coup on March 8, 1963, soon after restoring and promoting most of the members of the Military Committee. Traditional political elites at this point were too demoralized to oppose the move while nationalist forces, particularly the Nasserites, welcomed the coup a month after the new government, with the blessing of the army, moved closer to Egypt and requested a trilateral union with it and its counterparts in Iraq, who had come to power a month earlier in a similar plot. However, with the failure of the earlier union experiment still fresh in his memory, this offer was turned down by Nasser.

With the success of the coup, al-Assad gained a military base command which ultimately became his fiefdom and a springboard to greater things. A twenty-man National Council for the Revolutionary Command (NCRC) was formed, made up of twelve Ba'thists and eight Nasserite nationalists and independents. The Nasserites took eye-catching civilian jobs while the Military Committee held the real power through their military posts, forming a junta within a junta. Importantly, the Homs Military Academy was placed under Ba'thist command, thus becoming a breeding ground for the party's future officers, including relatives of al-Assad and Jadid. These recruits were given crash officer-training courses to prepare them to fill the military posts vacated by the hundreds of army officers suspected of disloyalty by the junta. Al-Assad emerged as the *de facto* chief of the air force, the most powerful branch of the Syrian armed forces; Jadid was promoted to general and put in charge of the officer corps personnel of the chiefs of staff, giving him complete control over promotions, transfers and dismissals.

From April 28 to May 2, fifty Nasserite officers were purged, leading two of the three Nasserite members of the junta to resign in protest, and soon after Nasserite members of the cabinet followed suit. A couple of months later, the Ba'thist trio in the Military Committee had eliminated all opposition in the army and controlled Syrian politics, even though they were a fraction of what itself was a minority – a military splinter group of a semi-defunct party without a popular base.[5]

On July 18, the Nasserites retaliated with an abortive putsch, resulting in heavy casualties. Afterwards, there was a wholesale purge of Nasserites in the army. On July 22, Nasser denounced the Ba'thists and formally withdrew from the trilateral union agreement that he had signed with them and Iraq three months earlier. Thus began an era of tension that flared up periodically, and resulted in a further purge of Nasserites from the cabinet and the army. Independents and nationalists would soon meet the same fate.

With the failure of the Nasserite coup, Jadid became chief of staff in August, a post he held until September 1965, freeing al-Assad to turn his attention to building his own political power base in the country, first by eliminating his rivals in the Military Committee, and then by moving into the party leadership apparatus in the eight-man Regional Command in September 1963. In the Ba'th Party structure, the Regional Command was the highest Syrian party authority, although the National Command theoretically directed all Regional (Country) Commands. Further, while al-Assad was not initially embroiled in the confrontation between Umran and Jadid, his support of the latter proved decisive in its outcome – the eventual removal of Umran and the rise of Jadid and Amin al-Hafiz in Syrian politics. The new clique of the Military Committee needed a high-ranking officer to become its figurehead and turned to Lieutenant Colonel Amin al-Hafiz, a disciplined and respected Sunni who three months after the breakup of the union had been sent to Buenos Aires as military attaché. Though he had never been a Ba'th Party member, he had become an acquaintance of the Military Committee members and a friend of Umran while in Cairo as an instructor in the Military Staff College during the union years. He was promoted to lieutenant general, made minister of the interior and distinguished himself in the eyes of the Military Committee by his brutal suppression of the nationalist and Nasserite riots in Aleppo and Damascus in May 1963. Two months later, because of his loyalty and success, he was also entrusted with the sensitive Ministry of Defense and brought into the inner circle of the NCRC to become its chairman. Eventually, he became prime minister, army commander-in-chief, secretary of the party's Regional Command and chairman of the Presidential Council. All this gave him a false sense of security which led him to challenge Jadid and al-Assad in the summer of 1965. He enlisted the support of the traditional party leadership, including Michel Aflaq, the secretary general and party founder, for this push for power.

Jadid who was now officially the assistant secretary of the Regional Command, but in reality its chief, seemed to have the upper hand in the struggle. However, the National Command of the Ba'th Party, led by Aflaq, passed resolutions annulling the decisions of the Regional Command, Jadid's power base, and dissolving it, effectively restructuring the leadership of Syrian politics and dropping the Military Committee from the NCRC. Soon after, Umran was reinstated and appointed minister of defense and commander-in-chief. He proceeded to replace key Jadid supporters in the army on February 21, 1966. Two days later, however, al-Hafiz, Umran and their followers were arrested by Jadid, and the civilian leaders of the Ba'th Party, including Aflaq, were imprisoned. Meanwhile, al-Assad moved to support Jadid by putting the air force at his disposal. At this point, al-Assad was rewarded with the Ministry of Defense, giving him his first cabinet seat.

A pattern of power sharing developed, with Jadid controlling the party apparatus and government while al-Assad continued to nurture his power base within the military. These two power centers would inevitably clash as their jurisdictions overlapped. Jadid looked upon al-Assad as a member of the Regional Command, and even as minister of defense, merely one member of the cabinet whose policies would be formulated by the Regional Command, namely himself, as its secretary. Thus, he insisted that the Regional Command was the sole legitimate authority and that al-Assad was bound to its dictates. Al-Assad, however, viewed his power as the reason why the party was able to maintain control.

With the Six Day War of 1967, Minister of Defense al-Assad lost his prized air force and Syria lost the Golan Heights. The civilians blamed the military and al-Assad became the focal point of their criticism. However, he maintained his post and grip on the military. Soon after the war, the traditional leaders, imprisoned fifteen months earlier along with purged senior army officers, were released and encouraged to leave the country. However, the rift between the party's Regional Command and the cabinet, headed by Jadid, and the rest of the army, headed by al-Assad, developed, with the two sides formulating contrasting ideological positions. The former called for the transformation of Syrian society to socialism and rejected any cooperation with the conservative regimes of the region, such as Iraq,

Lebanon, Jordan and Saudi Arabia, while calling for closer cooperation with the Soviet Bloc. The al-Assad group, on the other hand, believed the most important mission of Syrian society was to reclaim the land seized by the Israelis, which required full coordination between all Arab countries, including the conservative ones, even if that required delaying the socialist transformation of Syria. The dissension between al-Assad and Jadid now moved into a phase of confrontation between the party and the military. The issue came to a head at the party's 4th Congress in September and October 1968, in which all of al-Assad's proposals were rejected, and the army's prominence in Syrian party affairs was questioned by the delegates. Al-Assad, sensing the loss of his power, ordered his army officers to cease all contact with the party, which had the effect of turning the Ba'th into two parallel and competing structures – a military one with allegiance to al-Assad, and a civilian one whose loyalty was to Jadid.

Between 1969 and 1970, power gradually shifted to al-Assad's camp. By September 1970, he had emerged as the dominant power broker in Syria. However, in a final attempt to hold on to power, on October 30 Jadid mobilized his forces in the Regional Command to curtail al-Assad's control of the military. Al-Assad responded in what was termed the "Corrective Movement" by installing a fourteen-man Provisional Regional Command, made up of his most trusted supporters, who appointed him secretary general of the party and the Regional Command, as well as prime minister, on November 12. Soon after, the Provisional Regional Command nominated 173 members to fill the People's Assembly. Eighty-seven of them were Ba'thists, thirty-six were members of the General Union of Peasants and the rest were nationalists and independents, all of whom were vetted by the party. Jadid was arrested and remained in jail until his death in 1994.

Soon after his takeover, al-Assad embarked upon an ambitious, although less formally socialist, economic plan. He also paid more attention to real public policy, inviting old faithful Ba'thists who had been purged by Jadid to rejoin the party and build a new Syria. On February 22, 1971, he formally assumed the presidency; and two weeks later, in a plebiscite, he was confirmed in the role for a seven-year term.

Hafez al-Assad: the new regime

Born into a poor peasant family in 1930, al-Assad's rise to the highest office in the country symbolized the ascendancy of Syria's minorities and downtrodden masses, and the corresponding loss of power of the majority Sunni population, particularly in Aleppo and Damascus, the traditional centers of power. Also, since his success came at the expense of the civilian wing of the Ba'th Party, his assumption of power marked the complete subjugation of the party to the military, and of the country and the entire political process to the rule of one individual.

The immediate preoccupation of the new leader was to break Syria's political isolation in the Arab world and restore its credibility at home. He was successful in the first of these tasks. Ties with Egypt and Libya improved to the extent that, in 1972, proposals were floated for the federation of the three countries. However, the proposal was never seriously considered by Syria's partners and, in fact, later years witnessed a worsening of ties with these and other Arab countries. Nevertheless, the initial moves helped to bring Syria back into the Arab fold.

At the party level, al-Assad moved to consolidate his authority under a guise of allowing more cadre input into the leadership selection process, first through the election of delegates to the 5th Regional Congress in May 1971, in which his most trusted allies filled the new Regional Command. Then, at the 11th National Congress in August, the National Command was selected from the delegates, all of whom were also faithful to al-Assad. On March 3, 1972, al-Assad instituted yet another layer in the centralization of his control, through what was billed as popular input into the Syrian political system through elections to local councils. The formal function of these municipal councils was to aid the fourteen governors of the provinces in the administration of their duties. In the meantime, a parallel party structure supervised both the councils and the governors, and reported to the central government and the party.

Once he had control over his own party, al-Assad moved to tame the most active opposition parties, initiating a reign of terror against all other political organizations through arrests, assassination and harassment. On March 7, 1972, he gave his political opponents the impossible choice of joining an umbrella organization that the regime had instituted, the Progressive National Front, or being eliminated. The five most active political parties, including the communists, joined the Front, which caused all of them to fragment and weakened their popular appeal. In addition, as a condition of joining the Front, they were prohibited from any recruitment activities in the army or among students, and forced into a subservient position to the Ba'th, which turned them into instruments of the state. All other political parties were banned, which drove many of them underground. There were harsh reprisals for anyone caught participating in these groups: for instance, in March 1980, a law came into effect that authorized the death penalty for anyone belonging to the Muslim Brotherhood. Before long, the Front members were entirely dependent on the regime and virtually all opposition to the government had been neutralized.

In 1973, the People's Assembly completed its main task and drafted a permanent constitution that embodied the basic principles of the Ba'th Party, provided for a republican presidential system in Syria, and stipulated that the party was the vanguard of the state and society as the head of the Progressive National Front. The document declared Syria to be a democratic, popular socialist and sovereign state and proclaimed that the country was an integral part of the Arab homeland and its people were part of the Arab nation.

According to the constitution, the president would hold office for a seven-year term, was to be nominated by the party and the parliament and then approved by a popular plebiscite, held ultimate power as commander-in-chief of the armed forces, and had the right to appoint and dismiss the cabinet, dissolve the People's Assembly and assume its power. It was approved in a plebiscite in March 1973. Given the conditions of the constituion, it is hardly surprising that al-Assad won over 99 percent approval in each of the five presidential plebiscites that took place between 1971 and 1999. In 1974, he moved to take control of all professional associations and labor unions (whose right to strike had already been removed ten years earlier), on the premise that the state represented the interests of the working classes.

Al-Assad consolidated state power through the administration of a corporatist economic policy. The Ba'th Party apparatus created a multitude of corporatist associations for teachers, doctors, lawyers and other professional groups. These organizations were administered from the top down and were dominated by Ba'th Party representatives. This corporatist policy focused on consumption rather than accumulation. In other words, the party distributed resources and benefits throughout society – driven by oil revenues – in exchange for loyalty. As a function of these economic and political policies, the most significant institutions of Syrian society were progressively brought within the fold of the Ba'thist administration.[6]

While al-Assad received some semblance of legitimacy from the elections, these did nothing to increase the people's participation in the running of the country. During his time in office, the presidency was transformed into the undisputed focus of power, subordinating the party and all other elements in society to him. As president, secretary general of the party and commander of the armed forces, he occupied the three most poweful positions in Syria, and he maintained his power by appointing a close clique of his kinsmen, the Alawi, to key military, security and intelligence positions. However, fearing that his regime might be labeled sectarian, he also appointed a number of Sunnis to prominent positions in the government in order to undermine the threat of Islamic radicalism and to bring the Sunni aristocracy into the state system.

Al-Assad introduced a new style of leadership. A realist rather than an ideologue, he pursued a pragmatic approach to running the country, something that the old guard of the party detested. He was cautious but always ready to be ruthless, as could be seen in his responses to both internal and external threats. In Lebanon, his opponents were subjected to brutal reprisals; and at home he used harsh measures against all his foes. Most prominently, the regime brutally suppressed an uprising by the Muslim Brotherhood in February 1982, when 12,000 troops sealed off the city of Hama, systematically pummeled it with artillery, tanks and helicopter gunships, and caused the deaths of between 5,000 and 10,000 civilians during three weeks of bloody fighting.[7] Another uprising in Aleppo met the same fate. The regime's toughness, and some of its controversial foreign policy decisions, can be explained by its desire – or obsession – to maintain its grip on power.[8] As one scholar has pointed out, under al-Assad, the more isolated the regime felt, the more paranoid and militant its behavior became.[9]

However, when faced with international isolation, al-Assad always managed to reposition Syria, such as when he was faced by the loss of his main Cold War ally, the Soviet Union. In the new international environment, al-Assad maneuvered closer to the US, the only remaining superpower, when Iraq invaded Kuwait in August 1990. Diplomatically and economically, this realignment proved rewarding for Syria. In addition to easing tensions with the US, it increased Syria's influence within the region. (It had previously been regionally isolated as a result of its support for Iran during the Iraq–Iran War.)

During al-Assad's presidency, Syria became a regional power, and all sides now agree that any resolution of the Arab–Israeli conflict will be impossible without the Syrians' involvement. However, stability based on one individual is always fragile. When al-Assad suffered a heart attack in 1983, serious rivalry surfaced among aspirants to the leadership of the country. Having recovered, al-Assad settled the matter by exiling his brother, Rif'at, for some years. Then he groomed his elder son, Basil, for future leadership. However, this plan came to an abrupt end when Basil died in a car accident on his way to Damascus airport.

Bashar al-Assad

Ultimately, power was inherited by another son, Bashar, who was elected unopposed as president in 2000. An ophthalmologist by profession, Bashar was initially not thought to be "presidential material," although he managed to preside over a smooth transition of power and continues to rule. Contributing to his unimpeded rise to power was a societal desire for stability, the absence of a suitable alternative and the acquiescence of the army and security forces.[10] (Hafez al-Assad had previously replaced any members of the army and the security services whom he considered a threat to the succession.)

In the early 2000s, Syria underwent an intense period of social and political debate – the "Damascus Spring." In this milieu, dozens of "dialogue clubs" convened, with Syria's intelligentsia meeting to discuss the social and political matters concerning their country. Prominent in this period was the "Manifesto of 99," which was signed by prominent intellectuals. It called for the cessation of emergency rule, the abolition of martial law, the release of political prisoners, the safe return of exiles, and the right to form political and civil organizations. However, the "Damascus Spring" proved short-lived when the regime cracked down on the burgeoning civil society organizations in the second half of 2001, citing security concerns. This was followed by the passage of a restrictive press law. Within a year, continued arrests had erased all hope for political and social reform.[11]

However, beyond the perpetuation of Syria's closed political system and the suppression of dissent, Bashar al-Assad's presidency has been marked by a cautious liberalization of the economy, which has paid some dividends, and an attempt to control corruption within state institutions. Bashar has also presided over a rapid influx of refugees from war-torn Iraq, which has put a strain on the state's social services. In addition, he has been forced to maneuver the country's regional politics in light of the departure of its army and security forces from Lebanon in the aftermath of the assassination of former Lebanese Prime Minister Rafik al-Hariri and the subsequent emergence of the March 14 Movement. Lastly, Bashar is faced with an occasionally restive Kurdish population, numbering about 2 million, who have been denied cultural rights and face occasional harassment from the security services.

Following his father's geopolitical realignment in the early 1990s, Bashar has deftly maneuvered between accommodations with the United States and Israel – as seen in occasional collaborations with the US in its "war on terror" and informal peace dialogues with Israel – and Arab nationalist policies vis-à-vis Lebanon and Palestine, even though the latter have frequently put Syria at odds with the West and Israel. This pattern of cautious, pragmatic politics is likely to persist; and, barring outside interference, it seems that the Syrian regime will remain both stable and a force in regional politics.

Economy

Syria has the potential resource base to establish prosperity for its citizens. Relative to other Arab states, it is economically fortunate: it has fertile agricultural lands, oil and other mineral resources, and a growing textiles sector. Moreover, it is strategically located on trade routes to the Arab Peninsula and the Indian Ocean. Oil pipelines and road links between Western and Eastern Europe cross its territory. Also, because of its dominant position in Arab politics, it has benefited from aid and investment from the oil-rich countries of the Gulf.

In spite of these advantages, though, the country's economic performance has tended to be dismal, particularly in the 1990s. The country's preoccupation with security has been a major drain on its resources: the military budget consumes about 50 percent of national spending. Also, the economy is burdened by a huge and inefficient public sector and its dependence on oil revenues. However, there have recently been moves to revitalize the private sector, albeit in a slow way. Bashar al-Assad's move toward economic liberalization has been articulated as the development of a "social market economy," inspired by the experiences of other countries, such as China.

The economic picture seems to be improving. Syrian citizens working abroad have helped by remitting portions of their earnings back to the country. Agriculture has dramatically improved as a result of good weather and prudent policies. And the government has taken steps to reform the economy at a more fundamental level. Owing to a reform program initiated in 2004, most economic sectors have been opened to private investment, with a dynamic private banking sector now leading financial sector growth. The Damascus stock exchange was reopened in March 2009, albeit under strict controls: it operates only two days a week and for a few hours per session; stocks cannot be bought and sold on the same day; and stocks are not allowed to exceed 2 percent growth in any one day.[12] Nevertheless, after being shut down for forty years, the reopening of the exchange was emblematic of Syria's economic liberalization. The International Monetary Fund projects steady GDP growth over the coming years, particularly as excess liquidity from Gulf countries pours into the local economy to take advantage of new investment opportunities.

Notwithstanding the country's economic growth over the last few years, the most significant long-term threat remains the unstable regional environment. The rapid influx of Iraqis has contributed to "inflationary pressures, particularly in rental and real estate prices . . . [T]he surge in refugees [strains] government expenditures, particularly on energy and food subsidies, and spending on health and education. "[13] At the time of writing, the Iraqi refugee population in Syria stood at over a million. Syria is also increasingly being exposed to regional economic competition generated by its various bilateral and multilateral trade agreements with neighbouring countries. The influx of refugees and the opening up of the economy are just two of the many factors that will continue to shape Syria's domestic economy in the coming decades.

Foreign relations

The Arab–Israeli conflict dominates the foreign policy thinking of the regime. Syria, part of whose land is still under Israeli occupation, has traditionally been at the forefront of the Arab states allied against the common enemy, Israel. The leadership of the country strove to maintain a united Arab front against Israel. However, inter-Arab wrangling put paid to this, most significantly when Egypt broke away from the Arab fold to sign a separate peace deal with Israel. Syria then became the center of opposition to the Camp David Accord. By 1996, Arab unity in confronting Israel jointly had been almost totally shattered. Jordan normalized its relations with Israel, and the Palestinians signed their own separate deal with their former enemy. Syria could do nothing to halt these moves, so it has since pursued its own separate talks while continuing to maintain support for political actors that have rejected peace agreements with Israel. Negotiations between Syria and Israel are routinely bogged down by the refusal of the former to define the kind of peace it is willing to offer unless the latter has fully committed itself to a total withdrawal from the Golan Heights.

During the Cold War, Syria and the US harbored a mutual enmity. The Syrians viewed the US's unfailing support for Israel with bitterness, while the US was suspicious of Syria because of its links to the Soviet Bloc. During the Reagan era, Syria came to be seen as a Soviet satellite state that had to be countered, with Israel promoted as a valuable asset in this confrontation. Direct action was taken against the Syrians: the country was put on a list of states which the US claimed sponsored international terrorism[14] and some international moves were made to isolate it.

The collapse of the Soviet Union was a serious challenge to the rulers in Syria, who witnessed the collapse of their largest and most powerful military and diplomatic partner. However, the first Gulf War soon gave al-Assad the opportunity to reestablish Syria's position as a powerful regional player. Syrian forces joined the multinational coalition that drove Saddam Hussein's forces out of Kuwait, allowing Syria to shed its pariah status in the world. US hostility to the regime was mollified, and Syria came to be viewed as an essential participant in any peace talks, such as those that began in Madrid in 1991. Visits by key US politicians to Damascus increased, symbolizing the importance they accorded the regime. This was also reflected in the fact that Syria was granted a freer hand to deal with the Lebanese situation (see below).

Initially, the peace process after 1993 presented some difficulties for Syria. Whereas other Arab states – Jordan, the Maghrib countries and even the Gulf states – rushed to improve relations with Israel in order to enhance their economic prospects and relations with the United States, this was difficult for Syria as its soldiers had faced Israeli troops as recently as 1982. The relationship between the two countries was still marked by severe distrust, and while the US was willing to look more favorably on Syria due to its participation in the anti-Iraq coalition, Israel certainly was not. There was also the problem of Syria's cordial relations with Iran, which had initially been formed for pragmatic reasons: mutual enmity toward Hussein's regime in Iraq as well as toward Israel and the US.

Israel was quite happy to keep Syria isolated. Al-Assad, for his part, did not seem in any rush to alter Syria's longstanding position. The country's economic situation, while hardly booming, was not dire, and the flow of military equipment from the USSR had already been replaced by smaller but astute purchases from Russia, China and Iran. Meanwhile, Syria gradually solidified its hold over Lebanon to the point where the latter was accepted as a *de facto* annex of the former, as all political and administrative processes had the Syrians as final arbiters.

In April 1996 Hizbollah guerrillas based in refugee camps in southern Lebanon began to launch rockets over the border into northern Israel in response to Israeli attacks against civilians. These attacks had little effect, even in comparison to the day-to-day violence in the region, but Israeli Labor PM Shimon Peres was in the middle of a difficult election campaign, facing charges from the hawkish Likud Party that he was soft on Arabs. Therefore, his response, Operation Grapes of Wrath, was a calculated move to shore up his domestic credibility. However, it backfired tremendously when the plane, helicopter and artillery bombardments designed to flush out Hizbollah fighters instead killed hundreds of Lebanese civilians and Palestinian refugees. In one attack, direct artillery hits against a UN-protected refugee camp killed over a hundred men, women and children as well as four Fijian soldiers serving as peacekeepers. The damage to Israel's international image was instant and severe, and international moves to secure a ceasefire followed.

Due to its position as *de facto* power in Lebanon and its links with Hizbollah, Syria now took center stage. Al-Assad played his cards very carefully, meeting with the Russian and French foreign ministers during their trips through regional capitals while, at one point, refusing to meet with US Secretary of State Warren Christopher. Syrian troops in Lebanon took no action against Israeli forces, but they did aid in the evacuation of civilians and refugees. Of course, this greatly enhanced Syria's international image, especially in comparison with Israel's.

Subsequent to Israel's sixteen-day attack against Lebanon, a Likud government led by Benjamin Netanyahu rose to power. In the diplomatic tension that followed the election, Syria took a hard line on Arab unity against Israel. As successive Israeli governments have refused to compromise, mutual enmity between the two countries remains, although this has recently cooled somewhat. In mid-2008, Israel and Syria conducted informal peace talks through the good offices of Turkey, with the agreement of the US. For the Syrians, all diplomatic relations ultimately hinge upon the return of the occupied Golan Heights – which Israel's leadership at least seems willing to consider. Meanwhile, Israel demands that Syria cease its support for Hizbollah in Lebanon and Hamas in Palestine, and loosen its ties to Iran. These points have already stymied several negotiations, while Nentayahu's reelection as prime minister in 2009 – as well as his appointment of the belligerent Avigdor Lieberman as foreign minister – has set back the peace process. Israel has now officially dismissed Turkey from its role as mediator between the two countries, with Lieberman claiming: "So long as I am foreign minister and Yisrael Beiteinu [his party] is in the government, there will be no Turkish mediation . . . The Syrians want to talk? Then direct negotiations, only."[15] Syria, for its part, seems resigned to the stalemate, with Bashar al-Assad highlighting the "absence of a serious Israeli partner who aims to achieve peace."[16]

US–Syrian relations have likewise been difficult of late. The bellicose environment that followed the attacks of September 11, 2001 prompted the US to increase its diplomatic pressure on Syria, given the latter's sponsorship of US-designated "terrorist groups," namely Hizbollah and Palestinian militant organizations. These tensions were only exacerbated by the Anglo-American invasion and occupation of Iraq in 2003. Since then the US has repeatedly accused Syria of turning a blind eye, or even sponsoring, militants crossing its border into Iraq. However, the failure of the Anglo-American occupation forces to stabilize Iraq has encouraged limited discussion between the US and Syria, in the interest of securing peace in the beleaguered country. Likewise, the election of President Barack Obama, and his rhetorical dedication to engagement, has opened the possibility for a thaw in relations. Indeed, the Obama administration signaled its intention to reinstate an American ambassador to Syria in 2010, in the spirit of a "consistent and concerted outreach to the Arab world."[17]

In the modern independent era, Syria's foreign policy has been dominated by its uncompromising opposition to Israel, its attempts to be a leader of Arab nationalism within the region, and its delicate maneuverings in international diplomacy. However, perhaps its most significant foreign policy role has been played in neighboring Lebanon, sometimes in contravention of both Lebanese and international law, but at other times – as in the post-Ta'if era – with the full support of regional and international powers.

Republic of Lebanon

On September 1, 1920, the state of Greater Lebanon was established under a League of Nations French mandate. While elements of the Maronite community welcomed the fulfillment of a hard-fought dream, the new state's creation added fuel to Arab nationalism. Some of the dominant Sunnis, the most vehement opponents of the border changes, felt threatened by the inevitable dwindling of their influence in the new arrangement. While the state of Greater Lebanon formally ceased to exist in 1926, giving way to the Republic of Lebanon, the early period established underlying political–sectarian dynamics that have persisted to this day, and have occasionally erupted into war.

Lebanon's social fabric consists of more than eighteen known sects and religious groupings, which make peace within the country difficult but not impossible, as the Lebanese people proved when they created a political equilibrium in which all groupings found themselves precariously coexisting. However, the balance between these groups is so delicate that any internal, regional or international stimulus can upset the status quo. On the basis of a questionable 1932 census, representation in the parliament and the government was subject to the numerical strength of the various sects. A few years later, in November 1936, a Franco-Lebanese treaty was signed recognizing the independence of Lebanon in the wake of a similar one that had accorded the same status to Syria. However, events in France during the Second World War interfered with the implementation of the accord.

At the end of the war, the domestic scene was united in bringing the French mandate to a close. De Gaulle called for elections and these brought to power a new government headed by a Maronite, Bishara Khoury, as president, and a Sunni, Riad Solh, as prime minister. The new government hastily adopted reforms which never met with French approval. In a controversial move, the French detained members of the new regime and suspended the constitution. In its place, a puppet government was installed under the leadership of Emile Eddé. However, this move proved counter-productive for the French, since it united and strengthened domestic opposition to their rule. The French could not hold back the rising tide of discontent and they quit Lebanon in 1946. The country they left behind was dominated by the Maronites but divided over which path to pursue, pro-West or pro-Arab. Even more significantly, the dominant sectarian communities remained deeply distrustful of each other.

Political development

From the outset, independence for Lebanon was destined to be a bitter harvest. Building a single country whose past had been dogged by periods of extended acrimony among myriad sectarian communities was obviously going to be an uphill task. Although there have been ingenious attempts to reconcile the antagonistic groups, such as the National Pact, pressures of discord have proved insurmountable in certain periods of the country's independent era. Indeed, violence became a sinister and inextricable component of the nation's political development. Lebanon has always been a sanctuary for wandering marginals, vividly described as "victims of collapsing empires, of revolutions, and struggles to integrate new nations . . . solitary individuals who, exiled from their homes, have rootlessly wandered the globe over, pathetic but fascinating in their talents at survival."[18] It is this character that gives the country its uniqueness and, at times, its traumas.

The founders of Lebanon, the Maronites, still form a powerful sectarian community in the country. This Uniate Christian community escaped persecution in Syria in the second half of the seventh century and found a safe haven in Mount Lebanon. During the crusades, they formed a strong communion with Rome, a relationship that has since solidified. In 1861, they comprised 76 percent of the population of Mount Lebanon.[19] According to the 1932 census, they were the most dominant single sect in Lebanon.

Second, in numerical terms, to the Maronites among the Christian sects are the Greek Orthodox, whose political leadership has had tenuous, and often difficult, relations with its Maronite equivalent. Contrary to the Maronites, they do not form a compact community, being dispersed over the country, with many of them in Syria, too. This, in addition to the historical absence of a foreign patron, has made them receptive to the ideas of pan-Arabism and pan-Syrianism. The community is known for bringing forth prominent leaders of the Arab world, such as Antun Sa'ada, the founder of the Syrian Social National Party; Michel Aflaq, one of the founders of the Ba'th Party and its ideologist; and George Habash, father of the Arab Nationalist Movement and later leader of the radical Popular Front for the Liberation of Palestine. Smaller Christian groups include the Roman Catholics, the Armenian (Gregorian) Orthodox, Nestorian Assyrians and a few Protestant sects. There are also a small number of Jews in the country.

Among Muslims, the Sunnis are the dominant sect, although Shi'ites are now numerically larger. The Sunnis are more educated and prosperous than the Shi'ites, who remain a disadvantaged group. There are also Alawites, or Nusayris, but most of them are in Syria, where they wield enormous political influence, far in excess of their numerical size. The Druze form an additional sect in Lebanon. A closed community, they have played a crucial role in the making of modern Lebanon. Historically, they have proved adept at organizing themselves into fierce and disciplined fighting groups.

The Palestinians were the most recent marginal group to flock to Lebanon in search of sanctuary. These were refugees from the Arab–Israeli wars of 1948 and 1967, as well as the Jordanian civil strife of 1970. While some of them have since left Lebanon for other destinations, the bulk still live in the seventeen camps set up with the help of the United Nations Relief and Works Agency (UNRWA), which was specially created to cater for their humanitarian needs. The total number of Palestinians in Lebanon is in dispute, but the UNRWA puts their figure at 370,000.[20]

Many indigenous Lebanese, particularly the Maronites, resent the Palestinian presence. They have introduced a new demographic element since many of them are Sunni Muslim, threatening the power-sharing arrangements in the country. Moreover, Lebanon has now become an active front in the Arab conflict with Israel, with the Lebanese bearing the brunt of the cost of this.

Confessional state

The country's various Christian and Muslim sects live together, forming a precarious balance. The different, and often contradictory, positions adopted by the sects and communities are an ever-present menace to this balance. Disagreements between the groups translate into political rivalry. Thus, religion is a permanent feature of politics.

When independence came in 1943, within artificial borders arbitrarily fixed by the French, there were six large religious sects and about a dozen smaller ones, all with different traditions, cultures and loyalties. The Maronites had close affiliation with France and the West, while the Sunnis, who had benefited little from the mandate, looked to the East and the emerging trend of Arab nationalism.[21] It was through the wisdom and statesmanship of Bishara Khoury, the Maronite president, and Riad Solh, the Sunni prime minister, that a consensus was found. The basis of their cooperation was the unwritten National Pact. Principally, this limited the ambitions of the various sects in pursuit of foreign policy desires. Domestically, positions of authority were reserved only for members of designated sects. Accordingly, the president, prime minister and speaker of parliament were to come from the Maronite, Sunni and Shi'ite communities, respectively. Also, ministerial and top posts in the civil service were allocated with regard to the sectarian composition of the country. In the legislature, Christian and Muslim representation was fixed in the ratio of 6:5. Therefore, in the beginning, the Christians, and particularly the Maronites, wielded enormous power over the other communities. This was initially justified by the fact that the Maronites were more numerous than other sects. However, over time, the population balance tipped in favor of Muslims, which brought more pressure on the confessional system as resentment over the Maronites' power grew. The Shi'ites are especially disgruntled by their marginalization, particularly as they now outnumber the Sunnis. Likewise, the Druze resent the status quo since they are automatically disqualified from holding one of the three top positions of authority in the country.

These tensions have contributed to the volatile political climate in Lebanon. The fragile balance of power was first tested in 1958 when President Camille Chamoun allied the country with the West against the wishes of Arab nationalists who favored Nasserism. US forces were brought in to quell the crisis, and the problem was finally solved when Chamoun was replaced with Fouad Chehab, an army commander who had refused to use force against the Muslim rebels. Nevertheless, this crisis highlighted the fact that the system was not flexible enough to accommodate the demands of discontented communities, a state of affairs which escalated into civil war in the 1970s.[22] Eventually, though, civil strife exhausted all of the various communities, and the political dominance of the Christians was curtailed for the sake of peace.

Party politics and elections

Constitutionally, Lebanon is a parliamentary democracy, with a president whose term of office lasts six years. A prime minister is the head of government. Initially, he or she was appointed by the president, subject to the approval of parliament, but in the reformed system the prime minister is now directly appointed by parliament. Although, on the surface, this comprises a Western model, in practice the situation is rather different.

Politics preceding the civil war was dominated by a closed elite, historically embodied in the *zu'ama* (singular: *za'im*). Each *za'im*, the head of a sectarian clientele, owed his position to ancestry and wielded enormous power in his constituency. He might not have been a government minister himself, nor even a deputy, but his power gave him control over groups of deputies and ministers.[23] Because inheritance is a central element in the *zu'ama* system, politics in Lebanon came to be dominated by just a few families. Some of these families owe their dominance to the wealth and power accumulated during the feudal past, while others have risen through success in business and finance. A glance at the power brokers in the country clearly illustrates the continued centrality of these families. For instance, the Eddie, Solh, Karami, Jumblatt and Gemayel families have all provided a number of high-ranking politicians since independence.

Beside these historic *zu'ama*, the ecclesiastical hierarchies have played important political roles. The Maronite patriarch is a political force in the country due to his large following, and Maronite militias have historically exerted formal and informal pressure on the political system. The Muslim clergy has also played a pivotal role in the politics of the country, especially through organizing Shi'ite activists into potentially violent groups such as Amal and Hizbollah.

Given the political evolution of Lebanon, it is not surprising that the country's democracy is unique, and a far cry from what is practiced in the West. While the *zu'ama* have largely receded as the preeminent shapers of Lebanese politics, the sectarianism they embodied has not. Formally there are elections, but these could never be described as "free," any more than the resulting parliament could be described as "representative." Lebanon continues to be fractured along disputed lines and dominated by sectarian associations, authorities and, in some cases, paramilitary forces.

Civil strife and the search for national reconciliation

Conflict, in some cases catastrophic, has consumed a good portion of the country's independent era, characterized by sectarian violence, foreign intervention and failed efforts at reconciliation. Between 1975 and 1976, the country entered into a devastating civil war, which was followed by the arrival of Syrian forces. The Syrians became active combatants and their efforts to reconcile the belligerents ended in failure. Arab peacekeeping forces were sent in with the hope of bringing about peace, but again with no success. Complicating the situation further was an Israeli military intervention in 1977–1978 and a larger-scale one from 1982 to 1985, followed by successive overt and covert military operations against enemies based on Lebanese soil.

The civil war of 1975 can be traced back to events that took place in the wider region. The creation of Israel in 1948 initiated a massive exodus of Palestinians seeking refuge in neighboring countries, followed by more from the West Bank following the Six Day War of 1967. Resistance groups sprang up to fight for the rights of these people. The League of Arab States established the PLO in 1964 to organize the Palestinian people. Initially, however, many Palestinians were skeptical of the new organization and chose to organize autonomously. However, over time, it became the sole representative of the Palestinian people as the armed factions, particularly Yasser Arafat's Fatah group, gained control over it. The armed groups operated from their bases in Jordan and Lebanon, which invited Israeli retaliatory attacks. In Syria the guerrillas were organized by the army, but this was not the case in Lebanon, owing to its weak government. The Lebanese-based guerrillas were therefore free to do largely as they pleased, which resulted in increased tension in the south of the country. When, in 1970, the Jordanians evicted the militias, they shifted their operations to Lebanon, turning it into an operational base.

Some groups, especially the Maronites, were unhappy with the way in which the Palestinian militias were turning their country into a front line with Israel. On the other hand, the country's Arab nationalists, inspired by Nasser's nationalism, were keen for the militias to enjoy freedom of action. Under the prompting of the Maronites, the army was ordered to take limited action against the guerrillas, which resulted in paralysis of the government when Prime Minister Rashid Karami resigned in protest. The government then found itself isolated as Arab states rallied behind the guerrillas, albeit hypocritically, since it had been their expulsion of the militias from their territories that had caused the situation in Lebanon. A compromise was reached in November 1969 between General Bustani, the Lebanese army commander, and Arafat. However, this agreement was one-sided, legitimizing the Palestinian position at the expense of the interests of the Maronites. Animosity between the two groups deepened, particularly as Israeli retaliation against continued guerrilla attacks caused massive devastation in south Lebanon. Against this background, tensions within the Lebanese body politic exploded into intercommunal violence in 1975.

The ambush of a bus and the killing of its twenty-eight (mostly Palestinian) occupants on April 13 at Ain Rummaneh, a Christian suburb of Beirut, by Maronite militias is generally considered as the starting point of the civil war. (However, this attack was itself in retaliation for an earlier shooting at a Maronite church meeting attended by the *za'im* Pierre Gemayel in which several people died.) Clashes between the Maronites and the Palestinians spread quickly throughout the country. The fighting paralyzed Beirut. Politically, Rashid Solh's government collapsed and President Suleiman Frenjieh called on Noureddin Rifai to form a new cabinet. However, the Muslim establishment forced the resignation of the new prime minister, who was succeeded by Rashid Karami, their choice.

A ceasefire was announced but it did not hold. Instead, the fighting resumed in a more intense manner. The original combatants, the Maronite Phalanges and Palestinians who were outside Arafat's Fatah movement (which kept out of the conflict at first), were joined by other militias. By September, the dividing lines between the two groups of combatants were apparent. On one side there was a coalition comprising Gemayel, ex-President Chamoun, Frenjieh and Father Charbel Qassis, calling itself the Lebanese Front. Except for Qassis, all of these men headed their own militias. The largest Christian militia group was the Phalanges, with a force of about 10,000 men, followed by Chamoun's Tigers and

Frenjieh's Zghorta Liberation Army. Against them was the Lebanese National Movement, nominally under the leadership of Kamal Jumblatt, the Druze leader. This loose group included Jumblatt's Progressive Socialist Party, two communist parties and some Nasserist organizations. Militarily, it was weak and disorganized, and no match for the Maronite alliance. Meanwhile, the Palestinians remained divided, but many of them got drawn into the conflict, against Arafat's advice.

He could not even keep his own militia out of the war for long. When Phalanges forces attacked and massacred Palestinians in camps and slums around Beirut (with the worst attack occurring on January 18, 1976 at Karantina, where about 1,000 Palestinians and Lebanese Muslims were killed and nearly 20,000 more were expelled[24]), all Palestinian groups entered the conflict. The balance of power therefore shifted against the Maronites. The Palestinians sent reinforcements to back up National Movement forces attacking Maronite coastal districts south of Beirut. This was made possible by the dispatch by Syria of Palestinian Liberation Army (PLA) fighters – regular PLO forces stationed in Syria and technically under Arafat's command. The Syrian support for the National Movement and the Palestinian guerrillas included the supply of weapons and other *matériel*, which led to an escalation in the fighting.[25] Chamoun's fiefdom at Damour eventually fell and his militia surrendered in a major defeat for the Lebanese Front. Meanwhile, the army was thrown into disorder as sectarian loyalties emerged. Lieutenant Ahmad Khatib (a Sunni) mutinied to form the Arab Army of Lebanon in protest against the use of the air force against National Movement and Palestinian forces. This fracture in army ranks was not the last. By January 1976, the war had become more sectarian, and Christians moved to "their" sector in the east of the Beirut while Muslims relocated to the west.

A ceasefire was arranged after Syrian mediation that month, and an outline peace agreement was drafted. On February 14, a program of reforms known as the "Constitutional Document" was made public by President Frenjieh. The key elements of the document were that parliamentary seats were henceforth to be allocated on a 50:50 basis, the prime minister was to be elected by parliament, and civil service appointments were to be made on merit alone. However, implementation of these reforms was aborted in light of the army's disintegration, something that both the National Movement and the Palestinians were thought to have fomented. Muslim and Maronite soldiers battled for control of garrison towns and weaponry. Meanwhile, Jumblatt reiterated his determination to achieve a military victory. Druze campaigns threatened the presidential palace and Frenjieh fled to the safety of Mount Lebanon. A ceasefire was achieved only after intense Syrian pressure, backed by the entry of Syrian armor into Lebanon and the blockade of National Movement ports (Tyre, Sidon and Tripoli).

This marked a change of Syrian policy toward Lebanon: it was now actively pursuing a military solution to the crisis. The offensive specifically targeted Jumblatt, whom the Syrians blamed for the collapse of the Constitutional Document.

Syrian military involvement

The Syrian invasion commenced on May 31, 1976 and a ceasefire was enforced on June 9, although Palestinian forces offered stiff resistance. In the Arab world, the Syrian move was heavily criticized, particularly by Iraq. In light of this, its next move against the Palestinians comprised an attempt to wear down the militias' fighting capacity. In concert with Christian forces, the Syrian army exerted gradual pressure on the Palestinian guerrillas and their leftist allies. However, the Palestinians remained resolute. Consequently, the Syrians launched decisive military actions between September 28 and October 17. These offensives, again carried out jointly with Christian forces, forced the Palestinians to reach an accommodation with the Syrians.

Earlier, on May 8, 1975, the Syrians had engineered the election of their nominee, Elias Sarkis, to replace President Frenjieh, who had become very unpopular. Thus, it was clear that peace could not be achieved without considerable Syrian involvement. The Riyadh mini-summit of October 15, 1976 subsequently brought about a *de facto* ceasefire, and the Syrians called for the formation of a 30,000-man peacekeeping force, known as the Arab Deterrent Force (ADF). All parties agreed to this on the understanding that the bulk of the ADF's troops would be Syrian, thereby legitimizing Syria's continued presence in Lebanon. Following the Riyadh agreement, 6,000 Syrian troops and 200 tanks, now under the banner of the ADF, took up positions in Beirut, while other Syrian forces entered Maronite and National Movement territories.[26] Meanwhile, the Palestinians shifted their forces to the south – a move that would soon heighten tension with Israel.

The first two years of the civil war exacted an immense toll on Lebanon. Officially, 50,000 people were killed, twice that number wounded, and 600,000 displaced.[27]

The Israeli invasion

In its struggle against Palestinian guerrilla groups and their backers, Lebanon increasingly became a cause for concern among Israeli leaders. And their worries were exacerbated when Palestinians turned the country into an operational base and Syria's role in Lebanon expanded. Initially, the Israelis provided support to groups allied to them, particularly in Maronite villages along the border, where there was a small force under a rebel Lebanese officer, Major Sa'd Haddad. Known as the South Lebanese Army (SLA), this group was formed to fight Palestinian and National Movement militias in the south of Lebanon.

With the defeat of the Labor Party by Likud in the 1977 general election, Menachem Begin came to power in Israel and instantly toughened his country's policy toward Lebanon. Begin, who was known for his aggressive stance toward the Palestinians, set out to liquidate the threat posed by the guerrillas operating out of Lebanon, and in 1978 he ordered Israeli troops to cross the border.

The invasion came after the seizure of an Israeli bus on March 11, which resulted in the deaths of thirty-seven Israelis and nine Palestinian guerrillas in a gun battle. A few days later, 25,000 Israeli soldiers, supported by air and naval power, crossed into Lebanon, occupying the south up to the Litani River. The operation aimed to strike at Palestinian guerrilla infrastructure and eliminate their bases along the border. Casualties among civilians were predictably high and many Shi'ites had to leave their homes. However, the guerrillas had time to relocate to the north, so their casualties and loss of equipment were minimal.

On March 19, the UN Security Council met to adopt two resolutions, 425 and 426. Resolution 425 called on Israel to withdraw its forces from Lebanese territory and authorized the setting up of a peacekeeping force; 426 outlined the mandate of the force. A few weeks later, the force – known as the United Nations Interim Force in Lebanon (UNIFIL) and comprising contingents from Canada, France, Iran, Norway and Sweden – had been mustered. Reinforcements from Nepal, Nigeria and Senegal joined UNIFIL at the end of April, bringing the total number to 4,000. In response, Israel pulled back its force to within six miles of its border – an area it called the "security zone." On June 12, Israel decided to hand this strip of territory to Haddad, whose SLA forces controlled the area. Suddenly, therefore, Haddad acquired complex military facilities and hardware, which, in the future, he would put to effective use against his foes.

The Israeli withdrawal and the deployment of the international force never calmed the situation in Lebanon. In the south, tensions remained high and nothing could be done about them since the government remained weak and ineffective. Haddad's militia, with the tacit approval of their Israeli sponsors, continued to harass the peacekeepers and frustrate any efforts to spread government control to the south. (At the beginning of March 1983, they even fired on UN positions, and a number of peacekeepers lost their lives.)

In the spring of 1981, Israel was gearing up for elections later in the year. Likud's poor domestic record weakened its chances at the polls. Thus, the decision was made to contest the election on foreign policy, which had a strong anti-Arab content. Attacks on Palestinian targets in southern Lebanon, Beirut and Syrian-controlled areas intensified. In addition, there were aerial confrontations with the Syrians. For instance, Israeli planes went into action against Syrian helicopters on April 28 in support of Christians battling Syrian forces at Zahle. The next day, Syria deployed surface-to-air missiles in the Bekaa, and in response Israel demanded their immediate removal. In the summer elections, a group of hard liners came to power in Israel, namely Ariel Sharon (defense minister), Yitzhak Shamir (foreign minister) and Moshe Arens (ambassador to the UN). Further afield, Ronald Reagan had come to power in the United States in January, and the early signs were that he was more sympathetic to Israel than his predecessor, Jimmy Carter, had been.

Against this background, Israeli leaders met on June 5, 1982 and gave the go-ahead for a second invasion of Lebanon, in an operation codenamed Peace of Galilee. Its main aims were the destruction of the Palestinian infrastructure in Lebanon and the establishment of a government that would sign a peace treaty with Israel.

The very next day, Israeli Defense Forces (IDF) entered Lebanon. Palestinian positions were subjected to attacks from land, air and sea. UNIFIL forces were pushed aside as the IDF swept past. Clashes in the Bekaa Valley were minimal, although the Syrian air force sustained high losses. On June 9, Israeli air strikes destroyed missiles deployed by the Syrians in the Bekaa. Thereafter, diplomatic efforts intensified in a bid to contain the conflict, and a ceasefire was agreed between Syria and Israel on June 11. The IDF then shifted their focus from the Bekaa to the Beirut–Damascus highway, which it soon occupied, before laying siege to Beirut between June 26 and September 1. Massive bombardments by planes and artillery were brought to bear on the Palestinian guerrillas and Syrian forces trapped in Beirut in an effort to force them to leave. One of Israel's main objectives was met in August, when American envoys received word that the Palestinians and Syrians had agreed to quit the capital. The withdrawal was to be supervised by a multinational force, including the US. On August 21, the first of about 8,000 Palestinians left by sea, and the whole exercise came to a close on the 31st, by which time about 6,000 Syrian soldiers and PLA brigade members had also left. The multinational force, including units from Italy and France as well as the US, left between September 10 and 12, its task complete.

Alongside the departure of the Palestinians, the election to the presidency of the pro-Israeli Bashir Gemayel on August 23, 1982 and the signing of the Lebanese–Israeli agreement of May 17, 1983 seemed big achievements for the Israelis. However, the Syrians were determined to counter these setbacks. Unable to launch direct attacks themselves, they relied on proxies to carry out their plans. These included Jumblatt's Druze militia as well as those of Amal (Shi'ites), the Syrian Social Nationalist Party (Greek Orthodox and Druze), the Syrian Ba'th Party, and supporters of Suleiman Frenjieh (Maronite) and Rashid Karami (Sunni). The Syrians, who were well schooled in the use of guerrilla and underground violence,[28] depended on these groups to eliminate opponents and undermine policies contrary to their interests. Bashir Gemayel was assassinated on September 14, 1982 and his brother, Amin, was elected a week later to replace him. In the wake of the assassination, Israeli and Israeli-supported Lebanese soldiers massacred hundreds of Palestinian refugees in the Sabra and Shatila refugee camps in southern Lebanon, ostensibly as part of an offensive against "terrorists." The following year, the May 17 agreement was abrogated. Arafat (who had fallen out of favor with the Syrians) was forced out of Lebanon by Palestinian guerrillas supported by the Syrians on December 19, 1983. By then, the Israelis, facing the prospect of a general uprising of the Shi'ite community in the occupied southern territories, had already started to withdraw to the Awwali River. They went all the way back to the international border at the end of May 1985.

Pro-Khomeini fundamentalist groups sprang up in the course of the war and established a strong foothold among the Shi'ite community, threatening the dominance of Amal. Playing an important role in the transformation of these groups were the 1,500 or so Iranian Revolutionary Guards who, during the war, reached Baalbek. The Islamic groups strove to establish an Islamic republic in Lebanon on the Iranian model. Although incompatible with the Syrian model, strong mutual interests between the Syrians and the backers of these groups gave them freedom of action. In the summer of 1983, the groups carried out a number of suicide operations against the Israeli occupation forces and Western targets: for example, a suicide attack on the American Embassy left sixty-three Americans dead, and another suicide attack killed twenty-eight Israelis at Tyre. In February 1984, the Americans finally withdrew their force from Beirut following a suicide bomb in October 1983 which killed 241 American soldiers at a barracks. All of these attacks aided the Syrians, with minimal direct involvement or cost.

To capitalize on this situation, the Syrians launched a peace initiative which resulted in the December 28, 1985 Tripartite Agreement signed in Damascus by three major militias: the Amal, Lebanese Forces and the Druze Socialist Progressive Party. However, this agreement soon ran into trouble when the leader of the Lebanese Forces, Eli Hobeika (who had been instrumental in its drafting), was deposed by Samir Geagea. Sporadic communal violence and assassinations continued, and Amin Gemayel's government was too fragile to do anything to rectify matters.

The situation worsened when Gemayel's term of office came to an end. The Syrians, whose troops had returned to Beirut in 1986, used their influence to sway the presidential election in favor of a candidate of their choice, which caused much confusion and resulted in no one officially holding the post for over a year. On September 22, 1988, fifteen minutes before his term as president expired, Gemayel appointed Michel Aoun, commander-in-chief of the Lebanese army, as prime minister, but the Syrians refused to recognize him. Instead, they backed Selim al-Hoss. Thus, two rival governments emerged.

Aoun was a dynamic personality who cultivated considerable support within the Christian camp. His crusade against the Syrians caused further destruction in Beirut, but he had some initial success against them. However, he soon got locked in a conflict between the Lebanese army loyal to him and Geagea's Lebanese Front militia, and made more enemies when he tried to close down the illegal ports on which many guerrilla groups relied for supplies. Logically, the Syrians exploited these difficulties to defeat Aoun. In the middle of the confrontation, Aoun declared a war of liberation from Syrian occupation on March 14, 1989.

The confrontation between the Lebanese army and the Syrians that ensued attracted more inter-Arab and international pressure on Syria to seek a peaceful settlement. The heads of state of Algeria, Morocco and Saudi Arabia (at the behest of the League of Arab States) developed a framework for talks between the Lebanese factions at Ta'if in Saudi Arabia that was endorsed by the US, the USSR and the European Community. The result was the Ta'if Accord of October 1989.

The Ta'if Accord

Arab countries were jolted into action when the conflict between Aoun and the Syrians took a dangerous turn, threatening to escalate into a wider war. Iraqi military support for Aoun could bring Damascus and Baghdad into a head-on collision. At the Casablanca Summit of May 1989, the League of Arab States created the Tripartite High Commission, consisting of the leaders of Algeria, Saudi

Arabia and Morocco, to resolve the conflict. Under the auspices of this committee, sixty-two members of the Lebanese parliament met in Ta'if from September 30 to October 22, 1989. The parliamentarians were split evenly between Christians and Muslims. From this meeting emerged the Document of National Understanding, whose salient features were similar to reform efforts of the past. In essence, the document upheld the central features of the National Pact of 1943, conceding that it was futile to try to rid the country of political sectarianism. The UN backed the accord on October 31. In Lebanon, the Chamber of Deputies approved constitutional reforms based on it.

The key reform was the loss of some of the Maronite president's powers in favor of the Sunni prime minister and the legislature. The speaker of the People's Assembly would be elected for a four-year term, and the prime minister would be nominated by the president only after consultation with the speaker. The cabinet would be the executive authority, and the position of prime minister would be the single most important in the system. Distribution of seats in the People's Assembly would be on the principle of Christian–Muslim parity. "There is no question that the Maronites and the Shi'i Muslims were the big losers in Ta'if. The political predominance of the Maronites, symbolized notably in the prerogatives of the president, became history."[29]

However, implementation of the accord was delayed due to Aoun, who had rejected it on the grounds that it was silent on the withdrawal of Syrian forces from Lebanon. By mid-1989, it was estimated that more than one million people had fled Beirut due to the exchange of artillery fire between the eastern and western sectors of the city, and more than 800 people had been killed.[30] Meanwhile, the Syrians engineered the election of Rene Muawad to the presidency on November 5, but seventeen days later he was assassinated. The Lebanese parliament met to fill the vacant post, and Elias Hrawi was elected. He had no domestic power base but had close links with the Syrians and soon won the support of the Arab countries and the world in general. El-Hoss's government was recognized and the Syrians resolved to push Aoun out of the Ba'abda Palace by force, if necessary. Under the cover of the Gulf crisis, the Syrians made a decisive move against Aoun in the autumn of 1990, which led to his defeat on October 13. He took refuge in the French Embassy, and later fled to France.

Implementation of the Ta'if Accord could now proceed. 'Umar Karami (Rashid's brother) formed a government of national unity on December 24, 1990, with the cabinet of thirty individuals, split equally between Christians and Muslims, made up of militia leaders. The various militias had all withdrawn from Beirut a week later. The parliament declared the dissolution of all militias, except for Hizbollah. The army expanded its deployment in the country. In September 1992, elections brought to power Rafiq Hariri – a wealthy Sunni supported by the Saudi royal family – as prime minister and Nabih Berri as speaker of parliament. The process of reconciliation and reconstruction was consolidated, but Syrian influence remained overwhelming. Syria had disregarded the agreement that its troops would withdraw to the Bekaa region by 1992, and the 1995 presidential election was canceled when Hafez al-Assad indicated that he wanted

Hrawi to remain in power. Eventually, parliament approved a constitutional amendment extending his term by three years, thereby legitimizing the Syrian intervention. Hrawi was succeeded by Emile Lahoud in 1998. Under the precedent set by Hrawi, parliament extended his term by an additional three years in 2004.

The March 14 Movement and the degradation of Lebanese politics

Simmering opposition to the Syrian presence in Lebanon and the underlying sectarian logic of the country exploded with the killing of Rafiq Hariri on February 14, 2005. After that, Lebanon saw a resurgence of sectarianism and a violent internal politics, a process which culminated in the Israeli invasion of summer 2006. Hariri was killed when a massive explosion ripped through his motorcade in Beirut. While the perpetrators of this act have never been identified, the anti-Syrian political bloc immediately laid blame on the Syrian regime of Bashar al-Assad and demanded a full withdrawal of Syrian forces from Lebanon. The United Nations Security Council, in turn, adopted Resolution 1559, calling for the removal of Syrian forces and the disbanding of Hizbollah. Then, under Resolution 1595, an investigative team led by the German judge Detlev Mehlis was sent to Lebanon to investigate the circumstances of Hariri's killing. The team's initial report was released on October 20, 2005 and pointed the finger at the Syrian regime and its Lebanese proxies. Subsequent reports have maintained this position. The United States and France also blamed Syria.

Whatever the exact circumstances of Hariri's killing, the event created fissures in Lebanon's already fragile polity. On March 8, 2005 Hizbollah organized a pro-Syrian demonstration. In response, on March 14, a massive anti-Syrian protest took place at the site of Hariri's grave in Beirut, demanding an end to Syrian influence and an international inquiry into the assassination. The anti-Syrian alliance was labeled the "March 14 Movement," and its nominal leader was Sa'd Hariri, Rafiq's younger son.

The combined pressure of the anti-Syrian alliance and international allies forced the withdrawal of some 14,000 Syrian troops, which culminated on April 26. By then, the pro-Syrian government of 'Umar Karami had collapsed (on April 13). The anti-Syrian bloc would subsequently win 72 out of 128 seats in parliament. Fouad Siniora, a former advisor to Rafiq Hariri and a close associate of his son Sa'd, was appointed prime minister.

While the success of the March 14 camp was widely celebrated, particularly in the American press (who labeled it the "Cedar Revolution"), its rise to power saw a resurgence of political sectarianism and an associated campaign of violence against Syrian laborers: scores of guest workers were killed or beaten.[31] Of even more concern was the marginalization of the country's Shi'a population, and the concurrent empowering of Hizbollah. A popular Shi'a militia founded during the Israeli invasion of 1982, Hizbollah became a major political force representing the country's whole Shi'a population. It has historically held a Khomeinist vision of politics, and has been supported by both Iran and Syria. Ever since its formation, it has sustained a paramilitary campaign against Israel, particularly against the latter's presence in the disputed Shebaa farms region.

On July 12, 2006 ongoing skirmishes between the IDF and Hizbollah developed into a full-scale war[32] when eight Israeli soldiers were killed and two were captured in a cross-border tussle. Using the missing soldiers as a pretext, Israel launched an air and land campaign into Lebanon, ostensibly to eliminate Hizbollah as a military and political force. Ultimately, the Israeli bombardment would kill over 1,000 Lebanese civilians and devastate its infrastructure, causing billions of dollars' worth of damage. A UN-brokered ceasefire came into effect August 14 (although Israel continued to launch sporadic raids into Lebanon's Bekaa Valley). In the aftermath of the war, a tenuous peace was maintained by the United Nations Interim Force in Lebanon, comprising over 13,000 troops representing nearly 30 countries.

Israel's military campaign in Lebanon, for all its potency, failed to end Hizbollah as a force in Lebanon. Moshe Arens, three time defense minister of Israel, opined: "as the war they so grossly mismanaged wore on . . . gradually the air went out of them . . . The war, which according to our leaders was supposed to restore Israel's deterrent posture, has within one month succeeded in destroying it."[33] This failure resulted in a massive political controversy within Israel, while Hizbollah's resistance was celebrated throughout the Arab world, where it was lionized as a rare victory against Israel.

In the aftermath of the Israeli invasion, Lebanon continued to be plagued by political sectarianism and tension, and risked returning the abyss of a civil war. Hizbollah – and its patrons in Syria and Iran – stood against the Lebanese government – backed by the US and Saudi Arabia. In the spring of 2008, the government attempted to shut down Hizbollah's private communication network, which Hizbollah justifies as a defensive and necessary infrastructure in its struggle against Israel. In response, on May 8, Hizbollah instigated street-fighting in Beirut which quickly got out of hand.

However, a week of negotiations in Doha under League of Arab States auspices reached an agreement on May 21. Under the terms of this agreement, General Michel Suleiman – commander of the Lebanese armed forces, and respected for his perceived neutrality during the May fighting – succeeded Emile Lahoud as president of Lebanon. He was sworn into office four days later. The next task was to form a national unity government, with Hizbollah given the power of veto over key cabinet positions. Additionally, Lebanon's political districts were redrawn into smaller enclaves in the lead-up to the 2009 parliamentary elections, in order to give fuller representation to the country's various sects. Finally, each side "agreed to refrain from accusations of treason or other language that can incite sectarian violence, and from resorting [to] violence, armed or otherwise."[34] The accord was approved by Iran, with that country's Foreign Ministry spokesman Mohammad 'Ali Hosseini characterizing it as an "example of regional integration for achieving stability and tranquility." Syria likewise applauded the agreement, and in October 2008 the two countries signed a joint document formalizing relations between them, which paved the way for full diplomatic ties for the first time since they won independence in the 1940s.[35] In the West, the US publicly welcomed the Doha Accord, although it expressed concern over Hizbollah's new veto power.

However, the high-minded aspirations of the accord were quickly undermined by the realities of Lebanon's sectarian and political infighting. According to the accord, "16 seats in the new 30-member cabinet were allocated to members of the parliamentary majority, the March 14 bloc. An additional 11 portfolios were slated for the March 8 opposition bloc, with the remaining three to be chosen by the president."[36] Predictably, given the multi-denominational composition of the March 8 and March 14 blocs, the parties within the two groups bickered for months over the distribution of cabinet positions, and this back-room politicking has only reinforced the sectarian competition in the country's polity.

Nevertheless, the basic power-sharing contours of the Doha Agreement were reinforced in the 2009 Lebanese general election. The American- and Saudi-backed March 14 coalition won 61 out of 128 parliamentary seats, while the March 8 coalition took 57 seats, with the Progressive Socialist Party taking the remaining 10. Following the election, Sa'd Hariri – with the backing of 86 members of parliament – was asked by President Suleiman to serve as prime minister and Nabih Berri, "an ally of Hizbollah and Syria and head of the Amal movement, was reelected speaker of parliament."[37] Though the election was conducted without violent incidents and a government was duly formed, the political tripwires in Lebanon remain fundamentally the same. For the Hariri government, "the most precarious issues [remain] whether to give veto power to the minority alliance in parliament [and] whether to disarm Hizbollah."[38]

Hizbollah is now a permanent fixture in the Lebanese political environment – a multifaceted socio-political movement representing the country's Shi'a population. The evolution of Hizbollah from paramilitary force into influential political actor can be understood in an analysis of its 1985 and 2009 political manifestos. The first of these documents defined the movement as part of a "nation" led by Ayatollah Khomeini and called upon "Lebanese to adopt Islamic rule." Hizbollah was, in other words, an expressly revolutionary Shi'a movement which, aside from its immediate objective of opposing Israeli occupation, saw its ultimate objective as the Islamic project. The 2009 document, beyond offering a critique of American foreign policy and restating Hizbollah's antipathy toward Israel, provides some revealing comments on Lebanese politics, declaring:

> We want Lebanon for all Lebanese alike, and we want it unified. We reject any kind of segregation or federalism, whether explicit or disguised . . . Our vision of the state that should build together in Lebanon is represented in the state that preserves public freedom, the state that is keen on national unity . . . [A] state that depends on qualified people regardless of their religious beliefs . . . applies balanced development between all regions.

While one may doubt the full sincerity of this statement, the 2009 manifesto (the organization's first since 1985) is a marked step back from Hizbollah's original orientation, indicating a desire to work within the bounds of normal politics.

However, the fundamental questions of disarmament and Hizbollah's status as a parallel state within Lebanon remain largely unanswered.[39]

Through 2009, Lebanon's precarious balance was maintained, and, indeed, showed signs of further stabilization. In December, Sa'd Hariri made a landmark visit to Syria, where he was hosted by Bashar al-Assad. The two men held a private meeting that lasted over three hours, followed by a public embrace. Hariri suggested that "skies are blue between Syria and Lebanon" and promised a new phase of cooperation and good relations between the former foes. While this certainly overstates the two countries' accord, it is nevertheless remarkable, given the March 14 Movement's suspicion of Syrian complicity in the killing of Hariri's father. Analysts have additionally suggested that Hariri's rapprochement with Syria represents an attempt to mend relations with Hizbollah. However, he will have to be very careful not to alienate his March 14 backers if he continues down this route.[40]

Lebanon and the Palestinians

Lebanon's most significant obstacle to peaceful development remains the presence of thousands of Palestinians in the south of the country, in Israel's self-declared "security zone." This was most graphically demonstrated in April 1996, when Israeli strikes against "Hizbollah guerrillas" near refugee camps killed hundreds of Lebanese citizens and Palestinian refugees. Lebanon had not been extensively involved in the Palestinian–Israeli peace negotiations, ongoing since 1992, as most of its policy was controlled by Syria, with Israel regarding the southern portion of the country as its private military preserve. The resolution of the Israeli–Hizbollah conflict indicated Lebanon's lack of influence and even legitimacy – despite the fact that the conflict took place on Lebanese soil, negotiations were undertaken with Syria.

In the conflagrations that followed the emergence of the March 14 Movement, the Palestinian population, marginalized and destitute, continued its meager existence. According to UN statistics, of the 400,000 Palestinians living in Lebanon, some 215,000 live in camps. Nahr al-Bared, a camp in the north of the country housing some 30,000 Palestinian refugees, came under attack from the Lebanese army in May 2007. (This was in direct contravention of the 1969 Cairo Agreement, which prohibited the entry of the Lebanese army into all Palestinian camps.) The justification for this attack was the supposed presence of Fatah-al-Islam, an Islamic militant group, in the camp. Unsurprisingly, this group has been linked to al-Qa'ida and the Syrian regime by Israel and the United States. Elsewhere, however, it is reported that it is actually a splinter movement of Fatah al-Intifadah – a Palestinian group – and had been propositioned by "people [representing] the Lebanese government's interests . . . presumably to take on Hizbollah."[41] Whatever the truth, Palestinian civilians have again suffered the most. Moreover, political divisions have only hardened. Hizbollah, no ally of hardline Sunni movements, initially supported the government offensive, although it subsequently condemned the attack. Hasan Nasrallah, its leader, was quoted as saying: "The Nahr al-Bared camp and Palestinian civilians are a red line . . . We will not accept or provide cover or be partners in this."[42] While the Palestinian issue persists in Lebanese politics, the preeminent domestic political drama remains the conflict between Hizbollah and the March 14 Movement.

Economy

Lebanon before the civil war of 1975–1990 was more prosperous than many developing countries. Its per capita income was higher than those of all countries in the Asian region except for Japan, Singapore, Israel and Kuwait. This prosperity was powered mainly by the private sector, contrary to the situation in most Arab countries. In particular, trade and banking were the key areas in the economy, overshadowing industry and agriculture. The strategic position of the Levant coast between East and West was conducive to commercial pursuits. Moreover, the growth of oil production in the Middle East and the associated expansion of links with markets in Europe increased the significance of the Levant. The region also attracted tourists; malaria and smallpox had been eliminated; and 80 percent of the country's population were literate. Nevertheless, the country was plagued by serious ills that needed addressing. The wide division between the rich and the poor was a grave matter, and might have contributed to the building of tensions that led to the civil war. For example, the outskirts of Beirut, where the affluent led luxurious lives, housed a mass of poor Shi'ites who had been displaced from the south by war and conflict. The numbers of the disadvantaged swelled as migrants from the countryside came to seek better lives or security.

The generally positive economic profile of the country was destabilized when the country was swallowed up by civil strife. Sixteen years of destruction exacted a high toll on the economy. The final cost was estimated at $25 billion, and 150,000 deaths.[43] Many more Lebanese were forced to desert their homes. However, with the conflict finally over, the Lebanese are devoting their energies to the restoration of their country to its previous preeminent position in the region.

In the post-conflict era, the government of the late Rafiq Hariri (1992–1998) spearheaded efforts to reconstruct Lebanon. To achieve this, a ten-year program, dubbed Horizon 2000, allocated $11.7 billion to rebuilding damaged or destroyed infrastructure, rehabilitating institutions and rejuvenating the private sector.[44] The international community was also encouraged to contribute to the reconstruction efforts. Hariri's government went a long way to meeting the objectives of the plan. The Lebanese pound was stabilized, inflation was brought down from 131 percent to 10 percent, and Beirut's infrastructure started to be repaired.[45] However, the reconstruction efforts were dealt huge blows by the Israeli attacks of 1996 and 2006. Israeli bombing caused billions of dollars' worth of infrastructure damage, and the international community has so far provided a pittance in reconstruction funds. According to the most recent figures, Lebanon also now has a massive external debt of $21.11 billion.[46] Additionally, the reconstruction efforts have failed to address underlying socio-economic distinctions and mass poverty, particularly as most of them have focused on Beirut's center, leaving outlying parts of the city (and the rest of the country) in disrepair.

Foreign relations

Foreign policy in Lebanon is a contentious matter, principally because of the identity problem that the country has faced. While some communities have been keen to be fully integrated into the Arab camp, others have been resentful of taking this course. After the civil strife resulting from one president's attempts to move the country closer to the West, leaders have been careful not to repeat the same mistake. A balance between maintaining a close relationship with the Arab world and keeping traditional links with the West has therefore been sought for the sake of peace.

After Hafiz al-Assad assumed the role of "godfather" to Lebanon, the country could not countenance adopting a position contrary to that of Syria, so it was difficult to talk of an independent Lebanese foreign policy while this relationship was in place. This situation was most clearly demonstrated in the aftermath of Operation Grapes of Wrath in 1996, when Lebanon's role in the peace settlement was assumed by Syria. Recent developments, precipitated by the events of March 2005, freed Lebanon from Syrian tutelage as the March 14 Movement seized power and international pressure forced the evacuation of Syrian troops. The internal politics of Lebanon now sit at a crossroads, as jockeying for power between the March 14 Movement (supported by the US and the Saudis) and the forces affiliated with Hizbollah in the March 8 Movement (backed by Syria and Iran) almost guarantee an unsteady and turbulent future. Notwithstanding the recent Doha Accord and Hariri's apparent rapprochement with Syria, the domestic and regional dynamics of the Lebanese conflict are far from resolved and will remain at the forefront of the country's problematic political environment.

Notes

1 Patrick Seale, *The Struggle for Syria: A Study of Post-war Arab Politics, 1945–1958* (London: Oxford University Press, 1965), p. 25.
2 Valerie Yorke, *Domestic Politics and Regional Security: Jordan, Syria, and Israel; the End of an Era?* (Aldershot: Ashgate, 1988), p. 101.
3 Seale, op. cit., pp. 310–311.
4 Patrick Seale, *Assad: The Struggle for the Middle East* (Berkeley: University of California Press, 1988), p. 67.
5 Ibid., p. 85.
6 Ray Hinnesbusch, *Syria: Revolution from Above* (Oxford: Routledge, 2002), p. 83.
7 Alasdair Drysdale & Raymond A. Hinnebusch, *Syria and the Middle East Peace Process* (New York: Council on Foreign Relations, 1991), p. 34.
8 Juzif Abu Khalil, *Lubnan wa-Suriya: mashaqqat al-ukhuwwah* (Beirut: Sharikat al-Matbu'at lil-Tawzi' wa-al-Nashr, 1991), p. 84.
9 Ibid., p. 85. *Lan ans'a: mudhakkirat* (Beirut: Dar al-Farabi, 1996).
10 Martha Kessler, Helena Cobban & Hisham Melham, "What About Syria?," *Middle East Policy*, Vol. 9, No. 1 (1999). URL: http://www.mecp.org/public%5/5Fasp/journal_vol7/9910_syria.asp.

11   Human Rights Watch, *False Freedom: Online Censorship in the Middle East and North Africa: Syria*, November 2005. URL: http://hrw.org/reports/2005/mena1105/6.htm.
12   Al-Jazeera English Television Broadcast, March 10, 2009.
13   International Monetary Fund, *Syrian Arab Republic, IMF Article IV Consultation, Mission Preliminary Conclusions*, May 16, 2007. URL: http://www.imf.org/external/np/ms/2007/051607.htm.
14   Other perennial members of this list include Iran and the Sudan, and, until 2006, Libya. Iraq, once a staunch US ally, joined the club during the first Gulf War and was removed following the 2003 Anglo-US invasion and occupation of the country.
15   Barak Ravid, "Lieberman: Turkey Cannot Mediate between Israel, Syria," *Haaretz*, December 28, 2009.
16   Reuters, "Israel Not Interested in Peace: Syria's Assad," *Reuters*, December 23, 2009. URL: http://www.reuters.com/article/idUSTRE5BM4FJ20091223.
17   Josh Rogin, "New Ambassador Could be on the Road to Damascus," *Foreign Policy* December 10, 2009. URL: http://thecable.foreignpolicy.com/posts/2009/12/10/new_ambassador_could_be_on_the_road_to_damascus.
18   David C. Gordon, *The Republic of Lebanon: Nation in Jeopardy* (Boulder: Westview Press, 1983), p. 30.
19   David C. Gordon, *Lebanon, The Fragmented Nation* (Stanford: Hoover Institution Press, 1980), p. 38.
20   Andrew Lee Butters, "Palestinians in Lebanon," *Time*, February 25, 2009. URL: http://www.time.com/time/magazine/article/0,9171,1881651,00.html.
21   David Gilmour, *Dispossessed: The Ordeal of the Palestinians 1917–1980* (London: Sidgwick & Jackson, 1980), p. 27.
22   P.S. Khoury, *Syria and the French Mandate: The Politics of Arab Nationalism 1920–45* (Princeton: Princeton University Press, 1987), p. 20.
23   Gilmour, op. cit., p. 34.
24   Walid Khalidi, *Conflict and Violence in Lebanon: Confrontation in the Middle East* (Cambridge, MA: Harvard University Press, 1981), p. 51.
25   Reuven Avi-Ran, *The Syrian Involvement in Lebanon since 1975* (translated by David Maisel) (Boulder: Westview Press, 1991), p. 27.
26   Khalidi, op. cit., p. 64.
27   Gilmour, op. cit., p. 142.
28   Avi-Ran, op. cit., p. 151.
29   Augustus Richard Norton, *External Intervention and the Politics of Lebanon* (New York: Foreign Policy Association, 1991), p. 464.
30   Ibid., p. 466.
31   See, for example, Amnesty International, *Lebanon: Stop Attacks on Syrian Workers and Bring Perpetrators to Justice*, April 21, 2005. URL: http://web.amnesty.org/library/Index/ENGMDE180042005.
32   See Gilbert Achcar & Michel Warschawski, *The 33-Day War: Israel's War on Hizbollah and its Consequences* (Boulder: Paradigm, 2007).
33   Moshe Arens, "Let the Devil Take Tomorrow," *Haaretz*, August 13, 2006, quoted in ibid.
34   Jim Quilty, "Lebanon's Brush with Civil War," *Middle East Report*, May 20, 2008. URL: http://www.merip.org/mero/mero052008.html.
35   "Syria and Lebanon Formalize Ties," *Agence France-Press*, October 15, 2008. URL: http://english.aljazeera.net/news/middleeast/2008/10/200810158435920158.html.
36   Stacey Philbrick Yadav, "Lebanon Post-Doha," *Middle East Report*, July 23, 2008. URL: http://www.merip.org/mero/mero072308.html.
37   Jeffrey Fleishman, "In Lebanon, Sa'd Hariri Assumes Prime Minister's Post," *LA Times*, June 28, 2009. URL: http://www.latimes.com/news/nationworld/world/la-fg-lebanon-hariri28–2009jun28,0,6290466,print.story.

38 Ibid.
39 Paul Woodward, "Hizbollah's New Manifesto," *The National*, December 2, 2009. URL: http://www.thenational.ae/apps/pbcs.dll/article?AID = /20091202/GLOBAL BRIEFING/912029997/1009?template = globalbriefing. Meris Lutz, "LEBANON: New Hezbollah Platform Reflects Party's Shift to Domestic Politics," *LA Times*, November 30, 2009. URL: http://latimesblogs.latimes.com/babylonbeyond/2009/11/lebanon-new-hezbollah-charter-casts-group-in-global-struggle-against-imperialism.html.
40 Zvi Bar'el, "The Lebanese Test Lab," *Haaretz*, December 27, 2009. URL: http://www.haaretz.com/hasen/spages/1137850.html. Sami Moubayed, "Hariri's Syria Visit Sets Lebanon on Track," *Asia Times*, December 23, 2009. URL: http://www.atimes.com/atimes/Middle_East/KL23Ak02.html.
41 Seymour Hersh, "The Redirection," *The New Yorker*, March 5, 2007. URL: http://www.newyorker.com/reporting/2007/03/05/070305fa_fact_hersh.
42 Al-Manar TV, May 26, 2007. Transcript at URL: http://www.manartv.com.lb/News Site/NewsDetails.aspx?id = 17777&language = en.
43 *Time*, January 15, 1996, p. 17.
44 *Middle East Economic Digest*, June 17, 1994, p. 10.
45 *Time*, op. cit., p. 18.
46 *CIA World Factbook: Lebanon* (2010). URL: https://www.cia.gov/library/publications/the-world-factbook/geos/le.html.

Further reading

The following is a representative sample of both seminal texts on Syria and Lebanon as well as items of more recent interest, including the 2006 Israeli war against Lebanon.

Fawwaz Traboulsi's *A History of Modern Lebanon* and Hanna Ziadeh's *Sectarianism and Inter-Communal Nation Building in Lebanon* provide historical background for Lebanon. The former provides a broad historical sketch of Lebanon over five centuries, in its pre-modern and modern forms, while the latter provides a history of Lebanon's "confessional state" and the sectarianism that has come to define its political culture. Youssef Chaitani and Patrick Seale's *Post-Colonial Syria and Lebanon: The Decline of Arab Nationalism and the Triumph of the State* examines the historical development of Syrian and Lebanese politics and society since independence, examining how both countries became increasingly divided, rather than united, in the post-colonial era.

The sectarian culture of Lebanon and the successive foreign interventions in the polity gave rise to Shi'a militia parties Amal and Hizbollah. Augustus Richard Norton has provided the most accessible English-language accounts of both: *Amal and the Shi'a: Struggle for the Soul of Lebanon* and *Hezbollah: A Short History*. Each text provides a history of the social origins of the respective movements and their multitude of functions within Lebanon. Naim Qassem, the deputy-secretary of Hizbollah, has published an ostensible "insider's account" of the organization – *Hizbullah: The Story from Within* – which, while undoubtedly self-serving to some degree, is remarkable for its frankness and insights.

Useful accounts of the Israeli assault on Lebanon include Gilbert Achcar and Michel Warschwski's *The 33-Day War: Israel's War on Hezbollah in Lebanon and its Consequences*, a short but comprehensive and informative summary of the events surrounding Israel's military campaign and the accompanying human consequences. Likewise, a valuable edited collection by Nubar Hovsepian and Rashid Khalidi, *The War on Lebanon: A Reader*, includes analysis by a variety of distinguished academics and journalists, investigating the causes and consequences of the campaign.

As relates to Syria, Hanna Batatu's *Syria's Peasantry, the Descendants of its Lesser Rural Notables, and their Politics* is a dense but penetrating piece of political sociology that examines the political culture of Syria, and the politics of its classes. Raymond A. Hinnebusch's *Authoritarian Power and State Formation in Ba'thist Syria: Army, Party, and Peasant* provides a fascinating academic insight into the consolidation of power by the Ba'thist clique in the early 1960s and their subsequent state-building processes.

Syrian politics has been dominated for decades by the al-Assads, first Hafez and then Bashar. Patrick Seale's *Assad: The Struggle for the Middle East* provides a political portrait of Hafez, detailing his rise from peasant to national leader. Accessible and journalistic, Seale's book has interesting insights. David W. Lesch's *The New Lion of Damascus: Bashar al-Assad and Modern Syria* and Flynt Leverett's *Inheriting Syria: Bashar's Trial by Fire* provide sketches of Bashar al-Assad's ruling style and the politics of post-Hafez Syria. Volker Perthes's *Syria under Bashar al-Assad – Modernization and the Limits of Change* and Raymond Hinnebusch and Søren Schmidt's *The State and the Political Economy of Reform in Syria* provide detailed and balanced accounts of the contemporary economic environment in Syria and the challenges therein.

References

Achcar, Gilbert & Warschwski, Michel (2007) *The 33-Day War: Israel's War on Hezbollah in Lebanon and its Consequences*, Paradigm Publishers.

Batatu, Hanna (1999) *Syria's Peasantry, the Descendants of its Lesser Rural Notables, and their Politics*, Princeton University Press.

Chaitani, Youssef & Seale, Patrick (2007) *Post-Colonial Syria and Lebanon: The Decline of Arab Nationalism and the Triumph of the State*, I.B. Tauris.

Hinnebusch, Raymond (1990) *Authoritarian Power and State Formation in Ba'thist Syria: Army, Party, and Peasant*, Westview Press.

Hinnebusch, Raymond & Schmidt, Søren (2008) *The State and the Political Economy of Reform in Syria*, Lynne Rienner.

Hovsepian, Nubar & Khalidi, Rashid (eds) (2007) *The War on Lebanon: A Reader*, Olive Branch Press.

Lesch, David W. (2005) *The New Lion of Damascus: Bashar al-Assad and Modern Syria*, Yale University Press.

Leverett, Flynt (2005) *Inheriting Syria: Bashar's Trial by Fire*, Brookings Institution.

Norton, Augustus Richard (1987) *Amal and the Shi'a: Struggle for the Soul of Lebanon*, University of Texas Press.

—— (2009) *Hezbollah: A Short History*, Princeton University Press.

Perthes, Volker (2006) *Syria under Bashar al-Assad – Modernisation and the Limits of Change*, Routledge.

Qassem, Naim (2009) *Hizbullah: The Story from Within*, Saqi Books.
Seale, Patrick (1990) *Asad: The Struggle for the Middle East*, University of California Press.
Traboulsi, Fawwaz (2007) *A History of Modern Lebanon*, Pluto Press.
Ziadeh, Hanna (2006) *Sectarianism and Inter-Communal Nation Building in Lebanon*, Hurst & Company.

8 Israel and the Palestinian National Authority

With Glenn E. Perry

The rival claims of the indigenous population of the country historically known as Palestine (today's Israel proper, the West Bank and the Gaza Strip) and of the Zionist movement originating in Europe in the late nineteenth century have produced one of the world's most intractable conflicts. Formerly part of the Ottoman Empire, this land between the Mediterranean and the Jordan River fell under British occupation in 1917 and had the status of a British mandate between 1922 and 1948.[1] All other political issues in Israel/Palestine – from land ownership to relationships with the world – revolve around the Palestinian–Zionist struggle.

Several factors add unusual fuel to this conflict. Struggles involving European settler populations implanted into a country as a part of Western colonialism that reject the equality of the indigenous population tend to be particularly acute, as in the case of South Africa or Algeria – or Palestine/Israel. This is particularly true when the indigenous people remain too numerous to be completely overwhelmed, as in the case of North America or Australia, or not susceptible to religious, linguistic and cultural assimilation. The severity of the problem in the case of Palestine/Israel is compounded by some Jews' perception of themselves as returnees after an absence of roughly two millennia (and sometimes even a belief in divine right) and also by the extent to which their people's ordeal in the lands of "exile" in Europe reached new levels of persecution in the twentieth century. The location of Palestine at the heart of the Arab/Islamic world, whose peoples see the Palestinians' cause as their own, provides a unique factor, as has been the intervention of Western countries, notably the United States, to bolster the Jewish state's military power and enable it to continue its intransigence.

Israel proper and the territories it rules

Extending from the Mediterranean Sea between Egypt and Lebanon eastward to the Jordan River and the Dead Sea (and southward like a wedge to the Red Sea – that is, the Negev Desert), the pre-1948 Palestine mandate is now divided into three entities. About 78 percent of the territory, defined by a so-called "Green Line" – frontiers established by a series of armistice agreements in 1949 – makes up the Jewish state of Israel in the narrow sense of the term ("Israel proper"). With the displacement of the bulk of Israel's Arab Palestinian population during

1948–1949 (who constituted two-thirds of the population of Palestine and a majority within the future Green Line as late as 1948, after decades of Zionist settlement), and the ingathering of Jews from other countries, Israel was transformed into an overwhelmingly Jewish society. At the time of its establishment in 1948, it had a population of 806,000 (not including those Palestinians who would soon take refuge outside). As of 2009, it had grown to 7.4 million (apparently including Jewish settlers in occupied territories, the Palestinians of East Jerusalem, and perhaps half a million Israeli citizens living abroad). Nearly 5.6 million of this total were Jewish (although the Jewish religious authorities do not recognize all of them as such), and 1.5 million (20.2 percent) were Arabs,[2] while foreign residents made up 4.3 percent of the population. In 1967, Israel conquered the rest of the country (inhabited by Arab Palestinians, a majority of whom were refugees from Israel proper after the events of 1948–1949), that is: east-central Palestine (including East Jerusalem), which had come to be called the "West Bank" (with a Palestinian population that had reached 2.345 million, including 208,000 in East Jerusalem, by 2008) since its incorporation into the Kingdom of Jordan (whose original territory became the "East Bank") eighteen years earlier; and the small but crowded Gaza Strip (with a population that has now reached 1.5 million), which had been administered, but not annexed, by Egypt since the armistice of 1949. In addition, Israel conquered southwestern Syria (the Golan Heights, depopulated except for members of the Druze sect, who now number about 20,000, and about 18,000 Jewish settlers) and the Egyptian region of Sinai.

Except for Sinai, which was returned to Egypt in 1982 as a largely demilitarized territory in accordance with the 1978 Camp David Agreement, small adjustments on the Syrian front in 1975, and Israeli occupation of parts of Lebanon between 1978 and 2000, the *de facto* frontiers of the state of Israel have remained the same since the 1967 conquests. Admittedly, the Israelis moved all their troops as well as Jewish settlements from the Gaza Strip in 2005, but they continue to control the skies and borders of this territory – and engage in a policy of economic strangulation – and periodically (as during December 2008–January 2009 on a massive scale) bomb targets there and make incursions, meaning it remains a territory within their military frontiers, evoking comparisons with the Warsaw Ghetto during the Second World War. In the words of Gideon Levy,[3] Gaza's "occupation . . . has simply taken on a new form: a fence instead of settlements. The jailers stand guard on the outside instead of the inside." Aside from a broadly defined East Jerusalem as part of Greater Jerusalem (usually no longer counted by the Israelis as part of the West Bank) and the Golan Heights, the Israelis have not officially annexed the territory beyond the Green Line. But they have established large settlements there that – temporarily or permanently – have consolidated these territories' status as integral, *de facto* parts of the Jewish state.

An autonomous Palestinian National Authority (PNA or PA) has governed parts of the West Bank and Gaza (each recently controlled by a separate political group) since the 1990s and aspires to evolve into an independent Palestinian state. The Israelis are divided on how much of these territories they will insist on eventually keeping and on what limitations would be put on such a state. Consequently, the

Israeli/Palestinian territory includes one state and a partially self-governing Palestinian subordinate entity. In terms of the "prosaic proposition" that "the existence of a state in any given political unit is an empirical question"[4] relating to a *de facto* situation rather than to juridical, normative principles, the state of Israel ("Greater Israel") whose frontiers include all of historic Palestine (as well as Syria's Golan) is a longtime reality. If, in the future, a Palestinian entity acquires formal sovereignty, one can expect it – barring a fundamental transformation in the regional and global distribution of power – to remain subordinate to Israel and thus effectively still a part of Greater Israel.

Whether we treat Israel as another "oppressive state" depends on whether the focus is on the Jews (both within and outside the Green Line) or on the whole territory it rules. The Jewish Israelis govern themselves in a liberal, democratic manner, and to that extent the state might even be considered a model democracy. However, the Arabs within the Green Line belie the state's classification as non-oppressive, because they have citizenship and are enfranchised but are denied full equality. And the Palestinians in the occupied West Bank and Gaza Strip are clearly a subject people – ruled by an oppressive, subaltern Palestinian elite acting as surrogates of the occupiers in the former, and suffering economic strangulation as well as armed attacks and incursions in the latter. In 2008, comparing the situation in Hebron to that of Jews in Czarist Russia and noting the soft treatment of offenders by the courts, some Israelis began to use the term "pogroms" for the attacks by Jewish settlers on Palestinians. (The millions of Palestinians in diaspora who claim the right of return constitute a special category in relation to the question of oppression, but in important ways they lie outside the scope of our study of the domestic politics of Israel/Palestine within its *de facto* frontiers.) Several terms have been proposed for such a political system. With specific reference to Israel, Oren Yiftachel uses the term "ethnocracy,"[5] while Meron Benvenisti harshly speaks of "herrenvolk [master race] democracy."[6] Israelis themselves talk of "a Jewish and democratic state," implying that these adjectives complement each other, but to others the phrase exposes a limitation on, if not a contradiction of, the principle of democracy. Many observers have called this a form of apartheid. With specific reference to the modern highways connecting the settlements in the West Bank to Israel proper that deny access to Palestinians (in December 2009, in the case of one such road, the Israeli Supreme Court called for an end to this kind of discrimination within five months,[7] but it was unclear whether this decision would be implemented), a prominent Israeli commentator coined the term "distilled apartheid," in which "the Jews on top" constitute "the lords of the land," with the Palestinians "going on foot . . . through a dark, moldy tunnel."[8]

Center and Periphery

The relationship between the Palestinians and the Israelis can be understood in relation to the terms "Center" (or "Core") and "Periphery." The territories that have been occupied since 1967 (though not including the Jewish settlers, who fully form a part of the Center) can be treated – at least for now – as the Periphery of the Israeli state, with the Jewish population on both sides of the Green Line constituting its Center. The Palestinian minority in Israel proper can be described as the "internal Periphery." The total number of Palestinians worldwide was estimated at well over 10 million in 2005.[9] Most of them live outside Israel/Palestine as refugees – many of them, as is also true in the West Bank and Gaza, still living in camps set up by the United Nations – but might also be considered as an Outer Periphery, as they invoke United Nations resolutions and broad principles of human rights to claim the right to return to their homeland.

The terms "Center" and "Periphery" apply to Palestine/Israel in a broader sense. As they are used in dependency and world system theory, the Palestinians are part of the underdeveloped world (Periphery, Third World or Global South) along with other parts of Asia and Africa as well as Latin America. On the other hand, the Jewish Israelis, particularly those of European origin who established the state (although most of them came from semi-Peripheral regions such as Poland and Russia), constitute a part of the developed world (the First World, the Global North, or the Center of the world system). (The Mizrahi – "Eastern" – Jews (those originating in Middle Eastern and other African and Asian countries) show some characteristics of membership of the Periphery, but for the most part they are treated here as part of the Center.) On a global scale, this gap between the Center and the Periphery began to emerge roughly half a millennium ago and it widened as one part of the world developed by "underdeveloping" the rest – at least according to such writers as Immanuel Wallerstein, Andre Gunter Frank, Walter Rodney and Johan Galtung.[10] The way in which the Palestinians have progressively been dispossessed by the Center country – whether or not this is representative of the worldwide relationship between Center and Periphery – will permeate much of this chapter, although, of course, their position in the global Periphery long antedated – and facilitated – the rise of Zionism and of Western colonialism in the Middle East in general.[11]

As for the political sphere, Israel's Center is like other Center countries in recent times in having a democratic political system. On the other hand – in accord with what Galtung[12] shows in relation to Periphery countries in general – a Palestinian elite (the "center of the Periphery") now has formed an alliance with the rulers of Israel ("the center of the Center"), in close association with much of the Center in general, particularly the United States, in which the latter bolsters the authoritarian rule of the former against the potential and real opposition of the "periphery of the [Palestinian] Periphery." Still, the Center nation treats its client as the enemy and conducts wars on its territory.

Israel proper (except for its Arab Palestinian minority) and the Jewish settlements in the West Bank and the Golan Heights constitute part of the developed world (First World or Center). It is true that its 20 percent Palestinian minority, somewhat like the case of the African-American minority in the United States, pulls Israel's statistical rankings down. However, in some ways, Israel proper demonstrates elite status even among other Center countries, as it has the largest number of engineers and scientists per capita and ranks second in publication of books per capita and near the top in physicians per capita.[13] *The Times* Higher Education Survey of 2008 ranked Hebrew University among the world's top 100 institutions of higher learning, while two other Israeli institutions, the Technion and Tel Aviv University, came in at 109 and 114, respectively.[14] In its report for 2007/2008, the United Nations Development Program (UNDP) gives Israel a Human Development Index (HDI) ranking of 23rd (with a score of 0.932 out of a possible 1.0), just below Germany and outranked in Asia by only Japan and Hong Kong. In 2005, life expectancy at birth was 80.3 years (the same as Canada's), and the adult literacy rate was 97.1 percent. GDP per capita (purchasing power parity) was $25,864, somewhat lower than the highest-ranking countries. The structure of its trade provides further telling testimony to its Center status, with only 4 percent of its exports being primary products (one of the lowest figures for any country) and 83 percent manufactured goods (including cut diamonds, weapons and software), with 13.9 percent of the latter in the hi-tech category,[15] which has grown fast since 2003.[16]

Several factors converged to produce this high level of development. First, the state was established by settlers from Europe who generally had high levels of education. Israeli scholars today are disproportionately represented among the high achievers in many, perhaps most, academic disciplines, just as Jews in the United States, according to a Pew survey, have the highest level of income and, aside from Hindus (mainly immigrant professionals), the highest level of formal education of any religion.[17] Even the Mizrahi ("Eastern," primarily from the Middle East) immigrants of the 1950s had benefited from the Alliance Israelite Universelle schools financed by their Western co-religionists from 1860 onward, and most of them, unlike the majority of people in their home countries or Periphery countries in general, could read and write.[18] Second, vast amounts of wealth have been transferred to Israel since its establishment, including reparations from Germany that totaled 100 billion Deutsche Marks by 2000[19] as partial compensation for the crimes of Hitler's Nazi regime. Also, the Absentee Property Law of 1950 provided for the confiscation of the land and other property of Palestinian refugees. And the amount of foreign aid the country has received from the United States since 1948, and particularly since 1973, is astonishing: an annual average of some $3 billion in economic and military assistance. This is in addition to massive private donations through the United Jewish Appeal. Admittedly, military expenses, previously long the highest in the world relative to GDP and still among the highest, have been a severe drain, but even this is partially offset by Israel's sale of weapons abroad. The ability to combine one of the best-funded welfare systems in the world with extraordinary military expenditure (both "guns and butter") is unique for a state of such limited resources.

High rates of inflation and budget deficits used to plague Israel, but economic reforms inspired by global neoliberal trends starting in the 1980s successfully combated these problems, although there was a price to be paid in higher levels of unemployment and inequality. Israel experienced remarkable rates of economic development during much of the 1990s but underwent slowdowns later, notably after the renewal of the Palestinian uprising (the Intifadah) in 2000. However, its growth rate later climbed to about 5 percent. The global economic crisis that started in 2008 brought only a moderate slowdown in the Israeli economy, which bucked the worldwide trend and grew by 0.5 percent in 2009.[20]

By contrast, the Palestinians are typical of the global Periphery, ranking 106th in the HDI with a score of 0.731, which puts them between Vietnam and Indonesia (although this is in the "medium" rather than "low" development category). Even the economic benefits resulting from providing manual labor for the Israelis, as well as the sale of agricultural produce, which grew rapidly following the beginning of the occupation in 1967, ended with the outbreak of the second Intifadah in 2000, and particularly with the construction of the "security wall." Having become dependent on this subordinate but, in some ways, beneficial economic relationship with the Center, Palestinians in the West Bank, and even more so in Gaza, are now largely destitute. Today the Israelis depend on manual laborers from places such as Thailand and Romania instead.

One remarkable indicator of the unequal relationship between the Israelis and the Palestinians is the way the former consume the water from the aquifers in the West Bank. In a pattern that has been called "water apartheid," only Israeli settlers are allowed to have deep wells, so they get the lion's share of water while the Palestinians' share has fallen "well below the threshold for absolute scarcity."[21]

Israeli measures designed to suppress the post-2000 Intifadah have intensified the poverty of these areas, especially the Gaza Strip, where an Israeli military assault brought devastation in 2008–2009, making them extreme examples of the impoverishment of the Periphery. Some Israelis stress that the costs of the occupation are further impoverishing the poor in the Center, too.[22] The West Bank and Gaza had an estimated average GDP per capita of $1,100 (purchasing power parity) in 2006, and their growth rate was 8 percent.[23] Benvenisti points to "the dramatic gap in gross domestic product per capita between Palestinians and Israelis, which is 1:10 in the West Bank and 1:20 in the Gaza Strip (even before the assault at the end of 2008), as well as the enormous inequality in the use of natural resources [that] cannot exist without the force of arms."[24] In reference to Gaza in particular, Avi Shlaim concludes that it "is not simply a case of economic underdevelopment but a uniquely cruel case of deliberate de-development," in which "Israel turned the people of Gaza into the hewers of wood and the drawers of water, into a source of cheap labour and a captive market for Israeli goods," destroying "the underpinnings essential for real political independence."[25] This "de-development" had been forced on Gaza for over a decade before the 2008 assault.[26]

In addition to the drop in Palestinian income in the West Bank and Gaza, there has been the shrinking of Palestinian physical space. An Israeli statistical report in 2008 showed that the settler population in the West Bank had increased by 107 percent in just twelve years (and by 5 percent in the previous three years), compared with a 29 percent increase within the Green Line.[27] More than 500 military checkpoints have been built since September 2000. As a result of such policies, the West Bank has been dissected into fifty disconnected pockets, a fragmentation that has been exacerbated by the construction of the security wall.

The two peoples claiming the land

The Jews

We need to look at the two peoples involved in order to understand how each views Palestine/Israel as its homeland and often rejects the claims of the other. Far from being "age old," as is sometimes imagined, the conflict between Palestinians and Jews is strictly a product of the past century, although the roots of the dispute extend back four millennia. Perhaps in no other conflict in the world do the "burden of history" and historical/religious mythology play such prominent roles.

Like other lands in the Fertile Crescent, Palestine/Israel's ethnic makeup has been shaped by successive waves of tribes known as Semites (that is, speakers of a closely related family of Semitic languages) who migrated from the Arabian Peninsula over a period of several millennia. In the Old Testament, the country is called the "Land of Canaan," for the Semitic people who inhabited it during the Bronze Age. Non-Semitic "people of the sea," or Philistines, appeared on the coast around 1200 BCE. Although the Philistines became extinct as a people, the country eventually came to be known as Philistia or Palestine (in Arabic: Filastin). At about the same time, according to the biblical account, another Semitic people, the Israelites, entered the country from the east and fought with both the Philistines and the Canaanites. However, Israeli "biblical revisionists" have recently suggested that the Israelites were simply a faction of the Canaanites. Either way, while the Philistines long prevailed in the coastal region, the Israelites gained control of the hill country to the east.

According to the biblical account (again disputed by biblical revisionists), the Israelites ruled an empire that extended as far as Damascus. Following King Solomon's death, the northern Israelite tribes broke away to form the Kingdom of Israel (the Northern Kingdom), while the two southern Israelite tribes constituted the Kingdom of Judaea (the Southern Kingdom), with Jerusalem as its capital and extending over the southern part of today's West Bank. The term "Jew" was applied only to the Israelites of the Southern Kingdom. The Kingdom of Israel was conquered by the Assyrian Empire in 722 BCE, and part of the population was uprooted, while those who remained – along with other people brought in by the Assyrians and eventually assimilated – were known as Samaritans (only a few hundred of whom have retained this identity).

The Israelites of Judaea – i.e., the Jews, whose own kingdom ended with conquest by the Chaldean Empire in 568 BCE – were to play a larger role than their northern counterparts in subsequent millennia. With the Achaemenid Persian Empire allowing their exiles to return to Judaea, they enjoyed some autonomy under Persian and, later, Macedonian rule. Many of them migrated to other parts of the world, such as Alexandria, while other people in various countries converted to Judaism. The Aramaic language (representing another wave of Semitic peoples) replaced Hebrew as the spoken language of the Jews in Palestine centuries before the Christian era, with Hebrew relegated mostly to religious use. The Jews of Judaea revolted against the Macedonians in the second century BCE and established another kingdom under the Hasmonaean dynasty that expanded their territory and forcibly converted two groups of Arabs, the Ituraeans of Galilee and the Idumaeans south of the Dead Sea, to Judaism. This kingdom was conquered by Rome in the first century BCE, even though fanatical Jewish rebels, the Zealots, recurrently resisted foreign domination until the Romans destroyed the Jewish Temple in Jerusalem in 70 CE. Following another Zealot uprising, the Romans engaged in brutal ethnic cleansing – killing, enslaving or exiling much of the Jewish population of Judaea in 135. However, not all Jews were removed from Palestine, nor even from Judaea, and there was an increase in the Jewish population of Galilee,[28] while some of the exiles from Judaea were assimilated by their fellow Israelites in Samaria. It seems that a small Jewish community always remained in the country, numbering perhaps 10,000 in 1860, but most of the indigenous Jews (and Samaritans), like others in Palestine and adjacent countries, converted to Christianity and then to Islam.[29]

The Jews constituted a minority religion throughout much of the world for well over two millennia. Unjustly accused of collective responsibility for killing Jesus Christ, they were often persecuted in Christian Europe, especially in Czarist Russia, where they were perpetual victims of ugly, organised attacks (pogroms). Elsewhere, they were forced to live in special quarters (ghettos). In spite of this discrimination, by the nineteenth century there were many flourishing Jewish communities throughout Europe. However, the persecution reached unprecedented levels when approximately 6 million Jews were killed in the Holocaust of the Second World War.

Jews have played an important role as a minority community throughout the history of the Islamic world. Today, this group is known as the Mizrahim ("Oriental" or "Eastern" Jews), to differentiate them from those from Europe. It would be wrong to idealize their condition in so many countries over so many centuries. Nevertheless, their Islamic rulers designated them as *dhimmi*s (protected people), and they were able to practice their religion freely and live under their own law (although a poll tax was imposed on them because they were exempt from the military service expected of Muslims). In the Ottoman Empire, each religious community was organized in a non-territorial way as a *millet* (or "nation") under its own religious leader, such as the Grand Rabbi. When Jews were expelled from Christian Europe, they often took refuge in the more tolerant world of Islam. Indeed, while the bulk of European Jews are called Ashkanezi (literally "German" as most used a German dialect, Yiddish, written in the Hebrew alphabet), most of the contemporary Mizrahim are known as Sephardic ("Spanish"), as they were driven out of Spain after the Christian reconquest in 1492. While the crusaders massacred or expelled Jews when they conquered Jerusalem, they were allowed to live there again once the Muslims regained control. Indeed, the Islamic conquest of Palestine in the seventh century had saved the Jews from the Roman/Byzantine Emperor Heraclius's decree ordering their forced conversion to Christianity.

The Palestinians: the indigenous population

One of the slogans of the early Zionists, "A land without a people for a people without a land," perhaps best epitomizes the politics of historic Palestine. The problem Zionism faced was that Palestine was not an empty land at all, although Europeans tended to think of African and Asian peoples as mere "natives" who did not really count. Palestine's history had not ended in 135 CE. The dispersal of the Jews of Judaea left Palestine as a whole still substantially populated by Jews and others. Most of the Palestinian people, including the Jews, eventually converted to Christianity, as did the Roman Empire, of which it remained a part until the seventh century. Indeed, some of the early Zionists, particularly David Ben-Gurion, believed that the Arab Palestinians were of Jewish descent and, for a while, fancied that the peasants in particular would revert to Judaism. Ironically illustrating an extreme version of pan-Arabism, another constant theme of Zionism has been that, although there were non-Jews in Palestine, they did not constitute a distinct Palestinian people but merely Arabs who happened to live there and whose homeland was really Syria, Iraq, Egypt or somewhere else.

In the seventh century another wave of Semites, Arabs under the banner of Islam, conquered Palestine. Most of its population eventually converted to the new religion, although the process took centuries. There seems to have been a relatively small infusion of the Arab conquerors into the local population, but Palestine became an Arab country in the sense that it adopted the Arabic language and other aspects of Arab culture. Aside from the interlude of crusader rule (and momentary intrusions by the armies of Hulagu Khan and Napoleon Bonaparte), Palestine then continued as part of the territory of a succession of Islamic states until the First World War. Although there were glimmers of Arab nationalist separatism in the nineteenth century, it did not matter to most Muslim Palestinians (and other Arab subjects of the Ottoman Empire) that their rulers for several centuries were Turkish, for Muslims historically considered themselves as a single community or Ummah. The reach of the Ottoman state varied in strength over time, and in some periods the country gained considerable autonomy. For instance, in the eighteenth century, a local notable, Zahir al-'Umar, ruled a *de facto* state that included much of Palestine, although it is simplistic to portray this as representing any sort of Palestinian nationalism. Palestine was sometimes called "southern Syria," but by the nineteenth century there were signs of a specific Palestinian identity. On the other hand, the location of Palestine at the center of the Arab world during the twentieth century, as Arabs overwhelmingly aspired to unite, helped propel it to the center of pan-Arab national consciousness. The centrality of Jerusalem to the Muslim faith further contributed to Arab and Muslim identification with Palestine.

Palestine was not a particularly sparsely populated country. In 1880, just before the beginning of Zionist settlement, its slightly more than 10,000 square miles (with the largely barren Negev Desert in the south comprising almost half of this) contained 456,929 people – including 399,334 Muslims, 42,089 Christians and 14,731 Jews.[30]Almost all of them were Arabic speakers, including the Jews.

Whereas the Zionist claim to Palestine was based on the idea of Jews "returning" to the "Land of Israel," the Arab Palestinians considered the country to be their own, primarily on the basis of being the people who currently inhabited it. They invoked the idea of self-determination, a principle that acquired increasing moral and legal status during the twentieth century, to claim the right to rule themselves as an independent state or to join a larger Arab state. Like other Arabs, Palestinians also share with Jews the myth of descent from Abraham, to whom the land is said to have been promised by God. Furthermore, Jerusalem is a holy city for Muslims and Christians as well as for Jews. But such religious ties of the Muslim world as a whole should not be confused with the specific attachment of the Palestinians to their homeland. The idea that they could be expelled (which they believed was implicit in the idea of a Jewish state) seemed absurd to them and evoked extreme hostility to the Zionist project. Zionists did not publicly call for the expulsion of the Arab Palestinians, but it seems certain that they viewed it as an essential precursor to the founding of their Jewish state.

The Arab Palestinians are overwhelmingly Sunni Muslims. Only seven villages near the Lebanese border before 1948 were Shi'ite Twelver sub-sect.[31] As in Lebanon and Syria, there is also a small minority of Druze, a heterodox branch of Ismaili Shi'ism. At least 10 (some say as many as 25) percent of the Arab Palestinian people in the early twentieth century were Christian, mostly Greek Orthodox, and towns such as Nazareth and Bethlehem historically were primarily Christian. However, dramatic increases in emigration to Western countries since 1967 have reduced the Christian presence in historic Palestine, while a higher birth rate for Muslims has further reduced the overall proportion of Christians among the Palestinian people generally. While both Islamist and secular ideologies have mobilized Palestinian opposition to Zionism and Israel over the years, there has been a remarkable degree of solidarity between Christian and Muslim Palestinians. Indeed, some of the most militant Palestinian opponents of Zionism have been Christians. By contrast, the Zionists from an early date collaborated with some of the Druze population and divided them from their fellow Arab Palestinians. (Today in Israel, the Druze are officially – and bizarrely – defined as a totally distinct ethnicity and faith, neither Arab nor Muslim.)

The emergence of Israel and the erasure of Palestine

Political Zionism emerged as a new nationalist movement alongside other European nationalisms during the late nineteenth century. While Jews over the centuries repeated the slogan "Next year in Jerusalem" and looked forward to an eventual return to the Land of Israel, attempts to pursue this actively before the coming of the Messiah had been forbidden. However, in response to renewed pogroms following the assassination of Czar Alexander II in 1881, a group of Russian Jews formed a new movement, Lovers of Zion, and the following year they established a few small settlements in Palestine. This eventually developed into the First Aliya (literally "going up"), which continued until 1903.

However, this was only a prelude to the emergence of a movement to establish a Jewish state – that is, political Zionism – which was initiated by a prominent Jewish journalist based in Vienna, Theodor Herzl, in the 1890s. Previously optimistic about life in Europe, Herzl was shaken by the infamous Dreyfus Affair in France, in which a Jewish army officer was convicted on false charges. Herzl published a book titled *The Jewish State* in 1896, which led to the convening of the 1st Zionist Congress in Basle, Switzerland, the following year and the formation of the World Zionist Organization (WZO). Avoiding the controversial word "state," the Basle Program called for the establishment of a Jewish "home in Palestine secured by public law" and for "colonisation" of the country as a means of achieving that goal. However, attempts to secure international support for the movement, such as Herzl's meeting with Ottoman Sultan 'Abd al-Hamid II in 1901, long came to naught, and some political Zionists discussed establishing the Jewish national home somewhere other than Palestine.

The Zionist movement did not appeal to most Jews at the time. Orthodox Jews saw the movement as "profane," led by nonobservant people who often tended toward atheism, for which the Jewish community was merely a nationality. Most Reform Jews saw it as a threat to their status as patriotic citizens of the countries in which they lived. Immigration to the United States was more attractive to Russian and Eastern European Jews than settlement in Palestine. A few rejected the idea of a Jewish state in favor of cultural or humanitarian Zionism,[32] which aimed at establishing a center of Jewish culture in Palestine. In later years, such people – notably the theologian Martin Buber and Hebrew University president Judah Magnes – favored a binational state in which Arab Palestinians and Jews would share the land.

Settlement in Palestine continued on a small scale as new institutions such as the Jewish Colonial Trust and the Jewish National Fund (JNF) facilitated the acquisition of land to be owned collectively by the Jewish people. The Second Aliya (1904–1913) brought in several thousand more settlers, primarily from Russia. In many ways, this provided the nucleus of the future state, introducing socialist ideas – at least as "a mobilizing myth, perhaps a convenient alibi," subordinated to nationalism and used for building power and strengthening a "capitalist economy"[33] – and the beginnings of organized labor and political parties, along with individuals (such as David Ben-Gurion) who would remain dominant until the 1960s. The vast majority of the Jews settled in cities, but the Zionists of the Second Aliya also glorified establishing ties to the land, particularly through setting up collectivist settlements called kibbutzim – long publicized as purely egalitarian, communistic communities, although this now is disputed,[34] and the somewhat less collectivist moshavim. The collective settlements, which have now evolved into big industrial enterprises employing cheap foreign labor, were particularly important in the early days in creating a Jewish presence in what were remote parts of the country. Later, Israeli military leaders would disproportionately emerge from them.

The Jewish population had grown to 60,000 by 1914; and even after some Russian nationals were expelled as enemy aliens by the Ottomans at the beginning of the First World War, Palestine still had a Jewish population of more than 56,000.[35] However, the newcomers were often resented by the indigenous Jews, while some Muslim and Christian Palestinians – then numbering 700,000 – started to see the Zionist movement as a serious threat.

The war provided new momentum for the Zionists. When the Ottoman Empire allied itself with Germany, the Allied powers began to make plans for its demise. In the famous Hussein–McMahon correspondence of 1915–1916, Britain promised to support Arab independence within frontiers that (at least in the Arab reading) included Palestine. Secretly, however, in 1916 Britain entered into the Sykes–Picot Agreement with France, according to which much of the territory of the Ottoman Empire was to be divided between these two powers, while most of Palestine would be internationalized. But in November 1917, in response to lobbying by the Zionist movement, the British government made yet another commitment in the form of a letter from Foreign Minister Arthur Balfour to the head of the British Zionist Federation, Lord Rothschild, stating its commitment to "the establishment in Palestine of a national home for the Jewish people." The so-called Balfour Declaration was carefully worded, so it did not call for a "state" or say how much of Palestine would constitute this future "home," and it went on to clarify that "nothing shall be done which may prejudice the civil and religious rights of existing non-Jewish communities in Palestine" – hardly consistent with the idea of an ethnically based entity – or, as reassurance to anti-Zionist Jews, "the rights and political status enjoyed by Jews in any other country."[36] While this did not provide all that the Zionists would have liked, it provided the foundation for the future establishment of a Jewish state and the erasure of the Arab Palestinian presence.

British forces occupied Palestine the following month, and Jewish immigration soon resumed. At the Paris Peace Conference in 1919, the Zionists called for a Jewish national home within boundaries that would extend far beyond what ultimately became the borders of Palestine. The following year, the Allied Supreme Council, meeting in San Remo, awarded Palestine to Britain as a mandate under the League of Nations, with the words of the Balfour Declaration incorporated into the document almost verbatim. London appointed a dedicated Zionist, Sir Herbert Samuel, as high commissioner. The Council of the League of Nations formally approved the mandate in 1922. By then, small-scale clashes had been taking place between Arabs and Jews for at least two years.

Great Britain's commitment to the Balfour Declaration created a new demographic situation in Palestine that increased the likelihood of the eventual establishment of a Jewish state. At first, Jewish immigration was slow, but it increased drastically after Hitler came to power in Germany in 1933. The British largely cut off the flow of immigrants in 1939 when it set up a naval blockade, but by the end of the mandate, in 1948, there were approximately 600,000 Jews in Palestine, nearly a third of the country's total population. Almost all were Europeans, including some whose presence there predated the Zionist movement.

A set of political institutions emerged that provided the nucleus for the Jewish state. With the League of Nations asserting that the mandatory power should work with "an appropriate Jewish agency" to create the national home, the WZO was given the role, although it later set up a distinct organization called the Jewish Agency to perform this function. In addition, an elected National Council was established to supervise the affairs of the Yishuv, as the Jewish community in Palestine was called.

The socialist coloring of the Second Aliya resulted in the creation in 1920 of the Histadrut (General Federation of Labor), which became a powerful Yishuv institution. More than just a union, the Histadrut – with its funds provided by the WZO – had its own industries and provided healthcare, education, housing and other vital services for its members. It was, in effect, the core of the Yishuv's autonomous government, because the same socialist parties that held power in the less significant National Council were even more dominant in the Histadrut (a situation that would continue during the first decades of the Israeli state). Two labor factions, Ahdut Haavodah (Unity of Labor), known until 1919 as Poale Zion (Workers of Zion), and Hapoel Hatzair (Young Worker), contended with each other but joined together to create the Histadrut, and they united again to form the Mapai (Workers') Party in 1930. David Ben-Gurion, the party leader, used his position to allocate jobs and other benefits – and to screen prospective immigrants – in order to establish tight control over the Yishuv and the WZO. The Mapai-dominated Histadrut also gained control of a military force, the Haganah (Defense), which would transform itself into the Israel Defense Forces (IDF) after independence. Joel Migdal shows how this began a process of creating a strong Israeli state, one that is not caught up in a web of more powerful social forces.[37]

Nevertheless, the dominant Mapai leadership was challenged by other groups. First, there was the Agadut Israel, anti-Zionist Orthodox Jews who at first attacked the Balfour Declaration and contemplated working with the Arab Palestinians.[38] Then there was a small leftist faction – known as Ahdut Haavoda by the early 1940s – that was predominant in some kibbutzim and favored a binational rather than a Jewish state. On the other hand, there were several capitalistic, "bourgeois" factions, beginning with pre-Third Aliya farmers who depended on Arab labor, while the Fourth Aliya (1924–1930 and heavily Polish) and the Fifth Aliya (1932–1939 and largely German) included many immigrants with money to invest. Forerunners of the post-1948 Liberal Party, these groups gravitated toward the general Zionists, some of whom took an anti-British and anti-socialist position. Another faction, known as Progressives and headed by Chaim Weizman (who led the WZO for most of this period and complemented Ben-Gurion's role in Palestine by directing the movement's "external strategy"[39]), was willing to work with the labor Zionists.[40]

The biggest challenge to Mapai was the right-wing, anti-socialist Revisionist Party, founded by Vladimir Jabotinsky in 1925. The Revisionists went so far as to establish a separate "New Zionist" movement ten years later. The Revisionists' youth group, the Betar, emulated various fascist practices of the time, including donning brown shirts. Demanding that the national home must include all of the original Palestine mandate, including Transjordan, the Revisionists pursued a militant policy that decried "paying attention to the mood of the natives," who would have to be kept "behind an iron wall [i.e., a Jewish military force] which they will be powerless to break down." While this seemed to differentiate the Revisionists from the socialist Zionists, an important study has recently shown that there was no basic difference between Jabotinsky and Ben-Gurion on the idea of the "iron wall," although the latter was somewhat more inclined to depend on

British military force.[41] But the murder in 1933 of a leading labor Zionist, Chaim Arlosoroff, for which the Revisionists were blamed, intensified the mutual hatred of the two groups. The Revisionists eventually established their own military force, the Irgun (Organization), led by Menachim Begin, and an even more militant group later broke away to create the Lehi, better known as the Stern Gang. (One member of its leading triumvirate, Yitzhak Shamir, succeeded Begin as Israel's prime minister in the 1980s.) Both of these groups engaged in terrorist activities not only against the Arabs but, during the 1940s, against the British, and they sometimes clashed with the Haganah, too.

By contrast, the development of countrywide self-government – or of Arab Palestinian institutions comparable to those of the Yishuv – was lacking. This was largely because Britain's commitment to the Jewish national home prevented it from supporting any plan that would be acceptable to the Arab Palestinians. When, in 1923, London proposed setting up an Arab Agency to parallel the Jewish Agency, this seemed to imply that the Arabs, who made up nearly 90 percent of the population at the time, were merely one of two equal communities.

Unlike many other colonial situations, no national representative institutions emerged in Palestine in the inter-war years. Of course, this suited the Zionists, who were busy creating the nucleus of a future Jewish state, which would have been scuppered by anything approximating majority rule. Moreover, Britain's commitment to the Balfour Declaration stood in the way of creating any institution in which the majority community would be represented in proportion to its size. Thus, while the British suggested establishing an advisory Legislative Council in 1922, the Arabs rejected it because its would have comprised eleven British and two Jewish members against only eight Muslims and two indigenous Christians, guaranteeing a pro-Balfour Declaration majority at every meeting. The Zionists did not like this proposal either, but they had no need to come into conflict with the British, as they knew the Arabs would veto it. Some Arabs later decided that such an advisory body might help them to promote their case for better representation, but by then the Zionists stood in the way of its acceptance.

Besides simply resenting British rule and fearing that they were losing their country to the flood of Jewish immigrants, the Arab Palestinian peasants were gradually deprived of their agricultural land. Most land historically had been collectively owned by the villagers and rotated to different families under the *musha* system. But the Ottoman Land Law of 1858 provided for private owner-ship. Thereafter, peasants who were mistrustful of the government tended to register the land they tilled in the names of people from important families. As a result, much of the land officially came to be owned by just a few people, some of whom, such as the Lebanese Sursuq family, had vast landholdings in northern Palestine that they were tempted to sell to the Zionists. Various landowners in Palestine, including some heavily indebted smallholders, sold land to the JNF, despite the shame they faced in their own community when such transactions became known. Even by the end of the British mandate, the Zionists had not acquired much more than 6 percent of the acreage, but this included some of the best land and perhaps 20 percent of the cultivatable land in general. In the Vale of

Esdraelon, close to Haifa, the sale of land in 1921 by the Sursuk family to the Zionists resulted in the displacement of eight Arab Palestinian villages, a phenomenon that occurred on a larger scale during the following decade.[42] As land held by the JNF was intended for use only by Jews and became the perpetual property of the Jewish people, it could not be resold to non-Jews. Arab Palestinian tenant farmers were uprooted from their villages in large numbers, which set the scene for a peasants' revolt.

There were many protests from the very beginning. A Palestine Arab Congress was held in Haifa in December 1920 and set up an Arab Executive Committee that sent delegations to London to protest against Britain's policies. Rival urban-based landholding families, the most important of which were the Husaynis and the Nashashibis, were at the center of Arab politics, each with a pyramidal structure of client families that reached various villages.[43] While all the Arab leaders (the center of the Periphery) denounced Zionism and the Balfour Declaration, they tended to be willing to cooperate with the British in the hope of wooing them away from support for a Jewish national home. However, they were outmaneuvered by the usual divide-and-rule tactics employed by colonial powers. Supported by High Commissioner Samuel, Hajj Amin al-Husayni succeeded his brother as mufti and headed the Supreme Muslim Council, two offices that gave him considerable authority in religious matters and more generally as the dominant spokesperson for the Arab Palestinians. He eventually became an uncompromising opponent of British rule, but the British took the office of mayor of Jerusalem away from the al-Husayni family and gave it to Raghib al-Nashashibi, who remained closely tied to them and to another British client, Emir (and later King) Abdullah of Transjordan.

In 1928–1929, Jabotinsky's followers attempted to widen Jewish use of the area facing the Wailing Wall (a Jewish holy site in Jerusalem), which led to several bloody clashes. Next, attacks by undisciplined mobs on the anti-Zionist Jewish community in Hebron deprived the Arab Palestinians of a potential ally against Zionism – the small community of indigenous Jews[44] – although Muslims saved most of the Jews by giving them refuge in their own homes.[45]

With popular anger against the British and Zionists intensifying, new leadership and renewed political activity emerged among the Arab Palestinian community. In 1932, the Arab Independence (Istiqlal) Party was formed, signaling the demise of the now-moribund Executive Committee two years later. Other pan-Arab bodies also arose during the decade, particularly among the youth, with the Arab Youth Congress the most influential. Around the same time, numerous clandestine armed groups formed, such as those headed by 'Abd al-Qadir al-Husayni and Izz al-Din al-Qassam, which advocated guerrilla warfare against the Zionists.

Arab Palestinian resistance to Zionism and British rule developed into outright revolt in 1936. Leaders of six factions formed an Arab Higher Committee, headed by Hajj Amin al-Husayni, which declared a general strike. Guerrilla warfare against the British and the Zionists accelerated, especially after September 1937. With the struggle for Palestine a popular cause throughout the Arab world, a Lebanese former Ottoman army officer, Fawzi al-Qawuqji, entered Palestine with 200 volunteers to participate in the guerrilla campaign.[46] In response, Orde Wingate, a British army officer whose belief that he was fulfilling biblical prophecies made him a passionate supporter of the Zionists, helped to turn the Haganah into a first-rate military force which joined British troops in organizing "night squads" that carried out anti-guerrilla raids. Arab Palestinians were subjected to mass arrests, demolition of houses, suppression of their newspapers, and collective fines. With their leaders exiled, the head of the rebellion was cut off, and it was all but crushed by 1939. Defense regulations imposed by the British to limit political activities and to allow arbitrary arrest and exile brought an oppressive state into existence that would long outlast the mandate, as the Hashimites and then, after 1967, the Israelis inherited the same rules.[47]

The conflict created a dilemma for the British. Although they were establishing the foundation of a new Jewish society in Palestine, they were often the objects of Zionist ire. Even Samuel, whose position demanded that he exercise some evenhandedness, became unpopular with his fellow Zionists. Several commissions were sent to study the situation and make recommendations, typically followed by a White Paper clarifying government policy. This had begun back in 1922, when the Churchill White Paper tried to reassure the Arab Palestinians that they were not to be subordinated, that the "national home" did not mean a Jewish state, and that the country's "economic absorptive capacity" would be taken into account in determining the extent of Jewish immigration. The Passfield White Paper of 1930 provided further assurances to the Arab Palestinians. However, these were virtually repudiated by Prime Minister Ramsay MacDonald in response to heavy Zionist pressure. Following the outbreak of the Arab revolt, a Palestine Royal Commission headed by Lord Robert Peel concluded that the mandate was not viable and proposed partition, with a small area, including Jerusalem, to continue under British rule; a Jewish state established in 20 percent of the country (and the Arab Palestinians, about half of this area's population, removed); and the remainder united with Transjordan (with a handful of Jews to be removed). Ben-Gurion thought this proposal was acceptable, given that it could lead to a larger Jewish state in the future, and the WZO authorized negotiations on the matter. However, among the Arabs, only the Nashashibis and Emir Abdullah – classic examples of the center of the Periphery allied with the center of the Center – favored it.

With war looming in 1939, the British government concluded that it was imperative to keep Palestine quiet for its duration. A new White Paper announced the limitation of Jewish immigration over the next five years to 75,000, with the Arab Palestinians to have a veto over all immigration after that. Palestine, still with a large Arab majority, was promised its independence in ten years. Although the Arab Higher Committee as well as the Zionists rejected the latest White Paper, the British finally seemed to have turned their back on Zionist aspirations. Unsurprisingly, Zionist ire again turned on the British.

Palestine remained relatively passive during the Second World War. Defeated in their recent revolt and with their leaders in exile (Hajj Amin al-Husayni eventually took refuge in Germany and engaged in anti-Allied propaganda), the

Arab Palestinians remained on the sidelines, although some of them served in the British army. While the White Paper was not deemed satisfactory, it probably helped to suppress unrest in the Arab world generally. The Jewish Agency announced that it opposed the White Paper but supported the British war effort, although it smuggled Jewish refugees from Europe into Palestine, which sometimes led to disaster. (The Agency blew up the refugee-filled SS *Patria* in Haifa harbor in 1942 in order to demonstrate their plight, and inadvertently killed 240 of the refugees.)

Seeing the war as an opportunity to gain military experience, the Zionists sought to create a Jewish Division. Although the British resisted this, a smaller Jewish Brigade came into existence and even participated in the British invasion of Lebanon in 1942. On the other hand, the Haganah raided British arms depots, thus building up their future military capacity. Among the Jewish militias, only the Stern Gang attacked the British during the early phases of the war. (It even proposed an alliance with Germany.) In fact, London was ready to drop the White Paper in favor of a new partition plan in 1944, but the Stern Gang's assassination of a top British official, Lord Moyne, in Egypt stopped this in its tracks.[48] Stern Gang gunmen also assassinated High Commissioner Sir Harold MacMichael in the same year. After the tide of war had turned in favor of the Allies in 1942, the Irgun also carried out terrorist operations against the British. During the last few months of the war, the Haganah joined with the British in combating the Stern Gang, and particularly the Irgun, which it saw as a dangerous rival. This poisoned the relationship between the labor Zionists and the Revisionists, and particularly that between Ben-Gurion and Begin.

Seeing the United States as the center of world power in the postwar era, the Zionist movement began to focus its activities there. At a special conference in the Biltmore Hotel in New York in 1942 that was dominated by Ben-Gurion, Zionist leaders called for the transformation of Palestine into an independent "Jewish Commonwealth." The Biltmore Program was subsequently approved by the Jewish Agency.

The immediate postwar period was characterized by demands from United States President Harry S Truman for the admission of more Jewish refugees into Palestine. The Irgun and Stern Gang continued their terrorist attacks on the British, and for a while the Haganah reached an agreement with them to coordinate such activities. Despite occasional disagreements with the two more extreme organizations on tactics as well as rivalry over future leadership, Haganah was fully in accord with them "in purpose: the expulsion of the British to achieve Jewish statehood in Palestine."[49] After a major crackdown on the Haganah in 1946, the Irgun retaliated by blowing up the King David Hotel in Jerusalem, which housed the British civil and military headquarters. Two Anglo-American commissions in that year failed to bring about a resolution of the conflict, inducing London to take the problem to the United Nations General Assembly in April 1947. In September, London announced that it would withdraw from Palestine by May 15 of the following year.

An eleven-member United Nations Special Commission on Palestine (UNSCOP) was created to study the situation. It eventually called for partition of Palestine into

Arab and Jewish states and an internationalized Jerusalem, with an economic union of the whole territory. With minor modifications, this report was approved by the General Assembly in November. Washington exerted much pressure to obtain this vote, while the members of the Soviet Bloc, in a reversal of their traditional opposition to Zionism, agreed to the proposal, too. It was mainly Arab and Muslim states, plus a majority of the few other independent African and Asian countries, that were opposed.

The plan awarded 54 percent of Palestine to the Jewish state, even though the Jews made up only a third of the population. The country was to be divided in a chessboard pattern. The "Jewish state," according to this plan, would have included areas with large Arab majorities and would barely have had a Jewish majority overall. Any further enlargement would have produced a "Jewish state" with more Arab than Jewish inhabitants. The Jewish Agency publicly accepted the plan, although the Zionists aspired to take more territory than it designated to them. Arabs overwhelmingly rejected it as unfair, although King Abdullah secretly reached an agreement with the Zionists.

As it happened, the plan had little influence on the final outcome. Instead, civil war broke out immediately after the UN vote. It is unclear who started the fighting, for when a Jewish bus came under fire in November (the event that many Zionists cite as the beginning of the war), it was actually being attacked by bandits who targeted Arabs and Jews alike.[50] Many Arab Palestinians chose not to resist the Zionists at all, and whole villages entered into agreements with nearby Jewish settlements, but they still came under attack.[51] Both sides used terror against civilians. But the fight between the well-trained and well-armed Jewish forces – which thousands of American and other Jewish volunteers from abroad joined – and the pitifully unprepared and disorganized Arab Palestinians under 'Abd al-Qadir al-Husayni – aided by volunteers from other Arab countries, such as al-Qawuqji's Palestine Liberation Army – was a total mismatch. As the British gradually withdrew, the Yishuv institutions in effect constituted a well-organized state ready to proclaim itself as such, and the Haganah cooperated with the Irgun and the Stern Gang in regular military and terrorist operations. However, in June, the IDF, as the Haganah was now known, sank an Irgun ship that was laden with arms, thus guaranteeing that no Jewish group would be able to challenge Ben-Gurion's nascent state.[52] When the Haganah itself received a clandestine shipment of arms from Czechoslovakia in March 1948, the gap between the two sides widened.

Despite their proclaimed acceptance of the partition plan, the Zionist forces began to implement their "Plan D" on April 1, which involved invading areas allotted to the proposed Arab state. A joint operation by the Zionist military forces on April 9 that ended with the massacre of 115 people at the village of Dayr Yasin was used to frighten the whole Arab Palestinian population. By May 15, as the British completed their departure and the Jewish Agency declared the independence of Israel, at least 300,000 Arab Palestinians had been uprooted from their homes. This number had increased to 400,000 by the start of the following month.

The Arab Palestinians looked to the armies of adjacent Arab states to come to their rescue, but their hopes were never realized. Arab armies (those of Egypt, Transjordan, Syria, Lebanon and Iraq) tried to join the fight once the British had left, but they were unprepared and inadequately armed. Moreover, they did not send many troops: contrary to what is often imagined, Israeli forces greatly outnumbered them. Popular pressure made it incumbent on Arab leaders – the center of the Periphery – to demonstrate support for their fellow Arabs in Palestine, but really it was no more than that. King Abdullah of Transjordan had always been sympathetic toward the Zionists and secretly cooperated with them. So he did not send his British-officered Arab Legion into Palestine in 1948 to crush Israel (although his forces did fight for the Old City of Jerusalem), but rather to acquire the share of Palestine that the Israelis had already agreed to cede to the Arabs. As for King Farouq of Egypt, he had long seen the Hashimites as rivals and, aside from appeasing the Egyptian people, his main reason for intervening in Palestine was to contain King Abdullah.

By the early part of 1949, the Israelis had already occupied not just their allotted 54 percent but 78 percent of Palestine. A series of armistices between Israel on one side and each of the adjacent Arab states froze in place the military lines (aside from a 144-square-mile strip that King Abdullah's forces held but handed over to the Israelis), creating the "Green Line." After King Abdullah organized two congresses of Palestinians who were willing to cooperate with him, Transjordan (subsequently called simply Jordan) annexed what came to be called the West Bank, while Egypt administered the Gaza Strip. (Eighteen years later, these territories would come under Israeli occupation after the Six Day War.) Consequently, when the fighting ended, there was no Arab Palestinian state.

More remarkable than the territorial changes were the demographic ones. The end of the war left approximately 750,000 Arab Palestinians whose homes were within the Green Line as refugees on the other side of the line (and thousands of others displaced within the Green Line). An estimated 400 villages were depopulated, as were towns such as Ramle and Lydda and cities such as Jaffa and the Arab Palestinian sectors of Haifa. Visiting Haifa, Ben-Gurion described "A fantastic and terrifying spectacle. A dead city, a city-corpse . . . without a living soul save stray cats."[53] An Israeli Foreign Ministry report predicted that some of the refugees would "perish,"[54] and it may only have been the relief activities of the United Nations Relief and Works Agency (UNRWA), as well as efforts by Quaker groups and others, that prevented this. Arab Palestinians' homes were occupied by new Jewish immigrants from Europe and later from the Middle East or were left to decay or be razed. An Absentee Property Act confiscated all property owned by Arab Palestinians who were away from their homes in enemy-controlled territory at any time after November 29, 1947, and the land was transferred to the JNF for exclusive Jewish use. In Resolution 194, the UN General Assembly upheld the right of Palestinian return (and reaffirmed it year after year). However, virtually all Israelis adamantly reject this, as a return of the refugees would make it impossible for Israel to continue as a Jewish state.

Only a small minority of the Arab Palestinian population remained. Totaling about 160,000, the Arabs within the Green Line after the armistices included 30,000 who were expelled but slipped back in and managed to stay. About 75,000 of the total were "present absentees" – refugees from their own villages and not allowed to return or reclaim their property.[55] Although there was a massive influx of Jewish immigrants (nearly 700,000 by the end of 1951), the Arab population would never drop below 10 percent of the total Israeli population, a proportion that has now doubled because of the group's relatively high birth rate. With this exception, the whole physical and human landscape of old Palestine was replaced by a new one. Benvenisti poetically laments the land's "buried history,"[56] and a newcomer might not be able to imagine that such an Arab Palestinian world ever existed. When, in subsequent years, the Israelis would celebrate the birth of their state, the Arab Palestinians would simultaneously mourn the Nakba (Catastrophe).

A myth was long perpetuated that the Arab Palestinian flight was voluntary – that they just "chose not to live under Israeli rule" and that Arab radio broadcasts ordered them to leave. There was always an abundance of evidence to show that this was not true, but in the 1980s some Israeli historians professed astonishment when they discovered documentary materials in the Israeli archives that completely belied their old narrative.[57] Indeed, many Israelis still refuse to accept the truth, even though it is now indisputable that the flight was coerced, partly through fear and partly through outright expulsion by the IDF. Irrespective of whether there were written orders to expel the Arab population, Israeli leaders well understood the need to do so in order to have a Jewish state.

Israel: the formal institutions of the state

Israel proper has a set of formal institutions that generally parallels the typical organization of many modern parliamentary states. At the center of the structure – though by no means of power – is a parliament, known as the Knesset (Assembly). Like other modern national parliaments, it has supreme authority to enact legislation, and the government is responsible to it. Its membership is fixed at 120, elected for a four-year term, although elections can occur sooner in certain situations.[58] All citizens of the state who have attained the age of eighteen may vote in Knesset elections, and (aside from some specific disqualifications adopted in 1964) can stand for election at twenty-one. With the whole country constituting one constituency, each political party presents a list of candidates and – if it receives at least 2 percent (previously 1.5 percent) of the vote – is allocated a proportionate number of seats. In the past, party central committees drew up the lists, which made the process highly oligarchical. And it still is, to a large extent, even though most parties now conduct primary elections to decide their lists.

As in other parliamentary systems, the chief executive is the prime minister, who heads the cabinet. The president, elected by the Knesset for a five-year term, acts as the ceremonial head of state but exercises little real power. The president designates a member of the Knesset, normally the head of the biggest party, to form the government: that is, as a prospective prime minister. (A plan for direct election adopted in 1996 was scrapped five years later.) If one party were to hold an absolute majority of the seats in the Knesset, this would be a straightforward process, as various ministerial portfolios would simply be assigned to the leaders of that party. However, this has never happened in Israel (the Labor Party came closest, winning 56 seats in 1969), so coalition governments have always had to be constructed. The person designated by the president is obliged to negotiate with leaders of other parties, offering ministerial positions – the total varies, ranging as high as thirty, almost all of whom will be Knesset members – and policies to attract them. When a coalition finally gains the support of an absolute majority in the Knesset, the government is formed.

There is an increasing tendency for the prime minister to dominate the political process while in office, but there is always the potential danger of coalition partners breaking away to deprive the government of its majority and thus necessitating a new coalition to be formed or even a general election to be called. Unlike the British pattern of "collective responsibility," members of the Israeli cabinet often openly disagree with one another, and the party holding a particular portfolio tends to have a largely free hand within its ministry without much collective supervision by the cabinet. A recent innovation is the adoption of the principle of a constructive vote of no-confidence (as in the German Federal Republic), in which the government is not voted out unless another majority coalition comes into existence. However, this may prove academic, as only one government has ever received a vote of no-confidence.

An unusual feature of Israel's state structure – although one it shares with the United Kingdom's parliamentary system – is the absence of a single document called a constitution. This is explained by the difficulty of bridging the divide between religious and secular Jews and the more obvious desire of the leadership not to be restricted. The nearest thing to a constitution is a series of basic laws, some of which can be modified only by an absolute majority in the Knesset. Recently, the Supreme Court has also struck down a few legislative acts on the grounds that they are either unreasonable or violate one or other of the basic laws.

In many respects, the level of respect for civil liberties is high. There is much military censorship, but a much wider range of opinion – including harsh attacks by Arab members on concepts dear to most Zionists – is heard in the Knesset than would be imaginable in, say, the United States Congress. The same has been true for the press in the past, although the Press Freedom Index gave Israel a rank of only 46 (out of 175 countries) for 2008. But restrictions imposed as a result of the assault on Gaza at the end of the year caused its rank to sink to 93, lower than some authoritarian Arab states, in 2009.[59]

Armed forces constitute an important part of most states, and the IDF is no exception. An unusually high proportion of the state's GDP is spent on the military, and it has repaid this investment by becoming one of the world's most effective fighting forces. While some Israelis attributed their failure in the Second Lebanon War (2006) to a decline in both their preparation and their soldiers' fighting spirit, one must also take into account the unprecedented tenacity of their new enemy, Hizbollah. With all Israeli citizens – aside from rabbinical students, religiously observant women, Arabs and most of the Druze (some Bedouin are recruited as desert patrols) – officially required to serve, the IDF pervades Israeli society (even though many individuals gain exemptions in practice).

As the parliamentary regime possesses a high level of popular legitimacy, the idea that the IDF might ever carry out a coup seems preposterous. It would perhaps make even less sense in light of the military's centrality in running the state throughout its history. In the early days of the state, political leadership came from Mapai apparatchiks, not from army officers, and Ben-Gurion kept the military under his personal control, but this was done with close "interpenetration of the highest echelons of Mapai and the highest echelons of the army."[60] As the first generation of leaders faded away, retired army officers began to predominate in the political elite. Some students of Israeli politics argue that army officers have long played a major role in political decisions,[61] and Israel's role as a leading producer and exporter of armaments has been conducive to the growth of a powerful military–industrial complex.[62] Israel has never had "an apolitical, instrumentalist army under the absolute supervision of state institutions, but rather one that actively participates in setting goals and in which the line between civilian and military "spheres are porous and shifting" in a partnership where there are signs that "the military is the senior partner."[63] A study of thirty-six "democracies" published in 2006 put Israel bottom in terms of non-involvement of the military in politics.[64]

With the state engaged in a wide range of activities, it employs a large proportion of the population. Even with increasing economic liberalism (i.e., the growth of private enterprise), the transfer of functions such as health insurance from the Histadrut to the state has actually increased the size of the state sector.[65] Perhaps surprisingly for a society that in some respects is highly "modern," the merit principle is far from dominant, especially for higher-level positions. From all accounts, what Israelis call *protektzia* ("pull" or "connections" – the equivalent of the much-deplored *wasta* of the Arab world) is ever present. Transparency International gives Israel a low rating on political corruption compared with almost all other Western democracies.[66]The Civil Service Commission is part of the Finance Ministry and thus susceptible to political control.[67] The state is highly centralized, with towns and cities dependent on the central authorities for funds. Each local unit has its council, elected on the basis of party lists, with mayors elected separately since 1978.

In addition, some important organizations have been so interlinked with the state as arguably to constitute parts of it. Though recently weakened, the Histadrut, now renamed the New Histadrut, remains an important institution. Always controlled by Mapai/Labor until 1994, it once owned major economic enterprises – banks, stores, kibbutzim and moshavim, and industries. This constituted a mainstay of Mapai/Labor's electoral power by providing enormous patronage opportunities. Notably, one needed to be a member of the Histadrut in order to get health insurance, which it controlled; when that was taken over by the state in 1995, Labor's membership plummeted. The decline of the ILP and the weakening of the Histadrut have thus gone hand in hand.[68] Then there are the WZO and the Jewish

Agency, to which a major role in education and settlement is assigned. Also, the Jewish Agency is the partial or complete owner of many major business enterprises. Another WZO organ, the United Jewish Appeal, collects vast amounts of money that is spent in cooperation with the state.[69]

Also established by the WZO, the JNF has title to vast amounts of land. This includes some land that it acquired (or, in Zionist terminology, "redeemed") through purchase, but mainly it comprises Palestinian property that the state acquired through the Absentee Property Act and later turned over to the JNF.[70] The owners of this land are officially the Jewish people, and it makes up about 13 percent of the total within the Green Line. Land that is owned by the state *per se* – most of the land in Israel – is now administered by the Israel Land Administration (in which the JNF has almost half the votes). The JNF land is leased for long periods, but JNF rules – while not always enforced – ban its use by non-Jews. This policy has caused much controversy in recent years, with Adala (Justice), a Palestinian Israeli human rights organization, taking the issue to the UN Commission on Human Rights and to the Israeli Supreme Court. In 2007 the latter delayed final consideration of the matter.

Israeli society

Class divisions

No one now makes the long-touted claim that Israel is the most egalitarian country in the world. Even in the early days of the state, such a statement was dubious in light of the poverty of the Arab and Mizrahi populations. For that matter, Sternhell points to the contrast during the 1930s between the myth of egalitarianism and the "enormous gap between the managers and officials of the Histadrut economy"[71] and suggests that in the 1950s Israel's "inequalities" matched "and in some ways" exceeded those of Western Europe.[72]

Today it has been suggested – although this too is an exaggeration – that Israel leads the world in inequality.[73] Actually, Israel's Gini Index (a standard measure of inequality), according to the *2007/2008 Human Development Report*[74] shows that its income distribution is more equal than that of many Periphery countries, although it is worse than that of any other Center country, with the exception of the United States. By 2008, globalization and neoliberalism, involving tax cuts for the rich and reduced support for public services, pensions and the like, as well as growing corruption, had led to a situation in which just 500 people were worth a total of $75 billion in a GDP of only $130 billion. Furthermore:

> In 2005–7, Israel produced more millionaires per capita than any other country. But it also pushed more people back beneath the poverty line [$400 a month for one person and $1,100 for a four-person family] than any other western nation in the last decade . . . One and a half million people, or 20 percent of the population, live under the poverty line. That means thirty-four percent of Israeli children live in poverty.[75]

A survey in 2008 found that many of the people on food aid feared starvation or had contemplated suicide.[76]

By 2007, the number of dollar millionaires shot up by 13.6 percent, compared with 6 percent worldwide, while multimillionaires (those with at least $30 million) increased by 12 percent, compared with 8.8 percent around the world.[77] Considering that the lines between rich and poor do not cut across ethnic divisions at anything close to right angles (the average income for Arabs is half that of Jews,[78] while among the latter poverty is concentrated among Mizrahim and the ultra-Orthodox Haredim), this situation carries implications for future relationships between the various groups that make up Israeli society. A recent report shows that discrimination against poor students, notably Mizrahim and Arabs, by the school system is widening the social gap.[79]

Organized interest groups

Rather than concentrating on lobbying individual legislators in the American style, Israeli interest groups tend to be linked to whole parties. The parties, in turn

> colonize bureaucracies or public policy issues or both. The ruling party, either Likud or Labor, has dominated defense, Labor has run the Histadrut and has colonized the agriculture bureaucracies, and the NRP and haredi parties have nationalized the religious issue and made it their own. Pluralism is not in evidence; competing political parties are.[80]

Particularly on economic issues, the government brings representatives of key groups into the decision-making process in a corporatist pattern of interest representation[81] (such as that long associated with Latin America and much of Western Europe) as opposed to the "pluralism" of the United States and the United Kingdom. Quasi-governmental bodies that "include kibbutzim and moshavim; the Development Towns' Forum; representatives of West Bank settlers; ultra-Orthodox groups; you name it" are adept at securing scarce resources for their Jewish constituents, while the absence of comparable groups for Arabs has been offered as one explanation of why they are deprived of their share.[82] Jewish settlers in the post-1967 occupied territories, who tend to be associated with parties on the right, constitute an example of a powerful pressure group, one that could conceivably defy the state – some observers fear a "unilateral declaration of independence" that would establish a second Jewish state ruling over the Palestinian majority – if Israel ever decides to withdraw to the Green Line.

National cohesion

Despite important cleavages that divide some sectors of the population from the majority, Israel proper's political system has enjoyed the kind of cohesion necessary for it to have a highly effective political system. A sense of threat from the Arab/Islamic world may in part explain why potential centrifugal forces, including divisions between Europeans and Mizrahim and between secular and religious Jews, have failed to get out of hand. Recent polls show high percentages of the population demonstrating a strong identity as "Israelis." For instance, a 2008 survey revealed that 80 percent were "very proud to be Israeli."[83]

The party system in relation to cleavages

Existing cleavages would make it difficult to have a two-party system, even in the absence of proportional representation. However, there have been sufficient centripetal forces to avoid the kind of instability that has made some multiparty systems so notorious. Considering that as many as thirty-five party lists have competed in one election and that typically about a dozen win seats, this might be surprising. Some coalition partners come and go, and prime ministers often do not stay in office until the next scheduled elections. In recent years, no Knesset has survived until the end of its full term, with elections now typically held halfway through the term. But a recent study shows Israel's governmental stability during 1996–2006 was moderate, making it comparable to that of Great Britain or Germany.[84] During the whole history of the state, only once, in 1990, did a government receive a vote of no-confidence, and even then the prime minister (Shamir) stayed on as the head of a new coalition.[85] But attempts to cobble together new governments – which typically involve giving in to the demands of various small parties – when a prime minister resigns may go on for months and still fail, with the end result sometimes being that an election must be held. Such was the case when Ehud Olmert resigned (but continued on an interim basis) even after his Kadima Party chose a new leader, Tzipi Livni, in 2008. Following the election in February 2009, it seemed unlikely that a new government would be formed, and at least one observer saw the state as having become "well-nigh ungovernable, fragmented and paralysed."[86]

The absence of a major antisystem party – that is, one that fundamentally challenges the values on which the state is based – is a huge asset in the Israeli polity. It means that there is a consensus on the basic rules of the game, giving the democratic system the legitimacy it needs to be secure. Despite major ideological divisions, the major parties (and arguably most, if not all of the minor ones) are committed to the democratic process. Even the Herut, with its roots in the fascist-influenced Revisionist movement, never challenged the right of election victors to rule. Indeed, it and its successor, the Likud, eventually participated in coalitions with Labor. Aside from small Arab parties (including the partly Jewish-led Communists/Hadash), all parties in the Knesset are therefore potential partners in governing coalitions. And no large party has emerged that rejects the Jewish nature of the state, which would destroy the existing consensus on another crucial question, partly because the Arab Palestinian citizens have so far not been able to form a united anti-Zionist party. Another factor favorable to the stability of the existing system is the high level of economic development that has produced increasing prosperity (and, for a long time, relatively equal distribution), something that is essential to the success of democracy.

All of this said, there are several reasons to temper optimism. The secular–Haredi divide provides the potential for future conflict, especially in light of the growth of the latter group, and could create political instability, particularly if the conflict with the Palestinians and the wider Arab/Islamic world ever lost its salience. The gradual growth of the proportion of Palestinian Israelis will likely make it more difficult for Israel to be a "Jewish and democratic state," and the possible permanent incorporation of more Palestinians into the population would aggravate this problem. If economic inequality continues to increase – and particularly to the extent to which the rich–poor divide fails to cut across the Jewish–Arab, secular–Haredi and European–Mizrahi cleavages – increasing pressure could be put on Israeli democracy. Finally, it is difficult to see how a supposedly "democratic" state will be maintained if it continues to suppress another population, namely the Palestinians in the West Bank and Gaza Strip.

Already, the popular legitimacy of democracy – always an important basis for its survival – is showing some signs of decline. A poll conducted in 2003 indicated that the percentage of Israelis who consider democracy to be the best political system had dropped from about 90 percent to just 76 percent.[87] (Only a few other countries registered a lower response to this question.) Moreover, Israeli responses to questions about the need for strong leaders (61 percent in 2006, higher than in any other long-consolidated Western democracy)[88] and the primacy of maintaining security over the rule of law showed substantial majorities expressing what could be considered undemocratic attitudes.[89] By contrast, another survey revealed that Israelis increasingly feel that there is not enough democracy in their country. (However, the same survey seemed to indicate that most Israelis thought that democracy was entirely compatible with a Halakhic state.)[90] Other polls have revealed increasing anti-Arab racism, with only about half of Israelis believing that Arab citizens should have equal rights, 55 percent wanting the state to encourage them to leave, and 74 percent of Jewish youth describing Arabs as "unclean."[91]

Levels of trust, which many political scientists see as crucial to democracy, seem to be on the decline. According to a Pew Global Attitudes survey conducted in 2007, only 42 percent of Israelis consider most people trustworthy, compared with 71 percent in Canada, 79 percent in China, 58 percent in Egypt and 52 percent in Jordan.[92] Another study shows high levels of trust in the judicial system and the mass media but not in political parties.[93] Finally, one survey revealed a notable drop in interest in politics and a "growing mistrust of government institutions." Ninety percent see their state as "tainted with corruption," with 60 percent saying it is "very high," while 51 suggest that corruption is a prerequisite for top leadership positions, resulting in "support for solutions . . . that are not necessarily democratic."[94]

The rate of electoral participation used to be high, but has dropped significantly in recent years. A 63.2 percent turnout in 2006's general election put Israel slightly ahead of the United States and the United Kingdom, but well below that of most long-established democracies.[95] This is striking in light of the fact that Israel ranks first among Western countries in terms of citizen interest in and staying informed about and discussing politics.[96] The explanation seems to be a significant drop among Israeli Jews in the belief that ordinary people have any influence whatsoever over government (down from 49 percent in 1984 to 26 percent in 2006), with 62 percent opining in 2006 that politicians do not consider the public's views.[97] This meshes well with a study conducted by the World Bank in 2004 which showed that Israel did indeed rank low in terms of governmental accountability (32nd out of 36 countries).[98]

Labor parties: hegemony and after

The proliferation of parties notwithstanding, the Mapai Party – later enlarged and renamed the Israel Labor Party (ILP) and sometimes formally aligned with Ahdut Haavoda or Mapam) – remained in effective control of the Yishuv and then of the independent state of Israel until its "earthquake" loss to the rightist Likud in 1977. Founded by David Ben-Gurion in 1930, Mapai was closely tied to both the Histadrut and the WZO. The party was committed not only to Zionism but to a socialist ideology that included a major commitment to collective ownership – particularly by Histadrut – and control of the economy. This generally paralleled the positions of various parties of the non-communist left in Europe and elsewhere. However, the Mapai Zionists were not alone in supporting state ownership, and in fact long resisted the idea of national health insurance, supported by other parties in favor of keeping this under the control of the Histadrut.[99] Like other social democratic parties, the ILP has become more capitalistic over the years, but it is still perceived as representing a left-of-center position in relation to its principal opponents – vis-à-vis economic questions, but particularly because it is more flexible than the rightist parties on the matter of eventually withdrawing from the territories occupied in 1967.

Until 1977, Israel exemplified what political scientists call a "dominant party system." Mapai/Labor – by having a plurality but never an absolute majority in the Knesset – occupied a central, controlling role in every government. Admittedly, this was accomplished by providing important political plums for its minor partners in government and even kowtowing to them on particular issues. There was no effective opposition party or potential rival coalition, and it was usually assumed that this state of affairs would be permanent. This situation was exemplified during 1967–1970, when all of the country's political parties, with the exception of the Communists, united to form a national unity government.

The ILP has a complicated history involving numerous schisms, mergers and the drafting of joint lists with other parties, both during the period of its dominance and afterward. When the state of Israel was founded, two factions – Ahdut Haavoda and Mapam – had already split from Mapai, and they long continued to offer more left-wing alternatives to their parent party, including favoring closer ties with the USSR. Ahdut Haavoda and Mapam formed an alignment (a joint electoral list, which included candidates from each party) in 1965, and in the same year Mapai split again, when Ben-Gurion supported a group of rising politicians with military backgrounds, including Moshe Dayan and Shimon Peres, and formed a new party called Reshimat Poalei Israel (Rafi). By 1968, however, most of Rafi's senior members had rejoined the fold (although Ben-Gurion held out and headed the separate "State List" for a while). Mapai and Ahdut Haavoda went on to create the ILP. Mapam allied itself to the new party the following year to form the Labor Alignment, although it retained its separate identity while its candidates appeared on a joint electoral list alongside members of the ILP. However, Mapam withdrew from the Alignment after the 1984 elections in protest over the ILP's decision to form a national unity government with Likud. Thereafter, in 1992, it joined with two other groups to form a new party, Meretz, which later united with another small group to become Meretz–Yachad.

The post-1977 era produced more alternation of parties in power, though with a growing preponderance of the right wing. There was still no likelihood that any party would gain an absolute majority in the Knesset, but for the next three decades both Labor and Likud could aspire to win enough seats to form a ruling coalition. Following seven years of Likud-led governments, the Alignment gained 44 seats against Likud's 41 in the 1984 election, and thereafter there was a national unity government headed for two years by ILP leader Shimon Peres and for the next two years by Likud leader Yitzhak Shamir. Another national unity government, this time with Shamir as prime minister for the whole term, came to power in 1988. The ILP won the most seats in the elections of 1992 and 1996, but in the latter case direct election of the prime minister led to victory for Likud leader Benjamin Netanyahu. Subsequently, the ILP (campaigning as "One Israel") gained 26 seats against Likud's 19 in 1999, and its leader, Ehud Barak, defeated Netanyahu in the separate battle for the premiership. However, early prime ministerial elections held in 2001 led to a big victory for the Likud candidate, Ariel Sharon. This bipolar pattern of competition ended in 2006, when the Kadima (Forward) Party – a new grouping led at first by Sharon and bringing together former members of both Likud and the ILP – came to power. Three years later, Netanyahu's Likud gained the most seats (albeit just one more than Kadima). In the same election, the ILP was reduced to fourth place (with a mere 13 seats), indicating how far it had descended far from its former hegemonic position.

The Likud and its rightist predecessors: Mizrahi protest

Like the previously dominant Labor Party, the right-wing Likud bloc that came to power in the "earthquake" election of 1977 has roots going back to the mandate era. And its history is another complicated story of schisms and mergers. Likud itself was not even formed until 1973, through the merger of several older parties.

Today's Likud is primarily the continuation of Jabotinsky's ultra-militant, anti-socialist Revisionist branch of Zionism that emerged during the 1920s and developed into the terrorist Irgun and Stern Gang during the 1940s. This became the Herut (Freedom) Party under Menachim Begin following independence in 1948. Long peripheral to Israeli politics – gaining 14 seats in the 1949 election and only eight in 1951 – and considered beyond the pale by the mainstream, the Herut Party continued to call for the incorporation into the new state of the whole territory of the

Palestine mandate, including both banks of Jordan. It would become the second-largest party by the mid-1950s (with 15 seats in 1955).

Begin and Ben-Gurion nurtured an intense mutual hatred, hurling such insults as "totalitarian" and "fascist" at each other, while the latter denounced the former as "clearly a Hitler type."[100] All of this had its roots in a series of pre-1948 incidents, including the murder of an important labor leader in 1933 and the Haganah's cooperation with the British in capturing Jewish terrorists in 1945. Later, Begin launched bitter attacks on the government about the issue of reparations from Germany, which incited mob violence against the Knesset and for a time threatened the viability of the democratic order.[101]

In 1965, Herut combined with most of the Liberals – a small, pro-private-enterprise party which itself had suffered several splits – to form the Gahal (Gush Herut Liberalism) list, which ultimately participated in the government of national unity between 1967 and 1970. However, in reality, this government was far from united. Gahal was committed to keeping most of the territories that had been occupied in the recent Six Day War, while the dominant ILP expected to return most of them to Arab rule as part of a future peace agreement. (The Allon Plan, adopted in 1967, contemplated the return of most of the West Bank, except for Jerusalem or the strip adjacent to the Jordan River, to Jordan.) In 1973, the rightist coalition grew when two splinter groups (including the small State List) joined with Gahal to form Likud, which won 39 seats in that year's election, held in the immediate aftermath of the 1973 war. It went on to become the governing party, with 43 seats against Labor's 32, four years later. This victory resulted from several factors. One was the emergence of a new centrist political party, the Democratic Movement for Change, which drew votes away from Labor. Another was the growing support of the bulk of the Mizrahim for Likud because of bitterness over their treatment by successive Labor governments.

The immigration of large numbers of Jews from Middle Eastern countries (and a few from other parts of Africa and Asia) drastically changed the makeup of Israeli society. The Jews of European origin who had founded the state would eventually be outnumbered by these Mizrahim (although an influx of immigrants from Russia in the 1990s restored the European majority, at least for a while). There was a deep divide between the two groups, as the immigrants from the Arab world were fundamentally Arabs of the Jewish faith, and as such were often the victims of cultural and even racial prejudice in Israel. Immigration officials treated them with contempt as they arrived, spraying them with DDT with the implication that they might be dirty and lice ridden. Thereafter, they tended to be sent to remote parts of the country, often near the frontier, to "developmental towns." The Mizrahim were mostly poor and less educated than the European Jews, and the latter were almost totally dominant in running the state. A study of the Israeli political elite in 1974 showed that, of seventy people who had been cabinet ministers, only four had been of non-European origin.[102]

Mizrahi support for Likud has been paralleled by a hawkish attitude toward the Arab world. A case in point was the Lebanon War of 1982. When the largely Ashkenazi, dovish Peace Now organized demonstrations in February 1983, protesting against the IDF's involvement in the massacre of Palestinians in the Sabra and Shatila refugee camps, their sometimes violent confrontations with hecklers, who were almost entirely Mizrahim, took on an ethnic character. The hecklers shouted that the Europeans should not have been saved from Hitler, and that they should have been in the Palestinian camps. A prominent spokesperson for the anti-war demonstrators characterized the chants as "a roll of tom-toms in a savage tribe,"[103] a comment which itself seemed to carry racial overtones.

It is far from easy to explain Mizrahi hawkishness toward the Arab world and support for Likud. Just like Mapai/Labor, Likud has also been dominated by European Jews. And the widespread assumption that Mizrahi antipathy toward Arab nations is due to bad experiences in those countries is belied by studies showing that hostility to Arabs is largely a characteristic of those who were born in Israel, while their parents (the immigrants themselves) often have fond memories of friendships with Muslims. Some have suggested that Mizrahim, who had once been forced to work in menial jobs, liked the fact that Palestinians took on these roles after 1967 and feared that an end to the occupation would put them – the Mizrahim – back at the bottom of the social pile. Others explain the phenomenon in psychological terms: the Mizrahim hope to gain acceptance by the Ashkenazim by demonstrating that they are even more anti-Arab than the European Jews. However, the main reason why Mizrahim support Likud simply seems to be that they resent the contemptuous treatment they received when Mapai/Labor was in power.

There are some indications that the Mizrahi–European divide is slowly closing. Intermarriage between the two groups is increasing. Mizrahim have much more representation in the Knesset, with many holding ministerial portfolios. Amir Peretz, of Moroccan origin, even headed the Labor Party during 2005–2007, and two Mizrahim have held the largely symbolic office of president. But Mizrahim, on average, still have incomes that are only about two-thirds those of other Israelis. The Jews of Ethiopian origin (numbering 105,000 in 2005) are even worse off, with incomes even lower than those of Arab Palestinian Israelis, and they are often subjected to specific discrimination.[104]

Some observers found it surprising that the emergence of a Likud government in 1977 was followed by the sudden acceleration of negotiations with Egypt in response to dramatic diplomatic moves by Egyptian President Anwar al-Sadat later that year. The Camp David Accords of 1978 provided the framework for a peace treaty, which was concluded the next year, leading to full withdrawal of Israeli forces from Sinai in 1982. This resulted in the formation of some small parties to the right of Likud, such as Tehiya, Tzomet and Moledet, with the last calling for "transfer" – that is, expulsion – of Israel's Arabs. However, the accord with Egypt did not indicate a shift of Likud to a more dovish position. By giving up the Sinai, the Likud government simply hoped to be in a better position to resist pressure to relinquish any part of pre-1948 Palestine, particularly the West Bank, which Israeli nationalists saw as the historic heart of their homeland. Indeed, almost as soon as peace was concluded with Egypt, the government ordered an invasion of Lebanon that was designed to destroy the PLO, which was seen as the remaining obstacle to the formal annexation of the West Bank and Gaza. In later years, Likud attacked any moves that might have led to withdrawal from the Palestinian territories, including the Oslo Accord of 1994, and when Netanyahu headed the government he dragged his feet in a clear effort to thwart that agreement. When Sharon came to power in 2000, he continued to pursue this more traditional Likud policy as he suppressed the new Palestinian Intifadah. However – unlike many of Likud's members and supporters – he eventually came to acknowledge that the "demographic threat" posed by the Palestinians could be solved only through "separation" and the eventual establishment of a Palestinian state, leading him to break away from Likud and form Kadima.

Religious parties

A third force in the Israeli political system consists of a constantly changing constellation of religious parties. These carry political clout far beyond their numerical electoral strength because they are invariably key components of a coalition. Anyone aspiring to lead the government is dependent on the support of some or all of the religious parties. The coveted support of these parties can be gained by giving in to them on the issues that are close to their hearts and by awarding them certain cabinet portfolios. This explains why, although most Israelis are secular minded and not very observant of Jewish religious practices, their political system persistently perpetuates important theocratic patterns. It explains why in a place where a large proportion of Jews are of the non-practicing sort and even tend toward agnosticism, only Orthodox (as opposed to Reform or Conservative) Judaism has official recognition. It explains why there is no secular marriage or divorce, leaving the Orthodox rabbinate to apply Jewish religious law in such matters, including such anomalies as not allowing any Jew who was born as a result of his or her mother's adultery (called a *mamzer*) – nor even his or her descendants – from marrying any Jew aside from another *mamzer*.[105] It explains why interreligious marriages cannot occur in Israel. It explains why various dietary laws – such as forbidding the raising of pigs on Jewish-owned land and allowing municipalities to ban the sale of pork (although a 2004 Supreme Court decision overruled this in communities where the overwhelming majority want to allow it) – and restrictions on business activities on the Sabbath are still in force. It explains why yeshiva (Jewish seminary) students and Orthodox women are exempted from military service as well as the generous provision of state funds for religious schools.

This entrenchment of Orthodox Judaism evokes much resentment among the majority of Israelis, and there is mutual, intense ill-feeling between secular and Orthodox Jews. Secularists sometimes try to combat Orthodox influence, as in the formation of the citizens' rights movement of Shulamit Aloni in 1973, but to no avail so far. On occasion, this secular–Orthodox tension seems about to erupt into outright conflict.

There has always been a multiplicity of religious parties. In the first general election after independence, the Agada (Community) parties joined together in a common list and then proceeded to act as a bloc in the Knesset. In subsequent elections, some of them united to form the National Religious Party (NRP), which would long remain the major religious grouping, consistently securing between 10 and 12 seats in each election up to 1970, but later dropping to roughly half of that. The NRP might be regarded as the religious party that is closest to the Israeli mainstream, as it has fully come to terms with Zionism. Others religious parties have included those of the ultra-Orthodox Haredim: Agudat Israel (Community of Israel, which later united with another Haredi faction to form the United Torah Judaism) and Poalei Agudat Israel (Workers of the Community of Israel). The former movement accepted the establishment of the state of Israel as a fact, much like any other state in which Jews live, but continued to disassociate itself from the Zionist movement and its principles. It avoids ministerial positions while supporting various coalitions in the Knesset. Beginning in the 1980s, a new ultra-Orthodox party, Shas, emerged among the Mizrahim, who considered themselves underrepresented in Agada electoral lists. It eventually became the biggest religious party in the Knesset, securing 17 seats in 1999. Winning 11 seats in the 2009 election, Shas hoped to form a coalition with other ultra-Orthodox parties, including United Torah Judaism (with 5 seats), that would counter the secularist, right-wing Yisrael Beiteinu.

On the ultra-Orthodox fringe of the anti-Zionist Haredi factions – although not a political party – is a small faction known as Neturei Karta (Guardians of the Gate). Its members refuse to recognize the legitimacy of the state and continue to denounce Zionism in the strongest possible terms..

Totally unlike the traditional Orthodox opposition to Zionism, a new kind of messianic Orthodox Zionism – typically labeled "fundamentalist" or "extremist" and committed to a Greater Israel – arose after the Six Day War. It includes the Gush Emunim (Movement of the Faithful) – not a political party. Rabbi Meir Kahane's Kach (Thus) Party, which called for the "transfer" of Arabs from Greater Israel, was disqualified on the basis of being "racist" in 1988.

Following the 1996 elections, religious parties formed the third largest bloc in the Knesset and continued to sustain their political power and influence within the Likud-led coalition. Some secular Israelis fear that the Haredim – with their high birth rates in self-contained communities (notably in Jerusalem) that have little contact with the broader society and oppose the Zionist ideology on which the state was founded – will grow in numbers and power, pointing ominously to the fact that in 2007 they made up 23 percent of first-graders. (Meanwhile, the other anti-Zionist group – the Arab Palestinian citizens – constituted 22 percent.)[106]

Haredim often throw stones at cars passing near their neighborhoods on the Sabbath, which angers other Israelis. In 1986 militant secularists went as far as to burn a synagogue and paint swastikas on another in retaliation for the defacing of a bus station by ultra-Orthodox Jews who were angered by pictures of women in bathing suits. A poll of Israeli Jews that year found 67 percent of them considered Haredim "unacceptable," while only 14 percent called them "acceptable." (Notably, 23 percent were willing to apply the latter adjective to Arab citizens.)[107]

The Russians and Yisrael Beiteinu

With the Soviet Union and its successor states providing nearly a million immigrants after 1989, many of the new Israelis joined mainly "Russian" parties.[108] One example was Natan Sharansky's Yisrael B'aliya (Israel on the Rise), which ballooned for a while during the 1990s but later shrank before merging with Likud. An even more right-wing "Russian" party – but drawing much of its support from the broader population – emerged later in the decade under the leadership of a Moldavian immigrant, Avigar Lieberman, who had earlier ties to Meir Kahane and became part of the governing coalition under Ariel Sharon in 2001. Lieberman's party, Yisrael Beiteinu (Israel Is Our Home), won 11 seats in 2006 and fifteen in 2009, becoming the third largest in the Knesset. Adopting such campaign slogans as "Only Lieberman understands Arabic" and "No citizenship without loyalty"[109] in reference to the increasingly alienated Palestinian citizens of Israel, Yisrael Beiteinu called for protection of the Jewishness of the state by transferring Palestinian towns and villages to the PNA (and a future Palestinian state) – an idea that was generally anathema to them – while annexing Jewish-settled areas in the West Bank.

Arab parties: the internal Periphery

After the 1949 armistices, approximately 160,000 Arab Palestinians within the Green Line acquired Israeli citizenship and voting rights but not equality. Their high birth rate, typical of the Third World, has made them an increasingly large proportion of the population – about one-fifth today. Some projections suggest they will form the majority before the end of the twenty-first century, and they already do so in Galilee (particularly outside the coastal cities), despite sporadic calls to "Judaize" the region. Most of them live in exclusively Arab towns, the largest of which is Nazareth. The remainder are in towns or cities with a Jewish majority, such as Acre, where an attack on an Arab who entered the Jewish sector during Yom Kippur in 2008 led to a spate of violence. They are often called "dirty Arabs" or "dogs," and poor craftsmanship is referred to as "Arab work." Until 1966, they were subjected to military rule. As an example of the precariousness of their existence, in 1956 forty-seven people in the village of Kafr Qasim were shot and killed by the border police as they returned home from work. The only punishment was a ten-cent fine for the police commander. (Half a century later, President Shimon Peres apologized for the event and the education minister asked schools to mark it on their calendars.)

Like Palestinians who wound up outside the Green Line, those who were refugees from their villages in 1948 ("present absentees") lost their land on the basis of the Absentee Property Law. Other land was then progressively taken from them and assigned to the Jewish National Fund. By one estimate, 65–75 percent of all their land was eventually confiscated.[110] In 1976 protests and a general strike over this issue led to six Arab Palestinian Israelis being killed, and now they commemorate an annual "Day of the Land" on April 30 to express their grievances. Palestinian Israeli poets such as Samih al-Qasim and Mahmoud Darwish have focused on themes such as resistance and attachment to the land.

Their main complaint, though, is against severe neglect. A recent study shows that less than 1 percent of the $4 billion that the outside world transferred to Israel in the early 1960s reached the Arab minority.[111] Another shows that, on a per capita basis, Arab citizens now receive only 70 percent of the amount of government resources provided to the Jews, that the life expectancy of Jewish men is 3.5 years longer than that of Arabs, and that 65.7 percent of Arab children live below the poverty line, as opposed to 31.4 percent of Jewish children.[112] At the beginning of the twenty-first century, it was revealed that the average earnings of people in Jewish cities and towns were double those in Arab communities.[113] Human Rights Watch presented a picture of a school system in which Palestinian Israeli schools are not only separate – which few Palestinians or Jews object to – but divided from their Jewish counterparts by an "enormous" gap in every possible respect.[114] Attempting to explain the relative "quiescence" of the Palestinian Israelis that has "puzzled" some observers, Ian Lustick points to a "sophisticated system of control" that differs from South African apartheid in not being "explicitly recognized" legally but still involves "segmentation, dependence, and cooptation."[115]

For Israeli Palestinians, the basic underlying problem is the definition of the state in ethnic terms. There are many calls for Israel to be transformed into "a state of all its people." An Arab human rights group stirred up a furor in 2007 when it published a draft "Democratic Constitution" rejecting Israel's identity as a Jewish state. By contrast, Kadima leader Tzvit Livni called on Palestinian Israelis unwilling to accept Israel's Jewish character to migrate to a Palestinian state in the future. In addition, the repression of Palestinians in Gaza and the West Bank has increasingly embittered Palestinians within the Green Line.[116]

With the remnant of the Arab Palestinian community in disarray and near starvation after 1948, and with few of their former leaders left in Israel, there was much confusion. They clung to their towns and villages and were determined not to join their fellow Palestinians in exile. At first, they generally accepted the designation "Arab Israelis," but while insisting on their status as Israeli citizens and protesting against discrimination, they have increasingly come to identify themselves simply as "Palestinians."

Most of the Arab vote during the early decades went to Zionist-affiliated parties, as a hierarchy of coopted Arabs (the center of the Periphery) funneled patronage to heads of kinship units (*hamulas*) in return for their families' votes. As Arab nationalist parties (representing the periphery of the Periphery) were banned for many years, Arabs increasingly gravitated to the small Communist Party. In 1965, this split into a predominantly Jewish group, which soon faded away, and a strongly anti-Zionist New Communist List (Rakah), whose membership was mainly Arab, although most of the leaders were Jewish. It became the largest component of a joint electoral list known as Hadash (Front or, in full, the Popular Front for Peace and Equality), which, in addition to its communist core, included some Arab village leaders and what was left of the Black Panthers (a small group of young, radical Mizrahi Jews). Hadash generally tended to receive about half of the Arab vote in Knesset elections and dominated most Arab town councils, although Islamist candidates eventually cut into its support.

A strictly Arab party is the Sons of the Village (Balad) of Azmi Bishara, who resigned from the Knesset in 2007 following accusations that he had engaged in treason during the war in Lebanon the previous year. 'Abd al-Wahhab Darawsha, an Arab member of the Knesset formerly affiliated with Labor, broke away to form the Arab Democratic Party (ADP) in 1988, following the outbreak of the first Intifadah. The ADP later combined with some other factions to run as the United Arab List (UAL), which in 2006 formed a joint list with another Arab party, Ta'al (a splinter of Balad that had joined with Hadash in 2003), to form UAL–Ta'al. At the time of writing, Arab anger over ILP leader Ehud Barak's involvement as defense minister in the assault on Gaza in 2008–2009 seemed finally to be drying up any remnants of Arab support for his party. Nevertheless, with only a handful of seats (three for Balad and four each for Hadash and UAL–Ta'al in 2009), the Arab parties remain peripheral to Israeli politics and might even be excluded from the Knesset in the future if the threshold for seats is raised.

The broader Periphery: the Palestinians after the Nakba

For eighteen years following the 1949 armistices, 22 percent of Palestine remained outside Israeli rule. Refugees from the other side of the Green Line had flooded into the West Bank and the Gaza Strip, while hundreds of thousands of others had found themselves spread outside Palestine, especially on the other side of the Jordan River. The West Bank's population was suddenly doubled, while that of the Gaza Strip was multiplied many times over. Most would find temporary – but, for many, seemingly perpetual, even until today – homes in UNRWA-supported refugee camps and access to a meager 1,500 daily calories that would enable them to survive. Despite the efforts of the government and UN observers to keep the frontiers quiet, a few would succeed as "infiltrators" and return to their original homes, but most who tried to cross the armistice lines were not so lucky.

Responding to popular anger throughout the Arab world, Arab regimes tended to vie rhetorically with one another to voice their support for Palestinian rights, but the reality of Israeli power prevented them from taking any decisive action. Moreover, moves toward a peaceful settlement, for which many entertained high hopes at first, invariably came to naught. The situation nearly boiled over many times, and in 1956 the Gaza Strip (and Sinai) came under Israeli occupation, but international pressure resulted in an Israeli withdrawal soon afterward. Finally, in 1967, another crisis ended with the Israeli occupation of both Gaza and the West Bank. Thus far, this has persisted for more than four decades.

There were many controversies between 1949 and 1967 over the Palestinian lands remaining outside Israeli control. Under Jordanian rule, the West Bank suffered economic neglect, which propelled increasing numbers of Palestinians to migrate to the East Bank or beyond in search of work. With a congress of his Palestinian supporters providing a façade of legitimacy, King Abdullah was able to achieve his goal of annexing the West Bank in 1950, although this never gained international recognition and, as he was moving secretly toward formal peace with Israel, led to his assassination by a supporter of Hajj Amin al-Husayni soon afterward. Nevertheless, 900,000 Palestinians, including those indigenous to the West Bank and refugees from within the Green Line, were added to Jordan's population of just 400,000 and were given citizenship.

Jordanian rule was highly unpopular, especially with more nationalistic – and generally much more urbanized and educated – Palestinians. They saw the Hashimites as representing an unending British (and eventually American) imperialism and clandestine collaboration with Israel. The Jordanian parliament was enlarged to allow for West Bank representation, although the regime managed to get loyal, conservative figures elected, while radical groups were suppressed. Various Palestinian politicians joined the cabinet, but real power rested with the palace. Some local figures such as Mayor Mohammad 'Ali al-Ja'bari of Hebron eagerly alligned themselves closely with the Hashimite regime.[117] Only once, as nationalist sentiment inspired by Nasser in Egypt reached its zenith in October 1956, were relatively free elections held, resulting in a government headed by a nationalist leader, Sulayman Nabulsi. However, the king dismissed Nabulsi, along with the parliament, in April of the following year and restored palace domination. The growing number of educated middle-class Palestinians under Jordanian rule would remain a threat to the Hashimite regime, although they were aware that overthrowing it would lead to an Israeli occupation. They tended to steer away from separatism and stood alongside Jordanian revolutionaries – the Arab Nationalists, National Socialists, or Ba'thists in the pan-Arab camp; the Islamist Liberation Party or the Muslim Brotherhood in the Islamist camp; or the Communist Party – who opposed the neo-colonialist Hashimite regime.

In Gaza, the Egyptians went through the motions of supporting Palestinian independence, if only to thwart Amman's schemes. An "All-Palestine" government was set up in September 1948, with Ahmad Hilmi Pasha as prime minister, but this was never more than a formality, although it officially represented Palestine in the League of Arab States until 1963. The Gaza Strip was too sensitive an area for the Egyptians truly to allow it to govern itself, so it remained under military control. Nevertheless, in Gaza, and among the Palestinians generally, Nasser – even when he acted cautiously – was widely looked upon as a hero and a potential liberator of Palestine. Responding to a series of Israeli military attacks on the Gaza Strip during 1955, the Egyptian army organized groups of Palestinian *fida'iyin* ("self-sacrificers," that is, guerrillas) who carried out raids within the Green Line. However, the temporary Israeli occupation of Gaza and Sinai in October 1956 was followed by the establishment of a United Nations Emergency Force on the frontier and by Cairo focusing on avoiding conflict for over a decade. In 1959, there were calls by Nasser and Iraqi President 'Abd al-Karim Qasim for the establishment of a Palestinian "entity" and a Palestinian republic, respectively, and these led to UAR-sponsored elections for a Legislative Council in 1961 and the adoption of a Palestinian constitution.[118] All of this must be seen in the context of Arab politics, with various leaders – some of whom genuinely wanted to help the Palestinians – having to defend their popular reputations as defenders of the Palestinian cause while undermining the reputations of their rivals but always fully aware of Israeli power.

In January 1964, a League of Arab States summit in Cairo established a Palestine Liberation Organization (PLO). Ahmad al-Shuqayri, who had previously served as the Palestinian representative in the League of Arab States as well as the Saudi representative at the UN, was designated as the new organization's chairman. The PLO was to have a Palestine Liberation Army (PLA), although this would be held on a short leash. While on the face of it this decision represented a militant reaction to Israeli plans to complete a canal to divert water from the upper reaches of the Jordan River, cynical observers saw it as a way for the League of Arab States to appease the Arab public while actually doing nothing substantial. Shuqayri's reputation for harsh but empty rhetoric bolstered this interpretation.

Simultaneously, more serious moves were afoot by Palestinians to take matters into their own hands. The Arab Nationalist Movement (ANM), which emerged in the early 1950s to pursue the liberation of the Arab world, gradually veered leftward, and by the mid-1960s it had adopted the Marxist idea of "scientific socialism." After the Six Day War, the Palestinian branch of the ANM, headed by a Christian physician, George Habash, merged with two smaller groups to form the Popular Front for the Liberation of Palestine (PFLP), which was committed to Marxism–Leninism. Two factions of the PFLP broke away to form the PFLP-General Command, led by Ahmad Jibril, and the Popular Democratic Front for the Liberation of Palestine (PDFLP), headed by a Christian of East Bank origin, Nayif Hawatmah.

Destined long to constitute the mainstay of the Palestinian guerrilla movement, the Movement for the Liberation of Palestine – better known by its Arabic initials (in reverse order), Fatah – had informal beginnings in Cairo among Palestinian students from Gaza who attempted to unite behind the single objective of liberation, despite their varied ideologies.[119] Some of these young men, including the engineer Yasser Arafat, were later united in Kuwait. By the end of 1964, they had formed a military wing called al-'Asifah (the Storm), which carried out its first raid on Israel on December 31. This was the first of many military actions over the following months. The radical Ba'thist regime that came to power in Syria in 1966 cooperated with them, although most of the raids on Israel were carried out from the Jordanian-ruled West Bank. Indeed, this helped precipitate the Six Day War and Israeli occupation of the rest of Palestine, something that some supporters of the Palestinian cause welcomed as it provided the opportunity for them to launch a guerrilla war.

The occupation of the West Bank and Gaza

Israel has ruled the whole of Palestine since 1967. However, aside from Jerusalem – including large nearby areas that were arbitrarily incorporated into the city and sometimes, as in the case of the Latrun salient, thoroughly "cleansed" of their Arab populations – the territories conquered in that year were not formally annexed.

Indeed, from the point of view of the most militant Israelis, there was no need for Israel to annex any part of what had always been the "Land of Israel." While the international community continue to consider all of Israel's new acquisitions as "occupied" territories, Israelis themselves refer to them as "liberated" or "administered," or sometimes as "disputed." They also contend, contrary to the consensus of the rest of the world, that the Fourth Geneva Convention of 1949, which establishes legal limits on occupying powers, does not apply in this case. But they have been incorporated into Israel in all respects except that the Palestinians are not citizens and, except for some local elections, are disenfranchised and subjected to military rule. In the recent words of an Israeli commentator, "Israelis have lived . . . in a binational reality, but the regime . . . has consistently remained unitary."[120]

Israel serves as a prime example of an internally democratic society that collectively rules another society in an authoritarian manner. In this case, the IDF has been the government, issuing legislation through a series of military orders, although there was an attempt (part of a plan to implement the Camp David Accord's proposals for autonomy) in 1981 to establish a "civilian administration" subordinate to the military with the cooperation of some Palestinians who were induced to form "village leagues." Deprived of the civil rights accorded to Israeli citizens, the Palestinians' condition increasingly evoked comparisons with that of black South Africans under apartheid. With the Emergency Regulations adopted by the British in 1945 revived, hundreds of Palestinians were subjected to detention without trial and often to torture. Others were expelled. Acts of collective punishment targeting civilians were numerous, such as when the IDF recurrently destroyed homes because members of particular families were accused of anti-Israeli activities. Sometimes Palestinians were confined to their homes or villages. Books and cultural activities were censored, while universities were closed for long periods.

Occupation was followed by a process of establishing Israeli settlements. In a process that was labeled "creeping annexation," legislation was enacted that ended the early ambiguity about whether the settlers were inside or outside Israel by making them subject to the same laws that applied within the Green Line in such matters as taxation, jurisdiction of Israeli courts, citizenship and voting.[121]

Occupation solidified the idea that Palestinians themselves would have to defeat Israel through guerilla war, rather than rely on rescue by Arab armies, hence bolstering Palestinian nationalism. Although nearly half a million additional Palestinians were uprooted in 1967 (many of them for the second time), the people of the West Bank and the Gaza Strip found themselves under Israeli control, a situation that seemed, for the first time since 1948, to present the possibility of guerrilla war from within. So Fatah leaders began to make new preparations. Arafat himself slipped through the lines during the summer of 1967, setting up secret headquarters, first in Nablus and later in Ramallah, and attempted to organize guerrilla activity. However, within a few months, the Israelis had hunted down the leaders, destroyed homes, and killed or imprisoned hundreds of Fatah members and supporters. Arafat just managed to escape. Thereafter, Fatah focused on commando raids launched from the East Bank, rather than rebellion inside Israeli-controlled territory.[122]

The guerrilla organizations, primarily Fatah, soon remade the PLO. They gained representation in the Palestine National Council (PNC), with Fatah allotted the lion's share of members. Shuqayri was removed as head of the organization in 1967, and Arafat was elected to this position two years later.

The PLO adopted a program calling for the defeat of Israel through "armed struggle" and the land's transformation into a unified, nonsectarian Palestine. The Israeli Jews (or at least those who had been in the country before the beginning of the "Zionist invasion"), so the proposal went, would remain as citizens of the new state. But as time passed there was a growing tendency to put aside this unattainable "rejectionist" goal in order to concentrate on what seemed to be the more realistic idea of establishing an independent Palestinian state in whatever areas from which Israel might withdraw. Thus, the idea emerged of a Palestinian state in the Gaza Strip and the West Bank that would leave Israel as a Jewish state within the Green Line, something that corresponded with the original expectation in 1967 that the Israelis would withdraw from the occupied territories as part of a peace settlement. For decades, almost all Israelis, including those who wanted to withdraw from the new territories, adamantly rejected the idea of a new Palestinian state on the grounds that this implied that there were two separate peoples in the former Palestine mandate whose rights to the country were symmetrical. Ingeniously pointing to the Palestinian majority there, they insisted that Jordan was already a Palestinian state, and that any part of the West Bank they relinquished would have to return to the Hashimite kingdom.

The "Jordan option" persisted for decades, as both Israel and the United States refused to deal with the PLO. UN Security Council Resolution 242, adopted in November 1967, called for withdrawal from the occupied territories as part of a peace settlement (although it was argued that this did not necessarily mean withdrawal from every inch), but it failed to deal specifically with Palestinian national rights (except for a vague call for justice for refugees). At least one implication of this was that withdrawal meant return of the West Bank to Jordanian rule, which King Hussein eagerly sought.

Palestinians described their strategy for coping with the occupation as one of "steadfastness" (*sumud*). They felt that outright resistance was not feasible – although there were hundreds of small-scale acts of violence against the occupation[123] – and that the only strategy left for them was to cling to their lands rather than subject themselves to the sort of expulsion that had occurred in 1948. Many observers foresaw the outbreak of a mass revolt and even wondered why it had taken so long to occur. A partial explanation for the delay is that political oppression was matched by significant improvements in the standard of living as Palestinians got jobs as day laborers working for Israelis, a new generation of whom grew up taking the equation of Arabs equals manual work as a given. Although the Palestinian workers were subjected to degrading rules (for instance, they were not allowed to stay overnight within the Green Line) and much discrimination in matters such as pensions, they earned much more money than before. Also, many other Palestinians took jobs in oil-rich Persian Gulf countries and sent remittances to their families.

From Intifadah to the Oslo Process

The first Intifadah (literally "casting off shackles") erupted on December 9, 1987, the day after an Israeli military jeep in Jubalya Refugee Camp in the Gaza Strip drove into a truckload of Palestinian laborers, killing four of them. That event precipitated spontaneous demonstrations in protest against Israel's military occupation and settlement policies, which quickly spread throughout the occupied territories. Popular committees, under an overall Unified National Leadership (UNL), organized community services denied to the population by the Israeli military authorities in the occupied territories (such as health, sanitation and security), and provided the organizational infrastructure and leadership for the Intifadah. The strategy rested on a campaign of civil disobedience, focusing on strikes and the boycott of Israeli goods, combined with acts of symbolic violence – such as burning tires, rock-throwing and graffiti – aimed at the economic, political and administrative disengagement of the occupied territories from Israel. The leaders explicitly rejected armed violence.

With the Intifadah, a political movement with Islamist coloring came to the surface and would eventually overshadow the PLO and its various components as an anti-Israeli resistance movement. Over the following decade, the Islamists would gain renewed strength as the spokespeople for the periphery of the Periphery as Fatah tended to take on the classic role of a center of the Periphery working in collaboration with the center of the Center (Tel Aviv and Washington). As in other parts of the Islamic world, a resurgence of Islamist movements as an anti-imperialist force was occurring. Palestinian resistance to Zionism in the 1930s sometimes took an Islamist form, as in the case of Izz al-Din al-Qassam's revolt, and the Muslim Brotherhood, particularly in Egypt, demonstrated its fervent opposition to the establishment of a Jewish state in 1948. Some of the founders of Fatah (including Arafat) once had ties with the Brotherhood, but a fundamentally secular pan-Arab (and then an equally secular Palestinian) identity long tended to overshadow Islamism. For that matter, the Muslim Brotherhood saw secular nationalists as a threat and had close relations with Western client regimes (the centers of the Periphery), such as those in Jordan and Saudi Arabia, and maintained a quietist position with regard to the occupation. The Palestinian branch of the Brotherhood was long favored by the Israelis as a common enemy of the PLO and of Arab nationalists. Apparently in part inspired by the Islamist Iranian revolution, a small, militant Palestinian group known as Islamic Jihad, founded in 1980, may have played a key role in the early days of the Intifadah and was represented on various local coordinating committees alongside Fatah and others.

In February 1988, the Palestinian Muslim Brotherhood established a front organization, the Islamic Resistance Movement, better known by its Arabic acronym, Hamas (Zeal), under the leadership of Sheikh Ahmad Yasin, which would organize strikes and other resistance activities independently of those planned by the UNL. While willing to acquiesce in the establishment of a Palestinian state in the West Bank and Gaza, Hamas proclaimed its determination to engage in *jihad* against Israel until the whole country was transformed into an Islamic state. With donations from individuals and other Islamist movements, as well as from both revolutionary Iran and conservative Arab states, it was able to finance charitable activities that earned the loyalty of people who otherwise would not have had access to such necessities as medical care. It began to seem likely that this new group would eventually take control of the PLO, but while Arafat offered it 20 percent of the seats on the PNC, it refused to accept less than 50 percent.[124]

The Israeli government responded to the Intifadah with force and intimidation in an effort to suppress public protest and restore military control. By January 1990, more than 1,000 Palestinians had been killed, with an estimated 80,000 wounded (many permanently). More than 50,000 had been held in administrative detention for up to a year. However, this iron-fist policy failed, and the Intifadah proved virtually irrepressible. Nevertheless, the Israeli government responded with even greater violence, precipitating a split at home and within the international community over the use of military force against an unarmed civilian population and widespread reports of human rights abuses. The Intifadah proved to be an entirely indigenous grassroots movement that gained new sympathy in the international community for the plight of the Palestinians. Its leadership threw its support behind Arafat and the PLO as the symbols of Palestinian nationalism in the international community. This support revived the PLO's legitimacy as the sole representative of the Palestinian people and reinvigorated Arafat's flagging leadership of the organization. He responded to the renewed mandate by attempting to articulate the aspirations of the people of the occupied territories for peace with Israel that would end Israeli military occupation and bring self-determination. As a result, at its November 1988 meeting in Algiers, the PNC declared "Palestine," comprising the occupied West Bank and Gaza, to be an independent state, and implicitly recognized the existence of Israel and Resolution 242 as the basis for peace negotiations. Israel's government rejected this approach and continued its iron-fist policy, but the domestic peace lobby started to grow ever stronger. In early 1990, a split over the issue of peace brought down the fragile coalition government.

In March 1991, after the termination of military operations in the Gulf area, President George Bush Senior addressed the US Congress and defined the basis of future US policy in the Middle East. With regard to the Arab–Israeli conflict, he declared that comprehensive peace should be based on Security Council Resolutions 242 and 338 (of November 1973, which called for a ceasefire and the implementation of the earlier resolution) as well as the principle of "land for peace," whereby Israel would be offered recognition and security in return for returning lands occupied since 1948 and recognizing the right to self-determination of the Palestinian people. While this represented a marked decline in US support for Israel, it still failed to mention the establishment of a Palestinian state.

This was the basic framework on which the Madrid Peace Conference was initiated at the end of October 1991. The conference included sixteen Arab countries (including the five directly involved in the conflict), Israel, the United States, the Soviet Union, the European Union and the United Nations. Negotiations were to follow both bilateral and multilateral tracks. The former involved direct peace talks between Israel and each of its immediate neighbors – Syria, Jordan and Lebanon – as well as with the Palestinians. The latter dealt with common regional issues: economic development, refugees, the environment, regional security and water.

This formula allowed the Palestinians to participate for the first time in direct talks with the Israeli government, a positive step in the eyes of many Arabs. However, this participation was initially very restricted, as Israel would not accept the presence of an independent Palestinian delegation, so a joint Palestinian–Jordanian delegation was created. Also, the Israelis refused to deal with Palestinian representatives except those who were residents of either Gaza or the West Bank (excluding Jerusalem). For twenty-two months – until August 1993 – the Israeli–Palestinian bilateral talks failed to produce concrete results as rounds of discussions were wasted in negotiating the nature and form of the Palestinian delegation and other procedural matters. It was only in the ninth round of talks that the issue of Palestinian representation was settled, and Israel agreed to deal with an independent Palestinian delegation. The obstacles then became the issues of Jerusalem, the ultimate fate of Palestinian refugees, the Jewish settlements in the occupied territories, and a timetable for complete Israeli withdrawal. The deadlock caused great disappointment on the Palestinian side and aggravated differences within the delegation. It also drove the PLO to try to undermine the role of the Palestinian representatives from the occupied territories, who had gained wide popular support at home during the Intifadah and posed a challenge to its uncontested leadership.

Secret negotiations between the Israelis and the Palestinians began in December 1992 in a meeting in London between Ahmad Qurai' (Abu 'Alaa), from the PLO, and an Israeli professor, Yair Hershfeld, a friend of the dovish deputy foreign minister, Yossi Beilin. The talks were arranged by Terg Larsen, the director of a Norwegian research center interested in studying the situation in the occupied territories. Although the meeting was informal and Hershfeld insisted that he represented only himself, the Palestinians knew of his relationship to Beilin and thus were encouraged to pursue the talks. Beilin had given Hershfeld permission to open this dialogue. In fact, he joined the Israeli team in this secret exchange and went to meet a Palestinian delegation in Oslo once the Knesset lifted the ban on negotiating with the PLO in January 1993. Negotiations between the three parties continued until August 20, when they agreed on a declaration of principles, formally signed in Washington on September 13. All of these negotiations were carried out without the knowledge of the official Palestinian delegation in the bilateral peace talks, whose role diminished after the conclusion of the Oslo Accords.

Two agreements were signed between Israel and the Palestinians. The first dealt with mutual recognition between Israel and the PLO and was also signed in September 1993. The second stipulated the establishment of Palestinian self-rule in Gaza and Jericho as a first step toward the final resolution of the Israeli–Palestinian conflict. This resolution was scheduled to take place in two stages (which in reality would be delayed for long periods in violation of announced deadlines). The first stage was to be the expansion of Palestinian self-rule in the West Bank, including: the redeployment of Israeli troops so as to force their withdrawal from densely Arab-populated areas; elections for a Palestinian Council (originally scheduled for July 1994, also to be the start of a five-year transition to a final settlement, with permanent status negotiations to begin in 1997) and the implementation of a further redeployment of Israeli troops to specified areas in the West Bank as soon as the Council was formed; transfer of certain authority to the Palestinian Authority; and the revision of active laws, regulations and military orders. The second stage, to start in May 1996, was to lead to a final settlement. The agreement avoided contentious core issues, such as the status of Jerusalem and the settlement of Palestinian refugees living outside the occupied territories. There were also major omissions in issues that had been agreed upon, for example the geographical limits of Palestinian authority in Jericho.

In accepting the plan, Palestinians agreed to defer consideration of demands that had been central to their struggle: creation of a Palestinian state; return of refugees expelled in 1948 and 1967; and Palestinian sovereignty over East Jerusalem. What they gained immediately from the agreement was control over the Gaza Strip and the West Bank city of Jericho. Elsewhere on the West Bank, Palestinians would be nominally allowed to take over such local functions as healthcare, education and tourism, with Israel retaining responsibility for security.

The Oslo Accords were followed by a series of other agreements that slowly allowed more scope for the PNA. With self-rule delayed until May 1994, the proposed Interim Agreement (Oslo 2) was finally concluded in September of the following year. This provided for the PNA to exercise "full responsibility" in six major population centers (Zone A), and limited authority in other areas (Zone B), with a third category of areas (Zone C) left for settlement in the permanent status talks. The Hebron Accord of January 1997 allowed Israeli troops to remain in the Israeli settlement there. The Wye River Memorandum of October 1998 provided, among other matters, that the PNA would suppress "terrorism" and work closely with the CIA. The Israelis agreed to implement the terms of the Hebron Accord, but the hawkish prime minister, Benjamin Netanyahu, refused to implement his part of the agreement.[125]

With the PLO now making peace with Israel, a Jordanian–Israeli peace treaty was concluded in October 1994. The Hashimite regime's longstanding collaboration with its official enemy seemed no longer to need the cover of secrecy. As far as Syria was concerned, though, progress stalled because the Likud government and then that of Ehud Barak favored a hardline approach toward Damascus, such as insisting on retaining control of the Golan. Success on this issue was considered an essential part of any solution to the problem of southern Lebanon until Israel's refusal to give up its self-declared security zone made way for unilateral withdrawal in June 2000.

With the establishment of the PNA, those who had been in the forefront of the liberation struggle now completed their transformation into an oppressive center of the Periphery, allied with the center of the Center. From Israel's point of view, the purpose of the PNA was to serve as its "surrogate in policing the Palestinians and guaranteeing Israeli security," particularly against groups such as Hamas that constituted threats to Israel and to "a PLO perilously close to collapsing" in the wake of the Gulf War, so that human rights groups would no longer be justified in condemning Israel.[126] The luxurious villas and lifestyles of the new Palestinian elite contrasted utterly with the poverty of the masses, and the opulence of the "crystal chandeliers, silk carpets" and the like astonished looters who finally entered their quarters is Gaza in June 2007.[127]

Elections were held for president and members of an 88-seat Palestinian Legislative Council (PLC). As the longtime symbol of Palestinian nationalism at a time when many people thought self-determination was finally on its way, Arafat won the presidential election against only nominal opposition. Fatah entered the parliamentary elections as a political party and won 50 seats (in reality 71, including supporters elected as independents).[128] However, while this looked like a democracy, the reality was quite different, as the parliament never attained any real influence over Arafat's regime. With both Arafat and his Israeli patrons fearful of actions by a popularly elected parliament, a Basic Law adopted by the PLC in 1997 failed to get presidential ratification until 2002.[129] A lack of popular commitment to democracy tends to be weak in the absence of a long democratic tradition (and in any case, the top priority of the people was clearly national liberation rather than democracy); moreover, various aspects of Palestinian political culture may not be conducive to democracy. However, one survey indicates the existence of a higher level of trust (an important signifier of a democratic political culture) in the West Bank and Gaza than in Israel proper.[130]

But the question is largely moot in that democracy would have interfered with the PNA's surrogate role (a center of the Periphery allied with the center of the Center), resulting in Israel's and the United States' need for authoritarianism.[131] Palestinians arbitrarily imprisoned by the PNA reported that the torture they experienced was worse than that carried out by the Israelis.[132] Heads of the PNA's various security agencies, such as Mohammad Dahlan and Jibril Rajoub, would gain notoriety for their repression of fellow Palestinians. These agencies were prompted to act by, and had a close relationship with, the Israelis[133] and with the CIA, which in the 1990s began to teach them "the uses of mental torture and coercion" at a supposedly secret "school for spies" at Harvey Point, North Carolina.[134] As for press freedom, the PNA territories ranked very low – between Uzbekistan and Laos – in a global survey.[135] With regard to corruption, Transparency International assigned the PNA a ranking of 108th (tying with Argentina and Albania) out of 145 countries in 2004,[136] while the rich lifestyle of the new ruling central class (known as "the Tunisians," as the PLO had relocated to Tunisia following the 1982 Lebanon War) stood in contrast to that of the impoverished Palestinian periphery.[137] In the words of Akiva Eldar, the PNA "has become a fig leaf covering the nakedness of a deluxe version of occupation [with] Mahmoud Abbas's police . . . the subcontractors for the Israeli security forces."[138]

Late in 1995, the whole peace process was threatened by the increased violence being perpetrated by Jewish and Islamic militants. The assassination of Rabin by a rightist Israeli, Yigal Amir, on November 4 dealt a significant blow to the Oslo Process. Although the more moderate Peres assumed the leadership, he did not command the level of trust that the Israeli public had placed in Rabin as far as security was concerned. Aiming to accelerate the peace process, Peres brought forward the date for the general elections to May 1996, in the hope of benefiting from the tarnished image of the opposition in the wake of Rabin's death. However, his position was badly weakened by four Hamas bombings in the heart of Israel, resulting in the loss of some fifty-five lives and further raising questions about the commitment of all sides to the peace process.

Failure of the Oslo Process

In 1996, in the closest election in Israeli history, Peres lost to Benjamin Netanyahu by fewer than 30,000 votes out of almost 4 million cast in the prime ministerial election. Peres had gained the support of many Israeli Palestinians, but their low voter turnout and the fact that over 90 percent of Orthodox Jews voted for Netanyahu allowed the Likud challenger to slip into power. The Knesset elections resulted in one of the most divided houses in Israeli history, with massive losses for both Likud and Labor, while the religious parties jumped from 16 to 24 seats and became essential allies in Netanyahu's coalition. Centrist groups, notably parties representing recent Russian and ex-Soviet republic émigrés, managed to gain 11 seats. The largest of these also joined the government.

One of Netanyahu's campaign planks, probably his strongest, was that he would continue the peace process but would never allow the establishment of a Palestinian state. He made it clear that Israel would negotiate only from a position of strength, dictating terms to the Palestinians and other Arab states rather than negotiating with them. He said shortly after his election that he would not even meet with Arafat unless it was "important to Israel's security and interests." Such hardline views were increasingly dictated by the need of the Likud government to maintain the support of the religious parties in the Knesset.

Although Ehud Barak of One Israel (the Labor-led list) replaced Netanyahu in 1999, hopes for a settlement soon dissipated, and new levels of violence ensued. United States President Bill Clinton, Barak and Arafat met at Camp David in July of the following year, at a time when the gap between the two sides showed no signs of narrowing and as divisions in the Israeli cabinet allowed the prime minister little leeway for negotiation. Barak made a vague offer – which he would not put in writing for fear of bringing down his government – of a Palestinian state, initially comprising 66 percent of the West Bank (excluding Jerusalem) but with an additional 14 percent to be added to this in stages over twenty years. With Israel retaining the bulk of Israeli-settled areas, including part of Hebron, as well as a strip of territory along the Jordan River, this would have resulted in a Palestinian state made up of four noncontiguous segments (including the Gaza Strip). The offer also stipulated Israel's retention of Jerusalem (which would have been enlarged to include settlements stretching halfway to the Jordan) in its entirety, with the Palestinian capital to be located in the nearby village of Abu Dis, to be renamed Al-Quds (the Arabic word for Jerusalem). Furthermore, there would be no right of return for Palestinians to areas within the Green Line.

Of course, Arafat could never accept such terms. And although Clinton apparently had some success over the next few months in persuading Barak to make a better offer, once the latter's government collapsed, the prospects of reaching an agreement dimmed even further.[139] Then, with a new Intifadah in full swing and a new administration headed by George W. Bush taking office in Washington, the prospect of reaching a compromise dried up altogether. (Bush had come to power with the backing of America's Christian right, who stressed the theological imperative of fully supporting Israel.) As the idea that Arafat had rejected Barak's "generous offer"[140] gained wide currency, he and the Palestinian cause suffered another major blow.

The collapse of faith in the Oslo Accords as a path to comprehensive peace created a combustible situation. But it was a political stunt by the new Likud leader and prime ministerial hopeful Ariel Sharon that had provided the spark to set off another Intifadah and brought the Israeli–Palestinian conflict to an historical nadir. On September 28, 2000, Sharon – along with other Likud leaders and hundreds of policemen – made a provocative, highly publicized visit to the Temple Mount/al-Haram al-Sharif. The next day, following Friday prayers, violent confrontations broke out between Palestinians and the thousand-strong police force Prime Minister Barak had deployed. The Palestinians started throwing stones at the police, who responded by firing into the crowds with live ammunition and carrying out targeted assassinations. Facing such violent repression, the demonstrators gradually switched from stones to their own bullets and suicide bombs.[141]

The second Intifadah was far more violent than the first. Hamas and offshoots of Fatah such as Tanzim (Organization) carried out suicide attacks against Israelis on both sides of the Green Line after Sharon became prime minister in 2001. Israeli forces indiscriminately fired on civilian neighborhoods and on unarmed demonstrators.[142] Roadblocks multiplied in order to restrict movement. Israeli military forces bombed and reoccupied various Palestinian-controlled areas. A brutal assault on Jenin in 2002 destroyed much of the refugee camp there. More than three thousand Palestinians and about a thousand Israelis had been killed by 2006.

In a bid to find a solution to the violence, the Sharon government began constructing a massive wall to separate much of the West Bank and Gaza from Israel. It cut arbitrarily through Palestinian property, often leaving Palestinians cut off from their places of work and virtually imprisoned between the Green Line and other parts of the West Bank. In an advisory ruling, the International Court of Justice determined that this was a violation of the Fourth Geneva Convention, but generally to no avail (the Israeli Supreme Court ordered some minor changes).

Intended for ultimate annexation, large chunks of territory in the West Bank, including Israeli settlements in the heart of the region, ended up on the Israeli side of the wall, as did the Jordan Valley in the east.

As expected, the Bush administration's policy in the Middle East came to be aligned ever more closely with Israel. Bush praised Sharon as "a man of peace" and lauded his "sense of history." A report by former United States Senator George Mitchell (who had been sent to assess the situation and make recommendations during the last days of the Clinton administration) called for an end to terrorism and a halt on settlement activity, but this was disregarded by the new president. Although the Intifadah appears to have been directed, at least at first, against Arafat as well as the Israelis, the Bush administration placed responsibility for the violence squarely on him (particularly after the Israelis presented questionable evidence that he was involved in a shipment of arms, allegedly from Iran, which they intercepted in January 2001) and demanded his replacement as president of the PNA "as a condition for American support of negotiations."[143] In June 2002, Bush called for the establishment of a Palestinian state, but only if the PNA came under new leadership.

Proposed by Bush in the same year, a "Road Map" was adopted by the United States, the European Union, the United Nations and Russia (the so-called Quartet), which called for an end to terror and violence and the establishment of Palestinian institutions with the aim of ending the conflict by 2005. But Sharon dragged his feet and, with Bush's acquiescence, ultimately abandoned the scheme. Only in November 2007, at a summit conference in Annapolis, did the Bush administration show signs of wanting to build up momentum for a two-state settlement.

In response to pressure from Washington and Tel Aviv to turn over power to someone else, the Palestinian Basic Law was amended in 2003 to provide for a prime minister who would head a government responsible to the PNA. Arafat subsequently designated Mahmoud Abbas, whom Washington considered acceptable, to fill the new office. This seemed to mean that the PNA was being transformed into a parliamentary system in which the president wielded little or no real power. In 2002, the IDF had destroyed the bulk of the compound in Ramallah in which Arafat resided, leaving him imprisoned, but eventually they allowed him to leave for medical treatment in France, where he died soon afterwards. Abbas was elected president in 2005 and extended his term for another year after it expired four years later.

Emergence of Kadima

Subsequent to his participation in the events that sparked the second Intifadah, Sharon was elected prime minister in February 2001, a position he held until January 2006, when a stroke put him in a persistent vegetative state. In the intervening years, he and his deputy prime minister and successor, Ehud Olmert, began to realize that Israel's "demographic problem" necessitated establishing a separate Palestinian state to save Israel's Jewish character in the long run. However, this was to be established unilaterally, on Israel's terms. The new policy, called "convergence," involved giving up all settlements in the Gaza Strip while enlarging and consolidating smaller ones in the West Bank. Despite the angry opposition of Gaza's Jewish settlers, they were evacuated and the IDF presence in the area ended. However, Israel retained control over the airspace and the frontiers, meaning that, in a new forum, the occupation continued.

In 2005, along with Olmert and others, Sharon broke away from Likud to form a new centrist party, Kadima, to support their two-state plan. Some members of the Labor Party, including Peres, joined the new group too. With Olmert having succeeded the comatose Sharon, Kadima won 29 Knesset seats in the general election of 2006 and formed a new government dedicated to the unilateral disengagement plan.

Earthquake election in the PNA: victory of Hamas

Having engaged in much rhetoric about its commitment to democratization in the Middle East, the Bush administration had difficulty opposing free elections for the PNA. Admittedly, it had been satisfied with cosmetic democratization in countries such as Egypt and Saudi Arabia that left intact the power of client regimes (the center of the Periphery, closely tied to the center of the Center), but it went ahead – despite the skepticism of many Israelis – with the idea of completely open, free elections for the Palestinians, assuming that Fatah would win. After all, it had become an axiom for some political scientists and politicians that democracies are peaceful toward one another, the upshot being that only a party committed to peace with another democracy could win a democratic election. However, the results were such that the rhetoric about democratization largely ended (Bush's "freedom agenda" was dead, it was said), as Hamas won a big victory, gaining 72 of the 132 seats. Accordingly, the PLC voted in a Hamas-dominated cabinet headed by Ismail Haniya, which was later enlarged to include Fatah in a government of national unity.

Washington was determined not to let this be the end of the matter. The Bush administration convinced the Europeans to join it in cutting off aid to the PNA. It convinced the Quartet to demand that Hamas end its commitment to resisting Israel. The Israelis withheld the customs duties and other taxes which, according to the Oslo Accords, it collected for the Palestinians. Israel and the United States demanded of President Abbas that, contrary to the provisions of the Palestinian Basic Law, he must replace Haniya and later called on him to declare a state of emergency and appoint an acceptable emergency government, with the Bush administration urging that Mohammad Dahlan should head it. Dahlan – sometimes seen as a prospective "Palestinian Pinochet" – was encouraged to use his own militia to attack Hamas, while the Egyptian and Saudi regimes were encouraged to arm him and later pledged to provide $86 million to strengthen units loyal to Abbas to enable him to defeat Hamas and call new elections. With further military aid from Egypt and Saudi Arabia in the works, the US-backed Dahlan (whom Bush proclaimed to be "our guy") planned a *coup d'état*, but this was preempted by Hamas forces, who crushed Dahlan's units in June 2007 in the Gaza Strip.

Meanwhile, Abbas and a new Fatah-dominated government (appointed by him without parliamentary approval) were in control of the PNA in the West Bank, largely because of Israeli backing. (Israel had imprisoned forty Hamas members of the PLC, including the speaker, in 2006.) In short, there were now two *de facto* Palestinian entities.[144]

Assault on Gaza, 2008–2009

After June 2007, the Gaza Strip was turned into a veritable concentration camp with the guards keeping watch from the outside. In an attempt to starve it into submission, the Israelis, in violation of commitments made in 2005, cut it off from other parts of the country and from the sea, while the Mubarak regime in Egypt collaborated with Israel by closing entry to Sinai. The Gazans broke through the wall separating them from Egypt in 2008, but Cairo soon resealed it. On other occasions, mercy ships risked interception by Israel. The main lifelines were secret tunnels into Egypt that provided some supplies and weapons. In order to bargain for an end to their suffering, the Gazans sometimes fired crude missiles across the Green Line, killing nine Israeli civilians between September 2005 and December 2008. Hundreds of Gazan civilians died from Israeli military attacks during the same period. A generally effective six-month truce was in place during 2008, although the Israelis violated it on a large scale in November and never respected the provision for ending the strangulation, leading the Gazans to refuse to agree to a renewal in December.

Instead, with full diplomatic backing from Washington as the Bush administration neared its end, a massive Israeli air assault began on December 27, followed by a ground invasion on January 3, 2009. Israelis calculated the flat terrain and the closed frontiers of Gaza would allow them to reassert the military prowess that had been tarnished in the Second Lebanon War (2006), while many politicians from various parties hoped that the assault would stand them in good stead in the approaching election. Aside from hoping to destroy the Gazans' military capacity, the Israelis apparently wanted to overthrow the Hamas regime and enable Fatah to restore its control, although polls later showed that Hamas's support actually increased.

Hundreds of Palestinians, including noncombatants, were killed. Gideon Levy wrote of "the frightening balance of blood – about 1,200 Palestinians dead for every Israeli killed."[145] The eventual death toll of Palestinians, mainly noncombatants, may have reached 1,400, although the precise number is disputed, while four Israelis were killed (by rockets) within the Green Line and nine Israeli soldiers were killed in Gaza, four of them by "friendly fire." Government buildings and the Islamic University were struck, and numerous Palestinian leaders were assassinated from the air, along with their families.

The aftermath of the assault left the people of Gaza in continuing despair. Thousands were disabled and the homes of an estimated 325,000 people were destroyed. Power cuts lasted most of each day, and the poor quality of drinking water resulted in many more deaths. Despite commitments of $3.13 billion in international aid, little reconstruction was possible, as the continuing blockade prevented materials such as cement and steel from entering. Violence dropped drastically as the Hamas-led government found it imperative to prevent armed groups from firing across the frontier. (By contrast, there were reports of increased prosperity in some parts of the West Bank during 2009, even though talk of another Intifadah was in the air.)

A fact-finding mission appointed by the UN Human Rights Council (HRC) and headed by an eminent South African jurist, Richard Goldstone, concluded that Israel had committed war crimes and possibly crimes against humanity, singling out such actions as "deliberate attacks against the civilian population" and "use of Palestinian civilians as human shields."[146] It found that Palestinian armed groups had also violated the law of war by firing inaccurate missiles across the Green Line, and recommended that the matter be referred to the International Criminal Court if the parties themselves failed to take legal action against individual offenders. The report also called for reparations. These findings were endorsed by major human rights organizations and by the HRC, but were contemptuously rejected by Israel and the United States. Nevertheless, the possibility of prosecution in domestic courts of other countries under the developing legal concept of "universal jurisdiction" began to worry some Israeli leaders, who were increasingly reluctant to travel abroad.

In another textbook case of the pattern of alliance between the center of the Periphery and the center of the Center, the Fatah-dominated regime in Ramallah and the client regimes in Cairo, Riyadh and Amman appeared hopeful that their *de facto* ally would prevail over Hamas but were fearful that accusations of collaboration would undermine them. Nevertheless, Mubarak told visiting European ministers that victory for Hamas must not be allowed.[147] With some Fatah sympathizers in Gaza said to be publicly celebrating the Israeli attack, there were reports of several Palestinians being executed as collaborators.[148] When Abbas, in order to appease Israel and the United States, called for postponing a vote in the HRC on the Goldstone report, his legitimacy among Palestinians suffered another blow.

The Israeli election of 2009

Israel's general election of February 2009 demonstrated a continuing movement of the state's politics to the right and provided little comfort to those who hoped for a two-state solution for the country. Kadima barely managed to maintain its position as the largest party in the Knesset, with 28 seats to Likud's 27, but parties to the right of Kadima secured 65 of the 120 seats, and President Perez called on Netanyahu to form a government. At first, it was unclear whether he would form a purely rightist coalition or try to bring in Kadima and others. For her part, Livni proclaimed her party's unwillingness to join a coalition that opposed moving toward peace. Kadima continued to resist offers to join the government, including Netanyahu's offer of two cabinet posts without portfolio in December 2009. Attempts to convince several members of Kadima to break with their party also failed.

However, some observers believed that the future danger to the Jewishness of the state presaged by perpetuating the occupation and the possibility of a clash with the new administration of President Obama in Washington, who was expected to be less compliant than his predecessor, would make pragmatic positions inevitable.[149] And conflicts between some right-wingers (e.g., the Orthodox Shas versus the secular Yisrael Beiteinu) seemed to necessitate a broader coalition. By a narrow margin, the ILP eventually decided to join the new government, and the party was given several portfolios, with Barak reinstated as minister of defense, a post he had held in the previous cabinet. However, the possibility of this Israeli government meeting the minimal demands of the Palestinian leadership seemed more remote than ever.

Palestinian optimism about the new administration in Washington soon subsided. At first, President Obama spoke in a different tone from that of his predecessor, which made Palestinians and other Arabs hopeful. For instance, in a major address delivered in Cairo, he called for a complete halt to Israeli settlements as the first step toward peace. However, he then backed down in the face of Netanyahu's opposition. In the meantime, the Israeli prime minister publicly accepted the idea of a Palestinian state, albeit a truncated one that would be demilitarized and would not include any part of Jerusalem. Following a period of accelerated building, he finally agreed to a six-month freeze on settlements. However, greater Jerusalem would be excluded from this, there would be no limit on various types of public building, and settlements that had been started could be completed. To Palestinians and others, these exceptions made the proposal nearly meaningless, but United States Secretary of State Hillary Clinton praised Netanyahu for making unprecedented concessions.

Imagining one state

With prospects for reaching a two-state solution growing more distant, the idea of a unified Israel/Palestine increasingly appeared as an alternative. A handful of Israeli Jews, notably Benvenisti, argued that a "Second Israeli Republic" had already been established with the conquest of the West Bank and Gaza Strip in 1967 and subsequently made permanent by the planting of Jewish settlements, so the problem was now one of transforming the "Herrenvolk democracy" into a truly democratic state by extending citizenship and the franchise to the Palestinians.[150] In short, Benvenisti was saying that Israel had unwittingly set the stage for its own transformation from a Jewish state to a binational one. One of the few Israelis to share his opinion was Avraham Burg, former Knesset speaker and JA chairman, who declared in 2003 that his state had become "strange and ugly," and rested on "corruption" and "oppression."[151]

Even those who continued to push ardently for the sort of two-state solution that would save Israel from binationalism were sometimes forced to admit that it was possibly too late.[152] Others increasingly defied moral condemnation and evermore signs that history was working against them in the long run through increased bellicosity. At least until it came to power again in 2009, Likud claimed that a

Jewish-dominated "Greater Israel" was still viable, and Netanyahu declared that the Palestinians would acquiesce to the continuing occupation if their economic situation could be improved. Others saw this as a kind of wishful thinking that would ultimately destroy the Jewish state. For instance, Sharon and Olmert both began to see an Arab Palestinian state as an urgent priority, precisely in order to head off the danger of accelerated calls for binationalism, yet there remained an unwillingness on the part of most Israelis to accept the minimum demands of the Palestinians for real independence in 22 percent of the country. Olmert painfully concluded that the threat of future demands for binationalism would necessitate withdrawal from virtually all of the areas conquered in 1967. But what degree of real independence would he or his successor as Kadima's leader, Tzipi Livni, have been willing to concede to a Palestinian state, even if their party had remained in power?

At least a few Palestinians started to consider the alternative of one democratic state. This would involve acceptance of Israeli rule over all of historic Palestine as a fact, but only as a starting point for democratizing it: that is, by gaining equality for themselves and bringing to an end the specifically Jewish state (a peaceful version of the earlier goal proclaimed by the Palestinian Resistance Movement). Some Palestinian leaders occasionally brought this up, if only to taunt the Israelis with the danger of not accepting their terms for a separate state. Palestinian leaders had a vested interest in becoming the ruling class of a nominally independent state – that is, a center of the Periphery allied with the center of the Center – even if that would continue Israeli domination in a way that would be analogous to the Bantustans established by the apartheid regime in South Africa as a "solution" to that country's racial problem. And most Palestinians did not look with equanimity at the prospect of giving up the two-state option in favor of starting at square one with a movement for equality within Israel. Still, some are beginning to think that a democratic Israel/Palestine might not only be a better choice but a more realistic one in the long run.

Notes

1 Transjordan, the area east of the Jordan River (i.e., today's Jordan), was included as part of the Palestine mandate but was governed separately as a Hashimite emirate from the beginning and officially became independent in 1946.
2 Moti Bassok, "Israel at 61: Population Stands at 7.4 Million, 75.5% Jewish," *Haaretz*, April 27, 2009. URL: http://www.haaretz.com/hasen/spages/1081532.html.
3 Gideon Levy, "An Open Response to A.B. Yehoshua," *Haaretz*, January 18, 2009. URL: http://www.haaretz.com/hasen/spages/1056269.html.
4 Lisa Anderson, "The State in the Middle East and North Africa," *Comparative Politics*, Vol. 20, No. 1 (October 1987), p. 2.
5 Oren Yiftachel, "The Shrinking Space of Citizenship: Ethnocratic Politics in Israel," *Middle East Report*, No. 223 (2002). URL: http://www.merip.org/mer223/223_yiftachel.html.
6 Meron Benvenisti, "The Second Republic," *Jerusalem Post* (international edition), January 11–17, 1987, pp. 8–9.
7 Ethan Bronner, "Israel Court Rejects Barrier to Palestinians on Road," *New York Times*, December 30, 2009, p. A8.

8   Gideon Levy, "28 Kilometers of Distilled Apartheid," *Haaretz*, December 30, 2009. URL: http://www.haaretz.com/hasen/spages/1138665.html.

9   See Samih K. Farsoun & Naseer H. Aruri, *Palestine and the Palestinians* (2nd Edition) (Boulder: Westview, 2006), p. 111.

10 For a convenient introduction to these theories, see Ronald H. Chilcote, *Theories of Development and Underdevelopment* (Boulder and London: Westview Press, 1984).

11 On the incorporation of the country into the global economic system, see Farsoun and Aruri, op. cit., pp. 25ff.

12 Johan Galtung, "A Structural Theory of Imperialism," *Journal of Peace Research*, Vol. 8, No. 2 (1971), pp. 81–117.

13 Matthew Krieger, "Israel Leads World in Per Capita Scientists and Engineers," *Jerusalem Post*, December 5, 2007. URL: http://www.jpost.com/servlet/Satellite?c = JPArticle&cid = 1196834823747&pagename = JPost%2FJPArticle%2FShowFull.

14 "*The Times* World University Rankings 2008." URL: http://www.timeshigher education.co.uk/hybrid.asp?typeCode=416&pubCode=1&navcode=137.

15 United Nations Human Development Program (UNDP), *Human Development Report 2007/2008: Fighting Climate Change: Human Solidarity in a Divided World* (New York: UNDP, 2007), p. 285. URL: http://hdr.undp.org/en/media/HDR_20072008_EN_Complete.pdf.

16 See *CIA World Factbook* (2010). URL: https://www.cia.gov/library/publications/the-world-factbook/geos/is.html.

17 *Religion in American Culture – Pew Forum on Religion & Public Life*. URL: http://religions.pewforum.org/?pos=list.

18 Meyrav Wurmser, "Post-Zionism and the Sephardi Question," *Middle East Quarterly*, Vol. 12 (2005). URL: http://www.meforum.org/707/post-zionism-and-the-sephardi-question.

19 See Ghada Hashem Talhami, *Palestinian Refugees: Pawns to Political Actors* (New York: Nova Science Publishing, 2003), p. 45.

20 Moti Bassok, "GDP, Jobs Figures End 2009 on a High," *Haaretz*, January 3, 2010. URL: http://www.haaretz.com/hasen/spages/1139253.html.

21 UNDP, *Human Development Report 2006: Beyond Scarcity: Power, Poverty and the Global Water Crisis* (New York: UNDP, 2006), p. 216. URL: http://hdr.undp.org/en/media/HDR06-complete.pdf.

22 See Shlomo Swirski, *The Cost of Occupation: The Burden of the Israeli–Palestinian Conflict, 2008 Report* (Tel Aviv: ADVA, in partnership with Oxfam and Action Against Hunger, 2008). URL: http://www.israelsoccupation.info/files/costofoccupation 2008fullenglish(1).pdf.

23 *CIA World Factbook*, op. cit.

24 Meron Benvenisti, "Moot Argument," *Haaretz*, August 21, 2008.

25 Avi Shlaim, "How Israel Brought Gaza to the Brink of Humanitarian Catastrophe," *Guardian*, January 7, 2009. URL: http://www.guardian.co.uk/world/2009/jan/07/gaza-israel-palestine.

26 See Sara Roy, *The Gaza Strip: The Political Economy of De-Development* (Washington, D.C.: Institute for Palestine Studies, 1995).

27 Nadav Shragai, "Settler Population Growing Three Times Faster than Rest of Israel, Study Says," *Haaretz*, December 15, 2008. URL: http://www.haaretz.com/hasen/spages/1046766.html.

28 Salo Wittmayer Baron, *A Social and Religious History of the Jews*, Volume II: *Christian Era: The First Five Centuries* (2nd Edition) (New York: Columbia University Press, 1952), p. 123.

29 For a fuller analysis, see Shlomo Sand, *The Invention of the Jewish People* (translated by Yael Lotan) (London: Verso, 2009).

30 Justin McCarthy, *The Population of Palestine: Population History and Statistics of the Late Ottoman Period and the Mandate* (New York: Columbia University Press, 1990), p. 10.

31 See Asher Kaufman, "Between Palestine and Lebanon: Seven Shi'i Villages as a Case Study of Boundaries, Identities, and Conflict in the Middle East," *Middle East Journal*, Vol. 60 (October 2006), pp. 685–706.

32 See Dr. Norton Mezvinsky,"Humanitarian Dissent in Zionism: Martin Buber and Judah Magnes," in Eaford & Ajaz (eds), *Judaism or Zionism: What Difference for the Middle East?* (London: Zed Books, 1986), pp. 98–119.

33 Zeev Sternhell, *The Founding Myths of Israel: Nationalism, Socialism, and the Making of the Jewish State* (translated by David Maisel) (Princeton: Princeton University Press, 1998), especially pp. 20, 32.

34 Ibid., especially pp. 32, 43.

35 Justin McCarthy, *The Population of Palestine: Population History and Statistics of the Late Ottoman Period and the Mandate* (New York: Columbia University Press, 1990), p. 24.

36 Charles D. Smith, *Palestine and the Arab–Israeli Conflict* (6th Edition) (Boston and New York: Bedford/St. Martin's, 2007), p. 103.

37 Joel S. Migdal (1988) *Strong Societies and Weak States: State–Society Relations and State Capabilities in the Third World* (Princeton: Princeton University Press, 1988), pp. 142ff.

38 Smith, op. cit., p. 124.

39 Migdal, op. cit., p. 152.

40 Asher Arian, *Politics in Israel: The Second Republic* (Washington, D.C.: CQ Press, 2005), p. 148.

41 Avi Shlaim, *The Iron Wall: Israel and the Arab World* (New York and London: W.W. Norton, 2000), pp. 12–13.

42 Ann Mosely Lesch, *Arab Politics in Palestine, 1917–1939* (Ithaca and London: Cornell University Press, 1979), pp. 67–69; William R. Polk, "The Arabs and Palestine (Part III)," in William R. Polk, David M. Stamler & Edmund Asfour, *Backdrop to Tragedy: The Struggle for Palestine* (Boston: Beacon Press, 1957), pp. 236–240.

43 See Joel S. Migdal, *Palestinian Society and Politics* (Princeton: Princeton University Press, 1980), pp. 21, 27. On the previous development of indigenous industry and a bourgeoisie, see Beshara Doumani, *Rediscovering Palestine: Merchants and Peasants in Jabal Nablus, 1700–1900* (Berkeley: University of California Press, 1995).

44 Yehoshua Porath, *The Emergence of the Palestinian–Arab National Movement 1918–1929* (London: Frank Cass, 1974), pp. 6–62.

45 Tom Segev, *One Palestine Complete: Jews and Arabs under the British Mandate* (New York: Holt Paperbacks, 2000), pp. 225–226.

46 See Ghada Hashem Talhami, *Syria and the Palestinians: The Clash of Nationalisms* (Gainseville: University of Florida Press, 2001).

47 Shaul Mishal, *West Bank/East Bank: The Palestinians in Jordan, 1949–67* (New Haven: Yale University Press, 1978), pp. 34–35.

48 Smith, op. cit., pp. 177–178.

49 Eugene Rogan, *The Arabs: A History* (New York: Basic Books, 2009), p. 250.

50 Meron Benvenisti, *Sacred Landscape: The Hidden History of the Holy Land Since 1948* (translated by Maxine Kaufman-Lacusta) (Berkeley, Los Angeles and London, 2000), pp. 3ff.

51 Amnon Kapeliouk, "New Light on the Israeli–Arab Conflict and the Refugee Problem and Its Origins," *Journal of Palestine Studies*, Vol. 16 (Spring 1987), p. 17.

52 Migdal, *Strong Societies*, op. cit., pp. 48–49.

53 Benny Morris, "Diligent Diarist," *Jerusalem Post* (international edition), April 22–28, 1986, p. 19.

54 Kapeliouk, op. cit., p. 21.

55 Ian Lustick, *Arabs in the Jewish State: Israel's Control of a National Minority* (Austin and London: University of Texas Press, 1980), pp. 51, 55.

56 Benvenisti, *Sacred Landscape*, op. cit.

57   See, *inter alia*, Simha Flapan, *The Birth of Israel: Myths and Realities* (New York: Pantheon, 1987), pp. 81ff; Benny Morris, *The Birth of the Palestinian Refugee Problem Revisited* (2nd Edition) (Cambridge and New York: Cambridge University Press, 2004); Ilan Pappe, *The Ethnic Cleansing of Palestine* (Oxford: One World, 2006); and Eugene L. Rogan and Avi Shlaim (eds), *The War for Palestine: Rewriting the History of 1948* (Cambridge: Cambridge University Press, 2001).
58   See, for example, Arian, op. cit., for details.
59   Reporters without Borders, "Press Freedom Index 2009." URL: http://en.rsf.org/press-freedom-index-2009,1001.html.
60   Arian, op. cit., pp. 329, 330.
61   See Yoram Peri, *Generals in the Cabinet Room: How the Military Shapes Israeli Policy* (Washington, D.C.: US Institute of Peace Press, 2006).
62   See James A. Bill and Robert Springborg, *Politics in the Middle East* (5th Edition) (New York: Longman, 2000), p. 196.
63   Arian, op. cit., pp. 330, 336.
64   Asher Arian, Nir Atman & Yael Hadar, *The 2006 Israeli Democracy Index: Auditing Israeli Democracy: Changes in Israel's Political Party System: Dealignment or Realignment? (*Jerusalem: Guttman Center of the Israel Democracy Institute, 2006), p. 24. URL: http://www.idi.org.il/SITES/ENGLISH/PUBLICATIONSCATALOG/Pages/The_2006_Israeli_Democracy_Index/Publications_Catalog_7774.aspx.
65   Arian, op. cit., p. 69.
66   Arian et al., op. cit., p. 23.
67   Arian, op. cit., p. 378.
68   Ibid., pp. 53–58, 369–376.
69   Ibid., pp. 50–53.
70   See Israel Harel, "Mazuz versus Herzl," *Haaretz*, May 25, 2008. URL: http://www.haaretz.com/print-edition/opinion/mazuz-versus-herzl-1.221372. Meron Benvenisti, "With All Due Respect for the 'Blue Box,'" *Haaretz*, May 29, 2007. URL: http://www.haaretz.com/print-edition/opinion/with-all-due-respect-for-the-blue-box-1.221682. Editorial, "Who Needs the JNF?," *Haaretz*, September 23, 2007. URL: http://www.haaretz.com/print-edition/opinion/who-needs-the-jnf-1.229832.
71   Sternhell, op. cit., p. 43.
72   Ibid., p. 327.
73   Dan Ben-David, "A State of Inequality," *Haaretz*, January 8, 2008. URL: http://www.haaretz.com/hasen/spages/942112.html.
74   UNDP *2007/2008*, op. cit.
75   Yossi Melman, "Equality's Last Gasp in Israel," *Newsweek*, December 2007. URL: http://newsweek.washingtonpost.com/postglobal/yossi_melman/2007/12/equalitys_last_gasp_in_israel.html.
76   Ruth Sinai, "Charity: One in Five Israelis on Food Aid Has Considered Suicide," *Haaretz*, December 10, 2008. URL: http://www.haaretz.com/hasen/spages/1045057.html.
77   Michal Ramati, "Israel Bred 1,000 Millionaires in 2007," *Haaretz*, June 25, 2008.
78   Ruth Sinai, "Study: Jews Earn Nearly Twice as Much as Arabs," *Haaretz*, April 19, 2004. URL: http://www.haaretz.com/hasen/pages/ShArt.jhtml?itemNo = 417018.
79   Or Kashti, "College Entry Exams Show Money Counts – and Roots," *Haaretz*, July 21, 2008. URL: http://www.haaretz.com/hasen/spages/1003781.html.
80   Arian, op. cit., p. 316.
81   Ibid., p. 320.
82   Shalom Dichter, "Ensuring Them Their Rightful Share," *Haaretz*, August 22, 2008. URL: http://www.sikkuy.org.il/english/docs/haaretz22_8_08.htm.
83   Israel Democracy Institute, "The 2008 Democracy Index." URL: http://www.idi.org.il/sites/english/ResearchAndPrograms/The%20Israeli%20Democracy%20Index/Pages/2008PressRelease.aspx.
84   Arian et al., op. cit., pp. 30–33.

85 Arian, op. cit., p. 279.
86 Carlo Strenger, "Israel's Age of Fragmentation," *Guardian*, February 11, 2009. URL: http://www.guardian.co.uk/commentisfree/2009/feb/11/israeli-elections-2009-israelandthepalestinians1.
87 See Arian et al., op. cit., pp. 12, 43.
88 Ibid., pp. 83, 84.
89 "Democracy on the Retreat," *Haaretz*, December 26, 2008. URL: http://www.haaretz.com/hasen/pages/ShArt.jhtml?itemNo = 376204.
90 Sever Plotzker, "We Want Democracy but Don't Understand It," *Yediot Ahronot* (Shabbat Supplement), August 6, 1999, p. 21 (published in English translation by the Israeli Ministry of Foreign Affairs). URL: http://www.mfa.gov.il/MFA/Archive/Articles/1999/We+Want+Democracy+But+Don-t+Understand+It+-+06-Aug.htm.
91 Yuval Yoaz and Jack Khoury, "Civil Rights Group: Israel Has Reached New Heights of Racism," *Haaretz*, December 16, 2007. URL: http://www.haaretz.com/hasen/spages/932384.html; Avrima Golan, "Study: Israeli Jews Becoming Increasingly Racist Toward Arabs," *Haaretz*, March 19, 2008. URL: http://www.haaretz.com/hasen/spages/966014.html.
92 Richard Wike and Kathleen Holzwart, "Where Trust is High, Crime and Corruption are Low," Pew Research Center Publications, April 15, 2008.
93 Plotzker, op. cit.; Arian et al., op. cit., p. 41.
94 Israel Democracy Institute, op. cit.
95 Arian et al., op. cit., p. 55.
96 Ibid., pp. 59, 60.
97 Ibid., pp. 862, 63.
98 Ibid., p. 25.
99 Ibid., p. 373.
100 Tom Segev, *The Seventh Million: The Israelis and the Holocaust* (New York: Hill and Wang, 1994), p. 375.
101 Arian, op. cit., p. 143.
102 Emanuel Gutmann and Jacob M. Landau, "The Political Elite and National Leadership in Israel," in George Lenczowski (ed.), *Political Elites in the Middle East* (Washington, D.C.: American Enterprise Institute, 1975), p. 186.
103 "Marcher Is Killed in Israeli Protest,", *New York Times*, February 11, 1983, p. A10.
104 Ruth Sinai, "Labor MK: Put Ethiopian Children in Secular Schools," *Haaretz*, August 19, 2007. URL: http://www.haaretz.com/print-edition/news/labor-mk-put-ethiopian-children-in-secular-schools-1.234566. Moti Bassok, "Report: Ethiopian Immigrants Earned Half of Average Salary Last Year," *Haaretz*, April 5, 2007. URL: http://www.haaretz.com/hasen/spages/845435.html.
105 Aryeh Dayan, "Better to Be a Mamzer or to Grow up without a Father?," *Haaretz*, November 7, 2006. URL: http://www.haaretz.com/hasen/spages/756433.html.
106 Nehemia Shtrasler, "The End of Zionism," *Haaretz*, July 19, 2007. URL: http://www.haaretz.com/hasen/spages/883868.html.
107 "Smith Poll for 'The Jerusalem Post' Finds: 67 per cent Find Ultra-Orthodox Unacceptable," *Jerusalem Post* (internatonal edition), July 5, 1986, p. 19.
108 See Vladimir (Ze'ev) Khanin, "Israel's 'Russian' Parties," in Robert O. Freedman (ed.), *Contemporary Israel: Domestic Politics, Foreign Policy, and Security Challenges* (Boulder: Westview, 2009), pp. 97–114.
109 See Zvi Bar'el, "Who Here Speaks Arabic?," *Haaretz*, February 15, 2009. URL: http://www.haaretz.com/hasen/spages/1064180.html.
110 Ian Lustick, *Arabs in the Jewish State: Israel's Control of a National Minority* (Austin and London: University of Texas Press, 1980), p. 276, note 26.
111 Sarah Ozacky-Lazar, "Their Willful and Continued Exclusion," *Haaretz*, June 27, 2008. URL: http://www.haaretz.com/hasen/spages/991919.html.
112 Yoav Stern, "Study: Israeli Jews Live Nearly 4 Years Longer than Israeli Arabs," *Haaretz*, July 9, 2008. URL: http://www.haaretz.com/hasen/spages/1000595.html.

Also see *The Sikkuy Report 2006: The Equality Index of Jewish and Arab Citizens in Israel* (Jerusalem and Haifa: Association for the Advancement of Civic Equality in Israel, 2007). URL: http://www.sikkuy.org.il/english/home.html.

113 Sinai, "Study: Jews Earn Twice as Much," op. cit.

114 Human Rights Watch, *Second Class: Discrimination against Palestinian Arab Children in Israel's Schools* (New York: Human Rights Watch, 2001). URL: http://www.hrw.org/reports/2001/israel2/.

115 Lustick, op. cit., pp. 25–27.

116 See Yoav Stern, "This Time It Was Gaza, but We're Next," *Haaretz*, February 2, 2009. URL: http://www.haaretz.com/hasen/spages/1063764.html; Gideon Levy, "The Court Arabs," *Haaretz*, September 22, 2008. URL: http://www.haaretz.com/hasen/spages/1022177.html.

117 Migdal, *Palestinian Society*, op. cit., pp. 37ff.

118 See Moshe Shemesh, *The Palestinian Entity 1959–1974: Arab Politics and the PLO* (London: Frank Cass, 1988), pp. 1ff.

119 Helena Cobban, *The Palestinian Liberation Organisation: People, Power and Politics* (Cambridge: Cambridge University Press, 1984), p. 11.

120 Ibid., p. 21.

121 Meron Benvenisti, with Ziad Abu-Zayed & Danny Rubinstein, *The West Bank Handbook: A Political Lexicon* (Jerusalem: Jerusalem Post and Boulder: Westview Press, 1986), pp. 37–38.

122 Cobban, op. cit., pp. 36ff.

123 See Benvenisti et al., op. cit., p. 221.

124 F. Robert Hunter, *The Palestinian Uprising: A War by Other Means* (Revised and Expanded Edition) (Berkeley and Los Angeles: University of California Press, 1993), pp. 37–38.

125 Smith, op. cit., p. 476.

126 See Cheryl A. Rubenberg, The *Palestinians: In Search of a Just Peace* (Boulder: Lynne Rienner, 2003), pp. 48, 54.

127 Robin Wright, *Dreams and Shadows: The Future of the Middle East* (New York: Penguin Press, 2008), p. 62.

128 Rubenberg, op. cit., p. 69.

129 Ibid., p. 249.

130 Wike and Holzwart, op. cit. On broader support for democracy, see Mark Tessler and Jodi Nachtwey, "Palestinian Political Attitudes: An Analysis of Survey Data from the West Bank and Gaza," *Israel Studies*, Vol. 4, No. 1 (1999), pp. 22–43; William B. Quandt, "The Urge for Democracy," *Foreign Affairs*, July/August 1994, pp. 11–43; and Palestinian Center for Policy and Survey Research, "Public Opinion Poll No. 6, 2002. URL: http://www.pcpsr.org/survey/polls/2002/p6b.html.

131 See Rubenberg, op.cit., pp. 240ff; and Akiva Eldar, "Border Control/Democracy in the West Bank? Not if It's up to Israel," *Haaretz*, December 16, 2008. URL: http://www.haaretz.com/hasen/spages/1046960.html.

132 See "Palestinian Jailers Can be Worse than Israelis, Ex-Prisoners Say," *Haaretz*, December 4, 2008. URL: http://www.haaretz.com/hasen/spages/1043720.html.

133 See Rubenberg, op.cit., pp. 265–268.

134 Tim Weiner, "CIA is Teaching Tricks of the Trade to the Palestinians," *New York Times*, March 5,1998, pp. A1, A9; Tim Weiner, "Is That Base a CIA School for Spies? Base? What Base?," *New York Times*, March 20, 1998. URL: http://www.nytimes.com/1998/03/20/world/is-the-explosion-noisy-base-a-cia-spy-school-what-base.html. Also see "The Palestinian Authority and the CIA: Who Will Protect the Guards?," *International Institute for Strategic Studies*, Vol. 4, No. 10 (December 1998). URL: http://www.iiss.org/publications/strategic-comments/past-issues/volume-4—-1998/volume-4—-issue-10/the-palestinian-authority-and-the-cia/.

135 Reporters without Borders, op. cit.

136 Transparency International, "Corruption Perceptions Index." URL: http://www.transparency.org/policy_research/surveys_indices/cpi/2004.

137 Juliane Hammer, *Palestinians Born in Exile: Diaspora and the Search for a Homeland* (Austin: University of Texas Press, 2005).

138 Akiva Eldar, "The Balkans Have Arrived," *Haaretz*, October 5, 2008. URL: http://www.haaretz.com/print-edition/opinion/the-balkans-have-arrived-1.254955.

139 See Smith, op. cit., pp. 509–512.

140 See Hussein Agha and Robert Mallely, "Camp David: The Tragedy of Errors," *New York Review of Books*, Vol. 48, No. 13 (2001). URL: http://www.nybooks.com/articles/14380.

141 Smith, op.cit., p. 512.

142 Ibid., p. 515.

143 Ibid., p. 514.

144 See Gareth Porter, "Politics: Bush Plan Eliminated Obstacle to Gaza Assault." URL: http://ipsnews.net/news.asp?idnews = 45297; David Rose, "The Gaza Bombshell, *Vanity Fair*, April 2008. URL: http://www.vanityfair.com/politics/features/2008/04/gaza200804); Mike Whitney, "The CIA and Fatah: Spies, Quislings and the Palestinian Authority," June 21, 2007. URL: http://www.globalresearch.ca/index.php?context = viewArticle&code = WHI20070621&articleId = 6104.

145 Gideon Levy, "The Time of the Righteous," *Haaretz*, January 9, 2009. URL: http://www.haaretz.com/hasen/spages/1054158.html.

146 Human Rights Council (2009), "Human Rights in Palestine and Other Occupied Arab Territories: Report of the United Nations Fact-Finding Mission on the Gaza Conflict," Twelfth Session, Agenda Item 7, General A/HRC/12/48, September 25, 2009, United Nations General Assembly. URL: http://www2.ohchr.org/english/bodies/hrcouncil/docs/12session/A-HRC-12-48.pdf.

147 Zvi Barak Ravid, Avi Issacharoff, and Zvi Bar'el (2009), "Egypt's Mubarak to EU: Hamas Must Not Be Allowed to Win in Gaza," *Haaretz*, January 6, 2009. URL: http://www.haaretz.com/hasen/spages/1052974.html.

148 Amira Hass, "Hamas Executes Collaborators and Restricts Fatah Movement," *Haaretz*, January 8, 2009. URL: http://www.haaretz.com/hasen/spages/1053825.html.

149 See Gideon Levy, "Netanyahu, Put Your Money Where Your Mouth Is," *Haaretz*, February 19, 2009. URL: http://www.haaretz.com/hasen/spages/1065367.html.

150 Benvenisti, "The Second Republic," op. cit.

151 Avraham Burg, "The End of Zionism," *Guardian*, September 15, 2003. URL: http://www.guardian.co.uk/world/2003/sep/15/comment.

152 Gershon Baskin, "Encountering Peace: The Emerging Bi-national Reality," *Jerusalem Post*, December 15, 2008. URL: http://www.jpost.com/servlet/Satellite?cid = 1228728209241&pagename = JPost%2FJPArticle%2FShowFull.

Further reading

The Israeli–Palestinian conflict remains one of the world's most intractable disputes, with the ideological and nationalist claims of two movements, Zionism and Palestinian nationalism, standing in seemingly irresolvable opposition. Scholarship on this conflict, and on the larger Arab–Israeli conflict, is abundant. However, due to the rawness of the struggle, scholarship on the subject has itself become an ideological arena, unusual for its intensity and mobilization of interest groups.

The Israeli–Palestinian conflict ultimately represents a clash of two national visions, Zionism and Palestinian nationalism. One recent attempt to document the origins and development of the conflict is Shlomo Ben-Ami's *Scars of War, Wounds of Peace: The Israeli–Arab Tragedy*. Though critical of Palestinian interlocutors, Ben-Ami, a former Israeli foreign minister, makes a responsible effort to provide a critical account of the barriers to a peace settlement. He diagnoses Israeli policies that have aggravated the conflict, characterizing the Israeli security wall, for instance, as a cynical strategy to increase costs on the Palestinian population and to forestall the emergence of Palestinian demands for a one-state solution. Drawing upon Revisionist school scholarship, Ben-Ami additionally criticizes widespread conceptions of Israel's origins and ideology.

Rashid Khalidi's *Palestinian Identity: The Construction of Modern National Consciousness* evaluates the historical evolution of Palestinian nationalism. Central to Khalidi's argument is that a distinct Palestinian nationalism, contrary to the standard narrative, did not emerge as a reaction to the 1948 Nakba but had a longer lineage, dating to the eighteenth century and crystallizing during the British mandatory period of 1917–1923. Khalidi's text serves as a refutation of ideological attempts to delegitimize Palestinian nationalism as a phenomenon distinct from Arabism. Likewise, Samih Farsoun and Nasser H. Arubi's *Palestine and the Palestinians* is a sweeping survey of Palestinian history, covering the history of the Palestinian diaspora, nationalism, the political and armed responses to Israeli occupation, and inquiries into future development. Khalid Hroub's *Hamas: A Beginner's Guide (2010)* is a good and credible primer on the Hamas movement, while Sara Roy's *Between Extremism & Civism: Political Islam in Palestine* is the culmination of her extensive research into the political, economic and social conditions of the Gaza Strip, and principally an evaluation of the social function of the Islamic movements (chiefly Hamas) within the territory.

Ilan Pappe's *A History of Modern Palestine: One Land, Two Peoples* is a provocative work of scholarship from the "New Historian" school that documents the history of Palestine and Zionism from the early 1800s to the establishment of Israel in 1948, challenging the once-hegemonic narrative of Israel's emergence. Likewise, Pappe's *The Ethnic Cleansing of Palestine* concerns itself with the facts related to the Palestinian exodus of 1948, provocatively accusing Israel of a deliberate campaign of ethnic cleansing, whose strategic underpinnings persist in present-day Israeli policies. It is a controversial but provocative argument. In this vein, Walid Khalidi's *Before Their Diaspora: A Photographic History of the Palestinians 1876–1948* provides a harrowing account of the Palestinian life and culture that was violently disturbed by the 1948 war; *All the Remains: The Palestinian Villages Occupied and Depopulated by Israel in 1948*, by the same author, is an authoritative account of the 400-plus Palestinian villages that were destroyed or depopulated. Sylvain Cypel's *Walled: Israeli Society at an Impasse* is a passionate critique of the way Israel, in its treatment of Palestinians, has succumbed to a "cult of force" that threatens a degradation of Israeli society and morality. Cypel further attempts to evaluate Israel's historic and contemporary policy toward the Palestinians in terms of its underlying ideological content.

Relating to the present, Asher Arian's *Politics in Israel: The Second Republic* is a useful survey of the parameters and environment of Israeli domestic politics, identifying and evaluating Israel's political elites and parties, historic and contemporary electoral patterns, public policy and administration. Moreover, Arian provides extensive statistical data of past elections, historical composition of the Knesset, and public polling on the range of issues concerning Israelis. This is a very useful political survey. Likewise, Robert O. Freedman's *Contemporary Israel: Domestic Politics, Foreign Policy, and Security Challenges* is a thorough analysis of Israel's political landscape, covering domestic politics (a survey of Israel's political parties, as well as analysis of state institutions), foreign policies (relations with the Arab world and the United States, as well as India and Turkey), and strategic considerations (the 2006 Lebanon War). This is a primer for the predominant political questions in contemporary Israeli society.

In the Israeli–Palestinian conflict, even archaeology is a disputed domain. Nadia Abu El Haj's award-winning *Facts on the Ground: Archeological Practice and Territorial Self-Fashioning in Israeli Society* studies the relationship between Israeli archaeological science and the construction of social and historical narratives of Israel, arguing that Israeli archaeology has been used to generate territorial claims in often spurious fashion. Likewise, Meron Benvenisti's *Sacred Landscape: The Buried History of the Holy Land since 1948* is a compelling account of a post-1948 project to reconstruct the landscape of the country to serve the ideological claims of Zionism.

References

Arian, Asher (2005) *Politics in Israel: The Second Republic*, CQ Press.

Ben-Ami, Shlomo (2007) *Scars of War, Wounds of Peace: The Israeli-Arab Tragedy*, Oxford University Press.

Benvenisti, Meron (2002) *Sacred Landscape: The Buried History of the Holy Land since 1948* (translated by Maxine Kaufman-Lacusta), University of California Press.

Cypel, Sylvain (2006) *Walled: Israeli Society at an Impasse*, Other Press.

El Haj, Abu (2001) *Facts on the Ground: Archeological Practice and Territorial Self-Fashioning in Israeli Society*, University of Chicago Press.

Farsoun, Samih K. & Arubi, Nasser (2006) *Palestine and the Palestinians: A Social and Political History* (2nd Edition), Westview Press.

Freedman, Robert O. (ed.) (2009) *Contemporary Israel: Domestic Politics, Foreign Policy, and Security Challenges*, Westview Press.

Hroub, Khalid (2010) *Hamas: A Beginner's Guide*, Pluto Press.

Khalidi, Rashid (1997) *Palestinian Identity: The Construction of Modern National Consciousness*, Columbia University Press.

Khalidi, Walid (2004) *Before Their Diaspora: A Photographic History of the Palestinians 1876–1948*, Institute for Palestine Studies.

—— (2006) *All The Remains: The Palestinian Villages Occupied and Depopulated by Israel in 1948*, Institute for Palestine Studies.

Pappe, Ilan (2006) *A History of Modern Palestine: One Land, Two Peoples* (2nd Edition), Cambridge University Press.

—— (2007) *The Ethnic Cleansing of Palestine*, One World Publications.

Roy, Sara (2010) *Between Extremism & Civism: Political Islam in Palestine*, Princeton University Press.

West and east of the Red Sea

9   The Arab Republic of Egypt

The Nile River gave birth to Egyptian civilization. Its rich silt deposits began to nourish settlement along its banks more than 5,000 years ago. At that time, a civilization emerged whose predominant social feature was a peasant-tributary taxation system from which the pharaohs were able to appropriate an enormous surplus. The tributary system evolved into a highly centralized form of government. Under the pharaohs, Egypt made considerable progress in architecture and science and thus developed into a highly sophisticated culture. During the Hellenistic, Byzantine, Roman and Arab empires, Egypt was reduced to a province whose agricultural surplus, which had once supplied the pharaonic ruling class, was appropriated by foreign courts. Then, between the tenth and sixteenth centuries (Tulunid, Fatimid, Ayubid and Mamluk dynasties), Egypt once again benefited from the profits that accrued from the southern trade route through the Red Sea, which supplemented the revenue from the countryside and supported the emerging urban centers. In the towns, wage labor and various forms of mercantilism developed, along with an increasing number of artisan guilds. Arabic literature flourished just as literature tends to thrive in most sedentary cultures. Nevertheless, with the Ottoman conquest in 1517, Egypt lost its economic and literary prominence. The countryside, in turn, became impoverished and landlords were forced to squeeze greater surpluses from the peasants.[1]

Emergence of modern Egypt

In 1798, Napoleon invaded the Ottoman province of Egypt, intending to use the territory as a base from which to threaten the British Empire by attacking India. His plan was unsuccessful, and Napoleon departed, leaving behind an occupying French army, which in 1801 was compelled to withdraw by the collaborating Turkish and British armies. When the British departed in 1803, Mohammad 'Ali, an Albanian junior officer, was left in control of several thousand Albanian and Bosnian troops. He competed for power with four groups: the 'Ulama, which he was able to coopt; the Turkish garrison, which he was successful in controlling; the Ottoman governor, whom he deposed with the help of the 'Ulama; and various warring factions of Mamluks, which he eliminated. Thus he neutralized all opposition to his rule and became pasha (governor) of Egypt between 1805 and

Map 9.1 Egypt
Drawn by Ian Cool

1849 and is hailed as the founder of modern Egypt. However, he recognized that the socio-economic structure was incapable of sustaining comprehensive reforms that would combine European science and technology with a revived Arab-Egyptian heritage. Accordingly, Mohammad 'Ali launched a state-driven program in which his primary objectives were to build a modern industrial infrastructure, promote economic diversification, develop a strong national army, and create a modern state bureaucracy. Resources were drawn from assessed taxes on a peasantry, composed of small landholding families. The surplus was used to finance factories and irrigation, and to expand agriculture, transportation, education and the army. In the political arena, he set up three-tier political councils with members to be elected without religious or racial discrimination.[2] It is astonishing how this unlettered officer was able to modernize Egypt to the extent that state workshops and factories employed tens of thousands of workers, producing steam engines, cannons, iron and more cotton goods than most European countries. All of this was achieved with the adoption of foreign technology.[3]

Mohammad 'Ali's vision of a modern, powerful and interdependent Egypt extended to a sphere of influence that the Egyptian army acquired in a campaign in the Arabian Peninsula, against the Wahhabbis, in 1828 and in Greater Syria in 1836. The expansion of Egyptian influence into these regions was seen as a serious threat to Britain's trade interests. In Britain, it revived an urgent concern about the region that had first been roused by Bonaparte's invasion of Egypt.[4]

Some argue that, in time, Egypt could have become an autocentric capitalist power because Mohammad 'Ali's modern reforms were quite similar to those of both Japan's Meiji Restoration government, which occurred around the same time, and Peter the Great's reforms in Russia, a century and a half earlier.[5] Egypt's arrested development can be traced to forces that Japan did not face. The first was the proximity of Egypt to Europe and the threat that it apparently posed to Britain's strategic and economic interests. This apprehension about Egypt's intentions culminated in the Anglo-Ottoman military campaign of 1840, which defused Egyptian ambitions. Moreover, it subjected the country to Ottoman rule and resulted in the country being flooded with imported goods while bestowing extrajudicial privileges on foreigners. The second force was that local social conditions had not sufficiently matured, meaning that there was no significant Egyptian middle class or intelligentsia. Furthermore, Mohammad 'Ali's successors – such as Ismail (khedive (viceroy), between 1863 and 1879) and Tawfik (khedive, 1879–1892) – who were absolute rulers, were much less capable than he had been, and they abandoned his economic policy of self-reliance in the hope of Europeanizing Egypt with European capital. This, however, ultimately turned the country into a cotton plantation for Lancashire and integrated it into the world markets by way of lopsided development.[6] As a consequence, the country fell into ruinous debt that resulted in the imposition of the European Debt Commission, known as the Dual Control, in 1876. The Commission acquired such financial and economic power that it was described as "veiled colonial administration."[7] In this context, the ruling class, with the help of the state, seized land and transformed itself into an oligarchy of agrarian capitalists or landowners whose prosperity was now dependent on global markets.

Egypt was thus polarized between the landed aristocracy and an urban middle class consisting of clerks, artisans, merchants, administrators and intellectuals, along with their rural equivalents – village notables. Together, these latter two groups formed the mainstay of a rekindled renaissance seen in an adaptation to cultural and technical innovation and in a renewal of a generally critical spirit, which, in the environment of imperial economic domination and the expansion of a modern education system, awakened a spirit of nationalism and patriotism that came to be symbolized by the movement led by Colonel Ahmad 'Urabi. However, the urban middle class and village notables failed to develop sufficiently along capitalist lines and remained shackled by a pre-capitalist culture and clinging desperately to tradition in an attempt to preserve their identity.[8]

'Urabi was an army officer from a peasant background who became a symbol of Egyptian discontent with the ever-increasing European influence in his country. In May 1880, he presented a petition to the government in an attempt to redress several grievances. He was immediately arrested but then freed in an army revolt and installed as minister of war. 'Urabi's followers in the National Party gained control of parliament and eventually forced Tawfik to create a constitution. The party then drew up a moderate reform program. In 1882, however, Britain and France protested the formation of a constitutional government. The British stated that "no satisfactory or durable arrangement of the Egyptian crisis was possible without the removal of 'Urabi." Subsequently, they presented two ultimatums to the Egyptian government, and when both were rejected they invaded. On July 11, 1882, they defeated 'Urabi's forces and the nationalist movement in the Battle of el-Tel el-Kabir, north of Cairo. Although declaring that they had no intention of staying longer than was necessary to restore financial stability and good government, the British installed themselves as the true power in Egypt and imposed their rule for the next seventy-two years.[9]

British occupation

British rule in Egypt was strict, although it involved a political tug-of-war between the British proconsul (or high commissioner) and Egyptian politicians. As a general rule, the British opposed national demands and only grudgingly made concessions under pressure. A case in point is that of the third British proconsul, Lord Kitchener, who in 1913 allowed the establishment of an Egyptian legislative council while continuing to maintain control of the executive branch. The British reorganized Egypt's administration and reduced its debt but such improvements were made at a cost: social and political problems were almost entirely ignored, as was the development of an educational infrastructure. The British refusal to allow an increase in self-government led much of the nationalist movement to develop independently. This was especially true after Abbas Hilmi II became khedive in 1892 and allied himself with the nationalist forces against the British. He was ultimately deposed in 1914 and the eldest member of the line, Hussein Kamel, was appointed Sultan. That year, Britain declared Egypt a protectorate and all progress on institutional development was arrested.

Between 1900 and the outbreak of the Second World War, the Egyptian political elite had been systematically eliminated, both politically and economically, and replaced with petty bureaucrats who unquestioningly accepted foreign domination. The landed aristocracy gradually became agro-capitalists and then, from 1919 onward, segued into commercial and industrial business elites. The working class eked out a bare existence and the rest of the population was forced to struggle for survival. The reaction of the intelligentsia – represented by Mustafa Kamel and Mohammad Farid, who launched the National Party – was to appeal to the sympathies of European public opinion. However, when the nation rose in revolt in 1919, the National Party withered away as more revolutionary groups rose to prominence. The emerging rural landowning middle class, represented by the

Ummah Party, was ideologically conservative, sharing the aristocracy's fear of a revolt from the landless peasantry, and so supported the continuation of British administration.[10]

During the First World War, Egypt had been used as a military base. Labor was conscripted and substantial numbers of British forces (whose arrogance and ethnocentrism antagonized the native population) were brought into the country. The British were able to pay higher prices for commodities, which resulted in rampant inflation. Restrictions on the production of cotton were imposed and confiscated crops were sold at huge profits. Thus, all levels of Egyptian society grew embittered toward the British. However, nationalist leaders were determined to hold their forces in check for the duration of the war.

Two days after the armistice, however, a prominent nationalist, Sa'd Zaghlul, and his followers formed an Egyptian delegation (known as Wafd) to present a demand for independence to the British proconsul, Sir Reginald Wingate. Although Wingate urged his government to allow Zaghlul to proceed to London, permission was refused. This gave rise to a popular revolt in 1919 throughout Egypt. In response, the British authorities were forced to allow the Egyptians to attend the Paris Peace Conference, but Zaghlul's delegation failed to secure Egyptian independence and the protectorate status was recognized by the attending nations.

The road to independence

Despite Zaghlul's failure in Paris, the British decided to take steps to redress Anglo-Egyptian antagonism and drew up a treaty of alliance with Egypt in 1920. However, Zaghlul and the Egyptian people rejected the treaty, as it guaranteed a continuation of British occupation. The British deported Zaghlul, realizing the threat he posed, and in March 1922 unilaterally terminated the protectorate. In the same year, Egypt was granted "formal" independence as Britain agreed to grant the country a form of self-rule in which the Egyptians were given responsibility over civil administration and local governance while the British reserved for themselves communications, defense and the protection of foreign nationals. In 1923, a constitution was adopted, establishing a democratic parliamentary system. It designated the people as the source of all power and referred to many important democratic principles as well as to a wide range of civil and individual liberties. In addition, it recognized two main elements of government – the legislative and executive authorities – and emphasized a separation of powers between the two. Freedom of the press was also granted. Egypt became a monarchy under King Ahmad Fouad I, but Britain continued to hold real power.[11]

Between 1919 and 1935, there were twenty governments and eight rounds of negotiations during which the Egyptians tried to reduce British control. In 1936, Britain, fearing the Italian threat from Libya and Ethiopia and the looming war in Europe, compromised with an Anglo-Egyptian treaty, which was intended to last for twenty years. The treaty granted Egypt a substantial degree of independence while Britain retained control of the Suez Canal as well as the right to station troops there.[12]

At the beginning of the Second World War, Egypt was once again turned into a British base of operations. Although the upper echelon of Egyptian society prospered as a result of a 200 to 300 percent increase in the value of land and buildings, the masses suffered severe deprivation, analogous to their experiences in the First World War, because wholesale commodity prices mushroomed by 330 percent between 1939 and 1944. In the meantime, the British took drastic measures to keep Egypt neutral. Axis sympathizers were purged from the government, the palace was barricaded, and Fouad's successor, Farouk, was forced to hand over the reins of government to Mustafa al-Nahas, who, as leader of the Wafd Party, was perceived as a representative of the people and able to handle a turbulent national situation during the war.

The Wafd Party was ousted from power at the end of the war and a long period of domestic instability and disquiet began, capped by Egyptian demands for a revision of the Anglo-Egyptian treaty of 1936. To be sure, the creation of the state of Israel in 1948 drastically altered Egypt's perception of Britain because Egypt, as a whole, considered Britain to be responsible for its creation. In 1948, Egypt joined the war against the new state. The poor performance of its army against Zionist forces as well as corrupt government practices humiliated the Egyptian people and notably junior army officers. Against this background of unease and anguish, the Wafd Party regained power in 1950. On October 8, 1951, it unilaterally abrogated the 1936 treaty and declared Farouk king of Egypt and Sudan, thereby also laying a territorial claim to unity with Sudan (which technically was jointly ruled by both Britain and Egypt at that time).

The abrogation of the treaty was of inestimable political significance. The political institutions of the regime rested on a delicate balance of cooperation between the British and the palace against the national popular movement, represented by the Wafd Party. The British presence in the Suez Canal was legal under the terms of the treaty, signed earlier by the Wafd. The new document of abrogation, signed by the Wafd and Farouk, broke the alliance with Britain. The Wafd had historically pursued peaceful struggle toward independence and democracy but changed its strategy by adopting a popular armed struggle. This may explain why, after declaring the abrogation of the treaty in parliament, al-Nahas declared: "The government has done its duty; the decision is now for the people."[13] Hostilities broke out between Egyptians and the British authorities on October 13, 1951. On January 25, 1952, forty-three Egyptian policemen were killed during a British attack on the police barracks of Ismailia. Riots erupted in Cairo the following day – "Black Saturday" – and most of the foreign quarter was burned.

Between October 1951 and Black Saturday, all socio-economic strata, political organizations, professional societies and segments of the rural centers united in a popular uprising. For example, on November 14, 1951, demonstrators in Cairo were estimated to number a million. The socialist, communist and Wafd presses launched daily attacks on the palace and on British imperialism, urging the people to bring down the regime.[14] Spontaneous attempts to organize a reformist "national front" to include national political movements, such as the Wafd, the National

Party, the Socialist Party, the Muslim Brotherhood, the Muslim Youth and others were undertaken as early as October 20, 1951.[15]

The period from late 1951 to the launch of the *coup d'état* on July 23, 1952 was one of widespread militant radicalization in opposition to monarchical despotism and the British use of naked force. On January 27, 1952, the king removed the Wafd from office and asked the pro-palace 'Ali Maher to form a new government. However, this failed.[16] Instead, another government was formed and led by Najib al-Hilali. He suspended the constitution, censored the press and exercised extra-judicial power. However, he was forced to resign in late June 1952.[17] The political paralysis continued for four days and tension mounted. The king then appointed one of his most trusted aides, Hussein Serry, to form a pro-palace government on July 2, but this also met with popular scorn.[18] The palace then attempted to impose its will on a highly rebellious population utilizing the only remaining forces at its disposal: the army and the state security police.

The opposition to the ruling regime comprised organizations supported by large segments of society, articulated platforms of ideology, and widespread political mobilization of the large middle class. Both the salaried and the self-employed sectors of the middle classes were politically significant because they worked in the education system and the mass media. Furthermore, changes in the global balance of power had major repercussions on Egypt. As a result of the Second World War, Britain and France were financially exhausted and their imperial status was in rapid decline. They were already being superseded by the neocolonial superpowers – the USSR and the United States. The latter was striving to contain rising Soviet influence and to consolidate its position as the new "leader of the free world." It was the era of "Pax Americana" when the incorporation of the Middle East into Western capitalist markets was high on the agenda.

As early as January 1951, the Egyptian daily *Al-Gomhour al-Misri* had reported anti-American demonstrations staged by communist groups as well as a plan to create an anti-communist office staffed by Westerners and Egyptians to counteract growing anti-Americanism in Egypt.[19] After the abrogation of the 1936 treaty, national mass movements did indeed systematically employ anti-American (as well as anti-British) slogans and called for a treaty of cooperation with the USSR.

Egypt in revolution

On the night of July 22, 1952, a group of young Egyptian army officers – the Free Officers' Movement – led a successful coup against the monarchy. King Farouk abdicated four days later in favor of his son and went into exile. The Egyptian monarchy came to a formal end on June 18, 1953, when a republic was proclaimed.

The Free Officers' Movement came into being for a number of reasons. Egypt's socio-economic problems had become so extreme by 1952 that the existing political structure could not adequately deal with them. At the time of Mohammad 'Ali's suzerainty over Egypt, the country had a population of 3 million; by 1952, it had grown to about 20 million. This tremendous increase had severe economic and social consequences. In spite of the country's modernization, there had been none of the expected "trickle-down" to raise the standard of living among a significant proportion of the population. In fact, income inequality actually increased, which exacerbated poverty, which in turn fueled a population boom. Egypt remained a desperately poor and underdeveloped nation whose masses were thoroughly and hopelessly impoverished.

Their poverty was compounded by the concentration of landownership in the hands of very few families. Absentee landowners were largely based in the cities and were out of touch with the conditions in the countryside, where 80 percent of the population lived. However, this minority invariably shaped Egypt's political, social and economic life. The monarchy had lost all vestiges of popular support, while the nationalist movement, headed by the Wafd, had lost its dynamism and credibility. Conservative politicians were not prepared to undertake essential economic or political reform, and other factors exacerbated an already tense situation: the humiliating defeat of the Egyptian army in Palestine; the personal experiences of failure among many of the officers in that war; and their belief that the defeat had been mainly the result of widespread corruption in the palace. All of these factors, combined with the British refusal to withdraw their forces from Sudan or the Canal Zone, paved the way for the army takeover.

The Free Officers' Committee was primarily a group of lower- and middle-ranking army officers who had attended military college together. The acknowledged head of the secret organization was Lieutenant Colonel Gamal 'Abdul Nasser, the son of a post office clerk. However, in order to obtain wider support, the group had chosen as their symbolic leader a respected and distinguished higher officer, General Mohammad Naguib. The Committee consisted of about twenty officers, four of them descended from the upper classes (major landowners, merchants and bureaucrats) and about sixteen from the petit bourgeoisie and the salaried stratum.[20]

In the first months after the coup, the Free Officers, under the leadership of their thirteen-man executive committee, the Revolutionary Command Council (RCC), attempted to reorganize the political system and restore order to Egyptian life. Politically, this meant controlling the political environment sufficiently to make the economic and social goals of the revolution come about more rapidly. Within months of the revolution, the political parties of pre-revolutionary Egypt were dissolved and a new constitution was proclaimed. However, resistance to the revolution remained, of course. The Muslim Brotherhood, the only remaining substantial political organization to survive the dissolution of the parties, was one source of resistance and was powerful enough to delay the RCC from consolidating the revolution.

Naguib was replaced by Nasser in April 1954 after a short power struggle. The two men had different visions of the political path that the country should follow at that time. Whereas Naguib was in favor of restoring democracy and civilian rule, Nasser wanted the army to remain in power, arguing that socio-economic development should take precedence over democracy and political liberalization. Naguib was subsequently placed under house arrest in October after an attempted assassination of Nasser. The attempt was sponsored by the Muslim Brotherhood, which gave Nasser the perfect excuse to disband it with force. Thus, by late 1954, Nasser had reached the pinnacle of power, and he consolidated it with the revocation of the Anglo-Egyptian condominium over Sudan and by the evacuation of British troops from the Canal Zone in 1956. In June 1956, a national plebiscite endorsed his presidency with the support of 99.9 percent of the electorate, thus formalizing his power and laying the foundation for a new political ideology: Nasserism.

Nasserism

The practical concerns of building a viable political order and maintaining the position of the RCC colored Nasser's initial approach to politics. His main concern before the Suez Crisis of 1956 was the domestic security of his regime. Even positive neutralism and seizing control of the Suez Canal were pragmatic responses to threatening circumstances, while also being important tenets of his ideology.

The notion of stability and order dominated the thinking of the RCC. For Nasser and his close associates, political instability was fomented by plurality. They believed that the different orientations of political parties and other civic organizations provoked chaos. The RCC's remedy was to dissolve all such organizations. It followed that freedom of expression, free elections, majority rule, constitutional guarantees and the rule of law were all revoked, too. All significant social forces – large landowners, big merchants, the private industrial sector, top executives, unionized labor, religious organizations, the intelligentsia, students, peasants' societies and even ethno-sectarian associations – were closely monitored and controlled. However remote the threat might be, Nasser brooked no opposition.

Nasserism is associated with a historical epoch that commenced after 1956, when the magnetic personality of Nasser personified popular feelings in the Arab world via nationalist and anti-Western slogans. The nature of the discourse engendered a quest for a national dynamic identity and a common culture that would transcend conflicting interests, reduce the misery of the oppressed, and bring about a collective bond and solidarity. Nasserism was articulated as a discourse of grand principles and fostered fervent national pride during a time of revolutionary intensity that reached its zenith in the mid-1960s, with nationalization and a five-year economic plan to showcase Egyptian economic independence.[21]

Nasser's domestic policy was founded on systematic acquisition of organizational power, numerical power and capital-resource power. The phases in the process of monopolizing this power tend to overlap, but a rough scheme is as follows:

1   The RCC was a parallel body to the state organs whose top decision-making positions – from ministries to executive posts in organs of local government, the bureaucracy and the press – were immediately filled by army officers. All

decisions were made within the RCC, which acted as a military corporate structure.

2 The use of the oppressive power of the state was intensified to eliminate all opposition. A transitional phase of three years was declared in which the regime enforced martial law and exercised legislative, executive and quasi-judicial functions. As a result, the regime transformed itself into a body with unlimited political power. It also established a reserve mass organization, the Liberation Rally, under Nasser's direction, in 1953, when the struggle with Naguib was fermenting.[22] In 1956, the Liberation Rally was superseded by a more elaborate body, the National Union, intended to be a vehicle for mass mobilization and indoctrination.

3 Prior to the new constitution, which was promulgated on January 16, 1956, the military had already gained control of the civil sources of power: organized labor, student unions and civil associations such as the Muslim Youth Society, and professional organizations. By monopolizing the content of information media and recruiting a large segment of the intelligentsia to become regime ideologues, the state was able to assume total control.

4 Concurrent with the above phases, Nasser had deprived traditional groups and classes of their power bases: ownership of large economic assets in both land and capital. A number of sweeping new laws, initiated by the Land Reform Act, were promulgated in 1952 and followed by a series of nationalization measures in 1961. These measures transferred the financial, industrial, agrarian and service sectors to state control.

Despite the slogans celebrating "social justice," the first Land Reform Law of 1952 was politically motivated to liquidate the power of the landed aristocracy. It targeted ninety-three landowners and confiscated 118,748 feddans (1 feddan = 1.038 acres).[23] Those who owned less than five fedans, the small landholders, who constituted 94.3 percent of the farming population, were not affected. Between 1961 and 1965, with further confiscations and an increase in the gross cultivatable area, the percentage of landowners remained the same while the percentage of Egypt's area that was farmed increased to 57.1 percent. Distribution of confiscated and reclaimed land (478,000 feddans) into small peasant ownership did not entail legal proprietorship but only the right to utilize the land, regarded as state property. In effect, the state decided what was to be produced, the buying price of the crop and its selling price.

On January 16, 1956, a new constitution was promulgated and Nasser was elected president of the Republic of Egypt. Accordingly, a legislative assembly was created in 1957. However, Article 192 of the constitution stipulated that anyone running for parliament was to be vetted by the National Union, while Article 8 mandated the National Union to arrange and approve the list of candidates. The mission statement of the National Union read:

> The National Union is not a government. It is an organization of the rulers and the people, which makes possible mutual cooperation to solve domestic

problems within the framework of the Socialist Democratic Cooperative society. It is the instrument of genuine democracy and makes people feel that they govern themselves.

The National Union ultimately rejected 1,188 out of 2,058 candidates put forward for the National Assembly in 1957. Consequently, regime loyalists and officers filled the parliament's seats. Despite the depth of his control, Nasser was unwilling to accept even a modicum of dissent in the Assembly. He suspended it following some criticism in 1958, ostensibly to create a more relevant legislature in 1960, especially in light of the union with Syria. However, a new legislature did not materialize because the union fell apart in September 1961.[24]

In November 1961, Nasser appointed the Preparatory Council to organize a Congress of the Popular Forces to draft the national charter for Egypt, to create the Arab Socialist Union (ASU) to replace the defunct National Union, and, finally, to prepare for the election of the 350-member National Assembly.[25] The deliberations of the Preparatory Council were broadcast live on radio and tele-vision. The structure of the ASU was developed in fourteen months between 1963 and 1964 and membership was open to all, including women, except for members of the police force and the army. Membership of the ASU became a prerequisite for running for a position in the National Assembly and even for promotion to top positions in the public and private sectors. The ASU claimed to represent the interests of the popular forces but peasants and workers were assigned only half of the seats in the National Assembly and the definitions of "peasant" and "worker" were questionable. Thus, only the rural notables were allowed into the ASU and subsequently the Assembly. Moreover, there were no representatives of the workers and peasants on the ASU's Supreme Committee during its lifetime.[26]

The pyramidal structure of the ASU lacked a defined role and a coherent ideology, and its relationships with other institutions, such as labor unions and the army, were never defined. In fact, the attempt to use the ASU to control all civilian life led some to infer that Nasser was actually attempting to check the increasing power and popularity of Marshal 'Abdul Hakim Amer, his vice-president, who enjoyed the loyalty of the army.[27] Amer committed suicide after the defeat of the Egyptian army in the Six Day War, whereupon Nasser regained control of the army, and the ASU, to all intents and purposes, became irrelevant.

Nasser's economic policy

The initial economic success between 1957 and 1965 coincided with a favorable international Cold War environment for Egypt. After the Second World War, the region became the focus of US investment and trade. This resulted in a loosening of the ex-colonial powers' grip on the Third World, including Egypt.[28] Nasser understood that political independence was inseparable from economic autonomy, a conception that was realized in large-scale industrialization projects. His economic strategy was based on import substitution, the commonly accepted economic paradigm of the time. However, his policy of centralizing power deprived him of the bureaucracy necessary for the success of these projects, even though this policy provided the necessary capital base for his visionary economic program.

Between 1961 and 1966, sequestration and nationalization contributed 33 million Egyptian pounds in cash, 7,000 properties and 293 enterprises to the state's treasury and asset portfolio.[29] In addition, Egypt received $50 million from Western countries and other financial institutions between 1955 and 1960; another $200 million from 1961 to 1966; and a further $16 million from 1967 to 1969.[30] However, the development strategy of import substitution entailed inherent contradictions. First, it relied on having a "Developed World" economy without the corresponding developmental stage or infrastructure. Second, it favored the allocation of scarce resources to the production of capital goods, neglecting the production of basic goods, such as subsistence foodstuffs. In fact, agricultural production stagnated, relative to the increase in total population with its high rural density. Third, it forestalled the creation of an adequate technological and research base which, in effect, created a technological dependency on others.[31]

The economic policies of Nasser's regime can be understood in terms of étatism and dirigisme. The first refers to centralized administration and economic management; the second to the state as an essentially interventionist agent of economic transformation.[32] We shall refer to the combined effect of these two instruments, henceforth, as state-planned capitalism (SPC). Nasser employed two main devices to achieve what he called economic self-sufficiency and social justice: expansion of the civil service and the establishment of a huge public sector that was in charge of 91 percent of total investment between 1961 and 1966, and in control of 83 percent of all production tools: finance, insurance, extractive and processing industries, and all import and export activities.[33]

There were four layers of power within the civil service and the public and para-public sectors. The loyal military personnel and members of the original 1952 coup were at the apex of power. The middle and lower management of these sectors was staffed by the pre-revolutionary private sector groups, who possessed business expertise. This second layer, the traditional bourgeoisie, served as intermediaries between the military figures at the apex. The third layer was the technocrats – professors, technicians and professionals – whose expertise was necessary for an advanced economic transformation. The fourth layer consisted of rural notables who controlled local governments and village councils and transformed themselves into powerful pressure groups whose interests seemed to be congruent with those of the other layers.[34]

Within ten years, state employees, possessing special privileges, increased by 400 percent, and between 1961 and 1965 they expanded by another 150 percent.[35] The expansion of the public sector created its own complex array of bureaucratic checks, discretionary procedures, and rules that allowed for the emergence of what Gunnar Myrdal called "the norm of corruption." Corruption was comprehensive, ranging from large-scale graft by politicians, high-ranking army officers and civil servants to extensive petty bribery at lower levels.[36]

Thus, Nasser's SPC generated a corporatist salaried stratum, or a "bureaucratic bourgeoisie," whose principal interest was to exploit the power of the state apparatus for personal gain. In the mid-1960s, this group had become so powerful that some observers referred to it as a "counter-developmental stratum."[37] Despite initial financial success, SPC could not generate and satisfy basic material needs: sufficient food, clothing, shelter, mobility, quality education and health insurance. In the process of building his new society, Nasser did not protect human rights or provide democratic access to policy-making processes, despite his good intentions.[38] The military defeat of June 1967 put an end to the SPC, but it also coincided with Europe's burgeoning economic growth and its growing interest in Third World markets as important outlets for Euro-American products and as transfer points for capital. Of course, Third World markets were especially attractive to American transnational corporations that were facing a tripartite problem of significant wage increases, scarcity of some raw materials and legal constraints on environmental and industrial pollution at home.[39]

Foreign policy

Nasser's foreign policy focused on three issues: the Palestinian–Israeli conflict, the Cold War and the macro-political dynamics of the Middle East. Needless to say, Israel was regarded throughout the Arab world as a creation of Western imperialism that was detrimental to the interests of the Arab people.[40] By repeatedly denouncing Israel as a foe, one which all Arabs could easily reject, Nasser could extend Egyptian identity by conferring on it a regional legitimation: Nasserism. This became a new brand of Arab nationalism, the epithet of Arab unity. The rallying point was the Palestine problem, which spawned a sense of "Arabness" and solidified anti-Western sentiment. Yet, the solution to the Palestine problem, from Nasser's perspective until the defeat of 1967, was based on the UN Partition Resolution of 1947.[41] Palestine, therefore, was a legitimating contrivance of Nasserism and of little real concern to Egyptian foreign policy.

The emergence of the international dimension of Nasser's foreign policy is usually pinpointed to the Suez Crisis of 1956. In fact, it had been shaped the year before, with Israel's raid on Gaza, which revealed Egypt's military vulnerability. It was also heavily influenced by the American refusal to sell arms to Egypt, a state of affairs that forced Nasser to distance himself from the United States and seek military assistance from Czechoslovakia. These circumstances coincided with the halcyon days of the non-aligned movement, as expressed by the Bandung Congress of April 1955, and they were also influential in the creation of the Afro-Asian Solidarity Movement.[42]

Nasserism, as a discourse and a theory, did not die with the Egyptian military defeat in June 1967 and the Israeli occupation of Sinai. In fact, the defeat brought the Arab world together in a rallying call for Arabism. Furthermore, the main goals of Nasserism, especially Arab unity, proved to be unachievable because of international, regional and Egyptian political realities. Externally, the international system is founded on asymmetrical power relations that allow the powerful to impose, to various degrees, their strategic interests on the weak. Such a feature, given the asymmetry of power, may be viewed as legitimate within the international context. The sustained confrontation between the dominant Western powers and the Middle East has been unmatched in the history of colonialism in terms of power relations. At the regional level, the incorporation of the Arab states into the world capitalist system has made the region vulnerable to exploitation by Western powers.

Egypt under Sadat

Anwar al-Sadat, Nasser's last vice-president, assumed power after Nasser's death in September 1970. His accession to office was a matter of chance, rather than merit. Between September 1970 and May 1971, he promised to pursue Nasser's policy in form and content. However, a power struggle erupted, and Sadat cemented his position by appointing a loyal army chief of staff as commander of the presidential guard. In early May, Sadat rounded up more than ninety members of the old Nasser regime and initiated an about-face against Nasserism.[43] The country witnessed a comprehensive reorientation process in both domestic and foreign affairs that many analysts have termed the de-Nasserization of Egypt.[44] This process was the outcome of several factors, perhaps most importantly Sadat's lack of a charismatic personality. Despite his success in overcoming his main political opponents from the left and consolidating his political authority, he never truly appealed to the Egyptian public. He had not been well known to most of them during the time of Nasser because he had not occupied any key positions until the very end. Even when he was appointed vice-president, he did not have much influence in the decision-making process and he was certainly overshadowed by Nasser's overwhelming charisma. Sadat appeared to recognize his lack of popular appeal, so sought to establish his legitimacy on different grounds: success in domestic and foreign affairs.

He has been credited with making peace with Israel and liberalizing Egypt. As early as 1971, he declared the permanent constitution, which created an elected legislature, the People's Assembly. Nevertheless, this constitution gave the president great powers over other state institutions, including the ability to make laws and dissolve the People's Assembly. It maintained the single-party arrangement of the Arab Socialist Union under Nasser, and continued to present dubious definitions of "peasant" and "worker," whose combined representation in the People's Assembly was set at 50 percent. The ASU was then reorganized into three forums: the Right, the Center and the Left, each of which was somewhat pointlessly transformed into a party in 1977. After all, as early as 1973, according to Yahia al-Gamal, a professor of law and a Sadat cabinet minister, the only political reality in the decision-making process was the person of the president. All others were simply there to legitimize his decisions.[45]

Eager to win American support and to show his change of direction, Sadat ordered the expulsion of Soviet military personnel from Egypt in July 1972, and by the end of August all 7,725 had left. However, American support never materialized because Sadat's diplomatic démarche did not correspond with US interests in the region at the time – to replace the USSR and thus become the only superpower in the region.[46] Frustrated by American inaction in the region, Sadat decided to launch a limited war that had been conceived by the military during the Nasser era. The idea was to break the diplomatic deadlock and steer both superpowers, particularly the United States, toward a peaceful settlement.

The October War and peace with Israel

On October 6, 1973, Egypt and Syria launched a war that was essentially a diplomatic gambit. Egyptian forces were to cross the Suez Canal, advance for only about 15 kilometers and remain within the protective umbrella of the surface-to-air missiles installed on the western side of the canal in order to minimize the risk of retaliation from the Israeli air force. Up to October 15, Israeli forces were required to fall back and its counteroffensive was halted. Sadat, without any real frontline military experience, decided at this point to change the strategy and send the army into the open desert, despite strong objections from his army commanders. This resulted in Israel pinning down Egypt's Third Army on the canal's eastern bank. The initial victory had turned into a stalemate. The demilitarization of Sinai and Sadat's consistent mismanagement of the war prompted the Egyptian general chief of staff, Sa'd al-Shazli, to file a court case with the prosecutor general against the president in July 1979, accusing him of treason.[47]

The political outcome of the war, and the consequent Egyptian–Israeli peace in what came to be known as the Camp David Accord, entailed related domestic, regional and international repercussions. Domestically, Sinai became demilitarized, and Egypt became indefinitely bound by the terms of an American memorandum that was attached to the accord. This held that in the event of Egyptian violation of the treaty, the US could take "such remedial measures as it deemed appropriate, which may include diplomatic, economic and military measures."[48] Egypt, thus, became unable to engage in an active role in Arab regional politics lest it be construed as a violation of the terms of the accord. For instance, Egypt could not intervene when Israel invaded southern Lebanon in 1982. Regionally, as the Egyptian negotiators sat face-to-face for the first time with their Israeli counterparts (previously an unthinkable situation), their sense of Arabness began to break down and ultimately disintegrated with the conclusion of the Camp David negotiations. Furthermore, the separation between the "Framework for Peace" signed in 1978, and the bilateral Egyptian–Israeli agreement, signed in 1979, left the problem of Palestine to be negotiated between concerned parties. In effect, resolution of the Palestinian problem was postponed, and Egypt's membership of the League of Arab States was suspended in 1979.

Sadat's economic policy

Between 1971 and 1975, the Egyptian commodity sector as a percentage of GDP slid from 55.6 percent to 51.3 percent, and the service sector rose from 44.4 percent to 48.7 percent. The government continued to rely on short-term commercial loans, which by 1974 represented 36 percent of its current operating account, in order to compensate for reduced domestic private sector savings that had declined from 12.7 percent to 4.5 percent. In the same period there was also a deficit in the current operating account of 21 percent of GDP.[49] The net outcome was a sharp increase in inflation and a reduced ability to supply basic needs. Between 1973 and 1976, Egypt received soft loans from the oil-rich Arab countries totaling $4.4 billion.[50] In 1976, it was compelled to conclude an agreement with the International Monetary Fund (IMF) for an economic stabilization program which required that the deficit be reduced by controlling wages and cutting state subsidies for staples and other goods. As a result, riots broke out in 1977, although most of those arrested were released by a court which ruled that the protest was justifiable. Nevertheless, Sadat described the riot as a "thugs' action."

By 1974, the government had moved toward liberalizing the economy by measures that came to be called the "open-door policy," or *infitah*. Investment Law 43/1974 for Arab and Foreign Capital was passed and then amended by Law 32/1977. The goal of these two laws was to give privileges and legal protection to imported Arab and foreign capital. Thus, the pre-1952 revolution bourgeoisie reemerged in alliance with the civil service technocrats and military officers to establish import agencies and to speculate in the brokerage and financial sectors. By 1982, there were more than 1,800 import agencies, forming a pressure group powerful enough to incorporate the Egyptian economy fully into world capitalist markets.[51]

Between 1975 and 1981, the annual average growth in agriculture was 1.8 percent; in mining and industry it was 6.2 percent; in transportation and storage it was 7.6 percent; in government civil services it was 9.9 percent; and in the finance sector it was 17 percent.[52] Between 1970 and 1975, the average annual growth in wages was 33.1 percent, but the average increase in the urban food basket was 46.6 percent; and in clothing it was 34.7 percent.[53] On the other hand, the open-door policy did not attract new capital, as most investment funds came from the public sector or from domestic groups. In 1980, the external debt was $19.1 billion, and debt service was 13.4 percent of GDP. Between 1981 and 1990, rural poverty rose from 16.1 percent to 28.6 percent and urban poverty rose from 18.2 percent to 20.3 percent. The bottom 80 percent fared worse than previously, while the top 20 percent was better off.[54]

Political liberalization

One Egyptian scholar has argued that political plurality normally embodies three main principles: freedom of expression and tolerance for difference of opinion; commitment to a peaceful transfer of power in accordance with the majority vote; and the supremacy of law.[55] In 1974, concomitant to the open-door policy, Sadat issued his "October Paper," in which he outlined a strategy for the development of Egypt until the year 2000. He criticized the Arab Socialist Union and called for structural and organizational reform within it. While he supported the ASU as the only political organization in the country, he also recognized the presence of different political trends within this organization. Four months later, he issued another paper that addressed in detail the issue of ASU reform. This recognized the presence of three major political trends, as follows:

> There are those who tend to be conservative. They suspect the new and prefer to move gradually . . . There are others who are motivated by the desire for radical change, and between these two groups there is a majority which aspires towards progress but which does not wish to lead into the unknown . . . It is desirable that the Arab Socialist Union, which represents the alliance of people's forces, should reflect these various trends in its leadership.[56]

The two papers triggered intensive debate inside the ASU, which ended with the adoption of a resolution accepting plurality within the organization. The establishment of political forums or platforms (*manabir*), reflecting different ideological and political trends within the ASU, was approved. Sadat then established a national committee to discuss the future of political organizations in Egypt. This met for sixteen sessions between February 1 and March 19, 1976, with four major trends emerging from the discussions in its final report. The first trend, which was adopted by a majority inside the ASU, opposed a multi-party system and called for the establishment of fixed forums within the organization. The second trend supported the continuity of the ASU while allowing for more freedom of expression through the establishment of opinion forums. The third trend advocated the establishment of political parties. Finally, the fourth trend called for the establishment of forums inside and outside the ASU. Sadat adopted the first trend and agreed to the establishment of three forums within the frame-work of the ASU: the Liberal Socialist Forum represented the right; the Arab Socialist Forum represented the center – that is, the regime; and the Nationalist Progressive Unionist Forum represented the left. Other major political forces in the country, such as the Wafd, the Nasserites, the Muslim Brotherhood and the communists, were not granted representation within the ASU. In 1976, the three political forums competed for seats in the People's Assembly. This was the first plural parliamentary election to be held in more than two decades. The Arab Socialist Forum achieved an overwhelming victory, winning 81.8 percent of the total vote; 3.6 percent went to the Liberal Socialist Forum; just 0.06 percent went to the Nationalist Progressive Unionist Forum; while 14 percent went to inde-pendent candidates.[57]

The same year, Sadat decreed the final transformation of the forums into independent political parties. On November 11, 1976, he asked the People's Assembly to issue a law permitting the establishment of political parties and for all laws to the contrary to be abolished. In 1977, the Political Parties Law 40/1977 was issued and five political parties were established: three representing the political forums already established within the ASU (the centrist Egypt Arab Socialist Party, headed by Sadat (which later became the National Democratic Party – NDP), the rightist Socialist Liberal Party and the leftist National Progressive Unionist Party – NPUP), the Socialist Labor Party and the New Wafd Party.

Despite the significance of Law 40/1977 in reintroducing pluralist party politics to Egypt, the law placed major restrictions on the formation and operation of these parties. All of them had to:

> uphold the constitution; not be established on an ethnic, religious, class or racial basis; justify their creation by showing that their basic program differs substantially from any of the already existing parties; obtain prior official permission for meetings outside their own premises; refrain from accepting any foreign funding or forming cooperative alliances with parties in other countries; and should not advocate or engage in any street demonstrations or public rallies.[58]

Another serious restriction in the law was the formation of the so-called "Committee for Political Parties' Affairs," with the purpose of reviewing and approving the establishment of the parties. The law stipulated that any political party must gain the approval of the Committee, which was to be chaired by the Secretary of the Central Committee of the Arab Socialist Union (although this was later changed to the Chairman of the Shura Council) and composed of the ministers of justice, of the interior and of state, along with three independents. The Committee was required to examine applications for the establishment of political parties and had the right to request any documents it deemed necessary. It also had the authority to ban the activities of existing political parties if it was proven that the party as a whole or some of its members had violated the constitution or had not abided by its declared program (Articles 8 and 17). In this respect, the law gave the regime full control over the process of establishing and abolishing political parties.

Sadat's ultimate aim was to set up a limited process of liberalization under his full control for the purpose of achieving certain political ends. He wanted to project Egypt as a liberal, democratic country to the West but he was not ready to surrender his grip on domestic politics. Thus, he strictly controlled a fragile democratization process. This fragility was soon evident. In November 1977, Egypt suffered the massive food riots (referred to above) in protest against Sadat's economic policies. The riots escalated in various parts of the country and began to threaten the regime itself. Sadat responded by announcing a series of decrees that repressed the modest civil liberties that had been initiated earlier. In addition, the signing of the Egyptian–Israeli peace treaty in 1979 triggered extensive criticism from several Egyptian political forces, including the Muslim Brotherhood, the communists and the Wafd. Sadat went on the offensive. In June 1979, he called for new parliamentary elections with the purpose of securing an overwhelming majority in the People's Assembly for the National Democratic Party. After relentless government intervention and electoral violations, Sadat's party received an 88.7 percent majority. The following year, he amended the constitution by introducing a clause that allowed for the reelection of the president for an indefinite term. Also in 1980, Sadat introduced the Shura Council, the upper house of the bicameral Egyptian parliament, comprising 264 individuals. Similar to the House of Lords in Britain and the Canadian Senate, the Shura Council's powers are limited. Two-thirds of its members are elected, while the remaining eighty-eight are appointed by the president. Finally, in 1981, he rounded up all of his leading political opponents (reportedly 1,519 dissidents) and detained them in prison, where they remained until his assassination in October of that year.

Mubarak: continuity and change

As soon as Hosni Mubarak assumed power following the assassination of Sadat, he made several statements that emphasized his concern with political continuity and stability. One of his earliest moves was to deal with the acute economic problems facing the country that had resulted from the open-door policy. He called for a meeting of Egyptian economists to examine and offer suggestions to solve Egypt's economic challenges. Mubarak himself also readjusted the open-door policy and stressed that it should concentrate on productive projects. Nevertheless, the economic situation deteriorated after 1981 because of a lack of will on the part of the political leadership to implement these recommendations. As a result, housing, transportation and inflation problems increased and foreign debt continued to rise. Under Mubarak, the Egyptian economy maintained its course and the basic tenets of the open-door policy have remained in operation.

In domestic politics, Mubarak initially set out on a path of political liberal-ization, immediately releasing political prisoners and rehabilitating opposition forces. He also declared a new policy of open discussion, with respect for the opposition. The Wafd Party returned, and the Islamic-oriented Ummah Party was established in 1983. Despite such early efforts, subsequent developments, notably reinstitution of state controls, now prevent opposition forces, including Nasserites, leftists and activist religious groups, from participating in the Egyptian system. On a regional level, Mubarak has succeeded in returning Egypt to the Arab fold.

The fundamental components of political life in Egypt are, first, a legally enforced restriction of public activity and, second, a "policy of exception in which those responsible for human rights violations usually escape punishment amid a climate of impunity intentionally created and fostered over several decades."[59] These conditions were aptly summarized in a recent joint report by a coalition of Egyptian human rights non-governmental organizations. Fundamental to this political environment are the "state of emergency" laws passed in 1981 which have continued uninterrupted ever since, creating a culture of impunity for state authorities and an absence of legal transparency. Consequently, the role of the security apparatus has continued to expand, interfering in the cultural, political and religious domains. As an example, the "University Laws" subject academies of higher education to state security control, with university presidents appointed by presidential degree; the appointment, promotion and even travel of academics is likewise subject to security control.

Egyptians have no protection against the use of torture by the state security forces; and this has developed an international dimension in the post-9/11 era, as Egypt has served as a destination for "war on terror" "extraordinary rendition."

The Egyptian government has resisted all attempts to conform its extremely narrow definition of torture to the standards declared by the United Nations and human rights organizations.

Under the state of emergency laws, Egypt has operated a system of "emergency courts" that are allowed to consider cases typically assigned to common courts. Constitutional amendments in 2007 provide legal protection for the use of these emergency courts to prosecute a wide range of offenses. The Egyptian legal system applies the death penalty to a host of offenses, while offering very limited recourse to appeal. Since 1992, "military tribunals and emergency courts have issued at least 137 death sentences in terrorism cases,"[60] 67 of which have been carried out. Moreover, under the rubric of the state of emergency laws, the Egyptian government has suspended constitutional protections since 1981, thereby severely restricting basic freedoms: Egyptians are prevented from forming political parties, organizing independent trade unions and assembling peacefully. There are other restrictions relating to media and communications, while warrantless arrests and searches are routine.[61]

In 1983, a new electoral system was established by amending the electoral law of 1972. The new system established three major rules. First, it decreased the number of electoral constituencies from 175 to 48 large constituencies. Second, elections were to be held under proportional representation. This meant that they were to be conducted on the basis of party lists, as distinct from the 1979 elections, when all candidates, regardless of party affiliation, had to run as "independents." Third, political parties had to obtain at least 8 percent of the vote to be eligible to take seats in the parliament. In 1984, Mubarak's first parliamentary elections were contested by five political parties, with the Muslim Brotherhood allowed to participate under the auspices of the Wafd Party. There were numerous allegations of violence and forgery, and the results were challenged. However, the NDP won 73 percent of the votes, while the new Wafd/Brotherhood alliance received 15 percent, making it the main opposition.

In February 1987, Mubarak dissolved parliament and held elections in April on the basis of the Supreme Constitutional Court's (SCC) decision to declare the state's electoral law prohibiting independents from running for election illegal. The SCC decision resulted in a second amendment to the electoral law. This amendment stipulated that independent candidates could run, while also maintaining the principle of party list-based elections. Each electoral constituency was to include one independent candidate in addition to the party lists, and voters could cast one vote for an independent candidate and one for a party. This meant that the election would have 48 independent candidates for the 48 constituencies.[62] The elections resulted in better representation of the opposition parties, although the NDP retained a large majority. Meanwhile, a trilateral alliance between the Labor Party, the Liberal Party and the Muslim Brotherhood enabled it to win 60 seats (22 for Labor, 34 for the Brotherhood, and 4 for the Liberals) and thus become the main opposition force. The Wafd won only 12 seats.

These opposition parties accused the government of violating the constitution by not abiding fully by the SCC's ruling. They also continued to question the legality of the electoral law, which, from their viewpoint, still gave limited opportunity to independent candidates. Accordingly, the issue was raised again in the SCC, which in 1990 issued a ruling that declared all election laws that limited the right of Egyptian citizens to run in elections as independents unconstitutional. This ruling resulted in a return to the system based on a two-round majority vote with individual candidates contesting in two-member constituencies. The country was divided into 222 constituencies, with each electing two deputies.

However, this was a hollow victory for the opposition. The state of emergency remained in effect, so the major opposition parties decided to boycott the 1990 elections and sought to establish a united front against the regime. Of course, the elections resulted in an overwhelming majority for the NDP, which gained 85.94 percent of the seats. Independent candidates won 12.50 percent and the NPUP won 1.34 percent.

By 1993, the nomination of Mubarak to a third six-year term as President was being vigorously challenged by the terrorist activities of the Jihadi groups. In that year, a secularist writer, Farag Fouda, who reiterated the government's position on Islamic activism on a weekly television show, was assassinated. Assassination attempts were also made against the Information Minister, the Interior Minister and the Prime Minister. Although all of these failed, they resulted in the deaths of several innocent people. In 1994, Mubarak initiated a national dialogue involving the government and opposition parties in an attempt to forge agreement on basic issues facing the nation and, especially, to mobilize widespread political support to confront the Islamic militants. The dialogue proved fruitless because the government refused to discuss such issues as constitutional and political reform, which were major bones of contention for the opposition groups.

Other steps were taken by the government to consolidate its power and eliminate threats from the Islamic militants as well as the legal opposition, no matter how moderate. In 1992, Law 40/1977 was again amended to place onerous restrictions on political party activity. The amendment stipulated that founding members of new parties were not allowed to act on behalf of their party if that party was not sanctioned by the Parties Committee. Violations would be punished with greater severity than previously. For example, prison sentences of one to five years replaced the old LE500 fine.[63] In the same year, the Penal Code (Law 97/1992) was amended to allow for harsher penalties for any acts of "terrorism" carried out by individuals or groups. Terrorist acts would be referred to the Supreme State Security Court (a court of the Egyptian security establishment that is not "civilian" in nature and adheres to a separate set of judicial rules) as well as to military courts (whose rulings are not subject to appeal, only to modification or dismissal by the president).[64] Then, in 1993, a new unified law for professional syndicates was passed, authorizing the judiciary to supervise syndical elections. The government used this law to curb the increasing Islamic influence in professional syndicates. Finally, in 1994, the government banned the Muslim Brotherhood, accusing it of illegally supporting terrorist Islamic groups, thus alienating even the moderate elements within the Islamist movement. (Officially, the Brotherhood had been banned since 1948, but its existence had been tolerated in practice.)

The legal restrictions were matched by stringent security measures. In late 1993 the government began to pursue a more aggressive policy against Islamist opposition groups, leading to a sharp drop in terrorist attacks, but with significant sacrifice of certain human rights. Prominent journalist and writer Mohammad Heikal claimed that in 1994 an average of fifty Egyptians were detained daily, while five were killed every week – either by the government or by the Islamic groups – and three Egyptians were hanged by the government every month. Heikal commented that while Islam cannot be preached by murder, just laws could not be implemented by having the police announcing the killing of suspected Islamic fanatics. Even the pro-government *Arab Strategic Report*, in a rare admission, warned that the problem of "thousands of detainees" could undermine Egypt, even though detentions might seem necessary to counter terrorism.[65] While the government strengthened its political control, it tried to present an image of fostering democracy and mass participation by claiming to encourage the establishment of non-governmental organizations (NGOs).

According to political scientist Ahmad Abdallah, although Egypt has 15,000 NGOs that are active in many fields, severe regulations prohibit them from forming the basis of a sound civil society. First, a single department in the Ministry of Social Affairs supervises NGOs, all of which are subject to the same close scrutiny despite differences in purposes and activities. Second, they are regulated by a complex set of rules and regulations originating from 1964 onward that preclude the emergence of an independent civil society. As per Law 84/2002, no civil society association can be formed without the express approval of the Ministry of Social Affairs. Moreover, the very scope of potential NGOs is regulated by Article 25 – which nominally regulates the activities allowable by political parties but has the potential to influence NGO activity, too, as it prevents them from cooperating with established political parties to investigate matters of mutual concern. The laws regulating NGOs not only decide which of them may exist but continue to regulate their activity after formation. Article 34 gives the Ministry of Social Affairs the power to "disqualify at will candidates for the membership of governing bodies" within NGOs, where Article 23 allows the ministry to force an NGO to rescind any decision or decree issued by the association where it is deemed to violate the law. Finally (as per Article 42), the Ministry of Social Affairs may dissolve an NGO at any moment, should it: disperse funds in a way violating the initial charter granted to the NGO; receive funds from foreign bodies or collect donations without prior approval; establish institutional ties with organizations/NGOs outside Egypt; or commit any "grave" violation of the law or public morals ("grave," of course, is left highly ambiguous).[66] Finally, these organizations are established and administered by an elite that is somewhat alienated from the average citizen. All of these factors work to undermine effective participation in the political system.

The next parliamentary election was held in 1995. Realizing the failure of the boycott to trigger the popular support they had expected, this time the opposition parties decided to participate. Opposition to the government centered on the outlawed Muslim Brotherhood, which contested the election despite its illegal status. Mubarak responded by ordering a massive detention of its members and their trial by military courts. One Brotherhood candidate was arrested twice at his own rallies, despite a court order allowing him to campaign freely. Pre-election violence between opposition supporters and security forces at rallies claimed twelve lives and over a thousand people were arrested. Fifty-four Brotherhood leaders were found guilty of sedition and sentenced to hard labor in the week before the election. The results of the poll were predictable: of 444 parliamentary seats, Mubarak's supporters claimed over 400.

The regime's lack of commitment to true democracy is coupled with its flagrant disregard for the constitution. By 1997, the Supreme Constitutional Court had invalidated 121 laws. Six of these had been proclaimed before the 1952 revolution, 27 in Nasser's regime, 38 in Sadat's, and 50 under Mubarak's government. Thirty-two of them had been enacted in 1996–1997. As overwhelming as these figures may be, not all alleged unconstitutional laws are challenged in court.

In July 2000, the Supreme Constitutional Court invalidated the 1990 parliament on the grounds that a clause in the law that governed its election was unconstitutional. The ruling, although specifically aimed at the 1990 parliament, meant that the parliament currently in session was also illegitimate. Mubarak stepped in and issued two decrees. The first introduced amendments to the law on practicing political rights, and the second summoned parliament from its summer recess. The changes, contained in Decree 167/2000, were unanimously endorsed by parliament during an extraordinary session on July 16, and the constitutional crisis was averted. These amendments satisfied a key opposition demand, validated by the court's decision, that elections at all the main and branch polling stations should be supervised by judges rather than public sector officials. They further obliged the government to stagger elections over three weeks instead of holding them all on one day.[67]

Observers have claimed that the real danger of Mubarak's crackdown is that it will accelerate the radicalization of the Islamic opposition by denying it any role in the legitimate political life of the country. The Brotherhood and its splinter groups are very well connected, especially in academic and professional circles as well as among businessmen in small and medium-sized enterprises. It also enjoys tremendous support with thousands of Egyptians who are based abroad, many of whom provide financial support. Like most Islamist groups, the Brotherhood is more than a political organization. It has managed schools, medical facilities and media outlets, and it has had strong connections with groups monitoring human rights abuses. Many of its operations were crippled by the government crackdown in the run-up to the 1995 elections. Amnesty International (AI) claims that Brotherhood supporters or activists are regularly rounded up and detained, either without charge or on false charges. While detained, they are often beaten, tortured and threatened with the rape or abuse of their female relatives. On numerous occasions, Amnesty has expressed concern over the repeated arrest, detention and prosecution on terrorism-related charges of leading members of the Muslim Brotherhood, apparently because of their peaceful exercise of their right to freedom of association and assembly. AI also considers that military courts should not have jurisdiction to try civilians, whatever charges they may face, so the organization has criticized the military trial of forty members of the Brotherhood. It made three attempts to send international observers to these trials, but on each occasion the observer was denied access to the military court. AI has also criticized the amendment of Article 179, which allows the president to interfere in the judiciary and bypass the ordinary criminal courts, including referring people suspected of terrorism-related offenses to the military courts.[68]

Although Mubarak and his supporters won the 1995 elections with over 94 percent of the popular vote, voting irregularities led to approximately one-third of those elected having their seats challenged. As of June 1998, the appeal court had nullified the elections of some 170 members of the People's Assembly.[69] However, the Assembly was still decidedly in the NDP's clutches when it nominated Mubarak for a fourth six-year term as president. According to the *Arab Strategic Report* of 1998, his government faced a huge credibility problem at the beginning of the parliamentary session in 1998, despite Mubarak's landslide electoral victory.[70] Because of the loss of a large number of seats due to electoral irregularities and a high level of absenteeism in the People's Assembly, new elections were needed to reestablish legitimacy. The Assembly had seemingly abdicated its legislative role to the executive, limiting itself to a rubber stamp for government programs. This was evident in the sporadic activity conducted during the Assembly's third session in 1997. A paltry eleven laws were passed with practically no discussion, while the Assembly enacted twenty-nine pieces of legislation giving the government emergency powers, despite a decline in religious terrorism.

The general election in 2000 saw a significant shift in Egyptian politics. Throughout the 1990s, the judiciary had increasingly served as "the opposition" by performing a number of political tasks, such as the promotion of democracy and political liberalization. In fact, a number of the political parties who gained seats in the People's Assembly in 2000 acquired them only through court orders. With judges now overseeing the voting, the elections were evidently conducted to the satisfaction of many in the opposition as well as international observers.

There were gains for a number of opposition parties and a dramatic ousting of incumbent NDP deputies. Of the 444 contested seats, only 132 incumbents secured victory. The allocation of seats again favored the NDP, with 388 deputies, down from 410 in the previous election. Some 218 of these were actually elected as independents (out of a total of 256 independents). Opposition members rose to 35, an increase of 21 seats from the previous Assembly, with the major parties represented as follows: Muslim Brotherhood (17), Wafd (7), Tagammu (the new name for the NPUP – 6), Nasserites (2), Liberal Party (1), with two opposition deputies remaining independent.

The government's clampdown on the Muslim Brotherhood was seen as one of the principal reasons for the latter's success. The unremitting harassment of Brotherhood members and supporters created sympathy for their platform. As its senior members were detained, it was forced to run a list of young and relatively unknown candidates, which meant it was less susceptible to government scrutiny. Fifty-seven Christian candidates ran for office, with seven winning election (six

Copts and one Roman Catholic). A record 120 women candidates ran for office, with five winning election, and a further six were appointed by Mubarak among the ten members he is constitutionally required to select. This provided the highest level of female representation since 1979.

The post-2000 façade of democracy and the question of succession

Mubarak's authoritarian tendencies throughout the 1990s have been increasingly resisted from within and outside the country since the turn of the century. The regime has been subject to robust domestic and external pressures to allow for greater political participation, with the latter playing the most important role. The prototypical US policy toward regimes in the region is to do whatever is necessary to ensure stability, so that the various regimes will protect its interests. The US therefore allocated the larger portion of its democracy-oriented aid – around $250 million during the 1990s – to projects that were not likely to undermine local authority. In the aftermath of 9/11, however, America's attitude changed, with US officials holding authoritarian regimes in several Arab countries responsible for nurturing extremism among their peoples. It was believed that political reform – democracy – could rectify the situation.

The Mubarak regime fully grasped the change in US policy and so adopted a number of measures designed to accommodate the West. However, in reality, these produced merely a façade of democracy. In 2002, the National Council for Human Rights, a government-appointed body, was established. The system of state security courts was canceled, and a dialogue with opposition forces was initiated. These measures were largely the result of the growing influence of Mubarak's son, Gamal, within the ranks of the NDP. And the reforms were likely intended to propel him to the forefront of the Egyptian politics by depicting him as a catalyst for reform or a representative of youthful aspirations for change. Such speculations proliferated when the young Mubarak was thrust into the political limelight at the General Congress of the NDP in September 2003. During the Congress, he was appointed Secretary of the NDP Policies Committee, making him responsible for shaping the party's general policies at home and abroad.

In 2004 opposition and civil society groups joined forces to call for genuine democratic reform, having recognized that the government's program was merely cosmetic. In March of that year, the Muslim Brotherhood formulated a comprehensive initiative for political, economic, religious and social reform in Egypt. Announced by "Supreme Guide" Mahdy Akef, this manifesto demanded a parliamentary, constitutional, republican system; called for the respect of public freedoms and the principles of democracy; urged that steps be taken to ensure the independence of the judiciary; and demanded that laws be made more compatible with Islamic *Shari'a*. In the economic sphere, it called for the promotion of the private sector through a well-thought-out program and closer cooperation with the rest of the world. In the religious sphere, it called for the formation of a committee of senior religious scholars; for the grand imam of al-Azhar to be elected; and for

Muslim endowments to be separated from the state budget. It also voiced commitment to freedom of belief and worship and urged national unity. This initiative received mixed reactions from the various political forces. Both the regime and Tagammu Party denounced it, albeit for different reasons. Whereas the regime rejected it on the basis that the question of reform should be discussed by legal parties, not illegal organizations, Tagammu rejected it due to its longstanding ideological conflict with the Muslim Brotherhood. The Wafd, Nasserite and Labor parties all gave the initiative a cautious welcome.

In line with the Brotherhood's initiative, in August 2004 the Egyptian Movement for Change – Kefaya (Enough) – came together. It included nearly 300 Egyptian intellectuals and political activists of all political stripes – pan-Arabists and Nasserites as well as Islamists, Marxists and liberals. Kefaya has emerged as the most vocal opposition movement, denouncing the NDP's political monopoly and calling upon Mubarak to step down. It also rejected Gamal Mubarak as a candidate for high office. In October, it held its first conference, where its founding document was presented by a highly respected former judge, Tariq al-Bishrî, who called upon Egyptians to withdraw their "long-abused consent to be governed" and to engage in civil disobedience.[71] It also urged immediate political and constitutional reform, the independence of the judiciary, and the abrogation of emergency and extraordinary laws.

In December, Kefaya organized its first demonstrations in Cairo, demanding an end to Mubarak's rule. These protests represented a remarkable break with tradition. Over the past two decades, popular demonstrations in Egypt had been directed at foreign affairs, such as the war in Iraq and the Palestinian question, while domestic issues had been confined to debates in the press, seminars and party headquarters. However, Kefaya managed to organize public rallies on domestic issues without prior consultation with the authorities. In addition, the three principal legal opposition parties, Wafd, Tagammu and the Arab Nasserist Party, have joined in an "Alliance of National Forces for Reform" with the Islamist Labor Party, which has not been allowed to operate or publish its newspaper since 2000. The alliance presented its agenda in September 2004 to coincide with the annual congress of the NDP and called for six main reforms: an end to the state of emergency; a constitutional amendment to allow for the direct election of the president from among competing candidates and a limit of two five-year presidential terms; free elections under judicial supervision; greater freedom to establish political parties; a loosening of the government's controls over unions, syndicates and civil society groups; and an end to the ruling party's dominance in the state media.

In 2005, opposition forces amplified their demands for political reform, and in February Mubarak called for a change to Article 76 of the constitution to allow for competition in presidential elections. Although this initiative likely came in response to outside pressure, it triggered an unprecedented level of unrest and civil activism within Egypt. In the months following the announcement, a disparate collection of opposition movements across different sectors of society converged with one message: opposition to the status quo. Thousands regularly took to the streets, demanding more political freedom and democratic reform. In March, for the first time in decades, thousands of Muslim Brotherhood protesters demonstrated outside the People's Assembly and called for constitutional reforms and the lifting of the emergency laws. In April, the Brotherhood organized demonstrations at universities, mobilizing thousands of Islamist students to call for the cancellation of emergency laws. In the same month, fifteen of its parliamentary deputies presented a memo on Article 76 to the speaker of the People's Assembly, listing the following demands: that the president should be elected through direct, multi-candidate elections under full judicial supervision; that candidates must secure the signatures of 20,000 voters to be nominated; that a commission, headed by the chairman of the Supreme Constitutional Court and including four counselors from the Court of Cassation, should be established to supervise the electoral process; and that the successful presidential candidate should give up any party affiliation.[72] Meanwhile, Kefaya and other political forces organized vociferous protests in many Egyptian cities, demanding an end to Mubarak's rule and the implementation of reform.

However, optimism for genuine political reform faded quickly as the drafting of the constitutional amendment continued to conform to the overall interests of the regime. The NDP set terms that were intended to maintain its monopoly over political life. The amended article reads as follows:

1. For nomination to the presidential elections, independent candidates need the approval of at least 250 elected members from the People's Assembly, Shura Council, and local councils, all together. Out of this figure, the approval of at least i) 65 members from the People's Assembly, ii) 25 members from the Shura Council, and iii) 10 local councilors in 14 of the 26 provinces, must be secured.

2. Political parties, which were founded at least 5 years before the date of nomination to the presidential elections, and which have at least 5 percent of the number of seats inside the People's Assembly and Shura Council – 5 percent for each – have the right to nominate one of their senior members to the presidential elections.

3. Candidates of political parties to the presidential elections are exempted from the 5 year and 5 percent conditions for the September 2005 elections.

4. An oversight commission – the Committee of Presidential Elections – is to be established with the task of supervising all stages of the electoral process. The committee is chaired by the chief of the Supreme Constitutional Court, and consists of five senior judges, including i) the chief of the Supreme Constitutional Court, ii) the chief of Cairo's Court of Cassation, iii) the oldest member among the deputy-chiefs of the Supreme Constitutional Court; iv) the oldest member among the deputy-chiefs of the Court of Cassation, and v) the oldest member among the deputy-chiefs of State Council; plus five public figures, three of which to be chosen by the People's Assembly, and two by the Shura Council.

5. The President of the Republic is elected by 50 plus 1 majority. If none of the candidates receives this required majority, the election is repeated after at least

seven days between the two candidates who received the largest number of votes.[73]

These terms effectively excluded independent candidates from competing with Mubarak or with any future NDP presidential candidate. Furthermore, independent candidates would have virtually no chance of even running in the elections, given that approval had to be secured from 250 members of the lower and upper houses of parliament and nationwide local councils. After all, the NDP is dominant in all these institutions. Similarly, opposition political parties would have little chance of nominating candidates for future elections, given that the 5 percent representation condition has never been attained by any opposition party. None the less, the NDP-sponsored amendment was approved in June by both the People's Assembly and the Shura Council.

In September, the first "competitive" presidential election was held in Egypt. There were ten candidates: Hosni Mubarak of the NDP, Noman Gomma of Wafd, Ayman Nour of al-Ghad, Usama Shaltut of al-Takaful, Ahmad al-Sabbahi of al-Ummah, Wahid al-Oqsury of Egypt's Arab Socialist Party, Rif'at al-'Agroudy of the National Conciliation Party, Ibrahim Turk of the Democratic Unionist Party, Mamdouh Qinawi of the Constitutional Party and Fawzy Ghazal of Egypt 2000. Mubarak obtained about 88 percent of the vote, followed by Ayman Nour (8 percent) and Noman Gomma (3 percent).

One month later, the parliamentary election was held in three stages. During the first stage, there was an unprecedented level of violence that left ten people dead and dozens injured. The violence escalated during the second and third phases after the Muslim Brotherhood had managed to secure 34 parliamentary seats in the first phase. Scores of polling stations were sealed off by large contingents of police to prevent opposition supporters from voting. Hundreds of machete- and club-wielding gangs were directed by security agents to attack supporters of opposition candidates. The regime also arrested about 700 Brotherhood members and supporters. Despite these draconian measures, the election's results came as a surprise to most observers and political analysts. The NDP won 311 seats after receiving 71.9 percent of the vote – its lowest majority since 1976. al-Wafd won 6 seats, al-Tagammu two, and al-Ghad and al-Karama one each. Independents won 112 seats, but many of these were actually Muslim Brotherhood candidates, who had been forced to run as independents. Therefore, once the Assembly formed, it contained eighty-eight Brotherhood deputies (20 percent of the total), making them by far the largest opposition force inside parliament.

Since 2005, repression and persecution of political dissidents has become commonplace, with the Brotherhood and judges the main targets. In early March 2006, the regime arrested twenty members of the Brotherhood, including Mohammad Rashad El-Bayoumi, Professor of Geology at Cairo University and a member of the Brotherhood's Guidance Bureau, on charges of possessing anti-government publications. Additionally, dozens of Islamist students and professors from al-Azhar University were arrested for protesting the disqualification of Brotherhood-affiliated students from running in student union elections. "Deputy

Supreme Guide" Mohammad Khayrat al-Shater was also detained. Similarly, the relationship between the regime and the judiciary soured when, on March 6, 2006, Fathi Khalifa, the government-appointed president of the Court of Cassation, referred two senior judges in Alexandria for interrogation allegedly for accusing the Supreme Judicial Council of falsifying the 2005 election results in favor of the ruling party. In April, the government–judiciary confrontation escalated when two more senior judges accused the government of rigging the election and some members of the Court of Cassation of committing fraud or ignoring serious irregularities while supervising the election. The Supreme Judicial Council denounced these accusations and referred the two judges to a disciplinary panel on charges of insulting the judiciary. This triggered a strong reaction by the Judges' Club, which on April 27 held an extraordinary meeting in support of the two accused judges. The meeting concluded with a final statement demanding genuine reform through free elections and the abolition of all exceptional laws.

In May, thousands of Egyptians of various political persuasions took to the streets to protest the disciplinary action against the two judges and demand real political reform. Their demonstrations were met with overwhelming force. Large sections of central Cairo were sealed off to traffic while state security forces assailed the protesters. Hundreds were arrested, while others were severely beaten, including one judge. Legislation was drafted ostensibly to ensure independence of the judiciary, but the deputy-chairman of the Court of Cassation, Ahmad Mar'i, described this as a "conspiracy" against the judiciary. In addition, the Ministry of Justice suspended all financial subsidies to the Judges' Club to force its members to back down on their demands for reform.

The government's onslaught did not stop there. In March 2007, justified by the need to modernize the constitution, thirty-four articles were amended. For example, Articles 4, 12, 24, 30, 33 and 56 were all amended, supposedly to reflect the changed economic and social situation in Egypt since the 1970s. References to socialism, the alliance of working forces and the leading role of the public sector in development were eliminated.[74] Some of the amendments aimed at expanding the powers of the prime minister.[75] For instance, there was a stipulation that the prime minister must approve or be consulted with regard to the president's exercise of their vast executive and quasi-legislative authorities. Other amendments strengthened the Shura Council and gave additional powers to parliament.[76] The People's Assembly was granted the right to vote article-by-article on the general budget and withdraw confidence from the cabinet, which would force the president to accept the government's resignation.[77] These amendments, however, did not fundamentally alter the distribution of power because the president continues to enjoy sole authority over the appointment and dismissal of the prime minister and, more importantly, still has the authority to dissolve parliament without a referendum. Consequently, the amendments were clearly designed to shore up executive power. A third clause was added to Article 5, which stipulates that the Egyptian political system is based on party pluralism. The new clause stipulates that "any political activity or political parties shall not be based on religious authority or foundation, or on any discrimination on the basis of race or gender."[78] Effectively, this gives the regime the constitutional right to accuse any institution or civil organization of involvement in religiously inspired political activity. It was clearly introduced to curb the growing influence of the Muslim Brotherhood. Moreover, Article 62 was amended to allow for a change in the Egyptian electoral system from an individual candidate system to a mixed one that "combines the individual district and party list systems in any ratio that it specifies." This amendment has led to the narrowing of the margin available for electoral candidates to run in the general elections as independents and further restricts electoral opportunities for the Muslim Brotherhood, which has benefited from the individual candidacy system. Article 88 was amended to minimize judicial scrutiny of general elections by establishing a supreme supervisory commission whose membership includes, but is not limited to, current and former members of judicial bodies. However, the amendment did not identify the broader monitoring functions of this commission and did not provide guidelines for hundreds of auxiliary polling stations. This means that, in practice, the auxiliary stations will be supervised by state employees. The amendment also stipulates that the election should take place on a single day, thus making it practically impossible to rely primarily on members of the commission to supervise the voting process. Finally, Article 179 was amended to give the executive – specifically the president and the security forces – unprecedented powers. The state was given the right to suspend proscriptions for arbitrary arrests and requirements for judicial warrants for home searches and technological surveillance of citizens. In addition, the president was given the right to refer crimes of terrorism to exceptional courts, such as military or state security courts (in violation of Article 68 of the constitution, which stipulates that all citizens have the right to a "natural judge").[79] All this led Amnesty International to describe the amendments as "the greatest erosion of human rights in 26 years."[80] Hassiba Hadj Sahraoui, the deputy director of Amnesty's International Middle East and North Africa Program, asserted that such amendments

> would simply entrench the long-standing system of abuse under Egypt's state of emergency powers and give the misuse of those powers bogus legitimacy . . . Instead of putting an end to the secret detentions, enforced disappearances, torture and unfair trials before emergency and military courts, Egyptian MPs are now being asked to sign away even the constitutional protections against such human rights violations.[81]

In the midst of all of this, the NDP took further steps to promote Gamal Mubarak within the ranks of the party. This process had begun in earnest in early 2006, when he was appointed assistant secretary-general, in addition to his post as chairman of the Policies Committee. In March, he was portrayed by the state media as a senior official when he opened a social rehabilitation center in Cairo. Then, in August, one of his close associates, Husam al-Badrawi, admitted for the first time that Gamal Mubarak was one of the candidates to succeed President

Mubarak. In an interview with the *al-Wafd* opposition newspaper, al-Badrawi said, "The ruling party seeks to maintain power and present candidates for the presidency, whether it is President Mubarak or other figures who will succeed him in the future . . . [and] Gamal Mubarak is one of those figures, as long as this takes place within a legal framework and according to free presidential elections."[82] In September, the young Mubarak received a significant endorsement from President George W. Bush, who praised him in the *Wall Street Journal* as the leader of "a new group of reformers who are now in government." The same month, the NDP held its Annual Congress, in which Gamal overshadowed other senior party members, including the secretary-general himself, by playing the lead role in all discussions on domestic and foreign issues.

Despite the growing civil opposition to Gamal Mubarak's succession, it is unlikely that opposition forces will be able to prevent it on their own. However, the military might yet come to their aid. Should the young Mubarak succeed his father, this would mark a departure from the usual method of succession in republican Egypt, which has always taken place with military approval. Despite the apparent demilitarization of Egyptian society over the last two decades, the armed forces remain the most influential institution in the country. Accordingly, high-ranking military personnel must be unified in their support for Gamal Mubarak, otherwise his succession could fail.

Structural adjustment

Between 1984 and 1988, external debt increased progressively from $37.8 to $45.7 billion. The debt service from the US sources alone was $2.4 to $3.4 billion, while the export value of goods and services dropped from $3.4 to $2.7 billion. The obvious conclusion was that the Egyptian government was not able to pay even the necessary debt service charges.[83] The liberalization of the economy thus impoverished the majority while enriching the well-off few who had supported the close ties between foreign capital and the regime. In sum, the few simply depleted economic resources instead of becoming a genuine national bourgeoisie that was engaged in economic development and political reform.[84]

The rapidly increasing gap between rich and poor in Egypt is a major factor contributing to the rise of Islamic militancy and the delegitimization of the regime. In 1993–1994, Egypt ended the first stage of its structural adjustment program, initiated in 1991 through agreement with the IMF and the World Bank. Egypt agreed to embark on policies to lower inflation and reduce the balance of payments deficit. Meanwhile, it would implement policies to improve the efficiency of the public sector and to privatize public assets.

The structural adjustment program has had some success. The deficit as a percentage of GNP decreased from 17 percent in 1989 to 3.5 percent in 1993, and inflation declined from 21.2 to 11.1 percent in the same period. However, austerity measures have come at a high cost to the middle and lower classes. According to a World Bank Report, average individual income in Egypt has fallen from $670 a year in the early 1960s to $610 a year in the early 1990s.[85] Yet the government simultaneously adhered to World Bank injunctions to minimize social subsidies to the poor for subsistence and education. Prices increased by almost 300 percent, excluding new taxes. New economic policies also led to higher unemployment, estimated by the World Bank in 1994 to be 17.5 percent, and by other sources as high as 20 percent.[86] Furthermore, unemployment in Egypt is not cushioned by social insurance or social welfare.

The upper classes have profited from corruption, arms sales commissions, widespread bribery and commercial services. As if to add insult to injury, their wealth tends to be invested outside of Egypt, with a double indemnity for the country: there is little domestic investment in developmental infrastructure and taxes are avoided. According to a study by Mohammad Heikal, there are 50 Egyptians whose wealth is $100–200 million; 100 with $80–$100 million; 150 with $30–$50 million; 350 with $15–$30 million; 2,800 with $10–$15 million; and 70,000 with $5–$10 million. If Heikal is correct, then over the last twenty years almost 1,000 individuals have accumulated over $50 billion, more than the foreign debt of Egypt, and all of them have accumulated this wealth from within the country – through estates, by setting up monopolies for essential goods, or as agents of international companies.[87]

The sharp deterioration of economic conditions for the vast majority of Egyptians over the last two decades has recently led to the emergence of the "new social strikes."[88] These strikes have been largely apolitical and focused on one major issue: the fall in wages and salaries.[89] In the beginning, they were limited to factory workers, especially textile workers, but they spread to the professional classes, including public sector employees. The first strike took place in February 2007, when thousands of workers from the Misr Spinning and Weaving Company in al-Mahalla al-Kubra occupied their factory and adjacent streets to demand a wage increase. They wanted payment of overtime, an increase in basic pay and basic medical and transport services, but also insisted that the company's chairman should be suspended pending investigation into alleged misuse of funds and that union officials attached to the state-controlled General Federation of Trade Unions should be impeached. Perhaps surprisingly, the government agreed to the workers' demands, which inspired workers in other industries across the country to strike, too. In almost every confrontation between workers and the government, the result was the same. In November 2007, university professors protested against poor salaries and the security forces' intervention on campuses. Pharmacists, lawyers and civil servants have all followed suit, and the strikes were still ongoing at the time of writing.[90]

In political and economic terms, Egypt is ossified. In April 2008, the cost of food staples doubled and incited protesters to storm the "City Hall in Mahalla, burn[ing] tires in the street, smash[ing] chairs through shop windows . . . The police responded with tear gas and detained more than 500 protestors."[91] The government has continued to jail opposition figures, and is now employing a new tactic of closely scrutinizing the internet to identify dissenters.[92] Fundamental restrictions were again imposed on the democratic process prior to the 2008 municipal elections, when 800 Muslim Brotherhood members and supporters were rounded up. In response, the Brotherhood boycotted the election, allowing the NDP to claim 92 percent of the vote.

Foreign policy under Mubarak

In the mid-1980s, Egyptian–Israeli relations started to warm, as official visits were exchanged and Israel participated in the Cairo Book Fair. Since then, though, Egypt has been careful not to appear too close to Israel, with Mubarak keeping relations formal. By the late 1980s, the relationship was focusing on the issue of elections in the occupied territories, and a degree of genuine cooperation was achieved here. However, this has never looked like developing into anything that could be described as "friendship."

Mubarak has also moved to enhance bilateral relations with other Arab countries and emphasized that Egypt's return to the Arab fold was only natural. He ordered the cessation of propaganda attacks against Arab regimes, even if they had previously attacked his regime. Officially, he asserted that any restoration of relations with Arab states should be based on an Arab initiative, because they had broken off relations with Egypt. Behind the scenes, however, Egyptian diplomats and Mubarak himself worked feverishly to regain Egypt's credibility. As a result, Egyptian troops on the Libyan border were relocated and Mubarak cultivated ties with Oman and Jordan while emphasizing Egypt's historic links with Sudan.

Egypt finally regained its dominant role in the Arab and Islamic world when, in 1984, its membership in the Organization of the Islamic Conference was restored, five years after it had been rescinded. Meanwhile, bilateral relations between Egypt and Arab/Muslim countries began to improve. Moreover, in late 1987, the League of Arab States allowed Arab countries the right to restore bilateral relations with Egypt (although this was a mere formality because they had never been completely terminated). In February 1989, Egypt, Iraq, Jordan and North Yemen established the Arab Cooperation Council, and by the following year Egypt had restored formal diplomatic relations with all of its Arab neighbors.

With the liberation of Kuwait in 1991, in which Egypt participated with troops in the Coalition forces to evict Saddam Hussein, and the initiation of the Middle East peace process, Egypt's political leadership pursued a more aggressive foreign policy, especially at the regional level, taking an active role in bilateral negotiations in the peace process. It also became an active partner in international peacekeeping operations both inside and outside the region. Mubarak attempted to solidify regional political blocs, detach Egypt from certain US policies and present his country as a sovereign entity, free from the suzerainty of the US.

The Madrid peace process, initiated by the United States after the 1991 Gulf War, allowed Egyptian representation only in the multilateral negotiations which discussed general regional issues, not in the bilateral peace negotiations. However, Egypt insisted on carving a vital role for itself in the bilateral talks because it was the only Arab party that had good relations with both Israel and the Arab countries involved in the process. It therefore became a hybrid of mediator and partner in the negotiations: in some instances, it tried to mediate between the Israelis and the

Palestinians or between the Israelis and the Syrians; at other times, it championed the Arab position and abandoned its previous "neutrality."

In this context, Mubarak met with Yitzhak Rabin, Hafez al-Assad and Yasser Arafat whenever there was a deadlock in negotiations. However, Egypt decided not to interfere in the Israeli–Palestinian Oslo negotiations. Nevertheless, Mubarak, at Arafat's request, persuaded Rabin to add part of the West Bank to the self-rule area, so that the PLO leader could not be accused of trading the West Bank for Gaza. Consequently, Jericho was included in the Palestinian domain. Later, Cairo hosted the Israeli–Palestinian negotiations for the implementation of the Declaration of Principles and was involved in last-minute negotiations to get the implementation agreement signed on May 4, 1994.

Egypt had also been consulting closely with Syria, and on December 1, 1994, Mubarak visited Syria to promote bilateral relations and to discuss the peace process with al-Assad. The Israeli reaction to this suggested that Egypt should take a stronger stand for peace between Israel and the Arabs, which highlighted Egypt's significance in the peace process. Later that month, though, Egypt hosted a trilateral summit with Syria and Saudi Arabia that was designed to slow the normalization process with Israel until a comprehensive peace had been achieved. Al-Assad was concerned that the Arab states would end their economic boycott of Israel before the latter agreed to withdraw from the Golan Heights, which would leave Syria in a weakened position in future peace negotiations. This would have been ironic, because Egypt had opened the door for normalization with Israel at Camp David and had paid dearly with almost ten years as a pariah in the Arab world. Egypt pursued its active involvement in the peace process to convince the Western world, especially the United States, that it, not Israel, was the key to stability in the region. By doing this, Mubarak hoped to secure the economic benefits of peace.

In the upsurge of violence that followed the assassination of Rabin in November 1995 and the Palestinian elections in January 1996, Egypt again seized the chance to act as a regional mediator. It hosted the March 1996 "Summit of the Peacemakers" in the Red Sea town of Sharm-al-Sheikh, with US President Bill Clinton, Russian President Boris Yeltsin and Israeli Prime Minister Shimon Peres as well as King Hussein of Jordan and Yasser Arafat all in attendance. While the leaders presented a united front in condemning terrorism, deep divisions were evident. Egypt took the opportunity to advance itself at Israel's expense by blaming the spate of Hamas suicide bombings on Israeli intransigence in the occupied territories and succeeded in isolating Israel in its endeavors to win united condemnation of Iran for its role in sponsoring terrorism. However, both Syria and Lebanon, key players on the Arab side of the Palestinian issue, boycotted the conference. Nevertheless, for Egypt, hosting the conference was an end in itself, and the domestic press and government trumpeted the return of the country to prominence in regional affairs.

Subsequent to the May 1996 election of Benjamin Netanyahu and the Likud government in Israel, Mubarak seized the opportunity to make further diplomatic gains. In response to Arab concerns about the direction of the new regime in Tel Aviv, Mubarak, King Hussein and King Fahd of Saudi Arabia called for an Arab summit to be held in Cairo in late June. This summit strengthened Egypt's position, as has its continued efforts to maintain communication channels with Israel, although Mubarak has never expressed support for the Likud interpretation of the peace process.

With the outbreak of Intifadah in September 2000, relations between Egypt and Israel spiraled downward, with the former accusing the latter of employing excessive force against the Palestinians. The Egyptian regime turned a blind eye to the country's press (both opposition and official) depicting Israeli Prime Minister Ariel Sharon as a "Nazi" and a "butcher" who only understood the language of blood.[93] Relations deteriorated further when Mubarak recalled the Egyptian ambassador in Tel-Aviv in response to Israel's escalation of military force in the occupied territories. However, the two countries began to reach an understanding on several issues in the aftermath of the Anglo-American invasion of Iraq in 2003.

In that year, the "Road Map" peace plan was released by the International Quartet for Middle East Peace (United States, the European Union, Russia and the United Nations). This plan divided the resolution of the conflict into three phases. The first phase focused on Palestinian reform, recognition of Israel and an end to the Intifadah. The second related to Israel's withdrawal from the Palestinian self-rule areas occupied after September 2000. The third focused on the establishment of an interim Palestinian state and on the normalization of relations between Israel and the Arab states. In June 2003, an Arab–American summit was held in Sharm-al-Sheikh with the aim of securing Arab support for the Road Map. The summit was attended by President George W. Bush, the leaders of Egypt, Jordan, Saudi Arabia and Bahrain, and the new Palestinian prime minister, Mahmoud Abbas.

The first significant improvement in Egyptian–Israeli relations came in May 2004 when Mubarak and Sharon agreed to set up political, security and economic committees to improve all aspects of the bilateral relationship. The move was augmented with the conclusion of the biggest economic deal ever signed between the two countries: a contract worth $2.5 billion for Egypt to supply Israel with natural gas. Mubarak then surprised the Arab world by asserting that Sharon was the Palestinians' "best chance for peace."[94] The following month, Mubarak affirmed Egypt's readiness to help keep the peace in Gaza after Israel's planned withdrawal. Finally, in December, he sent both his intelligence chief and foreign minister on an official visit to Israel, during which the two countries signed a protocol for the deployment of 750 Egyptian troops along the Egypt–Gaza border in advance of Israel's planned withdrawal from the territory. The protocol, which was finalized in August 2005, would make Egypt responsible for preventing arms smuggling into the Gaza Strip.

The same month, bilateral relations warmed even more. First, Egypt returned an imprisoned Israeli spy, Azzam Azzam, who had been in an Egyptian prison since 1996, in exchange for six Egyptian students who had been arrested in Israel a few months earlier on suspicion of terrorism. Then, the two countries signed the Qualified Industrial Zones (QIZs) Agreement, according to which Egyptian goods would gain free access to US markets only if 11.7 percent of the content originated in Israel. This agreement, although largely welcomed by the Egyptian business community, triggered significant opposition from a cross-section of Egyptian society, including lawmakers, economists and activists, because it gave Israel a *de facto* veto over Egyptian exports to the US. Galal Amin, a prominent economist, said the agreement "has put Egyptian industries under the mercy of Israel, which could now decide upon which types of industries would be allowed to develop and flourish, and which ones would stagnate and diminish."[95]

Other measures enhanced the new relationship. In February 2005, Egypt hosted the first Israeli–Palestinian summit in four years. Highlighting Egypt's indispensable role in the mechanics of peacemaking in the Middle East, this was held amid hopes of reviving the peace process in the wake of Arafat's death and the election of Abbas as Chairman of the PNA. More importantly, the two countries agreed to reestablish formal diplomatic ties. Later in the year, Mubarak stunned Egyptian and Arab public opinion amid the military confrontation between Israel and Hizbollah. In a joint statement with King Abdullah of Jordan, he blamed Hizbollah for the outbreak of the war in Lebanon and referred to "uncalculated adventures that do not serve the interests of the region."[96] The statement also made indirect reference to UN Security Council Resolution 1559, which calls for the deployment of the Lebanese army in southern Lebanon and the disarmament of Hizbollah. Mubarak's remarks fueled angry demonstrations in many Egyptian cities in support of Hizbollah. Thousands of protesters waved Hizbollah flags and held aloft pictures of its leader, Hasan Nasrallah, while demanding the expulsion of the Israeli ambassador from Egypt and calling for the termination of all aspects of cooperation with the Jewish state. From 2007 onward, Mubarak again antagonized Egyptian and Arab public opinion when he joined with Israel to impose an economic blockade on the Gaza Strip in light of the internecine conflict between Abbas and the Hamas-led government of Ismail Haniya. The aim of the blockade was to topple the Hamas government in Gaza. All crossings to the Strip, including humanitarian supply lines, were blocked. Then, in December 2008, Israel launched a massive assault on Gaza which resulted in the deaths of more than 1,300 Palestinian civilians.

In late 2009, Egypt confirmed that it was constructing an underground barrier on its border with the Gaza Strip in order to disrupt "tunnel traffic." The 1.5 million residents of the Strip have relied on a network of tunnels to import everything from food and cars to cigarettes, as well as weapons.[97] In response to construction of the barrier, and the death of a Palestinian during the excavation, Palestinians protested against the Egyptian government.[98] Likewise, Hizbollah protested against the Egyptian action, with Nasrallah telling a crowd of tens of thousands that "Egypt should be condemned if it does not stop building the wall." This development comes in conjunction with Egypt's prosecution of twenty-six men "suspected of links with Hizbollah and accused of planning attacks inside the country."[99]

Relations with the United States

Egypt still maintains a special relationship with the US – it is the second-largest recipient of US aid in the region. However, the Egyptian government has demonstrated an inclination to be more independent of its American patron, mainly as a result of misperceptions between the two nations beginning in late 1994. It was bad enough, from Egypt's perspective, that the American press criticized Mubarak for violating UN sanctions against Libya, but this was followed by an American report on human rights abuses in Egypt. In both these instances, the Egyptian press and intellectuals attacked the Americans for distorting Egypt's image and adopting double standards. The government was upset at US interference in Egypt's domestic politics, and denied the allegations. It was suspected that the reports were published in retaliation for Egypt's stance on the extension of the Nuclear Non-Proliferation Treaty. The treaty, signed in 1970, was up for renewal in April 1995, but Egypt declared that it would not approve any extension unless Israel joined. The Egyptian position was that Israel had been justified in keeping its nuclear arsenal when it was at war with the Arab states, but now that the region was moving toward peace, Israel should not be exempt. Egypt tried to rally the Arab states and the developing world in opposition to the US proposal to have a collective vote on an indefinite extension of the treaty. However, the American proposal succeeded and the treaty was renewed indefinitely.

In spite of this, the United States found itself increasingly dependent on Egypt to assist in sorting out the complex difficulties pertaining to the peace process of the mid-1990s. As we have seen, Egypt hosted both the "Summit of the Peacemakers" in 1995 and the Arab Summit the following year. It also led the Western-aligned Arab states in trying to arrive at a lasting settlement of the Palestinian issue. There is also domestic concern in the United States about the continued cost and dubious benefit of $3 billion per year in foreign aid to Israel (most of it military assistance), especially if the peace process collapses and a more militant Israel emerges. Egypt is now the US's best contact in the Middle East and must be carefully supported if moderate Arab states are not to abandon the peace process.

In 2004, Egyptian–US relations warmed with the appointment of Ahmad Nazif's cabinet. Nazif recruited a number of pro-Western business executives to head key government departments, such as the Ministries of Industry, Foreign Trade, Investment, Agriculture, Housing and Tourism. As strong advocates of economic liberalization and integration into the global economy, the new ministers were influential in accelerating the implementation of the World Bank and IMF structural adjustment programs in Egypt. They also adopted policies that complemented US interests in Egypt, especially in terms of normalizing relations with Israel. This was manifested in the decision to sign the QIZs Agreement and to export Egyptian natural gas to Israel at prices below international levels. However, these ministers have not formulated these policies on their own initiative. Rather, they have implemented policies dictated to them by forces close to the president.

Egypt and the invasion of Iraq

The Anglo-American invasion of Iraq in 2003 marked a turning point in Egyptian–US relations, as it posed a dilemma for the Egyptian regime, which had opposed the use of military force against Iraq from the start. On the one hand,

Egypt considered itself to be a close ally of the United States, a status that Cairo did not wish to jeopardize. On the other, Egypt had commitments to its Arab neighbors and could not be seen to favor the invasion of an Arab country. Even more importantly, the Egyptian regime had developed a favorable trading relationship with Iraq toward the end of the 1990s. Notwithstanding the UN Security Council's economic embargo, the terms of trade with Iraq steadily favored Egypt following the launch of the UN Oil-for-Food Program, which allowed Iraq to export oil in return for importation of basic essentials. In January 2001, Egypt and Iraq had signed a free-trade agreement. This was signed in Cairo by Egyptian Prime Minister Dr. Ebeid and Iraqi Vice-President Taha Yassin Ramadan, the highest-ranking Iraqi official to visit the capital since the 1991 Gulf War. The pact called for an immediate end to all customs barriers between the two countries, and this was realized shortly thereafter. Moreover, in late 2001, the Egyptian minister of foreign trade visited Baghdad with a large delegation to lay the foundations for strong bilateral cooperation between the two countries. Their subsequent accord forged a working partnership on industrial, trade and technical issues, bolstering the free-trade agreement. Thus, Egypt had become Iraq's most important trading partner in the Arab world (and its fifth biggest overall, after Russia, China, France and India) prior to the invasion.

In response to domestic outrage over the invasion, Egypt formally rejected the US's action in principle and refrained from taking part militarily. However, once the invasion was over, Egypt gradually shifted its position from condemnation to acceptance. Consequently, it recognized the US-appointed Governing Council of Iraq; it provided training for Iraqi security forces; and it sent an ambassador to Baghdad. However, in July 2005, a few weeks after his arrival, this ambassador was kidnapped and assassinated by a militant group. Egypt refused to send a new envoy to Iraq until 2009, when it yielded to American pressure and thus initiated the process of renewing diplomatic representation in the country.

Notes

1 Samir Amin, *The Arab Nation* (London: Zed Press, 1978), pp. 18–20.
2 Samir Amin, *Unequal Development* (London: Monthly Review Press, 1976), p. 302.
3 Amin, *The Arab Nation*, op. cit., p. 30.
4 Khaldûn H. al-Naqîb, *Al-Mujtama' wa al-Dawlah fî al-khalîj wa al-Jazîrah al-'Arabiyyah* (Beirut: Centre for Arab Unity, 1987), pp. 105–106.
5 Amin, *The Arab Nation*, op. cit., p. 31.
6 Amin, *Unequal Development*, op. cit., pp. 302–304.
7 Derek Hopwood, *Egypt: Politics and Society, 1945–1981* (London: Allen and Unwin, 1982), pp. 11–12.
8 Amin, *The Arab Nation*, op. cit., pp. 31–32.
9 Hopwood, op. cit., pp. 11–12.
10 Amin, *The Arab Nation*, op. cit., pp. 35–36.
11 Hasan Youssef, "The Democratic Experience in Egypt, 1923 – 1952," in 'Ali Dessouki (ed.), *Democracy in Egypt: Problems and Prospects* (Cairo: The American University in Cairo, 1978), p. 25.
12 Galal Amin, *Al-Mashriq al-'Arabî wa al-Gharb* (Beirut: Center for Arab Unity Studies, 1979), pp. 16, 35.

13 Târiq al-Bishrî, *Al-Ḥarakah al-Siyâsiyyah fî Miṣr, 1945–1952* (Cairo: al-Hay'ah al-Maṣriyyah al-'Âmmah lil Kitâb, 1972), pp. 481–498.

14 Ibid., pp. 488–508.

15 Ibid., p. 492.

16 Ibid., pp. 559–563.

17 Ibid., pp. 567–577.

18 Ibid., pp. 578–579.

19 Ibid., p. 417.

20 Khaldûn H. al-Naqîb, *Al-Dawlah al-Tasalluṭiyyah fî al-Mashriq al-'Arabî* (Beirut: Center for Arab Unity Studies, 1991), pp. 133–135.

21 Ibid., pp. 149–50.

22 Ibid., p. 140; see also Aḥmad Ḥamrûsh, *Al-Inqilâbât al-'Askariyyah* (Beirut: Dâr Ibn Khaldûn, 1980), p. 80; and Roger Owen, *State, Power, and Politics in the Making of the Modern Middle East* (London: Routledge, 1992), p. 267.

23 Al-Naqîb, *Al-Dawlah al-Tasalluṭiyyah fî al-Mashriq al-'Arabî*, op. cit., p.102.

24 Ḥamrûsh, op. cit., pp. 82–83.

25 Owen, op. cit., p. 267.

26 Ḥamrûsh, op. cit., pp. 84–86.

27 Owen, op. cit., p. 268.

28 Gamal Amin, op. cit., pp. 48–49.

29 Samia Sa'id Imam, *Man Yamluk Miṣr, 1974–1980* (Cairo: Dâr al-Mustaqbal al-'Arabî, 1986), pp. 57, 86.

30 Galal Amin, op. cit., p. 74.

31 Samir Amin, *Classes and Nations, Historically and in the Current Crisis* (London: Monthly Review Press, 1980), pp. 137–139.

32 Nazih Ayubi, *Over-stating the Arab State: Politics and Society in the Middle East*, (London: I.B. Tauris, 1995), p. 13.

33 Sa'id Imam, op. cit., pp. 83–84.

34 Ibid., pp. 87–93.

35 Ibid., pp. 97, 92.

36 Gunnar Myrdal, *The Challenge of World Poverty* (New York: Random House, 1970), pp. 233–234. For examples of corruption, see Sa'id Imam, op. cit., pp. 90–91, 97.

37 Sa'id Imam, op. cit., p. 99.

38 Galal Amin, op. cit., p. 54.

39 Ibid., pp. 57–60.

40 Mohammad H. Heikal, *Secret Channels* (London: HarperCollins, 1996), pp. 29–49.

41 Ibid., p. 132.

42 Ibid., pp. 106–109.

43 Ibid., p. 168.

44 See, for example, Hamied Ansari, *Egypt: The Stalled Society* (Albany: State University of New York Press, 1986); Raymond Hinnebusch Jr., *Egyptian Politics under Sadat: The Post-Populist Development of an Authoritarian-Modernizing State* (London: Cambridge University Press, 1985).

45 Yahyâ al-Gamal, "Al-Ta'addudiyyah al-Ḥizbiyyah fî Miṣr," in Sa'd al-Ibrâhîm (ed.), *Al-Ta'addudiyyah al-Siyâsiyyah wa al-Dîmuqrâṭî fî al-Waṭan al-'Arabî* (Jordan: Arab Thought Forum, 1989), p. 220.

46 Sa'd Eddîn al-Shazlî, *Ḥarb October: Mudhakkarât* (London: n.p., 1988), p. 164.

47 Ibid., pp. 304–305.

48 Heikal, op. cit., p. 286.

49 Galal Amin, op. cit., pp. 84–86.

50 Ibid., p. 99.

51 Sa'id Imam, op. cit., p. 59.

52 Ibid., p. 192.

53   Galal Amin, *Al-'Arab wa Nakbat al-Kuwait* (Cairo: Madbouli Bookshop, 1991), p. 145.
54   Eberhard Kienle, "More than a Response to Islamism: The Political Deliberalization of Egypt in the 1990s," *Middle East Journal*, Vol. 52, No. 2 (Spring 1998), pp. 231–232.
55   Yaḥyâ al-Gamal, op. cit., p. 215.
56   See "Documents on Constitutional and Parliamentary Life in Egypt 1952–77 (Appendix 1)," in 'Ali Dessouki (ed.), *Democracy in Egypt: Problems and Prospects* (Cairo: The American University in Cairo, 1978), p. 83.
57   Sayed Marei, "Political Evolution from the One-Party to the Multi-Party System," in 'Ali Dessouki (ed.), op. cit., pp. 40–42.
58   Moheb Zaki, *Civil Society & Democratization in Egypt, 1981–1994* (Cairo: The Ibn Khaldoun Center, 1994), p. 76.
59   Cairo Institute for Human Rights Studies, *Individual Report on the Universal Periodic Review (UPR) of* Egypt, December 2009. URL: http://www.anhri.net/en/?p=64.
60   Ibid.
61   Cairo Institute for Human Rights Studies et al., *A Joint Report by a Coalition of Egyptian Human Rights Non-governmental Organizations (NGOs) on the Universal Periodic Review (UPR) of Egypt*, December 3, 2009.
62   Eberhard Kienle, *A Grand Delusion: Democracy and Economic Reform in Egypt* (London: I.B. Tauris, 2001), p. 26.
63   Ibid., p. 68.
64   The emergency laws grant the government the right to establish exceptional courts, such as the state security courts and the Supreme State Security Court of Emergency, to hear cases related to crimes committed in violation of rulings made by the president or his deputy (Article 7/1) and the right to include members of the military in the formation of the courts (Article 7/4). These powers clearly violate constitutional and international principles relating to the separation of powers, the independence of the judiciary and the immunity of judges (Articles 165–173 of the constitution and Article 14 of the International Covenant on Civil and Political Rights). International Federation for Human Rights, *The Emergency Law in Egypt*, November 17, 2001. URL: http://www.fidh.org/THE-EMERGENCY-LAW-IN-EGYPT.
65   Mohammad H. Heikal, *Bâb Miṣr Ilâ al-Qarn al-Wâḥid wa al-'Ushrûn* (Cairo: Dâr al-Shurûq, 1995), p. 28.
66   Cairo Institute for Human Rights Studies, *Individual Report on the Universal Periodic Review (UPR) of Egypt*, December 3, 2009.
67   Hala G. Thabet, "Egyptian Parliamentary Elections: Between Democratisation and Autocracy," *Africa Development*, Vol. 31, No. 3 (2006), p. 14.
68   Amnesty International, *Egypt: Continuing Crackdown on Muslim Brotherhood*, November 30, 2007. URL: http://www.amnesty.org/en/library/asset/MDE12/028/2007/en/30d4ef42-d36d-11dd-a329-2f46302a8cc6/mde120282007en.html.
69   *Al-Taqrîr al-Istirâtîjî al-'Arabî 1999* (Cairo: al-Ahram Center for Political and Strategic Studies, 2000), pp. 295–298.
70   "Mubarak Wins 94 Percent in Plebiscite," *Globe and Mail*, September 28, 1999, p. A15.
71   Quoted in Mona El-Ghobashy, "Egypt Looks Ahead to Portentous Year," *Middle East Report Online*, February 2, 2005. URL: http://www.merip.org/mero/mero020205.html.
72   Michaelle Browers, "The Egyptian Movement for Change: Intellectual Antecedents and Generational Conflicts," *Contemporary Islam*, Vol. 1, No. 1 (June 2007), pp. 69–88.
73   Nathan J. Brown, Michele Dunne & Amr Hamzawy, "Egypt's Constitutional Amendments," Carnegie Endowment for International Peace, March 23, 2007. URL: http://www.carnegieendowment.org/publications/index.cfm?fa=view&id=19075.
74   See the text of the revised constitutional articles. URL: http://weekly.ahram.org.eg/2007/837/eg13.htm.

75 Before the amendment, Article 82 extended power only to the vice-president.
76 See the text of the revised constitutional articles. URL: http://weekly.ahram.org.eg/ 2007/837/eg13.htm. The process of strengthening the Shura Council had actually begun some time earlier. For instance, on June 3, 2000 the Supreme Constitutional Court had ruled that the Law on Private Associations and Institutions (Law 153 of 1999) was unconstitutional on the grounds that it had not been referred to the Council before adoption by the People's Assembly. Euro-Mediterranean Human Rights Network, *Court of Egypt Rules the NGO Law of 1999 Unconstitutional*, September 6, 2000. URL: http://en.euromedrights.org/index.php/news/emhrn_releases/emhrn_statements_2000/3 329.html.
77 URL: http://weekly.ahram.org.eg/ 2007/837/eg13.htm.
78 Ibid.
79 Ibid.
80 Amnesty International Press Release, March 18, 2007. URL: http://www.amnesty. org/en/library/asset/MDE12/008/2007/en/c74b5428-d3a5-11dd-a3292f46302a8cc6/ mde120082007en.pdf.
81 Cited in ibid.
82 *Al-Wafd* (Cairo), August 28, 2006. URL: http://www.alwafd.org/front/detail.php? id=3704&cat=invest&PHPSESSID=26da628160397994cec97a79681d77b5.
83 Galal Amin, *Al-'Arab wa Nakbat al-Kuwait*, op. cit., p. 65.
84 Sa'id Imam, op. cit., p. 230.
85 See Tareq Y. Ismael, *Middle East Politics Today: Government and Civil Society* (Gainesville: University of Florida Press, 2001), p. 448.
86 Ibid.
87 *Al-Taqrîr al-Istirâtîjî al-'Arabî 1997* (Cairo: al-Ahram Center for Political and Strategic Studies, 1998), p. 20; Heikal, *Bâb Miṣr Ilâ al-Qarn al-Wâḥid wa al-'Ushrûn*, op. cit., p. 20.
88 *Al-Taqrîr al-Istirâtîjî al-'Arabî 2007/2008* (Cairo: al-Ahram Center for Political and Strategic Studies, 2008), p. 421.
89 Ibid., p. 422.
90 For a detailed review of the social strikes over 2007 and 2008, see ibid., pp. 423–432.
91 Paul Schemm, "High Prices, Bread Shortages Trigger Protests in Egypt," *Seattle Times*, April 8, 2008. URL: http://seattletimes.nwsource.com/html/nationworld/2004333929_ egyptriots08.html.
92 James Blitz, "Amnesty Links Rise in Rights Abuses to Downturn," *Financial Times*, May 28, 2009. URL: http://www.ft.com/cms/s/0/090b9796-4b1f-11de-87c2-00144 feabdc0.html.
93 Editorial, "Invitation to Sharon Draws Angry Reaction in Pro-Palestinian Egypt," *SPME* Digest, February 27, 2003. URL: http://spme.net/cgi-bin/facultyforum.cgi? ID=1578.
94 Mona el-Ghobashy, "Egypt Looks ahead to Portentous Year," *Middle East Report Online*, February 2, 2005. URL: http://www.merip.org/mero/mero020205.html.
95 Galal Amin, *Miṣr wa al-Maṣriyyîn fî 'Ahd Mubarak (1981–2008)* (Cairo: Dar Merit, 2009), p. 93.
96 Editorial, "Cairo Draws the Line," *Al-Ahram*, July 20–26, 2006. URL: http://weekly. ahram.org.eg/2006/804/re91.htm.
97 AFP, "Gaza Barrier a 'Sovereign Right': Egyptian Daily," *AFP*, December 17, 2009. URL: http://news.yahoo.com/s/afp/20091217/wl_mideast_afp/mideastconflictgaza egyptsmuggling.
98 "Palestinians Protest Egyptian Steel Barrier," *PressTV*, December 25, 2009. URL: http://www.presstv.ir/detail.aspx?id = 114655&sectionid = 351020202.
99 "Hezbollah Chief Asks Egypt to Stop Building Gaza Border Wall," *Haaretz* December 26, 2009. URL: http://www.haaretz.com/hasen/spages/1137967.html.

Further reading

The following represents a collection of texts covering the historical development of Egypt as a nation state, including economic analysis.

As historical backdrop, Juan Cole's *Napoleon's Egypt: Invading the Middle East* and Afaf Lufti al-Sayyid Marsot's *Egypt in the Reign of Mohammad Ali* provide, first, a historical primer on the Egyptian experience under French military occupation and emergent sources of resistance, and, second, a historical narrative of the emergence of Egypt as a modern nation state under the towering leadership of Mohammad 'Ali during the early nineteenth century.

Michael Ezekiel Gasper's *The Power of Representation: Publics, Peasants, and Islam in Egypt* traces the development of Egypt's national identity from the mid-1870s through to the 1910s by focusing on the development of a "new class" of Egyptian urban intellectuals: teachers, lawyers, engineers, clerks, accountants and journalists.

P.J. Vatikiotis's *The History of Modern Egypt: From Mohammad Ali to Mubarak* serves as a comprehensive historical survey of Egypt in the nineteenth and twentieth centuries. Two major works on Nasser's Egypt and his revolution are: R. Hrair Dekmejian's *Egypt under Nasir: A Study in Political Dynamics* and Peter Mansfield's *Nasser's Egypt*. Each provides a compelling insight and portrayal of Nasser and his policies.

The signing of the Camp David Accords in 1978 was a profound demarcation point in Egypt's modern history. It marked the first Arab state to declare official relations with the state of Israel, and, consequently, saw Egypt sacrificing its ideological leadership role within the region. This period and its consequences are examined in William Quandt's *Camp David: Peacemaking and Politics* and *The Middle East: Ten Years after Camp David*. Raymond William Baker's *Sadat and After: The Struggle for Egypt's Political Soul* is a lucid and well-documented text that examines the debates within Egyptian society concerning national identity and Egypt's place within the Arab world.

Beginning with the reign of Anwar Sadat, and accelerated under Hosni Mubarak, Egyptian society has undergone profound shifts owing to a neoliberal realignment of its economy and the abandonment of any socialist pretense. On this theme, Nadia Ramsis Farah's *Egypt's Political Economy: Power Relations in Development* provides a broad overview of the political and economic transformations of the modern Egyptian state from the appointment of Mohammad 'Ali as governor in 1805 to today, with a special focus on the neoliberal economic shift between 1990 and 2005. M. Riad el-Ghonemy's *Egypt in the Twenty-First Century: Challenges for Development* is an investigation of neoliberal economic reform in Egypt and long-term challenges. Ninette S. Fahmy's *The Politics of Egypt: State–Society Relationship* probes along similar lines, investigating the nature of the relationship between the Egyptian state and society, and how this relationship could aid development.

The Muslim Brotherhood has persisted as the most influential non-state organization within Egypt since its advent in 1928. Bruce K. Rutherford's *Egypt after Mubarak: Liberalism, Islam and Democracy in the Arab World* examines the ideological battlefield on which Islamists feature prominently and considers the democratization of the country. Denis Joseph Sullivan and Sana Abed-Kotob's *Islam in Contemporary Egypt: Civil Society vs. the State* examines the ideological and organizational struggle between the authoritarian state and the Muslim Brotherhood, and provides a descriptive sketch of the heterogeneity and diversity of the Islamic movement in Egypt. Finally, Raymond William Baker's *Islam without Fear: Egypt and the New Islamists* is the most significant recent work examining the contours of Islamic political thought and Islamist movements within Egypt, identifying a centrist, accommodationist trend.

References

Baker, Raymond William (1990) *Sadat and After: Struggle for Egypt's Politics*, Harvard University Press.
—— (2006) *Islam without Fear: Egypt and the New Islamists*, Harvard University Press.
Cole, Juan (2008) *Napoleon's Egypt: Invading the Middle East*, Palgrave Macmillan.
Dekmejian, R. Hrair (1971) *Egypt under Nasir: A Study in Political Dynamics*, State University of New York Press.
El-Ghonemy, M. Riad (ed.) (2003) *Egypt in the Twenty-First Century: Challenges for Development*, Routledge.
Fahmy, Ninette S. (2002) *The Politics of Egypt: State–Society Relationship*, Routledge.
Farah, Nadia Ramsis (2009) *Egypt's Political Economy: Power Relations in Development*, The American University in Cairo Press.
Gasper, Michael Ezekiel (2008) *The Power of Representation: Publics, Peasants, and Islam in Egypt*, Stanford University Press.
Mansfield, Peter (1965) *Nasser's Egypt*, Penguin.
Marsot, Afaf Lufti al-Sayyid (1984) *Egypt in the reign of Mohammad Ali*, Cambridge University Press.
Quandt, William B. (1986) *Camp David: Peacemaking and Politics*, Brookings Institution Press.
—— (ed.) (1988) *The Middle East: Ten Years after Camp David*, Brookings Institution Press.
Rutherford, Bruce K. (2008) *Egypt after Mubarak: Liberalism, Islam, and Democracy in the Arab World*, Princeton University Press.
Sullivan, Denis Joseph & Abed-Kotob, Sana (1999) *Islam in Contemporary Egypt: Civil Society vs. the State*, Lynne Rienner.
Vatikiotis, P.J. (1991) *The History of Modern Egypt: from Mohammad Ali to Mubarak*, Johns Hopkins University Press.

10 The Gulf Cooperation Council

The Gulf Cooperation Council (GCC) countries of Saudi Arabia, Kuwait, Oman, Bahrain, Qatar and the United Arab Emirates, also termed here the Arab Gulf states, are grouped together because their patterns of politics and government are sufficiently similar to justify collective treatment. Furthermore, the same forces of history, geography and economics shape these patterns of political behavior. The region contains the largest concentration of conservative, non-constitutional monarchies remaining in the world, and controls 39 percent of the world's proven oil reserves and 23 percent of the world's proven natural gas reserves.[1] The Gulf regimes reflect a political tribalism that allows for a highly hierarchical society and unrepresentative rule.

The "age of oil," and the politics that it has produced, began in the 1930s, although the rentier state did not materialize until after the Second World War and more specifically in the 1950s.[2] The majority of oil discoveries occurred in the 1930s as a number of Western multinational corporations explored the region.[3] Joint projects with Iraqi, Saudi and Bahraini oil companies saw the first production and exportation of crude oil through new sea terminals and pipelines across Syria and Palestine. With the outbreak of the Second World War in 1939, oil exploration and production were interrupted, with some areas halting altogether. The huge increase in oil production and the increased income to the region mostly came in the form of rentier taxes paid by the international oil companies to the ruling families. Almost like a foreign subsidy, the income from oil was continuous and organized in such a fashion that it altered the power structures in the region by firmly entrenching those royal dynasties who happened to be in place when the international cartels arrived, permanently casting them in the form and with the apparatus of the modern state.[4]

Khaldûn al-Naqîb, the distinguished Kuwaiti sociologist, sees the prime feature in the development of this rentier state as:

> the national economy of this kind of state does not depend directly on oil but indirectly on the state expenditure arising from oil concessions. Public spending becomes the primary channel through which oil revenues are distributed to society in the Gulf monarchies. Here the central role of the state becomes evident . . . in the social and economic life of the population. The

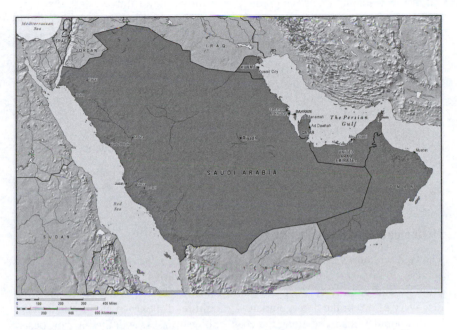

Map 10.1 The Gulf Cooperation Council

Drawn by Ian Cool

state possesses a great deal of surplus capital ... which leads to heavy interference in the economy through a monopoly of financing which sees the monarchies, in the guise of the state, initiate and guarantee the majority, if not all, commercial and industrial projects [in the region].[5]

The most dynamic sectors of the economy, export/import, construction and contracts, also depend heavily on the state's ability to guarantee bids for such business. This role of the state, both customer and guarantor, is clear; and by extension the role of the royal families and traditional elites, frozen by the imperial protectorate treaties, sees them cast as the central authority for state control and monopoly of the economy. Al-Naqîb explains:

For that reason the ruling families appear as if they are political associations who own the state by birthright, rather than having ascended to authority through popular election or choice. The relationship with imperial powers [and the business elites of the Western world] meant the adoption and adaptation of the modern capitalist state to the requirements of sectarian tribal demands and the necessity of the traditional conservative ruling elite to protect the traditional relations within the framework of the modern political system and new economic conditions [which had been adopted from the West].[6]

All of these adaptations have predictably resulted in a ruling system that safeguards the existing political conditions as they have existed since the beginning of the "oil age." The immense wealth which oil has brought to the region has not upset the traditional balances of society's social and economic class structure, though the vast infusion of wealth created an array of welfare arrangements, with the effect of reducing the labor force. As a result of this change in society's views of work, a new division of labor pushed citizens to attempt political change, and governments to give a higher priority to the instruments of political oppression, in order to secure their place at the apex of a hierarchical society. The further adoption of such measures increased these governments' dependence on external sources of security against internal dissent.[7]

We first look at the common forces that bind the region together, then at features that are unique to individual countries.

Historical legacies

The GCC countries lay along the world's most ancient sea routes, and have been centers of intense commerce and trade for centuries. Pearling, fishing, boat building and commerce were the main industries of the Gulf region until the discovery of oil. In the desert climate, agriculture, if it existed at all, was limited. Settled populations lived along the coast and near oases, with the interior, desert Gulf region inhabited by nomads. The Gulf has played a significant role in the West's domination of the Orient since the initiation of the age of imperialism. The hegemony of the British East India Company over India by the end of the eighteenth century prompted Britain's increasing efforts to dominate the Gulf in order to protect and expand its imperial interests.

Between 1820 and 1899, Britain achieved colonial control over the entire Gulf through a series of treaties with local leaders (1820 with the Omani Coast; 1891 with Muscat; 1892 with Bahrain; and 1899 with Kuwait). In 1915, Britain signed the Treaty of Dir'iyya[8] with 'Abdul-Aziz Ibn 'Abdul-Rahman Ibn Sa'ud (Ibn Sa'ud), in which Britain promised to provide protection for his expanding territory and pay him £5,000 each month in return for refraining from attacking British interests in Kuwait and the southern part of the Gulf. In the Treaty of al-'Aqeer (1922), Britain formally drew new boundaries between Kuwait, Iraq and Najd, for the first time demarcating the Arabian Peninsula. The borders were established to control the movement of the nomadic peoples of the interior, and to keep them from switching political loyalty from the leaders now established as the heads of the newly created sheikhdoms. Bedouin society had always been based on sociopolitical relationships, which had focused upon interpersonal relationships rather than geographical constraints. So the treaty limited political movement, tying the people of the region, through tribal elites, to Western-sponsored rulers.[9]

Between 1902 and 1926, Ibn Sa'ud conquered the area of what is known today as Saudi Arabia. In 1927, in the Jeddah Treaty, Britain lifted his protectorate status and recognized the newly formed Saudi Arabia, which now incorporated the Hejaz, Najd and al-Ahsa', while simultaneously altering its legal borders with contemporary Iraq and Kuwait. The political motive behind this treaty was to use the ambition of Ibn Saʻud as a counterbalance to the newly created Hashimite dynasties of Transjordan and Iraq.[10]

By the beginning of the twentieth century, the Gulf and the Arabian Peninsula were politically and economically under the control of the British Empire. However, rather than administering the region directly as a colonial possession, Britain institutionalized its control by exploiting the historical tribal relations that had existed in the region for centuries. Within the framework of these tribal relations, government and politics were largely undifferentiated from the institution of kinship. Rulers, while holding authority, had no fixed lines of succession within the ruling family. The British subverted the tribal institution so it would function as a surrogate for British colonial administration.

Britain accomplished this subversion by aiding and abetting the transformation of the Gulf's ruling families into royal families. This was achieved by concentrating economic and political power in the hands of one ruler – one who was favorable to Britain, of course, and who readily exchanged authority based on community consensus for power based on British support. Succession was then limited to direct lines of descent from this ruler. The British guaranteed royal families' rule against internal and external challenges in return for their support and loyalty. This structure remained in effect even after the British formally withdrew from the entire Gulf region in 1971.

The impact of British imperialism on the patterns of government and politics in the region has been twofold: all the states of the region have royal families as the central and most powerful institutions in their political structures, and the region is politically fragmented into independent states. Before the British replaced the institution of ruling families with that of royal families, political organization was based on tribal alliances, and divisions between polities were consequently loose, informal and fluid.

As British hegemony waned and Cold War rivalry set in, the United States became the leading Western power in the Gulf region. The need to secure Gulf oil resources from hostile forces become the preeminent American concern, as the survival of Western economies depended on the uninterrupted flow of oil. The strategic prerogative continued with the eventual collapse of the Soviet Union. The rich but militarily weak states straddle powerful yet envious neighbors – Iran and Iraq – a reality that came into sharp focus with the 1991 Gulf War.

The Gulf Cooperation Council

The power relations of Egypt and Iran have affected the geopolitics of the Arabian Peninsula since time immemorial, as the peninsula was a bridge between the Egyptian and the Persian/Iranian civilizations. When the respective status of those two countries weakens, Iraq has traditionally emerged as the significant regional power.[11] In 1979, both Egypt and Iran declined in regional status, the former as a result of the Camp David Accords and the latter as a result of post-revolution turmoil. The same year witnessed a shift in Iraq's regional interests – away from the Fertile Crescent and Greater Syria to the Gulf area. This was affirmed in a national declaration on February 8, 1980. Iraq's regional ambitions led it to declare war on Iran in September 1980, to regain concessions it had made to Iran in 1975 and, thus, assert its leadership in the Gulf.

The GCC was formed in direct response to the Iraq–Iran War in March 1981, when the constituent members signed the twenty-two-provision Incorporation Charter. The following month, the GCC held its first summit and declared its goal to be protection from foreign interference.[12] This meeting in Abu Dhabi empha- sized that the GCC comprises only states that are homogeneous in their political, economic and social orientations, which virtually guaranteed the permanent exclusion of Iraq and Yemen.[13] As such, the GCC was a closed sub-regional organization whose strategic orientation was mainly fear of domination by regional neighbors, particularly Iraq and Iran, and, to some extent, Egypt. However, the GCC lacked concerted military plans, integrated economies, boundary stability and, most importantly, approved modalities for conflict resolution.

The military weakness of the GCC was dismally highlighted with the Iraqi invasion of Kuwait in August 1990. When Kuwait requested military assistance from its fellow GCC members, as per the founding charter, no other GCC member responded with force, nor did any of them even call for military action to help Kuwait.[14] This was because all of the member states relied on foreign military protection rather than a collective defense strategy, largely because they could not agree on concrete criteria of what constituted an enemy. (This remains the case today.) For example, during the Iraq–Iran War, Saudi Arabia and Kuwait severed relations with Iran, while the United Arab Emirates (UAE) and Oman maintained (and occasionally improved) relations with that country. After the war, the GCC formally restored relations with Iran, despite its hostility to revolutionary Shi'ism. Following the liberation of Kuwait by the international coalition, in December 1992 Qatar restored diplomatic relations with Iraq, to the consternation of both Saudi Arabia and Kuwait. Meanwhile, Oman had never cut relations with Iraq in the first place.[15]

After more than two decades, economic integration of the member states of the GCC remains little more than a dream. First, the member states' economies are competitive rather than complementary. Second, they are all oil-based (with oil exports accounting for about 80 percent of each state's GDP), a fact that makes these economies highly incorporated into the world capitalist market. This situa- tion is complicated further by disagreements among the GCC states over oil quotas, which practically leaves each state to produce oil according to its own discretion, and consequently weakens a unified economic front. Third, the low level of diversification and the small domestic markets of the GCC makes integration almost impossible. This has become most evident in light of the fact that the GCC has consistently failed to unify its customs tariffs or to present a unified front in economic negotiations with the European Union.[16]

In December 2005, the GCC held its twenty-sixth summit to discuss three main issues: the need to push ahead with economic modernization; the formulation of unified commercial policy; and the ongoing violence in Iraq. The summit approved a plan for unifying customs tariffs and reiterated the GCC's desire for a common market. Nevertheless, after the thirtieth summit in December 2009, one Saudi journalist wrote wearily:

> the GCC charter talks about "coordination, integration and inter-connection" in "all fields in order to achieve unity." This sentence has not been made up, but is part of Article 4 of the GCC charter. If we truly try to compare these words to the reality on the ground we will see that these words do not accurately or sincerely reflect the true state of affairs. Despite some wonderful examples of cooperation, there have also been many incidents that represent a lack of coordination, and there are inconsistencies in some important fields.[17]

Despite declining oil revenues in the 1990s, GCC members spent more and more on defense, purchasing billions of dollars' worth of tanks, warships and aircraft. However, the devastation of Iraq and the apparent shift of Iran's foreign policy designs northward left many in the GCC believing that they no longer face any obvious or immediate threat. Moreover, in spite of the billions that have been spent, it seems likely that they will still not be able to defend themselves without Western support.[18] Neverthless, recent developments have reinvigorated security concerns. With the collapse of the Iraqi state – Iran's primary foe and counter-vailing power – Iranian regional ambitions and influence have grown. This has stoked the fears of the Arab Gulf countries, who view the ascent of Iran with nervousness for both geopolitical and religious reasons. Iran has done little to ease this tension as it pursues its nuclear program. However, the GCC has yet to formulate a consistent policy against its northern neighbor: it has vacillated between confrontation and accommodation, criticizing Iran's activities in Iraq while entertaining an Iranian proposal for a free trade pact.

At the twenty-eighth summit of the GCC in 2007, President Mahmoud Ahmadinejad – the first Iranian president to attend a GCC summit – presented a twelve-point plan that included cooperation on scientific, cultural and economic issues, and most importantly opened the door for security cooperation between the GCC and Iran. "We are proposing the conclusion of a security agreement," said Ahmadinejad. "We want peace and security . . . based on justice and without foreign intervention."[19] This tone was echoed in the final communiqué of the GCC, which reiterated a desire for peace and reconciliation, and this sentiment was echoed in the subsequent summit held in Bahrain.

The GCC was initially fraught with disputes over territorial boundaries: Saudi Arabia versus Oman; Saudi Arabia versus Bahrain; Saudi Arabia, UAE and Oman over the area of Buraimi; Saudi Arabia versus Kuwait over the neutral zone; Saudi Arabia versus Yemen; Kuwait versus Iraq; and Oman versus Yemen. However, all of these disputes were resolved by 1995, leaving just two rancorous wrangles: one between Qatar and Bahrain; the other between Qatar and Saudi Arabia. The first of these was referred to the International Court of Justice, which issued its verdict in March 2001. Both sides accepted and implemented this ruling immediately.[20] The second dispute was resolved in the same month, when the two sides signed a border delineation agreement that was also fully implemented.

The economy

The economy of the region is reliant on oil exports. Individual states have accumulated vast wealth as a result of oil sales, and each has invested according to its individual development plans. As a legacy of the British era, control over oil revenues was invested entirely in the ruler's hands, and until recently there was little distinction between state budgets and the private purses of the rulers. Even now, once the revenues have gone to the Ministry of Finance, the emirs and kings can skim off a percentage for their personal use. Under British influence, communal ownership was transformed into private ownership, and with the discovery of oil the power of the royal families throughout the Gulf became entrenched.

The economies of the Gulf are all narrowly specialized around the production of oil and management of the resulting financial capital, which is far greater than their absorptive capacities can accommodate. The net result is high consumption in both public and private spheres and service-oriented economies based on consumption rather than production. The indigenous population of the Arab Gulf states constitutes a pampered leisure class, with labor predominantly performed by

Table 10.1 Estimated proven world crude oil reserves: twenty leading nations (thousands of barrels), 2007

1.	**Saudi Arabia**	**264, 251, 000**
2.	Canada	178, 800, 000 (includes oil sands)
3.	Iran	138, 400, 000
4.	Iraq	115, 000, 000
5.	**Kuwait**	**101, 500, 000**
6.	**United Arab Emirates**	**97, 800, 000**
7.	Venezuela	87, 035, 879
8.	Russian Federation	74, 400, 000
9.	Libya	41, 464, 000
10.	Nigeria	36, 220, 000
11.	United States	21, 317, 000
12.	China	16, 100, 000
13.	Mexico	12, 500, 000
14.	Algeria	12, 200, 000
15.	Angola	9, 035, 000
16.	Norway	8, 500, 000
17.	**Oman**	**5, 238, 000**
18.	United Kingdom	5, 002, 795
19.	**Neutral Zone**	**5, 000, 000**
20.	Indonesia	4, 979, 710
	Total	1, 293, 000, 000

Source: Organization of the Petroleum Exporting Countries, World Oil Outlook 2007. URL: http://www.opec.org/opec_web/static_files_project/media/downloads/publications/WorldOilOutlook.pdf

migrant workers. Indeed, the high number of foreign workers in the region only increases the populations' dependence, as they are not participating in the maintenance of their own societies but relying on the foreign workers for both manual labor and technical expertise. Such dependence has increasingly led to political instability, as manifested in mass protests of foreign workers in Kuwait and UAE in 2008, which resulted in mass deportations. The numbers are staggering: foreign workers were estimated to comprise 80 percent of the labor force in Kuwait prior to Iraq's invasion in 1990, and today only an estimated 11 percent of the UAE's 4.5 million population are citizens.[21] In the private sector foreigners form almost the entire workforce, reaching 98.6 percent in Kuwait and 99 percent in the UAE. Although dominated by construction and services, the private sector also employs foreign labor in agriculture and industry, especially in the intermediate and lower-level positions, while Gulf citizens maintain control of upper management. In Saudi Arabia foreign workers constitute some 55 percent of the population, while in Qatar the figure is 90 percent.[22] Most foreign workers come from South Asia, with an estimated 65 percent of the total from India and Pakistan. The second major grouping are fellow Arabs, comprising 25 percent, mostly from Egypt, Syria, Jordan (although Palestinians have been excluded due to their support of Saddam Hussein's invasion of Kuwait) and the Sudan. A further 5 percent are from Southeast Asia (Indonesia and Philippines), with 5 percent from Europe, too.[23]

The guest workers of the Gulf sheikhdoms, although fundamental to these countries' economies, work in the absence of firm legal protection and/or labor rights, and are frequently subjected to abuse and low pay. These difficult conditions were aggravated in 2008 with a worldwide rise in food prices. Accordingly, on March 19, over 1,500 low-paid workers in the UAE staged a violent wage protest, going "on strike and [rioting] in their living quarters in the industrial area of Sagaa in Sharijah . . . [They stoned] and [torched] dozens of cars and buses in the parking lot, and tried to attack police and Labor Ministry officials."[24] This most recent explosion of labor strife was preceded six months earlier by a similar incident in which thousands of construction workers – primarily of South Asian origin – went on strike, some engaging in violence. In the aftermath, the UAE detained 4,000 workers, laid charges against 159 and deported most of the remainder.

This predicament was replicated in Kuwait, where in late July 2008 an estimated "80,000 mostly Bangladeshi, cleaning workers joined a work stoppage,"[25] citing "poor wages, poor working conditions, overtime without pay, lack of sick leave and time off, etc."[26] In the subsequent week, the Kuwaiti government expelled 800 guest workers. On August 17, over 6,000 Bangladeshis resumed their protest "over non-payments and unlawful deductions of their salaries."[27] Again, the Kuwaiti government responded with mass expulsions, deporting as many as 1,286 Bangladeshi workers at the end of the month.[28] Many of the deported workers claimed to have been tortured by Kuwaiti police prior to their expulsion.[29]

Two weeks before the riots, an important Gulf state official had told the editor of *Al-Quds Al-Arabi*:

we reached the conclusion that the problem [of guest-worker discontent] was virtually impossible to resolve. Half of our citizens are naturalized. Do you want us to be transformed into a minority? If we continue to grant citizenships to [guest workers] . . . we prefer Indians. They are cheaper, more obedient and accept low wages. Who of the Arabs would agree to work for $100 a month or even $200 under difficult living conditions?[30]

A July 2008 report by the US-based National Labor Committee reported that Kuwaiti companies subcontracted to US military bases subjected South Asian guest workers to rampant abuse and exploitation. In one harrowing account, a Bangledeshi guest worker at the US Camp Arifjah said that he earned a paltry $34.72 for working a seventy-two-hour week. This endemic mistreatment of South Asian guest workers is cruelly ironic, given that Bangladesh contributed 2,300 soldiers to the international coalition that liberated Kuwait in 1991.[31]

Recognizing the severity of the labor situation, the Kuwaiti government made the tentative gesture of compelling errant firms to pay back-wages to the guest workers; that is to say, it merely enforced the terms of the workers' contracts. On September 10, 2008, the Kuwaiti parliament called an emergency session to study the question of labor strife in the guest-worker population, which ultimately resulted in the passage of labour law amendments in 2009.

The economies of the Arab Gulf states are integrated into the global economy as high-powered consumer economies: "high powered" not because of the size of the market but because of the size of the bankroll. They are economically independent of each other, which increases their absorptive capacities for the renewal of infrastructure technologies. Socially, economically and politically, oil has been the dominant factor in the Gulf's development. The revenues deriving from its extraction have fundamentally transformed the Gulf. With this wealth at their disposal, governments in the region have overseen great changes in the socio-economic situations of the GCC countries, which have kept their populations tranquil. Oil revenue also provides the greatest aid in maintaining power – control of the royal purse, the rulers' share of oil sales, which amounts to several billion dollars annually even in the case of tiny Qatar. The figure in Saudi Arabia may be up to $7 billion a year, out of estimated oil revenues of perhaps $50 billion. These tremendous financial resources allow the rulers of the Gulf states to run their economies essentially as private households.

However, although the GCC countries remain affluent, since the 1980s they have increasingly had to deal with economic problems. Sharp declines in the price of crude oil in the 1980s had a negative influence on their economies: the GCC's annual earnings declined from a high of $180 billion in 1981 to a low of $70 billion eight years later.[32] Attempts to compensate for this by developing industrial bases have thus far failed.

The 1991 Gulf War added to the GCC countries' economic problems. While the conclusion of the war was a victory for the GCC, particularly Kuwait, the economic dimension proved painful. Footing the cost of the war was a major financial burden to these states. The Saudi contribution, estimated at $60 billion,[33] exacerbated the endemic budgetary difficulties already facing the country. The situation was grave in Kuwait, too, since its oil exports had been halted. The Kuwaiti government had utilized income surpluses throughout the 1970s to build up investments abroad, so it was able to meet its financial obligations during and after the occupation. However, the requirements were still daunting. Indicative of the unfavorable economic environment, both Saudi Arabia (for the first time in its modern history) and Kuwait were forced to borrow money on the international markets to ease their immediate financial strains.[34]

Conscious of the drawbacks of over-reliance on one source of income, the GCC states are all trying to develop other sources of national income. At the forefront of this endeavor are the member countries that are facing early depletion of their oil reserves. Bahrain, with a burgeoning population, tried to shift the focus of its economy to financial services, but its efforts to promote itself as the commercial center of the Gulf were frustrated by the Iran–Iraq War. Now, it is pursuing industrialization through foreign investment. In addition to other concessions, it has relaxed ownership rules to allow foreign investors to own up to 100 percent of any business. Oman has also publicized a series of incentives to attract capital. The UAE has been the most successful in shifting its economy to the non-oil sector, which is an increasing source of revenue for the federation. Nevertheless, the federal budget still depends heavily on Abu Dhabi's oil revenues: it contributes about 60–75 percent of the total, Dubai about 15–20 percent, with the remainder coming from federal revenues such as taxes. Dubai, one of the wealthiest emirates, is becoming the principal gateway for the entry of business and trade to the Gulf region.[35] Qatar, with limited oil revenues, is becoming a major player in the world's liquefied natural gas market.

Deficit problems experienced by the GCC countries have called into question the role of the government in the economy. It has been suggested that a reduction in government spending and reactivation of the private sector offer long-term solutions to the problems of budget and balance of payment deficits. Most GCC states have adopted a series of reforms aimed at cutting government spending and boosting private enterprise. However, these policies have been implemented cautiously to avoid social unrest, given the high standard of living and parasitic reliance of the general economy on the oil sector.

Like much of the world, the global credit crunch of 2008–2009 adversely affected the Arab Gulf states. During the first three months of 2009, property values in Dubai contracted by 41 percent, which led to a mass exodus of speculative finance.[36] Moreover, thousands of foreign laborers – primarily Indians – exited at this time: 5,277 Indians left in the first four months of 2009, compared with just 894 in the same period the previous year. At the end of 2009, the government-owned Dubai World investment group asked creditors for extensions on its $59 billion debt, raising the specter of the largest government default since the Argentinian crisis of 2001. This led Moody's and Standard & Poor's to downgrade six Dubai-owned enterprises to "junk" status.[37] On December 14, the Dubai government was bailed out by Abu Dhabi, with a loan of $10 billion. Dubai immediately transferred $4.1 billion of that to service its debts.

Nevertheless, at the time of writing, Dubai's economy remained extremely precarious.[38]

Domestic affairs

The discovery of oil brought a social revolution to the nomad tribes of the region. The tiny, uneducated populations of the Gulf states were unable to meet the labor needs of the oil industry, so there was a tremendous influx of workers from Lebanon, Egypt, Palestine, India, Pakistan and East Asia. These expatriates have come to dominate the labor forces in all of the Gulf states. Since independence, the majority of Gulf workers in all sectors of the economy have generally been expatriates. The only significant sector of indigenous labor is the public sector, the second most important economic sector in the region, and even this has become possible only recently, as education levels of Gulf citizens have risen dramatically.

The first Gulf War totally distorted labor and population flows in the region, creating untold suffering to individuals and disrupting the economies of poor nations. But for some countries, it provided a welcome opportunity to effect drastic demographic changes. Kuwait openly expressed its desire to reduce its total population. Before the occupation, non-Kuwaitis made up 73 percent of the population and 86 percent of the workforce, and the government had made no secret of its plans to increase the proportion of Kuwaiti nationals in the workforce to at least 40 percent by 2015.[39] The Iraqi occupation caused two-thirds of Kuwaiti nationals and 90 percent of non-nationals to flee. In the aftermath of the war, Saudi Arabia expelled 800,000 Yemenis, while Kuwait expelled its Palestinian non-nationals.

However, the fallout of the war extended far beyond this. The domestic politics of the Gulf states were permanently altered. Citizens of these countries became more concerned with the manner in which they were being ruled. The gradual loss of faith in the leadership of the Gulf states, as well as in other states in the Arab Middle East, had commenced before the war, but the crisis hastened the process. Increasingly, people called for more say in politics and for more accountable leadership. This trend became so disturbing for some leaders that they gradually started to embrace a degree of political liberalization in their countries.

Table 10.2 Recent demographic information on GCC countries

Country	Year	Source	Nationals	Non-Nationals	Total
Saudi Arabia	2007	Estimate	22,024,962	5,576,076	27,601,038
Bahrain	2007	Estimate	473,465	235,108	708,573
Qatar	2007	Estimate			907,229
UAE	2005	Census			4,444,011
Oman	2007	Census	2,627,604	577,293	3,204,897
Kuwait	2007	Estimate	1,214,205	1,291,354	2,505,559

Source: CIA World Factbook. URL: https://www.cia.gov/library/publications/the-world-factbook/

Kuwait's ruling family reluctantly submitted to several demands of the opposition. Political developments there appear to be pointing toward more openness, but away from familiar patterns of democracy.[40] In 1992, the ruling family honored a pledge it had made while in exile to return the country to the 1962 constitution. Some 81,000 Kuwaitis, out of a population of 650,000, went to the polls on October 5 to elect 50 representatives (from 278 candidates) to a four-year national assembly. Only males over the age of twenty-one whose family background could be traced to a pre-1920 Kuwait were eligible to vote. The franchise was extended to naturalized Kuwaiti citizens of thirty years' standing in 1996. In June 2006, after a lobbying campaign that had begun in 1999, women went to the polls for the first time in Kuwait's history, having been granted the vote on May 16 the previous year. However, no woman was elected to parliament that year.

Resistance to the Iraqi invasion had been founded on an active civil society that existed before the war. More than fifty associations, including trade unions, and professional and politically oriented groups, had been registered in the country before the occupation.[41] These associations and non-associational groups played pivotal roles in organizing service provision and mobilizing civil disobedience. The non-associational groups, particularly the *diwanniya* – private rooms where men meet to socialize and exchange views – came to prominence when the formal associations could not function effectively owing to Iraqi restrictions. Kuwaiti women also played an important role both during and after the war. Several women lost their lives during demonstrations at the height of the anti-occupation campaign.

The fact that Kuwaiti society, rather than the state, organized resistance to the Iraqis laid the foundation for changes in the relationship between state and society in post-war Kuwait. For instance, education is now available to all, although disparities remain. Male literacy rates continue to surpass those of women, while urban women are generally better educated than their rural counterparts. Tradition and societal norms still have significant influence on levels of educational achievement, irrespective of what the law or official policy might say.

The parliamentary tradition in Kuwait is embedded in the socio-political life, which can be traced back to 1752, when the al-Sabahs, the present ruling family, migrated to Kuwait from al-Zubara, adjacent to the coast of Qatar. An alliance was formed between the indigenous community, comprising merchants and notables, and the al-Sabahs that was founded on consultation as the basis of the decision-making process. This pattern continued until 1896, when Sheikh Mubark al-Sabah came to power, ended the consultation process and initiated tribal domination of the political process.

In 1921, a reform movement requested the reinstitution of the consultation process, including the right of the community to have a say in the selection of the ruler. But this failed in the face of the intransigence of Sheikh Ahmad al-Jaber. In 1938, having been inspired by the Palestinian uprising of 1936, and under the influence of King Ghazy of Iraq, the reform movement demanded a constitutional regime and the building of a modern country, and insisted that Sheikh Ahmad create instruments to allow the people to have direct access to him. A legislative assembly was duly established and declared the Document of the Basic Law. However, the ruler dissolved it just six months later, and leading reformers were either jailed or exiled.

The declaration of the Kuwaiti constitution of 1962 was both a concession by the tribal regime in the face of Iraqi claims to Kuwaiti territory and the culmination of the political demands of the 1938 movement. According to Abdullah Fahd al-Nafisi, a respected Kuwaiti political scientist, the declaration was an attempt to shift opposition attention away from the al-Sabah royal family and made "the parliamentary experiment in Kuwait an instrument to protect British interests in that country."[42] The spirit of the constitution is based on the allegiance of the Kuwaiti people to the ruling family in return for the complete allegiance of the ruler to the constitution. However, over the next two decades, the ruling family and the government showed little tolerance for free expression or criticism, and in 1982 the ruler dissolved parliament and suspended popular political participation on the pretext of the Iraq–Iran War. Thereafter, he governed as a tribal chieftain.[43]

The return of parliamentary politics in 1992 was mainly due to the Western pressure, especially from the US, and the fact that the Kuwaiti people had struggled alone against the Iraqi invasion. Yet the elections of 1992,[44] 1996,[45] 1999, 2003, 2006 and 2008–2009 did not change the old political pattern of "compromise politics" that has been typical of Kuwaiti political life for almost a century. In this pattern – the modern form of traditional tribal politics – policies are rarely formed on the basis of the demands of the majority; rather, they are the result of manipulation by the ruling regime, which ends in a compromise between parliament and government and breeds factionalization in the opposition which works to the advantage of the rulers.

The 1992 election, which was generally considered to have been fairly contested, gave the opposition (a host of factions and independents who held a wide variety of views) a clear victory: 35 out of the 50 seats in the national assembly. The new assembly moved fast to assert its authority by passing legislation that aimed to promote more openness and accountability in the government and widen citizen participation in running the country. However, its overall performance disappointed many Kuwaitis, who were exasperated by the deputies' lengthy theoretical debates, particularly between Islamists and secularists, while the practical concerns of the electorate were ignored.[46] This served the interests of the government very well, given that the next elections were not far off; and the rulers were especially pleased to see the strength of the Islamists (their staunchest critics in the assembly) on the wane.

The political status of the Islamists has varied. While from 1996 to 2006, the Sunni Islamist bloc maintained a plurality of seats, this never resulted in the establishment of an Islamic legislative agenda. For instance, a bill supported by the Islamists to segregate male and female students in Kuwait University was never passed. The June 2006 elections saw a near tie and, in the most recent parliamentary elections of 2009, the Independent bloc won a decisive plurality of seats. Sixteen women ran in those elections and four were successful in becoming representatives.

In Saudi Arabia, the first Gulf War never seriously threatened the dominance of the royal family. Nevertheless, it had to contend with a rising tide of dissent and opposition, especially from the Islamic movement. The weakness of the ruling family and its dependence on the West were exposed as the crisis unfolded. Underwriting part of the cost of the war and the subsequent purchase of military hardware claimed a sizable proportion of Saudi wealth, which worsened the country's deficit difficulties. Tackling the debt problem had political ramifications, since public discontent was likely to increase if cuts were made to the extensive welfare system.

The Saudi regime is founded on the parallel authorities of the Wahhabbi religious establishment and the ruling family of al-Sa'ud. This historical equal-power relationship is manifested in the former's complete control over all social institutions (schools, press, religious foundations and all cultural establishments) and its hegemony in shaping socio-cultural norms. The Wahhabbi establishment is a collective hierarchical organization, comprising tens of thousands of members, and it exercises a degree of power over the populace that is comparable in magnitude and effect to that of the Vatican in Europe in the Middle Ages. Because the Wahhabbi organization is the source of religious legitimization for the regime, it possesses complete autonomy and the power of self-regulation.[47] As an indication of its power, during the Second World War, President Roosevelt asked King 'Abd al-Aziz for permission to deploy some American troops in the kingdom, but the king refused after the Wahhabbi establishment – who consider all non-Muslims to be infidels – made their objections clear.[48]

Political planning and policy formulation, and the whole process of maintaining his family's rule, is the domain of the ruler, without interference from Wahhabbism, which in terms of social control is independent of the political regime. However, there are a few issues that must be tackled bilaterally, such as deciding whether to open dialogue with non-Muslim entities; declaring emergency laws; public information policy; and declaring war. The last needs the input of the Wahhabbi establishment because of the religious implications of waging "holy war."[49]

The first Gulf War exposed the various currents within the Wahhabbi establishment and the conflicting views of different generations within society. The Wahhabbi leader, Ibn Baz, and his high-ranking entourage supported the foreign coalition by issuing edicts without any religious justification. However, as soon as the war began, opposition voices within Wahhabbism were loud and clear. This opposition comprised large sections of the Wahhabbi rank and file, including prominent figures like Mohammad Abdullah al-Massari, former president of the Grievance Board, Abdullah Bin Jabrin, a member of the Edict Authority, and Abdullah Bin Ku'ad, a member of the Supreme Council of the 'Ulama.

Following the war, the religious opposition submitted a 400-signature petition calling for reform of the army, an obvious slight against the royal family, whose members dominate the army and the air force. A year later, the same group submitted a "Petition of Counseling" to King Fahd, this time signed by forty-seven prominent Wahhabbi figures and university professors. This very public opposition, emphasizing the break with the tradition of holding secret meetings with the king to resolve points of contention, as well as the religious hard line of the splinter Wahhabbi group, threatened both the Wahhabbi establishment and the palace. The crisis deepened when the American Embassy in Saudi Arabia held meetings with the splinter group in the hope that it might be used to exert pressure on the regime over human rights abuses. Later, the opposition group opened offices in Britain and the USA.

A number of demonstrations were held, mainly organized by activist Muslims demanding the release of jailed opposition figures, but these precipitated a crack-down by the authorities during which several protesters were jailed.[50] The detained Islamic leaders had issued a petition to the king criticizing the deviation of the country from purist Islam in its foreign and domestic dealings. This underlines one facet of the Saudi opposition – it is fragmented between Islamist and liberal bases, who are unlikely to agree on anything besides a vague anti-Americanism and a desire for "democracy," a word which means very different things to the two parties.[51] Although this wave of opposition did not constitute a major problem for the regime, it could not be ignored. The significance of al-Massari as an opposition figure was hard to determine, but he certainly succeeded in demonstrating the existence of a front upon which the regime might be challenged.[52]

In response to unprecedented Western pressure, the Saudi regime reluctantly initiated a so-called liberalization process.[53] In March 1992, King Fahd announced the establishment of the Majlis al-Shura (Consultative Council) to help in governing the country. The Majlis, with its appointed members, would simply formalize the system of consultation that was already in place.[54] This consultation involves the holding of regular *diwans* (public audiences) by senior Saudis during which any citizen, in theory, can air his views and grievances. The sixty-member Majlis finally convened for the first time on December 29, 1994. King Fahd used the occasion to caution that pluralism, democracy and other alien ideas were not for Saudi Arabia. The delay in convening the Majlis may have been due to the rise in domestic Islamic activism. The king had been keen to balance the influence of religious and secular elements in society. Perhaps to tame the increasing influence of the Islamic forces, he had reshuffled the Supreme Council of the 'Ulama in November 1992, ousting ten of its eighteen members.[55]

Also in 1992, the king adopted by decree the "Basic Law of Saudi Arabia," which serves as an exposition of the country's formal constitution (the Qur'an and the Sunnah). This law was drafted by an ad hoc committee of the Interior Ministry and reinforced the political dynamics of the kingdom, affirming the country's Islamic basis and the unchallenged rule of the monarch. It provided the basis for the creation of the Majlis while leaving oligarchic rule intact and denying the basic freedoms of an open society (freedom of expression, freedom of assembly, freedom of association, religious freedom, and so on). Apostasy is a capital crime in Saudi Arabia, and if the "guilty" person does not recant, he is liable to capital or at least corporal punishment. Christian and Hindu guest workers have been harassed and/or deported on occasion. For instance, in March 2005, a makeshift

Hindu temple was razed by the religious police, and the worshipers were deported. Even Shi'a Muslims have been harassed by the authorities and have frequently been identified as errant or deviant in their beliefs. They are often denied state positions and the more visible aspects of Shi'a celebration are banned.

Since the creation of the Majlis, Saudi Arabia has made very few moves toward democracy. Even when there is a glimmer of hope that some progress is being made, it is snuffed out. For instance, the 2005 municipal elections saw half of each council elected by popular vote for the first time (the other half was, as usual, formed by royal appointment). Women were excluded from this process, but it was rumored that they would be eligible to vote in the next round of elections, due to be held in 2009. However, this became a moot point in early 2009, when the regime quietly postponed the municipal elections "for a few years" for "consultative purposes."[56] Thus ended Saudi Arabia's brief flirtation with political liberalization.

Other countries of the GCC have established their own consultative councils. Oman's Majlis al-Shura, established in 1991, is an elected body that allows women's participation (the first time that any GCC women were allowed to play an active role in politics). The Majlis is now an 83-member body, but unfortunately its legislative power extends little further than proposing laws and offering suggestions to the still-unchallenged monarch. The process of filling the 83 seats involves the selection of elders, prominent businessmen and intellectuals in each of the 59 provinces, who vote for 2 or 4 nominees (depending on the population of the province) and thereby create a pool of 160 people, out of whom the sultan picks the members of the Majlis. The council has no say in foreign, defense or security affairs.[57]

Likewise, Bahrain set up an appointed Majlis with limited powers in November 1992. However, this was no replacement for the elected assembly that was dissolved in August 1975. Consequently, demands for the restoration of the liberal constitution that had been adopted after independence intensified. In December 1994, clashes between the police and protesters left a number of people dead and many others detained, leading to concern over human rights abuses in Bahrain.

In 1999 Sheikh Hamad bin Isa Al Khalifa became emir on the death of his father, Sheikh Isa. He initiated social and political reforms and ended the political repression that had defined the 1990s by scrapping state security laws, releasing all political prisoners, instituting elections, giving women the right to vote, promising a return to constitutional rule, and inviting all of Bahrain's exiles, irrespective of their political beliefs, to return home. Some of the returnees were subsequently appointed as cabinet ministers.

In 2001 Sheikh Hamad proposed the National Action Charter (NAC), which presented a vision of Bahrain moving toward a more democratic society. It was supposed to represent the Bahraini political consensus on future reform. The following year, Hamad promulgated a new constitution, which was actually an amended version of the 1973 one. It asserted that Bahrain is a constitutional monarchy ruled by a king; that the king is succeeded by his son; and that the elected and royally appointed chambers of parliament have equal legislative power. The opposition rejected this from the outset. As a result, the parliamentary elections held on October 26, 2002 were boycotted by four "political societies" labeled as the "Quadruple Alliance," primarily in protest against the powers of the appointed Shura Council.

The elections to the Council of Representatives witnessed the participation of women as both voters and candidates for the first time in Bahrain. However, none was elected, and the Council of Representatives was dominated by Islamists. King Hamad responded by appointing six women to the Shura Council. (The first female cabinet minister was appointed two years later, when Dr. Nada Hafadh became minister of health.) Hamad also appointed a number of liberals to the Shura Council, to counterbalance the Islamist influence in the Council of Representatives. The second elections to the Council of Representatives were held in November 2006. Most of the opposition groups that had boycotted the 2002 elections took part this time. The turnout was 72 percent, and Islamist political societies, both Shi'ite and Sunni, made major gains.

According to the 1971 constitution of the UAE, legislative power is invested in the forty-member Federal National Council, a consultative body whose members are appointed by the emirates' rulers. This provision was later amended to inject an element of public choice. The first elections to the council were held in 2006, with twenty of the forty members now elected to serve two-year terms. (The other half continues to be appointed by the rulers of the seven constituent emirates.) The council has only advisory powers.

Qatar's constitution, approved in April 2003 by popular referendum, created a Shura Council, a legislative body with forty-five members, thirty of whom are to be elected by universal suffrage, with the other fifteen appointed by the emir. According to the constitution, the council has the power to approve (but not prepare) the national budget; to monitor the performance of ministers and censure them through no-confidence votes; and to draft, discuss and vote on proposed legislation, which becomes law only with a two-thirds majority in the council and the emir's endorsement. However, the first elections to the Shura Council had yet to be held at the time of writing.

All of the GCC states ban the formation of political parties. However, "political societies" are now allowed in Bahrain, while in Kuwait certain political forces act as political parties. The most important of these is the Ummah Party, representing some Islamists. Freedom of the press is severely restricted in Saudi Arabia, the UAE and Oman, but the other GCC states allow a little more freedom of expression.

Foreign affairs

Western, especially American, intervention during the first Gulf War checked potential Iraqi incursion into other GCC countries after its occupation of Kuwait. More importantly, it eventually restored Kuwaiti independence. Although the GCC countries remain dependent on Western protection against potential adversaries, this status quo does not answer the long-term security concerns of these states. Rather than strengthening the position of the ruling families, it seriously undermines it. Reliance on a Western security umbrella is never popular with some sectors of these conservative societies, especially the Islamists. Viewed from the context of rising Islamic activism, it is indeed a sensitive issue. Saudi opposition to the presence of foreign troops on their soil after the war highlights the gravity of the matter. Some Western analysts have raised doubts not only about rivalries within the house of al-Sa'ud, but about a troubled regime that is under serious challenge. Among its problems are the growth of an Islamist opposition movement; a middle-class seeking to break the princely monopoly on decision-making; cuts in the vast welfare system; high-level corruption; and foreign policies that are widely seen as subservient to the economic and political interests of the United States.[58]

Perceived threats to the GCC countries are a cause for concern. The Saudi and Iranian regimes have been implacably hostile to one another for political, economic and ideological reasons for over thirty years. The Saudis are clients of Iran's greatest enemy, both states are massively dependent on oil exports, and the Wahhabbi and Shi'ites regard each other as heretical. However, it would not be in the Saudis' interests to see the fundamentalist regime toppled, as it seems certain that a Western-leaning Iran would quickly replace the Gulf state as the leading American client in the region. This is unlikely to happen, though, as Washington has displayed no appetite for any thaw in its relations with Tehran. Nevertheless, hostile ideological and political ideas are on the rise; and internal differences among the GCC countries themselves could flare up into open conflict.

Individually, these countries lack the capacity to build formidable armies that could resist an Iranian military onslaught, so they have been forced to find other ways to guarantee their security. For instance, a mutual defense pact between Egypt, Syria and the GCC was signed in Damascus in March 1991. It envisioned the provision of a permanent force of between 100,000 and 150,000 Syrian and Saudi Arabian troops to support the defense forces of the other GCC countries. This would be funded by the GCC. However, this pact had run into difficulties before the year was out. As an alternative, the GCC countries explicitly expressed their desire for Western protection. A series of defense pacts with Western and other powers duly followed. Kuwait signed a ten-year pact with the USA in 1991, followed by agreements with the other permanent members of the UN Security Council. Other members of the GCC also increased their cooperation with the world's major powers. The effectiveness of this policy was tested when threatening Iraqi forces were deployed close to the Kuwaiti border in October 1994. The UN and the Americans responded promptly and decisively, and the Iraqis were forced to withdraw under threat of military action.

On another front, fresh efforts were devoted to revitalizing defense cooperation between the GCC member states. Oman proposed the establishment of a force of 100,000 men, with the clear intention that most of them would be Omani. There was no enthusiasm for this plan among the other GCC states. Instead, Saudi Arabia proposed a gradual expansion of the peninsula shield force based on its territory. However, this was rejected, too. Thus, lack of consensus on a concrete course of action continued to undermine hopes for a unified defense among the GCC countries. Unresolved border disputes and national pride remain divisive factors, which thwart the attainment of meaningful defense integration. Even where some form of cooperation has been achieved, difficulties often crop up. During the course of joint military exercises in 1992, planned maneuvers had to be canceled because the Omani forces refused to take orders from Saudi commanders. Likewise, Kuwaitis have been reluctant to serve under Omanis. This national pride has extended to the acquisition of military equipment. Generally, each country has gone to great lengths to purchase hardware that is radically different from whatever has been bought by its neighbours.[59] Of course, this makes the prospect of establishing an effective, unified defense force even more remote.

Nevertheless, a GCC defense ministers meeting in Abu Dhabi on November 8, 1993 reiterated the members' determination to establish a Gulf defense force. Individually, these countries had invested a lot to enhance their defensive capabilities. Immediately after the cessation of hostilities in 1991, there had been panic buying of military equipment. Saudi Arabia put in large orders for arms to strengthen its ground forces as well as its air defense. It also rapidly expanded its manpower – from 40,000 at the time of the war to 73,000 by the end of 1993. Similarly, Kuwait embarked on building a massive army from scratch. However, the worsening economic climate soon put the brakes on both countries' military expansion. For instance, Saudi Arabia was forced to suspend an order of 150 M1A2 tanks from the USA because of cash-flow problems. Furthermore, the Kuwaiti government had to contend with constant probes into its military spending by its opposition-dominated national assembly. Worse yet, these large purchases of military equipment have not been absorbed by the two countries' armed forces; and as they lack the technical expertise to service it, much of the hardware is maintained by American and European contractors.

The UAE has historically been better off as far as the question of liquidity is concerned, and it may end up spending more on defense than all of the other GCC countries combined. However, whether that spending is based on any semblance of rationality is another thing entirely. The UAE can field fourteen different kinds of armored vehicle in its federal army of 65,000 troops, due to the rather whimsical procurement policies of various officials. In March 2000, the UAE ordered eighty F-14 fighter jets, at an approximate cost of $6.4 billion, from Lockheed Martin.[60] However, the UAE already had ninety-seven modern aircraft that were of dubious utility because none of the emirates had the ground facilities or associated infrastructure required for modern air operations.

Kingdom of Saudi Arabia

Saudi Arabia is the largest of the GCC states at 1,226,480 square kilometers, most of which is desert. The two most notoriously extensive desert parts are al-Rub' al-Khali (about 647,000 square kilometers) and al-Nofud (about 56,580 square kilometers).[61] The population is about 27.6 million. The harsh geography has had a strong impact on the socio-demographic structure of the country. It is mainly nomadic pastoralist, with a portion of quasi-nomads who settled in the few oases. The traditional tribe was the principal social constituency until the 1930s. The production of oil, and the incorporation of the Bedouin into the oil industry, led to the decline of pure Bedouin, and by 1989 they had completely disappeared.[62] Up to the discovery of oil, and the accumulation of wealth, the economy was based on pasture, agriculture-based oases and Hajj trade (pilgrimage).[63] From the fall of the Abbassid dynasty in 1258 until 1744, when the first Saudi/Wahhabbi state was established, the peninsula did not experience any central authority. It was characteristically in a state of fragmentation in which tribal traditions and way of life dominated.[64]

History

The al-Sa'ud family dominates the history of Saudi Arabia. Over the years, this family has skillfully employed religion and later oil to build a state from groups that have little in common. However, the road to this has not been smooth, and there have been a lot of failures along the way. The founder of the modern state of Saudi Arabia was 'Abdul-Aziz Ibn 'Abdul-Rahman Ibn Sa'ud, commonly known as Ibn Sa'ud. However, to understand fully how he managed to do this, it is necessary to look at the Saudi dynasties that preceded his kingdom.

The al-Sa'uds established the town of Dir'iyya, located at the heart of the Najd region in the central Arabian Peninsula, as their capital. This Najd homeland was isolated for centuries because of its geography. Crucial to the consolidation of the rule of al-Sa'uds in the extension beyond Najd was the role played by Imam Mohammad Ibn 'Abd al-Wahhab, who founded the Wahhabbi movement. Ibn 'Abd al-Wahhab, born in 1703 in Najd to a family deeply rooted in Islamic law, received religious education in several Islamic cities. He was dismayed by what he considered deviations from the Islamic faith, and hence decided to advocate a return to the true faith and the strict application of its laws (as he deemed fit). His preaching, however, never sat well with his people and he was soon expelled. In 1744, he took refuge in Dir'iyya under the protection of Mohammad Ibn Sa'ud, the first ruler of the house of al-Sa'ud, where the climate was more accommodating. Eventually, his ideas led to the establishment of a theocratic state, the first Saudi state, and gave rise to the military expansion of that state beyond the borders of Najd.[65] Wahhabbism provided the moral and ideological basis for uniting various tribes in the Arabian Peninsula under the al-Sa'uds. Macca and Medina were occupied, the Shi'a holy places of Najaf and Karbala in Iraq were attacked, and taxes were levied in Aleppo in northern Syria. This expansion incurred the wrath of the Ottoman sultan, who decided to act. The viceroy in Cairo, Mohammad 'Ali, was asked to put an end to the Wahhabbi state and a military offensive ensued from 1811 to 1818,[66] which culminated in the destruction of Dir'iyya and the capture and execution in Constantinople of the state's ruler, Abdullah. Thus ended the first realm of the Saudi/Wahhabbi state (1744–1818).

In spite of this defeat, the al-Sa'ud family soon regained political control over central Arabia. Abdullah's uncle organized his forces and established Riyadh as his capital, then extended his control over the whole of Najd and the eastern areas. The Egyptians were forced to withdraw to Hijaz. Faisal succeeded his deceased father, Turki, in 1834 and ruled for the next four years, when Mohammad 'Ali defeated and imprisoned him in Egypt. Khalid Ibn Sa'ud, a rival claimant to Saudi leadership, who himself had been in custody in Egypt since the defeat of Abdullah, was installed as the new ruler under the supervision of the Egyptian forces. Later, Mohammad 'Ali withdrew the overextended Egyptian forces following the signing of the Treaty of London in 1840, which had downsized his rule. Three years later, Faisal al-Turki escaped from jail and regained control in Najd, ushering in his second reign (1843–1865), a period described as the "golden age of the second realm."[67]

Faisal's death in 1865 was followed by a long period of civil war among his sons. The instability provided the Turks with the opportunity to occupy the eastern region in 1871. Also, the growing strength of the al-Rashids, who had been put in power by the al-Sa'uds in Jabal Shammar, was a looming threat. Eventually, Mohammad Ibn Rashid, the tribal leader of the Shammar tribe, extended his control over the whole of Najd. The Battle of Mulaida, in 1891, between the forces of Mohammad Ibn Rashid and the al-Sa'uds under the command of Faisal's youngest son, 'Abdul Rahman, dealt the final blow to the second Saudi/Wahhabbi state, although 'Abdul Rahman and his family escaped to Kuwait. A witness to this defeat and the exit of his family from their homeland was the fifteen-year-old son of 'Abdul Rahman, 'Abdul-Aziz Ibn 'Abdul-Rahman Ibn Sa'ud, who would later establish the kingdom of Saudi Arabia. In exile, the defeated father prepared his son for a future that would restore the glory of the family. He received a strict religious education, thorough tutelage in the art of war, and, by attending Kuwait's Majlis, a grounding in governance.

In 1902, leading a small force of between forty and sixty relatives and retainers, Ibn Sa'ud attacked and overran Riyadh, killing nearly every member of the garrison, including the governor of the town. The news of this success pleased Sheikh Mubarak of Kuwait, who immediately dispatched warriors to support Ibn Sa'ud's position. Meanwhile, Mohammad Ibn Rashid was furious and vowed revenge. To consolidate his hold of the town, Ibn Sa'ud raided the neighboring Bedouin tribes. When he felt strong enough, he called his father to join him. On May 11, 1902, 'Abdul Rahman left Kuwait to do just that. For Ibn Sa'ud, the main factor motivating his struggle, particularly up to the time of Mohammad Ibn Rashid's death, was the desire to avenge their familial honor.[68] However, this would soon prove insufficient to build a kingdom.

The al-Rashids lost territory and soon they sought military support from the Turks, which was provided because the Turks were wary of the friendship between Ibn Sa'ud and Mubarak, who, in turn, was a friend of the British. In July and August 1904, a series of battles took place between the opposing groups, with the Turk–al-Rashid alliance finally being defeated. Mohammad Ibn Rashid was killed near Burayda, and was succeeded by Mitab Ibn 'Abdul Aziz Ibn al-Rashid.

Ibn Sa'ud's experiences in this period of conflict convinced him that professed loyalty to his leadership would be insufficient to hold his followers together. For instance, on many occasions, the Bedouin, having promised their support, had melted away at first sight of battle. Hence, he conceived the idea of fostering loyalty not only to him but to an ideology – Wahhabbism – which would be spread by the "Hafr." This refers to the departure of Wahhabbi preachers into the desert to teach the Bedouin the true and pure word of Islam. These religiously zealous preachers transformed the Bedouin into a loyal, formidable force who were prepared to fight as Ikhwan (Brothers) under Ibn Sa'ud in order to spread the true Islam.[69] By 1916, all of the Bedouin were members of the Ikhwan, and the tribal sheikhs were required to attend an Islamic law school in the mosque in Riyadh.[70]

This gave the struggle a truly religious dimension. The Ikhwan were good fighters and helped Ibn Sa'ud to take al-Ahsa' on May 9, 1913. Its Turkish defenders were then allowed safe passage to Bahrain. In what amounted to international recognition, Ibn Sa'ud concluded a treaty with the British in 1915 (the Darin Treaty), in which Najd, al-Ahsa', al-Qatif and al-Jubayl, as well as their dependencies and territories, were all recognized as falling under his suzerainty.[71] Ibn Sa'ud was given a subsidy to encourage him to fight Ibn al-Rashid and the Turks, and to discourage him from starting a war with Hussein bin 'Ali, the ruler of Hijaz, who was on the Allied side. However, Ibn Sa'ud's actions jeopardized this agreement, and Hussein audaciously declared himself "king of all Arabs" after receiving an arms consignment. In 1919, he was bold enough to attack Wahhabbi territory, but his forces were quickly annihilated.

After a three-month siege, the defenders of Ibn al-Rashid's headquarters of Hail surrendered, bringing to an end the house of al-Rashid as a rival family. Meanwhile, Hussein suffered a series of defeats in battles aimed at securing his territory. In December 1925, Jeddah, the last town to fall in Hijaz, came under Ibn Sa'ud's control. By 1927, he was being hailed the king of Hijaz and the sultan of Najd.

Hijaz was more sophisticated than Najd, with both its government and its educational system organized along modern lines. "Purifying" the region became a serious point of contention between the Ikhwan and Ibn Sa'ud. The zealous Ikhwan were determined to apply their brand of Wahhabbism, but they were never allowed a free hand to do so. It was their insistence on equating Wahhabbism with a simple lifestyle that caused problems in Hijaz.[72] This was also the core of the disagreement between the Ikhwan and townspeople. The Bedouin considered the telephone, telegraph and radio works of the devil that should be eliminated. Over time, they began to undermine the leadership of Ibn Sa'ud, and sought ways of provoking an open conflict with him. By 1928, Faisal al-Dawish of Mutayr, Sultan b. Humayd b. Bijab of 'Utayb and Didan b. Hithlin of al-'Ujman were aligned against Ibn Sa'ud and his loyal forces. Secretly, they had agreed to carve up Saudi territory among themselves. Following a series of clashes, the final battle was fought and won by Ibn Sa'ud on September 9, 1929. Faysal ad-Dawish died in jail on October 30, 1931, having been extradited from Kuwait to Riyadh by the British. Sultan Bijab surrendered and later died in jail in al-Ahsa. Matters regarding religion would henceforth be referred to the 'Ulama, and the Ikhwan movement came to an end.

On September 18, 1932, a decree was issued changing the name of the realm to the Kingdom of Saudi Arabia. The future unity and development of the kingdom would be based on modernization, which was assured by the discovery of oil. In 1938, after years of exploration, oil was discovered in large quantities, which immediately led to the formation of the Arabian American Oil Company (ARAMCO). Oil transformed the kingdom into a financial power and tremendously increased its influence around the world. Massive development programs and improvement of the living conditions of the people kept the population happy and maintained the unity of the country.

Ibn Sa'ud died on November 9, 1953, and was succeeded by his son, Prince Sa'ud. However, the latter lacked the extraordinary leadership qualities of his father. He could not arrest the social and moral disintegration of Saudi society, despite colossal oil revenues. To mollify discontent, the royal family and the Wahhabbi leaders transferred executive power to Crown Prince Faisal in 1958. King Sa'ud regained power in 1960, only to be deposed once again in 1964. Thereafter, Faisal restored Saudi political legitimacy. In March 1965, he appointed his half-brother, Khalid Ibn 'Abd al-Aziz, crown prince and indulged in a regional power struggle with Nasserism. He shrewdly used Islam to counterbalance Arab nationalism, and established the Organization of the Islamic Conference.

On March 25, 1975, Faisal was assassinated by one of his nephews, and Crown Prince Khalid ascended to the throne. However, he died suddenly on June 13, 1982, and his younger brother, Fahd, took over. Abdullah Ibn 'Abd al-Aziz, a half brother to the king, became crown prince and first deputy prime minister. Fahd turned out to be a shrewd political operator who was capable of balancing conflicting secular and clerical interests, and maintaining at least an appearance of independence from Saudi Arabia's American patrons. In early 1996, after a long period of failing health, he suffered a stroke and Prince Abdullah performed his duties without officially replacing him. Abdullah is viewed as more of a traditional conservative than Fahd, favoring Arab self-reliance over overtly pro-American policies,[73] but there was no immediate change in Saudi policy. The ailing monarch increasingly faded into the background, leaving functional rule to Abdullah. King Fahd finally died on August 1, 2005, and was formally succeeded by Abdullah.

While Saudi Arabia remains in the US camp, King Abdullah's regime has proven less compliant than those of previous monarchs. For instance, in March 2007, at the Arab League Summit, he lamented the sectarian violence in Iraq and condemned the US presence there as an "illegitimate foreign occupation."[74] This prompted much US consternation, as could be expected.

Politics and government

Saudi society is traditional, and Islam is strictly observed. The old social networks, such as the tribe, the extended family and other sectarian connections, are bound by and into the state.[75] These relationships form the core of societal cohesion and shape the political culture of the kingdom. The extended family is the central unit of the community, within which the different sexes are assigned their separate roles. The male plays a dominant part in the life of the community, while the female is subjected to onerous restrictions. Women are barred from public office, never allowed to travel unaccompanied without the written permission of a spouse or father, banned from driving, and required to wear a veil and long black robe in public. Protesting against their treatment, some veiled women defied the ban and drove themselves around central Riyadh during the first Gulf War, which drew a swift response from the government: the ban was transformed into a civil law. Women are compelled to devise survival strategies, and alternative methods of expression and communication, to cope in this stifling environment. Access to information sources is entwined within the kingdom's efforts to modernize while maintaining traditional social values, and Saudi women have proven resourceful in their efforts to access information through any means possible, including the internet.[76] They are also successfully turning to business and the professions. It is reported that 40 percent of private wealth in Saudi Arabia is in the hands of women, and that women now outnumber men in some of the sciences and medicine.[77] However, full female emancipation is still a long way off.

Despite its massive spending on armaments, Saudi Arabia does not maintain a large armed force by regional standards. The ruling family may well have limited the army's size specifically to stop it becoming an internal threat to their power. Perhaps also for this reason, a National Guard consisting entirely of Bedouin with strong tribal and religious loyalty to the al-Sa'ud family is maintained. This is nearly as large and as well equipped as the regular army.

The distribution of power in the kingdom is skewed in favor of the ruling family. *Forbes* estimated the personal wealth of King Abdullah as \$21 billion in 2008.[78] From the founding of the kingdom up to the time when oil revenues started to flow into Saudi coffers, the affairs of state were managed just like those of a household. Ibn Sa'ud kept a tight grip on the running of the country, including management of its income. He dispensed funds according to his will, mainly to win the support of others. However, with the oil bonanza and the accompanying affluence, a proliferation of institutions and a network of responsibilities gradually emerged. There was therefore a need for an administrative capability to handle the government machinery. The management of the oil economy especially required new administrative and management inputs. Initially, foreigners met this demand, but as the education of Saudi nationals progressed, they assumed an increasing role in the running of their country.

In a token response to demands for change, in March 1992 a Majlis al-Shura was established to function as a purely consultative council. It was initially composed of 61 members, but this was increased to 90 in 1996 and thereafter to 150. All members are appointed by royal decree, and they are all men. Before the Majlis's formation, the leadership of the kingdom managed public affairs single-handedly, with little input from the public. A council of ministers manages the socio-economic, administrative and political affairs of state, but the powers of the monarch remain supreme. Executive power rests with him, so he has the exclusive jurisdiction to pass laws, initiate policies and oversee their implementation.[79] He also holds the position of prime minister, which means the members of the council are directly accountable to him. But members of the royal family hold most of the crucial portfolios in the council anyway. The sole experiment in democracy, and a hollow one at that, comprised the municipal elections of 2005, involving 178 of Saudi Arabia's municipalities. This sop to the regime's domestic and international critics did not alter the regime's autocratic principles a whit. Needless to say, women were excluded from the whole process, a decision that was lamely justified on logistical grounds.

Saudi Arabia has increasingly attempted to play the role of regional leader since the first Gulf War, especially once the Middle East peace process began to collapse in late 1995. An Arab leader largely by default, because of its tremendous wealth, Saudi Arabia has joined Israel and Egypt in jockeying for position as the chief American deputy in the region. However, while it has the closest involvement in the pivotal American interest in the region – oil – Saudi Arabia lacks a commitment to developing a strong military and has the specter of a difficult succession and accompanying instability in the near future. Also, it has proved increasingly reluctant to act as a base for American troops. By 2003, reflecting changing regional dynamics and exposing the latent pressures in US–Saudi relations, US troops left the country. US–Saudi relations deteriorated further with the invasion and occupation of Iraq, which destroyed the traditional buffer between Saudi Arabia and Iran.

Saudi relations with Iran have oscillated between accommodation and confrontation. After the diplomatic chill that dominated the late 1980s and much of the 1990s, relations warmed in 1997 when Crown Prince Abdullah visited Tehran, becoming the highest-ranking Saudi official to do so since the Islamic revolution. Subsequently, Iranian President Khatami visited Saudi Arabia in 1999, and the countries signed a security pact in 2001. However, this diplomatic thawing was halted with the US invasion and occupation of Iraq, which bolstered Iran's power in the region. Since then, all of the Arab Gulf states, with Saudi Arabia at the forefront, have criticized Iran's activities in Iraq. They are likewise suspicious of the country's nuclear program.

Saudi Arabia has recently intervened in neighboring Yemen's "Houthi insurgency." A rebellion by the Shi'a Zaidiyyah under the leadership of dissident cleric Hussein Badreddin al-Houthi has been raging since 2004, primarily in the Sa'dah Governorate. While the Houthi rebels have long accused Saudi Arabia of collaborating with the Yemeni government, Saudi Arabia's direct intervention in the conflict began only in November 2009, when Houthi rebels killed a Saudi border guard and captured villages within Saudi territory. This initial clash culminated in Saudi Arabia launching heavy air strikes against the rebels in northern Yemen. In December 2009, the Saudi government announced that seventy-three of its soldiers had been killed and that its major combat operations were now over. In response, the Houthi rebels promised continued resistance. The Saudi media has repeatedly accused Iran of having a hand in the Houthi rebellion, threatening further degradation of Saudi–Iranian relations.[80] The role of the United States in the Yemeni conflict remains ambiguous. From December 14, 2009 onward, the United States launched a series of air strikes in northern Yemen, claiming al-Qa'ida activity in the region and stating that an "imminent attack against a US asset was being planned."[81] This was an odd justification as the targeted regions, the northern Shi'a provinces, would be an inhospitable environment for al-Qa'ida sympathizers. In light of these attacks, the Houthi rebels have claimed that the US is collaborating with the Saudi regime against them.[82]

Kuwait

Kuwait today is a far cry from its beginnings as a trading and fishing center in the eighteenth century. Oil revenues have turned it into one of the wealthiest states in the Gulf, and indeed the entire world. The oil boom after the Second World War transformed Kuwait into a welfare state with a rapidly expanding economy. Welfarism has not been without its drawbacks, though, as dependence on oil has placed Kuwait in a vulnerable position. It is also geographically vulnerable, given its proximity to the Gulf's most prominent powers – Iran, Iraq and Saudi Arabia – all of which have had dramatic effects on Kuwaiti development.

Kuwait entered the international arena as an independent state in June 1961, upon terminating its treaty ties with Great Britain. According to al-Nafisi, "Kuwait hasn't achieved yet the full and complete transformation from tribalism into the state," although it emphasizes the formality of its statehood. Anyone living in Kuwait for any length of time soon learns the truth: all public affairs are conducted in a wholly tribal way.[83] All political parties are banned and there is no genuine opposition. Even those members of parliament who are officially in opposition to the government do not challenge the status quo. Al-Nafisi says, "Kuwait is now in an extraordinary condition because, since the liberation from the Iraqi invasion, it has experienced administrative decay, social chaos, corruption, cultural and intellectual confusion and increased foreign domination."[84]

Kuwaiti statehood was challenged early on. In the 1960s, Iraq renewed its historical claims to Kuwait based on the fact that it had fallen under the jurisdiction of Basra during the long period of Ottoman rule. To retain their sovereignty, the Kuwaitis enlisted the support of the British and, later, the League of Arab States. In 1968, when the Ba'th regime came to power in Iraq, the basis of its threat shifted from historical territorial claims to ideological challenges. Despite its attempts at government reform, Kuwait remained a conservative monarchy that was the antithesis of the Ba'thist ideology. However, Kuwait managed to dilute its northern neighbor's hostility to some extent by adopting an Arab nationalist stance in regional issues, such as the Arab–Israeli conflict. It was one of the first Arab states to sever relations with West Germany after Bonn initiated relations with Israel; it sent troops to Egypt during the Six Day War; and it was a strong supporter of the Palestinian cause. Aside from these issues, however, Kuwait has more or less adopted a pragmatic approach to its foreign policy – for instance, maintaining its British accounts after the 1967 and 1973 Arab–Israeli wars rather than moving them elsewhere.

Despite its small size, Kuwait was an important player in the Arab world throughout the 1970s and 1980s because of the Kuwait Fund – a foreign aid fund made possible by its massive oil revenues. The fund was distributed throughout the Third World by an arm of the Kuwaiti Foreign Ministry. In the Arab world,

Kuwait aided states at all points on the ideological spectrum, but it was also prepared to withdraw funds if necessary, as it did from Egypt after the Camp David Accords.

While the Iran–Iraq War never really threatened Kuwaiti territory (save for Iraqi mining of Kuwaiti waters in 1987), it did affect its ability to secure access routes into and out of the Gulf. Iran attacked a number of Kuwaiti tankers, and the pressure was such that the Kuwaitis grew concerned about their continued ability to trade. They therefore approached the Soviet Union and the United States for help in keeping open the export routes through the Gulf. The Soviets lent the Kuwaitis a small number of vessels and agreed to provide naval protection to Kuwaiti ships. The US responded in kind and even reflagged a number of Kuwaiti tankers. Kuwait thus managed to ensure the safety of its oil exports through the Gulf.

Political situation

Kuwait has a longer and deeper history of political involvement than any other Gulf state, save Bahrain, and it is home to the longest-running national assembly in the region. Early Kuwait was ruled by an oligarchy of noble families, all of which were Sunni Arabs, who selected a political leader from among themselves. One of these leaders was Sabah al-Jaber, whose family has since ruled Kuwait. The process demanded that the man chosen as leader was to rule in accordance with the endorsement of the leaders of the other families. There was therefore a high degree of consultation. However, at the turn of the twentieth century, Sheikh Mubarak al-Sabah, who came to power in 1896, and his son Selim abandoned these informal lines of communication and sought to expand the family's authority throughout Kuwait. Unsurprisingly, these attempts met with considerable opposition. Sheikh Selim was highly unpopular because of disputes with Ibn Sa'ud that negatively affected Kuwait's relationship with Arabia. The decline in trade with Arabia and the resulting economic problems prompted the merchant class to pressure the al-Sabah family to establish some kind of formal consultative body after Selim's death in 1921. The family agreed and a council was formed with twelve representatives from the merchant class. However, it proved to be ineffectual and inefficient.

By 1928, the council no longer existed, but demands for more democratic institutions rose to challenge the ruling family. Kuwait was exposed to the nationalist ideals that were so common in the Arab world at the time, and by 1938 demands for a new consultative council were being renewed. Sheikh Ahmad (Selim's successor) was unpopular in Kuwait, and his family's rule was challenged by elements in Iraq. In addition, a Saudi blockade that had been initiated in 1923, the absence of any kind of development plan, and charges of financial incompetence led to a great deal of popular dissatisfaction. Kuwaiti exiles in Iraq formed opposition groups – the al-Shabiba and the National Bloc – and other groups of all ideological persuasions began to spring up both outside and within the country. A number of Kuwaitis were arrested, and discontent was exhibited by some important notables, which aroused the suspicions of the British. The pressure was such that Sheikh Ahmad was forced to agree to form the Majlis al-Ummah al-Tashri'i. The fourteen members of this council were elected by eligible voters from 150 Kuwaiti families.

The council was very active during its six months of existence: it drafted an interim constitution, fought to reform the economy, and attempted to check the power of Sheikh Ahmad. However, it attempted too much too soon, and was opposed by conservative elements in society, who were still quite powerful. The council was replaced by a new twenty-member council (chosen from an electorate of four hundred), but then it returned under a new definition – it was no longer a legislative council, as it had been previously, but an advisory council. In the meantime, Sheikh Ahmad had rewritten the constitution to give himself veto rights. This met with heavy opposition from the new council, which refused to convene until its original status had been reasserted. Sheikh Ahmad rejected this demand, and the council was dissolved four months later.

The democratic movement remained in hiding until the 1950s, when, after a number of elections to ineffectual councils, political opposition once again proliferated. Egyptian expatriates began a Kuwaiti branch of the Muslim Brotherhood in 1951, which later gave rise to the Social Reform Society. Movements such as the Teachers' Club, the pan-Arabist Cultural Club and the Graduate Club also emerged in the 1950s. Syrian and Palestinian workers imported Ba'thist ideology, and Iraqi and Iranian communists were instrumental in starting the Kuwait Democratic Youth. However, it was only after independence in June 1961 that an assembly of any value was established. Political parties were still banned, but "political currents operate openly and the political system deals with them, and takes them into account when forming governments, which indicates that they have political power, but there is also a fear of officially recognizing their existence and loyalty."[85]

Constitution

Emir Abdullah al-Salim, who replaced Sheikh Ahmad in 1950, established a constituent assembly. It comprised twenty elected members and eleven cabinet ministers, and its principal role was to draft the country's permanent constitution. That constitution, adopted in 1963, declared Kuwait a hereditary monarchy under the al-Sabah family, whose ruler had to be a direct descendant of Emir Mubarak. However, it placed restrictions on the ruler's power and guaranteed personal liberties, the right to social and economic welfare, and freedom of the press, residence and communication. Executive power would rest jointly in the hands of the emir and the national assembly. The latter was to consist of fifty secretly selected members as well as all non-elected cabinet ministers, who were to serve four-year terms. It could question ministers, who could also be subjected to votes of no-confidence, although only the emir was allowed to call for the resignation of the entire cabinet.

The national assembly

Theoretically, the constitution is a contract between the ruler and the people, represented by the national assembly. (The emir must swear an oath to respect the constitution.) While political parties are banned, and thus all candidates run as "independent," it is possible to identify loose coalitions representing different interests (conservative and pro-government, Shi'a, Arab nationalist, liberal). The national assembly has been suspended by the emir on four occasions after severely criticizing government policies and the integrity of its ministers. The first time this occurred was in 1975, when the emir determined that the existence of the assembly was contrary to the interests of both his government and the country. The assembly remained suspended until 1981 – four years after the emir's death and his replacement by Sheikh Jabir al-Ahmad. Emir Jabir was more open to the concept of the national assembly, which, throughout its suspension, had remained a popularly supported institution. The new national assembly had a different character from its predecessors, as electoral "reforms" had increased the number of voting districts from ten to twenty-five, with two members per district, for a total of fifty elected members. In addition to these elected members, the sixteen (unelected) members of the Kuwaiti cabinet also held seats in the assembly. The electoral reforms were a reaction to the Iranian revolution of 1979 and growing fear of Shi'a militancy, and they had the desired effect: Shi'a interests were under-represented in the new parliament; while conservative, Bedouin interests were greatly over-represented. There were similar results in the 1985 election, when the pro-government National Center Group (composed of Bedouins and conservatives) maintained control of the assembly. When combined with the cabinet members who sat in the assembly, the pro-government bloc held a comfortable majority.

The 1981 and 1985 assemblies both had to deal with the difficult economic situation in which Kuwait found itself in the 1980s. The latter assembly proved to be more vigorous in its examination of the governmental and bureaucratic systems and managed to force the resignation of Justice Minister Sheikh Salman al-Dua'yj al-Sabah. (It also came close to forcing the resignation of the oil minister, Sheikh 'Ali al-Khalifa al-Sabah, because of financial mismanagement and impropriety.)

The assembly was so successful in its attacks on the government that it was suspended on July 1, 1986. However, the public demanded a restoration of democracy, and Emir Jabir consequently announced the formation of a national assembly with consultative powers as an interim step to the resumption of parliamentary democracy. On June 10, 1990, elections to this new assembly took place. It consisted of seventy-five members: fifty elected by secret ballot and twenty-five appointed. This weak assembly was widely (and correctly) recognized as a step backwards, and the elections were boycotted by twenty-seven members of the 1985 parliament as well as a number of other political groups.

Following the liberation of Kuwait from Iraqi occupation, Jabir promised restoration of the national assembly, and a new one was duly elected in 1992. Seventeen members of the 1985 parliament were reelected, sending "a serious message regarding the people's determination to restore the 1985 parliament's full powers over the executive authorities."[86]

Further elections were held in 1996, 1999, 2003, 2006, 2008 and 2009. The trend has been toward controlled competition between Islamists and (pro-government) "independents," with the former generally having the upper hand. In the 2003 elections, the Islamists won 21 seats and the "independents" 12; in 2006, the Islamists won 17 seats while the "independents" won 16. Ultimate power still rests with the emir – the head of state and effectively the prime minister, too – but the legislature has proved to be a reasonably effective advisory and consultative body, and, on occasion, it has exercised meaningful power. For instance, in early 2006, the assembly voted to remove the ailing Emir Sa'd al-'Abdullah al-Sabah from power, to be replaced with Jabah al-Ahmad al-Sabah.

Abdullah Fahd al-Nafisi attributes the creation of the parliamentary system in Kuwait to British pressure rather than any indigenous democratic instinct. The parliamentary experiment was intended to divert the population's attention away from any problems caused by the al-Sabah family, tribal elites and the governments appointed at their behest in order to protect both their rule and Western interests in Kuwait. Thus, the assembly was not invested with any significant political power, parliamentary reform accomplishes little, and the elected members of the assembly cannot alter government policy or the national structure. As Fahd al-Nafisi says, "Parliament is like a retail shop . . . the government can close it at any time."[87] This happened for the third time in 1999, when the assembly was suspended in order to halt its increasingly embarrassing probe into graft and the enormous disappearance of state assets and investments during the Iraqi invasion.[88]

Two major political trends have appeared in Kuwaiti electoral campaigns, although they cannot be defined as "parties" in the Western sense. The first is Islamic, which is different to the Islamist activist trend that is prevalent in the rest of the region. Gulf Islamists can more accurately be described as "Gulfists," due to their deep-rooted commitment to the Gulf and its way of life as opposed to Muslim society the world over. They may be broken down into three major groupings: the Islamic Constitutional Movement, the nearest thing to a true political party in Kuwait, whose roots go back to the Egyptian Muslim Brotherhood of the 1950s; the Salafiyyah Movement, which began in the 1970s, looks to Mecca for guidance and follows the Saudi Wahhabbi; and the National Islamic Coalition, which is predominantly Shi'a and as such is associated ideologically with Iran, although it is more liberal than the Islamic republic. The second trend comprises liberal and secular political groupings: the Democratic Forum, which is progressive and somewhat leftist; and the National Democratic Grouping, which is largely made up of moderates from the commercial and academic strata of Kuwaiti society.[89] The lack of parliament's formal power to oversee the government – beyond questioning ministers, and even this is viewed by the royal family as an infringement on its prerogative to appoint the government – has resulted in gains for liberal reformers at the expense of both Islamics and government supporters.[90]

Kuwait and the Iran–Iraq War

Iran's initial successes in the Iran–Iraq War – driving toward Basra and occupying the Fao Peninsula – alarmed the neighboring Kuwaitis. Kuwait had put aside its suspicions of the Ba'th regime in Iraq and was fully supporting and financing its war effort against the Islamic republic. Iran had made it clear that it would not stand for such support and began to vilify the Kuwaiti ruling family for its treatment of its Shi'a citizens. An Iranian victory over Iraq, or merely in the Fao, would surely have spelled disaster for Kuwait. In late 1983, Iran began to provoke the regime by sponsoring attacks against Kuwaiti oil installations and other targets. A pro-Iranian group – the Iraqi Da'wa Party – bombed the US and French embassies in Kuwait. (Ironically, Da'wa later emerged as a powerful political party in US-occupied Iraq.) Tehran began to mine Kuwaiti waters, fired a number of missiles into Kuwaiti territory, and, in 1985, even made an (unsuccessful) attempt on the emir's life. Over the next two years, its assaults on oil installations, other parts of Kuwait's economic infrastructure and Kuwaiti shipping intensified.

Around the same time, the key port of Mina al-Ahmadi and a number of cafés in Kuwait City were bombed. Those responsible for these and other acts against the state were found to be Kuwaiti Shi'as opposed to al-Sabah rule. Also involved was a Kuwaiti army officer and an employee of the Kuwait Petroleum Company, as well as several other important members of Kuwaiti society. The bombers were motivated not only by their opposition to the ruling family but by the harsh treatment they had traditionally received in Kuwait. In repsonse, Shi'as were immediately attacked in the press, tens of thousands of Shi'as from other Islamic states were deported, and Shi'as were removed from sensitive positions in the oil industry.

Kuwaiti occupation and liberation from Iraq

On August 2, 1990, Iraqi forces invaded Kuwait, sparking a crisis of immense proportions for the Gulf region and the world as a whole. The emir fled to Saudi Arabia, where he set up a government in exile as the Iraqis deployed over 100,000 soldiers in the neutral border area between Saudi Arabia and occupied Kuwait. UN Security Council Resolution 660 condemning the assault was adopted, and all of the major powers followed suit unilaterally. President George Bush Senior ordered the deployment of US forces to defend Saudi Arabia on August 6. After a few days, France and Britain augmented the American forces in the Gulf region and soon Arab countries, including Syria and Egypt, sent troops to defend Saudi Arabia, too. Thereafter, the build-up of forces against Iraq continued while possible diplomatic solutions were pursued. A coalition of twenty-eight nations under US leadership had formed by the end of the year.

On November 29, UN Security Council Resolution 678 was adopted, authorizing the use of force to liberate Kuwait if the January 15 deadline for withdrawal was not heeded. The day after the expiry of the deadline marked the onset of the war to liberate Kuwait, with the ground offensive starting toward the end of February. On February 28, Kuwait was liberated after just two days of land fighting, and the Iraqi leadership was forced to accept all twelve relevant Security Council resolutions.

Before then, some six hundred oil wells had been set ablaze in Kuwait by the Iraqis, devsastating the oil-dependent economy until reconstruction efforts could clean up and repair the damage. Reconstruction began in earnest when the royal family returned, and this largely proved to be a resounding success. By contrast, reconstruction of the governmental structure has not been pursued nearly so vigorously. The political system can still boast no true opposition that might challenge the ruling elite and alter its decisions. Furthermore, parliament is not always represented in the government. The national assembly remains merely a watchdog without any teeth that operates at the behest of the emir.

Democracy in Kuwait

After the Iraqi invasion of 1990, reforms were promised to allow Kuwaitis more participation in the political process and decision-making within their own state. The first elections, in 1992, saw the Islamics gain ground at the expense of the liberal and nationalist Democratic Forum, and they maintained their dominance of the opposition in the 1996 elections. In May 1998, Islamic MPs forced the resignation of the (royal) minister of information after books deemed unkind to Islam were published in Kuwait. In March 1999, following the publication of an edition of the Qur'an that contained several typographical errors, the assembly rounded on the minister of religious affairs. This hounding of his ministers contributed to the emir's decision to disband the national assembly.[91]

In the summer 1999 election that followed, the Sunni Islamist representation fell in parliament while its Shi'a counterpart increased. The Islamist trend in Kuwait is unique in that it is not predominantly fundamentalist but rather more traditionalist in character, capitalizing on those dissatisfied members of Kuwaiti society who oppose both the modernist trend and the hierarchical tribal power structure.[92] Islamists appear to be assuming the role previously played by liberal and leftist reformers in advocating social justice while the traditional tribal leadership maintains its support of government policy.[93] The liberal reform trend did gain some seats, but not the large increase they had expected, or that was predicted in the international media. This tendency was reinforced with the 2006 election, where the Islamic bloc actually lost seats, securing only seventeen, while the pro-government bloc closed the gap. However, in the May 2008 elections, the trend against reform was at least temporarily reversed as the Islamic bloc won 21 seats. Once the assembly had convened, the opposition began a campaign of firing questions at the prime minister. Eventually, in early 2009, the emir grew exasperated and dissolved the assembly, saying that the constant quizzing of the prime minister was personally motivated and not in the best interests of the people.[94] In the subsequent elections the Islamists were punished (partly because of their opposition to the participation of women), with "independent" candidates winning 21 of the 50 seats, while both Sunni and Shi'a Islamists lost ground.

The 2009 election seems to confirm the historical reality of Kuwaiti society, whereby ideological leanings are subservient to sociological differences, such as urban versus Bedouin. Support for most political trends is along the lines of tribal affinity. The parliament is stratified along two distinct lines: the first being urban society, which is dominated by business groups and intellectual elites; and the second rural, based upon the tribal or Bedouin society which divides along geographical lines north–south. Both strata stress an individual's background rather than current political, ideological or issue-specific leanings. And identifying with tribal or other sociological identities is only strengthened by the appearance of weakness, inefficiency or failure in the Kuwaiti government. The nature of the welfare state, with its constitutional guarantees for housing, education and public health, presents such opportunities. The cost, size and location of public housing, not to mention the backlog of available new homes, make the government appear weak and inefficient. This notion is enhanced by the government's exclusivity of membership and its unrepresentative nature. For example, Kuwait's cabinets – all eighteen of them – have drawn 43 percent of their membership from the wealthiest strata of society, with a further 25 percent coming from the royal family (which has also provided all of the prime ministers).[95]

These impediments to an efficient government will create further difficulties as the new government tackles three of its most pressing issues: the future role of the welfare state; the orientation of the economy; and the inclusion of women in the political process. Article 25 of the constitution guarantees compensation to Kuwaitis when they are injured by an "act of God," such as a war or a natural disaster destroying their home or business. However, after the incalculable costs of reconstruction following the Iraqi occupation, and with the burgeoning cost of the social aspects of the welfare state, the government would like to reduce social services and introduce personal taxation to raise funds. Opposition groups, however, say that taxes should apply only to corporations and to the capital gains of the wealthiest members of Kuwaiti society. Meanwhile, the government, under pressure from the World Bank and the IMF, as well as its close allies in Washington and Western Europe, is being forced to open up the economy. Of course, this increases the prospect of foreign influence and will reduce the control of the ruling elite.

Finally, the inclusion of women within the political process has proven to be consistently divisive – supported by opposition groups with liberal and moderate leanings and actively opposed by the traditionalist and Islamist groups. The franchise was finally extended to women on May 16, 2005, when the national assembly approved it by a vote of thirty-five to twenty-three, with one abstention. However, in the 2006 parliamentary elections, when women could vote for the first time, they accounted for only 35 percent of the votes cast, even though they now made up 57 percent of the electorate.[96]

In the 2009 elections, four women were elected to the assembly for the first time. This caused some consternation among conservative Islamics, as in the lead-up to the election ultra-conservative forces had argued that the participation of women was a "sin" and thus urged a boycott. Furthermore, two of the elected women chose not to wear the *hijab* during the first session of parliament, leading fourteen conservative members to walk out in protest. Moreover, the conservative

MPs Faisal al-Muslim, 'Ali al-'Umair and Jam'an al-Harbash argued that the women's refusal to wear the headscarf violated Kuwaiti electoral law. However, "The liberal MP Saleh al-Mulla was quick to defend the women, saying that the men should respect the will of the Kuwaiti people who elected them according to the constitution. His remarks earned him a round of applause from members of the public attending the session."[97]

An editorial in the *Khaleej Times* summed up the current state of the Kuwaiti polity: "Kuwait's democracy has a long way to go – and several shortcomings need to be addressed immediately: the absence of political parties; the appointment of ministers at the sole pleasure of the prime minister; and the inability of the government to take in criticism."[98]

Bahrain

Bahrain is unlike any other Gulf state: it is a group of small islands twenty miles from the coasts of Saudi Arabia and Qatar. This geography has greatly affected its political and economic development, as has the composition of its society. Iran has historically laid claim to Bahraini islands for both strategic and nationalistic reasons. In addition, the emergent Arab nationalist movement of the 1950s and 1960s was an even greater threat to the Bahraini monarchy than it was to the monarchies of the other Gulf states. Thus, Bahraini development took place in an atmosphere of hostility from outside powers and challenge from ideologies that disputed the hegemony of the ruling family.

Bahraini society consists of four principal groups. Members of the traditional aristocracy, centered on the ruling al-Khalifa family, are Arab Sunni Muslims. The Hawala are also Sunni, but came to Bahrain from Persia over the last several centuries. These two groups constitute the bulk of the upper and commercial classes of Bahraini society. The lower classes are mostly Shi'a Muslims. Constituting a majority of the population (estimates range between 55 and 70 percent), this stratum is divided into Baharna and Ajam: the Ajam migrated to Bahrain in significant numbers only in the last century, while the Baharna, who are more numerous, are the native descendants of the original inhabitants of Bahrain, with the majority of them living in Bahrain's rural areas. Though constitutionally equal to their Sunni countrymen, Bahraini Shi'as have long complained about the political, economic and social stratification between the sects that has seen them dominated by the Sunni minority.

The al-Khalifa family migrated to Bahrain from central Arabia (al-Zubara, a village in the west of Qatar) in 1783 and seized control after the collapse of Persian influence. They have ruled Bahrain ever since, imposed control over the remaining Shi'a population, and extended their influence throughout the islands. By the time the British turned the Gulf into a British lake, their supremacy was unchallenged. However, the people of Bahrain have a long history of political activism and they have staged anti-government protests. These took two forms in the first half of the twentieth century: anti-British demonstrations by members of the merchant community who were dissatisfied with reforms undertaken at Britain's request; and demonstrations by Shi'as who were unhappy about the treatment they received at the hands of the Sunni minority. These protests gave rise to a Bahraini nationalist movement that formed the Bahrain National Congress in 1923 to demand a reduction in British influence in internal affairs and the establishment of a consultative council that would make the emir more accessible to the public. The Shi'a protest movement included demands for proportional representation on municipal and educational councils. However, the British refused to act on the demands of all parties and made it clear that they firmly supported the status quo. Nevertheless, demand for reform continued.

In the 1950s and 1960s large numbers of Bahraini students returned home from abroad, where they had invariably been exposed to progressive and pan-Arabist ideologies. The British were particularly despised because of events in Palestine and their unwillingness to initiate reform, and strikes by Bahraini workers were common in British commercial interests. The pressure exerted by the strikes and the growing politicization of society forced the government to establish a number of committees to study the demands of the opposition. This inquiry resulted in the formation of three councils (health, education and municipal) that were to be half elected and half appointed. To the government's embarrassment, members of the Higher Executive Committee (HEC), formed by 'Abd al-Rahman al-Bakir (a student activist), received massive support in the voting for the health and education councils, which led the government to suspend voting for the municipal council. However, the councils proved to be unworkable because of conflicts with the government. Al-Bakir was forced to leave the country, and the HEC changed its name after a police crackdown following an HEC-led general strike in protest against the political stalemate. The HEC became the Committee for National Unity, with 'Abd al-Aziz al-Shamlan as secretary general, but the stalemate between the government and the reform movement persisted. Throughout 1955 and 1956, the reform movement tried to force change through more general strikes. These culminated in the return of al-Bakir to Bahrain. He, al-Shamlan and others were subsequently arrested and the Committee for National Unity was declared illegal.

Political opposition was driven underground by the regime's repression, which also solidified al-Khalifa control, though there is evidence that numerous Ba'th, Marxist and Arab nationalist cells were operating in Bahrain at the time. These cells eventually formed the National Liberation Front of Bahrain and the Bahraini branch of the Popular Front for the Liberation of Oman and the Arabian Gulf. However, these small groups were unable to challenge the dominance of the al-Khalifas.

The British withdrew from the Gulf in 1971, whereupon the formal independence of Bahrain was declared. This finally precipitated the reform of government structures. Bahrain's rulers initially signaled their desire to join the proposed federation of nine emirates, but they subsequently decided to go it alone. Despite the creation of an administrative council during the turmoil of the 1950s, the executive power of the al-Khalifa family remained supreme. A number of ministries were added, and the administrative council was renamed the council of state. The council then became the cabinet, with members appointed by the sheikh and representing the interests that were most supportive of him. Local officials chosen by the sheikh administered outlying, mainly Shi'a, areas.

Also accompanying independence was the formation of a constituent assembly that had as its primary duty the ratification of a newly drafted constitution. The ratification of the constitution by Emir Isa bin Salman al-Khalifa (1933–1999) in 1973 was followed by the formation of a 44-member national assembly that same year: 30 of the members were elected through a national election, and 14 were appointed by the emir. In practice, though, the assembly acted as an advisory council rather than a formal legislative body. Indeed, its attempts to acquire legislative powers drove the emir to dissolve it in 1975. He then instituted emergency law and suspended the reform principles of the constitution.

Bahrain persisted in this state until a reform campaign was initiated by the new emir, Hamad Ibn Isa al-Khalifa, in 1999. He became King of Bahrain in 2002 upon the introduction of a new constitution, broad political reforms and the election of a second national assembly. However, the al-Khalifa extended family still dominates politics in Bahrain, just as it has since the eighteenth century. While there is a separation of executive, judicial and legislative powers, the king and the national assembly share legislative functions. The king can veto any bill passed by the assembly and has the right to appoint members of the cabinet. He can ratify laws, while those he vetoes are sent to the assembly.

Under the terms of the 2002 constitution, the national assembly is bicameral, with an elected 40-member lower house (council of representatives) and a 40-member upper house (consultative council), which is appointed by the king. The assembly has the right to question any government minister, and ministers are responsible to the assembly. Individual assembly members may initiate legislation, and the assembly as a whole must ratify the annual budget. The assembly may also challenge any principle of the constitution – except for the concept of hereditary rule – if a two-thirds majority supports the motion.

All of this constituional reform came eight years after the US State Department's Human Rights Committee issued an important report summarizing Bahrain's repressive practices. The main allegations concerned the inability of Bahrain's citizens to change their government; the occasional practice of arbitrary and incommunicado detention; the absence of impartial inspection of detention and prison facilities; restrictions on the right to a fair public trial, especially in the Security Court; and restrictions on freedom of speech, the press, assembly and association, women's rights and workers' rights. [99]

Since coming to the throne, King Hamad, a career soldier who previously commanded Bahrain's armed forces, has continued his father's policy of pursuing close links with the West. However, whereas Isa was renowned for his ties to Britain, Hamad has moved closer to the princes of Saudi Arabia. He has also made overtures to Bahrain's Shi'a population, increasing optimism that full democracy may well come about under his reign.[100] However, progress has been uneven on that front, with final power remaining firmly in the hands of the executive. Moreover, the government has failed to institutionalize the basic democratic rights of freedom of assembly, association and expression.

Bahrain faces an internal challenge from its dispossessed Shi'a majority. The Shi'a live mainly in rural villages and are separated from the abundant prosperity of the rest of Bahraini society. Between 1994 and 1997, isolated acts of violence became more frequent. The Bahraini regime accused Iran of fomenting unrest among the Shi'a, and began arresting leading Shi'a figures. As one astute observer of Gulf politics says, soon after Bahraini independence in 1971, the Saudis began treating the country

> as if it were part of its eastern district. Soon after the Iranian revolution of February 11, 1979, Saudi Arabia was concerned with the Shi'a Islamic tide represented by the revolution . . . in Tehran and began pressing the Bahraini regime – whose Shi'ites make up a huge percentage of its 350,000 population, to isolate the Shi'ites from the political and economic life of the country and exclude them from participating in senior government positions, fearing their sympathy for Iran. In this unwise action, they pushed the Shi'as in Bahrain into the lap of Iran . . . Saudi Wahhabbism is a social doctrine antagonistic to anything that is not Wahhabbi and one of the most important features of Wahhabbism is to regard Shi'ism as totally heretical . . . but instigating the Bahraini Sunni regime . . . and inciting it against the majority Shi'a population is contrary to the historic class evolution of the intimate Bahraini society . . . the Shi'as in Bahrain participated in the nationalist movement against Britain during the colonial period . . . Through this Saudi policy, the social fabric of Bahrain was torn and the Bahraini government, after 26 years of independence, followed a new policy of exiling or expelling its Shi'a citizens.[101]

While Bahrain continues to marginalize its Shi'a majority, there has been some movement on the political front. In the parliamentary elections of 2006, the Shi'a opposition party, al-Wefaq, won 17 of the 40 seats. Owing to the party's success, the Bahraini regime was forced to appoint Nizar Baharna, a founder of al-Wefaq, as a minister of state for foreign affairs. It also appointed Jawad Oraied, a Shi'a supporter of the government, to the position of deputy prime minister, making him the first Shi'a ever to hold that post.

Qatar

Like the other Gulf states, Qatar's political development since independence has been dominated by its ruling family, and its economic expansion has resulted from its oil wealth. Its development, however, has followed a slightly different path to those of its neighbors, Kuwait and Bahrain, because of socio-cultural differences. These differences have resulted in Qatar's political development being marked by stability and a general lack of political activity among Qataris. Qatari society is marked by tremendous homogeneity – the indigenous population is entirely Sunni – and it is bound together by centuries-old social networks that combine with the powerful influence of Wahhabbism to make it politically and socially stable.

Unlike other Gulf states, Qatar has not emerged from a commercial tradition centered on coastal regions; rather, it has grown out of a Bedouin tradition with its center of influence in the interior. The tribes migrated to Qatar from today's Saudi Arabia. Among them was the Maadhid, to which the current ruling family – the al-Thanis – belonged. First emerging as a powerful force during the introduction of Wahhabbism to Qatar, the al-Thanis rose to prominence by tying themselves to the interests of foreign and regional powers who were shaping the region's development. By the late nineteenth century, when Kassim al-Thani managed to defeat a superior Ottoman force sent to overthrow him, the position of the family was unchallenged.

At various times in its history, Qatar has been tied by the al-Thanis to the interests of the Saudis, the Ottoman Empire and, finally, the British. These linkages resulted from two factors. The first is that Qatar is small, devoid of natural defenses and lacks the basic capabilities necessary for self-defense. Historical enmity between Qatar and its neighbor, Bahrain, caused Qatar to turn to outside powers for protection against al-Khalifa claims. Ultimately, the interplay between the foreign and regional powers prompted the al-Thanis to agree to formalize their relationship with the British in 1916, when Qatar became a British protectorate.

The second reason why the al-Thanis aligned themselves with foreign powers was to increase their influence within Qatar itself. Indeed, by the time that the treaty with Britain was signed, the position of the family was largely unchallenged. They had managed to play off foreign powers against one another to gain the best possible deal for Qatar and, in the process, had begun to construct the infrastructure through which they would rule the country to the end of the century.

When the British government announced its intention to quit the Gulf by 1972, Qatar did not join the other Gulf emirates in the UAE, opting instead for sovereignty. This necessitated the formation of some kind of governmental structure, but the structure chosen was, in reality, no different from the one that had existed under the British.

A provisional constitution was drawn up in 1970 and was subsequently amended in 1972 after the succession of Sheikh Khalifa to power. Though it was intended to be a purely transitional document, it remains in force to this day. In it, Qatar is described as a democratic Islamic Arab state that derives its laws from the *Shari'a*. Executive and legislative power rests in the hands of the emir. The constitution, however, provides for the creation of a council of ministers and an advisory council, which are designed to discuss issues and make recommendations to the emir on legislative matters. Constitutionally, the advisory council should consist of twenty appointed members in addition to the cabinet, but membership was expanded to thirty in 1975. There has never been an election to the council, and there has been only one council since the constitution came into effect; it is regularly extended by emiri decree. The council elects its own president, vice-president and standing committee.

Sheikh Khalifa was careful to use the composition of the council as a means of extending his personal and familial influence. Members of the merchant community and important tribes held 17 of the 30 seats and thereby constituted a majority. The most important constituencies in the state were well represented in the council, and its members were well respected and would likely have been elected, should an election ever have been called. The council's reputation spoke well for Khalifa's political acumen and showed the lack of interest in reform in Qatar.

However, events in Qatar took a surprising turn in June 1995, when Khalifa's son, Hamad, apparently with the promise of a $2.5–5 billion "buyout," deposed his ruling father peacefully. Hamad has since displayed an inclination for reform. In 1999, direct elections for the Central Municipality Council took place. Hamad also promised the preparation of a permanent constitution and a freely elected Shura Council. Moreover, he enfranchised women, who not only voted but ran as candidates in the 1999 civic elections. The 29-member Municipality Council is responsible for municipal affairs, agriculture, infrastructure and public health. An estimated 22,000 people registered to vote for the 227 candidates who ran for office.

Hamad appears quite willing to continue Qatar's role as the "black sheep" of the GCC, by opening even closer ties with Iran and, even more surprisingly, with Israel, including a $5.5 billion natural gas joint operation with an Israeli consortium. In November 1997, a number of Arab governments, including Saudi Arabia and Egypt, "boycotted a United States backed business conference in Qatar designed to cement the ailing Middle East peace process."[102] The former sheikh has been an honored guest in several GCC capitals, and the Saudis, especially, have spoken of the need to bring his son "into line." However, they have taken no action against Hamad; in fact, his foreign relations policies have generally been cautiously followed by the rest of the GCC states. He broke new ground once again when, on Sunday, August 8, 1999, he became the first GCC head of state to visit the Palestinian territories, a sign of warming relations between the Palestinians and Gulf states. A true rapprochement between the Palestinians and the Gulf states, whose leaders were angered by the Palestinians' support for Iraq during the first Gulf War, would reintegrate the Arab world.

In matters of foreign policy, the Qatari regime is now firmly in the US camp. US–Qatari relations, though officially beginning with the construction of a US Embassy in 1973, did not truly coalesce until the aftermath of the first Gulf War. In 1992, the US and Qatar finalized a defense cooperation pact, providing US access to Qatari bases and initiating joint military exercises. Subsequently, in 1996, Qatar built the al-Udeid airbase at a cost of more than $1 billion for use by US military aircraft. The activities of this base stepped up with the onset of the "war on terror."[103] Camp as-Sayliyah, "the largest pre-positioning facility of US equipment in the world, served as the forward command center for CENTCOM personnel during Operation Iraqi Freedom"[104] and has since served as the hub of US military activities in the Middle East.

Qatar, an embryonic constitutional monarchy, has a 35-member consultative assembly, whose members are appointed. While relatively free regional elections occur, participation is limited to males over eighteen, and national elections have yet to occur. For all its deficiencies on questions of democracy and human rights, Qatar has nevertheless distinguished itself by hosting the al-Jazeera satellite news channel, undoubtedly the most unimpeded and forthright news service in the Arab world. Despite the pro-US orientation of the ruling regime, al-Jazeera has been permitted to provide unflinching and critical coverage of both the Palestinian and the Iraqi crises.

Oman

The sultanate of Oman stretches over some of the most strategically important territory in the Middle East. Lying at the entrance to the Persian Gulf and the Gulf of Oman, the strategically vital Straits of Hormuz lie just off the tip of Oman's Ras Musandam. The hostile climate and geography of the region have determined much of Oman's history, and its development has been constrained by sea and desert. Historically, Oman was not a wealthy state because of its hostile climate and accompanying lack of resources, as well as its poor and often corrupt rulers. Throughout much of their history, Omanis were led by an elected imam. Most Omanis belong to the Ibadhi sect of Islam whose leader (the imam) heads the state. The present dynasty (the Al Bu Saids) dates back to 1744, when the family managed to expel the Persians from what is now Oman. The family has managed to retain control despite opposition from within and from early Wahhabbi interference from what is now Saudi Arabia, and despite the separation of the functions of the imamate and the sultanate, which occurred in 1783. The sultanate, the seat of real political power in Oman, has remained in the hands of the Al Bu Saids, while the imamate is in the hands of the Hinawi tribe.

This arrangement, brought about largely through British influence in the nineteenth century, has had dramatic effects on Oman's politics. The sultanate had to fight very hard to extend its influence inland and into the southern reaches of the state while also trying to prove itself the real seat of power at the expense of the imamate. However, until recently, the Hinawi have resisted Al Bu Said attempts to control Oman – even going so far as to apply for League of Arab States recognition of their control of the interior of the country in 1954. The sultanate eventually managed to increase its influence among the outlying tribes, but the imamate's opposition has not ceased entirely.

As with other Gulf states, the discovery of oil marked a critical period in Omani history. The rapid wealth accumulation after oil was discovered in 1962 led to societal demands for modernization. By 1968, these demands were so irresistible that Sultan Said Ibn Teimour began to draft a development and planning program. However, he was a conservative man and was determined to proceed slowly. At the time, Oman was one of the least developed parts of the Gulf: it lacked medical facilities (it had just one hospital, plus a number of dispensaries) and schools (it had just three, with 100 students), and its infant mortality rate was among the highest in the world. Moreover, the sultan was not only conservative but authoritarian. His inability to meet the needs of Omanis resulted in the formation of the Dhufar Liberation Movement, whose goal was to free southern Oman from the rest of the sultanate. Though the rebellion in Dhufar lasted well into the 1970s, the political situation changed with the overthrow of the sultan in July 1970 by his son Qabus Ibn Said, who had been under house arrest since returning from school in England.

Qabus pledged to modernize government structures and the economy, and to liberalize society. While this proceeded in fits and starts through the 1970s, Qabus managed to increase his personal influence within the ruling family and within Oman itself. By the end of the Dhufar rebellion in 1975, he had managed to extend the power of the sultanate throughout the state – an accomplishment his father had never been able to achieve. While Sultan Qabus was autocratic and initially ruled without any sort of consultative body, he was more open than his father had been. He ruled on the basis of personal and tribal relationships that had developed before he came to power and which he then fostered. During the 1970s, he succeeded in introducing basic socio-economic infrastructure to Oman.

The situation changed in 1981 when the State Consultative Council (SCC) was established after Sultan Qabus had summoned a small ministerial committee to report on the feasibility of introducing a formalized consultative body. Initially, the SCC had forty-three appointed members, though that number was increased to fifty-five in 1983. The original SCC committee selected members, whose names were then forwarded to the sultan. He accepted every nomination presented to him. The SCC president, a figurehead, was the only SCC member who was directly chosen by the sultan, and he had always been a member of the cabinet, too. Of the fifty-five members, nineteen were members of the government, while the Chamber of Commerce elected another nineteen, eleven of whom were chosen by the committee. The remainder represented each of Oman's seven geographic regions, with their numbers varying according to population.

The SCC developed into a government watchdog, and its members were encouraged to criticize government policy. Ministers, chosen by the sultan and tending to represent all regions of Oman, were held responsible by the SCC and were expected to appear before it when called. However, the government could not be subjected to a vote of non-confidence, and no one could question the ultimate rule of the sultan.

The success of the SCC in fostering unity among the Omanis encouraged the government to further the people's participation in politics. On November 18, 1990, at a time of increased Islamic activism, Qabus announced the formation of a Majlis al-Shura (consultative council) to replace the SCC. Around that time, the *New York Times* called Qabus "America's most reliable ally in the Persian Gulf,"[105] and it seems that his creation of the Omani Consultative Council (OCC) was an attempt to curry favor with the United States while also undermining the complaints of domestic activists by increasing political participation.[106] (The first Gulf War led all GCC leaders to seek more concrete domestic support and stronger external alliances, and increasing political participation was a means to achieve both of these ends.)

The OCC was the first political institution in the Gulf to boast women members, when the sultan appointed two women as regional representatives in 1994. In 2003, universal suffrage was extended to everyone over the age of twenty-one, and two women were elected. Nevertheless, Oman does not allow political parties, members of the upper house are still appointed by the sultan, and all members of the lower house stand as "non-partisans." The new constitution of November 1997 paved the way for the creation of an appointed "state council," which, when combined with the Majlis, would comprise a new supreme consultative council called the Council of Oman.

These political reforms have been accompanied by a substantive program to reform the economy, and over the last twenty-five years the sultanate has been able to transform the economy from traditional to modern through the development of its petroleum resources. Oil has come to generate 37 percent of Oman's GNP, 75 percent of the state's revenues, and 76 percent of its total exports. In an effort to diversify its economy and reduce its dependence on oil, the sultanate has invested in an infrastructure to take advantage of its large reserves of natural gas. With exports beginning in the year 2000, Oman has estimated proven reserves of 849.5 billion cubic meters of natural gas. In 2008, it was estimated that Oman exported over 10 billion cubic meters of natural gas.[107]

Oman has pursued economic links with nations around the globe, especially through its championing of the Indian Ocean Group for Economic Cooperation. Initially advocated by Mauritania, this economic bloc would increase cooperation and stimulate growth between economies as diverse as South Africa, Singapore, Kenya, Australia, New Zealand, Indonesia, Malaysia, Sri Lanka, Mozambique, Madagascar, Yemen and India.[108]

Recent political developments in Oman allow for some legitimate, if guarded, hope. On October 27, 2007, there was a parliamentary election which, by regional standards, appeared to be reasonably fair. Close to 63 percent of eligible voters cast their vote, an encouraging figure by any standard. However, political parties were still banned and all candidates were still elected as "non-partisans." Furthermore, this time, no women were elected to the Majlis. Therefore, the limitations of the Omani democratic experiment continue to be exposed. For instance, anyone elected to the OCC is prevented from speaking to the public about their activities and achievements in the Omani parliament, so – on this basis – incumbent candidates are unable to justify their reelection as it is impossible for them to highlight what legislation (if any) they enacted in their previous term.

Nevertheless, Oman's experiment with democratic institutions suggests a gradual shift toward a conservative constitutional monarchy. Furthermore, at a rhetorical level, Oman's rulers have given much credence to liberal reform and the democratic process, acknowledging that further changes and reforms need to be implemented. They have also exhibited what seems to be genuine regret that there are now no women in parliament, perhaps indicating a continued expansion of women's roles and relevance in Omani society.[109]

United Arab Emirates (UAE)

The UAE was formed as a federation of the Omani-coast emirates on December 2, 1971. These emirates and others had previously attempted to unify under British auspices but failed because of several obstacles. However, when the British government announced in 1968 that it would quit the Gulf by 1972, the rulers of

Abu Dhabi and Dubai signaled their intention to unite. Soon other Gulf leaders expressed their desire to join the union, and in December 1971 Abu Dhabi, Dubai, Sharjah, Ajman, Umm al-Qaywayn and Fujairah united to form the United Arab Emirates. Ras al-Khaymah joined the federation on February 10, 1972. A provisional constitution was promulgated for the union, but later the word "provisional" was removed, and the constitution was declared permanent on May 20, 1996. Abu Dhabi was also declared the official, permanent capital of the UAE.

The union is, in many ways, a strange one. Despite the ethnic and social ties that bind the people of the UAE together, the emirates differ vastly in size, wealth and economic strength. Historically, Abu Dhabi (the largest and richest of the emirates) and Dubai (the most populous) have dominated the union. Abu Dhabi's Sheikh Zayid Ibn Sultan al-Nahyan has served as the UAE's only president and he is considered one of the most powerful leaders in the Gulf region. Dubai's late ruler, Sheikh Rashid Ibn Sa'id al-Maktum, was the UAE's vice-president, and he also held the post of prime minister from 1979 until his death in 1991. His son, Sheikh Rashid al-Maktum, then assumed all of his father's posts, which he held until his death in 2005, whereupon he was succeeded by his brother, Sheikh Mohammad bin Rashid al-Maktum. By contrast, the smaller emirates are hamstrung by their small sizes and populations and insufficient economic bases, which limit their ability to influence the direction of UAE policy.

Theoretically, there is a separation of power in the UAE. The executive consists of the supreme council, the presidency and the council of ministers. The supreme council, composed of the sheikhs of each emirate, is the highest executive body in the federation and is chaired by the president. Each sheikh has one vote on issues before the council; a simple majority suffices on ordinary matters, but five of the seven members must approve substantial matters, and two of those votes must come from Abu Dhabi and Dubai. Therefore, although the power of Abu Dhabi and Dubai has been constitutionally balanced to some extent, they remain in positions to dominate the union. They also dominate because of the tremendous power vested in the president. He signs laws, convenes sessions of the supreme council, appoints the prime minister, deputy prime minister and cabinet, can end the tenure of any minister, and can veto all motions brought before him. Sheikh Zayid's reelection at the end of each five-year term and the powers vested in the presidency reflect both his role and Abu Dhabi's position as the most powerful of the seven member states. However, this concentration of power has not gone unopposed: one of the reasons why Ras al-Khaymah did not initially join the UAE was because of the veto power that would be possessed by Sheikhs Zayid and Rashid. Sheikh Saqr, ruler of Ras al-Khaymah, has been outspoken on this and other issues concerning the dominance of the two largest emirates. However, on the whole, the sheikhs of the smaller members seem to have accepted the dominance of Abu Dhabi and Dubai.

There have been differences among the sheikhs, though. The UAE is a federal state, and the constitution gives the federal government exclusive jurisdiction over defense, finance, foreign affairs, the use of the armed forces (both externally and internally) and other important areas. (However, defense was not unified until

1978, and Dubai's forces do not form part of the federal defenses.) All powers not included in the federal constitution are controlled by the emirates, which have, through this arrangement, retained many of the political and economic institutions that existed prior to union. Though the powers of the federal government are explicitly stated, this did not prevent it from trying to expand its areas of influence. It has also not stopped the emirates from squabbling among themselves.

The leaders of the smaller emirates must carefully balance their federal and local commitments. The sheikhs are hereditary rulers who rely on tribal support to stay in power. They must satisfy local needs in order to secure a local base of support, a difficult feat in a federal setting where federal policies often infringe on local interests. Such was the case in Sharjah in November 1972, when Sheikh Sultan moved to merge all his local institutions with the federal institutions. Earlier, on January 25, 1972, his predecessor Sheikh Khalid had been killed in *coup d'état*.[110] More recently, the federal government proved its willingness to interfere in the internal affairs of the emirates, when, on June 17, 1987, Sheikh 'Abdul Aziz al-Qassimi moved to depose his younger brother, Sheikh Sultan, as ruler of Sharjah because of financial profligacy and Sharjah's $1 billion debt. The supreme council refused to recognize 'Abdul Aziz's rule, Sultan was reinstated, and he agreed to reorganize Sharjah's administrative structure.

The federal national council is a consultative body of forty members. Abu Dhabi and Dubai both have eight members, Sharjah and Ras al-Khaymah six each, and the remaining three emirates four each. Half of the members are appointed, with the other half elected. The first election was held in 2006, but the franchise was extremely limited, with only 2,000 dignitaries, sheikhs and the like – chosen by the country's leaders – allowed to vote. The UAE also does not allow organized political parties, and the majority of members are representatives of the commercial classes, with many from Dubai, Sharjah and Ras al-Khaymah coming from prominent merchant families. Members from the other emirates tend to represent the dominant tribes. Furthermore, the national council is purely advisory, with final power remaining with the monarchs. Real democracy in the UAE therefore still seems far off.

The UAE has a mixed record on civil rights. "Freedom of speech" is enshrined in the constitution, but in practice the Ministry of Information governs press content and unapproved articles can be punished by imprisonment (although this has rarely occurred). The UAE is relatively tolerant of religious difference, allowing non-Muslim religious practice and hosting dozens of Christian churches, one Hindu temple and two Sikh temples. It even has a Bah'ai cemetery, despite the fact that Bah'ai is often considered a heretical offshot of Islam.

While the UAE has accumulated vast wealth and has diversified its economy beyond the traditional oil sector, it maintains very questionable labor practices. Approximately 80 percent of the UAE's resident population is made up of migrant workers, particularly South Asians. They form a permanent underclass, hidden from the glamor and prestige of the tourist and commercial sectors, and they are frequently abused. It is common for employers to seize migrant workers' passports and even withhold wages. While migrant workers can theoretically appeal to the Labor Board for redress, employers maintain a definite and unyielding advantage over their employees, some of whom compare their situation to indentured servitude.

Labor tension exploded in March 2006 when workers at the construction site of Burj Dubai revolted in protest over low wages and poor working conditions, causing significant property damage. Responding to this protest, and international scrutiny over its labor practices, the UAE is in the process of passing labor reform legislation, including requiring "employers to pay the expenses of migrant workers' travel, employment permits, medical examinations, and other required administrative costs."[111] Furthermore, in March 2006, the UAE's labor minister announced a measure to legalize labor unions in the construction sector.

Foreign affairs

The UAE's main foreign concern is its defense. Iran claims significant portions of UAE territory, especially two strategic Gulf islands – Tunb and Abu Musa – which it actually occupied on November 30, 1971. The UAE's odd, mainly mercenary military force is supplemented by large amounts of American equipment, and it makes no secret of its willingness to allow large numbers of US and British troops to base themselves on its soil, should the need arise.

The US and the UAE maintain close relations, corresponding with the UAE's rise as a major financial center in the world economy. The US is the primary arms supplier to the UAE, and US corporations have heavily invested there. For instance, Exxon-Mobil is a strategic partner of the Abu Dhabi National Oil Company. With the onset of the "war on terror" and the invasion and occupation of Iraq, the UAE has proven to be a junior, and silent, partner of the US enterprise. It hosts scores of US naval ports and provides over-flight clearance for US military aircraft. Likewise, the UAE has publicly pledged support for the fragile Iraqi governments and shares with the US a suspicion of Iranian activities, especially the latter's alleged nuclear development.

Notes

1 Christof Ruhl, *BP Statistical Review of World Energy* (London: British Petroleum, June 2008).
2 Khaldûn H. al-Naqîb, *al-Mujtama' wa al-Dawlah fî al-khalîj wa al-Jazîrah al-'Arabiyyah* (Beirut: Center for Arab Unity, 1987), pp. 119–120.
3 Anthony Sampson, *The Seven Sisters: The 100-Year Battle for the World's Oil Supply* (4th Edition) (New York: Bantam, 1991), pp. 56–136; Daniel Yergin, *The Prize: The Epic Quest for Oil, Money and Power* (New York: Simon & Schuster, 1991), pp. 134–302.
4 Al-Naqîb, op.cit., pp. 120–125.
5 Ibid., pp. 122–123.
6 Ibid.
7 Ibid.
8 Said K. Aburish, *The Rise, Corruption and Coming Fall of the House of Saud* (New York: St. Martin's Press, 1996), pp. 20, 152.
9 Al-Naqîb, op.cit., pp. 112–114.
10 Ibid., p. 113.

11 Riyâḍ Najîb al-Raiyyis, *Riyâḥ al-Sumûm* (London: Riad al-Raiyyis Books, 1994), pp. 46–47.

12 Ibid., pp. 58–59.

13 Ibib., p. 59.

14 Ibid., p. 61.

15 Ibid., pp. 309–310.

16 *Al-Taqrîr al-Istirâtîjî al-'Arabî* (Cairo: al-Ahram Center for Political and Strategic Studies, 1996), p. 193.

17 Mshari al-Zaidi, "The 30th GCC Summit," *Asharq Alawsat*, December 17, 2009. URL: http://www.aawsat.com/english/news.asp?section = 2&id = 19184.

18 "The Gulf: Won't You Buy," *The Economist*, March 20, 1999, p. 50.

19 "Iran Proposes Gulf Security Pact," *BBC News*, December 3, 2007. URL: http://news.bbc.co.uk/2/hi/middle_east/7125268.stm.

20 *Al-Taqrîr al-Istirâtîjî al-'Arabî* (Cairo: al-Ahram Center for Political and Strategic Studies, 1995), pp. 285–296.

21 *Al-Wasat*, No. 105 (January 1996), pp. 15–19.

22 Ibid., p. 14.

23 Ibid., p. 13.

24 "Guest Workers Stage Violent Wage Protest in UAE," Agence France-Presse, March 19, 2008.

25 The National Labor Committee, "Guest Workers Trafficked to Kuwait," July 21, 2008. URL: http://www.nlcnet.org/article.php?id = 601.

26 "Hundreds of Thousands Get Half the Promised wages," *Daily Star* (Bangladesh), August 25, 2008. URL: http://www.thedailystar.net/story.php?nid = 51797.

27 Ibid.

28 Porimol Palma, "Dhaka to Seek Compesentation for Innocent Workers," *Daily Star* (Bangladesh), September 3, 2008. URL: http://www.thedailystar.net/story.php?nid = 53105.

29 Ibid.

30 *Al-Quds Al-Arabi*, December 3, 2007. URL: http://www.nlcnet.org/reports?id=0012.

31 The National Labor Committee, op. cit.

32 See Tareq Y. Ismael, *Middle East Politics Today: Government and Civil Society* (Gainesville: University of Florida Press, 2001), p. 349.

33 *Middle East Economic Digest*, November 8, 1991, p. 4.

34 Ibid.

35 *The Middle East*, December 1994, p. 17.

36 "Dubai Property Prices Fall 41%," *BBC News*, April 28, 2009. URL: http://news.bbc.co.uk/2/hi/business/8022578.stm.

37 Elena Moya, "Six Dubai Companies Downgraded to Junk Status," *Guardian*, December 8, 2009. URL: http://www.guardian.co.uk/business/2009/dec/08/dubai-companies-downgraded-rating-action.

38 John Irish, "Transcript – Abu Dhabi gives Dubai $10 bn Bailout," Reuters, December 14, 2009. URL: http://www.finanznachrichten.de/nachrichten-2009-12/15695664-transcript-abu-dhabi-gives-dubai-dollar-10-bln-bailout-020.htm.

39 *Middle East Economic Digest*, October 4, 1991, p. 6.

40 Paul Aart, "The Limits of Political Tribalism: Post War Kuwait and the Process of Democratisation," *Civil Society*, Vol. 4, No. 37 (January 1995), pp. 16–18.

41 Shafeeq Ghabra, "Voluntary Associations in Kuwait: The Foundation of a New System?," *Middle East Journal*, Vol. 45, No. 2 (Spring 1991), p. 200.

42 Interview with Abdullah Fahd al-Nafisi, al-Jazeera, June 22, 1999.

43 Al-Raiyyis, op.cit., pp. 265–269; J.S. Ismael, *Kuwait: Dependency and Class in a Rentier State* (Gainesville: University Press of Florida, 1994).

44 Sa'd Eddîn Ibrâhîm, *al-Mujtama' al-Madanî wa al-Taḥawwul al-Dîmuqrâṭî fî al-Waṭan al-'Arabî* (Cairo: Ibn Khaldoun Center, 1996), pp. 179–188.

45 *Al-Taqrîr al-Istirâtîjî al-'Arabî* (1996), op. cit., pp. 252–253.
46 *Middle East Economic Digest*, February 24, 1995, p. 10.
47 Anwar 'Abd-ul-lah, *al-'Ulamâ' wa al-'Arsh: Thunâ'iyyat al-Sulṭah fî al-Sa'ûdiyyah* (London: Mu'assasit al-Râfid, 1995), pp. 373–375.
48 Ibid., p. 381.
49 Ibid., pp. 284–386.
50 *New York Times*, October 8, 1994, p. 41.
51 Mahan Abedin, "The Face of Saudi Opposition," *Asia Times*, April 20, 2006. URL: http://www.atimes.com/atimes/Middle_East/HD20Ak02.html.
52 *Guardian Weekly*, January 14, 1996, p. 53.
53 'Abd-ul-lah, op. cit., pp. 390–406. See also Hrair Dekmejian, "Saudi Arabia's Consultative Council," *Middle East Journal*, Vol. 52, No. 2 (Spring 1998), p. 217.
54 *The Economist*, November 17, 1990, p. 53.
55 *Middle East Economic Digest*, December 3, 1993, p. 26.
56 Brian Whitaker, "Hello, Democracy – and Goodbye," *Guardian*, February 24, 2009. URL: http://www.guardian.co.uk/commentisfree/2009/feb/24/saudiarabia.
57 *The Middle East*, November 1994, p. 24.
58 Michael Sheridan, "Ailing Saudi King Hands over to Prince," *Independent*, January 2, 2006, p. 10.
59 *Middle East Economic Digest*, December 10, 1993, p. 12.
60 Office of International Information Programs, "Text: Vice President Lauds Sale of F-16 Jets to UAE" (Washington, D.C.: US State Department, March 6, 2000).
61 Anwar 'Abd-ul-lah, *al-Betrûl wa al-Akhlâq* (Dubai: Dar al-Dhuha, 1990), p. 18.
62 Ibid., pp. 19–20.
63 Ibid., pp. 21–23.
64 Ibid., p. 24.
65 Hamid Algar, *Wahhabism: A Critical Essay* (Oneonta: Islamic Publications International, 2002), pp. 21–25.
66 Roy Lebkicher, George Rentz & Max Steineke, *The Arabia of Ibn Saud* (New York: Russell F. Moore, 1952), p. 28.
67 Ibid., p. 29.
68 Lawrence Goldrup, "Saudi Arabia, 1902–1932: The Development of a Wahhabbi Society," Thesis, University of California, 1971, p. 37.
69 'Abd-ul-lah, *al-'Ulamâ' wa al-'Arsh: Thunâ'iyyat al-Sulṭah fî al-Sa'ûdiyyah*, op.cit., pp. 30–32.
70 Masood Rashid, *Industrialization in Oil-Based Economies: A Case Study of Saudi Arabia* (Delhi: ABC, 1984), p. 25.
71 Goldrup, op.cit., pp. 106–161.
72 Ibid., p. 395.
73 Hirst, op. cit.
74 Lee Keath, "Saudi King Blasts US in Iraq," *Milwaukee Journal Sentinel*, March 29, 2007, p.13A.
75 Nazih N. Ayubi, *Over-Staffing the Arab State* (London: I.B. Tauris, 1995), p. 133.
76 Mariam Sami, "Web Opens up World for Saudi Women," *Austin-American Statesman*, August 16, 1999, p. D5.
77 *The Economist*, February 4, 1995, pp. 59–60.
78 Tatiana Serafin, "The World's Richest Royals," *Forbes*, August 20, 2009. URL: http://www.forbes.com/2008/08/20/worlds-richest-royals-biz-richroyals08-cz_ts_0820 royalintro.html.
79 Venkateswarier Subramaniam, *Public Administration in the Third World: An International Handbook* (New York: Greenwood Press, 1990), p. 190.
80 "Saudi Says 73 Soldiers Slain in War on Yemen Rebels," *New York Times*, December 22, 2009. URL: http://www.nytimes.com/reuters/2009/12/22/world/international-uk-saudi-yemen-rebels.html.

81 Brian Ross, "Obama Ordered US Military Strike on Yemen Terrorists," *ABC News*. URL: http://abcnews.go.com/print?id = 9375236.
82 "Yemen Rebels Say Air Raid Kills 120," Reuters, December 15, 2009. URL: http://www.reuters.com/article/idUSTRE5BE5G220091215.
83 *Kuwait: al-Ra'y al-Akhar* (London: Taha Advertising, 1978), p. 13.
84 Interview with al-Nafisi, op. cit.
85 See 'Ali al-Tarah, "The Kuwaiti Democracy Equation," *Al Ittihad* (Abu Dhabi), April 1, 2009, p. 39.
86 Jasem M. Karam, "Kuwaiti National Assembly – 1992: A Study in Electoral Geography," *GeoJournal*, Vol. 31, No. 4 (December 1993), p. 391.
87 Interview with al-Nafisi, op. cit.
88 "A Bolder Kuwait," *The Economist*, July 10–16, 1999, p. 39.
89 For more details on these movements, see Falâh 'Abd-ul-lâh al-Midîris, *al-Tajammu'ât al-Siyâsiyyah al-Kûwaitiyyah: Marhalat mâ ba'd al-Tahrîr* (2nd Edition) (Kuwait: Matâbi'al-Manâr, 1996).
90 "A Bolder Kuwait," op. cit., p. 39.
91 "Kuwait: An Unholy Row," *The Economist*, May 8, 1999, p. 49.
92 *Al-Wasat*, No. 389 (1999), pp. 24–26.
93 "Peace Allows Kuwaitis to Tackle Domestic Concerns," *Globe and Mail*, July 3, 1999, p. A15.
94 URL: http://www.upi.com/Top_News/2009/03/19/Kuwaiti_parliament_dissolved/UPI-75111237444712/.
95 *Al-Wasat*, No. 389 (1999), p. 25.
96 "Reformists Sweep Vote in Kuwait; Women Lose," *New York Times*, June 30, 2006. URL: http://www.nytimes.com/2006/06/30/world/africa/30iht-kuwait.2093689.html.
97 James Calderwood, "Women Arrive in Kuwait's Parliament, and Some Male MPs Walk out," *The National*, May 31, 2009. URL: http://www.thenational.ae/article/20090601/FOREIGN/705319845/1011/NEWS.
98 "Impetus to Kuwait Democracy", *Khaleej Times Online*. URL: http://www.khaleejtimes.com/DisplayArticleNew.asp?section = editorial&xfile = data/editorial/2009/may/editorial_may36.xml.
99 Aart, op.cit.
100 "Suddenly, It's Time for Charm," *The Economist*, July 17, 1999, pp. 41–42.
101 Riyâd Najîb al-Raiyyis, *Riyâh al-Shamâl* (London: Riad al-Rayyes Books, 1997), pp. 251–253.
102 Kathy Evans, "Gulf Summit: Discord and Disunity," *The Middle East*, Vol. 263 (January 1997), pp. 5–7.
103 Jeremy M. Sharp, "Qatar: Background and US Relations," Congressional Research Service (March 14, 2004).
104 Ibid.
105 Bob Hepburn, "Once-Isolated Oman Assures Strategic Position in Gulf," *Toronto Star*, March 28, 1993, p. F3.
106 *Al-Wasat*, No. 105 (1996), p. 14.
107 *CIA World Factbook: Oman* (2010). URL: https://www.cia.gov/library/publications/the-world-factbook/geos/mu.html.
108 *Al-Wasat*, No. 283 (1997), p. 12.
109 Pat Lancaster, "Oman Elections: Democracy at Our Own Pace," *Middle East*, December 2007, pp. 18–20.
110 Sa'd Eddîn Ibrâhîm, op. cit., pp. 179–188.
111 Human Rights Watch, *The UAE's Draft Labor Law: Human Rights Watch's Comments and Recommendations*, March 2007. URL: http://www.hrw.org/en/news/2007/03/24/uae-draft-labor-law-violates-international-standards.

Further reading

There is a relative paucity of scholarship on the countries of the Gulf Cooperation Council, with the exception of Saudi Arabia. Nevertheless, in the developing body of literature, there are several accomplished works.

At the general level, Kiren Aziz Chaudhury's *The Price of Wealth: Economies and Institutions in the Middle East* is a useful text for those interested in the Arab Gulf states and examines the recurring problems of oil-rich Gulf regimes, the nature of state and market institutions in these countries, and the reaction of these institutions to external shocks. Jill Crystal's *Oil and Politics in the Gulf: Rulers and Merchants in Kuwait and Qatar* is similarly useful as an inquiry into the political economy of the contemporary oil-rich Gulf states and an examination of the impact of oil wealth on political culture and state-building, using Qatar and Kuwait as case studies.

The United Arab Emirates represents the paradigmatic case of rapid economic expansion in the oil-rich Arab Gulf. Nevertheless, this has occurred at some significant cost, particularly in the arena of labor abuses. Nor has the UAE's policy of economic liberalization been accompanied by significant political liberalization. Neil Davidson's *Dubai: The Vulnerability of Success* and *The United Arab Emirates: A Study of Survival* are two of the more significant academic works on the UAE. Beyond providing an historical sketch of the development of the UAE, Davidson examines the seemingly anachronistic combination of a traditional political system and a highly modern economic sector. He also looks into contemporary issues within the UAE, especially Dubai, including labor abuse, criminal syndicates and economic corruption.

Academic literature on Oman is relatively scarce. Among the more significant works is Patricia Risso's *Oman and Muscat: An Early History*, which provides an historical overview of Oman and Muscat in the second half of the eighteenth century, as Oman developed a measure of economic independence and power. Risso discusses the development of tribal customs and patterns, the role of religion, and Oman's relationship with its neighbors. John E. Peterson's *Oman in the Twentieth Century* covers more ground, providing an historical survey of Oman's political, economic and social development in the twentieth century.

Serious Western academic inquiries into Kuwait are similarly lacking. However, H.R.P. Dickson, a British colonial officer between the 1920s and the 1940s, published *Kuwait and Her Neighbors* in 1956 and, while dated, this remains a fascinating and intimate portrait of nomadic life. Peter Mansfield's *Kuwait, Vanguard of the Gulf*, while brief, is an accessible survey of Kuwaiti history and culture. Jacqueline S. Ismael's *Kuwait: Social Change in Historical Perspective* and *Kuwait: Dependency and Class in a Rentier State* study the application of dependency theory to a capital surplus economy, emphasizing the social and class dynamics and their human consequences through the historic evolution of the state from its colonial origin through independence.

Fred H. Lawson's *The Modernization of Autocracy* and Rosemarie Said Zahlan's *The Creation of Qatar* represent broad historical overviews of Qatar's development, covering a period from the settlement of Zubarah in the late eighteenth century to the end of the twentieth century.

Tim Niblock's *Saudi Arabia: Power, Legitimacy and Survival* provides a concise yet instructive account of the development of the Saudi state, and the subsequent emergence of the oil rentier economy and its role within the region. As'ad Abukhalil *The Battle for Saudi Arabia* is a highly critical analysis of the Saudi state's relationship to its "subjects," its role within the Muslim world, and the highly textured nature of its relationship with the United States.

References

Abukhalil, As'ad (2003) *The Battle for Saudi Arabia*, Seven Stories Press.

Chaudhury, Kiren Aziz (1997) *The Price of Wealth: Economies and Institutions in the Middle East*, Cornell University Press.

Crystal, Jill (1995) *Oil and Politics in the Gulf: Rulers and Merchants in Kuwait and Qatar*, Cambridge University Press.

Davidson, Christopher M. (2005) *The United Arab Emirates: A Study in Survival*, Lynne Rienner.

—— (2008) *Dubai: The Vulnerability of Success*, Columbia University Press.

Dickson, H.R.P. (1956) *Kuwait and Her Neighbours*, George Allen & Unwin.

Ismael, Jacqueline S. (1982) *Kuwait: Social Change in Historical Perspective*, Syracuse University Press.

—— (1993) *Kuwait: Dependency and Class in a Rentier State*, Gainesville: University Press of Florida.

Lawson, Fred H. (1989) *The Modernization of Autocracy*, Westview Press.

Mansfield, Peter (1988) *Kuwait, Vanguard of the Gulf*, Hutchinson.

Niblock, Tim (2006) *Saudi Arabia: Power, Legitimacy and Survival*, Routledge.

Peterson, John E. (1978) *Oman in the Twentieth Century*, Barnes & Noble.

Risso, Patricia (1986) *Oman and Muscat: An Early History*, Croom Helm.

Zahlan, Rosemarie Said (1979) *The Creation of Qatar*, Croom Helm.

Index